The Varieties of Pension Governance

The Varieties of Pension Governance

Pension Privatization in Europe

Edited by
Bernhard Ebbinghaus

OXFORD
UNIVERSITY PRESS

OXFORD
UNIVERSITY PRESS

Great Clarendon Street, Oxford OX2 6DP

Oxford University Press is a department of the University of Oxford.
It furthers the University's objective of excellence in research, scholarship,
and education by publishing worldwide in

Oxford New York

Auckland Cape Town Dar es Salaam Hong Kong Karachi
Kuala Lumpur Madrid Melbourne Mexico City Nairobi
New Delhi Shanghai Taipei Toronto

With offices in

Argentina Austria Brazil Chile Czech Republic France Greece
Guatemala Hungary Italy Japan Poland Portugal Singapore
South Korea Switzerland Thailand Turkey Ukraine Vietnam

Oxford is a registered trade mark of Oxford University Press
in the UK and in certain other countries

Published in the United States
by Oxford University Press Inc., New York

British Library Cataloguing in Publication Data
Data available

Library of Congress Cataloging in Publication Data
Data available

Typeset by SPI Publisher Services, Pondicherry, India
Printed in Great Britain
on acid-free paper by
MPG Books Group, Bodmin and King's Lynn

ISBN 978–0–19–958602–8

3 5 7 9 10 8 6 4

Preface

While drawing a pension may seem far away for many working people, the financial crisis dramatically emphasized the importance of early planning and saving for one's own retirement. Especially given the twin demographic trends of increasing longevity and ageing populations, the maintenance of sustainable and adequate old age retirement income has become one of the most important concerns on the political agenda. This project developed during the mid-2000s as I completed my monograph on *Reforming Early Retirement in Europe, Japan and the USA* (Oxford, 2006) that explored the role of employer-provided or collectively negotiated occupational pensions as private pathways to early exit from work. Of important consequence for social inequality, the apparent cross-national differences in the public–private pension mix as well as the current trend towards privatization remained puzzling, demanding a more in-depth comparative study. Having moved from the Max Planck Institute for the Study of Societies (MPIfG) in Cologne to the University of Mannheim, I found in the Mannheim Centre for European Social Research (MZES) an ideal environment to conduct such an international research project.

In developing the collaborative project on the 'Governance of Supplementary Pensions in Europe' (GOSPE), discussions with Giuliano Bonoli (then Fribourg, now IDHEAP, Lausanne) were very fruitful. With the financial support of the MZES, Isabelle Schulze assisted the writing of the project application to the German Research Foundation (DFG) while finishing her dissertation. She also, with Karen Anderson and Ellen Immergut, co-edited *The Handbook of Western European Pension Politics* (Oxford, 2007), which provided an important stepping stone for our new project. Unfortunately, by the time that the GOSPE-project was granted its initial external funding in early 2007, Isabelle Schulze had moved on to the University of Konstanz.

Since summer 2007, Mareike Gronwald, a sociologist, and Tobias Wiß, a political scientist, have conducted their doctoral research within the project and contributed throughout this project in multiple ways, often going beyond the call of duty: they co-organized the two project workshops, assisted the process of turning papers into final chapters, and most importantly contributed to the Germany chapter (which served as a model for the other country studies) and also to two comparative analyses. Alongside her own dissertation on institutional change in pension systems, Mareike Gronwald contributed to the comparative-historical Chapter 2 on the changing public–private pension mix in Europe. Tobias Wiß co-authored the comparative Chapter 13 on pension governance while writing his dissertation on the role of the social partners in German public and private pensions. Jörg Neugschwender, an economist, joined the Mannheim team first as a trainee for part of 2007 and since September 2008 as doctoral researcher. He contributed to the comparative Chapter 14 on income inequality in old age while developing his own Ph.D. thesis on the same topic at the University of Mannheim's Graduate School of Economic and Social Sciences (GESS).

The authors of the country and comparative chapters of *The Varieties of Pension Governance* profited from intensive discussions at the two Mannheim workshops in February and December 2008. For the constructive criticism and comments, we all thank Dirk Hofäcker (University of Bamberg), Jürgen Kohl (University of Heidelberg), Lutz Leisering (University of Bielefeld), Katharina Müller (Hochschule Mannheim), Christine Trampusch (University of Bern), and Noel Whiteside (University of Warwick). Jean-Marie Jungblut of the MZES Eurodata unit (now at Eurofound, Dublin) also contributed to the first workshop with a preliminary analysis of SHARE data. At the MZES, our team has also profited from collegial exchange with Thomas Bahle, Jan Drahokoupil, Paola Mattei (now Oxford University), Timo Weishaupt, Claus Wendt (now University of Siegen), and the doctoral researchers in the welfare state research area 'A1'. I am grateful to my long-time companion, Justin Powell, who helped me in too many ways to elaborate here.

The GOSPE-project would have been impossible without the support by student assistants who helped in the research process in manifold ways. Particular thanks to Annette Krieger, Judith Langbein, and Annabell Zentarra at the MZES, and for the SHARE-analysis of Chapter 14 to André Schaffrin (now at the University of Cologne). The final copy-editing of the various chapters was patiently and smoothly organized first by Julian Brückner and later Agnes Orban at the Chair of Macrosociology, with additional help by Michael Becker. Language editing of non-native contributions was reliably conducted by Christi Smith while she completed her own dissertation at Indiana University in Bloomington.

This project would not have been possible without the generous resources granted by the German Research Foundation (DFG). Especially since it is difficult to receive funding for internationally collaborative projects from a national research funding agency, I am grateful for the two grants provided by the DFG to finance not only three doctoral researchers in Mannheim for several years but also the workshop participation and contributions of nine country experts across

Europe. Additional support was provided by the *Forschungsnetzwerk Alterssicher-ung* (FNA), the research network of the German statutory pension insurance (*Deutsche Rentenversicherung*), for the completion of the dissertation projects of Mareike Gronwald and Tobias Wiß. Finally, the MZES supported the GOSPE-project with a start-up grant and it continues to provide a well-functioning research infrastructure for cross-national research.

Finding a publisher for scholarly edited volumes is increasingly difficult in today's world of commercial publishing, so I am very grateful to Dominic Byatt and his team at Oxford University Press for their continued support. This collaborative project would not have been possible without the contributors' efforts to meet the project's demands in content, form, and schedule, and I appreciate the contributors' dedication to this scientific collaboration these past three years. We hope that our efforts to provide an up-to-date account of current pension policies in Europe will provide social policy experts, students, and scholars a valuable guide for understanding the achievements and chal-lenges in providing not only sustainable but also adequate pensions today and in the future.

Bernhard Ebbinghaus

Mannheim, June 2010

Contents

Contents

List of Figures

List of Figures

List of Tables

List of Tables

List of Abbreviations

ABP	Algemeen Burgerlijk Pensioenfonds / General Old-Age Pensions Act
ACAM	Autorité de Contrôle des Assurances et des Mutuelles / Insurance and Mutuals Supervisory Authority
AFP	Folkpension / Basic State Pension
AGIRC	Association Générale des Institutions de Retraites des Cadres / General Association of Cadres' Pension Institutions (France)
AHV/AVS	Alters- und Hinterlassenenversicherung / Assurance Vieillesse et Survivants / Pension insurance (Switzerland)
AKAVA	Akateeminen alojen keskuslitto / Confederation of Unions for Academic Professionals in Finland
ANBO	Algemene Nederlandse Bond voor Ouderen / Dutch Association of Senior Citizens
AOW	Algemene ouderdomswet / Basic state pension (the Netherlands)
AP	Originally Andelspensionsforeningen / Cooperative Pension Association
ARP	Anti-Revolutionaire Partij / Anti-Revolutionary Party
ARRCO	Association des Régimes de Retraite Complémentaire / Association of Supplementary Pension Schemes (France)
ASLK	Algemene Spaar en Lijfrente Kas / General Savings and Pension Annuities Fund
ASPA	Allocation de solidarité aux personnes âgées / Solidarity Benefit for Elderly People
ATP	Allmänn tilläggspension / Supplementary Pension (Sweden)
ATP	Arbejdsmarkedets Tillaegspension / Supplementary Labour Market Pension (Denmark)
BaFin	Bundesanstalt für Finanzdienstleistungsaufsicht / Federal Financial Supervisory Authority
BAV	Betriebliche Altersversorgung / Occupational pensions
BetrAVG	Gesetz zur Verbesserung der betrieblichen Altersversorgung / Occupational Pension Act
BMAS	Bundesministerium für Arbeit und Soziales / Federal Ministry of Employment and Social Affairs

BMF	Bundesministerium der Finanzen / Federal Ministry of Finance
BMGS	Bundesministerium für Gesundheit und Soziales / Federal Ministry of Health and Social Affairs
BNP	Banque Nationale de Paris / National Bank of Paris
BSP	Basic State Pension
BSV / OFAS	Bundesamt für Sozialversicherung / Office fédéral des assurances sociales / Federal Office of Social Insurance
BVG / LPP	Bundesgesetz über die berufliche Alters-, Hinterlassenen- und Invalidenvorsorge / Loi fédérale sur la prévoyance professionnelle / Federal Law on Occupational Retirement, Survivors' and disability pensions
CAO	Collectieve Arbeidsovereenkomst / Collective wage agreement
CBFA	Commissie voor Bank-, Financie- and Assurantiewezen / Banking, Finance and Insurance Commission
CCMIP	Commission de contrôle des mutuelles et des institutions de prévoyance / Supervisory Authority of Mutuals and Provident Institutions
CDC	Caisse des Dépôts et des Consignations / French Public Investment Institution
CDU	Christlich Demokratische Union Deutschlands / Christian Democratic Union of Germany
CHU	Christelijk Historische Unie / Christian Historical Union
CME	Coordinated Market Economies
CNPF	Conseil national du patronat français / National Council of French Employers and Entrepreneurs
CNV	Christelijk Nationaal Vakverbond / Christian Trade Union Federation
CONSOB	Commissione Nazionale per le Società e la Borsa / National Commission for Securities and Stock Exchange
COVIP	Commissione di Vigilanza sui Fondi Pensione / Pension Fund Supervisory Commission
CP	Collectieve pensioentoezegging / Collective pension plans
CPF	Fondi pensione negoziali / Closed pension funds
CREF	Complément de retraite de la fonction publique / Civil Service Retirement Supplement
CRH	Complément retraite des hospitaliers / Hospital Staff Retirement Supplement
CRPB	Caisse de Retraite de la Profession Bancaire / Banking Employees Pension Institution
CSG	Contribution sociale généralisée / Special general supplementary income tax
CSO	Centrale Samenwerkende Ouderenorganisaties / Association of Elderly Organizations

CSU	Christlich Soziale Union in Bayern / Christian Social Union in Bavaria
DB	Defined benefit
DC	Defined contribution
DC	Democrazia Cristiana / Christian Democratic Party
DKK	Dansk krone / Danish Kroner
DRV	Deutsche Rentenversicherung / German Pension Insurance
EDF-GDF	Electricité de France – Gaz de France / Electricity of France – Gaz of France
EET	Exempt contributions – exempt returns – taxable benefits
EK	Elinkeinoelämän keskusliitto / The Confederation of Finnish Industries
EL / PC	Ergänzungsleistungen / Prestations Complémentaires / Means-tested supplementary pensions
ELSA	English Longitudinal Study of Ageing
ETK	Eläketurvakeskus / The Finnish Centre for Pensions
ETT	Exempt contributions – taxable returns – taxable benefits
EU	European Union
EU-SILC	European Union Statistics on Income and Living Conditions
FDP	Freie Demokratische Partei / Free Democratic Party
FFSA	Fédération française des sociétés d'assurance / Federation of French insurance companies
FI	Finansinspektionen / Swedish Financial Supervisory Authority
FIN-FSA	Finanssivalvonta / Financial Supervisory Authority
FNV	Federatie Nederlandse Vakbeweging / Dutch Trade Union Federation
FONPEL	Fonds de Pension des Elus Locaux / Locally Elected Politicians' Pension Fund
FPG	Försäkringsbolaget Pensionsgaranti / Pension Guarantee Mutual Insurance Company
FTK	Financiële Toetsingkader / Financial Assessment Framework
FZG-LLP	Bundesgesetz über die Freizügigkeit in der beruflichen Alters-, Hinterlassenen- und Invalidenvorsorge (Freizügigkeitsgesetz)/Loi fédérale sur la prévoyance professionnelle vieillesse, survivants et invalidité/ Federal Law on the portability of occupational retirement, survivors' and disability pensions
GERP	Groupement d'épargne retraite populaire / Popular Retirement Savings Group
GMP	Guaranteed Minimum Pension
Greens	Die Grünen / Green Party
GRV	Gesetzliche Rentenversicherung / Statutory pension system
GV	Groepsverzekering / Group insurance contract

IBP	Instelling voor bedrijfspensioenvoorziening / Autonomous pension fund
IMF	International Monetary Fund
INPDAP	Istituto Nazionale di Previdenza dell'Amministrazione Pubblica / National Institute for Social Insurance of Civil Servants
INPS	Istituto Nazionale della Previdenza Sociale / National Institute for Social Insurance
IORP	Institution for Occupational Retirement Provision
IP	Individuele pensioentoezegging / Individual pension plans
IRCANTEC	Institution de Retraite Complémentaire des Agents Non Titulaires de l'État et des Collectivités Publiques / Supplementary Pension Institution for (non tenured) State and Local Employees
ISVAP	Istituto per la Vigilanza sulle Assicurazioni Private e di Interesse Collettivo / Insurance Supervision Authority
ITP	Industrins och handelns tjänstepensionsavtal / Supplementary pension plan for salaried employees in industry and trade
ITPK	ITP komplettering / ITP supplementary pension plan
JØP	Juristernes og Økonomernes Pensionskasse / Pension Fund for the Legal Profession and Economists
Kåpan	Kompletterande ålderspension / Supplementary old age pension for public employees
KAP-KL	Kollektivavtalad pension – kommuner och landsting / Collective bargained pension – municipalities and county councils (Sweden)
KBO	Katholieke Bond Ouderen / Catholic Elderly Association
Kela	Kansaneläkelaitos / Finnish Social Insurance Institution
KEVA	Kommunernas pensionsförsäkring / Municipal Pension Institution
Kok	Kansallinen Kokoomuspuolue / National Coalition Party
KP	Kommunernes Pensionsforsikring / Pension Insurance of Municipalities
KVP	Katholieke Volkspartij / Catholic People's Party
KvTEL	Kunnallisten viranhaltijain ja työntekijäin eläkelaki / Pension Law for Municipal Employees
LD	Lønmodtagernes Dyrtidsfond / Wage earners' deferred wage fund (Dänemark)
LEL	Lyhytaikaisissa työsuhteissa olevien työntekijöiden eläkelaki / Pension Law for Temporary Employees
LIS	Luxembourg Income Study
LME	Liberal Market Economies
LO	Landsorganisationen i Sverige / Swedish Trade Union Confederation
MEL	Merimiesten eläkelaki / Seamen's Pension Law

MHP	Vakcentrale voor middengroepen en hoger personeel / Managerial and Professional Staff Union
ML	Maalaisliitto / The Agrarian Party
MNTs	Member Nominated Trustees
MP	Pensionskassen for Magistre og Psykologer (previously Magistrenes Pensionskasse)/Pension fund for M.A. graduates and psychologists
MyEL	Maatalousyrittäjien eläkelaki / Pension Law for Self-employed in Agriculture
NCW	Nederlands Christelijk Werkgeversverbond / Dutch Christian Federation of Employers
NDC	Notional defined contribution
NISBO	Nederlandse Islamtische Bond voor Ouderen / Dutch Association for Older Migrants
NKBP	Nationale Kas voor Bediendenpensioenen / National Pension Fund for Salaried Employees
NKV	Nederlands Katholiek Vakverbond / Netherlands Catholic Trade Union Federation
NP	Kansaneläke / National Pension
NPM	Nationaal Pensioenfonds voor Mijnwerkers / National Pension Fund for Miners
NPT	Normale pensioentoezegging / Standard pension plan
NVV	Nederlands Verbond van Vakverenigingen / Netherlands Trade Union Federation
OCMW	Openbaar Centrum voor Maatschappelijk Welzijn / Social Assistance Centre
OECD	Organisation for Economic Cooperation and Development
OMC	Open Method of Coordination
ONP	Ondernemingspensioen / Company pension plans
OPCVM	Organismes de placement collectif en valeurs mobilières / Mutual fund
OPF	Fondi Pensione Aperti / Open pension funds
Opf	Vereniging van Ondernemingspensioenfondsen / Association of Company Pension Funds
PA03	Pensionsavtal 03 (för anställda i statlig sektor)/Pension agreement 03 (for employees in the central government sector)
PAYG	Pay-as-you-go
PCI	Partito Comunista Italiano / Italian Communist Party
PCOB	Protestants Christelijke Ouderen Bond / Protestant Christian Seniors Association
PEF	Fondi Pensione Preesistenti / Pre-existing pension funds

PERCO	Plan d'épargne retraite collectif / Company Retirement Savings Plan (France)
PERE	Plan d'épargne-retraite d'entreprise / Company Retirement Savings Plan
PERP	Plan d'épargne-retraite populaire / Individual pension saving plans (France)
PFA	Pensionsforsikringsanstalten / Pension Insurance Institution
PIP	Polizze Individuali Pensionistiche / Personal pension plans through life-insurance contracts
PKA	Pensionskassernes Administration / Administration of Pension Funds
PLI	Partito Liberale Italiano / Italian Liberal Party
PME	Pensioenfonds van de Metalektro / Pension Fund for the Mechanical and Electrical Engineering Industries
PMT	Pensioenfonds Metaal and Techniek / Pension Fund for the Engineering, Mechanical and Electric contracting sector
PPF	Pension Protection Fund (UK)
PPM	Premiepensionsmyndigheten / Premium Pension Authority
PREFON	Caisse Nationale de Prévoyance de la Fonction Publique / National Civil Service Provident Society
PRI	Partito Repubblicano Italiano / Italian Republican Liberal Party
PSDI	Partito Socialista Democratico Italiano / Italian Social Democratic Party
PSI	Partito Socialista Italiano / Italian Socialist Party
PSV	Pensions-Sicherungs-Verein auf Gegenseitigkeit / Pension Protection Fund (Germany)
PSW	Pensioen en spaarfondswet / Pension and Savings Law
PTK	Privattjänstemannakartellen / The Council for Negotiation and Co-operation (former Federation of Salaried Employees in Industry and Services)
PvdA	Partij van de Arbeid / Labour Party
PVK	Pensioen en Verzekeringskamer / Pension and Insurance Authority
PW	Pensioenwet / Pension Act
RAFP	Régime Additionnel de la Fonction Publique / Civil Service Additional Scheme
RKSP	Rooms-Katholieke Staatspartij / Catholic Party
RMZ	Rijksdienst voor Maatschappelijke Zekerheid / National Social Security Office
RPR	Rassemblement pour la République / Republican party founded by Chirac
RSZ	Rijksdienst voor Sociale Zekerheid / National Office for Social Security
SACRA	Société d'Assurance de Consolidation des Retraites de l'Assurance / Insurance Company for the Consolidation of Pensions in the Insurance Sector

List of Abbreviations

SAF	Svenska Arbetsgivareföreningen / Swedish Employers Confederation
SCP	Sectorpensioen / Sector pension plans
SDP	Suomen Sosialidemokraattinen Puolue / Finnish Social Democratic Party
SDS	Stichting Dienstverlening Samenwerkingsverband / Foundation for Co-operative Service Provision
SER	Sociaal-Economische Raad / Social and Economic Council
SERPS	State Earnings Related Pension Scheme (UK)
SHARE	The Survey of Health, Ageing and Retirement in Europe
SKG-N	Kommission für soziale Sicherheit und Gesundheit des Schweizerischen Nationalrates / Commission de la sécurité sociale et de la santé publique du Conseil national / Commission for social security and health policy of the National Council (lower chamber of the Federal Parliament)
SKL	Sveriges Kommuner och Landsting / Organization of municipalities and county councils
SN	Svenskt Näringsliv / Confederation of Swedish Enterprises
SNCF	Société Nationale des Chemins de Fer / National Railway Company
SOKA-BAU	Sozialkassen der Bauwirtschaft / Supplementary social insurances of the construction industry
SPD	Sozialdemokratische Partei Deutschlands / Social Democratic Party of Germany
SPI-CGIL	Sindacato Pensionati Italiani-CGIL / Pensioners section of the Italian union confederation CGIL
SPS	Særlige Pensionsopsparing / Special pension saving scheme
SPT	Solidaire pensioentoezegging / Solidaristic pension commitment
SPV	Statens pensionsverk / The National Government Employee Pensions Board
S2P	State Second Pension (UK)
STAR	Stichting van de Arbeid / Bipartite Labour Foundation
STTK	Suomen Toimihenkilökeskusjärjestö/Finnish Confederation of Salaried Employees
SVP / UDC	Schweizerische Volkspartei / Union Démocratique du Centre / Swiss People's Party
TaeL	Taiteilijoiden eläkelaki / Pension Law for Artists
TEL	Työntekijäin eläkelaki / Pension Law for the Private Sector Employees
Tfr	Trattamento di Fine Rapporto / Severance pay (Italy)
TUC	Trades Union Congress
TyEL	Työntekijän eläkelaki / New Employees Pensions Act (Finland)
UDF	Union pour la Démocratie Française / Union for French Democracy

UMP	Union pour un Mouvement Populaire / Union for a Popular Movement
VB	Vereniging van Bedrijfstakpensioenfondsen / Dutch Association of Industry-wide Pension Funds
VBL	Versorgungsanstalt des Bundes und der Länder / Supplementary public-sector pension agency (Germany)
VDB	Vrijzinnig Democratische Bond / Progressive Liberals
VDR	Verband Deutscher Rentenversicherungsträger / Federation of German Pension Insurance Institutes
VEL	Valtion eläkelaki / Pension Law for the State Employees (Finland)
VNO	Vereniging van Nederlandse Ondernemingen / Federation of Dutch Industry
VNO / NCW	Vereniging van Nederlandse Ondernemingen-Nederlands Christelijk Werkgeversverbond / Confederation of Dutch Industry and Employers
WAP	Wet op de Aanvullende Pensioenen / Occupational Pensions Act
WKA	Wet koppeling met afwijkingsmogelijkheid / Conditional Indexation Act
YEL	Yrittäjien Eläkelaki / Pension Law for Self-Employed (Finland)
ZVK	Zusatzversorgungskasse / Supplementary pension fund in construction industry

Contributors

Karen Anderson, Associate Professor at the Department of Political Science, Institute for Management Research, Radboud University of Nijmegen, the Netherlands.

Giuliano Bonoli, Professor at *Institut de hautes études en administration publique* (IDHEAP) in Lausanne, Switzerland.

Paul Bridgen, Senior Lecturer at the School of Social Sciences, University of Southampton, United Kingdom.

Johan De Deken, Lecturer at Department of Sociology and Anthropology, University of Amsterdam, the Netherlands.

Bernhard Ebbinghaus, Professor of Sociology at the School of Social Sciences, and Director of the Mannheim Centre for European Social Research (MZES), University of Mannheim, Germany.

Jørgen Goul Andersen, Professor at the Department of Political Science, University of Aarhus, Denmark.

Mareike Gronwald, Researcher at the Mannheim Centre for European Social Research (MZES), University of Mannheim, Germany.

Silja Häusermann, Researcher and Lecturer (*Oberassistentin*) at the Department of Political Science, University of Zurich, Switzerland.

Matteo Jessoula, Assistant Professor at the Department of Social and Political Studies, University of Milan, Italy.

Olli Kangas, Professor and Head of the Research Department of the Social Insurance Institution (KELA) in Helsinki, Finland.

Gabriella Sjögren Lindquist, Assistant Professor of Economics at the University of Stockholm and Deputy Director of the Swedish Institute for Social Research (SOFI) in Stockholm, Sweden.

Päivi Luna, Research and Development Manager at the Federation of Finnish Financial Services in Helsinki, Finland.

Traute Meyer, Reader at the School of Social Sciences, University of Southampton, United Kingdom.

Marek Naczyk, DPhil candidate at the Department of Politics and International Relations, University of Oxford, United Kingdom.

Jörg Neugschwender, Researcher at the Mannheim Centre for European Social Research (MZES) and PhD candidate at the Graduate School of Economic and Social Sciences (GESS), University of Mannheim, Germany.

Bruno Palier, Senior Researcher at the Centre for Political Research (CEVIPOF), Sciences Po, Paris, France.

Eskil Wadensjö, Professor of Economics at the Swedish Institute for Social Research (SOFI) and Director of Linnaeus Centre of Integration Studies (SULCIS), Stockholm University, Sweden.

Tobias Wiß, Researcher at the Mannheim Centre for European Social Research (MZES), University of Mannheim, Germany.

Part I

Comparing Pension Privatization in Europe

1

Introduction: Studying Pension Privatization in Europe

Bernhard Ebbinghaus

The increased privatization of pensions – the shift from state to private responsibility for old age retirement income – raises fundamental issues of participatory stakeholder rights and social inequality. International organizations and national policymakers advocate for a policy shift away from pay-as-you-go (PAYG) financed public pension schemes towards private, mainly prefunded, pensions. This is largely motivated by an economic logic of financial *sustainability* in ageing societies under fiscal austerity and of boosting financial capital markets to create economic growth. Pension reforms over the last two decades cut back public pension benefits, gradually extended the official retirement age, and fostered privately funded pensions. While the sustainability endeavour was driving much of these pension reforms, the *adequacy* of retirement income has often been neglected from current public debates, partly because poverty in old age seems no longer to be such a pressing concern in Europe's advanced welfare states. Yet poverty and income inequality vary across pension systems in Europe; they are also on the rise due to the continued retreat of public pensions and the larger reliance on voluntary prefunded private pensions. The recent financial market crises during the 2000s reveal the problematic nature of funded pensions that fall short of expected returns. These developments pose major questions with respect to the increasing role of private pensions: Does the retreat from public responsibility lead to more private initiative that fills the gap in future old age income provision? How are these private pensions that are invested for the benefit of future pensioners governed and regulated? To what extent are the risks of old age income security shifted onto individuals, and will income inequality grow larger?

Although some countries have a long tradition in pension fund capitalism, others have only recently decided to change from dominantly public to multipillar pension schemes. 'Private' pensions are not the same everywhere across

Europe. There is much cross-national and temporal variation that provides important insights. For this collaborative international study, we chose ten (Western) European countries of established Liberal, Nordic, and Continental welfare regimes.[1] These represent varying forms of public–private pension mix following either a more Bismarckian tradition of maintaining income through earnings-related state pensions or a Beveridge model of combining public basic pensions and (mainly private) supplementary pensions. The chosen countries are also at different stages in privatizing old age income responsibility: some have long traditions of multipillar systems with pension fund capitalism, while others have moved in this direction in various ways, and yet some Continental systems are still dominantly public pension systems. Using these cross-national variations, we will be able to explore several policy-relevant questions. What can we learn from the past development of the public–private mix for the division of responsibility today and in the future? And how do differences in regulation and governance of private pensions affect the participatory rights and income situation of those dependent on such pensions?

Addressing these pertinent questions, *The Varieties of Pension Governance* provides comparative analyses of the trend towards privatization and the cross-national variations in public–private pension mix, of the variations in governance and regulation of private pensions, and it investigates the impact of pension systems on the income situation of older people. This edited book combines a standardized analysis of each country experience besides the three systematic comparative analyses. In the country chapters (Chapters 3–12), the volume analyses the development and particular features of each of the ten European countries. Each chapter provides an overview of the main features of the pension system and the evolution of the public–private pension mix, while in the second part of the chapter the country experts discuss the private supplementary pension systems in more detail. This Introduction provides a short guide to the relevant literature, the main concepts used, the rationale for the selection of countries, and summaries of the content of the subsequent chapters.

1. Comparative welfare regime analysis and Varieties of Capitalism

The origins of pension systems date back more than a century when governments began to establish mandatory social insurance against social risks such as

[1] Although the new Member States of the European Union in Central and Eastern Europe have adopted in recent years important reforms that fostered private pensions, these pension systems are still in process of transformation and thus difficult to compare with the established (Western) European pension systems considered here. For important comparative studies on Central and Eastern Europe, see Müller, Ryll and Wagener (1999) and Orenstein (2008) as well as the international organizations OECD (2004) and World Bank (Holzmann et al. 2003).

old age and disability (Flora and Heidenheimer 1981). The choice between two different goals – poverty alleviation versus status maintenance – led to the post-war development of flat-rate 'Beveridge' basic pensions or earnings-related Bismarckian social insurance that left more or less developmental scope for supplementary private pensions. Private occupational welfare was an important defining criterion of Esping-Andersen's (1990) influential welfare state regime typology. In particular, he distinguished the Liberal regime due to its residual public welfare and extended private self-reliance from Social-democratic universalism and Conservative status-maintaining goals (Esping-Andersen 1996). As an instrument of poverty alleviation, the Liberal welfare state provides only flat-rate basic pensions and expects individuals to save privately. In contrast, the Social-democratic welfare state guarantees universal income security to all citizens, financed largely by taxes and relying on full employment. Finally, the Conservative welfare regime reinforces status differences due to its earnings-related and employment-based social insurance, although social contributions drive up labour costs and lead to welfare without work problems.

Many scholars consider these welfare regimes to be largely frozen, and any subsequent transformation to follow a regime-dependent logic: The Liberal regime leans towards retrenchment and privatization, whereas the Social-democratic and Conservative regimes favour re-calibration or rationalizing (Pierson 2001a). Such a regime approach aims to explain the (trans-)formation of welfare states as relatively inert institutional arrangements in which the pension system is only one – although a fiscally important – component. According to this line of argument, the reforms of pension systems, in particularly public pensions that are PAYG financed, are largely a product of earlier institutionalized decisions; hence, changes can only take place within certain 'paths' (Myles and Pierson 2001). Since private pensions are largely seen as a hallmark of Liberal regimes, this regime perspective fails to account for the growing importance of occupational welfare in Social-democratic and Conservative welfare regimes (cf. Shalev 1996).

In a similar vein, much of the Varieties of Capitalism approach (Hall and Soskice 2001) assumes different political economy logics for the linkage between social policy and economic governance (cf. Ebbinghaus 2006b; cf. Ebbinghaus and Manow 2001). While Liberal Market Economies and pension fund capitalism coexist, Coordinated Market Economies tend to rely more on patient capital, including on the book reserves for occupational pension commitments by firms (Jackson and Vitols 2001). With changes towards a service economy and Anglo-Saxon shareholder orientation, a reorientation of private pensions provided by firms occurred from defined-benefit (DB) towards defined-contribution (DC) pensions (Bridgen and Meyer 2005). In this study, we show that not only Liberal but also some Coordinated Market Economies, in particular the Netherlands (see Chapter 10) and Switzerland (see Chapter 11), developed mature multipillar pension systems and pension fund capitalism (see Chapter 13). We also investigate to what degree these regimes have departed from state pension reliance in recent years, thereby challenging arguments of the welfare regime literature about institutional inertia and path dependence.

2. Two models of public–private mix

Recent empirical studies on pension reforms seek to go beyond time-invariant fixation of welfare regimes and adopt a more differentiated analysis that also focuses more closely on pension systems. 'Two worlds' have been distinguished in retirement income systems: the Beveridge-type basic pensions and Bismarckian social insurance schemes (Bonoli 2003; Palier and Bonoli 1995). Adopting an institutionalist perspective, the timing and sequence of events is of importance for subsequent development, particularly for pension systems with PAYG financing that creates acquired social rights and thus binds future generations to past decisions (Myles and Pierson 2001). As our comparative-historical account indicates (see Chapter 2), different trajectories of public pension development had important consequences for subsequent development of the public–private mix. Bismarckian systems decided early on to establish earnings-related benefits to achieve status maintenance for different occupational groups. Beveridge-type systems shared an initial orientation towards a basic income but later embarked on two different paths: some were 'early-birds', others 'latecomers' in publicly mandating earnings-related supplementary pensions (Hinrichs 2000: 358). Since the mid-1980s, demographic, economic, and budgetary pressures have brought about a further transformation. Contrary to the 'path dependence' thesis of Esping-Andersen and others, retrenchment efforts and reform directions varied greatly even within countries of the same regime, leading to 'path departure' (Ebbinghaus 2006a, 2009).

A multitude of comparative politics approaches attributed the success or failure of structural pension reforms to the 'veto points' provided by political institutions (Bonoli 2001) and the electoral competition between political parties (Immergut and Anderson 2007; Kitschelt 2001). In order to limit electoral repercussions, the 'New Politics' (Pierson 1996, 2001b) approach assumes that politicians use strategies of 'obfuscating' retrenchment efforts or of diffusing blame through political consensus building (Pierson 1997; Weaver 1986). In addition, societal consensus building through social pacts with unions and employers has been used by governments to facilitate parliamentary passage and to overcome non-parliamentary resistance (Ebbinghaus and Hassel 2000; Schludi 2008). These comparative political analyses focused on the big reforms that instigated political debates if not conflicts, whereas the gradual privatization and smaller subterranean changes remained often neglected. While these comparative politics studies shed light on the causes for welfare state reform in general, the development of occupational pensions was treated rather as a

Table 1.1 Conceptualizing institutional change

	Intended	Unintended
Public policy (top-down)	*Policy-driven*: Private pensions receive preferential tax treatment	*Policy drift*: Non-adaptation of public pensions leads to retirement income gap
Private action (bottom-up)	*Self-regulation*: Collective bargaining partners seize opportunity	*Negative externalities*: Private actors failure leads to aggravated problems

by-product of the politically induced public pension reforms. Although building upon the insights of these New Politics studies, in this book we look more closely at the interaction between 'top-down' public reforms and 'bottom-up' responses by non-state actors (see Table 1.1), thereby applying and further developing the theory of institutional change (Streeck and Thelen 2005).

Building upon but also going beyond previous policy-oriented studies that have analysed government-induced pension reforms (Immergut et al. 2007; Natali 2008; Schludi 2005), this study explores the consequences and interaction of pension reforms that alter the public–private mix. While the state partially retreated from its responsibilities to finance adequate state pensions, the scope for public regulation and control of private pensions increased. Consequently, the debate on restructuring and recalibrating pension systems has increasingly concentrated on regulation. Prominently, Lutz Leisering (2002, 2010) claims that the need for regulation and the political relevance of pensions has increased due to privatization. By adopting a *governance* perspective (Merrien 1998; Rhodes 1996) that investigates who regulates what, this study enhances the policy-focused analyses by considering the role of non-state actors, especially employers, trade unions, financial institutions, and the individuals (contributors and retirees). It also combines the study of policymaking, its implementation, and outcomes (cf. Arza and Kohli 2008).

While previous comparative studies have focused on the political process, this study builds upon these documented pension reforms 'from above' and concentrates on the potential adaptive changes 'from below'. Even if the state induced reforms, these depend on the adaptation of private actors to these public policies (see Table 1.1). Public policy can set up a conducive regulatory environment for private pensions, in particular through tax incentives or public mandates, thereby aiming to foster or impose private pensions. Political retrenchment of public pensions might lead to lower benefits in the future, thereby indirectly increasing the need for private initiatives to fill the gap. Even non-action by the state can have major consequences due to 'policy drift' (Hacker 2005). For instance, when governments do not raise pension benefits in line with wages, the replacement rate will slowly erode. An example of a 'bottom-up' process that is not controlled by the state is the withering away of DB plans in Britain as more and more employers replace them by DC plans in order to meet a more competitive environment and follow the moves by others (Bridgen and Meyer 2005), thereby undermining their former personnel policy to bind skilled workers to their firm. Finally, the failure of self-regulation of private pensions may lead to increased state intervention. This so-called 'paradox of privatization' (Leisering 2010; Leisering et al. 2002) led to more state intervention despite the aim to retreat from public pension responsibility. Therefore, the governance mode of private pensions will be crucial for the impact of the public–private mix (Clark 2003). The question for the future is whether self-regulation can guarantee sufficient social responsibility or whether the social consequences of failures in pension governance will call for further state intervention, collective negotiations by the social partners, or better self-regulation by 'codes of conduct' of the pension funds.

In this study, we investigate two major sets of hypotheses, more or less explicitly advanced in the literature (Pedersen 1999; Shalev 1996), in the comparative-historical account of the changes in public–private mix (Chapter 2) and in the comparative analysis of income inequality (Chapter 14). The 'crowding-out' thesis postulates that Bismarckian state pensions have limited the developmental scope for private occupational pensions because they provide for sufficient earnings-related benefits (except for very high-income groups due to contribution ceilings). Moreover, the 'social partners', trade unions and employers, are involved in the self-administration of Bismarckian social insurance (Ebbinghaus 2010), thus they are less interested in setting up an additional collective pension scheme. Even if this thesis holds for the past, the question arises whether a retrenchment of public pensions will automatically lead to the reverse process: the 'crowding-in' of the formerly suppressed historical alternative. The 'inadequate state pension' (or pension gap) thesis postulates that Beveridge-type basic pension systems, particularly those 'lite' systems that did not develop mature earnings-related state pension (Hinrichs 2000; Myles and Pierson 2001), leave more room for non-state activities, thereby potentially 'crowding in' private pensions. This was particularly the case in Britain, where employers or individuals were given the opportunity to 'opt out' from the state earnings-related system. In addition, the strategy of the social partners matters a great deal. Unions tended to push for better state pensions first, but when employers were willing to negotiate occupational pensions in return for wage moderation, an opportunity for collective schemes emerged.

3. Studying the public–private pension mix

As early as the 1950s, Richard Titmuss (1958) emphasized the occupational side of welfare activities. Thirty years later, Rein and Rainwater (1986) demanded to bring labour relations back into the analysis of social policy, emphasizing the role of firms and social partners. Seminal comparative studies highlighted the role of occupational pensions provided by non-state actors (Rein and Wadensjö 1997; Reynaud et al. 1996; Shalev 1996). In times of austerity, the tax subsidies for private pensions, the 'hidden side' of the welfare state (Howard 1997), expanded, often unnoticed from official statistics (cf. Adema 1999). Different concepts have been used to describe the newly transformed arrangement such as the 'welfare producing state' or 'enabling welfare state' (Gilbert 2002). As discussed in this study (see particularly Chapter 2), the *public–private mix* of national pension systems has been shifting over time, but the dividing line between state responsibility and that of private actors varies across countries (cf. Clark and Whiteside 2003; Rein and Schmähl 2004). In order to compare the shifting public–private mix and to analyse the private supplementary pensions more in detail, we need a comparative analytical typology of the different pension systems.

Following common practice in pension policy analysis (Immergut et al. 2007: 24), we distinguish *pillars*, that is, the question: 'who provides a pension?', from *tiers*, that is, the question: 'what function does a pension serve in old age income security?'. In contrast to the comparative typologies based on 'welfare regimes' that describe the underlying institutionalized principles of welfare provision as most prominently propagated by Esping-Andersen (1990), the concept of 'pillars' (Goodin and Rein 2001) provides an analytical tool to delineate the different institutionalized providers (or sponsors) responsible for the production of welfare: the state, a single employer, the social partners, and/ or the individual (see Chapter 13). In addition to pillars, pension systems assume different functions with respect to income security or maintenance which is referred to with the concept of 'tiers' – different layers of income protection (see Chapter 14). The first, basic social security aim is either a guaranteed minimum to all in need (e.g. social assistance) with a means test or a basic pension for all residents independent of any means test, what T.H. Marshall (Marshall 1950) referred to as a 'social citizenship right'. The second tier aims at status maintenance through earnings-related benefits, following the 'equivalence' principle of paid contribution record and expected benefits. This is common in Bismarckian pensions but also possible to achieve by a second (earnings-related) state pensions in Beveridge-type systems or through occupational pensions. The final tier is only a 'topping-up' of retirement income thanks to the expected returns on invested savings, for instance a fringe benefit offered by an employer to high-skilled employees or a voluntary personal saving schemes offered by financial institutes.

Under *supplementary* pensions, we thus consider all non-state pensions sponsored by firms, negotiated by the social partners (employers and trade unions), or individual decisions to save for old age in addition to mandatory state-provided pensions. For our analysis we divide (see Table 1.2), in addition to

Table 1.2 Pillars and tiers in pension systems

Tiers	(I) Public pillar	(II) Occupational pillar		(III) Personal pillar
	State	Social partners	Employer	Individual
Third tier (topping-up)				(3) Personal savings
Second tier (earnings-related)	(a) Earnings-related (b) Second tier	(1) Collective agreement	(2) Firm-level pension plan	
First tier (minimum income)	(a) Social assistance (b) Basic pension			

Notes: (a) Bismarckian pension, (b) Beveridge pension; (1–3) alternative private pensions (grey box), sometimes coexistent.

the public pension's first pillar (I), between the second pillar (II) *occupational* pensions (collective schemes governed by the social partners or firm-level pension schemes set up and sponsored by an employer) and the third pillar (III) *personal* pensions (individual saving plans). Thus private pensions can be an alternative or a complement to second-tier state pensions.

The ten countries considered in this study were chosen from a variety of pension systems with varying public–private mixes (see Table 1.3). Four countries represent dominantly public pension systems of the Bismarckian tradition (Belgium, France, Germany, and Italy) with important earnings-related state pensions for most occupational groups, and rather limited private pension development. The Nordic countries (Denmark, Finland, Sweden) represent not only different variations of the Beveridge-tradition with basic income security but also different public or private solutions for earnings-related supplementary pensions. And finally, we consider three mature multipillar pension systems (Britain, the Netherlands, Switzerland) with basic pension provisions for all and rather developed private pensions, in particular (quasi-) mandatory occupational pensions. However, there are two borderline cases (marked in boxes) of schemes that share public and private features: they are both mandatory quasi-public schemes but are also partly administered by the social partners. This is the case in Finland for the public and private sector as well as in France for private sector employees. Although they are often considered to be first (public) pillar schemes, we consider these as second (collective) pillar schemes in the comparative analyses. In two cases, we include public personal pensions as part of supplementary pensions: the Danish and Swedish mandatory personal pensions are included as third-pillar personal pensions since they are fully funded and allow individuals choices as to their portfolio. Although these are integral part of the public pensions, we consider them here

Table 1.3 First and supplementary pension pillars

Country	Statutory pensions		Supplementary private pensions		
	I. State (SP)		II. Occupational (OP)		III. Personal (PP)
	First tier	Second tier	Collective	Firm	Individual
Dominantly Bismarckian public pension systems					
Belgium	Min.	Earnings	*Sector-wide*	–	*Voluntary*
France	Min., Mixed	Mandated earnings OP		*Voluntary*	*Voluntary*
Germany	Tested	Earnings	*Sector-wide*	Larger firms	*Voluntary*
Italy	Min.	Earnings	–	*(Tfr)***	*Voluntary*
Nordic emergent hybrid multipillar systems					
Denmark	Basic+	Flat	Sector-wide	–	*Mandated SP*
Finland	Tested	Mandated earnings OP		*Voluntary*	*Voluntary*
Sweden (a)	Basic+	Earnings	Nation-wide	–	–
Sweden (b)	Tested	Earnings	Nation-wide	–	*Mandated SP*
Mature multipillar pension systems					
Britain	Basic	Earnings*	–	Opt-in*	Opt-in*
Netherlands	Basic	–	Sector-wide	Larger firms	–
Switzerland	Mixed	–	*Mandated*		*Voluntary*

Notes: Underlined: main income systems; *italics*: reformed since 1980s; (a) Sweden until 1998 reform, (b) since 1998 reform; SP: integral part of first public pension pillar, grey box: supplementary private pensions. *Opt-out of mandatory state second pensions possible;

**Tfr: mandatory end-of-service pay, partly transferred to personal pensions.

because they are similar to the voluntary schemes such as in Britain or Germany, except for being mandated.

Each country chapter provides an in-depth analysis of the development towards a multipillar pension system as well as the governance and regulation of the private pensions. The first part provides an overview over the current pension system. The development of the public–private mix is analysed with respect to the country's welfare regime, labour relations, and market economy. The emergence and changes of the public–private pension mix before and after 1945 is provided with the help of chronologies that provide a quick guide for the reader to understand the main steps in the path-dependent development but also the more recent path departures. The second part of each country chapter focuses on the governance and regulation of supplementary pensions of both occupational and personal pensions. All country chapters are organized around four leading questions. 'Who is covered?' analyses the overall coverage and its mechanisms (mandate, collective bargaining, employer or individual decisions). 'What kind of benefits?' describes the specific rules for benefits deriving from occupational/personal pensions, whether these are DB or DC systems. 'Who pays?' looks at the financing of the contributions and possible deficits (underfunding) of private pensions. The final section 'who governs, decides and manages?' analyses the problems of governance and regulation, the modes in which employees' interests are represented, and how supervision is regulated.

4. Bismarckian latecomers to multipillar pension systems (Part II)

In Chapter 3, Johan J. De Deken argues that Belgium's public–private pension mix can be considered a paradox: despite the conservative-corporatist welfare regime and rather limited Bismarckian social insurance for old age, voluntarist occupational pensions remained underdeveloped. Until recent pension reforms, the comparatively low replacement rates of public pensions did not lead to the development of extensive occupational plans, even if several institutional conditions that elsewhere advanced the expansion of supplementary pensions were given. The chapter also reviews the governance of private pensions, discussing how recent attempts to broaden access to occupational pensions have been facilitated and frustrated by the decision to embed those schemes into the neo-corporatist system of collective agreements. Although this allows to extend coverage of private pensions for lower-income groups, at the same time it also severely limited the possibility to mobilize funds that are necessary to guarantee adequate income maintenance for the general population.

In Chapter 4, Marek Naczyk and Bruno Palier discuss the French efforts to promote funded pensions in Bismarckian Corporatism. Following its social insurance tradition, the post-war pension system of France has been characterized by occupational fragmentation, its strong reliance on PAYG financing, and by the direct involvement of employers and trade unions in their management. Generous benefits offered a combination of statutory public pension and mandatory occupational pensions, initially crowding out any funded private pensions. However, pension reforms that promoted retrenchment both in the two PAYG-financed statutory public and occupational pension schemes since the 1990s have resulted in the gradual development of funded private pensions. In recent years, the governance of mandatory occupational schemes has been harmonized, and inequalities between different occupational categories have been reduced. While the regulatory framework governing voluntarily funded plans (both occupational and personal pensions) has been largely unified, access to these schemes remains mostly limited to high-skilled employees.

Chapter 5 by Bernhard Ebbinghaus, Mareike Gronwald, and Tobias Wiß discusses to what degree Germany has departed from its Bismarckian public pension tradition. The chapter first reviews the emergence and change of the public–private pension mix in Germany, emphasizing the path-dependent but recent path-departing developments from the Bismarckian social insurance tradition. The politically contentious pension reforms of the 1990s and subsequent reforms in the 2000s followed a strategy of institutional layering by introducing a voluntary personal ('Riester') pension, while fostering coexisting occupational pensions. At the same time, the reforms of public pensions made voluntary private pensions necessary for status maintenance in old age. The second part analyses the structure and governance of occupational and personal pensions in Germany, highlighting the new instruments for the design of occupational pensions such as collective agreements and collective pension institutions self-administered by employers and trade unions. The chapter concludes with an outlook on the future, discussing potential scenarios for institutional change and its consequences for old age income in Germany.

Finally, among the Bismarckian pension systems, Chapter 6 by Matteo Jessoula discusses Italy's efforts towards multipillarization under adverse conditions. In Italy, the move from a dominant public pension pillar based on a PAYG-financed Bismarckian social insurance towards a multipillar system is an instructive example of a 'top-down' process pursued by governments in order to compensate for the far-reaching pension reforms in the 1990s. Change began during difficult socio-economic and financial conditions when policymakers opted to exploit the pre-existing severance-pay scheme as an 'institutional gate' in order to boost private supplementary pensions. However, this strategy ruled out compulsory affiliation to the new funded schemes, thereby limiting their potential coverage. The establishment of supplementary pensions has recently given rise to a 'new politics' putting pressure on policymakers, employers, and trade unions for regulatory harmonization between occupational funds and personal pension schemes.

5. Emergent Nordic multipillar pension systems (Part III)

Jørgen Goul Andersen describes Denmark's silent revolution towards a multipillar pension system in Chapter 7. Denmark developed a multipillar pension system, adding private pensions to its universal flat-rate, tax-financed 'people's pension'. Following the failure to introduce a public earnings-related supplementary pension, fully funded 'labour market' pensions were added through collective agreements between employers and trade unions, extending these occupational pensions to nearly all employment groups since the early 1990s. Comprehensive institutional change took place almost without any legislation by non-state actors, except for the reform of the public basic pension which became increasingly means tested. Private pension governance is typically left to pension funds or to special life insurance companies jointly owned and controlled by unions and employers. Strict rules protect pension funds against financial shocks, but these were eased during the financial crisis to improve returns on these DC pensions. Nevertheless, the Danish pension system looks quite satisfactory from both an economic and social policy perspective.

Chapter 8 on Finland by Olli Kangas and Päivi Luna reviews the move from statutory pension dominance towards voluntary private schemes. Finland's pension system consists of income-tested 'national pensions' and statutory employment-related pensions. The latter are 'hybrid' public–private pensions that were legislated in the 1960s and partly funded through private insurance companies, while employers and trade unions participate in their administration. There is a strong corporatist element: the social partners have been owners of the statutory schemes, therefore they channelled improvements through 'their' own schemes, not via voluntary private pensions as elsewhere. Since the mandatory employment-related pensions are income-related with no ceilings, the high-income earners have had no incentives to contract voluntary supplementary pensions. However, this is changing through a piecemeal institutional change: as statutory pension promises are cut back, an expansion of voluntary occupational and individual pensions occurs.

Gabriella Sjögren Lindquist and Eskil Wadensjö argue in Chapter 9 that Sweden has a viable public–private pension system. The Swedish pension system developed through different stages from the establishment of the first statutory basic pension, the introduction of an earnings-related supplementary pension, and collectively negotiated occupational pensions to the most recent institutional change. A comprehensive pension reform was finally decided in 1994 which led to a switch to an earnings-related insurance with a notional defined-contribution (NDC) and a mandatory funded personal pension component (premium pension). In the second pillar, occupational pensions negotiated by employers and trade unions came under financial pressures due to the decline of industrial employment, which led to some restructuring such as the gradual switch from DB to DC pensions. The chapter also examines the governance and design of these occupational schemes as well as personal pensions.

6. Mature multipillar pension systems (Part IV)

Paul Bridgen and Traute Meyer argue in Chapter 10 that Britain has exhausted voluntarism. The British pension system – with a meagre basic pension in the Beveridge-tradition and coexisting private pensions that have increasingly been transformed from DB to DC pensions – has generally been viewed as consistent with the liberal welfare and production regime types. While this classification is appropriate for some elements, from the 1950s onwards a strong statist side was expressed through the role of the state as employer and as regulator, with important consequences for the scale of state provision and the coverage and governance of occupational provision. The dynamics set in place by these arrangements lie behind recent pension reforms. These serve to enhance the hybrid pension system, moving it in a clearly more social-democratic direction. However, the financial crisis and the change of government in 2010 mean that this movement may be halted before it had really begun.

Chapter 11 by Karen M. Anderson discusses the Dutch adaptation of a multi-pillar pension system to demographic and economic change. The Netherlands departed from the Bismarckian social insurance tradition by combining flat-rate public basic pensions with quasi-mandatory, funded occupational pensions with near universal coverage. The emergence, expansion, and reorganization of occupational pensions show their close integration with the public pension scheme. Many efforts helped expand coverage through collective agreements by employers and trade unions. Short case studies of pension funds in the public and private sector highlight the core features of the Dutch system as well as its institutional variation. In the wake of the financial crisis, occupational pensions were scaled back since DB pensions were threatened by underfunding. Current debates question the future viability of the Dutch system in an era marked by both demographic ageing and volatile financial markets.

Finally, Giuliano Bonoli and Silja Häusermann draw important lessons in Chapter 12 from the regulation of the multipillar pension system of Switzerland, which is considered a prototype. It includes both public and private, PAYG-financed social insurance and mandatory funded occupational pensions. As many European countries introduced supplementary funded pensions over the last several decades, Switzerland has become an instructive case for policymakers looking for lessons in pension fund governance, in particular concerning underfunding and guarantees in DC pensions during financial crises. However, the Swiss case does not provide a simple blueprint of effective regulation: governance of supplementary pensions not only involves employers and trade unions but it also entails continual political renegotiation. More-over, the Swiss case also demonstrates the difficulties of effective regulation because governance practice tends to deviate from the formal rules both to the detriment and to the advantage of the sponsors, the insured, and the benefit recipients.

7. The comparative analyses (Parts I and V)

In addition to the individual country chapters, this volume contains three comparative chapters that systematically examine the varieties of pension governance across Europe. As a first comparative overview, Chapter 2 by Bernhard Ebbinghaus and Mareike Gronwald maps the evolution of the public–private mix of old-age pension provision in the ten European countries. It describes the ways in which past decisions in expanding public pensions had major repercussions by defining the space of development for private (occupational and personal) pensions. The process of institutional change is examined by analysing three critical junctures in a comparative historical analysis. First, the early decisions leading towards a Bismarckian earnings-related social insurance for older workers or a Beveridge-type basic pension for citizens to prevent poverty had major implications for further reforms. The second juncture was the successful (or failed) expansion of public pension systems to safeguard the living standards of the middle classes by earnings-related state pensions, leaving less (or more) space for private initiatives that crowd 'out' (or 'in') non-state supplementary pensions. Finally, the more recent pension reforms are evaluated as to their impact on the public–private pension mix, indicating that 'path departure' has been possible in recent shifts away from state and towards private responsibility for old age income. Given the contemporary global economic crisis, the question of institutional change and reform potentials in these complex systems is more important than ever.

Following the country analyses, Chapter 13 by Bernhard Ebbinghaus and Tobias Wiß provides a comparative overview on the governance modes of supplementary pensions, the scope for collective or state regulation, and the different modes of financing mechanisms. It asks how these variations in governance and regulation impact the coverage, type of pension benefits, and its funding. The analysis of the selected European countries indicates a wide variety of supplementary pension governance types, which combine many different features in terms of coverage, benefit calculation, funding rules, super-vision, and administration. While the state has partially retreated from the public responsibility to finance sufficient state pensions, the need for and importance of state regulation and societal control of private pensions has increased. Societal actors like trade unions, employers' associations, and finan-cial service firms have become more important in regulating and governing pension systems. The ongoing changes of the public–private mix thus imply not only a privatization with decentralization of responsibilities on to private actors but also more self-regulation by collective bargaining partners as well as increased state re-regulation. The challenge is to balance both public and private responsibility for sustainable and adequate pension income in old age, especially as citizens' longevity extends and the economic situation remains more volatile.

Finally, Chapter 14 by Bernhard Ebbinghaus and Jörg Neugschwender ana-lyses the effect of public and private pensions on the incomes of retired people for the ten selected countries, using available international survey data on retirement income packages by individuals and households. Analysing overall poverty rates and income inequality indicators for older people (aged 65 and older), Chapter 14 discusses significant differences in pension systems and social inequalities. While the reduction of poverty risks is largely due to the minimum income protection in public pension systems, cross-national differ-ences in inequality are due to existing market income differences, the overall public–private pension mix that intervenes in redistribution, and the degree to which unequal protection arises from private pension arrangements. Focusing on private (occupational and personal) pensions, we then compare disparities in coverage as well as the degree to which pensioners receive private pensions and their share of transfer incomes. Analyses by gender, income group, and past employment career provide insights into the ways in which private pension systems may amplify market-generated social inequalities in old age. For the later third of the life course in the developed democracies, historically evolved pension systems determine who will age in relative security and who will face growing older with risks and fears.

8. Will Europeanization and globalization lead to convergence?

The reform of pension systems and the governance of private pension schemes are increasingly influenced by European political and economic integration (Natali 2008) as well as the globalization of financial markets (Clark 2003). Generally, European integration restricts the making of social policy on national level though 'negative integration' (Scharpf 1996), that is, market-making via deregulation. It is difficult to agree on redistributive policies at a supranational level. For instance, the European Court of Justice Barber ruling of 1990 imposed equal retirement ages for men and women in private pensions, but it led to a Maastricht Treaty amendment that limited its retroactive impact on past pensions (Pierson and Leibfried 1995). Most importantly, the European Monetary Union's deficit criterion provides a rationale for cost-cutting pension reforms since the 1990s. The Greek debt crisis in 2010 has increased pressures to cut back public pension, leading not only in Greece to social conflicts about pension retrenchment. Thus, other countries with large public debt followed suit, such as the French government's decision in June 2010 to raise official retirement age from 60 to 62. The European Union's Open Method of Coordination (OMC), by developing indicators and common objectives, invited EU member-states to adapt their policies in fighting social exclusion, achieve financial sustainability of social budgets, and foster welfare state modernization (de la Porte and Pochet 2002; Zeitlin et al. 2005). Most prominently, the EU's target to increase the employment rate among older workers aged 55 to 64 to above 50 per cent by 2010 has added pressures to the ongoing reversal of early retirement policies across Europe (Ebbinghaus 2006b). However, due to the high political salience and particular institutional conditions, pension reforms nevertheless remain largely within the national political realms and follow its own electoral political logic.

Where pension issue meets internal market rules, the EU also takes on direct responsibility: it regulates supplementary pensions through the passage of directives regulating the private insurance market. As early as 1998, Directive

98/49/EC guaranteed the portability of acquired pension rights. The Pension Fund Directive 2003/41/EC established a European market for pension funds. The directive regulates disclosure, cross-border administration of pension funds, principles of investment ('prudent investor rule'), and the calculation of actuarial reserves. Contrary to the first draft, the final directive did not include criteria for social, ecological, and ethical investments because it would lower the rate of return. Although the Pension Fund Directive liberalizes the pension market to some extent, Haverland (2007) argues that EU member-states largely succeeded in securing the national prerogative in social policy, while business and financial service interests were too fragmented to advance a more liberalized directive. Moreover, 'the preservation of national competence on social and labour law and the burden on individual IORPs (Institutions for Occupational Retirement Provisions) to conform with such a wide range of social, labour and tax rules have largely hindered the hoped for spread of pan-European pension plans' (Guardiancich and Natali 2009: 25).

The response to the financial crisis by international organizations such as the OECD (Organisation for Economic Co-operation and Development) has been rather cautious, suggesting that governance of private funded pensions should be improved not only by a more balanced portfolio and prudent investment rules but also it warned to backtrack on public pension reform and ongoing privatization (Antolín and Stewart 2009). The immediate impact of the financial crisis of 2008 was considerable losses in pension fund assets of 10–20 per cent not only in the mature multipillar pension systems of Britain, the Netherlands, and Switzerland but also in the emergent pension fund systems of Denmark and Sweden (OECD 2009: Figure 1.3). This led to considerable immediate underfunding of DB pension schemes or lowering of the short-term if not medium-term returns for those individuals expecting to draw on their DC plans soon. Those pension fund schemes with less risky investment strategies fared better, indicating the importance of oversight, if not quantitative portfolio restrictions.

The more long-term impact of the financial crises during the 2000s may be the disenchanting effect on individuals concerning the returns on saving for retirement after the sustainability problems of public pension have already led to a loss in confidence. These current economic problems increase the problems for social risk groups to contribute to voluntary private pensions (Meyer et al. 2007), while public pensions will collect less contribution to finance the acquired rights of pensioners. Moreover, the severe pressures on fiscal policies and public debt increase the pressure for governments to further control costs of public pension systems. While these long-term implications of the current financial crisis remained to be seen, the comparative analyses and country studies collected in this volume will provide a comprehensive overview of the current stage of public–private mix in retirement income responsibility and the different modes of private pension governance and regulation. Despite the long-term trend towards privatization and these pressing challenges, the cross-national varieties of pension governance discussed in the subsequent chapters will certainly remain important for the coming years.

Bibliography

Adema, W. (1999). 'Net Public Social Expenditure'. *OECD Labour Market and Social Policy Occasional Papers, 39.*

Antolín, P., and Stewart, F. (2009). 'Private Pensions and Policy Responses to the Financial and Economic Crisis'. *OECD Working Papers on Insurance and Private Pensions, 36.*

Arza, C., and Kohli, M. (eds.) (2008). *Pension Reform in Europe. Politics, Policies and Outcomes.* London: Routledge.

Bonoli, G. (2001). 'Political Institutions, Veto Points, and the Process of Welfare State Adaptation', in P. Pierson (ed.), *The New Politics of the Welfare State.* New York: Oxford University Press, 238–64.

——(2003). 'Two Worlds of Pension Reform in Western Europe'. *Comparative Politics*, 35: 399–416.

Bridgen, P., and Meyer, T. (2005). 'When Do Benevolent Capitalists Change Their Mind? Explaining the Retrench-ment of Defined-benefit Pensions in Britain'. *Social Policy & Administration*, 39/7: 764–85.

Clark, G. L. (2003). *European Pensions and Global Finance.* Oxford: Oxford University Press.

——and Whiteside, N. (eds.) (2003). *Pension Security in the 21st Century, Redrawing the Public–Private Debate.* Oxford: Oxford University Press.

de la Porte, C., and Pochet, P. (eds.) (2002). *Building Social Europe through the Open Method of Co-ordination.* Bruxelles: PIE-Peter Lang.

Ebbinghaus, B. (2006a). 'From Path Dependence to Path Departure in Welfare Reform Analysis'. *European Politics & Society Newsletter*, 5/2: 1–4.

——(2006b). *Reforming Early Retirement in Europe, Japan and the USA.* Oxford: Oxford University Press.

——(2009). 'Can Path Dependence Explain Institutional Change? Two Approaches Applied to Welfare State Reform', in L. Magnusson and J. Ottosson (eds.), *The Evolution of Path Dependence.* Cheltenham, UK: Edward Elgar, 191–212.

——(2010). 'Reforming Bismarckian Corporatism: The Changing Role of Social Partnership in Continental Europe', in B. Palier (ed.), *A Goodbye to Bismarck? The Politics of Welfare Reforms in Continental Europe.* Amsterdam: Amsterdam University Press, 255–78.

——and Hassel, A. (2000). 'Striking Deals: Concertation in the Reform of Continental European Welfare States'. *Journal of European Public Policy*, 7/1: 44–62.

——and Manow, P. (eds.) (2001). *Comparing Welfare Capitalism: Social Policy and Political Economy in Europe, Japan and the USA.* London: Routledge.

Esping-Andersen, G. (1990). *Three Worlds of Welfare Capitalism.* Princeton, NJ: Princeton University Press.

——(1996). 'Conclusion: Occupational Welfare in the Social Policy Nexus', in M. Shalev (ed.), *The Privatization of Social Policy? Occupational Welfare and the Welfare State in America, Scandinavia and Japan.* London: Macmillan, 327–38.

Flora, P., and Heidenheimer, A. J. (eds.) (1981). *The Development of Welfare States in Europe and America*. New Brunswick: Transaction Books.

Gilbert, N. (2002). *Transformation of the Welfare State: The Silent Surrender of Public Responsibility*. New York: Oxford University Press.

Goodin, R. E., and Rein, M. (2001). 'Regimes on Pillars: Alternative Welfare State Logics and Dynamics'. *Public Administration*, 79/4: 769–801.

Guardiancich, I., and Natali, D. (2009). 'The EU and supplementary pensions: Instruments for integration and the market for occupational pensions in Europe'. *ETUI Working Paper, 2009/11*.

Hacker, J. S. (2005). 'Policy Drift: The Hidden Politics of US Welfare State Retrenchment', in W. Streeck and K. Thelen (eds.), *Beyond Continuity. Institutional Change in Advanced Political Economies*. Oxford: Oxford University Press, 40–82.

Hall, P. A., and Soskice, D. (eds.) (2001). *Varieties of Capitalism: The Institutional Foundations of Comparative Advantage*. New York, NY: Oxford University Press.

Haverland, M. (2007). 'When the Welfare State Meets the Regulatory State: EU Occupational Pension Policy'. *Journal of European Public Policy*, 14/6: 886–904.

Hinrichs, K. (2000). 'Elephants on the Move: Patterns of Public Pension Reform in OECD Countries'. *European Review*, 8/3: 353–78.

Holzmann, R., Orenstein, M. A., and Rutkowski, M. (eds.) (2003). *Pension Reform in Europe: Process and Progress*. Washington, DC: The World Bank.

Howard, C. (1997). *The Hidden Welfare State: Tax Expenditures and Social Policy in the United States*. Princeton, NJ: Princeton University Press.

Immergut, E., and Anderson, K. (2007). 'Editors' Introduction: The Dynamics of Pension Politics', in E. Immergut, K. Anderson and I. Schulze (eds.), *The Handbook of West European Pension Politics*. Oxford: Oxford University Press, 1–45.

———— and Schulze, I. (eds.) (2007). *The Handbook of West European Pension Politics*. Oxford: Oxford University Press.

Jackson, G., and Vitols, S. (2001). 'Between Financial Commitment, Market Liquidity and Corporate Governance: Occupational Pensions in Britain, Germany, Japan and the USA', in B. Ebbinghaus and P. Manow (eds.), *Comparing Welfare Capitalism: Social Policy and Political Economy in Europe, Japan and the USA*. London: Routledge, 171–89.

Kitschelt, H. (2001). 'Partisan Competition and Welfare State Retrenchment: When do Politicians Choose Unpopular Policies?' in P. Pierson (ed.), *The New Politics of the Welfare State*. New York: Oxford University Press, 265–302.

Leisering, L. (ed.) (2010). *The New Regulatory State. Regulating Pensions in Germany and the UK*. Routledge, forthcoming.

Leisering, L., et al. (2002). *Vom produzierenden zum regulierenden Wohlfahrtsstaat: Eine international vergleichende und interdisziplinäre Studie des Wandels der Alterssicherung in Europa*, Regina Arbeitspapier Nr. 2. Bielefeld.

Marshall, T. H. (1950). *Citizenship and Social Class. The Marshall Lectures*. Cambridge: Cambridge University.

Merrien, F.-X. (1998). 'Governance and Modern Welfare States'. *International Social Science Journal*, 55/155: 57–67.

Meyer, T., Bridgen, P., and Riedmüller, B. (2007). *Private Pensions Versus Social Inclusion? Non-State Provision for Citizens at Risk in Europe*. Cheltenham: Edward Elgar.

Müller, K., Ryll, A., and Wagener, H.-J. (1999). *Transformation of Social Security: Pensions in Central-Eastern Europe*. Würzburg: Physica-Verlag.

Myles, J., and Pierson, P. (2001). 'The Comparative Political Economy of Pension Reform', in P. Pierson (ed.), *The New Politics of the Welfare State*. New York: Oxford University Press, 305–33.

Natali, D. (2008). *Pensions in Europe, European Pensions: The Evolution of Pension Policy at National and Supranational Level*. Brussels: P.I.E. Peter Lang.

OECD (ed.) (2004). *Reforming Public Pensions. Sharing the Experience of Transition and OECD Countries*. Paris: OECD.

——(2009). *Pensions at a Glance 2009. Retirement-Income Systems in OECD countries*. Paris: OECD.

Orenstein, M. A. (2008). *Privatizing Pensions. The Transnational Compaign for Social Security Reform*. Princeton, NJ: Princeton University Press.

Palier, B., and Bonoli, G. (1995). 'Entre Bismarck et Beveridge: "Crises" de la Sécurité Sociale et Politique(s)'. *Revue Française de Science Politique*, 4/45: 668–99.

Pedersen, A. W. (1999). *The Taming of Inequality in Retirement: A Comparative Study of Pension Policy Outcomes*. Oslo: FAFO.

Pierson, P. (1996). 'The New Politics of the Welfare State'. *World Politics*, 48/2: 143–79.

——(1997). 'The Politics of Pension Reform', in K. G. Banting and R. Boadway (eds.), *Reform of Retirement Income Policy*. Kingston/Ontario: School of Policy Studies, 273–93.

——(2001a). 'Coping with Permanent Austerity: Welfare State Restructuring in Affluent Democracies', in P. Pierson (ed.), *The New Politics of the Welfare State*. New York, NY: Oxford University Press, 410–56.

——(ed.) (2001b). *The New Politics of the Welfare State*. New York, NY: Oxford University Press.

——and Leibfried, S. (1995). 'Multitiered Institutions and the Making of Social Policy', in S. Leibfried and P. Pierson (eds.), *European Social Policy: Between Fragmentation and Integration*. Washington, DC: Brookings Institution, 1–40.

Rein, M., and Rainwater, L. (eds.) (1986). *Public/Private Interplay in Social Protection: A Comparative Study*. Armonk, NY: M.E. Sharpe.

——and Schmähl, W. (eds.) (2004). *Rethinking the Welfare State. The Political Economy of Pension Reform*. Cheltenham, UK: Edward Elgar.

——and Wadensjö, E. (eds.) (1997). *Enterprise and the Welfare State*. Cheltenham, UK: Edward Elgar.

Reynaud, E., apRoberts, L., Davies, B., and Hughes, G. (eds.) (1996). *International Perspectives on Supplementary Pensions*. Westport, CT: Quorum.

Rhodes, R. A. (1996). 'The New Governance: Governing Without Government'. *Political Studies*, 44: 652–67.

Scharpf, F. W. (1996). 'Negative and Positive Integration in the Political Economy of European Welfare States', in G. Marks et al. (eds.), *Governance in the European Union*. London: Sage, 15–39.

Schludi, M. (2005). *The Reform of Bismarckian Pension Systems. A Comparison of Pension Politics in Austria, France, Germany, Italy and Sweden*. Amsterdam: Amsterdam University Press.

——(2008). 'Between Conflict and Consensus: The Reform of Bismarckian Pension Regimes', in C. Arza and M. Kohli (eds.), *Pension Reform in Europe. Politics, Policies and Outcomes*. London: Routledge, 47–69.

Shalev, M. (ed.) (1996). *The Privatization of Social Policy? Occupational Welfare and the Welfare State in America, Scandinavia and Japan*. London: Macmillan.

Streeck, W., and Thelen, K. (eds.) (2005). *Beyond Continuity. Institutional Change in Advanced Political Economies*. Oxford: Oxford University Press.

Titmuss, R. M. (1958). *Essays on the 'Welfare State'*. London: Allen and Unwin 1976.

Weaver, K. R. (1986). 'The Politics of Blame Avoidance'. *Journal of Public Policy*, 6/4: 371–98.

Zeitlin, J., Pochet, P., and Magnusson, L. (eds.) (2005). *The Open Method of Co-ordination in Action: The European Employment and Social Inclusion Strategies*. Brussels: P.I.E.-Peter Lang.

2

The Changing Public–Private Pension Mix in Europe: From Path Dependence to Path Departure

Bernhard Ebbinghaus and Mareike Gronwald

1. Introduction

Current international and national public debates focus on the need to reform pay-as-you-go (PAYG)-financed public pension systems under the pressures of ageing societies and advocate for private funded pensions. This policy shift towards 'privatization' and multipillar systems has been advanced not only by national policy advisers but also by international organizations, from the IMF to OECD to the European Union (EU). However, contemporary pensions systems remain distinct with considerable country-level variation due to the historically specific development of the public–private mix and different reform trajectories across countries in recent years. We therefore present a comparative-historical account that reveals the cross-national similarities and differences in the shaping of private pensions in Europe in the context of earlier decisions concerning public pensions.

While comparative analyses of public policies have provided us with a better understanding of the major differences in welfare state regimes (most notably Esping-Andersen 1990), the evolution of the public–private mix needs closer scrutiny (for an early study, see Rein and Rainwater 1986; Shalev 1996*b*). Any definition of private pensions meets the largely soft, often historically shifting, and nationally specific borderlines of differences between public and private, universal and status group specific, mandatory and voluntary, collective and individual, state-regulated and self-regulated schemes (Shalev 1996*a*: 4–7). Comparative welfare analysis has largely focused on public policy (Immergut et al. 2007), while the firm-provided or collectively negotiated *occupational* welfare arrangements as well as voluntary personal pension savings have been the focus of less empirical scrutiny (Rein and Schmähl 2004; Rein and Wadensjö 1997), partly because they seem to be less widespread, more fragmented, and in a state of flux. In recent years, however, there has been renewed interest in the role of employers and unions in shaping not only public but also private social policy (Ebbinghaus 2006; Trampusch 2007). Despite these studies, we still lack a systematic comparative account that explains the different 'paths' of public pension developments and the shift towards private pensions.

Our comparative-historical analysis attempts to map the cross-national institutional diversity in the evolution of the public–private mix of old-age pension provision in ten European countries.[1] After a discussion of the main thesis on historical sequence, this chapter describes the way in which institutional arrangements in private (occupational and personal) pensions evolved over time and interact with the public system. In the following, the process of institutional change is examined by analysing *critical junctures* in the evolution of the public–private pension mix. First, the early legacy and path-dependent postwar dynamics in the formation of state pensions will be sketched in a comparative diachronical account. In particular, the early path-dependent decisions towards basic pensions (*à la* Beveridge) or earnings-related social insurance (*à la* Bismarck) will be compared. The second juncture compares successful versus belated or even failed expansion of public pension systems to include earnings-related second-tier pensions in Beveridge-type systems or versus the further expansions of earnings-related pension benefits in Bismarckian systems to secure living standards in old age. The main focus will be on the question of whether these public pension decisions had a stimulating or limiting impact on private pension development. Finally, the more recent pension reforms from above and evolution from below will be considered with regards to the changing public–private pension mix. Indeed, countries that had crowded out occupational and personal pensions have seen a recent shift towards adding such schemes, while those mature multipillar systems have faced the question of how to regulate the privatized pillars.

2. Critical junctures and path dependence

Historical institutionalists see *institutions* as enduring principles and rules emerging from more or less conscious choices by collective actors at critical junctures generating taken-for-granted expectations that govern behaviour (see also Ebbinghaus 2005). Even if it is often impossible to precisely predict a critical juncture, retrospective analysis can reveal the factors leading to changes

---

[1] The analysis of individual countries is based on the country chapters in this volume unless otherwise referenced.

of an existing or the emergence of a new institution as the result of the inter-actions of collective action by individual and corporate actors in a given histor-ical situation (Stinchcombe 1968). However, this does not imply that the institution was necessarily planned; it could also be the outcome of unintended consequences. The critical juncture model serves first and foremost as a working hypothesis that needs to be investigated by comparative-historical research.

Path dependence has been claimed for pension policy given the long-term commitment of PAYG systems, thus contributors expect to receive benefits in the future as a matter of acquired rights. Particularly, Conservative welfare states have been seen as reform-incapable due to status quo defence, leading to path-dependent inertia. Recent empirical studies on reform processes seek to go beyond time-invariant fixation of welfare regime analysis (*à la* Esping-Andersen) and adopt a more differentiated analysis that also focuses more closely on 'two worlds' of pension systems (Natali 2008; Palier and Bonoli 1995): the Bismarck-ian social insurance and the Beverdige-type basic pension. Adopting an institu-tionalist perspective, the timing and sequence of events is of importance for subsequent development. Bismarckian PAYG systems promised early on earn-ings-related benefits in return to deferring wage increases, binding future gen-erations to past decisions (Myles and Pierson 2001). Beveridge-type systems with less strict contribution-to-benefit expectations have more leeway to public inter-ventions, but this depends on whether earnings-related supplementary pen-sions were introduced as 'early-birds' or 'latecomers' (Hinrichs 2000: 358). In some countries, government's non-decisions (Hacker 2005) in the public pen-sion area 'crowded in' private schemes, compensating the income gap left by flat-rate state pensions.

The evolution of the public–private pension mix is characterized by two junctures that led to *path-dependent* regimes, and a more recent third juncture of *path departure*. Public policy, in particular social security, has an impact on the opportunities for private forms of old age provision, but this pattern also holds in the opposite direction. Moreover, the state-as-employer as well as the state-as-regulator shape occupational welfare in addition to its direct responsibility for the state schemes. In pension insurance, probably more than in other policy arenas, the national legacies weigh heavily in post-war development given the long-term consequences of pension commitments. In old age security systems, the early decisions towards a Bismarckian (earnings-related) social insurance or a Beveridge-type basic pension for all citizens have had major repercussions for private pension development (for similar approach, see Natali 2008). There are two major sets of hypotheses, more or less explicitly advanced in the literature (Hinrichs 2000; Whiteside 2006): the 'crowding-out' thesis which explains the limited scope for private pensions given the generous Bismarckian public pen-sions, and the 'crowding-in' thesis which predicts the rise of occupational pensions in systems with inadequate state pensions, particularly for higher-income groups.

The low degree of private pension development under Bismarckian systems is commonly attributed to the goal of status maintenance, guaranteed by the earnings-related public pensions, thereby crowding out private pensions (Øverbye 1996). The crowding-out thesis postulates that Bismarckian pension systems, such as in Germany, are limiting the scope for the development of private pensions because state pensions provide sufficient earnings-related benefits. Moreover, it is assumed that the involvement of trade unions and employers in the self-administration of social insurance, common in Bismarckian schemes (Ebbinghaus 2010), minimizes their interest in establishing additional collective pension schemes.

The crowding-in thesis suggests that Beveridge-type basic pension systems, particularly those 'lite' systems that did not develop a sufficient and mature earnings-related state second pension (Myles and Pierson 2001), have the largest potential for occupational pension development. This was the case in Great Britain, where an earnings-related supplementary pension was introduced much later, and employers or individuals were given the opportunity to 'opt out' from the state second pension. However, in Beveridge 'plus' systems, such as in Sweden that introduced earnings-related state pensions at an earlier stage, the need for additional private or occupational pensions is more limited. However, it is not only government inactivity in the area of public pension improvement that incrementally crowds in occupational and personal pension schemes. Trade union strategies and employers' actions also require analytical scrutiny. Unions have tended to push for state pension improvement first, but when employers are willing to negotiate occupational pension in return for wage moderation, an opportunity for collective schemes emerges.

More recent reforms, however, indicate that 'path dependence' in the sense of path stabilization may be overcome. Path departure becomes increasingly likely when more significant changes in the environment occur and the self-reinforcing mechanism provides sufficient resources for gradual adaptation (Ebbinghaus 2005). Here, the most relevant idea is of 'open' path dependence, in which earlier decisions narrow the choice set but do not determine the next adaptive step. Path departure lies between locked-in inertia, when nothing effectively changes the basic foundation, and radical system change, when everything is built *de novo*. Yet between these extremes, path departure also entails various forms and often occurs through a variety of simultaneous change processes (Streeck and Thelen 2005). First, there are long-term gradual changes that accrue over time to important reorientations (Pierson 2000). Second, functional conversion can lead to transformation whereby the same institution serves a different purpose than initially intended (Thelen 2003). Third, institutional layering occurs through adding (new) institutional arrangements with divergent orientations (Thelen 2003). These different processes of institutional change can be observed for the development of pension systems. Moreover, the private pension development can be linked to changes in the state pillar, particularly when the retrenchment of public pensions increases the need for private responsibility.

At the contemporary juncture of pension reform, there might be path departure in pension development such that laggards in multipillarization have recently fostered private schemes. To evaluate if pension policy has departed from its former 'path', we not only need to study the politically induced current transformation process but also scrutinize the effects of ongoing privatization 'from below'. A multitude of comparative politics approaches attributed the success or failure of structural pension reforms to the 'veto points' provided by political institutions (Bonoli 2001) and the electoral competition between political parties (Immergut et al. 2007). In order to limit electoral repercussions, the New Politics thesis assumes that politicians use obfuscating or blame-diffusing strategies through consensus building (Weaver 1986) or social pacts with unions and employers (Schludi 2005). These comparative political studies offer an explanation of the varying capacities for welfare state reform, but they also revealed the unintended consequences public policy could provoke in the responses of non-state actors. However, these comparative political analyses focused on the 'big' politically contentious reforms at the institutional level, whereas the gradual privatization advanced by collective actors and individuals remained largely neglected. While these studies treated the development of occupational and personal pensions rather as a by-product of the politically induced reforms, we aim here to look more closely at the interaction between 'top-down' public reforms and 'bottom-up' responses by private actors.

3. The first juncture and path dependence: Bismarck vs. Beveridge

While some company pension schemes predate state pension legislation, the introduction of mandatory public old age insurance had an important impact on the subsequent development. For understanding today's public–private mix, it will suffice to focus on the final outcome of the early development of retirement income systems that survived (or were reformed) after the Second World War. Viewed with the benefit of hindsight, our analysis summarizes the result of a longer (and sometimes inconsistent) history from 1880s up to the 1950s. This first juncture, in our analysis, was posed by the fundamental decision to introduce either a Bismarckian social insurance for major occupational groups such as in Germany in 1889 or a basic pension for older people ('Beveridge' *avant la lettre*) before or around the First World War (Flora and Heidenheimer 1981; see Table 2.1).

We classify those pensions that are contributory schemes that pay earnings-related benefits and are mandatory for particular occupational groups according to the 'industrial-achievement' model (Titmuss 1974) as *Bismarckian* systems.

Table 2.1 The first juncture: Bismarck vs. Beveridge public pensions

	Formation (before/around WWI)	Reconstitution (after WWII)
Bismarck social insurance path		
Belgium	1924 flat-rate pension (manual workers); 1925 earnings-related pension (white-collar)	1945 tax-financed pension complement
France	1910 workers and peasants insurance	1945 régime général
Germany	1889 blue-collar 'invalidity' insurance 1911 white-collar pension insurance	1949 restoration law (pre-war scheme)
Italy	1919 blue-collar insurance	1950 no income limit
	1939 white-collar insurance	1952 two-tier pension
Switch to Beveridge pension		
The Netherlands	1913 old age insurance for workers	1947 means-tested pension
		1956 universal flat-rate basic pension
Switzerland	1926 referendum, but 1931 law failed	1948 universal earnings-related pension
Beveridge basic pension path		
Britain	1908 means-tested flat-rate pension 1925 contributory old-age pension	1946 basic old-age and widow pension (contributory but flat-rate benefits)
Denmark	1891 means-tested old age assistance	1956 tax-financed basic pension
Finland	1937 general funded pension scheme	1956 universal basic pension
Sweden	1913 contributory basic pension, tax-financed means-tested supplement	1948 tax-financed basic old-age and widow pension

Source: Flora (1986): Appendix Vol. IV; Immergut et al. (2007); and country chapters this volume.

This definition entails three constitutive features: (*a*) it is a contributory social insurance paid by employers and employees (*parity principle*), (*b*) the benefits are related to former earnings (*equivalence principle*), and (*c*) it is mandatory for particular occupational groups, often organized into special schemes and self-administrated by these occupational groups (*occupational solidarity*). Although the Bismarckian pensions were providing limited benefits and restricted to some occupational groups, the later evolution led to more comprehensive coverage and benefits.

We group those public pensions that initially were means-tested benefits for the older poor but later developed into a universal basic pension based on citizenship rights as Beveridge-type. The British Beveridge report of 1942 tackling the giants of 'Want, Disease, Ignorance, Squalor and Idleness' had extended the idea of universal social benefits and public services as 'citizenship rights' (Marshall 1950). Beveridge assumed that under full employment, everyone (or at least every family breadwinner) would be able to gain income from work, and only those who could not work – for instance, due to old age – would receive basic subsistence. Constitutive for the Beveridge-model is: (*a*) a mandatory state pension for all citizens or residents (*universalism*), (*b*) the provision of flat-rate benefits (*basic pension*), and (*c*) financing through general taxes or non-credited payroll contributions (*publicly financed*). A major step was the removal of means testing for the basic pension, though basic pensions have often means-tested supplements for those with no sufficient second-tier pensions.

The decision to install an earnings-related contributory social insurance (Bismarck model) or a universal basic pension (Beveridge model) thus was the first crucial step in the long development of post-war old age income retirement systems. Decisions taken at this early juncture remained path dependent even through the immediate post-war reconstitution which reconfirmed and extended these early decisions in nearly all cases. Indeed, this path dependency prevailed despite two major world wars, the economic and political interwar crisis in many countries, and the extension of mass democracies. Among the ten countries studied here, four Continental European countries remained on a Bismarckian path, while Britain and the Nordic countries embarked on a Beveridge course. Although the Beveridge Report of 1942 was hotly debated on the Continent, only in one country, the Netherlands, can we observe a system change from Bismarck to Beveridge and in one other country, Switzerland, the belated pension development resulted in a mixed model.

3.1 The Bismarckian path

The early introduction of an 'invalidity' pension insurance for workers in Germany was part of Bismarck's strategy to respond to the ills of industrialization and tie the manual workers to the new nation-state, while repressing the rise of the labour movement (Alber 1982). Before the First World War, the German pension system already entailed its constituting future features: mandatory social insurance schemes organized into and self-administered by broad social 'status' groups, with parity contributions. Special pension benefits for white-collar employees (introduced in 1911) aimed already at status maintenance, in line with the (non-contributory, tax-financed) pensions for tenured civil servants (*Beamte*) which until today remain outside compulsory social insurance.

Other Continental European countries such as France, Italy, and the Netherlands were among the first countries to emulate the German social insurance model, albeit not as fast and as far reaching given their belated and more uneven industrialization. In comparison to Germany, Belgium was despite early industrialization quite delayed in developing Bismarckian pensions. Although special schemes for seamen and miners existed before, old age and 'invalidity' insurances were introduced in 1924 for manual workers (flat-rate pensions started in 1930) and for white-collar employees in 1925 (earnings-related pensions started immediately). By the Second World War, the occupationally divided Belgian pension schemes had become *de facto* flat-rate pensions, and only after several stop-and-go reforms during the 1950s, earnings-related pensions were re-established for manual workers and for salaried employees.

Late-industrializing Italy introduced a social insurance only in the interwar period, first for blue-collar workers (1919) and then for white-collar employees under the Fascist regime (1939). As a new nation-state, Italy also developed favourable special schemes in the civil service and public sector. Although there had been attempts to replace the occupational fragmentation by a more universalist social security system, these post-war efforts failed due to the still large agricultural labour force, small craft and commercial shops, a political patronage tradition, and a semi-feudal regime in the South. This led instead to particularist–clientelist Italian 'pensioner state' (Ferrera 1996).

In France, a contributory statutory workers and peasants pension scheme was installed in 1910 with rather small pensions. The Bismarckian model was introduced in France with the annexation of Alsace and Lorraine after the First World War. Despite the centralist state approach, the development of French social security is characterized by a strong corporatist tradition (Korpi 1995). Parafiscal schemes, rather than the state, are the main guarantor for old age security (Niemelä et al. 1996). Despite a debate on the Beveridge Report, French policymakers reconstructed a social security system in 1945 with a statutory pension scheme (*régime général*) that offered basic provision for blue- and white-collar employees. However, different occupational groups, such as civil servants, self-employed, and farmers – who have had their own schemes for several years – insisted on maintaining their privileged separate systems. Due to a rather low ceiling on pensionable earnings, labour market organizations were encouraged to create supplementary schemes based on collective agreements leading to the installation of AGIRC, an occupational supplementary pension scheme for private sector executives.

3.2 The Bismarck to Beveridge path

Two exceptional cases of pension development stand out on the Continent: The Dutch and Swiss. The Netherlands switched from Bismarckian corporatist to Beveridge-type basic pensions. An important feature of the Dutch society has been its cleavages along ideological and religious lines. Each of these groups had its own school systems, civic organizations, and voluntary social security arrangements. The first public pension scheme for manual and white-collar employees was introduced in 1913, although it was characterized by low coverage and small benefits. However, the Netherlands did not stay with its Bismarckian pension system after the Second World War; indeed the exiled-government in London was strongly influenced by the Beveridge model. A means-tested pension was introduced by the Emergency Law for everyone over 65 independent from the previous employment record, thereby switching towards a basic pension model. Eleven years later, the provisory was replaced by a universal flat-rate basic pension (AOW), completing the transition into a Beveridge system. However, long before the basic pension was legislated, the private industry had introduced voluntary pensions by individual firms or sector agreements. As benefits from and coverage by public pension had been rather low, occupational pensions developed and expanded in order to satisfy the social needs. Legally binding status for collective agreement in industries was provided to the Labour Ministry in 1949. When the statutory basic pension was introduced, policymakers had to solve the issue of how to treat wage earners already covered by occupational pensions, leading to the tight coupling between public and occupational pensions. Occupational pension rights accrue only for income above the AOW gross benefit and if public pensions decrease occupational pensions have to complement this gap (Anderson 2007).

Switzerland, due to its decentralized political system and uneven industrial development, was the other Continental country with a rather exceptional development. Although political efforts for a public pension existed since the late 1880s, the first referendum on old age security at the Federal level was passed in 1926, but the subsequent pension legislation failed. No final decision was made until the referendum of 1947 that led to the introduction of a mandatory public old age provision as of October 1948 that embraces Bismarckian earnings-related social insurance and Beveridgian universal basic pension principles. The contributory, earnings-related pension scheme (AHV/AVS) applies to all residents. Yet the difference between minimum and maximum benefits is insubstantial, thereby leaving much space for occupational and private pensions. Moreover, the lack of a public old age provision before 1948 had fostered the early expansion of occupational pension plans, thus a quarter of the population had already been covered by these private plans.

3.3 The Beveridge path

Although the German contributory social insurance scheme has been discussed at the time, Denmark decided as early as 1891 on means-tested, tax-financed 'relief' for people above 60 years in the tradition of the poor laws which emphasized poverty alleviation and the maintenance of a minimum living standard. In contrast to Germany, Denmark was a more agricultural society with only a small industrial workforce. Therefore, the first pension system primarily reflected farmers' interests (Niemelä et al. 1996). Denmark's tradition of a tax-financed public basic pension was renamed an old-age pension in 1922 and reconstituted for people above 65 in 1946. Finally, it was expanded into a universal (but earnings-tested) National Pension in 1956 under a Social Democrat-led government. At the same time, the attractiveness of private (occupational and individual) pensions increased through the introduction of generous tax incentives (Green-Pedersen 2007).

In Great Britain, a Bismarckian social insurance was also refuted after long political debates between Liberals and Conservatives, industrial and rural interests (Baldwin 1990). Despite Britain's flourishing 'friendly societies', poverty in old age became a pressing problem especially for the less skilled. In 1909, the Liberal government introduced a non-contributory, flat-rate, and means-tested pension financed by general taxes. Although contributory National Insurance was later introduced for health insurance and unemployment as well as a contributory pension for 'early' retirement at 65 in 1925, the constitutive element remained the basic pension. The Beveridge reform of the old age and invalidity pension in 1946 provided relatively low benefits. But neither poverty was eradicated, nor were the pensions sufficient for skilled workers and white-collar employees to maintain their living standard in old age, thus leaving much responsibility for private initiative.

Sweden also rejected Bismarckian social insurance proposals (opposed by farmers and employers), enacting in 1913 a universal contribution-financed basic pension with a tax-financed means-tested supplement for those who had no or only low basic pensions. In the interwar period, the financing principle was changed from funding to PAYG, and the eligibility criteria were expanded. In the 1940s, first discussions started about complementing the basic pension with an earnings-related pension, though some private occupational pensions already existed. In 1948, the Swedish state pension was restructured into a more generous tax-financed universal pension, abandoning the means test completely.

The agrarian social structure substantially influenced early Finnish social policies as farmers blocked the implementation of an insurance scheme demanded by industrial workers, proposing instead a universal pension scheme. Heated debates between Conservatives, who favoured a savings-based fully funded system, and Social Democrats, who preferred a tax-based PAYG system, preceded the introduction of the first public pension system in 1937. The final compromise between the agrarians, Conservatives, and Social Democrats was a nearly universal, premium-based, funded system with tax-financed supplements. After the war, pension fund assets were used to build up the economy and infrastructure. Low benefit levels, the exclusion of the majority of the elderly from receiving benefits due to the long maturation period, and the fear of post-war inflation led to the revised National Pension in 1956. A universal, contributory, PAYG basic pension was established, complemented by an income-tested flat-rate supplement for people in employment, thereby fostering universalism and equality but reducing the national pension funds financial contribution.

3.4 The extension of the two paths

The first juncture in the public–private pension mix in these European welfare states was the decision for a Bismarckian or Beveridge-type pension. This historical decision occurred before the 1950s for nearly all countries except Switzerland and the Netherlands. Continental European countries (Germany, Belgium, Italy, and France) institutionalized Bismarckian pensions long before 1945 and then reconfirmed this decision thereafter, whereas Britain and the Nordic countries (Denmark, Sweden, and Finland) installed Beveridge-type basic pensions and then extended these afterwards. The Netherlands remains the main exception in switching from a Bismarckian tradition to a Beveridge basic pension, while Switzerland was late in introducing what became a mix of universalism with earning-related benefits.

The difference between Bismarckian old age insurance and Beveridge-type basic pension is also evident from the expansion in coverage. The former schemes are only partially and stepwise inclusive as they extend to ever more occupational groups, whereas by definition the latter universal schemes extend to all citizens (or residents). Figure 2.1 provides the long-term development of

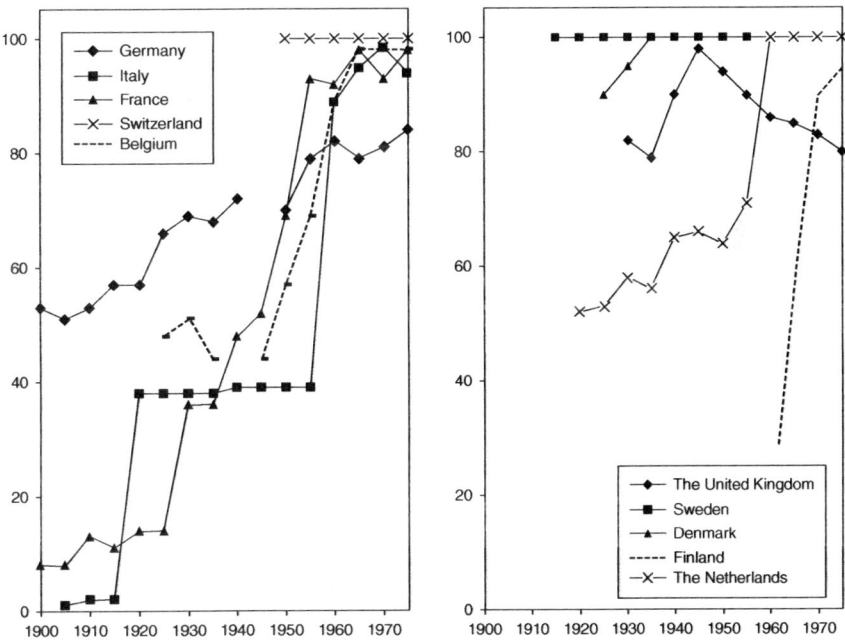

Figure 2.1 Coverage rate of state pensions (per cent labour force), 1900–75

Sources: Flora et al. (1983): I.7; Scruggs (2004): Finland: legislated occupational pension.

coverage of public pensions in relation to the labour force across these European countries from 1900 until 1975 (Flora et al. 1983). Given the occupationalism of social insurance, coverage in Bismarckian systems remained initially lower than for basic pensions that extended to the entire population. Among the Bismarckian systems, Germany had the highest coverage rate (above 50 per cent) already before 1914, covering all blue- and white-collar employees outside agriculture, and increasing over the interwar period to more than two-thirds of the working population, followed by the Netherlands with the second highest coverage level during the interwar period. Italy and France were much later in extending their bases of insured groups beyond one fifth, since the 1920s in Italy and in the 1930s in France. While France and Italy increased coverage by extension to all groups of employees and to the self-employed, Germany and the Netherlands increased the level of coverage only partly in the immediate post-war period. Among the Beveridge-type pension systems, coverage in Sweden, Denmark, Finland, the Netherlands (since 1957), and Switzerland (since 1948) is all inclusive with the exception of the United Kingdom, where contributory national insurance coverage varies across time and the Finnish statutory occupational pension that was stepwise introduced during the 1960s in addition to the universal basic pension.

4. The second juncture: post-war public or private income maintenance

Economic growth and increasing wages in the late 1950s inspired the debate about extending social security in order to find a solution for the growing gap between living standard during employment and retirement income. Thus, the concern for *income maintenance* in old age became the dividing issue of the second juncture in the evolution of the public–private pension mix. According to the crowding-out thesis, we would expect that to the degree that European welfare states developed generous basic pensions and/or earnings-related social insurance, occupational pensions played a less important role (Esping-Andersen 1996; Kangas and Palme 1996). These different choices in social solidarity, however, had important consequences for the emergence of a second system of supplementary pensions either as part of a second state pension or left to occupational private pensions. However, semi-public collective schemes negotiated by the social partners or mandatory occupational pensions assumed the function of public second-tier pensions in France, Switzerland, Finland, and the Netherlands, while negotiated supplementary pensions became common in Sweden, later in Denmark, and very recently partly in Belgium and Germany (see Table 2.2).

Table 2.2 The second juncture (1950s–80s): Bismarck vs. Beveridge-plus or -lite

	State pension	Private pension	OP
Bismarck systems			
Belgium	1950s phasing-out of funding principle for private sector schemes	1970s early retirement as part of industry-wide CA	L
	1967 unified system for all private sector employees	1984 reduced tax exemptions for OP	
France	1945 *régime général*: flat-rate	1947 CA (cadres); 1961 CA (workers)	H*
		1972 mandatory semi-public OP*	
Germany	1959 expansion (equivalence, PAYG)	Occupational pension: topping up	L
	1972 further social rights	1974 occupational pension regulation	
Italy	1960s expansion of pensions, minimum pension, public debt	Occupational pension secondary, but 1982 end-of-service pay (*Tfr*)	L
Nordic Beveridge systems			
Denmark	1956 tax-financed National Pension 1960 only flat-rate ATP supplement	Widespread voluntary OP: income maintenance	M
Finland	1957 basic pension, 1980s reforms	1961–6 OP becomes mandatory (funding within statutory pension)	L
Sweden	1948 tax-financed basic pension	1960 redesign of public and private white-collar CAs	(M)
	1960 second pension (ATP)	1970s CA for blue-collar workers	
Multipillar Beveridge systems			
Britain	1959 graduated pension	1979 opt-out OP	M
	1975 second pension (SERPS)	1986 opt-out PP	
The Netherlands	1947 means-tested pension 1956 universal flat-rate basic pension	1947 erga omnes CA	H
Switzerland	1946 universal earnings-related pension	1985 mandatory OP	H

Notes: CA: collective agreements; L = low; M = medium; H = high; *unfunded.
Source: Flora (1986): Appendix Vol. IV; Immergut et al. (2007); and country chapters this volume.

4.1 Bismarck-plus and crowding out

The aim of status maintenance attributed to Bismarckian pensions was closely tied to the German post-war pension reform of 1957 that introduced a new formula, increased contribution rates, and most importantly changed from funded to PAYG financing, allowing to provide better benefits to current pensioners, including the refugees from the East. After German unification in 1990, these PAYG pensions allowed the honouring of pension rights accumulated by East Germans under the state-owned economy. This meant financing a large share of transition costs through social insurance contributions but it also led to massive pressures on labour costs. Until recently, occupational pensions provided by many large firms (often on a book reserve basis) and negotiated public sector pensions were supplementary benefits that 'topped up' Bismarckian pension benefits, allowing to attract the better skilled employees. These pensions were largely unregulated until 1972 and remained rather neglected by German social policymaking.

Moving somewhat towards a Beveridge-orientation in the 1950s, Italy introduced two-tier benefits (flat-rate plus earnings-related) and a minimum pension for those without sufficient contribution records. The poverty problem became a pressing issue again in the 1960s, and in response social funds were allocated for improved minimum pensions. The expansion of pension insurance to agricultural labour and the self-employed had also helped in reducing poverty. With the exception of public sector employees and banking, special occupational pensions were not common in Italy until government efforts sought to foster private pensions since the 1990s. However, a functional substitute to occupational pension is the 'end-of-service pay' (*trattamento di fine rapporto* or *Tfr*), an accumulated portion of wages that is paid by the employer as a lump sum severance pay upon exit from work (Di Biase et al. 1997). First common as a deferred wage in collective bargaining, the *Tfr* was made mandatory for all employers in 1982.

Similar to the other Bismarckian systems, the Belgian public pension pillar has been expanded in order to achieve the goal of status maintenance, particularly for low-income groups (due to a rather low wage ceiling for the calculation of benefits) whereas higher-income groups would seek private insurance. Several reforms in the 1950s reinforced the equity principle by tightening the link between entitlements to welfare benefits and past labour market performances. Two other important measures were introduced in 1967. First, the separate schemes for private sector blue- and white-collar employees were merged into a single pension system, though schemes for civil servants and the self-employed continue to exist. Second, the guarantee of means-tested assistance for persons not covered by any of the compulsory schemes was introduced. In the arena of private pensions, there has been an extensive development of negotiated occupational pension schemes. Mutual benefits funds, group insurance schemes, and firm-based occupational pension plans have multiplied since the 1960s, though most have largely focused on white-collar employees with higher incomes.

4.2 Bismarck-lite and crowding in

The improvement of benefit levels and the expansion of coverage have also been on the political agenda in France. In the French case, these have focused attention most heavily on national occupational pension schemes. Next to AGIRC for managerial and professional 'cadres', a second national occupational pension scheme, ARRCO, was established for the majority of private sector employees in 1961, and the participation in these schemes has been made compulsory by state extension in the same year. Thus, for the private employees, the mandatory first-tier pension is supplemented by a quasi-public occupational pension that is, however, also a PAYG system as in the first tier. Although it is considered here as a private system, it is not completely comparable to funded private schemes.

4.3 Beveridge-plus early, late, or partially?

Among the Beveridge-type systems, the most exceptional development was the introduction of a second-tier earnings-related state pension in Sweden. The blue-collar union movement had called for a statutory superannuation scheme similar to the one that many white-collar employees enjoyed from company pension plans long in existence. The Social-Democratic government realized that, although manual workers were in favour of their proposal, the 'white-collar wage earners, in turn, were the wild card in the hand played for superannuation' (Baldwin 1990: 215). After a popular referendum on the issue in 1957, the break-up of the Left–Agrarian coalition, electoral gains into white-collar votes by the Social Democrats, and a one-vote majority in parliament, a supplementary compulsory pension scheme (ATP) for all wage earners (and self-employed with contracting-out option) was implemented in 1960. At that time, white-collar unions had negotiated occupational pensions, and the blue-collar unions followed in the 1970s, developing supplementary pension PAYG-financed by employers' contributions, though it was turned into a partially funded scheme in 1996 (Palme and Svensson 1997: 20). In the public sector, there are two other major collective schemes which have been negotiated for the central government and local public sector. The other Beveridge-type systems considered here did not include as far-reaching reforms as Sweden; they were either late or incomplete in adding supplementary state pensions, thus leaving more space for private pension development.

At the same time of the Swedish ATP reform, a 'graduated' (earnings-related) pension scheme was introduced in Great Britain (1959). However, 'the need to resolve with one blow the subsistence and superannuation issues' (Baldwin 1990: 211) limited the contributory 'graduated pension'. This insufficient supplementary scheme led many white-collar employees and some skilled workers to abstain from 'contracting in'. Instead, they relied on their more favourable occupational company pensions. With increasing inflationary pressures since 1973, the low flat-rate and insufficient supplementary state scheme required government action, leading finally to a reform in 1975. The graduated scheme became wounded up in 1978 with the phasing-in of the mandatory 'supplementary earnings-related pension scheme' or SERPS (Lynes 1997). The contribution to this second pension is paid by the employer, who can also decide to contract out of this general PAYG-scheme and join an occupational pension if it offers at least a 'guaranteed minimum benefit'. Except for the civil (and armed) services which have special schemes (non-contributory, tax-financed, and non-funded pensions), a larger share of wage earners (including public employees without civil servant status) had joined occupational pensions, and most were in opt-out schemes in the 1980s.

4.4 Beveridge-lite and crowding in

In the Netherlands, much like in Denmark, the role of the public pension pillar was mainly to provide a socially acceptable minimum income for everyone and not to provide earnings-related benefits. Beginning in the early post-war period, the Dutch society had become more secular and the societal division less important which made the development and expansion of the national social security system easier (Niemelä et al. 1996), and thus public pension benefits and coverage were improved. The Dutch pursued the goal of income maintenance by combining the generous public pension with the private occupational pensions through linking the defined benefits of the second tier to those of the first tier.

Switzerland is not only a hybrid between Bismarck and Beveridge, it is also *the* multipillar pension model. During the post-war years, the public pension was gradually improved with regards to benefit level and eligibility criteria. However, because pension benefits, in contrast to pension contributions, are only related to earnings between a narrow lower and an upper income ceiling, pension income from the public pillar resembles more a basic pension. With nine reforms of the AHV/AVS pension scheme between 1951 and 1976, the Swiss public pillar went through a comparatively high number of reforms. An attempt by the Communist Party to reform pensions in a Bismarckian manner failed as the right-of-centre government reacted with a counter-proposal favouring a multipillar solution. The government prevailed by suggesting that occupational pensions will be made mandatory for all employees, winning through this manoeuvre the national referendum in 1972. However, the mandatory occupational pension (*Obligatorium*) was delayed until 1985 due to legislative debate concerning the economic problems and uncertain impact of such compulsion (Queisser 2000).

Finland is a hybrid multipillar case since the 1960s when occupational pensions were legislated, yet they remain administered by the social partners and partially funded through the private insurance sector. The expansion of the Finnish old age security system focused primarily on the occupational pension pillar, while the public pension did not experience any larger reforms since its introduction in 1956. Since the late 1950s, a rapid growth of occupational pensions can be observed but coverage rates remained comparatively low because white-collar workers in big companies were integrated in the same plan and these were mostly bound to a specific employer. To advance guaranteed pension portability and extended coverage, especially for blue-collar workers, the trade unions demanded a legislated compulsory scheme. The employers' federation concluded that it was better to cooperate and suggested a legislated but decentralized partly funded scheme managed by private insurance companies. In 1961, employment-related occupational pensions were fully legislated and made mandatory for all private sector employees and short-term employees, followed by systems for municipal (1964) and state employees (1966), both PAYG systems, and finally by farmers and the self-employed (1970). The targeted first-tier pension is income-tested against other pensions, including the second-tier occupational pension, reinforcing the important income function of the latter.

The Danish 'golden years' of welfare development are characterized by two major trends following strong economic growth and full employment. First, there was a gradual extension and improvement of the existing National Pension. Extensive changes were made to the scope of coverage, entitlement rules (dismantling of means test) and benefits. Second, the importance of private occupational and personal pension schemes increased over time. The attempt to create a statutory earnings-related pension, akin to the Swedish model, was not successful. In 1964, a statutory funded pension (ATP) was introduced as a reaction to the demands of the blue-collar workers' union (LO) to supplement the basic National Pension, but this scheme remained rather limited as contributions were based on working hours and not income. For middle- and higher-income groups, the ATP pension did not provide a sufficient supplement to maintain the former living standard during retirement and some groups were already covered by occupational pension schemes. Thus, a two-pillar pension system emerged with a relative generous public basic pension and private quasi-mandatory supplementary pensions.

4.5 Crowding out/in revisited

The analysis of the second juncture reveals the different paths towards income maintenance through public or private means. After the introduction of a Bismarckian or Beveridge-type pension and its post-war reconstitution, the subsequent step was the general expansion in scope and benefits and the rise of supplementary schemes to fill the gap left by less generous statutory pension benefits, with long-term consequences for the development of occupational pensions (see Figure 2.2). The Beveridge-type welfare states, despite efforts to introduce social insurance elements, had first introduced a basic flat-rate pension scheme for all citizens, while the Bismarckian systems institutionalized an earnings-related social insurance based on occupational groups.

The basic decisions concerning public pensions (basic vs. earnings-related pensions) entailed important consequences for occupational pension

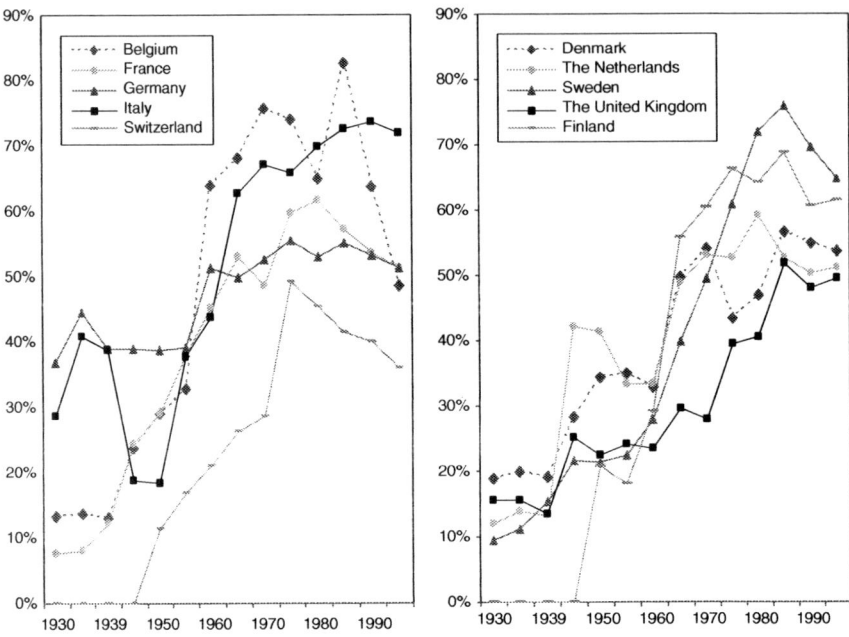

Figure 2.2 Net replacement rates of statutory pensions, 1930–95

Sources: Korpi, W. and Palme, J. (2008): SCIP Database 1930–95, http://hdl.handle.net/10102/1497Palme.

development. Given the low flat-rate basic pension and the 'opt-out' option of the incompletely developed superannuation schemes in Britain, the developmental niche left to non-state pensions was largest among the four Beveridge-type basic pension systems. Sweden, on the other hand, indicates that superannuation in combination with a basic pension system can take a different route, especially when trade unions of blue- and white-collar employees have the power to press and negotiate statutory supplementary and collective occupational plans.

In the Bismarckian systems, occupational pensions never assumed such an important role for old age income, nevertheless many employers provided occupational schemes in Germany and end-of-service payments in Italy. Today, all governments propagate private pension funds as a solution to the long-term financial problems of the PAYG systems, but whether such second-tier funded systems can actually fill the gap remains to be seen. Indeed, one needs to take a closer look at the interaction of coverage and benefits as well as other aspects of occupational pensions to understand the functional logic and the stratification impacts of private pension solutions.

Table 2.3 The third juncture: path departure?

	State pension	Occupational and personal pensions
Dominant public pillar		
Belgium	1990s parametric reforms of SP	1995 regulation of OP
		2003 collective OP fostered
France	1993 reform of private sector scheme	1990s agreement on OP reforms
	2003 reform of private and public sector schemes	2003 voluntary personal pension (PERP)
Germany	1990s/2000s reduction of state benefits; phasing-in age 67	2001–4 voluntary PP (Riester); Collective OP fostered
Italy	1990s NDC, phasing-in age 65, harmonization of private sector and public sector schemes, reduction of income maintenance role	2000 tax incentives for voluntary private pensions
		2004/5 compulsory *Tfr* transfer to OP
Emergent multipillar systems		
Denmark	No reform of national pension possible, except 'special pension' PP	1991 collective OP private, sector and firm OP
		1997/8 mandated PP (Special Pension as part of public pension pillar)
Finland	1990s earnings-test against income from other legislated pensions	1990s gradual cutbacks in mandatory occupational pensions, increased funding; efforts to increase personal pensions
Sweden	1994/9 Income Pension (NDC); transfer-tested Guarantee Pension, benefit cutbacks	1994 mandated PP (part of SP); Collective OPs change to DC
Mature multipillar systems		
Britain	2002 reform of SERPS into S2P	1995 regulation of OP
	2006 phasing-in age 68	2001 Stakeholder Pension (PP)
The Netherlands	1990s suspension of indexation of benefits	1997 OP regulatory framework + expansion of coverage
	1997 tax-financed AOW reserve fund	2006 further improvement of OP regulation
Switzerland	2003 failed pension reform	1985 mandatory OP
		1994/2003 regulatory changes

Notes: NDC: notional defined contributions; PP: personal pension; OP: occupational pension; BP: basic pension; SP: state pension.
Source: Immergut et al. (2007); GOSPE-Project country chapters.

5. Third juncture: institutional change and path departure

European welfare states have grown to their limits (Flora 1986). The rising mass unemployment, increased early retirement, and inflationary pressures following the first oil crisis in 1973 in conjunction with the ongoing ageing of societies have caused increasing public deficits. These economic and demographic problems challenge the financial sustainability of public pension systems. This affects the PAYG systems, predominant in the Bismarckian pension systems as well as in most of the countries with Beveridge-type systems. The retrenchment policies in the 1980s and early 1990s were introduced gradually, but even more radical approaches to reshape pension systems were constrained by the specific institutional structure already in place (Natali and Rhodes 2008; Pierson 1994). In particular, PAYG systems are seen as resistant to change if compared to a funded private pension system, given the double-payer problem of current payers who have to honour the acquired rights of current pensioners and save for their own future benefits (Myles and Pierson 2001).

The new pressures and challenges translated into different problems depending on their existing arrangements and governance institutions. We can distinguish three public–private pension configurations and subsequent problem loads: the Continental dominant public pension systems that are late in developing a multipillar system, the Nordic pension systems with hybrid privatization tendencies, and the mature mulitpillar systems (Britain, the Netherlands, and Switzerland). Countries with an expensive PAYG-financed Bismarckian public pension such as Belgium, France, Germany, and Italy engaged in introducing new pillars of occupational and/or personal pensions, while fostering cutbacks in the public pension. The Nordic countries combine universal public pensions with specific second-tier pensions that represent very hybrid multipillar solutions. Countries with developed multipillar pension systems such as Britain, the Netherlands, and Switzerland were mainly concerned with the improvement of the regulatory framework for private pension pillars under the new economic conditions. There are two concerns guiding recent private pension reforms: First, how to introduce private pension schemes and establish a multipillar system? And once established, how to regulate and govern existing occupational and personal pension schemes? Within each group of countries dealing with the same issues, somewhat different policy solutions can be detected that reflect the specific institutional design of the pension pillars (see Table 2.3).

5.1 Reforming dominant public-pillar systems: fostering private pensions

Germany's Bismarckian pensions, relying largely on social contributions and PAYG financing, faced the financial repercussions of an aggravated labour market and changing demographics since the late 1970s. The implications of the extensive use of the early retirement and the integration of East Germany after unification in 1990 posed additional challenges. While the pension reform decided in 1989 was still consensual in reducing early retirement pathways, pension reforms in the late 1990s remained politically contentious, including the new red–green government's reversal of retrenchment policies by its predecessor in 1999. However, the Schröder government soon realized the inevitability of reforms and reduced public pension benefits, while also introducing a new personal pension and fostering occupational pensions to make up for the future retirement income gap. The state subsidizes a new voluntary funded personal pension (called the Riester pension) that includes tax-incentives for lower-income groups. The reforms of the early 2000s also opened up new opportunities for unions to negotiate collective agreements on deferred wages. It also enabled the reorganization of the exiting firm-provided occupational pensions as well as the supplementary pension scheme in the public sector.

Although in the early 1980s Italy legislated a few measures to check inflationary pressures caused by pensions, major reforms were postponed until the 1990s, when the old party system was discredited and the financial markets and European Monetary Union required a drastic, overdue policy change. Given the long-term built-up public deficit and the fragmented but well-entrenched pension system, radical reform proposals were difficult to push through. In times of severe political crisis, the Left–Center and later technocratic governments negotiated a reform with the unions in 1995. This social pact decided on the major changes which were phased in: a gradual increase of retirement age to 65, less favourable benefit rules for newcomers to the system (adopting NDC), a rationalization of the multiple state pension plans, regulating the accumulation of pensions: Since the pension reforms of the 1990s, the severance pay arrangements are gradually converted to occupational pensions. New regulations for supplementary pensions were introduced giving rise to a number of collective agreements for defined-contribution (DC) schemes that partially incorporated the existing end-of-service allowances. Moreover, large parts of the public sector were brought under 'private law', following a government–union agreement.

Belgium suffered from similar problems as Italy: high public debt and a costly pension system due to early retirement, leading to a long-term cutback of the public pension benefits (due to an inadequate indexing of maximum reference income) and thus leaving more space for private responsibility. Following, reforms in 1985/6 book reserves and PAYG arrangements for private pensions were ruled out, thus fully funded group insurance gained in importance. The Occupational Pensions Act of 1995 regulated vesting, portability, and equal treatment rights of these funds, enhancing co-determination rights of employees. Following a social partner agreement (2001), a major advancement was legislated in 2003 by providing a framework for extending *erga omnes* sector-wide negotiated pension funds, which may include some risk sharing (including disability benefits and survivor benefits).

In France, the reaction to the increasing financial sustainability issues in the old age security system was to increase contributions as in Germany. Eventually, the government had to introduce incremental benefit cuts in the early 1990s by a *quid pro quo* strategy between the government and the social partners in the private sector but largely failed in the more contentious public sector. Since the late 1990s, the uncertainty about statutory pensions was used by policymakers to encourage individual pension savings, while launching further cutbacks in the statutory pillar. Early retirement incentives were cut back and the contribution period of the civil servants scheme was adapted to the required contribution period of the general pension system. Several agreements between the social partners aimed at stabilizing the PAYG supplementary pensions. The 2003 Raffarin Reform and a more recent reform of the special regimes (2007/8) aimed at further changes of the public pensions in both the private and public sectors to increase contribution periods and introduce DC elements, though these changes have not been completely introduced. A new voluntary personal pension (PERP) was introduced in 2003.

The reform efforts in countries with *dominant* Bismarckian pensions have been targeted on cutting back generous public schemes and fostering occupational and personal pension programmes. Italy introduced *notional* defined contributions (NDC) in public pensions to make benefits more dependent on contributions and the overall employment performance. The German state pensions had already a working-life contribution formula, and the new 'sustainability' factor will automatically cut benefits based on demographic developments. In nearly all Bismarckian pension systems, a process of conversion occurs in the public pillar that transforms the past goal of status maintenance into one of poverty alleviation by long-term reduction of statutory benefits. For instance, the introduction of a means-tested minimum old-age pension in Germany ('*Grundsicherung*'), replacing former social assistance, has the potential to become a quasi-income-tested basic pension as in Nordic countries. These cutbacks in public pensions have been made in order to make pension plans more sustainable for the future, yet they also increase the need for occupational and personal pensions to fill in the income gap.

In Germany and France, a process of institutional layering has taken place, although these two countries introduced *voluntary* and not mandatory personal pensions (Riester pension and PERP respectively). Italy has not introduced a funded personal pension but instead made use of an already existent institution, the mandatory end-of-service pay (*Tfr*), transferring it into a supplementary pension with the option for a closed or open fund. The collective bargaining partners took on the task to negotiate these new occupational pensions. New efforts to negotiate occupational pensions also gained momentum in several other countries. In Germany, favourable rules for negotiated occupational pensions were introduced in the 2000s. Similarly in Belgium, following a social partner agreement, an enhanced legal framework was introduced for occupational pensions that have gained momentum in the late 2000s. Thus, the third juncture has led to considerable path departure, not only changing the Bismarckian core of the public pillar but also fostering the development of occupational and personal pensions. The scaling back of the public pension from its status maintenance aims at crowding in the scope for private pensions to make up for the future income gap. Thus retrenchment and privatization have been twin reform processes.

5.2 Emergent multipillarization – the Nordic cases

Among the Nordic countries, Denmark is the latecomer in developing a multi-pillar system. Danish occupational pensions did not play such a large role in retirement income until the late 1980s, partly due to its generous tax-financed basic pension. Pension system changes have been introduced gradually from below, as evidenced by the dearth of pension reforms since 1964, by a process of 'institutional drift'. Since the early 1980s, the economic crisis and rising public deficits have increased pressure on the pension system, but efforts to cut back public pension or taxing private pensions failed. In 1997, the small Special Pension was introduced as a temporary new funded public pension in order to curtail consumption (it was made permanent in 1998). The link between contributions and benefits was tightened in 2001 in order to achieve actuarial fairness. While civil servants and other public employees were covered by tax-financed retirement pay or a collective occupational pension respectively, only one-third of private sector employees were covered by an employer-provided occupational pension in the 1980s. The Social Democrats and the blue-collar unions argued in favour of a mandatory central pension fund controlled by the unions, whereas the bourgeois government opposed such a plan. After long negotiations between the government, the main political parties, and unions, occupational pensions were introduced as part of private sector collective agreements. The metal workers' push for collective agreements in 1991 led to rapid spread of other earnings-related occupational pensions. Since the 1990s, collective bargaining led to a substantial increase in coverage thanks to strong trade unions, leading to a belated process of multipillarization. As such, Denmark is a case where financial sustainability, regulatory oversight, and governance issues did not (yet) play a role.

The Finnish pension system represents another special case among the multi-pillar systems. In the Finnish case, the employment-related second-tier pension is highly regulated by the state with regards to benefit and contribution levels, yet it is administered by the social partners and investments are managed by private insurance companies. Though classified here as a legislated (or statutory second pillar) occupational pension (different from the EU classification), this second-tier pension differs from other developed multipillar systems. Thus, recent restructuring processes in Finland did not primarily focus on regulatory issues but on financial sustainability, similar to the processes in systems with a dominant public pillar. At first, the National Pension was further developed in the 1980s (abolishment of means test and introduction of early retirement options). The economic crisis of the 1990s marked a turning point. The subsequent reforms introduced cutbacks and adjustments in the legislated occupational pensions.[2] In several reform steps, the National Pension became more or less a minimum pension especially by making it income-tested against the other pensions. The merger of the separate occupational pension funds in the private sector in 2007 was another step to simplify and reduce costs. As these employment-related pensions have been encompassing and generous (no income ceiling), there has not been a decline in demand for supplementary occupational or personal pensions to top up retirement income. However, recent cutbacks of statutory pension benefits and increasing competition among employers for skilled personnel have also increased demand for voluntary private pensions. Financial sustainability issues are more pressing than in the mature multipillar systems due to the special design and the hybrid structure of second-tier pensions.

The Swedish pension system was less affected by the economic crisis than many other countries. Several reform commissions that discussed proposals were inconsequential until the early 1990s, when the financial and unemployment crisis led to drastic changes of the 'Swedish model'. The early retirement for labour market reasons was abolished in 1991. However, the most far-reaching reform step was decided in 1994 by the government and opposition parties. This led to a systemic reform that replaced the basic pension by a transfer-tested Guarantee Pension, while the earnings-related state pension (ATP) was changed into an earnings-related Income Pension and a funded Premium Pension. In contrast to the former ATP scheme, the Income Pension is a notional defined-contribution (NDC) scheme that calculates benefits based on the principle of working-life income. The mandatory funded Premium Pension provides the individual with the choice of pension funds. It represents a new institutional layer, leading to a shift in risks towards the individuals. Sweden is unique in switching its path from a Beveridge-plus (basic pension plus earnings-related second pension) to a Bismarck-type contributory earnings-related system, yet it remains a universal pension system, given the safety net of the Guarantee Pension. In the second pillar, the negotiated blue-collar occupational pension was changed into a partially funded scheme in 1996 and switched to DC systems (Palme and Svensson 1997: 21).

5.3 Reforming multipillar systems: regulation of private pensions

In Great Britain, the Conservative government aimed in the mid-1980s to shift pension responsibility onto private actors. However, the efforts to turn the recently installed supplementary scheme (SERPS) from a PAYG to a funded

---

[2] These adjustments included introducing employee contributions (1993), harmonizing public and private sector schemes (1995), reversing early retirement incentives (1992, 2005), altering pension indexation and further adjustments to demographic changes (1996, 2005).

system faced opposition: 'Employees (and employers) were asked to continue making National Insurance contributions to pay for current retirees while making mandatory contributions to private schemes to fund their own retirement' (Pierson 1994: 61). Heeding the concerns of the middle-class electorate, large-scale employers, and pension fund managers, the government adopted a gradual strategy, phasing in diminished SERPS benefits and fostering opt-out occupational and private plans in the hope for a 'withering away of social insurance' (Erskine 1997: 140). With these reform measures, the British pension system returned to its liberal roots by emphasizing individual responsibility and the market as social security provider.

With increased importance of occupational and personal pension, regulatory issues came to the fore. The 1995 Pension Act, following the EU rulings on equal treatment in private pension, phased in equal pension age of 65 over the next two decades. It also established minimum solvency regulations for occupational pensions following the public outcry generated by the pension fund loss resulting from the Maxwell conglomerate bankruptcy. Coverage of private pensions among lower-income groups remained relatively low due to the high cost of personal pension plans. For this reason, the New Labour government introduced a more affordable Stakeholder Pension Scheme in 2001. It also reformed the SERPS into a state second pension (S2P) in 2002, incrementally introducing flat-rate benefits for earnings above a certain threshold. Moreover, employers increasingly turned defined-benefit (DB) into DC schemes, thus ever more people will receive DC benefits depending on personalized financial risks (Bridgen and Meyer 2005). The reforms of the 2000s were mostly targeted with the goal of improving the regulatory framework of the existing second and third pension pillars and the strengthening of the poverty alleviation function of the public pension pillar.

In the Netherlands, the government reacted to the increasing financial pressures by suspending basic pension increases in the 1980s and making them dependent on economic development in the 1990s, leading to a real-value decline in benefits. Besides resentment among pensioners, the social partners and pension fund managers vehemently criticized the suspension of benefit increases, especially due to benefit coupling, and occupational pensions were forced to compensate for basic pension decreases. However, this increased pension fund costs but it also increased the predictability of benefit expenses. Following pressures from the government in 1997, occupational schemes that allowed early retirement were transformed from unfunded DB schemes to funded flexible DC plans, lowering the financial incentives to exit from work early (Rein and Turner 2001). Since the mid-1990s, occupational pension funds also shifted to individual 'franchise', that is, decoupled from basic pension benefits.

In Switzerland, as a consequence of the broad agreement about the functionality of the existent three-pillar system, the public pension pillar did not experience a major restructuring process in contrast to most other European countries. The plan to cut back public pension benefits failed in 2003. More significant reforms were launched with regard to the occupational pension pillar. In 1994, the portability of pension rights was improved in order to adjust to growing labour market mobility. Another reform step carried out in 2003 included the adaptation of occupational pension benefits to increasing life expectancy. The extension of coverage for atypical workers was rejected, but instead, the earnings threshold which opens access to mandatory occupational schemes was lowered and coverage thereby expanded.

The analysis of recent reforms in these *mature multipillar* systems (Great Britain, the Netherlands, and Switzerland) shows that the problem load was largely a result of unintended consequences. Recent socio-economic changes such as the increase in atypical employment and unstable financial markets brought about 'new social risks' (Bonoli 2006) that the private pension pillars were unsuited to cope with. The reform responses since the 1990s can be described as path-dependent incremental adaptations to the changing socio-economic environment. The improvement of supervisory measures, the expansion of occupational pension coverage, and the adoption of pension rights to more flexible labour markets aim to support the survival of the multipillar model. The financial market crises of the 2000s have put particular stress on funded pension systems, especially in situations where the share of equities has been relatively high.

Whereas regulatory measures were introduced by the state, the increasing shift from DB to DC schemes in occupational pensions can be characterized as changes 'from below' introduced by non-state actors and passively facilitated by the inactivity of state actors, what can be labelled as 'policy drift' (Hacker 2005). Often unobserved by state actors, the employers, company by company, abdicate their former responsibility to guarantee certain DB levels due to increased competitive pressures and financial problems. As long as the state does not interfere, this might lead to significant changes in the original social security function of occupational pensions by shifting responsibilities and risks to the individual.

6. Conclusions

This comparative-historical analysis studied the long-term evolution of public and private pensions in ten European countries, suggesting three critical junctures that shaped the public–private mix until today (see Table 2.4). The *first* juncture was the initial evolution of the public pension, the first pillar. The major decision whether to introduce a Bismarckian contributory and earnings-related pension or to turn means-tested assistance into a Beveridge-type universal basic pension for all citizens (and residents) dates back prior to or around the

First World War. In all countries, except the Netherlands and Switzerland, the subsequent development was following a path-dependent logic, reaffirming the derived pension system after the Second World War. The Netherlands was unique in switching from a social insurance to a basic pension after 1945, acknowledging and integrating the parallel growth of occupational pensions into a Bismarckian-type income maintenance via private means. Switzerland introduced universal earnings-related old age insurance only in 1948, while the coexisting occupational pensions that were part of a multipillar structure were finally made mandatory as late as 1985. While the decision of Bismarck versus Beveridge was crucial for the way in which non-employed groups receive pensions and the consequences for poverty prevention, much depends on the level of the basic pension or earnings-related minimum pensions. Thus, both systems left some developmental space for supplementary occupational pensions, particularly for medium-to higher-income groups not satisfied with the then meagre public pensions.

Crucial for the further development of private pensions, however, was the *second* juncture: the extension of earnings-related pensions in *Bismarckian* systems or the addition of earnings-related second-tier pensions in Beveridge-type systems. Not all Bismarckian pensions developed into a 'Bismarck-Plus' system that allowed middle and upper income classes to maintain their living standards in old age without private pensions. Germany, Belgium, and Italy extended pensions thanks to PAYG financing and economic growth, though Italy and Belgium accumulated increasing public debt for its generous social benefits. The meagre first-tier pensions in France left much to the social partners to add earnings-related supplementary pensions in the post-war period,

Table 2.4 The three junctures

Type	First	Second	Third	Country
Dominant public systems				
Bismarck-Plus	SEP	SEP	SEP+qOP+vPP	Belgium
Bismarck-Lite	SEP	SEP+qOP	SEP+mOP+vPP	France
Bismarck-Plus	SEP	SEP+vOP	SEP+vPP/vOP	Germany
Bismarck-Plus	SEP	SEP	SEP+vOP	Italy
Emergent multipillar systems				
Beveridge-Lite	SBP	SBP+(SEP)+vOP	SBP+(2SEP, PP)+qOP	Denmark
Beveridge-Lite	SBP	SBP+qOP	(SBP) mOP, vPP	Finland
Switch→SEP	SBP	SBP+SEP, OP	(SBP) SEP+mPP, qOP	Sweden
Mature multipillar systems				
Beveridge	SBP	SBP+SEP/OP	SBP+2SEP/OP/PP	Britain
Switch→SBP	SEP→SBP	SBP+qOP	SBP+qOP	The Netherlands
Hybrid	—	SBP+vOP	SBP+mOP	Switzerland

Notes: SBP: state basic pension (means tested); SEP: state earnings-related pension; OP: occupational pension; PP: personal pension; opt-out; /: alternatives; m: mandatory; q: quasi-mandatory; v: voluntary.

the state made these mandatory in 1972. Belgium could also be grouped as a Bismarck-plus pension until more recent erosion, leading to a belated occupational pensions development.

Among the Beveridge-type systems, Sweden was exceptional in introducing a large-scale earnings-related second state pension in 1960 and transforming it into an earnings-related public pension (and a transfer-tested pension) that comes closer to the Bismarckian income maintenance principle. Denmark failed to do more than a flat-rate supplement in the 1960s, and later-funded personal pension remained rather minor, thus providing much space for occupational pensions. In Finland, the earnings-related pensions, with the help of the social partners, became the dominant second-tier pension, and the public basic pension was made means tested. Much later than Sweden, Britain introduced its second pension in 1978, by that time employer-induced occupational pensions had been widespread and were allowed to 'opt-out', and since 1986 individuals are also able to contract out a funded personal pension. Thus, Britain combines a meagre basic pension with a multipillar choice of supplementary pensions. In the Netherlands, public basic pension remained without a second state pension, and instead the Dutch social partners opted for negotiated and employer-led occupational pensions.

The *third* juncture is the recent transformation of the public–private pension mix, be it through increased fostering or regulation of private pensions. Some of these changes have been relatively path dependent in retrenching the public pillar, in particular the more generous pensions, and by introducing measures in reaction to the increased need to regulate occupational and personal pensions. Yet there were also important path-*departing* developments in the public pillar, most notably the pension reforms in Sweden and Italy introducing NDC benefits. Also notable were the introduction of funded personal pensions in public first pillars (Sweden, Denmark) and the introduction of voluntary personal pensions in Germany, Finland, and France. Institutional change occurred here often as twin processes in public and private pensions: reduction of the former increased the push for expansion of the latter. These new private pension arrangements add a new layer to the multipillar, multitier retirement income system. They bring about a transformative change without completely altering the public pillar, though there is a long-term conversion from the status maintenance to a basic income function in the Bismarckian systems. These reform steps indicate a gradual path departure moderated by institutional layering, conversion, or displacement depending on institutional capacities and preconditions. Yet, in the long run, these institutional changes may be the first steps towards a more substantial change in the public–private mix to come in the future.

Bibliography

Alber, J. (1982). *Vom Armenhaus zum Wohlfahrtsstaat: Analysen zur Entwicklung der Sozial-versicherung in Westeuropa*. Frankfurt: Campus.

Anderson, K. (2007). 'The Netherlands: Political Competition in a Proportional System', in E. Immergut, K. Anderson and I. Schulze (eds.), *The Handbook of West European Pension Politics*. Oxford: Oxford University Press, 713–57.

Baldwin, P. (1990). *The Politics of Social Solidarity: Class Bases of the European Welfare States 1875–1975*. Cambridge: Cambridge University Press.

Bonoli, G. (2001). 'Political Institutions, Veto points, and the Process of Welfare State Adaption', in P. Pierson (ed.), *The New Politics of the Welfare State*. New York: Oxford University Press, 238–64.

——(2006). 'The Politics of the New Social Policies. Providing Coverage Against Social Risks in Mature Welfare States', in C. Pierson and F. G. Castles (eds.), *The Welfare State Reader*. Cambridge: Polity Press, 389–407.

Bridgen, P., and Meyer, T. (2005). 'When Do Benevolent Capitalists Change Their Mind? Explaining the Retrenchment of Defined-benefit Pensions in Britain'. *Social Policy and Administration*, 39/7: 764–85.

Di Biase, R., Gandiglio, A., Cozzolino, M. and Proto, G. (1997). 'The Retirement Provision Mix in Italy. The Dominant Role of the Public System', in: M. Rein and E. Wadensjö (eds.), *Enterprise and the Welfare State*. Cheltenham: Edward Elgar, 149–94.

Ebbinghaus, B. (2005). 'Can Path Dependence Explain Institutional Change? Two Approaches Applied to Welfare State Reform'. *MPIfG Discussion Paper, 05/02.*

——(2006). 'The Politics of Pension Reform: Managing Interest Group Conflicts', in G. L. Clark, A. Munnell and M. Orzag (eds.), *Oxford Handbook of Pensions and Retirement Income*. Oxford: Oxford University Press, 759–78.

——(2010). 'Reforming Bismarckian Corporatism: The Changing Role of Social Partnership in Continental Europe', in B. Palier (ed.), *A Goodbye to Bismarck? The Politics of Welfare Reforms in Continental Europe*. Amsterdam: Amsterdam University Press, 255–78.

Erskine, A. (1997). 'The Withering of Social Insurance in Britain', in J. Clasen (ed.), *Social Insurance in Europe*. Bristol: Policy Press, 130–50.

Esping-Andersen, G. (1990). *Three Worlds of Welfare Capitalism*. Princeton, NJ: Princeton University Press.

——(1996). 'Conclusion: Occupational Welfare in the Social Policy Nexus', in M. Shalev (ed.), *The Privatization of Social Policy?: Occupational Welfare and the Welfare State in America, Scandinavia and Japan*. Basingstoke: Macmillan, 327–38.

Ferrera, M. (1996). 'The "Southern Model" of Welfare in Social Europe'. *Journal of European Social Policy*, 6/1: 17–37.

Flora, P. (1986). *Growth to Limits: The Western European Welfare States since World War II*. Berlin: W. de Gruyter.

——Alber, J., Eichenberg, R., Kohl, J., Kraus, F., Pfenning, W., and Seebohm, K. (1983). *State, Economy, and Society in Western Europe 1815–1975. Volume I: The Growth of Mass Democracies and Welfare States*. Frankfurt: Campus.

——and Heidenheimer, A. J. (1981). 'The Historical Core and Changing Boundaries of the Welfare State', in P. Flora and A. J. Heidenheimer (eds.), *The Development of Welfare States in Europe and America*. New Brunswick: Transaction Books, 17–34.

Green-Pedersen, C. (2007). 'Denmark: A "World Bank" Pension System', in E. Immergut, K. Anderson and I. Schulze (eds.), *The Handbook of West European Pension Politics*. Oxford: Oxford University Press, 454–95.

Hacker, J. S. (2005). 'Policy Drift: The Hidden Politics of US Welfare State Retrenchment', in W. Streeck and K. Thelen (eds.), *Beyond Continuity. Institutional Change in Advanced Political Economies*. Oxford: Oxford University Press, 40–82.

Hinrichs, K. (2000). 'Elephants on the Move: Patterns of Public Pension Reform in OECD Countries'. *European Review*, 8/3: 353–78.

Immergut, E., Anderson, K., and Schulze, I. (eds.) (2007). *The Handbook of West European Pension Politics*. Oxford: Oxford University Press.

Kangas, O., and Palme, J. (1996). 'The Development of Occupational Pensions in Finland and Sweden: Class Politics and Institutional Feedbacks', in M. Shalev (ed.), *The Privatization of Social Policy? Occupational Welfare and the Welfare State in America, Scandinavia and Japan*. London: Macmillan, 211–40.

Korpi, W. (1995). 'The Development of Social Citizenship in France since 1930: Comparative Perspectives', in B. Palier (ed.), *Comparing Social Welfare Systems in Europe: Vol. 1. Oxford Conference: France–United Kingdom*. Paris: MIRE, 9–47.

Lynes, T. (1997). 'The British Case', in M. Rein and E. Wadensjö (eds.), *Enterprise and the Welfare State*. Cheltenham, UK: Edward Elgar, 309–51.

Marshall, T. H. (1950). *Citizenship and Social Class. The Marshall Lectures*. Cambridge: Cambridge University.

Myles, J., and Pierson, P. (2001). 'The Comparative Political Economy of Pension Reform', in P. Pierson (ed.), *The New Politics of the Welfare State*. New York: Oxford University Press, 305–33.

Natali, D. (2008). *Pensions in Europe, European Pensions: The Evolution of Pension Policy at National and Supranational Level*. Brussels: P.I.E. Peter Lang.

——and Rhodes, M. (2008). 'The "New Politics" of Pension Reforms in Continental Europe', in C. Arza and M. Kohli (eds.), *Pension Reform in Europe. Politics, policies and outcomes*. London/New York: Routledge, 25–46.

Niemelä, H., Salminen, K., and Vanamo, J. (1996). *Converging Social Security Models? The Making of Social Security in Denmark, France, and the Netherlands*, Vol. 10. Helsinki: The Social Insurance Institution Finland.

Øverbye, E. (1996). 'Public and Occupational Pensions in the Nordic Countries', in M. Shalev (ed.), *The Privatization of Social Policy? Occupational Welfare and the Welfare State in America, Scandinavia and Japan*. London: Macmillan, 159–86.

Palier, B., and Bonoli, G. (1995). 'Entre Bismarck et Beveridge: "Crises" de la Sécurité Sociale et Politique(s)'. *Revue Française de Science Politique*, 4/45: 668–99.

Palme, J. (1990). *Pension Rights in Welfare Capitalism: The Development of Old-Age Pensions in 18 OECD Countries 1930 to 1985*. Stockholm: Swedish Institute for Social Research.

Palme, M. and Svensson, I. (1997). 'Social Security, Occupational Pensions, and Retirement in Sweden'. *Working Paper Series in Economic and Finance, no. 184*, Department of Economics, Stockholm University.

Pierson, P. (1994). *Dismantling the Welfare State? Reagan, Thatcher and the Politics of Retrenchment*. Cambridge: Cambridge University Press.

——(2000). 'Increasing Returns, Path Dependence, and the Study of Politics'. *American Political Science Review*, 94/2: 251–67.

Queisser, M. (2000). 'Pension Reform and International Organizations: From Conflict to Convergence'. *International Social Security Review*, 53/3: 31–45.

Rein, M., and Rainwater, L. (eds.) (1986). *Public/Private Interplay in Social Protection: A Comparative Study*. Armonk, NY: M.E. Sharpe.

——and Schmähl, W. (eds.) (2004). *Rethinking the Welfare State. The Political Economy of Pension Reform*. Cheltenham, UK: Edward Elgar.

——and Turner, J. (2001). 'Public–Private Interactions: Mandatory Pensions in Australia, the Netherlands and Switzerland'. *Review of Population and Social Policy*, 10: 107–53.

——and Wadensjö, E. (eds.) (1997). *Enterprise and the Welfare State*. Cheltenham, UK: Edward Elgar.

Schludi, M. (2005). *The Reform of Bismarckian Pension Systems. A Comparison of Pension Politics in Austria, France, Germany, Italy and Sweden*. Amsterdam: Amsterdam University Press.

Scruggs, L. (2004). *Welfare State Entitlements Data Set: A Comparative Institutional Analysis of Eighteen Welfare States, Version 10*.

Shalev, M. (1996a). 'Introduction', in M. Shalev (ed.), *The Privatization of Social Policy? Occupational Welfare and the Welfare State in America, Scandinavia and Japan*. London: Macmillan, 1–23.

——(ed.) (1996b). *The Privatization of Social Policy? Occupational Welfare and the Welfare State in America, Scandinavia and Japan*. London: Macmillan.

Stinchcombe, A. L. (1968). Constructing Social Theories. New York: Harcourt, Brace & World.

Streeck, W., and Thelen, K. (2005). 'Introduction: Institutional Change in Advanced Political Economies', in W. Streeck and K. Thelen (eds.), *Beyond Continuity. Institutional Change in Advanced Political Economies*. Oxford: Oxford University Press, 1–39.

Thelen, K. (2003). 'How Institutions Evolve: Insights form Comparative-Historical Analysis', in J. Mahoney and D. Rueschemeyer (eds.), *Comparative-Historical Analysis: Innovations in Theory and Method*. New York: Cambridge University Press, 208–40.

Titmuss, R. M. (1974). *Social Policy. An Introduction*. London: Allen & Unwin.

Trampusch, C. (2007). 'Industrial Relations as a Source of Social Policy: A Typology of the Institutional Conditions for Industrial Agreements on Social Benefits'. *Social Policy & Administration*, 10/3: 251–70.

Weaver, K. R. (1986). 'The Politics of Blame Avoidance'. *Journal of Public Policy*, 6/4: 371–98.

Whiteside, N. (2006). 'Adapting Private Pensions to Public Purposes: Historical Perspectives on the Politics of Reform'. *Journal of European Social Policy*, 16/1: 43–54.

Part II

Bismarckian Latecomers to Multipillar Pension Systems

3

Belgium: The Paradox of Persisting Voluntarism in a Corporatist Welfare State

Johan J. De Deken

1. Introduction

Belgium's retirement provision is paradoxical. Despite being embedded in a corporatist welfare state, Belgian public pensions were never generous enough to allow the middle and upper classes to maintain their former income status, while private provisions were until recently rather underdeveloped. Even if several institutional mechanisms which in other countries contributed to the expansion of supplementary pensions existed, the modest nature of statutory provision has not led to a co-evolution of occupational pensions. Only in the past two decades have these 'crowding-in' mechanisms and corporatist traditions come into play. Increasingly, we can see an attempt to transform voluntary private provision into more encompassing occupational pensions.

Following a description of the main features of the overall architecture of the Belgian pension system and its historical evolution, this chapter will analyse the governance of supplementary occupational and personal pensions. The analysis will demonstrate that recent attempts to broaden access to occupational pensions by embedding them into neo-corporatist wage bargaining have both facilitated and frustrated the development of mature second-pillar occupational pensions. While this allowed extending coverage towards lower-income groups, at the same time this institutional mechanism also severely limited the possibility to mobilize the funds that are necessary to guarantee adequate income maintenance to the growing population of future beneficiaries.

Part I: The evolution of the public–private pension mix

2. Pillars and tiers of the Belgian pension system

Belgium is commonly classified as a 'Bismarckian' or 'conservative-corporatist' welfare state, but its pension system qualifies only to a limited extent to what is considered to be distinct for such a regime. The earnings-related gradient of benefits for private sector employees is diluted by a guaranteed minimum benefit and a relatively low ceiling on benefits, whereas contributions are levied on total earnings. In other respects, the Belgian pension system seems to fit the ideal type of a 'conservative-corporatist' regime. In particular, public pensions consist of three occupationally distinct schemes: one for private sector employees, one for self-employed, and one for civil servants. The first two schemes are based on a 'watered down' version of earnings-related social insurance.[1] Employees and their employers jointly pay higher contributions and are entitled to more generous benefits than the self-employed. The public sector scheme is financed from general revenue. It closely follows the principle of a deferred wage and is therefore far more generous than the other two schemes.[2]

These three statutory schemes constitute the core of the Belgian pension matrix of pillars and tiers (see Figure 3.1). They all belong to the first pillar and their main function should consist of guaranteeing income maintenance. However, they effectively perform this second-tier function only for civil servants and for private sector employees with a low to median income. The self-employed and more affluent private sector employees cannot rely upon the first pillar to maintain their income position in retirement. The three schemes still form the most important part of the income package of the current generation of pensioners. For those with an incomplete or precarious work history, some programmes exist through a first-tier function that offers means-tested supplements to keep people out of poverty. These supplements are either financed out of the statutory pension scheme (this is the case for the so-called *inkomensgarantie voor ouderen*) or are paid by the general social assistance scheme (the so-called OCMW *bestaansminimum*).

---

[1] Benefits in the statutory scheme for private employees are based on a formula that includes three elements: (1) the employment career (including the so-called 'equivalent periods'), (2) the previous earnings and (3) the family status. For each year there is a maximum cap on to the reference earnings, which in 2008 amounted to about 120 per cent of the average production worker wage. For the period prior to 1955, a lump sum is used as a reference wage (which especially for older cohorts contracts the span of benefits). The family status is expressed in a weighting factor: for singles or spouses this is set at 60 per cent, whereas for heads of households at 75 per cent.

[2] It grants pensions that are calculated adding up fractions, the so-called *tantièmes*, which for each year of employment normally amount to 1/60 of the average earnings that the public employee enjoyed during the five years prior to his or her retirement.

	First pillar	Second pillar		Third pillar
	Statutory pension	Occupational pension		Personal pension
		Collective agreement	Employer commitment	
Third tier (topping up)				Individual life insurances *(individuele levensverzekering)* private pension savings plans *(pensioensparen)*
Second tier (income maintenance)	Wage earners (and their partners) *werknemerspensioen* compulsory social insurance: parity contributory financing with state subsidies and transfers to other social security branches; pay-as-you-go Self-employed *pensioen van zelfstandigen* similar to wage earner scheme; pay-as-you-go Civil servants *ambtenarenpensioen* deferred wage; general revenue financing	Wage earners: sectoral pension plans *sectorpensioen*	Wage earners group insurances *groepsverzekeringen* company pension funds *bedrijfspensioenfondsen*	
First tier (poverty alleviation)	Wage earners (and their partners) *inkomensgarantie voor ouderen* contributory financing (wage earner scheme with state subisdies)			
	means-tested social assistance *OCMW bestaansminimum* General revenue financing			

Figure 3.1 Pillars and tiers of Belgian pensions

Until a decade ago, the second pillar consisted only of voluntary company-based schemes that employers primarily offered as fringe benefits to a part of their white-collar employees. During the 1990s, attempts started to broaden access to these extra statutory pensions, by creating a framework for industry-wide occupational pension plans. But these attempts so far had only limited success and it is third-pillar schemes that experienced the most spectacular development. Given the inadequate income replacement for those with higher salaries, it might be problematic to categorize the individual life insurances and pension savings plans solely in the third tier, because for them those schemes perform more a kind of second-tier function.

Current pensioners are unequally distributed over the three main statutory programmes: about 60 per cent receive an old age benefit from the private employees' scheme, 20 per cent from the scheme for self-employed, and 14 per cent from the scheme for civil servants. The remaining 7 per cent receive means-tested assistance from the various public income guarantee schemes. In terms of current pension benefits, the second and third pillars in Belgium are surprisingly underdeveloped given the comparatively very low replacement rates for persons with an income above the median. Except for some collective life insurances, and some remnants of an aborted attempt of the 1950s to establish occupational pensions for salaried employees, the second occupational pillar is less appropriate for the majority of current pensioners. In 2004, about 35 per cent of all retired wage earners received an occupational pension benefit (Berghman et al. 2008).[3] The higher their first pillar public pension, the more likely it was for retirees to benefit from such a supplement: whereas amongst the poorest quintile of the statutory pension beneficiaries, only 5 per cent received a supplementary benefit; coverage amongst the richest quintile was more than 77 per cent. The average coverage amongst men was much higher (46 per cent) than amongst women (18 per cent). The amount of these supplementary benefits is very modest: the *median* benefit amounted to only about €125 per month. As the *mean* benefit amounted to €364, one can expect there to be a highly unequal income distribution *within* the population of occupational pension beneficiaries. To some extent, the second pillar does reduce the wide gulf that exists between statutory pensions in the private and public sectors (see Figure 3.2). But on average, civil servants still have significantly higher pensions – even compared to the minority of employees who do enjoy the privilege of a second-pillar pension.

There are little available data on the importance of private personal pensions. However, there is reason to believe that for those who built up their entitlements over the past decades, personal pensions cannot fulfil the role one would expect, given the weak income maintenance capacity of statutory pensions and the absence of an adequate second pillar. In the past, most Belgians relied upon other channels than the typical dedicated pension products to provide for their old age. This is reflected in the income packages of those currently in retirement. The alternatives include very widespread full home ownership, bank deposits, state bonds, participations in mutual funds, and possibly also savings accounts that are stashed away in tax shelters such as Luxembourg. Home ownership amongst the elderly has been estimated at 74 per cent, compared

---

[3] This study used data collected by the Federal Ministry for Social Security (using the tax declarations made during the period 2001–4 for determining health insurance contributions). It was based on a sample of 190,670 persons out of 2,179,167 contributors.

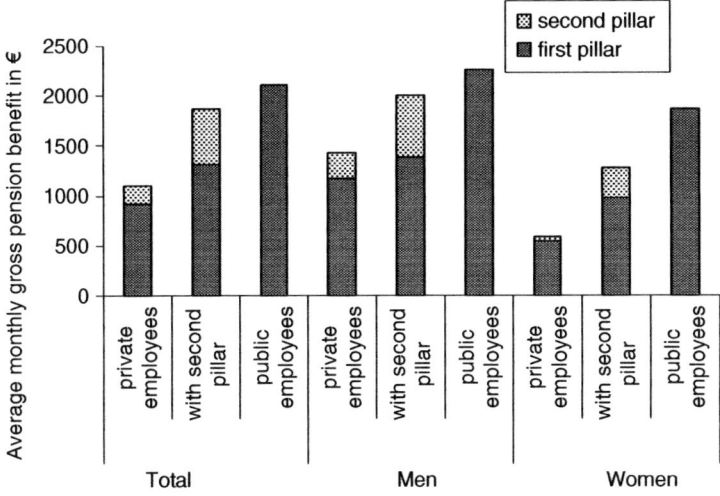

Figure 3.2 Average monthly gross pensions in 2004, Belgium

Source: Data from the *Pensioenkadaster* as reported in Berghman et al. (2008).

to only 19 per cent in the Netherlands, 28 per cent in Denmark – both typical countries with a much more mature second pillar (Dewilde and Raeymaeckers 2008). For the self-employed, renting out second or third homes also seems to have been a popular form of supplementing meagre public pensions. Belgium is known for its folklore of tax evasion, and the impressive wealth of neighbouring Luxembourg is most likely related to this. The volume of tax-declared savings is also substantial: in 2006, the registered assets of private households in deposit accounts amounted to some 73 per cent of the country's GDP, with stocks and bonds and participation in mutual funds amounting to another 129 per cent. Mortgage debts on the other hand only amounted to 35 per cent of GDP (and other debts such as consumer credits to a mere 8 per cent).[4] However, all these non-typical forms of the 'extended' third-pillar arrangements are beyond the scope of this analysis, even if they form an essential part in any attempt at explaining the Belgian paradox.

3. A corporatist welfare regime in a coordinated market economy?

Belgium is a country divided along class, ideological, and linguistic cleavages. These cleavages have been largely overcome by a system of consociational democracy that allows for a concertation between a series of ideologically

[4] Own calculation based on statistics from the Belgian National Bank (www.nbb.be).

integrated networks of organizations that intermediate political, social, and economic interests (Pasture 1996). Belgium's social security has traits of corporatist governance structure as it is administered by a series of tripartite institutions grouped around a central collecting agency, the National Office for Social Security (*Rijksdienst voor Sociale Zekerheid* or RSZ). This central agency is administered by a management board that includes five representatives of the employers' associations, the trade unions, and the state with equal voting rights. In addition, there are two members of the mutual benefit sickness funds who only have an advisory role. All the subsidiary agencies that implement the various branches of the social security system also have a bipartite or tripartite governance structure: in the field of pensions there is the National Pension Office (*Rijksdienst voor Pensioenen*) that is governed by a management board for which both employers' associations and unions each can put forward seven members who are appointed by the federal government, while the fifteenth member, the chairman, is directly nominated by the government.

Similar corporatist principles characterize the system of industrial relations. Wage bargaining occurs at three levels: (*a*) national or inter-sectoral, (*b*) industry-wide or sectoral, and (*c*) enterprise. There is a hierarchical relationship between these levels that implies that an agreement at one particular level cannot be less favourable than agreements on a higher level. National collective agreements are normally formalized in sectoral agreements that are almost always subject to administrative extension so that they tend to have the same effect as labour legislation and social legislation. The sectoral negotiations take place within the so-called joint committees (*paritaire comités*) which form the linchpin of Belgian industrial relations. The rate of unionization is amongst the highest in the world. This can, in part, be attributed to trade union involvement in the organization of unemployment insurance but it also reflects the system of union-nominated shop stewards (*délégués*) in individual companies, who play a pivotal role on the shop floor, and in some respects is a more important force to reckon with than the works councils.

The corporatist traits of the governance of social security and labour markets are one of the reasons why Belgium tends to be classified as a coordinated market economy. This is also reflected in the comparatively low stock market capitalization,[5] the dominance of small- and medium-sized firms (Traxler and Huemer 2007), and the prevalence of holding companies in the control structure of the larger listed companies. Several of the important financial service companies that offer second- and third-pillar products are closely integrated in the web of shareholding cascades that are typical of Belgian *haute finance*

---

[5] In 1995, the value of listed companies was only 38 per cent of GDP compared to a European average of 51 per cent; in 2001, it amounted to 81 per cent compared to 114 per cent (own calculations based on data from the World Federation of Exchanges (www.world-exchanges.org/statistics).

(see Becht et al. 2001) – even if towards the end of the twentieth century many parts of this network have been sold off to foreign players.

4. The emergence of the public–private pension mix

Belgium's first old-age pension arrangements (see Table 3.1) date back to the early nineteenth century when the Napoleonistic state and the provincial authorities started to grant occasional subsidies to encourage the creation of mutual benefit societies of miners. In 1850, the new Belgian state established the General Savings and Pension Annuities Fund (*Algemene Spaar en Lijfrente Kas* or ASLK) allowing workers to save for their own future under a state guarantee. Initially, neither the employers nor the state subsidized these individual forms of provision, but towards the end of the century, some employers started to contribute to the pension capital formation of their employees, and the state started to allocate bonuses on a systematic basis in order to encourage individual savings. A law was adopted to facilitate the members of the existing mutual benefit societies to affiliate to the new scheme.

At the beginning of the twentieth century, there were nearly 2,000 annuities or pension funds that started to associate on an ideological basis into national federations. In 1911, a first compulsory scheme for old-age pension insurance was legislated albeit only for miners. After the First World War, the Minister of Labour, a Social Democrat, introduced a provisional means-tested general-revenue-financed pension scheme as a first step towards the creation of a universalistic general-revenue-financed pension. However, after the Social Democrats were ousted from the government, work on the introduction of a Bismarckian system of contributory social insurance was resumed. This resulted in pension acts for manual workers (1924) and for salaried employees (1925). The new schemes were characterized by a very complicated benefit formula that combined elements of a defined-benefit (DB) and a defined-contribution (DC) approach. They were partly funded and in part run on a pay-as-you-go (PAYG) basis. The scheme for blue-collar workers granted flat-rate benefits, whereas the white-collar scheme had an earnings-related element built into it. The manual workers' scheme was administered by the ASLK (which was governed by a board nominated by the Ministry of Finance), whereas the white-collar scheme was administered by the National Pension Fund for Salaried Employees (*Nationale Kas voor Bediendenpensioenen* or NKBP), a semi-autonomous institution governed by a tripartite board.

In 1944, the National Social Security Office (*Rijksdienst voor Maatschappelijke Zekerheid* or RMZ) was established. The RMZ was set up as a public institution governed by the social partners with a representative of the Ministry of Labour and Social Affairs. The RMZ was responsible for collecting all social security contributions which it subsequently reapportioned over the various branches of the system, though different contributions and benefits for salaried employees, miners, and manual workers continued to exist.

In 1954, the blue-collar pension act was reformed, leading to the phasing out of funding. This was followed three years later by a similar reform of the white-collar scheme. In 1967, all schemes for private sector employees were finally merged into a unified system by a Christian Democratic and Liberal coalition. Long-term labour market shifts had made occupational fragmentation untenable: whereas the ratio between contributors and beneficiaries for the salaried employees' scheme was as low as 1:5, for manual workers it was 1:3, and for the miners scheme it was as little as 1:0.75. As a consequence, the latter scheme had been running large deficits. The new integrated private employee scheme completely abandoned funding and initiated a gradual convergence of contribution rates for blue- and white-collar employees (even if this would only be fully accomplished by the middle of the 1980s). But even after the 1967 reform, differences between blue- and white-collar employees continued to exist by different 'presumed wages' that were used for calculating entitlements built up in the period prior to the reforms of the 1950s, when no adequate records had been kept. In addition, separate schemes continued to exist for public employees and for the self-employed. The former continued to be run on a general-revenue financing and deferred wage model, whereas the scheme for self-employed started out as and still is a rudimentary version of the wage-earner schemes. In its present form, it dates back to the 1950s and consists of a combination of a funded DC system, with a means-tested flat-rate benefit paid out of a 'solidarity fund' that is largely financed by an annual state subsidy.

During the 1970s and 1980s, there were no important changes in the statutory pension scheme but a multitude of early exit routes were developed as part of industry-wide collective agreements. A decade later, the costs of the early retirement schemes became too high, and the government initiated various measures to limit their expansion. Budgetary concerns were also the main motive behind the introduction of a maximum reference income that was taken into account for the calculation of benefits, a measure that would remain in force for more than two decades. The ceiling would not again be linked to wage developments until 2003. As a consequence, the replacement rate for those who enjoyed an income above the median rapidly deteriorated.

In 1995, the government introduced the 'Integrated Management System': all social security contributions were to be collected by the National Office for Social Security (RSZ, the successor of the RMZ) and were accumulated into a single fund. The new central office redistributes these funds on the basis of the needs of each branch of the social security system.[6] Under the new system,

---

[6] Up to 1995, the various social security programmes were managed separately with each having its own autonomous financing mechanism, based on legally prescribed contribution rates for employers and employees. Some programmes were topped up by subsidies from the

the ad hoc transfers between the different branches of the social security system had become completely institutionalized. Since 1993, the distribution of the financial burden for the entire social security system between the state, the employers, and the insured has remained relatively stable: employer contributions account for about 43 per cent of the revenue, employee contributions 22 per cent, the wage moderation levy 7 per cent, the state's subsidies 19 per cent, and VAT the remaining 9 per cent. Only the share of VAT has seen a slow but steady increase from about 9 per cent in 2000 to 13.5 per cent in 2004 (NAR 2005: table 2).[7]

During the second half of the 1980s and the 1990s, there were only minor changes in the statutory pension scheme. Most of these parametric reforms sought to generate additional revenue for the system by imposing special contributions on early retirement benefits, or on combined benefits of first- and second-pillar pensions. On the expenditure side, the most important reform occurred in 1982 when the *wage* indexation of the caps on reference wages was replaced by a *price* indexation. This further diluted the already weak earnings-related nature of benefits and encouraged wage earners with an income above the median to seek supplementary pension arrangements. The link between wage and benefit developments would only be restored more than a decade later.

The last major reform of the statutory scheme occurred in 2001 with the introduction of a buffer fund to anticipate the peak of old age dependency (which in Belgium is expected to occur between 2010 and 2030). This so-called *Zilverfonds* is financed by specific fiscal revenues such as UMTS licences, surpluses in social security financing, and budget surpluses that are realized by reducing the state debt (the latter source of 'revenue' appears more to be a form of converting current debts into future debts). By 2006, the *Zilverfonds* managed assets of around €13 billion that were primarily invested in Belgian treasury bonds (see Table 3.1).

Although the replacement rates offered by the statutory pension scheme were rather low, even for wage earners with a median income, genuine income maintenance and topping up of the replacement gap have until recently remained the privilege of better-off white-collar employees. In part, this had been precisely the intention of some of the post-war reforms that sought to maintain status differences via the backdoor of privatization and voluntarism. In part, this was the result of effective lobbying during the 1950s by private and

central government. In case one programme would run a deficit, funds were transferred from those programmes that were running a surplus. This was done on an ad hoc basis. Later on, these transfers were formalized by establishing a fund for re-apportioning, the so-called Fund for Financial Balance in Social Security (*Fonds voor Financieel Evenwicht van de Sociale Zekerheid*).

[7] Source: Ministerie van Sociale Voorzorg (2004). It remains contested how to attribute the wage moderation levy, whether to the employers or to the employees.

Table 3.1 Chronology of major reforms of the statutory pensions in Belgium

Year	Reform	Political context[a]
1844	Civil Servants Scheme	*Catholic*
	• earnings-related deferred wage	
	• retirement age 65 (men and women)	
1850	ASLK voluntary savings plans	*Liberal*
1911	Miners Act	*Catholic*
	• compulsory insurance for miners	
	• flat-rate defined-contribution funding	
	• administered by mutual benefit societies and ASLK (as of 1930: tripartite NPM)	
	• retirement age: 55–60 years	
1920	Provisional Pension Act	*Socialist*
	• general revenue financed, means tested	
1924	Manual Workers Act	*Catholic*
	• compulsory insurance for manual workers	
	• flat-rate defined contribution funding	
	• parity financing with some state subsidies	
	• administered by state-controlled ASLK	
	• retirement age: 60 (women) and 65 (men)	
1925	Salaried Employees Act	*Catholic*
	• compulsory insurance for white-collar employees	
	• earnings-related defined contribution funding	
	• parity financing with some state subsidies	
	• administered by tripartite NKBP	
	• retirement age: 60 (women) and 65 (men)	
1944	Social Security Act	National Unity (*Socialist*)
	• National Social Security Office	
	• partial abandoning of defined-contribution funding	
1954	Reform of Manual Workers Act	*Christian Democratic*
	• National Office for Pensions of Manual Workers	
	• PAYG	
1957	Reform of Salaried Employees Act	*Socialist* & Liberal
	• mix DB funding and PAYG	
	• maximum ceiling for benefits	
1967	Merger of all wage-earner schemes	*Christian Democratic* & Liberal
	• unification of all wage-earner schemes	
	• complete phasing out funding	
	• benefit ceiling for manual workers as well	
1968	Guaranteed Minimum Income for the Elderly	*Christian Democratic* & Socialist
	• (low) means-tested basic pension	

1976	Uniform contribution rates for statutory pensions for all wage earners (manual workers and salaried employees)	*Christian Democratic* & Liberal
1982	Reference wage ceiling for benefit calculation only indexed for price inflation and no longer for wage developments.	*Christian Democratic* & Liberal
	Abolishing of wage ceiling for determining contributions (i.e. contributions are calculated on full wage).	
1994	Solidarity contribution (*solidariteitsbijdrage*) on combined statutory and supplementary pension benefits to finance topping up low pensions	*Socialist* & Christian Democratic
1995	Introduction of single social security contribution and integrated management system (*lobal beheer*)	*Socialist* & Christian Democratic
1997	Gradual convergence of retirement age for men and women to 65 completed in 2009	*Socialist* & Christian Democratic
2001	Establishing of Old Age Fund (*Zilverfonds*) to anticipate the peak of ageing of population between 2010 and 2030	*Socialist* & Christian Democratic
2003	Reinstatement of indexation of wage ceiling to wage developments; gradual equalization of retirement age for men and women	*Socialist*, Liberal, & Green

Notes: [a] Italicized is the party that controlled the ministry responsible for statutory pensions.

subsidiary insurance companies to maintain the low caps on reference wages in the statutory scheme, in order to safeguard a lucrative market of voluntary supplementary pension insurances and individual life insurance policies for more affluent salaried employees.

As early as the interwar period, white-collar employees had been given the possibility to 'top up' their public pension by contributing to a nascent supplementary occupational pension administered by the NKBP, the ASLK, and fifteen subsidiary insurance carriers. But the 1967 reform phased out this possibility of supplementary insurance. At the time, less than one out of ten white-collar employees was making use of that possibility. Most commercial insurance companies that underwrote the subsidiary schemes had lost interest in what they considered to be a too regulated form of extra-statutory coverage, and about half of the remaining accounts were administered by the only parity-

Table 3.2 Chronology of the antecedents of extra statutory pensions in Belgium

Year	Reform	Political context[a]
1930	Act regulating group insurances	*Catholic* & Socialist
1944	Premiums paid into group insurances become tax deductible	German occupation
1957	Supplementary insurance by subsidiary funds in salaried employees scheme	*Socialist* & Liberal
1967	Phasing out of supplementary insurance in statutory scheme	*Christian Democratic* & Liberal
1984	Limitation of tax deductibility of premiums paid into group insurances	*Christian Democratic* & Socialist

Notes: [a] Italicized is the party that controlled the ministry responsible for statutory pensions.

Table 3.3 Statutory pensions main indicators

	1955	1960	1965	1970	1975	1980	1985	1990	1995	2000	2005
Contribution rate % of wage (no income ceiling)											
Manual workers	7.00	9.00	12.00	13.63	14.00	14.00	16.36	16.36	16.36	Single integrated social security contribution	
Employees	3.50	4.50	5.25	5.88	6.00	6.00	7.50	7.50	8.86	—	—
Employers	3.50	4.50	6.75	7.75	8.00	8.00	8.86	8.86	8.86	—	—
Salaried employees	10.25	10.25	10.25	11.37	13.88	14.00	16.36	16.36	16.36	—	—
Employees	4.50	4.25	4.25	4.62	5.88	6.00	7.50	7.50	8.86	—	—
Employers	6.00	6.00	6.00	6.75	8.00	8.00	8.86	8.86	8.86	—	—
Minimum annual guaranteed benefit full career (€)	—	—	—	495	—	—	—	—	9,307	9,490	10,396
Maximum annual benefit for single man (€)	—	—	—	—	—	—	—	—	16,371	17,325	18,484
Income ceiling salaried employees (€)	1,545	2,716	3,055	5,579	11,624	16,595	27,020	29,992	33,372	36,835	43,315
Average macro-economic replacement rates (%)[a]											
Wage earners	—	—	—	—	—	—	—	32	31	30	31
Civil servants	—	—	—	—	—	—	—	—	—	—	82
Self-employed	—	—	—	—	—	—	—	—	—	—	24

Pension expenditure % of GDP

OECD: Public	—	—	—	—	5.9	6.3	6.5	7.1	6.9	7.2
Private (mandated + voluntary)	—	—	—	—	0.3	0.3	0.8	1.3	1.5	2.7
Tax expenditure	—	—	—	—	—	—	1.3	—	1.2	1.0
Eurostat total[b]	—	—	—	—	—	—	—	11.8	11.0	11.2

Notes: [a] Average pension benefits as a percentage of average gross earnings;
[b] Eurostat uses a broader definition of pension expenditure, including disability pension, early-retirement due to reduced capacity to work, old-age pension, anticipated old-age pension, partial pension, survivors' pension, early-retirement benefit for labour market reasons.
Source: Own calculations based on data from the *Rijksdienst voor Pensioenen* (www.rvponp.fgov.be), *Nationaal Instituut voor de Statistiek* (http://statbel.fgov.be), Belgostat database (www.nbb.be/belgostat), NAR (2005), Studiecommissie voor de vergrijzing (2002), Eurostat (2007).

controlled insurance institution: the only remaining subsidiary insurance carrier, the mutual benefit society l'Intégrale.

Another type of early second-pillar schemes took the form of 'group insurances', which date back to the 1920s and were first regulated in 1930 (see Table 3.2). After a hesitant start, these types of schemes proliferated during the period of the Second World War, when the German occupier made premiums paid into these kinds of insurances tax deductible. As a consequence, between 1938 and 1945, the size of liabilities of these schemes increased by a factor of ten. Initially, these insurances were only offered to executive employees, and in 1952 there were only about 52,000 of such contracts. Gradually, these fringe benefits were also granted to lower ranked white-collar employees and even to blue-collar workers in industries where loyalty was important. Thus, in 1968, some 500,000 wage earners were covered by a group insurance (Lewalle 1986). When in 1984 the state faced a fiscal crisis, the government decided to limit the tax exemptions for group insurances. In order to remain eligible for tax credits, contracts from then onwards were only allowed to contribute to a pension of maximum 80 per cent of the gross annual earnings of the last five years (the so-called 80 per cent rule that will be elaborated below). This measure effectively limited the possible scope of the second pillar, and in order to obtain a higher pension, compensation was sought after in the third pillar, as without fiscal stimuli employers were reluctant to make contributions to collective pension schemes (Gieselinck et al. 2002).

5. The changing public–private pension mix

The Belgian pension system never was 'Bismarckian' in the sense of an actuarially fair earnings-related scheme: the scheme for private sector employees offers comparatively high minimum benefits and low maximum benefits for all pensioners with a standard employment biography – irrespective of how much they actually earned during their working years.[8] The scheme is characterized by a sizeable degree of redistribution as there is no upper earnings limit for contributions, while the maximum wages taken into account to calculate benefits are capped at a very low level. Because during the period 1982–96, those caps were only indexed for prices instead of wages, replacement rates further deteriorated (see Table 3.3). Moreover, in contrast to theoretical replacement rates (based on a full-time career lasting forty-five years), the average statutory contributory pension benefit for men amounted to only 92 per cent of the minimum guaranteed benefit in 2006, while for women as little as 45 per cent

---

[8] In 2008, this minimum benefit for a single pensioner (family with one breadwinner) with a full career amounted to €920 (€1,149) per month while theoretical maximum benefit amounted to only €1,735 (€2,169).

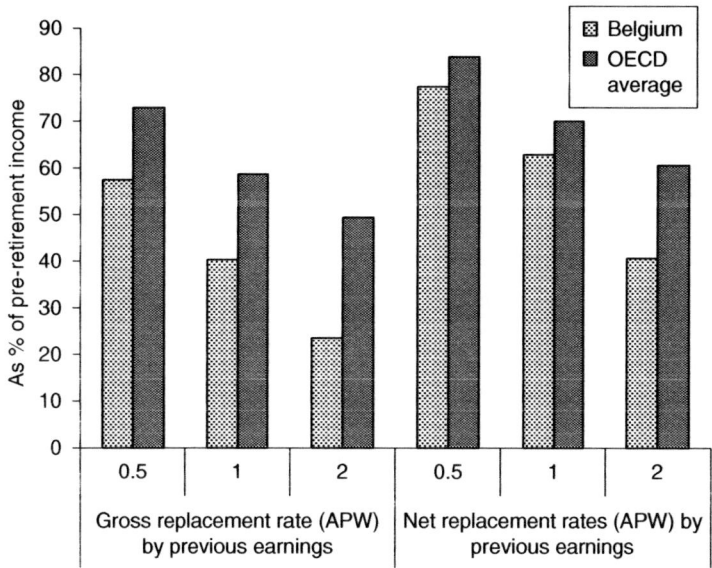

Figure 3.3 Gross and net replacement rates (per cent) for single persons in statutory pension schemes by previous earnings, Belgium

Notes: Gross replacement rates: Individual pension as percentage of pre-retirement gross earnings as multiple of APW; Net replacement rates: Individual pension as percentage of pre-retirement earnings net of taxes and contributions as multiple of APW.
Source: OECD (2007).

(Verbond van Belgische Ondernemingen 2006). Hence, a very large part of Belgian retirees, in particular women, has to apply for means-tested supplements. Compared to other OECD (Organisation for Economic Co-operaion and Development) countries, Belgian theoretical replacement rates of statutory pensions (i.e. for people with a full contributory record) are low across all income groups (see Figure 3.3) and these rates deteriorate quickly with increasing pre-retirement income.

Since these schemes are not tied to earnings, one would expect the second and third pillars would flourish. However, such schemes have failed to develop. Until recently, the occupational pensions have hardly been in the spotlight. However, fragmented empirical evidence on pension expenditure seems to indicate that during the past three decades, extra-statutory schemes might have reached sizeable proportions: according to the OECD, aggregate spending on private pension schemes in 2005 reached about two-thirds of the expenditure levels one can find in countries with the largest private pensions in Europe (the Netherlands and Switzerland), and was far more than what can be observed in typical 'Bismarckian' countries such as Austria, France, and Germany (De Deken 2009).

The Belgian legislator played a minor role in encouraging and regulating these extra-statutory forms of provision. The role foreseen for subsidiary funds in the 1955 reform of the white-collar scheme had effectively been phased out with the 1967 unification of all private sector schemes. In addition, the tax advantages for group insurances were scaled back during the 1980s as part of the state policy of fiscal consolidation. Not only was there a clear lack of consensus amongst the major political actors that had produced gridlock in political decision-making, and a succession of contradictory policy initiatives, there also prevailed an institutional fragmentation in the division of responsibility in the field of occupational pensions. Regulation of second-pillar pensions was not in the portfolio of the ministry and the civil service responsible for administering statutory pensions (a ministry that traditionally is staffed by Social Democrats or Christian Democrats with a trade union affinity). Rather, this regulation was considered to be the responsibility of the Ministry of Finance and its regulating bodies (a ministry traditionally held by Liberals or by Christian Democrats with a bourgeois affinity). Hence, public intervention in the second pillar was more focused upon financial issues, with only very little interest for such social concerns as the adequacy of benefits or the extent of the coverage.

Only over the last two decades an interest in the field of occupational pensions developed. During the 1980s, the coalition of Christian Democrats and Liberals had been working on legislative proposals to regulate occupational pensions, though this work was completed by a Socialist minister in a Centre–Left coalition government in 1995. The Occupational Pensions Act of 1995 (*Wet op de Aanvullende Pensioenen* or WAP) sought to reinforce co-determination rights in the second pillar and make occupational pensions more inclusive by regulating adherence rules and by facilitating the transition of acquired rights from one employer to another. This was followed by a revision in 2003 that sought to go much further in abandoning the voluntary nature of the schemes, which up to then had been the hallmark of private pensions in Belgium. The reform had been prepared in concertation with the social partners, who in 2001 had issued a common declaration at inter-industry level on the matter (Gieselinck et al. 2002: 58). The 2003 Act established a framework for making sectoral pensions mandatory and launched the so-called 'solidaristic pension' plans (see Table 3.4). The new pension schemes would be negotiated within the joint committees by trade unions and employers' associations. The new governance system would be subject to parity-based co-determination. The plans would no longer be based on orthodox actuarial calculations – now they would also insure additional risks such as disability and survival. The law made medical testing illegal and also foresaw tax incentives to allow plan participants to continue to accumulate entitlements during periods of inactivity such as sickness, maternity, and unemployment.

Table 3.4 Chronology of private pensions in Belgium

Year	Reform	Political context[a]
1985	Pension Fund Governance Act:	*Liberal* & Christian Democratic
	• terminating of possibility to use book reserve financing	
	• terminating of possibility of PAYG	
1995	First Occupational Pensions Act (WAP1)	*Socialist* & Christian Democratic
	• equal treatment of all employees of the same category (gender, age, full-time or part-time, medical records)	
	• limitation of minimum required adherence to 1 year at most	
	• transfer pension rights between funds in case of job change	
	• information rights and weak co-determination	
2003	Second Occupational Pension Act (WAP2) in consensus with social partners (national collective agreement of 2001)	*Socialist*, Liberal, & Green
	• framework for sectoral pensions (mandatory for all employers in a sector negotiated in joint committees by unions and employers' associations)	
	• introduction of SPT covering additional risks such as survivor benefits, disability benefits, as well as coverage during periods of inactivity (e.g. sickness, maternity, unemployment)	
	• limitation of possibility to grant individual pension commitments	
	• much stronger co-determination rights via joint committees (for sectoral pensions) and via parity-based supervisory board (for group insurances with insurance company)	
	• changes in fiscal regime encouraging annuitization	

Notes: [a] Italicized is the party that controlled the ministry responsible for statutory pensions.

Part II: The governance of supplementary pensions

6. Who is covered?

The present institutional architecture of the Belgian second pillar can be described by five aspects (see Figure 3.4):

- The initiator of the pension arrangement (*pensioenregeling*): individual employers can establish a pension arrangement at the level of the firm or the social partners can establish a sector pension at industry level

- The scope of the pension commitment (*pensioentoezegging*) defining *access* to the plan: which can be restricted to specific (categories of) employees of the firm (*individuele pensioentoezegging* or IP), or includes all employees (*collectieve pensioentoezegging* or CP).

- The type of pension plan: sector pension plans (*sectorpensioen*) cover all employees of all the companies in a particular sector, company pension

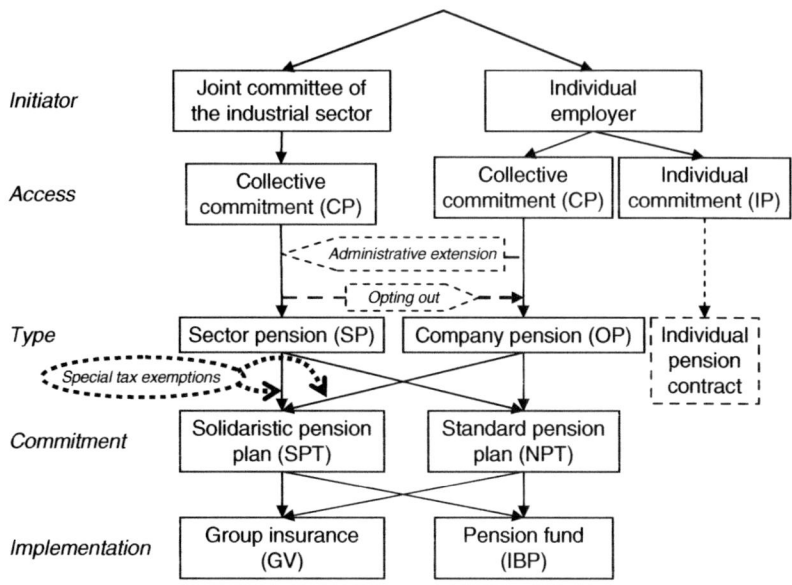

Figure 3.4 The institutional architecture of the second pillar in Belgium

plans (*ondernemingspensioen* or ONP) cover all the workers in one particular company and individual pension contracts are offered as fringe benefits for selected employees.

- The form of the pension commitment can be a standard pension plan in which the pension capital is solely dependent on contributions made by or on behalf of the individual pensioner; or a social solidaristic pension commitment in which additional labour market risks are covered, guaranteeing benefits even in case the participant is no longer able to work.

- The kind of pension institution (*pensioeninstelling*) that *implements* the pension plan, either an autonomous pension fund or a collective life insurance (a so-called group insurance) organized by an insurance company.

One of the main aims of the two WAP reforms was to enlarge access to occupational pensions: to include all employees of a company or the entire workforce of an industrial sector. With the adoption of the first WAP in 1995, the initiative to set up pension plans has started to shift from a unilateral voluntary decision by individual employers for (some of) their employees towards a collective agreement between the social partners at the level of the joint committee to cover all employees in an industry. These collective agreements are binding for all employers and employees in the sector covered by the joint committee. There is, however, one way for employers to 'opt out' when the sectoral collective agreement explicitly allows this possibility, and the employer's company plan offers at least as good conditions to its beneficiaries as the sector plan.

If the plan is initiated at the level of the firm, it is still allowed to offer an additional so-called individual pension commitment (IP). This type of pension plan was traditionally part of the remuneration package of executives and members of senior management. It used to consist of either an individual life insurance contract concluded by the enterprise for the individual employee, or it could be backed by book reserves on the firm's balance sheets. In case they were financed via book reserves, there was no insolvency insurance. The reforms of the late 1980s sought to discourage these types of plans and banned the book reserve method altogether, but it is still possible to set up the life insurance variant by relinquishing the tax exemptions that are granted to collective pension plans.

Table 3.5 gives an overview of the most important sectoral pension plans that existed in the beginning of 2007. For each industry, we also list the number of employed, both absolute and as a percentage of all private sector wage earners. In Table 3.6 are data from various sources that seek to estimate how many wage earners are covered by the second pillar. The figures for group insurances refer to the number of contracts rather than the number of persons. Hence, it is likely that there are double counts involved (e.g. of one person having two contracts with different companies). The 'corrected' figures result from a study of a government commission that sought to filter out these double counts.

Contrary to the politicians' expectations, the WAP reform seems only to have led to a moderate increase of the coverage rate of occupational pensions. Thus far only a handful of joint committees established genuinely new sectoral occupational schemes, while company occupational plans continue to cover about twice as many persons. Some of the largest sectoral plans listed in Table 3.5 already existed before the second WAP reform of 2003: they were simply converted so as to make them conform to the new standards. This often involved changing the method of financing (from PAYG to funding)[9] and modifying the benefit formula from a traditional DB (i.e. a percentage of average or final earnings) to a more DC-based system.

The sectors with a truly new plan represent little over 10 per cent of private sector employees,[10] though the subsequent increase in coverage seems to have

---

[9] Before the WAP reform, there were seven sectors covering about 10 per cent of wage earners that operated a sector plan on a PAYG basis (Assuralia 2005). Those plans were managed by the so-called *fondsen voor bestaanszekerheid* that in the Belgian neo-corporatist system are set up by joint committees to administer various social benefits agreed at the industry level (including training, measures to promote security in the workplace, and various extra statutory transfer payments such as early retirement benefits and, until recently, occupational pensions).

[10] New sector plans include the following parity committees (PC) in the private sector: PC112 (garage industry), PC118 (food processing), PC209 (metal industry) and a number of sub-committees within PC149 (machine tool industries) and PC106 (cement industries).

Table 3.5 Overview of some of the most important sectoral pension plans in 2007

Industrial branch joint committee	Plan participants absolute number	%	Year WAP	Type Plan	Type benefit	Contribution rates % of gross wages
Metal & Machine Tools	269,267	9.58				
111	149,695	5.33	2007 R	IBP	DC (GRR:3.25%)	Employer: 1.50% + flat-rate SPT
149.01	24,620	0.88	2002	GV (Dexia)	DC (GRR:3.25%)	Employer: 1.20%
149.04	16,493	0.59	2002	GV (Dexia)	DC (GRR:3.25%)	Employer: 1.50%
209	68,034	2.42	2002	GV (Intégrale)	DC (GRR:3.25%)	Employer: 1.10%
Construction	169,377	6.03				
124	161,774	5.75	2007 R	IBP	CB with GRR	Employer: 2.50%
Food Processing 118	59,435	2.11	2004	GV (AG)	DC (GRR:3.75%)	Employer: 1.32%
Transport & Logistics 226	41,979	1.49	2007	GV (ING/ P&V)	DC (GRR:3.25%)	Employer: 0.50%
Cleaning Services 121	37,525	1.35	2008	GV (Axa)	DC (GRR:3.25%)	Employer: 1.50%
Garage 112	27,726	0.99	2002	GV (Dexia)	DC (GRR:3.25%)	Employer: 1.40%
Wood and Textile 126	19,018	0.68	2007 R	GV (Allianz)	DC (GRR:3.25%)	Employer: 1.00%
Regional Public Transport 328	19,374	0.69	2007 R	IBP	CB (GRR:3.25%)	Employer: 2.50%
Market Gardening 145	20,125	0.71	2000		DC	Employer: 1.09%
Port of Antwerp 301.01	9,626	0.34	2004 R	IBP	DC	Employer: 0.50%
Notary Industry 216	6,503	0.23	2004 R	GV	DC (GRR:3.25%)	Employer: 4.20% Employee: 1.00%
Entertainment Industry 304	3,871	0.13	2006	GV (Ethias)	DC (GRR:3.25%)	Employer: 1.50%
Retail of Fuel & Combustibles 127	1,566	0.06	2003	IBP	DC	Employer: 2.00% Employee: 1.00%

Notes: IBP = autonomous pension fund; GV = group insurance (underneath is the insurance company mentioned that acts as pension institution for the plan); DC = defined contribution; GRR = guaranteed rate of return on contributions; CB = cash balance; SPT = part of contribution used to finance the solidaristic part of pension commitment; R = year that an existing sectoral scheme was converted into WAP conform one.

Source: CBFA (2007).

Table 3.6 Coverage of second-pillar pension arrangements

	2000	2001	2002	2003	2004	2005	2006	2007
Autonomous pension fund (1000s)	222.4	238.8	236.0	263.9	253.4	255.0	273.8	—
Group insurances contracts (1000s)	1,135.0	1,104.2	1,225.2	1,314.8	1,501.1	1,688.7	1,744.4	1,929.5
Company pension plans (estimate)* (1000s)	—	—	—	1,109.1	1,109.1	1,109.1	1,109.1	1,109.1
Sectoral pension plans (1000s)	—	—	389.0	434.5	488.0	488.0	491.5	511.4
Persons in second pillar (corrected) (1000s)	1,157.5	1,343.1	1,461.2	1,578.8	1,603.2	1,618.2	1,634.3	1,670.1
Wage earners (1000s)	2,655.8	2,711	2,695.5	2,691.7	2,705.7	2,741.9	2,772.5	2,811.2
Coverage rate: second pillar (%)	43.6	49.5	54.2	58.7	59.3	59.0	59.0	59.4
Coverage rate: sectoral plans only (%)	—	—	14.5	16.1	18.0	17.7	17.7	18.2

Notes: *After 2003, the CBFA has not published data on the number of participants in company pensions, but it seems reasonable to assume that the number has not changed that much because the number of pension funds (for which there are statistics available) has remained relatively stable over the period, evolving from 242 in 2002 over 245 in 2004, 238 in 2006 to 245 in 2007. The contributions also hardly changed during this period from 906 million in 2002 to 967 million in 2007.

Source: Own calculations based on data from Studiecommissie voor de vergrijzing (2007); and on statistical series of the financial services authority CBFA (www.cbfa.be). Data on number of private sector wage earners from Belgostat database (www.nbb.be/belgostat).

primarily benefited blue-collar workers. Whereas the ratio between blue- and white-collar employees in the workforce is about even, before the WAP reforms, the latter outnumbered the former by 1:4 in pension funds, and by 1:5 in group insurances (Assuralia 2005). As most of the genuinely new sectoral plans were concluded in joint committees for manual workers, their share is bound to have increased.

Third-pillar pensions include individual life insurances and personal pension savings plans. As was the case with second-pillar group insurances, one can make a distinction between DC schemes with a guaranteed rate of return, and DC schemes with returns on capital depending upon financial market performance. Personal pension plans closely resemble these individual life insurances, but whereas life insurances can only be provided for by insurance companies, personal pension plans can also be (and mostly are) administered by banks and other credit institutions. They are also subject to more tax exemptions because they can only be cashed in upon retirement.

Data on coverage by third-pillar schemes are even harder to obtain than for occupational pensions. According to the regulator, a total of 1.3 million individual life insurance contracts existed in 2007, though this again includes double counts. A study estimated coverage on the basis of tax return data of the late 1990s (Gieselinck et al. 2003). This approach did not allow estimating coverage at the individual level but had to differentiate between the coverage of married persons and that of singles as Belgian tax returns are made by households. In 1998, about 14 per cent of single households contributed to a personal pension plan, 17 per cent to a life insurance, and about 26 per cent to at least one of these two schemes. For married households, the respective figures were 34, 43, and 58 per cent. The study reports only a minor increase in coverage between 1992 and 1999. The problem with these kinds of estimates is that they only measure life insurances that are eligible for tax deductions and plans that are linked to an investment fund are not taken into account; and it is precisely those plans that during the 1990s have experienced a dramatic proliferation. During the early 1990s, those plans only represented a fraction of fixed capital life insurance policies, but by 2007 they became as important. Hence, it is likely that life insurances have become a far more important vehicle for old age provision than the reported estimates suggest.

With an occupational coverage rate of about 60 per cent of the dependent workforce, Belgium seems to develop a more inclusive second pillar, ending the anomaly of voluntarism in a corporatist welfare state. However, there is a major caveat: even though a majority of wage earners are now enrolled in an occupational pension plan (and the numbers are likely to increase), the level of the supplementary entitlements the participants in these plans are building up is very modest. At the aggregate level, this becomes evident when one relates the volume of contributions to occupational pension plans to the volume of payments for statutory pensions, and compares this with the total volume of premium payments to third-pillar arrangements.[11]

During the past two decades, the second pillar has experienced a steady growth. Compared to the first pillar, it is now almost twice the size it was in the early 1990s. But this growth seems to be only marginally related to the government's attempts to extend coverage by facilitating industry-wide arrangements. However, it might be too early to judge since the WAP reforms

---

[11] For statutory pensions expenditure data are used as a proxy for the contributions, because ever since 1995 the contributions to the public pension system are no longer separately registered. But as the statutory scheme operates on a PAYG basis, it seems reasonable to presume that the expenditures on benefits in a particular year form more or less the mirror image of the contributions that would have been made if the scheme was run independent of other branches of the social security system.

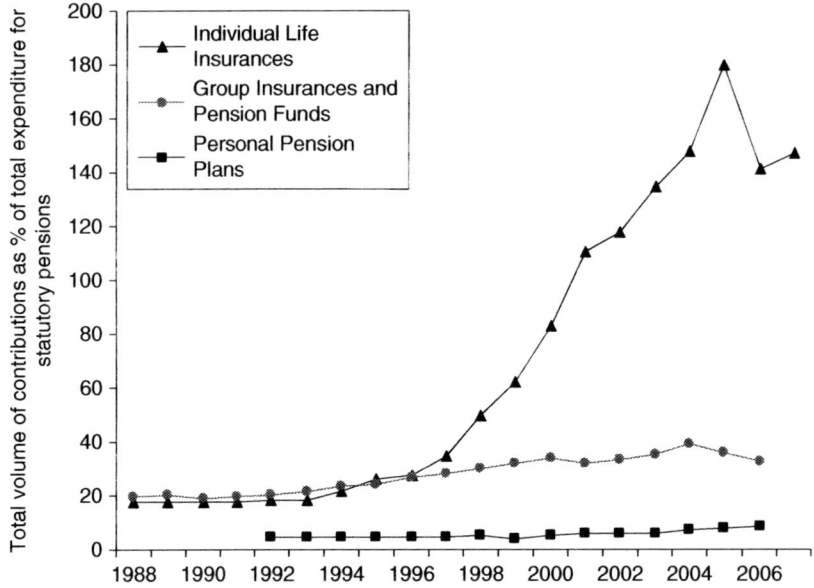

Figure 3.5 Contributions to the second and third pillars as a percentage of expenditure on statutory pensions, Belgium

Sources: Own calculations based on data from Belgostat database (www.nbb.be/belgostat); the association of insurance companies (Assuralia *Kerncijfers en voornaamste Resultaten van de Belgische Verzekering; Assurinfo* 31 2006; *Assurinfo* 33 2007); and annual reports and statistical series of the financial services authorities CDV and CBFA (www.cbfa.be).

are only gradually applied by sectoral collective agreements which provide the basis for the new more inclusive sectoral pension plans. On the other hand, some signs of stagnation, if not relative decline, can be observed following the adoption of the second WAP reform. One possible explanation may be that the new sectoral schemes are almost exclusively financed by employer contributions that are exchanged for potential wage increases during wage negotiations between the social partners. In the Belgian neo-corporatist system, the social partners are constrained by a government-mandated 'wage norm': a cap on the maximum wage growth that trade unions and employers associations are allowed to agree in collective wage agreements.[12] And the expansion of occupational pensions with respect to adequacy is thus constrained by the same

[12] This norm is determined for a period of two years by the tripartite consultation body, the Central Economic Council, composed of delegates from employers' associations and trade unions, plus six independent experts. It determines the wage norm by taking into account the expected wage developments in neighbouring countries.

institutions that allow expansion of coverage. Any attempt to develop the funding base at a faster pace than productivity growth inevitably has to be traded off for cuts in real wages. The expansion of the funded occupational pensions ends up being faced by similar problems as attempts to maintain the PAYG basis necessary for the adequacy of the public pension pillar.

Whereas the second pillar is only gradually gaining importance, compared to public pensions, third-pillar schemes have experienced an explosive growth since the mid-1980s. In 2007, Belgians contributed 1.5 times as much on voluntary than on statutory pensions. Again the impact of specific pension reforms appears to be limited because it is not the designated pension vehicles (the personal pension plans) that proved popular, but the standard individual life insurances. Belgians seem to prefer the higher liquidity of the former over the additional tax advantages offered by the latter. In terms of the total volume of contributions, the third pillar turns out to be four times as important as the second pillar (see Figure 3.5). A similar picture emerges when one compares the assets of the second- and third-pillar schemes relative to the country's GDP: during the past decade, the accumulation of the assets in the second pillar stagnated while the third pillar experienced an exponential growth (see Figure 3.6).

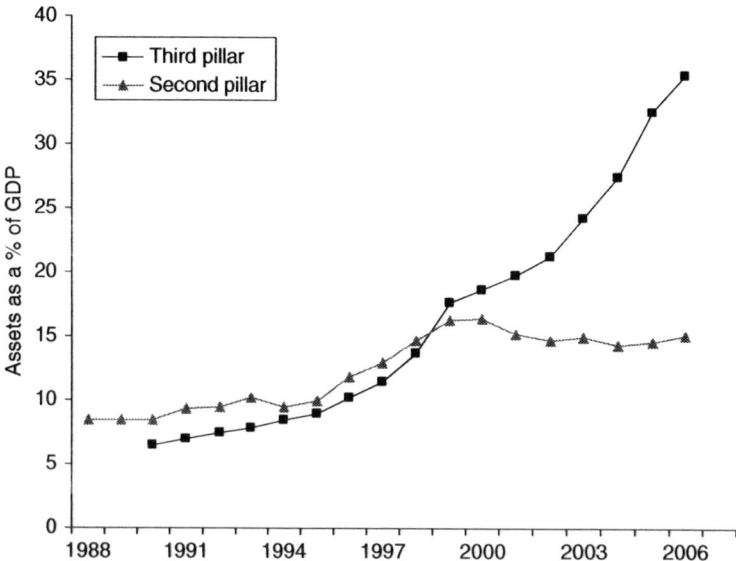

Figure 3.6 Liabilities of second and third pillars as a percentage of GDP, Belgium

Source: Own calculations based on same sources as Figure 3.8 and on data from the Belgian Banking Association (BVB) (www.febelfin.be).

7. What kind of benefits?

There are two main forms of collective pension plans: a standard promise that only guarantees an actuarially determined old-age pension benefit (*normale pensioentoezegging* or NPT) and a so-called solidaristic pension commitment (*solidaire pensioentoezegging* or SPT), which in exchange for certain additional tax exemptions has to cover a series of additional risks. The law distinguishes four categories of risks that a pension plan can cover in order to be recognized as 'social':

(1) continuing accrual of pension entitlements during periods of inactivity of the employee (such as temporary unemployment, sickness, disability, pregnancy, parental leave, educational leave, and sabbatical leave);

(2) survival benefits and benefits following income loss because of permanent disability;

(3) benefits in case of long-term sickness; and

(4) indexation of benefits.

In order to qualify as solidaristic, a collective pension plan must be initiated by a collective agreement and grant extra benefits resulting in at least two out of these four categories, and the costs of these benefits must equal at least the value of the tax exemption. An additional incentive for the social partners to fulfil the conditions of an SPT is that contributions to those plans are exempted from the wage norm.

The financial management of a pension plan can either be contracted out to a private insurance company in the form of a group insurance contract (*groepsverzekering* or GV), or the plan can be set up as an autonomous pension fund (*instelling voor bedrijfspensioenvoorziening* or IBP). Group insurances in turn come in two basic variants: one variant guarantees a certain lump sum of capital upon retirement, while in the other variant the capital at the end of the road depends upon financial market performance. This distinction only partly overlaps with the traditional division between DB and DC plans.

In Belgium, one rarely finds occupational pension plans that promise an indexed benefit expressed as a percentage of past earnings (average or final salary). Most extra-statutory pension plans lack an indexation mechanism linking benefits to wage developments. In most schemes, the prevalent benefit formula is that of an individual account with a guaranteed rate of return, supplemented by a share in the profits realized by the insurance company or the pension fund that implements the plan.

In terms of individualizing *labour market risks*, both the fixed capital and the contingent market capital variants operate like typical DC schemes. Benefits are dependent upon continuity of employment and the individual earnings history of the beneficiary. With respect to *capital market risks*, the fixed capital schemes, especially those with a guaranteed rate of return, have more in common with DB plans. The capital paid out upon retirement will be unaffected by turbulences on the capital market and might even grow at a steady pace of 3.25 per cent in the case of a scheme with a guaranteed rate of return. This return does not need to be achieved at the end of each calendar year. The settlement occurs at the time of the employee's retirement or upon the moment of his or her departure from the plan (e.g. because of a change of employer). In the event of poor investment performance of the pension plan, the guaranteed rate of return may end up requiring a back servicing of the pension obligation. In case of a group insurance, it is the insurance company which is liable to do so. In case the pension commitment is implemented in the form of an IBP, it is the sponsoring employer or all the employers of the sector who are liable for the back servicing.

The labour market risks in group insurances and in pension funds with a guaranteed rate of return are effectively reduced by incorporating a solidarstic component to the plan. Such an SPT normally has one part that guarantees the actuarially defined old age benefit (which since the WAP reforms has to be fully funded), and a second part that pools some of the individual labour market risks and is run on a PAYG basis with a sizeable reserve fund.

Finally, if one considers the *longevity risks*, until recently it was up to the individual pensioners to buy an annuity in the insurance market upon reaching the retirement age. Most of the time the occupational pension benefits were taken up as a lump sum and the individual life span risks were completely individualized (and insurance companies were free to charge different rates to the purchasers of annuities, reflecting their individual longevity risks). Only since the WAP reform can employees who retire demand that their collective pension is automatically converted into an annuity. The new regulations also require that the same annuitization rates are offered to men and women, thus favouring the longer life expectancy of women.

8. Who pays?

With the exception of two minor industries, employers almost always pay the full contribution of occupational pensions: thus in 2007, employee contributions were only 0.5 per cent of the total sum of contributions to sectoral plans (CBFA 2007). For company pension schemes, no comprehensive data are available, but scattered information suggests a similar practice. Contributions to sector pensions are very low, at best 1 or 2 per cent of gross wages. According to a spokesperson of Ethias, one of the largest Belgian insurance companies, contributions to company pensions are on average 2 per cent for blue-collar workers, 4–5 per cent for white-collar workers, and 7–8 per cent for middle and senior management staff (Vanthiemen 2006: 91). But there are apparently important differences between sectors: chemicals, car manufacturing, and the ICT sector are known to conclude very generous insurance contracts for their workforce.

Employers' contributions are exempted from income tax but are subject to the *80 per cent rule*, whereby pension entitlement cannot accumulate more than four-fifths of the employee's gross wage. Normally, contributions made for private pension products are liable to an insurance tax of 4.4 per cent, but solidaristic pensions are exempted from this tax, provided that this extra commitment at least equals the tax exemption. Over the past years, such sector pension plans contributed far more to the solidaristic component of the plan than required by law. On average, these contributions amounted to 5.8 per cent of total contributions in 2004 and even 11.2 per cent in 2005. Though these plans are allowed to operate partly on a PAYG basis, during their first years a reserve fund was being built up: benefits paid out of these schemes amounted to only about 20 per cent of contributions made in 2004, and 38 per cent in 2005 (CBFA 2007).

Benefits paid out as a lump sum are subject to a one-time tax of 16.5 per cent of the capital resulting from employers' contributions and 10 per cent of the capital accumulated via personal contributions. Annuity payments are subject to income tax, and to a reduced social security levy that covers health insurance. In addition there is a special crisis tax, the so-called solidarity contribution (*solidariteitsbijdrage*), that since the mid-1990s is levied on all larger income sources, thus also applying to more wealthy pensioners (it is progressively scaled from 0.5 to 2 per cent). Finally, employers can fully deduct pension contributions from the company's taxable profits. Before the WAP reforms, the tax regulations made it unattractive to take up occupational pensions as an annuity, as they were subject to the progressive marginal tax rates, and most pensioners preferred lump sum benefits that were only taxed once with a flat rate. The WAP reform has changed taxation so that pensioners no longer lose out when they convert their lump sum into an annuity.

9. Who governs? Who decides? Who manages?

In respect to governance of pension plans, it is important to bear in mind that Belgian law distinguished between the pension arrangement (*pensioenregeling*) and the pension institution implementing the plan (*pensioeninstelling*). In some cases this can be the same organizational entity, but more often it consists of two different organizations, particularly in cases where the pension plan is outsourced in the form of a group insurance managed by a commercial insurance company. Most occupational pension arrangements formally require some employee involvement in the governance of the pension institution. In the case of company plans, the employee influence is organized via the works council and shop steward in the company. They have to be *consulted* about the financing method, the application and interpretation of the pension agreement, and the choice of a pension institution in case the pension plan is contracted out. For autonomous pension plans without employee contributions and with no solidaristic component, employee influence can be circumvented. This is one of the reasons why many employers have decided to shoulder the entire funding of their company schemes.

One of the novelties of the WAP was that it sought to strengthen employee influence by requiring parity *control* for the sector and company plans with a solidaristic component. In case the pension institution and the pension arrangement are the same entity (i.e. no outsourcing), the fund is managed by a parity board. This board is comprised of employee representatives who are nominated by the unions (in case of sector plans) or by the works council (in the case of company plans). Most pension plans contract out the pension arrangement to commercial insurance companies such as Axa, KBC, Allianz or AG Insurance (formerly Fortis), or to mutual insurance companies like Ethias. There is only one pension provider in Belgium that is organized as a non-profit mutual benefit society with parity control: the Liège-based institution l'Integrale (the only remaining fund of the 15 subsidiary carriers that were established during the 1920s to implement the scheme for salaried employees). In case the implementation of the pension arrangement is contracted out to a commercial pension institution, parity control of this organization would be little more than an empty shell; therefore, the law requires the creation of a parity-based supervisory committee (*toezichtscomité*) to keep an eye on what the institution implementing the plan does. But in contrast to the management board of an integrated pension plan, this committee is not directly involved in the financial governance but only has an information right with respect to insurance company's investment policies. The insurance company has to submit annually a declaration of investment principles that explains the investment portfolio, asset management, and risk control; it also has to issue a transparency report that states the returns on the investments, the extent to which social and environmental criteria have been taken into account in investments, the cost structure and allocation of the profits sharing. Even when the pension plan is not outsourced, the parity-controlled pension fund board often does little more than choosing a consulting company, which in turn selects a fund manager.

Stakeholder influence is largely limited to formulating the conditions of the pension agreement during the collective wage bargaining that precedes the establishing of the plan, choosing a financial service company to implement that agreement, and specifying the conditions of the insurance contract. Employee involvement in determining the input for contracting out the pension plan may help to secure the long-term financial interests of scheme members, but it hardly gives them a voice in the way in which the funds, accumulated on their behalf, are invested. Control over investment remains solely in the hands of the financial service firm that occupies a key role in the complex chain of principal–agent relationships typical of externally funded occupational pensions. That is one of the reasons why supervision by the regulator is of central importance.

The Belgian pension industry is regulated and supervised by an independent agency, the Banking, Finance, and Insurance Commission (*Commissie voor Bank-, Financie-, and Assurantiewezen* or CBFA). The members of its management board and the supervisory board are nominated by the federal ministries of finance and of economic affairs. Two of the four members of the management board have to come from the Belgian National Bank. The CBFA can impose sanctions including the withdrawal of the licence of the pension institution that implements the pension arrangement, impose fines in case regulations are violated, or take the pension institution to court.

There is no special insolvency protection for pension funds or insurance companies. But in case an insurance company goes bankrupt and is not taken over by another company, its financial reserves cannot be used to settle general debts but have to be distributed between the beneficiaries of the insurance policies. In the advent of the financial crisis of 2008, the government decided to extent the coverage of the protection fund for deposits that guarantee bank-savings up to €100,000 to the life insurance policies with a guaranteed rate of return, even though all occupational plans (i.e. group insurances) were explicitly excluded from this extension. Thus, the guarantee only applies to a part of third-pillar savings, and even here it is up to the decision of each insurance company whether or not to join the guarantee system (Assuralia 2009).

10. Outlook

Belgium is an unusual case in the world of supplementary pensions. The Belgian public pension limits its aims to guarantee status maintenance in old age for employees with an income up to the median. According to the crowding-in thesis, this should have provided a fertile ground for the development of occupational pensions for higher-income groups. The corporatist system of wage bargaining and the relative high trade union density – both amongst blue-collar workers and white-collar employees – should have further facilitated the development of encompassing second-pillar pensions. Whereas other neo-corporatist regimes with statutory pensions not performing the second-tier income maintenance function developed, albeit in different ways, a supplementary system of adequate pensions for most of their wage earners, Belgium failed to do so. Despite the availability of several institutional mechanisms that facilitated the expansion of occupational pensions elsewhere, such as the administrative extension of wage agreements (as in the Netherlands), relatively high trade union density (comparable to Denmark), and a state that is quite capable of mandating labour market actors in other policy areas (similar to the *Obligatorium* in Switzerland). None of these institutional mechanisms came to effective use to promote the development of occupational pensions in Belgium.

Instead, the Belgian conservative-corporatist welfare state left an important part of income maintenance in old age to voluntaristic initiatives reminiscent of the practices prevailing in Liberal welfare regimes. Meanwhile, Belgians sought to secure adequate pensions via other individualized savings vehicles that are not specifically intended for retirement purposes alone. Only towards the end of the twentieth century, attempts were made to develop comprehensive occupational pensions resulting in a more encompassing second pillar. Yet the corporatist system paradoxically frustrated attempts to adequately fund the more widely available extra-statutory benefits. Embedding the occupational pension in the system of joint committees might have been a good strategy to make it more inclusive and to broaden coverage amongst manual workers and less well-to-do white-collar employees. At the same time, it also limited the room for mobilizing the funds that are necessary if the second pillar is to fulfil its role of safeguarding income maintenance in retirement at adequate levels. The system of wage moderation only allows the resources necessary for a well-funded mature second pillar to be exchanged for relinquishing wage growth or even accept cuts in real wages. This has now brought the country to a point where a majority of wage earners are covered but only by schemes that are underfinanced and therefore likely to produce meagre supplementary benefits for the future generation of pensioners. Those supplementary pensions will still fall short of performing the second-tier function of genuine income maintenance in old age.

Because neither the first nor the second pillar are capable of producing genuine earnings-related benefits for middle- and higher-income groups, third pillar voluntary arrangements in the form of life insurances have seen a spectacular development. They appear to have taken over the income-maintaining function from other non-tax-privileged individual savings instruments like state bonds, deposit accounts, and savings accounts stashed away in tax heavens. This shift might be partly due to a more effective fight against tax fraud, recently made possible by information exchanges between the tax authorities in Europe. It might also have to do with the low interest rates of the past years and European monetary integration that has affected the way the public debt is managed and the way it is being financed.

The guaranteed rates of return promised by life insurances in the individual and group insurance plans might initially have appeared an attractive alternative to state bonds and deposit accounts with their low yield. However, the financial crisis of 2008 seems to have put in jeopardy this popular private pension savings strategy. Several of the largest providers of group and individual life insurances came close to default and had to be bailed out by the state.

These included Dexia, Ethias, ING (the Dutch group that acquired the former Belgian national champion BBL), and Fortis (that rebranded its insurance branch back to the old name AG Insurance). In order to offer their attractive financial products, these financial service providers might have taken too high risks. There is a certain irony in that during the 1990s Fortis had acquired the ASLK, the once public savings and annuities fund that in the nineteenth century had formed the cradle of the Belgian pension system. Fortis, which controls about one-third of the life insurance market, recently had to be rescued by the Belgian state and was sold to BNP Paribas – one of the largest French financial groups operating in a country with a largely unfunded occupational pension system.

Bibliography

Assuralia (2005). *Les pensions complémentaires après la loi Vandenbroucke*. Brussels: Assuralia (www.assuralia.be).

——(2009). *Constat et perspectives 2008–2009*. Brussels: Assuralia (www.assuralia.be).

Becht, M., Chapelle, A., and Renneboog, L. (2001). 'Shareholding Cascades: The Separation of Ownership and Control in Belgium', in F. Barca and M. Becht (eds.), *The Control of Corporate Europe*. Oxford: Oxford University Press, 71–105.

Berghman, J. et al. (2008). 'Cartographie des retraites Belges. Partie 2: Pensions du premier et du deuxième pilier chez les travailleurs salariés retraites'. *Working Paper Sécurité Sociale no. 8*.

CBFA (2007). *Rapport bisannuel concernant les régimes de pension sectoriels*. Brussels: CBFA.

De Deken, J. (2009). 'Depoliticising the Financing of the Welfare State? Financial Profiling and the Hidden Costs of Privatised Retirement Provision'. Paper presented at the 2009 ESPANET Conference, Urbino, Italy, September 17–19, 2009.

——van Riel, B., Ponds, E. (2006). 'Social Solidarity', in G. Clarck et al. (eds.), *Oxford Handbook of Pensions and Retirement Income*. Oxford: Oxford University Press.

Dewilde, C., and Raeymaeckers, P. (2008). 'The Trade-off between Home-ownership and Pensions: Individual and Institutional Determinants of Old-age Poverty'. *Ageing & Society*, 28: 805–30.

Eurostat (2007). *European Social Statistics. Social Protection Expenditure and Receipts*. Luxembourg: Official Publications of the European Communities.

Gieselinck, G., Peeters, H., Van Gestel, V., Berghman, J., and Van Buggenhout, B. (2002). *Het Belgisch pensioenlandschap sinds 1980*. Leuven: Katholieke Universiteit Leuven.

——————(2003). *Onzichtbare pensioenen in België*. Gent: Academia Press.

Lewalle, H. (1986). 'Les pensions légales et complementaires'. *Courrier Hebdomadaire du CRISP no. 1131–1132*.

Ministerie van Sociale Voorzorg (2004). *Vademecum: begroting van de sociale bescherming*. Brussels: Federal Ministry of Social Affairs.

NAR (2005). *Rapport Nr.66 van de Nationale Arbeidsraad met betrekking tot de financiering van de sociale zekerheid*. Brussels: NAR.

OECD (2007). *Pensions at a Glance*. Paris: OECD.

Pasture, P. (1996). 'Belgium: Pragmatism in Pluralism', in P. Pasture, J. Verberckmoes and H. de Witte (eds.), *The Lost Perspective. Trade Unions between Ideology and Social Action in the New Europe. Vol. 1. Ideological Persistence in National Traditions*. Aldershot: Avebury, 91–135.

Studiecommissie voor de Vergrijzing (2002). *Jaarlijks verslag*. Brussels: Hoge Raad voor Financiën.

——(2007). *Jaarlijks verslag*. Brussels: Hoge Raad voor Financiën.

Traxler, F. and Huemer, G. (eds.) (2007). *The Handbook of Business Interest Associations, Firm Size and Governance: A Comparative Analytical Approach*. London: Routledge.

Vanthiemen, K. (2006). *De omvang van de pensioenen uit de tweede pijler voor arbeiders en lagere bedienden*. Thesis, University of Hasselt.

Verbond van Belgische Ondernemingen (2006). *Pensioenen: de financiële toekomst waarborgen*. Brussels (www.vbo-feb.be).

4

France: Promoting Funded Pensions in Bismarckian Corporatism?

Marek Naczyk and Bruno Palier

1. Introduction

For long, the French pension system has been characterized by its Bismarckian public pensions and its deliberate shunning of funded private pensions. While other countries have often complemented statutory pensions with funded occupational pensions, the French social partners have put in place encompassing supplementary pension schemes financed on a pay-as-you-go (PAYG) basis. The generosity of these schemes and their defence by trade unions and some of the business community have considerably limited the space for funded pensions. However, current reforms are leading to an increased harmonization of these occupational schemes and have been reducing replacement rates in the first and the second pillars. As a result, the development of pension savings has been promoted implicitly, albeit more on a voluntary basis than on a compulsory one. Meanwhile, the French economy has experienced important changes as the state's gradual withdrawal from the economy has resulted in the prevalence of market mechanisms in an increasing number of sectors. The promotion of French pension funds (*fonds de pension*) is thus considered by government officials and business groups as a means to strengthen the foundations of the changing French economy. After a presentation of the main features of the French pension system and of its historical evolution, this chapter will analyse the governance of mandatory PAYG supplementary schemes as well as the functioning of funded – occupational and personal – pension plans. In the second part, we first give an overview of who is covered by the different schemes. We then describe the type of benefits that are offered and how they are financed. Finally, we analyse the administrative and the regulatory governance of the different schemes.

Part I: Evolution of the public–private pension mix

2. The main features of the pension system

The French pension system is almost exclusively a social insurance system financed on a PAYG basis largely through social security contributions and, to a lesser degree, general taxes. It is managed by pension institutions (*caisses d'assurance vieillesse*) independent of the state budget and overseen by bipartite administrative boards with employee and employer representatives. Most employees are covered and the earnings-related benefits are provided to pensioners with sufficient contribution records. For older people who do not qualify for a contributory pension at all or whose retirement benefits are too low, the state provides a means-tested minimum pension.[1] As a result of a high degree of occupational fragmentation, different categories of workers are covered by particular mandatory pension arrangements. Private-sector employees (around 60 per cent of the workforce) have been traditionally covered by a public first-tier pension, *régime général*, and a mandatory occupational second-tier pension (*régimes complémentaires obligatoires*) whereas, until recently, farmers, most of the self-employed and public sector employees were covered by specific single-tier public pension schemes (see Figure 4.1).

The general scheme (*régime général*) provides a basic defined-benefit (DB) pension financed by social security contributions with a maximum gross replacement rate of 50 per cent of the annual average earnings (based on the twenty-five best years).[2] Contrary to the general scheme which was created by statute, the supplementary schemes (*régimes complémentaires*) were established by collective agreements, giving the social partners an exclusive responsibility for their day-to-day administration. These occupational pension schemes also operate on a PAYG basis. Employees receive points for their contributions, which later determine the pension level, therefore called 'points schemes'. Contributions are paid to independent pension institutions which must comply with rules set by two bipartite federations: *Association des Régimes de Retraites Complémentaires* (ARRCO), regroups all supplementary retirement institutions for all private-sector employees, and *Association Générale des Institutions de Retraites des Cadres* (AGIRC), supervises supplementary pension institutions for foremen, managers, and engineers (the 'cadres'). The principles regulating old-age pensions are roughly the same for farmers (3 per cent of the workforce) and the self-employed (12 per cent), but their schemes are managed by separate organizations. These occupational categories also receive a basic DB pension, calculated on the basis of an annual average income. However, these schemes

---

[1] *Minimum-vieillesse* and, since 2007, *allocation de solidarité aux personnes âgées*.

[2] The maximum replacement rate is offered after a minimum contributory period (37.5 years until the 1993 reform, 41 since 2008).

are much more heavily state subsidized than the *régime général*. Most of the self-employed did not draw a second-pillar pension, until the 2003 Fillon reform required all the self-employed (including farmers) to pay contributions to supplementary pension schemes.

In contrast to the private sector, tenured public employees have traditionally received more generous retirement benefits from the public pension pillar. Each category of public employees, that is, civil servants, local government employees, or employees of state-owned firms (in total 20 per cent of the workforce) must join specific pension plans that are PAYG and offer final-salary DB pensions with a maximum gross replacement rate of 75 per cent of the last six months earnings. A minimum contribution period of fifteen years is required, but the maximum benefit can be secured after a 37.5 or forty-year contribution period. However, these plans also differ in certain respects, notably the minimum retirement age spans from 40 years for dancers at the Paris Opera and 50 years for railwaymen to 55 or 60 years for civil servants. Public sector schemes have thus historically been more generous than private sector schemes. Nevertheless, the architecture of these schemes is rapidly changing.

The specific architecture of the French pension system has considerably hindered the development of fully funded pensions. Since all statutory benefits are earnings related, pensioners have been generally able to maintain their income status. Historically, only a few occupational categories have benefited from funded pensions: teachers (CREF), state employees (PREFON-*Retraite*), and a few employees in certain private companies (such as in banking and insurance). However, recent reforms have been systematically promoting funded private pensions. Since 1994, the self-employed have been offered tax incentives in order to sign up for voluntary pension savings plans. The 2003 Fillon reform established a mandatory funded points scheme for all civil servants. The reform also introduced two new instruments that are to counterbalance the future erosion of private employees' statutory pensions. On the one hand, social partners are encouraged to negotiate the creation of firm-level or sectorwide pension schemes with voluntary participation (*plan d'épargne retraite collectif* or PERCO). On the other hand, tax rebates are offered to individuals who will join a personal retirement plan (*plan d'épargne retraite populaire* or PERP). The popularity of life insurance contracts (Palier 2007) and the relative success of the newly introduced funded schemes (DREES 2009) seem to point to a gradual change in the public–private mix of the French pension system.

3. The French pension system in context

The post-war French pension system resulted from a compromise between left and centre-right forces. The dominant corporatist paradigm among bureaucrats led to the adoption of a welfare system aimed at providing male workers with

	First pillar	Second pillar			Third pillar
	State pension	Occupational pension	Funded occupational pension		Personal pension
		PAYG	Employer commitment	Collective agreement	
Third tier (topping up / replacement gap)				PERCO: voluntary fully funded DC with tax incentives	PERP: voluntary fully funded DC schemes with tax incentives
			Art. 39: mandatory fully funded DB pensions; tax incentives Art. 83: mandatory fully funded DC; tax incentives		
Second tier (income maintenance)		Mandatory PAYG 'points' schemes, financed by social contributions and managed by the social partners: • for all wage earners (ARRCO) • for 'cadres'/ executives (AGIRC)			
First tier (poverty alleviation)	Statutory PAYG DB pension scheme (*régime général*), financed by social contributions and managed by the social partners (controlled by the executive and the Parliament)				
Means-tested	Minimum income in old age (*ASPA* – formerly *minimum vieillesse*), tax-financed				

Figure 4.1 Pillars and tiers of French pensions for private sector employees

job security and income maintenance (Palier 2005a). However, following the 1970s economic crisis and after a period of hesitant Keynesian policy responses, policymakers decided to address the new economic conditions by adopting a 'neo-liberal modernization strategy' (Hall 2001: 176). Meanwhile, social policy expenditures increased in order to mitigate the effects of massive job loss. Economic, technological, and demographic shocks; a radical U-turn in economic policy; and fairly generous but costly social policies created several difficulties: a challenge of the functioning of the existing pension system, a worsening of already contentious labour relations, and a redefinition of the pension system's role within a changing political economy.

Like other Bismarckian welfare systems, France has been affected by the 'welfare without work' predicament. Early retirement programmes started to be used at the beginning of the 1970s and were expanded in the 1980s (Ebbinghaus 2006). Many large firms took advantage of these 'labour shedding' strategies which permitted the implementation of large-scale restructuring plans. As a result, employment rates among youths and elderly workers dropped considerably compared to the end of the 1970s. The pension system has also been challenged by other developments in the labour market. The growing use of atypical work arrangements, such as fixed-term and part-time contracts, has led to growing inequalities among different categories of workers and has particularly affected youths, women, and low-skilled workers. While the post-war welfare system relied heavily on job security and stable (full time) careers, the flexibilization and segmentation of the labour market means that in the future growing numbers of people will have uneven employment records and thus incomplete contribution records. Recent pension reforms have been tackling this problem by reinforcing the means-tested public pension. At the same time, the existence of multiple pension arrangements is considered to be a brake for labour market mobility because it may create incentives to stay within the same occupation.[3] Therefore, current reforms aim at harmonizing eligibility criteria and benefit formulas across different occupational pension schemes.

These tensions between labour market developments and social protection have led to more frequent conflicts between trade unions, business groups, and the state. After the Second World War, organized capital and labour were characterized by a strong degree of centralization and politicization. Trade unions in particular were unable to develop appropriate organizational capacities at the firm level because of three main factors: union fragmentation following political schisms, the ubiquitous role of the state that uses *erga omnes* extensions of collective agreements,[4] and finally the involvement of social partners in the joint administration of the welfare system. However, since the 1980s, a continuous trend of decentralization of industrial relations has been taking place (Lallemand 2006). These structural features of French

---

[3] About 40 per cent of French pensioners draw their benefits out of at least two different first-pillar pension schemes.

[4] The extension procedure allows the ministry to extend sector-level or nationwide collective agreements signed by at least one trade union and one employers' association to all firms active within the sector or country.

labour relations as well as the institutional characteristics of the French pension system have a threefold effect on current pension policy. First, the state is given the leading role in the reform of statutory pensions, while social partners mostly act as interest or veto groups. Second, the state has practically no influence on developments in private occupational pensions since their management lies exclusively with the social partners. Third, the poor organizational basis of trade unions combined with the 'crowding-out' effect of generous PAYG statutory and occupational pensions reduces the social partners' ability to negotiate sectorwide or firm-level fully funded occupational pensions in the private sector.

The French political economy has often been described as a 'state-coordinated' market economy (Schmidt 1996, 2009), but recent institutional changes suggest its transformation towards a more liberal market economy (Culpepper 2006; Hall 2006, 2007). Since the end of the 1980s, the still overwhelmingly Bismarckian welfare system has undergone incremental but also transformative changes, reflecting a growing reliance on market-based resource allocation (Palier 2005*b*). Economic institutions have been even more radically transformed: monetary policy has been devolved to the supranational level, product markets have been opened to international competition, and the state has gradually pulled out of the productive system. Deregulation of the financial system and changes in corporate law have made the Paris Stock Exchange a favourite destination for Anglo-American investment funds (Goyer 2007). The increasing dependence on short-term capital provided by financial markets and, as a result, the growing weight of foreign institutional investors have provoked a paradigm shift in pension policy among French political and business elites. The promotion of French pension funds has become a central priority and is presented, in political discourse, as a means of counteracting the strength of 'Anglo-Saxon' pension funds by giving back decision-making power to French investors in a globalizing world (Palier 2007; Palier and Bonoli 2000).

4. The emergence of the public–private pension mix

The French pension system developed in three main stages (see Table 4.1). The first pension arrangements were established not only to alleviate the growing problem of poverty among old workers but also to overcome manpower shortages in the industry. Historically, the earliest pensions instituted in France were employer initiatives. The state established special schemes for regular soldiers and for civil servants in the first half of the nineteenth century. Later in the century, railway and mining companies as well as firms in manufacturing created their own firm-level schemes. However, in 1898, only 10 per cent of private sector workers were entitled to receive private retirement benefits (Guillemard 1986: 37), while an ever larger part of elderly people was struck by

Table 4.1 Chronology of major pension reforms, 1905–82

Year	Reform	Political context
Nineteenth century	• state-sponsored pension schemes for civil servants and the military • employer-sponsored pension arrangements for workers in industry	Second Empire/Third Republic
1905	Social assistance for people in old age • covers men in old age (70+) and the disabled • financed and administered jointly by the state and local authorities	Bourgeois 'radical' government
1910	Old age insurance for workers and farmers (*Loi sur les retraites ouvrières et paysannes*) • mandatory social insurance for workers (up to an earnings limit) and voluntary social insurance for farmers and the self-employed • fully funded/DC benefits for people in old age (65+) • administered mainly by the national pension bank, mutual aid societies and funds managed by employers	Bourgeois parties allied with reformist Socialists
1928–30	Social Insurance Acts (*Lois sur les assurances sociales*) • mandatory social insurance for workers (up to an earning limit) • fully funded/DC benefits for people in old age (60+), between 20% and 40% replacement rate after a 30-year contribution record • administered by state-supervised local and regional funds	Left-wing initiative adopted under centre-right (corporatist – Laval and Tardieu) government
1945	*Régime général* • mandatory social insurance for all wage earners of the private sector (and, initially, for all members of the workforce) • PAYG/DB pensions for people in old age (flexible retirement age from age 60), with a 30-year contribution record • administered by public pension funds, supervised by the social partners	Post-war settlement between the left and the centre-right
1947	• Creation of AGIRC • System administered by the social partners	Collective agreement
1961	Creation of ARRCO (extended by the state to all firms in 1972)	Collective agreement
1971	*Loi Boulin*: Changes in benefit formula (*régime général*)	Centre-right government
1982	Statutory retirement age set at 60 years for all employees of the private sector	Socialist government

Source: Hatzfeld (1971), Guillemard (1986), Dutton (2002), Palier (2005a).

indigence. In 1905, parliament passed a law which compelled the central state and local authorities to offer assistance to poverty-stricken people who were at least 70 years old. Five years later, a social insurance scheme for workers and farmers was instituted, but contribution and benefit levels were low and implementation failed due to problems with the collection of contributions. After the First World War, attempts to set up a nationwide statutory pension as in formerly German Alsace and Lorraine met strong resistance from mutual aid societies, employers' associations, farmers' unions, and the dominant bourgeois political elites of the Third Republic (Dutton 2002; Hatzfeld 1971). A decade passed before legislation on social insurance was enacted: a first act was voted in 1928, but it was replaced by a new one in 1930. Yet only a minority of workers received appropriate pension benefits and many retirees whose income depended on their savings were hit by the monetary instability of the 1930s. The fully funded social insurance went bankrupt in 1941, under the Vichy regime. These events were largely responsible for the French citizens' and policymakers' lack of trust in funded schemes after the Second World War.

During the second stage of the pension system's development, the main objective was to provide most people in old age with earnings-related benefits. Influenced by the Beveridge report, policymakers intended to establish a single social insurance scheme for the entire workforce (including the self-employed). A *régime général de sécurité sociale*, which offered a very basic earnings-related DB pension with an income ceiling, was established by government legislation in October 1945 (Palier 2005*a*). Two very significant changes were introduced in the system's financing and management: statutory pensions were now financed on a PAYG basis, and trade unions were recognized as stakeholders on an equal footing with employers' associations. Despite this initial unification attempt, different occupational categories succeeded in keeping or establishing their own pension schemes. Public sector workers, both from the civil service and from recently nationalized companies, such as the railways (*SNCF*) and energy companies (*EDF-GDF*), managed to negotiate separate schemes which offered higher benefits than the *régime général*. Other occupations also struggled for separate pension schemes so as to pay lower contribution rates. Their efforts were rewarded after the communists left the government in 1947. Pension arrangements for the self-employed (craftsmen, tradesmen, manufacturers, and the learned professions) became compulsory in 1948, and those for farmers in 1952. As a result, French pensions were now mandatory for a much larger part of the population, but the system remained strongly fragmented along occupational lines.

More and more the focus shifted towards the problem of income maintenance in old age. Even though they offered DB pensions, statutory schemes did not guarantee generous benefits for all workers, particularly those with higher earnings (above the contribution ceiling). Discontented with their incorporation into the *régime général*, representatives of management staff in private companies (the 'cadres') were able to negotiate a collective agreement that established a supplementary PAYG 'point' scheme which would 'top up' their statutory first-tier pensions (Boltanski 1987; Friot 1996; Reynaud 1997): AGIRC was thus founded in 1947. From 1956, various firms and sectors created similar supplementary schemes for other occupations. In order to strengthen coordination between these multiple schemes and to improve coverage, the social partners established in 1961 the national federation ARRCO. In 1962, this collective agreement was extended by the state to all sectors encompassed by the main employers' association (CNPF). These agreements were a turning point in the transformation of pre-existing fully funded occupational schemes into PAYG ones as well as in the recognition of *paritarisme* (bipartite administration). In the 1970s, government policy focused on the reduction of the income gap between the working population and retirees and on the extension of pension coverage to groups that had been previously left aside. The Boulin Law of 1971 improved the benefit formula in the *régime général* by increasing the maximum replacement rate to 50 per cent (instead of 40 per cent) of the 'reference salary' (ten best years) and by granting pension credits to women with children. Craftsmen's and tradesmen's pensions were aligned with those of the *régime général* in 1972. In the same year, the state also intervened by making participation in ARRCO or AGIRC schemes compulsory for all private firms. Private employees drawing pensions from both the public and occupational pillars could now get a replacement rate between 70 per cent and 80 per cent of the reference salary, a level almost comparable with public employee pensions.

5. The changing public–private pension mix

After thirty years of remarkable expansion, French pension policy entered a new phase at the end of the 1970s, when successive governments started to restructure and reduce pension expenditure. Like other Bismarckian systems, the French pension system responded to demographic and socioeconomic pressures through a characteristic four-stage sequence of transformations, wherein each stage influenced the next (Bonoli and Palier 2007). First, the escalation in pension expenditures led to increases in payroll taxes, constituting the 'automatic' adjustment mechanism built into social insurance. In the *régime général*, employers' contributions were gradually raised from 5.5 per cent of gross pay (up to a ceiling) in 1970 to 8.2 per cent in 1979. They remained stable until 1991, when the government introduced a new contribution, without ceiling, of 1.6 per cent of gross pay. Employees' contribution rates increased from 3 per cent in 1970, to 4.7 per cent in 1979, to 6.55 per cent in 1991. In 1993 and 1994, contribution rates were also increased by the social partners in both ARRCO and AGIRC pension schemes, but these changes coincided with a reduction in benefits.

The second transformative stage took place in the early 1990s when concerns over rising contribution rates as well as the necessity to comply with the

Maastricht criteria provided a spur for a first wave of retrenchment. In 1993, the Balladur government implemented a reform that was limited to the *régime général*. Three measures aimed directly at a reduction in benefits and, indirectly, at an increase in retirement age. First, the contribution period required for a full pension was to be increased from 37.5 to forty years. Second, benefits were to be calculated on the basis of the twenty-five (instead of the ten) best years of earnings. These two changes were to be phased in over eleven years. Third, benefit indexation was linked to price inflation rather than to wage increases. Despite opposition from the Left and unions, the Balladur reform met surprisingly with little resistance, thanks to negotiations which resulted in a *quid pro quo* between the government and unions (Bonoli 1997). By creating an 'old-age solidarity fund' (*fonds de solidarité vieillesse*), the government acceded to the unions' persistent demand that means-tested pensions as well as pension credits for non-contributory periods be financed out of general tax revenues instead of being financed by social insurance funds. In 1995, Prime Minister Alain Juppé attempted to push through a similar reform in the civil servants' pension schemes as well as in the *régimes spéciaux*, that is, the pension schemes of employees of a number of state-owned firms or organizations (see Table 4.2), but he failed because he did not conduct prior negotiations with the unions (Bonoli 2000; Schludi 2005).

The Balladur reform, Juppé's failed attempt, the publication of several reports under the socialist government between 1997 and 2002, and the creation of a pension reserve fund (*fonds de réserve pour les retraites*) in 1999 contributed to dramatizing the French pension crisis. Due to this climate of insecurity and the new opportunities offered by financial deregulation, the 1990s saw a growing number of people 'save' for their pension, via financial products such as life insurance (Palier 2007). This relatively unexpected development facilitated more radical retrenchment in a second wave of reforms. In 2003, the newly elected Raffarin government brought about a major reform that affected most pension schemes. This reform, however, did not impact the *régimes spéciaux*. The most conspicuous change has been the gradual equalization of the contribution period required for a full pension between the civil servants' pension schemes and the *régime général* (see Table 4.2). A second key measure was intended to increase employment rates among the elderly: a system of disincentives to early retirement (*décote*, i.e. benefit cuts) as well as incentives to postpone retirement (*surcote*, i.e. augmented benefits) was created in all schemes affected by the reform. After fierce opposition and large demonstrations, the government made a few concessions to the unions concerning minimum pensions (85 per cent of minimum wage) and a retirement age of 58 for workers with long working lives. Left unaffected in 2003, *régimes spéciaux* were later modified by the Fillon government in 2007. In this second wave of reforms, retrenchment was tolerated by the public, arguably because of growing concerns over inequalities between different occupations (private vs. public

Table 4.2 Chronology of pension reforms since the 1980s

Year	Reform	Political context
1993	*Balladur* Reform (*régime général*)	RPR-UDF coalition
	• Reference salary calculated on the basis of 25 best years (instead of 10 best years)	
	• Contribution record for full pension increased from 37.5 years to 40 years	
	• Price indexation instead of wage indexation	
	• Establishment of the Fonds de Solidarité Vieillesse to finance non-contributory benefits (financed through CSG)	
1995	*Juppé* Plan (civil servants' pension schemes and *régimes spéciaux*)	RPR-UDF coalition mass strike
	• civil servants' pension schemes and régimes spéciaux to be 'aligned' with régime général. Notably, contribution record for full pension to be increased from 37.5 years to 40 years, in public sector schemes (abortive attempt)	
	• extension of governmental and parliamentary control over social security budget (Loi de financement de la sécurité sociale)	
1997	*Thomas* Law (not implemented and repealed in 2002)	RPR-UDF coalition (parliamentary initiative)
	• fully funded DC pension arrangements (*plans d'épargne-retraite*) to be established at the firm level or at the industry level, with voluntary participation	
1999	Introduction of statutory pension reserve fund (FRR)	Left-wing party government coalition
1993–4	AGIRC and ARRCO agreements	Collective agreements
	• increases in contribution rates	
1996	• price indexation of 'notional contributions' (points) as well as of current benefits	
2001	• clearing system between AGIRC and ARRCO	
	• simplified governance (fewer pension funds and greater cooperation between the two federations)	
2003	*Fillon* Reform (various pension schemes)	UMP majority
	• Contribution record for full pension in civil servants' pension schemes increased from 37.5 years to 40 years by 2008	
	• Contribution record for full pension in régime général and in civil servants' schemes to be increased from 40 years in 2008 to 41 years by 2012 (and 42 years by 2020)	
	• Disincentives to early retirement and incentives to postponed retirement (all schemes)	
	• Funded points scheme for civil servants and PAYG points scheme for the self-employed	
	• Legal framework for (voluntary) occupational and personal fully funded DC pension arrangements	
2007–8	*Régimes spéciaux* Reform	UMP majority
	• Contribution record for full pension in *régimes spéciaux* increased from 37.5 years to 40 years	
	• Price indexation instead of wage indexation	
	• Disincentives to early retirement and incentives to postponed retirement	

Source: Bonoli (2000), Palier (2005*a*), Palier (2007).

employees) and growing acceptance of fully funded pensions as a complement to public pensions.

The 2003 Fillon reform was also a breakaway from the existing public–private mix since it conspicuously planned to promote voluntary retirement savings plans. For the first time, a stable legal framework has been introduced for voluntary occupational (PERCO) and personal (PERP) fully funded defined-contribution (DC) pension arrangements. The same reform also introduced a mandatory pension fund for all civil servants which allows them to accrue pension rights on their bonuses (RAFP – see Table 4.4). Like in many Bismarckian systems, the first (1993) and the second (2003/2007–8) wave of reforms led more and more younger cohorts to join pension funds in order to save for their own retirement. The development of funded pensions, which constitutes a fourth sequence of transformations, is still at an initial stage, but the number of contributors to these schemes has been growing steadily since their introduction.

Part II: The governance of supplementary pensions

6. Who is covered?

French occupational pensions are unique since they are by and large not fully funded but are based on PAYG financing. National schemes were created for 'cadres' (managers and professional staff) in the private sector in 1947 (AGIRC) and for other private sector employees in 1961 (ARRCO), becoming mandatory for all private sector employees in 1972. While 'cadres' were initially covered only by AGIRC, they have also been paying contributions to ARRCO since 1972. Contributions in AGIRC and ARRCO are paid not only by employees having full-time and/or permanent contracts but also by workers in atypical employment (i.e. having part-time and/or fixed-term contracts). Their contributions, and consequently their benefits, are calculated on the same basis as those of standard workers. Although ARRCO schemes could be initially characterized as 'occupational' given that contribution levels and benefit formulas varied according to company or sector, the gradual harmonization of ARRCO schemes changed the meaning of 'occupational' to refer to differences in the socio-economic status of the beneficiaries: wage earners vs. the self-employed, managers vs. white-/blue-collar employees, public- vs. private-sector employees. Indeed, based on the AGIRC/ARRCO model, mandatory PAYG 'points schemes' have been gradually extended to other occupational categories. Thus, a special scheme was created in 1970 for public employees without tenure (IRCANTEC[5]) and another one for craftsmen in 1978. Other occupational

---

[5] *Institution de Retraite Complémentaire des Agents Non Titulaires de l'État et des Collectivités Publiques.*

categories were excluded until recently, but occupational PAYG points schemes were created for the self-employed and for farmers in 2003 (see Table 4.3). This part concentrates upon the ARRCO and AGIRC schemes since they cover approximately two-thirds of the workforce and provided a blueprint for similar schemes for other occupational categories.

Because, when combined, statutory and supplementary PAYG pension schemes have traditionally offered high replacement rates, funded pensions have been used mainly as a means to 'top up' retirement income. Given the high degree of occupational fragmentation within statutory pension schemes and therefore divergent needs among different categories of workers, the development of funded pensions has also been characterized by a very high degree of decentralization and, therefore, by multiple governance structures. Until the 1990s, funded schemes were established spontaneously for a limited number of occupational categories and did not operate under a unified regulatory framework. Public-sector employees have traditionally had the widest access to voluntary DC old age savings plans through schemes such as CREF, CRH, PREFON, or FONPEL. The 2003 Fillon reform has even extended coverage by public-sector pension funds by creating a mandatory funded points scheme which allows all civil servants to accrue pension rights on their bonuses. State intervention was necessary to promote special voluntary schemes for farmers (*exploitants agricoles* contracts) and for the self-employed ('Madelin' contracts) (see Table 4.4).

Private-sector employees have historically had more limited access to funded pension plans. Additional occupational pensions have been provided almost exclusively at the firm level, because collective bargaining is highly decentralized. Although no general legal framework exists governing the regulation of funded occupational plans, the French General Tax Code defines two main forms of firm-level or sectorwide pension plans: DB schemes (Art. 39) and DC schemes (Art. 83) with mandatory participation by a predefined group of employees of the firm or the sector. Art. 39 schemes are generally offered to a few senior managers employed in large companies[6] as a fringe benefit on top of mandatory AGIRC pensions. At retirement, top executives face a sharp decline in their income as the benefits provided to them by the *régime général* and ARRCO/AGIRC often attain an earnings replacement rate of only 25–35 per cent. Thus, additional DB schemes have been pervasive in major firms such as CAC 40 companies, since they are considered a useful human resource tool to improve recruitment and retention of the highly skilled. Until the mid-1990s, some larger firms, such as Saint-Gobain, Elf-Aquitaine, Usinor-Sacilor, Rhodia,

---

[6] No coverage data are currently available because companies often refuse to divulge this information considered confidential, given its strategic importance in human resources strategy. However, a recent survey carried out by Hewitt Associates shows that DB schemes are offered to a very limited number of employees, as 77 per cent of companies offered them to fewer than 250 employees (see Hewitt Associates 2007: 58).

Table 4.3 Mandatory PAYG occupational schemes (*retraite complémentaire obligatoire*)

Beneficiaries	Coverage[a] (in millions)	Occupational pension form	Initiators (year of enactment)	Sponsors (and financing mode)	Managers	Overseers	Benefit type
Wage earners of the private sector	Contrib.: 18[b] Benef.: 11.3[b]	ARRCO	Collective agreement (1961) extended by the state	Employers and employees (contributions)	1. 'paritarian' institutions 2. ARRCO	Bipartite supervisory boards (in 1. and 2.)	Points scheme
Managers of the private sector	Contrib.: 3.73[b] Benef.: 2.17[b]	AGIRC	Collective agreement (1947) extended by the state	Employers and employees (contributions)	1. 'paritarian' institutions 2. AGIRC	Bipartite supervisory boards (in 1. and 2.)	Points scheme
Wage earners of the public sector without tenure	Contrib.: 2.5 Benef.: 1.65	IRCANTEC	State (1970)	State as employer and employees (contributions)	IRCANTEC *and Caisse des Dépôts (CDC)*	Bipartite supervisory board	Points scheme
Self-employed farmers	Contrib.: 0.53 Benef.: 0.45	*Régime de retraite complémentaire obligatoire*	State (2002)	The insured (contributions) and the state (subsidies)	*Mutualité sociale agricole*	Supervisory board (members = representatives of the insured)	Points scheme
Craftsmen	Contrib.: 1.36 Benef.: 0.96	*Régime de retraite complémentaire obligatoire*	State (1978/ reformed and merged with tradesmen's scheme in 2003)	The insured (contributions) and the state (subsidies)	*Régime social des indépendants*	Supervisory board (members = representatives of the insured)	Points scheme
Tradesmen and manufacturers			State (2003)				

Notes: a: figures are for 2006; b: figures on 31 December 2007.
Source: AGIRC-ARRCO (2008); www.arrco.fr/chiffres-cles0/donnees-statistiques/

Rhône-Poulenc, or insurance companies offered Art. 39 final salary schemes to a larger segment of their employees than just management staff. However, because of changing accounting standards and the necessity to incorporate pension liabilities into company accounts, many of the DB schemes with wider coverage have been closed to new entrants and replaced by Art. 83 DC pension plans. Such DC schemes with mandatory participation cover a much wider number of wage earners, as they are generally accessible to a much larger pool of employees in the companies that provide them. Therefore, Art. 83 schemes are the most prevalent form of non-statutory occupational pensions. In total, approximately 3.0–3.2 million workers were covered by mandatory DC plans in 2007 (DREES 2009: 2), compared with 2.2 million in 2004 (DREES 2006: 3). Beneficiaries of Art. 83 schemes are generally workers with a stable employment history, as these schemes are usually accessible after a minimum length of service in the company (e.g. twelve months).

The Fillon reform also introduced DC collective retirement plans with voluntary participation (*plan d'épargne retraite collectif* or PERCO). Contrary to Art. 39 and Art. 83 plans which can be offered to a limited group of employees in the company, voluntary DC schemes (PERCO) must legally be open to all employees of a company or a branch covered by a PERCO collective agreement. Moreover, PERCO plans are in principle more accessible to atypical workers: the maximum length of service after which a worker is allowed to join the pension plan is three months. The number of companies offering such plans is steadily growing since 2004, particularly in very large companies.[7] 334,000 employees had joined such plans by 2007 (DREES 2009: 2).

Until 2003, legislation concerning personal pension savings plans was checked because of a long-standing opposition from left-wing parties and trade unions as well as dissensions within the business community, particularly between competing insurers, commercial banks, and mutual aid societies (see Palier 2003b, 2007). Therefore, since the 1980s, the dominant form of voluntary retirement savings among private-sector employees has been life insurance (Palier 2007: 101) since it offers generous tax incentives and relatively high rates of return. In 2003–4, 35 per cent of French households had subscribed to a life insurance contract and 27 per cent of these declared that they had done so to better prepare for their retirement (DREES 2006). It was only in 2003 that the government introduced the first 'popular' retirement savings product (*plans d'épargne retraite populaire* or PERP) available for all occupational categories, including for private-sector employees who had thus far had no access to personal pension plans. During the two years that followed its creation, PERP rapidly attracted many subscribers (1.7 million by 2005). However, this initial

---

[7] While 13 per cent of employees in larger companies employing 1,000 workers or more had access to a PERCO plan in 2006, less than 3 per cent were covered in companies employing less than 250 employees (DARES 2008: 2).

Table 4.4 Funded schemes

	Pension form	Coverage (in 1000s)	Beneficiaries	Initiators	Participation	Sponsors (contributions)	Managers	Overseers	Benefit type
Occupational pensions	*Régime Additionnel de la Fonction Publique* (RAFP)	4,600	Civil servants (all categories) and the military	State (2003)	Mandatory	State as employer and employees (contributions on bonuses)	*Etablissement de RAFP and Caisse des Dépôts (CDC)*	Bipartite supervisory board	Points scheme (lifetime annuity)
	Régime chapeau and *régime additif* (Art. 39 CGI)	—	Objectively defined groups of employees in private firms (mainly Executives)	Employer or collective agreement	Mandatory[a]	Employer	Mainly insurance companies, also provident institutions, mutual aid societies	Firm or *ad hoc* supervisory board + ACAM	DB (lifetime annuity)
	Group insurance (Art. 83 CGI)	Between 3,000 and 3,200	Objectively defined groups of employees in private firms	Employer or coll. agreement	Mandatory[a]	Employer (and possibly employee on mandatory basis)	Mainly insurance companies, also provident institutions, mutual aid societies	Firm or *ad hoc* supervisory board + ACAM	DC (lifetime annuity)
	PERE	131	Objectively defined groups of employees in private firms	Employer or coll. agreement	Mandatory[a]	Employer (and possibly employee – on a mandatory and/or voluntary basis)	Mainly insurance companies, also provident institutions, mutual aid societies	Firm or *ad hoc* supervisory board + ACAM	DC (lifetime annuity)
	PERCO	334	All employees of a private firm	Collective agreement	Voluntary	Employee (and employer on a voluntary basis)	Mainly insurance companies, also provident	Ad *hoc* board + ACAM	DC (lifetime annuity

Personal Pensions						institutions, mutual aid societies		or lump sum)
PREFON-Retraite	390	Civil servants (all categories)	Trade unions' initiative	Voluntary	Insured	PREFON and CNP Assurances	Supervisory board (members = trade union officials)	Points scheme (lifetime annuity)
COREM (ex-CREF)	299	All individuals (formerly reserved for teachers)	Consortium of mutual aid societies	Voluntary	Insured	Union mutualiste retraite (UMR)	Supervisory board and General Assembly + ACAM	Points scheme (lifetime annuity)
'Madelin Law' contracts	1,037	Self-employed	Individual decision	Quasi-mandatory	Insured	Insurance companies and mutual aid societies	ACAM	DC (lifetime annuity)
'Exploitants agricoles'	270	Self-employed farmers	Individual decision	Quasi-mandatory	Insured	Insurance companies and mutual aid societies	ACAM	DC (lifetime annuity)
PERP	1,994	All individuals	Individual decision	Voluntary	Insured	Insurance companies and mutual aid societies	GERP + ACAM	DC (lifetime annuity)

Notes: Coverage defined as number of people who contribute to a scheme. Data on coverage indicated for the end of 2007 (DREES 2009); a: applies to all employees of a participating firm. ACAM = *Autorité de Contrôle des Assurances et des Mutuelles* (Insurance and Mutual aid societies Supervisory Authority).
Source: Sénat (2006), DREES (2009).

growth has been slowed, falling short of 2 million contributors at the end of 2007 and only 1,000 beneficiaries (DREES 2009). Sign-up rates among PERP's target population (i.e. private-sector employees) are estimated at 8.6 per cent (FFSA 2008).

7. What kind of benefits?

ARRCO and AGIRC supplementary pensions are point schemes: In return for their contributions, participants earn pension points based on their individual earnings and on the current 'price' of the point. The pension points are recorded throughout the participant's career. At retirement, the scheme calculates the supplementary pension benefit by multiplying the accumulated pension points by the 'pension-point value'. Thus, the pension level depends on the earnings of the whole career. Although not DC plans per se, point schemes are comparable to notional defined-contribution (NDC) pensions (see Legros 2006).

The retirement age at ARRCO and AGIRC is normally set at 65, but given that the retirement age of the public first-tier pension (i.e. in the *régime général*) was lowered to 60 in 1982, social partners negotiated the possibility to draw a full supplementary pension at age 60. There is no minimum contributory period and benefits can be drawn even if the beneficiary lives abroad. As a result, vesting is automatic and the portability of pension rights is ensured by the fact that ARRCO and AGIRC are national – and not sector-level – schemes, thus applying to all wage earners in the private sector. Although the two supplementary schemes are much less redistributive than the *régime général*, 'free' pension points can be earned for non-contributory periods such as unemployment, maternity, sickness, or retirement. Moreover, both ARRCO and AGIRC offer pension credits to those retirees who raised three children or more during their career. Finally, both supplementary schemes offer benefits to the surviving spouse (or to orphaned children under the age of 21).

Although the benefit calculation principles have remained stable throughout the schemes' history, the purchasing power of supplementary benefits has been reduced in recent years, via alterations in indexation mechanisms. From 1993 onwards, the social partners increased the point price – thereby decreasing benefit levels – by indexing it to a much higher value than the price and wage developments. Moreover, they decided to decrease the point value by indexing it to price inflation rather than to wage growth. Between 2003 and 2008, the point price – used to calculate pension credits – was indexed again to wage growth, but the point value – used to calculate benefits – continued to be indexed to price inflation. Figure 4.2 shows how in recent years the price and the value of the point evolved in AGIRC. Developments concerning indexation were comparable in ARRCO and could lead to a considerable decline in

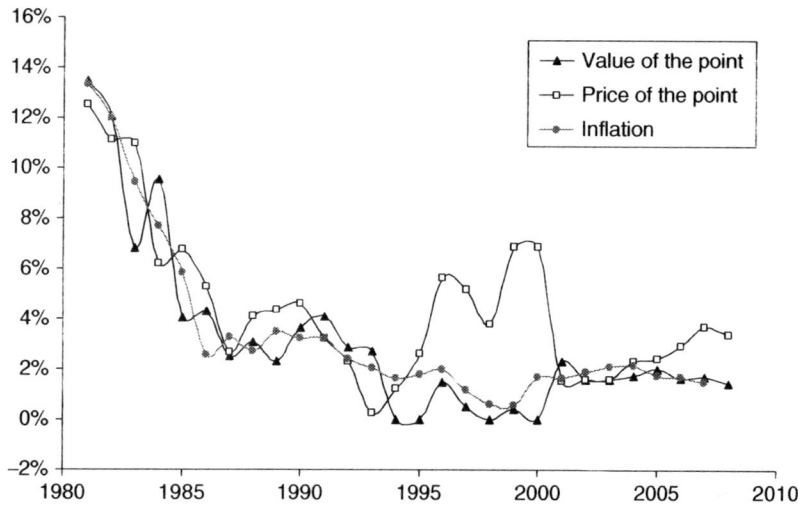

Figure 4.2 Benefit levels in AGIRC and prices (per cent change on previous year), France 1980–2008

Source: Own calculations; data gathered from Bozio (2006), from AGIRC website and from OECD Stat.

future replacement rates, if the social partners continue to follow the same strategy.[8]

Funded supplementary pensions still represent a very minor part of French pension expenditure. In 2006, only €4.2 billion was spent on pension annuities (less than 2 per cent of total pension expenditure).[9] French companies offer two types of Art. 39 DB pension plans: *'retraites chapeau'* and *'retraites additives'*. In the 'chapeau' schemes, the company commits itself to provide a guaranteed replacement rate (e.g. 50–70 per cent of the final salary), by paying the difference between this targeted replacement rate and the pensions offered by the statutory and ARRCO/AGIRC schemes. In the case of an 'additive' pension, the company generally guarantees an additional benefit whose level is independent of the social insurance pensions (e.g. 10 per cent of the final salary or 1 per cent of the final salary per year of service in the company). DB

---

[8] According to government estimations (COR 2007: 64), for a standard worker born in 1938 and with a forty-year contribution record, ARRCO pensions offered in 2003 a wage replacement of 27.6 per cent compared to 55.9 per cent in the *régime général*. Assuming a similar biography, a manager received a replacement rate of 11.8 per cent in ARRCO, 25.4 per cent in AGIRC and 26.9 per cent in the statutory scheme. The net replacement ratio will decline to about 76.8 per cent (51.8 per cent from *régime général* and 25 per cent from ARRCO) for a standard worker retiring in 2020 and 73.5 per cent in 2050, assuming a more generous indexation in AGIRC and ARRCO than the one introduced by the social partners in the mid-1990s.

[9] These figures do not include pension expenditures financed through book reserves.

pensions provided to senior executives in large companies are generally calculated on the basis of their salaries in the last years of their career, leading to very high benefits.[10] Because of the costs associated with 'chapeau' schemes, companies are increasingly transforming them into 'additive' schemes (e.g. BNP Paribas). Given that the objective of company-level DB plans is to develop staff loyalty, Art. 39 schemes do not have to guarantee the vesting of rights in case of a change of employer, thereby forcing employees to stay with the company until retirement.

Contrary to DB schemes, vesting is automatic in DC pension plans (Art. 83, PERCO and PERP). Benefits are entirely determined by the investment performance of the paid contributions. In the case of occupational DC schemes with mandatory participation for groups of employees (Art. 83), individuals' contributions depend on their earnings and the number of years of employment with the company. In the case of voluntary DC schemes (PERCO, PERP), they depend entirely on the individual decisions of the savers. These DC plans exclude any element of interpersonal solidarity. However, Art. 83 schemes often grant credits for non-contributory periods such as illness, maternity, or parental leave. Indexation of benefits can either be guaranteed by a contract (e.g. at 2.5 per cent) or it can be a function of the fund's performance. In general, DC pensions are paid in the form of a lifetime annuity. Lump sums are allowed only in case of low benefits. However, PERCO collective agreements can allow individuals to choose between a lump sum payment and periodic instalments. Although, in principle, contributions to DC schemes cannot be withdrawn before retirement age, legislation allows withdrawals in case of invalidity or loss of unemployment insurance benefits.[11]

8. Who pays?

A very striking characteristic of ARRCO and AGIRC schemes is that they are financed on a PAYG basis. Both occupational second-tier schemes are financed by joint contributions. While 'cadres' have to pay contributions to both ARRCO and AGIRC as they will draw pensions from both schemes, other private employees pay contributions only to ARRCO. The basis on which contributions are assessed is set according to the social security ceiling (€2,859 per month in 2009). Until 1999, 'cadres' paid higher contributions than other private

---

[10] In recent years, the *'retraites chapeaux'* received by CEOs or other senior managers have provoked uproar in the media, most prominently when in February 2005 it was revealed that Daniel Bernard would get as CEO of Carrefour a *'retraite chapeau'* with a replacement rate of 40 per cent of his last salary and that Carrefour had covered these liabilities with €29 million on its book reserves.

[11] PERP and PERCO also allow early withdrawals in case of excessive debt or if the insured buy their main home.

employees, thus receiving more pension points. However, the social partners subsequently agreed to harmonize benefit formulas between the two schemes: Both groups now pay the same total contribution rate, even though employer and employee rates are not necessarily the same.

In order to cope with possible financial imbalances within the occupational schemes, the social partners distinguished between different types of contribution rates when AGIRC and ARRCO were created. Given that pension points are calculated according to contributions, a simple increase in contribution rates would have led to more points earned. In order to mobilize more financial resources without automatically granting rights to higher benefits, different rates were distinguished: The 'contractual' contribution rate is used as a basis to calculate pension points, whereas the 'effective rate' is the contribution rate that is effectively paid by companies. The contractual rate and the effective rate are currently set at 6 per cent and 10 per cent respectively on income below the social security ceiling. Above the social security ceiling, the two rates are set at 16 per cent and 20 per cent respectively. For 'cadres', these contributions are paid up to eight times the ceiling into AGIRC, while for non-executives they are paid up to three times the ceiling into ARRCO.

While all DC plans (Art. 83, PERCO, and PERP) are funded, Art. 39 schemes have been forced to be either fully funded or guaranteed through book reserves on company balance sheets only since 1994. The implementation of these regulations was not entirely effective and has been strengthened by the 2003 Fillon reform as well as by the new IFRS accounting standards. Because many company plans moved into deficit following these regulatory changes and because book reserves are subject to an unfavourable tax regime, Art. 39 plans are increasingly being financed through group insurance contracts signed with insurance companies or with 'provident institutions'. These DB schemes are always financed exclusively by employer contributions. Art. 83 schemes have to be financed by employer contributions, but employee contributions are also allowed and can be fixed by occupational grade, particularly in plans created by collective agreement. While voluntary contributions to Art. 83 are not allowed, PERE (*Plan d'épargne-retraite d'entreprise*), a plan similar to Art. 83 schemes, allows for such an option.

Personal pension plans such as PERCO, PERP, and public-sector pension funds are exclusively based on voluntary contributions by individuals. However, PERCO is a peculiar product, because it is potentially offered only by an employee's firm or branch. As a result, contributions may come not only from individual savings but also from profit-sharing schemes[12] as well as from

---

[12] Two types of profit-sharing schemes are available in France: *Participation* is compulsory in companies that employ fifty people or more and has been introduced in 1967. *Intéressement* is optional and was created in 1959.

employees' 'working time savings accounts'.[13] Contrary to PERP or public-sector schemes in which contribution amounts are in principle unlimited, annual contributions to PERCO cannot exceed one-fourth of the worker's gross salary for the year. Employers must cover PERCO's management fees and they can offer matching contributions to their employees' payments, though this is always established through collective agreement. Former employees can continue to contribute to their PERCO if they do not have access to one in their new company but can then no longer benefit from employer-matching contributions and must cover the management fees. In order to promote funded pensions, the state has put in place tax incentives for both employers and savers. The global contribution to supplementary schemes (Art. 39, Art. 83, PERCO) may be exempt from corporate income tax,[14] while contributions to *régime général* and to AGIRC/ARRCO are totally tax-exempt. Moreover, employers are exempt from paying social security contributions on employer contributions to supplementary schemes up to 5 per cent of one annual social security ceiling. Individuals benefit from an 'exempt, exempt, tax' regime.[15] In the case of PERCO a different tax regime applies, because individual savings are not tax-exempt and no income tax is chargeable at exit if the individual decides to have his or her pension paid in the form of a lump sum.

9. Who governs? Who decides? Who manages?

The second-tier occupational schemes for private employees have a two-level governance system. They are administered locally by autonomous supplementary pension institutions and nationally by their respective federation (ARRCO or AGIRC). Both the pension institutions and the federations are supervised by the social partners. A remarkable feature of the AGIRC and ARRCO schemes is that responsibility for their financial governance lies entirely with representatives of trade unions and employers' associations. The social partners have the ability to change the different parameters that determine the financial equilibrium of the system. They have been using this capacity most notably by raising contributions and by changing indexation mechanisms. Efforts have also been made to generate annual surpluses, which are pooled into a reserve fund with the aim of dealing with future imbalances due to ageing. Recently, changes

---

[13] 'Working-time savings accounts' allow workers to opt out from working time reduction policies and to earn wages increased by 25 per cent for the foregone free time.

[14] Up to 8 per cent of a sum equal to eight times the annual social security ceiling (i.e. max. €21,296 in 2008).

[15] The global contribution to supplementary (occupational and individual) pension plans is exempted from personal income tax up to 10 per cent of taxable income (with max. 8 per cent of a sum equal to eight times the annual social security ceiling – i.e. max. €22,872 in 2008).

have been introduced in the administrative governance of both schemes in order to bring down management costs and centralize financial control over the schemes.

The administrative governance of the schemes has been undergoing considerable changes in the last two decades. Firstly, regulation has been harmonized within the ARRCO institutions since the beginning of the 1990s. Secondly, there has been increased cooperation between ARRCO and AGIRC, which results in a wave of mergers between the bipartite pension institutions. When AGIRC and ARRCO were established by collective agreements in 1947 and in 1961 respectively, they inherited an already elaborate network of various occupational schemes. Both collective agreements aimed at extending supplementary pensions to other categories of workers and the 'points' benefit calculation was adopted from their inception. While eligibility criteria, contribution levels, and benefit levels were unified within AGIRC, these rules remained relatively diverse across the ARRCO institutions. In 1996, the social partners signed an agreement that led to harmonization in ARRCO from 1999 onwards and a centralization of decision-making within the federation. At the time, ARRCO was composed of forty-five different schemes that were managed by ninety different pension institutions, whereas AGIRC was administered by fifty-five different funds.

In addition to the changes made in ARRCO, the social partners have encouraged a more effective cooperation between the two wage earners' schemes and a rationalization in their administrative governance. These developments are partly due to pressures coming from the European Union (EU) and partly due to a commitment to bring down management costs. In November 1998, the social partners agreed to comply with EU Regulation (EEC) 1408/71, which organizes social protection for migrant workers within the EU. This decision amounts to a quasi 'first-pillarization' of AGIRC and ARRCO, since both schemes have to implement a set of rules that normally apply to statutory schemes, even though they remain private (non-state) schemes. As a result, the schemes cannot be considered as potential competitors in the European market for supplementary pensions and will not be subject to anti-trust regulation. Nevertheless, it means that the pension institutions' commercial activities in the field of supplementary social protection must be kept separate from their 'quasi-statutory' activities.

Meanwhile, the local bipartite pension institutions have been encouraged to form 'clusters' that comprise at least one AGIRC and one ARRCO fund. By 2008, twenty-eight clusters had been constituted, comprising twenty-one AGIRC institutions and thirty-three ARRCO funds. These clusters have been building common information and management systems and should result in the creation of fully integrated bipartite groups (*groupes paritaires*). Besides reducing administrative costs in the mandatory unfunded schemes, the formation of strong bipartite groups also serves the purpose of fostering a 'competitive paritarianism'.[16] This strategy must enable the groups' commercial branches, the so-called 'provident institutions' (*institutions de prévoyance*), which are active for example in the retirement savings and complementary health insurance markets, to compete with commercial insurance companies and mutual aid societies in the emerging market of private supplementary social protection.

Because of the decentralized nature of funded plans, governance structures vary widely between different schemes. In firm-level schemes with mandatory participation by a group of employees (Art. 39 and Art. 83), beneficiaries have little to say about investment portfolios. These are chosen by the pension managers, who are supervised either by employers themselves or by bipartite supervisory boards. The organization of these schemes most often depends on how they were initiated. Art. 39 and Art. 83 plans can be established through three possible channels: a unilateral decision by the employer, a proposal of the employer put to all employees by referendum, or a collective agreement. Art. 39 DB plans that cover senior management staff are almost always created through a unilateral decision of the employer and are therefore usually overseen by the company's board of directors, which leaves no room for trade union control. These plans are managed either by the company itself (book reserves) or by an insurance company through a group insurance contract.

Since the more encompassing Art. 39 DB schemes were generally established through collective agreements, they used to be financed on a PAYG basis and were managed by specific bipartite institutions. However, due to the restrictions imposed on PAYG financing in 1994, the governance of these schemes has been profoundly modified in recent years. The managing 'paritarian institutions' frequently have been transformed into supervisory boards and the day-to-day running of the schemes delegated to insurance companies or to 'provident institutions'. Delegation of fund management is also very often the rule in Art. 83 DC schemes. However, a few companies (e.g. Société Générale and Nestlé) have established their own 'provident institutions', supervised by bipartite boards. In these type of plans, the employers and trade unions have in principle much larger decision-making powers concerning the running of the pension plan.

The pension funds that have been introduced by the Fillon reform have a different type of governance. Although PERCO are also occupational pensions, they are tightly linked to firm-level workers' participation plans and wage earners' savings programmes. They must always be established through a collective agreement and cannot be established unless a short-term savings plan (*plan d'épargne salariale*) is also available in the company. As PERCO are voluntary pension plans, the insured are given much more leeway to make their own investment decisions and must be presented with a choice between at least three mutual funds (*organismes de placement collectif en valeurs mobilière* or

---

[16] Guillaume Sarkozy quoted in *La Tribune de L'Assurance* (2007).

OPCVM), so that the insured may diversify their risks. PERCO plans can also provide access to firm-level investment funds, which are allowed to (re)invest part of the collected contributions into company assets.

PERP plans are managed by insurance companies, mutual aid societies, or provident institutions. However, they are supervised by non-profit 'popular pension savings groups' (*groupement d'épargne retraite populaire* or GERP) which are independent of pension managers and initiate plans through a group insurance contract with a financial company. The GERP's mission is to inform participants about developments in the PERP plan and to control the pension managers through a supervisory board and an annual general meeting of the insured, which is responsible for all necessary modifications in PERP contracts and the choice of pension managers. Although investment choices are more limited than in PERCO, because investment decisions are made by the pension managers, state regulation requires that accumulated personal savings be made more secure the closer individuals are to their retirement age.

Until the late 1980s, state supervision of supplementary pensions was limited to controlling insurance companies, but in 1989, an executive agency – the CCMIP[17] – was created in order to monitor mutual aid societies and provident institutions that are active in the market for supplementary social protection. As its control powers were limited due to understaffing, CCMIP has been merged with the insurance watchdog in 2005 (*Autorité de Contrôle des Assurances et des Mutuelles* or ACAM). State regulation concerning insolvency protection has also been strengthened in recent years. An insolvency fund was created for life insurance companies in 1999, while provident institutions have been running their own collective insolvency fund since 2003. Both funds are financed through contributions of the participating companies and insure savers' assets (€70,000 maximum). Although a similar fund for mutual aid societies was officially legislated in 2001, the implementation decrees had still not been issued by 2009. However, the French federation of mutual aid societies, an organization which represents the majority of mutuals, has been operating its own guarantee fund[18] since 2002. DB pensions that are financed through book reserves, however, are not protected against insolvency.

9.1 Case studies: the changing governance of supplementary pensions in the insurance sector and in the banking sector

Developments in insurance and banking illustrate the profound transformations that French supplementary pensions have been undergoing in the last two decades: further integration and harmonization of all supplementary PAYG

---

[17] *Commission de contrôle des mutuelles et des institutions de prévoyance* – loi Evin du 31 décembre 1989.
[18] *Système Fédéral de Garantie de la FNMF.*

schemes within the ARRCO/AGIRC framework, closure of 'chapeau' schemes to new entrants, and development of employer-provided Art. 83 DC plans. Similar to most private sector firms, insurance companies participated in the ARRCO/AGIRC pension schemes, but in 1978 they instituted their own sectorwide DB pension plan, which covered all employees and was financed on a PAYG basis. Since 1994, the scheme was under strain as Art. 39 pension schemes had to switch gradually to full funding or book reserves, and because its risk pool was limited to only 150,000 insured individuals. At the insistence of the federation of French insurers (FFSA), trade unions signed a collective agreement closing the 'chapeau' scheme to new entrants from 1996. The scheme's reserves as well as supplementary assets provided by the participating insurance companies were transferred to an ad hoc insurance company – the SACRA – which is supervised by the social partners. In compensation but also in an attempt to break the political taboo surrounding funded pensions in France, insurers pushed to create the first sector-level funded DC scheme, set up in 1999, despite opposition by the unions.

The insurers' pension fund is financed by employer contributions set at 1 per cent of gross earnings. This fund is managed by a consortium of insurance companies, which is supervised by a bipartite board. The scheme covers a very large majority of insurance companies and is open to employees with some seniority (twelve months for most employees and three years for lower grades). In addition, companies have also created their own firm-level pension schemes. For instance, Axa instituted two new pension plans for all its employees in 1999 (an Art. 83 plan and an Art. 39 plan). The Art. 83 DC plan is financed by employer as well as by employee contributions. Contributions start to be paid once the worker has been employed for twelve months. The Art. 39 DB plan is an 'additive' scheme and offers 4 per cent of the average gross salary of the five years preceding retirement. This scheme is offered only to employees who have a length of service of at least fifteen years and who are employed by the company at retirement. A PERCO plan has been added in 2005.

After the Second World War, supplementary pensions in banking were not integrated within the ARRCO/AGIRC schemes even though they were financed on a PAYG basis. Banks offered a DB 'chapeau' pension, based on wages earned just before retirement.[19] The system was managed by fourteen independent firm-level pension institutions as well as by a multi-employer one (CRPB), but their risk pools differed widely. From the mid-1980s, the number of pensioners increased very sharply, and demographic imbalances were projected to worsen during the following years. Therefore, the social partners decided to incorporate the company schemes into the ARRCO/AGIRC framework, and simultaneously to close the DB chapeau scheme to new entrants. A 'banking top-up'

---

[19] Benefits in banking were on average 15 per cent higher than in wage-earner schemes.

(*complément bancaire*) was granted to existing pensioners and people employed in banking for at least fifteen years at the time the collective agreement was signed (1993). This pension supplement is financed by the pre-existing firm-level pension institutions which have been transformed into Art. 39 schemes that are either fully funded or financed through book reserves. However, in order to partly counterbalance the loss of retirement income incurred by younger and new bank employees, many banks (including HSBC France or Banques Populaires) have set up mandatory DC schemes that cover most workers in the companies. At Société Générale, an Art. 83 plan has been established through a collective agreement signed in 1995. The scheme is managed by an ad hoc provident institution that is supervised by a bipartite board. Employee contributions are set at 0.5 per cent of gross salary,[20] whereas employer contributions are set at about 1 per cent. BNP Paribas has also been offering an Art. 83 DC scheme since 1997 and has transformed it into a PERE plan in 2006. The contribution rate is set at 1 per cent of the reference wage which is calculated up to a maximum of 110 per cent of the social security ceiling. Since the Fillon reform, both BNP Paribas and Société Générale have also set up PERCO plans whose funds are managed by the banks themselves.

10. The outlook for the French pension system

Funded pensions have traditionally been a delicate question in French politics. The negative experience with funded pensions during the interwar period led to a deep distrust of this mode of financing within French society. Intergenerational solidarity has become an integral part of the post-war social contract, both through the establishment of PAYG statutory pensions and the development of collective occupational pensions (AGIRC and ARRCO). In recent years, politicians have continued emphasizing their commitment to the PAYG mode of financing. However, by successfully framing reforms as attempts to 'consolidate' existing pensions and by skilfully sequencing reforms, successive governments have been able to tilt the balance towards an increased use of funded pensions. The numerous increases in the length of insurance that is required to get a full statutory pension promote a tighter link between contributions and benefits and will result in a very probable decrease in benefit levels in the future. This trend is reinforced by the changes that have been made by the social partners in the indexation of ARRCO and AGIRC benefits. By creating PERP and PERCO, the 2003 Fillon reform has given clear signals that younger workers are increasingly expected to save in voluntary retirement plans. Similarly, the introduction of a 'right to information' aims at helping employees to make

---

[20] Up to two (previously four) times the social security ceilings since 2006.

informed decisions about their retirement. Thus, since July 2007, different age cohorts have been regularly receiving statements with their accrued pension rights from the different compulsory schemes as well as simulations of their expected benefits.

However, the development of funded pensions is likely to be slowed down by the financial crisis that started at the end of 2007, because it may undermine confidence in funded pensions. The crisis has directly affected individuals through its negative impact on the value of the pension savings they have accumulated in occupational or personal pension plans. But the confidence of the public in funded pensions may also be affected by the highly publicized losses of the French pension system's buffer fund, the *'fonds de réserve pour les retraites'*, that is supposed to help financing the demographically imbalanced statutory pension schemes between 2020 and 2040. The ARRCO and AGIRC reserve funds have also posted significant losses. Consequently, their accumulated assets will have to be used to finance the deficits incurred during the crisis instead of being used to cope with future demographic imbalances as initially planned. The refusal of French employers to increase contribution rates in both schemes in order to compensate for these losses is likely to be met with a renewed unwillingness of trade unions to promote the expansion of firm-level funded schemes.

In the future, the reform agenda should focus on the pension rights of the increasingly numerous 'atypical' workers. The French labour market is characterized by a considerable degree of dualization: some workers enjoy strong employment protection and good salaries, while others are stuck in sectors marked by high job instability and low pay levels. Thus, a large group of workers are at a double disadvantage in terms of access to adequate pensions. First, job instability affects workers' contribution records and therefore the benefit levels that they can expect from the statutory and occupational schemes are limited. Second, it also affects workers' access to funded private pension plans, which are supposed to compensate for diminished replacement rates in public schemes. Workers employed on fixed-term contracts or in unstable jobs are not covered by employer-sponsored pension schemes, as they cannot reach the minimum length of service that is required to benefit from firm-level plans. Moreover, even if they are properly informed about their future benefit levels, they may not have the capacity to save for their pension.

Bibliography

AGIRC-ARRCO (2008). *La retraite en France – répartition, solidarité des générations et des professions*. Paris: AGIRC-ARRCO (www.agirc-arrco.fr).

Boltanski, L. (1987). *The Making of a Class: Cadres in French Society*. Cambridge: Cambridge University Press.

Bonoli, G. (1997). 'Pension Politics in France: Patterns of Co-operation and Conflict in Two Recent Reforms'. *West European Politics*, 20/4: 160–81.

——(2000). *The Politics of Pension Reform. Institutions and Policy Change in Western Europe*. Cambridge: Cambridge University Press.

——and Palier, B. (2007). 'When Past Reforms Open New Opportunities: Comparing Old-age Insurance Reforms in Bismarckian Welfare Systems'. *Social Policy and Administration*, 41/6: 555–73.

Bozio, A. (2006). *Réformes des retraites: estimations sur données françaises*, PhD thesis EHESS (supervised by T. Piketty).

COR (Conseil d'Orientation des Retraites) (2007). *Retraites: Vingt Fiches d'Actualisation pour le rendez-vous de 2008. Cinquième Rapport, Novembre 2007*.

Culpepper, P. (2006). 'Capitalism, Coordination and Economic Change: The French Political Economy since 1985', in P. Culpepper, P. A. Hall and B. Palier (eds.), *Changing France: The Politics that Markets Make*. Houndmills, Basingstoke: Palgrave Macmillan, 29–49.

DARES (2008). 'L'épargne salariale en 2006: plus de 15 milliards d'euros distribués'. *Premières Informations*, 25, 3, June 2008.

DREES (2006). 'L'épargne retraite en 2004'. *Etudes et résultats*, 518, September 2006.

——(2009). 'L'épargne retraite en 2007'. *Etudes et résultats*, 685, April 2009.

Dutton, P. V. (2002). *Origins of the French Welfare State. The Struggle for Social Reform in France, 1914–1947*. Cambridge: Cambridge University Press.

Ebbinghaus, B. (2006). *Reforming Early Retirement in Europe, Japan and the USA*. Oxford: Oxford University Press.

FFSA (2008). 'Les Perp en 2007'. *Enquête – Assurances de personnes*, May 2008.

Friot, B. (1996). 'The Origins of French Supplementary Pension Plans: The Creation of AGIRC', in E. Reynaud, L. Roberts, B. Davies and G. Hughes (eds.), *International Perspectives on Supplementary Pensions. Actors and Issues*. New York: Quorum Books, 41–8.

Guillemard, A.-M. (1986). *Le déclin du social: formation et crise des politiques de la vieillesse*. Paris: Presses Universitaires de France.

Goyer, M. (2007). 'Capital Mobility, Varieties of Institutional Investors, and the Transforming Stability of Corporate Governance in France and Germany', in B. Hancké, M. Rhodes and M. Thatcher (eds.), *Beyond Varieties of Capitalism. Conflict, Contradictions, and Complementarities in the European Economy*. Oxford: Oxford University Press, 195–219.

Hall, P. A. (2001). 'The Evolution of Economic Policy', in A. Guyomarch, H. Machin, P. A. Hall and J. Hayward (eds.), *Developments in French Politics 2*. Houndmills, Basingstoke: Palgrave Macmillan, 172–90.

——(2006). 'Introduction: The Politics of Social Change in France', in P. Culpepper, P. A. Hall and B. Palier (eds.), *Changing France: The Politics that Markets Make*. Houndmills, Basingstoke: Palgrave Macmillan, 1–26.

——(2007). 'The Evolution of Varieties of Capitalism in Europe', in B. Hancké, M. Rhodes and M. Thatcher (eds.), *Beyond Varieties of Capitalism. Conflict, Contradictions, and Complementarities in the European Economy*. Oxford: Oxford University Press, 39–85.

117

Hatzfeld, H. (1971). *Du Paupérisme à la Sécurité Sociale: 1850–1940*. Paris: Armand Colin.

Hewitt Associates (2007). 'Quantitative Overview on Supplementary Pension Provision'. Final Report. Prepared for the European Commission – Directorate General EMPL, November 2007.

Lallemand, M. (2006). 'New Patterns of Industrial Relations and Political Action since the 1980s', in P. Culpepper, P. A. Hall and B. Palier (eds.), *Changing France: The Politics that Markets Make*. Houndmills. Basingstoke: Palgrave Macmillan, 50–79.

La Tribune de l'Assurance (2007). 'Tendances – Groupes paritaires – La gouvernance au coeur des rapprochements', 1 November 2007.

Legros, F. (2006). 'NDCs: A Comparison of the French and German Point Systems', in R. Holzmann and E. Palmer (eds.), *Pension Reform: Issues and Prospects for Non-Financial Defined Contribution (NDC) Schemes*. Washington: The World Bank, 203–22.

Palier, B. (2003b). 'Facing the Pension Crisis in France', in G. L. Clark and N. Whiteside (eds.), *Pension Security in the 21st Century: Redrawing the Public–Private Debate*. Oxford: Oxford University Press, 93–142.

——(2005a). *Gouverner la sécurité sociale*. Paris: Presses Universitaires de France.

——(2005b). 'Ambiguous Agreement, Cumulative Change: French Social Policy in the 1990s', in W. Streeck and K. A. Thelen (eds.), *Beyond Continuity. Institutional Change in Advanced Political Economies*. Oxford: Oxford University Press, 127–44.

——(2007). 'Tracking the Evolution of a Single Instrument can Reveal Profound Changes: The Case of Funded Pensions in France'. *Governance*, 20/1: 85–107.

——and Bonoli, G. (2000). 'La montée en puissance des fonds de pension: une lecture comparative des réformes des systèmes de retraite, entre modèle global et cheminements nationaux'. *L'Année de la regulation*, 4/2000: 209–50.

Reynaud, E. (1997). 'France: A National and Contractual Second Tier', in M. Rein and E. Wadensjö (eds.), *Enterprise and the Welfare State*. Cheltenham: Edward Elgar, 65–98.

Schludi, M. (2005). *The Reform of Bismarckian Pension Systems. A Comparison of Pension Politics in Austria, France, Germany, Italy and Sweden*. Amsterdam: Amsterdam University Press.

Schmidt, V. A. (1996). *From State to Market? The Transformation of French Business and Government*. Cambridge: Cambridge University Press.

——(2009). 'Putting Politics Back into the Political Economy by Bringing the State Back in Yet Again'. *World Politics*, 61/3: 516–48.

Sénat (2006). 'L'épargne retraite en France trois ans après la « loi Fillon »: quel complément aux régimes de retraite par répartition?' Rapport d'information n° 486 (2005–2006) de M. Philippe MARINI, fait au nom de la commission des finances, déposé le 21 septembre 2006.

5

Germany: Departing from Bismarckian Public Pensions

Bernhard Ebbinghaus, Mareike Gronwald, and Tobias Wiß

1. Introduction

Germany is viewed as the hallmark of the Bismarckian social insurance tradition of status-maintaining statutory pensions. Although these mandatory public pensions reduced the need for private supplementary pensions, occupational pensions have been coexisting as German firms sought to retain their skilled workforce. Since the 1970s, Germany's conservative welfare state has grown to its limits with the rise of mass unemployment, the use of passive labour market policies, the social transfer to East Germany after unification in 1990, and the financial sustainability problem of pay-as-you-go (PAYG) pensions in an ageing society. After many parametric changes, pension reforms in the early 2000s have led to a more fundamental change, lowering and postponing the statutory old-age pensions, while fostering the development of voluntary private pensions. In contrast to the long-held view that Germany suffers from reform blockage due to too many veto points, these recent political reform efforts and institutional changes will transform the public–private mix of future retirement income provision.

The first part discusses the overall architecture of Bismarckian pensions, its traditional emphasis on income maintenance provided by the public pillar, and the secondary role of supplementary pensions. The second section reviews Germany's Conservative welfare state, social partnership tradition, and coordinated 'social market' economy. The following two sections review the emergence of the public–private mix and its more recent reforms, emphasizing the path-dependent but recent path-departing developments. Focusing on supplementary retirement income, the second part analyses the structure and governance of second-pillar occupational pensions and third-pillar personal pensions respectively. Four main factors are important for the governance of supplementary pensions: who is covered, what kind of benefits are offered, who pays, and who has control? In particular, we analyse the participatory and social rights of employees in these schemes. The final section concludes with an outlook on the future, discussing potential scenarios for institutional change and its consequences for old age income.

Part I: The evolution of the public–private pension mix

2. Germany's major public and minor supplementary pillars

The German pension system is traditionally dominated by the first (public) pillar. The contributory earnings-related statutory pension (see Figure 5.1) was initiated by the 'Bismarckian' social insurance reforms more than a century ago. The statutory pension scheme (GRV) is a mandatory PAYG system under a federal ceiling largely financed by parity social contributions of employers and employees, and a smaller government grant financed through taxes. The contribution rate is calculated as a percentage (currently 19.9 per cent) of gross income up until a statutory income ceiling (about 2.1 times the average salary). The public pension benefits are strongly linked to contributions paid during the individual's entire employment career, thus reproducing working life income differences and pursuing the goal of 'status maintenance' in old age (Riedmüller and Willert 2007: 141). A minimum qualifying period of five years is required, but also non-contributory periods for instance due to unemployment are recognized. Housewives receive benefits indirectly through their partner or as survivors, though child-rearing and care-giving years are partially credited in statutory pensions since 1986. Nearly all employees (those earning above a minimum) are covered by the public pension. In addition to the occupational fragmentation that existed for the statutory schemes (blue-collar workers, miners, and white-collar employees) until a merger in 2005, there are some special pension schemes for farmers and self-governing compulsory insurances for professional groups (*berufsständische Versorgungssysteme*). These systems represent a special type of professional (second tier) pensions that exist in lieu of the social insurance; they are mostly mandatory and partly publicly financed. Predating the Bismarck reforms, tenured civil servants (*Beamte*) obtained a privileged tax-financed retirement pay scheme in order to assure their loyalty to the state (Rothenbacher 2001). For pensioners with low-pension entitlements, a means-tested basic income (*Grundsicherung im Alter*) for old age and occupational disability was introduced in 2003, replacing the former social assistance rules by less stigmatizing claims procedure and a less strict means-test that limits next of kin responsibilities. In terms of overall retirement income, the first-pillar pensions are still dominant (86 per cent of pension income for people aged 65 and older), this holds particularly among East

	First pillar	Second pillar		Third pillar
	State pension (SP)	Occupational pension (OP)		Personal pension (PP)
		Collective agreement	Employer commitment	
Income (age 65+)	86% (East: 96%)	8% (1%)		6% (3%)
Third tier (topping up / replacement gap)		• public sector: special collective scheme for public employees (PAYG NDC); • private sector: 5 types of voluntary OPs (DB or DC) with tax incentives; • collective agreements in some private sectors; • Earnings-conversion (*Entgeltumwandlung*)		• *Riester pension* (2002-): voluntary earnings-related, subsidies for low income groups, funded DC • *Rürup pension* (2005-): tax incentives, DC
Second tier (income maintenance)	*Statutory pension system* (GRV): mandatory for employees; parity social contributions (with income limit); contribution period earnings-related PAYG DB (*equivalence*); child credits (tax-financed)	special statutory schemes: • civil servant pension pay (*Beamtenversorgung*) • farmers' income support • mandatory schemes for free professions (*Berufsständische Versorgungswerke*)		
First tier (poverty alleviation)	means-tested (social assistance, since 2003:) minimum income in old age (*Grundsicherung im Alter*), tax-financed			

Figure 5.1 Pillars and tiers of German retirement income system

Source: Adapted from synopsis in Schulze and Jochem (2007), income: Frommert and Heien (2006: 137).

Germans (96 per cent), whereas supplementary income is concentrated in West Germany for both occupational (9 per cent) and private pensions (7 per cent), albeit with considerable variations due to unequal coverage (Frommert and Heien 2006: 137).

The second-pillar occupational pensions 'top up' retirement income, particularly for those better paid employees (earning above the GRV contribution ceiling) either through voluntary occupational pensions (*Betriebliche Altersversorgung* or BAV) in the private sector or a quasi-mandatory scheme for all public employees (other than civil servants). While the public employee scheme aims at supplementing the statutory pension to come close to the civil servants' final-salary retirement pay, in the private sector, occupational pension coverage and benefit levels differ according to the firm size and branch. In the early 2000s, employer-provided voluntary occupational pensions are relatively widespread in the private sector among West Germans (34 per cent of men and 16 per cent of women) in contrast to East Germans (8 and 9 per cent respectively), who also have fewer years of contributions under the market economy (Frommert and Heien 2006: 137). Even if supplementary pension coverage is relatively large, occupational pension benefits have thus far been relatively unimportant except for top income groups.

Since 2001, employees have the right to convert a certain percentage of their wages into contributions (*Entgeltumwandlung*) to an occupational pension that has to be offered by their employer in line with a collective agreement. Thus, after a long period of stagnation following regulations in the mid-1970s, occupational pensions have revived in recent years. Although many Germans have additional savings and life insurances, the so-called Riester (2001) and Rürup (2004) pensions were legislated as voluntary personal pensions but with substantial state subsidies and tax benefits. These supplementary pensions will have to fill a growing income replacement gap, given the erosion of statutory pension benefits following parallel reforms which cut back benefits and increase retirement age from 65 to 67 until 2029. The recent reforms of the private pensions and a new boost in occupational pensions have to be understood in the context of the past public–private mix in retirement income provision and its recent changes.

3. Bismarckian pensions embedded in the social market economy

The Bismarckian pension legacy has to be placed in the larger context of Germany's Conservative welfare state, the social partnership relations between capital and labour, and the coordinated 'social market' economy. The Conservative welfare regime dates back to the paternalistic reforms of the Bismarckian authoritarian state in response to growing pressures from the labour movement (Esping-Andersen 1990). The Conservative welfare state was renewed after the Second World War under the Christian-Democratic Chancellors (1949–69) and expanded under the Left–Liberal coalition (1969–82). The maintenance of status differences results from the *equivalence* principle (linking benefits to contributions) and the occupational fragmentation into separate schemes (Kohl 2000: 130). Since the late 1950s, statutory pension benefits are relatively generous and function as *income replacement* rather than as *poverty alleviation*.

The traditional male breadwinner family model is reflected in the employment-related pensions. Examples of this are numerous and include indirect pension rights for housewives and widows, the subsequently introduced childcare credits, and the tax advantages for married couples (Pfau-Effinger 2004: 72ff).

Since its origins, the German welfare state relied largely on semi-public social insurances and subsidaristic social services through welfare associations. Although the state sets the main conditions by law, the principle of parity financing by employers and employees as well as self-administration provides the social partners with an institutionalized role in shaping social policymaking. In labour relations, the principle of autonomous collective bargaining (*Tarifautonomie*) between the well-organized employer associations and the encompassing trade unions limits the scope for direct state intervention. However, several co-determination laws provide employees with works councils with information and consultation right vis-à-vis employers, and unique for a market economy, the parity representation of employees' stakeholder interests on the supervisory boards of larger companies: first in the coal and steel sectors (1951) and then for stock market listed companies (1976). Although employer associations and trade unions have suffered from membership losses in recent years, sectorwide agreements (though in some cases with decentralized amendments) are still very common and state intervention via *erga omnes* extension remains rather exceptional. While the social partners are thus relatively autonomous in wage bargaining and participate in the self-administration of social insurance, there has been thus far a clear division between state intervention into public social security and voluntary firm-based occupational welfare.

The 'Rheinish'-coordinated capitalism has been based on a stakeholder model of corporate governance based on long-term patient capital provided by *Hausbanken* via credits and on-the-book-pension-reserves, and rather arms-length control of insider stakeholder interests (employees, banks, and other friendly business interests). Many export-oriented German firms maintain a diversified quality production strategy (Streeck 1997), they are relying on long-term employment relations even in terms of economic downturn, investing in skills via dual vocational training, and retaining skilled workers through firm-based occupational pensions. Firms have used available public early retirement pathways to downsize and restructure the workforce in a socially acceptable way, yet thereby externalizing these restructuring costs (Naschold and de Vroom 1994). In recent years, the pressure towards shareholder value has changed not only codetermination but also increased pressures on German companies to revisit their own occupational pensions. Under the red–green government, a paradigm shift to foster capital market investment through occupational and private pensions occurred. Moreover, employers' associations and other business interests have voiced increasing criticism about the high labour costs, stressing the need to cut public expenditure and reinforce incentives to work.

Germany faces particular challenges as a Conservative welfare state with the 'welfare without work' problem (Esping-Andersen 1996) or Continental dilemma (Scharpf 2001). Since the rise of mass unemployment following the oil shocks of the 1970s, Germany used passive labour market policies to finance long-term unemployment and early retirement, thereby increasing non-wage labour costs and thus pricing out unskilled labour even further.

The problems increased after unification: these included the particular labour market problems in the East German economy after the transition to a market economy and the need to finance the social security benefits for East Germans in the face of higher inactivity. Public debate on the viability of the German welfare state and social market economy in an ageing society and global economic competition proliferated (Manow 2000). The demographic changes, in particular Germany's very low birth rate, are seen as reducing the viability of statutory PAYG pensions in the future. An additional new challenge has been to adopt the German welfare state to the new social risks. Female labour force participation has increased over the last decade as a consequence of educational expansion, changing values, and improvements in childcare coupled with the earlier advances in East Germany. Despite these changes, however, many mothers with children still tend to work in part-time employment or even in mini-jobs, which result in low or no pension credits.

4. The emergence of the public–private pension mix

The German Empire was the first industrializing country to legislate social insurance against the social risks of income loss due to old age invalidity in 1889. To appease the growing working-class in the newly unified Empire and fight the labour movement during the anti-socialist laws, Chancellor Bismarck introduced a social insurance for old age and invalidity that was mandatory for blue-collar workers and white-collar employees (up to an earnings limit). Since plans to introduce a general consumption tax failed, parafiscal regional insurance funds were formed. Employers and employees paid contributions and in return their representatives were involved in self-administration. After thirty years of contributions, workers aged 70 (as of 1916: 65) received a relatively small but earnings-related pension (less than a third of former average earnings), though many industrial workers received 'invalidity' benefits at an earlier age. German white-collar employees successfully pressed for their own nation-wide pension scheme (1911) with higher contributions, an earlier retirement at age 65, less strict invalidity criterion, and status-maintaining pensions closer to those of civil servants. Also railway employees and miners had their separate schemes, adding to the occupational fragmentation. In 1911, a national insurance code was enacted to consolidate the three existing social insurances, introducing also widow and orphan pensions. Since benefits from the earnings-related statutory pensions were still comparatively low, several pater-nalistic employers continued to offer occupational pensions.

After the Second World War, which had depleted the public pension reserves and individual savings, the Bismarckian pension funds were continued first by the allied occupation forces, a favourable revaluation with the currency reform of 1947, and by ad hoc measures of the newly formed Federal Republic (1949). Poverty was still high among many workers, widows, and orphans despite increases in entitlements during the early 1950s. The 1957 Pension Reform under the Christian-Democratic Chancellor Adenauer proved a major juncture (Hockerts 1980) in expanding the Bismarckian pensions based on an intergen-erational contract (*Generationenvertrag*), introducing a full PAYG system (with only a small reserve fund). The principle of status maintenance and secure state pension benefits (above 60 per cent of prior earnings) in line with wage increases was affordable given the booming post-war economy. PAYG financing had immediate electoral advantages: it allowed extended pensions benefits to (non-)insured older people, including the refugees from the East and survivors of war victims.

The expectation of secure and sufficient public pensions made additional private provision less pressing, except for high-income groups as statutory benefits ended at 60 per cent above the average salary. Political benign neglect led to a rather uncontrolled co-evolution of occupational pensions and indi-vidual savings (in particular life insurance). From the employers' side, occupa-tional pension schemes were mostly seen as a means of re-financing the company after the war and later helped attract and bind skilled personnel (Jackson and Vitols 2001). The public employee unions were able to negotiate a collective agreement for supplementary pensions (VBL) in 1966 that was made mandatory by the Grand Coalition.

Under the new Left-Liberal Brandt government, the Pension Reform of 1972 improved statutory pension benefits, extended membership to some formerly excluded groups, and introduced flexible retirement at age 63 (without benefit reductions). With the subsequent economic crisis and mass unemployment, these various pathways to early retirement enabled firms to restructure their workforce in a socially accepted manner by using public pensions and circum-venting employment regulation for older workers (Jacobs et al. 1991; Rosenow and Naschold 1994). Nevertheless, the growing economic problems led to increased bankruptcy and restructuring of firms, leading to insolvency and transportability problems of occupational pension claims. The Federal Labour Court ruling on vesting rights led to the first federal regulation of occupational pensions in 1974 (aba 2005: 12) in order to protect employee rights, while leaving its voluntary basis. Although the law limited legal uncertainty for individual employment contracts, this regulation made it also less attractive to some employers.

The Varieties of Pension Governance

Table 5.1 Chronology of major pension reforms, Germany 1889–1974

Year	Reform	Political context
1889	Invalidity and Old Age Insurance (*Invaliditäts- und Alterssicherung*)	Bismarck's antisocialist strategy
	• mandatory social insurance for workers (up to income limit)	
	• self-administered parafiscal regional funds	
	• pension for old age (70+) or invalidity (2/3 incapacity)	
1911	White-collar Pension Insurance (*Angestelltenversicherung*)	Middle-class interests
	• mandatory social insurance for white-collar employees	
	• separate self-administered national fund (RVA)	
	• pension for old age (65+) or invalidity (1/2 incapacity)	
1934–45	Authoritarian measures:	Authoritarian Nazi regime
	• ending self-administration (1934)	
	• mandatory coverage for artisans (1937), voluntary insurance for self-employed (1938)	
	• reserve funds diverted to war efforts, depleted after war	
1948	• Association of pension funds (VDR) reinstalled	Allied occupation
	• DM currency reform (pension valuation at 1:1)	
1957	'Adenauer' Pension Reform (*Rentenneuregelungsgesetz*)	Conservative government (CDU/CSU/others)
	• expansion of statutory pension	
	• dynamic pension (wage indexed)	
	• PAYG financing (inter-generation contract)	
1966 (1967)	Supplementary Pension for Public Sector Employees (VBL)	Grand Coalition (CDU/CSU/SPD)
	• collective agreement on supplementary pension in public sector	
1972	Pension Reform (*Rentenreformgesetz*)	Left–Liberal government (SPD/FDP)
	• flexible retirement age without reductions (at age 63)	
	• voluntary insurance for certain groups of self-employed	
1974	Occupational Old Age Protection Act (BetrAVG)	Left–Liberal government (SPD/FDP)
	• voluntary employer decision	
	• regulation of four types of OPs	
	• vesting of pension claims	
	• OP cannot be lowered in line with SP increases	
	• insolvency protection	
	• inflation-proof adjustments	

Source: DRV (2006): Chronik, Alber (1986).

Table 5.2 Chronology of pension system restructuring since 1980s

Year	Reform	Political context
1989	Pension Reform (1992) • indexation based on net earnings • gradual increase of retirement age until 2014 • actuarial deductions for early retirement • credits for child rearing years improved • continuation of minimum pension	CDU/CSU and FDP government, consensus with opposition and social partners
1997	Pension Reform (1999, but not enacted) • reform of disability pensions (ending special disability rules for white-collar employees) • demographic (life expectancy) adjustment factor • credits for child rearing years improved • fixed contribution rate • federal grant for insurance unrelated benefits (e.g. child credits)	CDU/CSU and FDP government, no consensus with opposition and social partners; SPD has *Bundesrat* majority
1998	Revised Pension Reform (*Rentenkorrekturgesetz*) • abolishment of demographic factor • new regulations of disability pension (*Erwerbsunfähigkeitsrente*) • credits for child rearing years reevaluated • federal grant based on new 'eco' tax • contribution rate lowered to 19.3% • coverage of low wage earners and some self-employed	SPD & Greens
2001	Supplementary Old Age Income Provision (*Altersvermögensergänzungsgesetz*) (2002) • Pension formula no longer based on the development of average net earnings but only on average gross earnings similar to the principle from 1957 • Improvement of acknowledgement of child rearing times	SPD & Greens
2001	Old Age Income Provision (*Altersvermögensgesetz*) (2002) • voluntary private DC pension (*Riester-Rente*), tax subsidies for lower-income groups • employees can demand 'earnings conversion' to OP • DC schemes in OPs possible • tax exemption for contributions to OPs (*Pensionsfonds, Pensionskasse*)	SPD & Greens
2004	Pension Insurance Sustainability (*RV-Nachhaltigkeitsgesetz*) (2005)	SPD & Greens

(Continued)

Table 5.2 Continued

Year	Reform	Political context
	• sustainability adjustment factor (*Nachhaltigkeitsfaktor*) instead of abolished demographic factor	
	• later earliest possible retirement age	
	• educational credits abolished	

Source: DRV (2006): Chronik, Schulze and Jochem (2007).

5. The changing public–private pension mix

The crisis-ridden decades following the first oil shock of 1973 led to a series of reforms to control social expenditure and restructure pension systems. Increasing socio-economic and demographic challenges first led to some minor parametric reforms in order to consolidate public budgets. Since 1977 several 'pension adjustment' laws installed ad hoc cost saving measures (see Table 5.2), while early retirement was further facilitated by the possibility to retire after long-term unemployment at age 58, pre-retirement benefits (1984–8), and part-time pensions (1989). The public budget consolidation laws of 1983 and 1984 made benefits more conditional, subsequently pensions drawn at age 65 decreased considerably, particularly for women (Ebbinghaus and Schulze 2007). Several commissions and reports during the late 1980s questioned the sustainability of the state pension given increasing early retirement and demographic changes.

A major pension reform to gradually increase actual retirement age was decided in November 1989 just before unification. Beginning in 1992, the reform would phase in a new formula by which pensions slowly decrease and early retirement measures were to be phased out (Ruland 2007a: 34). This moderate reform was based on compromises between the government, opposition, and the social partners in order to avoid it as an election topic (Busemeyer 2006: 413; Schulze and Jochem 2007: 17). However, the reform had only induced incremental changes within the existing institutional framework, and private pensions were not part of the publicly framed welfare mix (Leisering et al. 2002: 86). The worsening economic situation of many companies since the 1980s had even made the employers' decisions to introduce or expand occupational schemes less likely (Schmähl 1997: 111).

During the mid-1990s, a major break with past consensus-tradition occurred when the intergenerational contract and the status-maintenance goal were undermined by the government, leading to intense conflicts. Following unification, the rising mass unemployment, particularly in the East, and the

Table 5.3 Statutory pension contributions, expenditure and benefits, (West) Germany 1960–2005

	1960	1970	1980	1990	1995	2000	2005
Contribution rate % wage (West)	14.0	17.0	18.0	18.7	18.6	19.3	19.5
Income ceiling in % average wage	167	162	171	180	185	190	213
Pension expenditure % GDP	—	5.4	7.1	6.8	8.2	8.7	8.8
Federal grant in % DRV revenues	21.3	13.9	15.6	14	17.8	16.2	16.7
Net replacement rate (45 years)	62.7	61.7	70.1	69.6	75.5	76.2	73.3

Source: BMAS (2007), DRV (2006).

financing of massive transfers to the East had put additional pressure on public expenditure and social contributions (see Table 5.3). Pointing at the high labour costs and the demographic sustainability problem of PAYG pensions, several expert commissions (e.g. Blüm Commission in 1996) advanced reform proposals in the public debate. A major effort to welfare retrenchment was undertaken by the Conservative–Liberal coalition in 1997, following previous unsuccessful Alliance for Jobs talks with the social partners. The opposition and trade unions criticized the automatic benefit reduction via a 'demographic factor' which would reduce net replacement rates from 70 to 64 per cent in the long term. After its successful election in 1998, the new red–green government reversed the demographic factor and watered down several retrenchment measures before these could take effect in 1999 (Leisering et al. 2002: 87; Schulze and Jochem 2007: 20–1). Yet the Schröder government soon realized that the immediate financial problems and long-term sustainability issues could not be denied.

A paradigm shift towards non-state pensions occurred under the red–green coalition; this was particularly remarkable given previous failures of the Conservative–Liberal government to do so (Hinrichs 2005). In order to circumvent a veto by the second chamber, the statutory pension changes were enacted separately from the non-state pension reforms. The Old Age Savings Act of 2001 fosters occupational and private pension plans, whereas the two other reforms modified the first-pillar state pension in 2001 and, more controversially, the government reintroduced an adjustment factor in 2004. Diverse social and fiscal policy goals were driving this policy change, including financial sustainability, reducing non-wage labour costs, the Maastricht public budget criteria, and capital market stimulation. The voluntary Riester pension added a third personal pension pillar, while the cutbacks in the first pillar will erode the status-maintenance goal in the long run. In particular, the sustainability factor (*Nachhaltigkeitsfaktor*) gradually decreases public pension benefits (Ruland 2007*b*: 37f).

A share of the labour income is expected to be voluntarily invested into occupational or personal pension plans (4 per cent by 2008), fostered by tax reductions and direct tax subsidies for lower-income groups (Mattil 2006: 105). The goal of maintaining adequate retirement income is gradually transferred from public to private responsibility, while the role of the state shifts from direct provider to regulator (Leisering et al. 2002: 92).

The red–green coalition introduced far-reaching changes, overcoming long-term consensual parametric reforms, though it has been debated whether this led to a paradigm shift. Seen from an institutional perspective, these parallel reforms combine a strategy of *institutional layering* of a voluntary new third pillar, indirectly fostering the development of the second pillar, and transforming the function of the first pillar as part of a new public–private pension mix. This also results in the conversion of the occupational pension function as these largely neglected private pensions assume new aims and actors. Whereas in the past, occupational pensions were merely a 'topping-up' for high-income earners and were employer-only financed, today occupational and personal pensions are needed to assure an adequate retirement income, and they are financed jointly or employee-only with tax concessions. Whether these reforms will lead to a long-term transformation away from the public pension pillar will depend on the political and social actors' reactions in the future, the politically intended and unintended consequences of these reform measures, and the future socio-economic developments as well as financial market performance. The recent financial crises at the beginning and end of the 2000s have led to some debate on the private funded pension strategy, though there seems to be no alternative.

Part II: The governance of supplementary pensions

Given the long-term crowding out through generous earnings-related public pensions and the neglect of public policymaking to foster private pensions, the occupational pensions developed rather unregulated until the 1970s, and the tax-subsidized personal pension took off only after 2001. In the second pillar, five forms of supplementary occupational pensions coexist in the private sector according to the law on occupational pensions (BetrAVG) of 1974 (reformed in 2001), while the collective agreement in the public sector added a special sixth form (see Table 5.4).

- Direct pension commitment (*Direktzusage*) by the employer is a pledge to their employees (and their survivors) that they get a pension payment upon retirement or disability, it is entirely financed by book reserves (BMGS 2004: 4–5).

- Support funds (*Unterstützungskasse*) are the oldest occupational pension form in Germany comprising legally independent funds of one or more employers providing old-age pension benefits.

Table 5.4 Overview of supplementary pensions in Germany

Supplementary pension	Coverage (mio.)	Funding	Sponsor (contributions)	DB/DC	Tax deductions/ subsidies	Liabilities (bn. €)	Limited investment	Insolvency insurance/ supervision
Direct pension commitment (*Direktzusage*)	} 4.6	Internal/ book reserves	Employer	DB	yes/no	238.5	None (book reserves)	PSV/none
Support fund (*Unterstützungskasse*)		Internal	Employer	DB	Yes/no	36.1	None	PSV/none
Direct insurance (*Direktversicherung*)	4.4	External	Employer and/ or employee	DC	Yes/possible	48.2	Yes	Protektor AG/ BaFin
Superannuation fund (*Pensionskasse*)	4.5	External	Employer and/ or employee	DC	Yes/possible	101.8	Yes	(Protektor AG)/ BaFin
Pension fund (*Pensionsfonds*, since 2002)	0.3	External	Employer and/ or employee	DC	Yes/possible	14.2	Marginal	PSV/BaFin
Supplementary pension for public sector employees (VBL)	5.2	PAYGO/ funded	Employer and employee	DB, 2002: DC	Yes	—	Non (PAYGO)	BMF and BaFin
Riester personal pension (*Riester-Rente* since 2002)	12.9	External	Individual	DC	Yes/yes	—	—	(Protektor AG)/ BaFin
Rürup personal pension (*Rürup-Rente* since 2004)	0.6	External	Individual	DC	Yes/no	—	—	BaFin

Notes: coverage includes multiple entitlements (in reality 17.5 mio. employees are covered). PSV: *Pensionssicherungs-Verein auf Gegenseitigkeit*, BaFin: *Bundesanstalt für Finanzdienstleistungsaufsicht*, BMF: Federal Ministry of Finance.

Source: aba (2005), BMGS (2005a), Schwind (2009), TNS Infratest (2005b), TNS Infratest (2008).

131

- Direct insurances (*Direktversicherung*) are particularly common among smaller firms due to low administrative costs and no employer liabilities as they are sponsors of a life insurance contract for their employees (aba 2005: 23f; TNS Infratest 2005*b*: 21).

- Superannuation funds (*Pensionskasse*) are independent funds tailored for one or more firms, similar to the direct insurance, though employees are more closely involved through membership in the fund (Ricken 2007: 371).

- Pension funds (*Pensionsfonds*) exist since 2002, allowing a more flexible and more risky investment portfolio with potentially higher rates of return than superannuation funds. These EU-compatible funds can offer occupational pensions across national boundaries.

- Supplementary public-sector pension agency (*Versorgungsanstalt des Bundes und der Länder*, VBL) has been a PAYG pension scheme dating back to 1929. It has been quasi-mandatory through collective agreements for public sector employees other than civil servants, providing advantages when compared to the private sector in respects to financial governance, benefits, and redistributive elements.

In the *third* pillar, personal pensions are of recent origin, except individual life insurances with some tax privileges that have been widespread for decades. Following the recent pension reforms, two new types of voluntary personal pensions emerged for two different clientele, both are voluntary and fully funded, but they are also regulated as they receive state subsidies and tax deductions:

- the so-called 'Riester'[1] pension (since 2002) is a guaranteed funded personal pension, fostered by subsidies for low-income earners and families with children;

- the so-called 'Rürup'[2] pension (since 2004) is a funded personal pension, devised for the self-employed who have otherwise no sufficient old age retirement income.

6. Who is covered?

Occupational pensions largely sponsored by employers for their employees as a fringe benefit have developed in a variety of forms prior to their first regulation in 1974. Thus, occupational pensions in both public and private sectors cover

---

[1] Walter Riester (ex-union leader) was Social Democratic Federal Minister for Labour and Social Affairs between 1998 and 2002.

[2] Economics Professor Bert Rürup was chair (2000–8) of the German Social Advisory Council (*Sozialbeirat*) and chair of the 'Rürup' pension commission (2002/3) as well as member of the German Council of Economic Experts (2000–9) until his move to the private sector.

17.5–19 million employees (about 65–70 per cent of 26–27 million employees covered by statutory social insurance), not counting the over 2.2 million civil servants (*Beamte*) with a final-salary pension and the 6.8 million mini-jobbers without mandatory social insurance (see Table 5.4). The occupational pensions have been largely voluntary commitments by employers in the private sector: the five private occupational schemes cover about 50 per cent of statutory insured employees (but including some double counts). Most of these are being divided between the three major schemes in the private sectors: the employer pension commitment, the direct insurance, and the superannuation fund (cover 16 per cent each). In the public sector, collective agreements led to a mandatory scheme for those public employees who were not civil servants (about 5.3 million or 20 per cent), while only about 1.2 million private sector employees (or less than 5 per cent) are covered by collective agreements declared mandatory by the Labour Ministry (BMGS 2004). Whereas in the private sector, mainly skilled male workers and higher level white-collar employees were insured by their employers until the 1990s, all employees in the public sector have been insured by the collective agreement of 1966 (BMAS 2006: 713–21). Although in comparison to other European countries occupational pension coverage in Germany is relatively high, the average *benefits* are relatively low, providing only a topping up of the earnings-related state pension.

Personal pensions are available for all members of the statutory system (and civil servants), that is about 30–35 million employees are entitled to sign Riester pension contracts (BMGS 2004). Initially, only 4.1 million contracts had been signed (2004), but after some regulatory improvement the sign-up rate increased to almost 13 million contracts by autumn 2009 or nearly every third eligible person (see Figure 5.2). Nevertheless, the government's initial

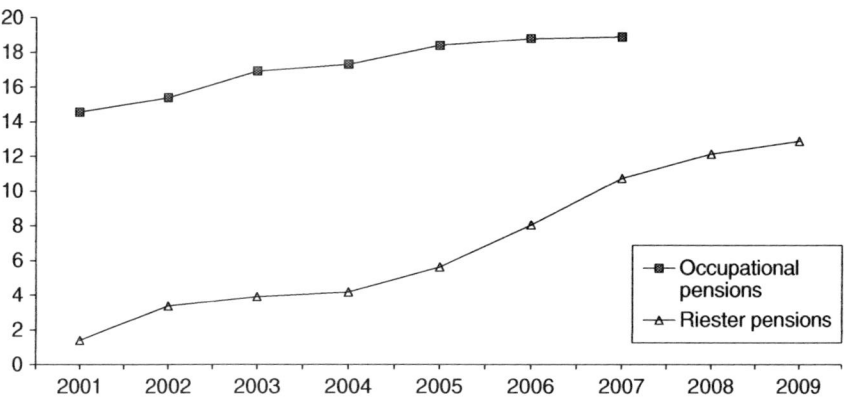

Figure 5.2 Development of occupational pension and Riester contracts (in million employees), Germany 2001–8

Source: BMAS (2009), TNS Infratest (2008).

high expectations that 85 per cent of the beneficiaries will receive state subsidies in 2008 did not materialize. Since 2005, all taxpayers are also entitled to the Rürup pensions, especially the self-employed who are excluded from occupational pensions (and Riester pensions), yet only about 0.6 million contracts have been signed thus far.

7. What kind of benefits?

Occupational pensions can vary in the way in which benefits are financed and calculated. In the case of *defined-benefit* (DB) pensions (whether financed by PAYG or partially funded), the sponsors take on the responsibility to guarantee supplementary benefits based on previous earnings (and contribution periods). On the other hand, *defined-contribution* (DC) pensions are funded and the returns depend on the investment portfolio, thus leaving the investment risk largely to the individual unless otherwise regulated. Among the five private sector occupational schemes, the direct pension commitments and support funds are traditional DB schemes, financed by book reserves of the sponsoring companies, thus there is an insolvency risk. The public sector occupational pension (VBL) is also traditionally a DB scheme financed on a PAYG basis.

A trend away from the more generous final-salary to average-working-life-salary DB schemes is evident. Most prominent are the changes of the public sector VBL scheme in 2002: it is now based on a point system of contributions and years, that is a notional DC of 4 per cent similar to the Riester pension (BMAS 2006: 715f). Most of the newly introduced occupational pensions since 2002 are DC schemes. Until 2002, all occupational pension schemes were DB, the shift of employers to DC plans is due to financial risks, liability exposure under international accounting standards, and cost containment pressures (Stevens et al. 2002: 31), thereby shifting risks to the employees and pensioners, leading often to lower benefits than under the former system. The Riester and Rürup personal pensions are designed to be DC schemes that are fully funded and benefits depend on contributions, albeit equal for men and women, as well as the rate of return on investments (but negative returns are not allowed).

In terms of benefits, an important issue is the regulation of pension adjustment of DB schemes: they are regulated to be adjusted by consumer price index or net wages of comparable employees in the firm, alternatively the employer commits to an annual increase by 1 per cent, except in cases of economic distress to the firm. However, not every scheme fulfils these obligations as employees are often unaware of their rights. Benefits from the public sector VBL scheme and earnings conversions must increase at least by 1 per cent per annum (Betriebsrentengesetz 2007). Since 1974, occupational pensions cannot be lowered in case of increasing state pension benefits. Benefits from non-public pensions are taxable, but public pensions will be taxed in the future too. Like all saving-plans, no automatic adjustments exist in DC-funded Riester or Rürup plans, thus capital returns need at least to exceed inflation rates to retain money value.

Occupational pensions can play some role in early retirement as there is no legal minimum age, though age 60 is common as a contractual minimum (Neise 2007); however, actuarial reductions commonly occur for early retirement (aba 2005: 37). The future rise of legal retirement age for the public pension to 67 will also apply to the state-subsidized personal pensions but it may not apply to occupational pensions (OPs) (see Rolfs 2007). The retirement age of the public sector VBL scheme is also increasing up to 67 and actuarial reductions (0.3 per cent per month up to 10.8 per cent for thirty-six months) apply for early retirement (BMAS 2006: 717). In the past, about 40 per cent of OP recipients have already received their pension before age 65 (TNS Infratest 2005a). Although pathways to early retirement were largely facilitated by the public transfers, occupational pensions have also facilitated labour shedding by firms as they could counterbalance public pension reductions. The policy change towards limiting public early exit pathways might again make occupational pensions gain in importance for firms, though early drawing would also lead to actuarial deductions.

Occupational pensions are by nature less redistributive than public schemes; however, there are some aspects in which intra- or intergenerational solidarity plays a role. Unlike saving plans, most German private pensions cover at least one of the risks (*ex post* balancing) of longevity, disability, or survivor benefits. Furthermore, many DB schemes ignore sex, health, age, and marital status for benefit calculations (*ex ante* redistribution). In times of longer absence from work, for example, due to sickness or childcare, OPs can voluntarily be continued through individual contributions (aba 2005: 35) and some private OPs pay benefits for surviving dependants (BMAS 2006: 716f). Notably, the public sector VBL grants credits in case of incapacity (reduction in earnings), death before 60 (survivor pension), and for maternity protection and parental leave. In contrast, redistribution plays no role in DC plans and schemes financed by employee contributions only (BMGS 2004: 14). One exception is the child credits that were introduced for Riester plans in 2002, and the state subsidy for low-income earners. Thus with a shift from DB to DC redistributive elements will largely disappear.

For European flexible labour markets, nationally and across borders, the possibility to change jobs while keeping social entitlements is an important factor for mobility. Portability of pension rights, however, may undermine the selective incentives for employers to bind skilled workers to their firm. German employer-financed occupational pensions become vested after five years of service for employees after age 30, though there are plans to lower the age limit to 25 (BMGS 2005a: 17, 39). Earnings conversions become already vested after the first paid contribution. These new vesting rules help less-skilled and short-term employees (including many women). Since 2005, employees are entitled to transfer vested benefits of new contracts to the new employer's insurance provider under certain conditions (BMGS 2005*b*: 64). Since 2005, portability in the public sector VBL scheme is only possible if entitlements are fully funded (BMGS 2005*a*: 74), this will hinder changes to the private sector since benefits in West Germany are still PAYG financed. Particularly with respect to transferability, we can find a conflict of interests: for employers higher portability means higher costs and no binding of employees to the firm, while social policy actors want to protect employees' benefits in times of reduced public pensions and economic rational of flexible labour markets (e.g. discussions about an EU Directive on portability). In the case of personal pensions, one can change the provider of the (subsidized) plan at any time and take one's savings along, albeit this portability may involve considerable losses.

8. Who pays?

Occupational pensions differ as to who pays contributions: the employer, the employee or both jointly (see Table 5.4). Generally, German employers finance the traditional modes of direct pension commitment and support funds, given that it is a voluntary fringe benefit to bind employees to the firm. There are no state subsidies for employees, but the book reserves with a nominal rate of return (currently 6 per cent) reduce a firm's pre-tax profits. After the war, large firms used these on the book reserves to refinance their investments, relying less on capital markets than Anglophone companies (Jackson and Vitols 2001). With increased importance of shareholder value and international accounting standards, these pension commitments are listed as liabilities (Clark 2003). Therefore, some employers have closed these schemes for new entrants or closed them in case of a merger (Ruppert 1997).

The other occupational pensions (direct insurances, superannuation funds, and pension funds) are largely financed by employees' voluntary contributions, though many superannuation and pension funds are still financed jointly (Leiber 2005: 318). A trend from employer-only towards jointly financed schemes is observable, but this may reduce the take-up rate by employees.[3] Normally, the question of who pays and how much is embedded within employer–employee negotiations. Since 2002, employees have the right to convert a certain percentage of their pre-tax earnings into a funded occupational

---

[3] The employee-only financed schemes are increasing (from 26 per cent in 2001 to 32 per cent in 2007) as well as jointly financed schemes (from 27 per cent in 2001 to 42 per cent in 2007), whereas the share of employer-financed schemes is decreasing (from 54 per cent in 2001 to 38 per cent in 2007) (BMAS 2008*a*).

pension. This should accelerate coverage particularly among small- and medium-sized firms. Since individual occupational pension contributions are exempt from income tax and social insurance contributions, they are favoured by many employees, but these lead to a reduction in overall payroll taxes (see Table 5.5).[4] Under some conditions, individuals covered by occupational pensions can convert part of their wages and profit from the Riester pension subsidies, though this has thus far been rarely used. The public sector scheme VBL was solely employer-financed until 1998 and remains thereafter still financed by four-fifths by the employer. VBL was a DB scheme (up to 92 per cent of final salary) but has been changed to a notional DC system in 2002 (BMAS 2006; Leiber 2005: 320). While VBL is still a PAYG system in the West, the Eastern scheme has been gradually transformed to a funded pension since 2004.

In terms of financial regulation, the direct pension commitment and support fund are forms of reinvestment and therefore need to be reinsured against the insolvency risk, while investment restrictions exist for superannuation funds and direct insurances to limit financial risks due to (foreign) stock market portfolios. Anglophone developments show that pension funds with a large percentage of equities may lead to underfunding, resulting in higher investments in fixed interest securities (Jackson and Vitols 2001: 184). An excess demand of fixed interest securities can in turn cause lower returns (Bundesverband deutscher Banken 2007: 18ff). The German pension fund reform and EU laws allow more investment in firms with registered offices in the European Economic Area, thereby fostering the German and European capital markets (BMGS 2002: 11).

Riester plans consist of tax deductions, state subsidies, and own contributions (free of tax but not free of social insurance contributions). In principle, tax deductions favour rather high-income earners, whereas low-income earners benefit more from state subsidies (Schmähl 2004).[5] To receive such subsidies, certain criteria must be fulfilled (e.g. payments from a minimum age, consumer information, and a minimum period of performance), indicating substantial state regulation. The level of subsidy for Riester contracts will not increase after 2008 given the contribution ceiling of the year 2000 (see Table 5.5), whereas the contribution ceiling for occupational pensions is linked to earnings development and thus will exceed the fixed ceiling in personal pensions in the future. Rürup pensions are fostered by tax deductions (but no subsidies), provided that annuities are not paid before age 60 and survivors' benefits are optional. Contributions can be paid within a year on a flexible basis (accommodating the

---

[4] The primary limitation of these exemptions until 2008 (because of the loss of social insurance contributions) was repealed.

[5] Since 2008, the minimum contribution to receive full subsidies is 4 per cent of last year income, and taxes are deductible up to €2,100 per annum. In addition to tax deductions, Riester pension contractors get a basic credit (€154) and a supplementary child credit (€185 per child, €300 for children born after 2007).

Table 5.5 Financial and tax regulation of occupational pensions

Occupational pension scheme	Tax deductions + social insurance contribution	State subsidies	Minimum return	Investment limits
Direct pension commitment	Employer payments are unlimited, free of tax and free of social contributions (up to 4% of ceiling)	No	DB	None (book reserves)
Support fund		No	DB	None
Direct insurance	Up to 4% of contribution ceiling + €1.800 and free of social contributions (up to 4% of ceiling)	Possible	Yes	Yes
Superannuation fund		Possible	Yes	Yes
Pension fund		Possible	No (0%)	Marginal
Supplementary insurance for public sector employees	No tax deductions	Possible (–2001 funded)	—	—

Source: aba (2005), BMGS (2004), OECD (2005), TNS Infratest (2005*b*).

unsteady income of many self-employed), supplementary payments are possible, and no minimum contribution exists – thus also makes it attractive to elderly people short before retirement (BMGS 2005*a*: 72).

The costs of supplementary pensions for the state are substantial. Forgone tax income and Riester subsidy amount to €11 billion in 2008 or 0.4 per cent of GDP (aba 2005: 15). Moreover, following the 2004 reform, public pensions will be automatically reduced if more and more people use earnings conversion, affecting also those persons who made no such savings. Since 2000s, voluntary supplementary pensions are largely a substitute for the reduction of the increasingly meagre public pensions, they are no longer a 'topping up' of generous benefits. Compared to before, individual contributions to finance the same overall retirement income now require a 4 per cent higher contribution to a personal pension plan (or about one-fifth higher contributions), though the tax benefits and subsidies for lower-income groups need to be considered too.

9. Who governs? Who decides? Who manages?

German employers decide whether or not to provide an occupational pension and in what form, though in some cases a collective agreement exists. Generally, all employees have the right, contingent on a collective agreement, to convert agreed earnings into an occupational pension. Direct pension commitments are governed by the management of the firm and in case of co-determination with equal representation of employees, the beneficiaries of direct insurances have no influence over asset management. The governance of pension funds is more complicated. Theoretically, employees can take part in decision-making in the board of trustees of pension funds via their representatives, but in reality it is questionable whether this matters. In addition, there may be conflicts of interests, for instance, between younger and older insured people, and some beneficiaries are more interested in high-return but risky investments, while others prefer lower risk and social or ecological investments.

Governance of pension funds creates a (multilevel) principal–agent relationship, since the insured person and the beneficiary rely as *principals* on an agent – the employer, a pension fund, or an investment manager. Asymmetric information (hidden knowledge) and unbalanced distribution of power need to be limited by appropriate governance structures. As sponsors of occupational pensions, employers can also act as the principal vis-à-vis the fund manager. Principals (especially the beneficiaries) can nominate their representatives to the boards and they are entitled to receive information on request (BMGS 2004: 33). Financial literacy is necessary in order to make well-informed choices between various available options. Employer or the pension fund is obliged to provide employees with written information on pension value and investment policies. Transparency is guaranteed by several information duties of the provider or employer in compliance with the European Directive (BMGS 2004: 33).

Supervision is particularly important in PAYG and DB schemes, in which the employer or financial institutions bears the risk of underfunding. Two EU Directives (2002/83/EC and 2003/41/EC) regulate the supervision of private pension insurances (BMGS 2005a: 39). According to German law, direct insurances, superannuation funds, and pension funds as well as Riester and Rürup contracts are supervised by the Federal Financial Supervisory Authority (BaFin), which is financed by a levy on the supervised entities. BaFin is a federal institution formally independent but the Finance Ministry is represented on the supervisory board and in exceptional cases can give ministerial instructions, while BaFin regularly consults the ministry concerning new regulations and guidelines (Pinheiro 2004: 43ff). The main functions of BaFin are to monitor the solvency of banks, insurance companies, and pension funds; to make on-site inspections; withdraw their authorization; and to ensure market transparency and consumer protection.

For the schemes with book reserves and pension funds, insolvency protection is compulsory and guaranteed by the Pension Protection Fund (*Pensions Sicherungs-Verein* or PSV, founded 1974) which is a self-help institution of the German (and Luxembourg) pension schemes insuring 5.8 million employees and paying currently about 1 million occupational pensions (TNS Infratest 2005b: 20f). As a risk reinsurer, PSV guarantees continued payment of benefits in case of bankruptcy of the firm (aba 2005: 13), an important social protection function. Direct insurances and the insurance-based superannuation funds are insured against bankruptcy by Protektor, a life insurance protection company. The (mainly) PAYG-financed public sector pension needs no insolvency protection due to state guarantees and *BaFin* supervision.

In the case of personal pensions, the insured alone decides to conclude a Riester or Rürup plan; however, the manifold offers are often complicated and not easy to understand. Choice and information overload require substantial financial literacy (Bundesverband deutscher Banken 2007: 14). Prior to signing a personal pension contract the clients have to be informed about the expected administration costs, which can be considerable particularly during the early phases of investment. The providers have to emphasize guaranteed benefits in compliance with the EU directive 2002/83/EG for life assurances (BMGS 2004: 33, 49ff). Furthermore, providers have to inform about investment possibilities and portfolio structure (taking into account ethnic, social, and environmental issues). The insurer is required to inform annually about the investments, saved assets, administrative costs, and achieved income (BMGS 2005a: 51f).

BaFin is responsible for the licensing of Riester pensions according to five criteria: pension payments only from the minimum age onwards, a minimum interest rate of 2.25 per cent in case of life insurance contracts or guaranteed security of invested savings (but not of returns), minimum period of performance, specified consumer information, and the possibility to pay out 30 per cent of the capital stock as a lump sum and 70 per cent as an annuity (BMGS 2005b: 65). Like all insurance contracts, the insurance-based Riester and Rürup pensions are protected by Protektor in the event of the insurance company's bankruptcy. Germany's personal pensions are thus relatively well secured by the minimum guarantee and bankruptcy protection compared to many funded DC schemes in other countries.

The current financial crisis of 2008/9 (as well as the earlier turbulences in 2001/2) has differential effects. For DC plans, the pension level is dependent on investment decisions (risky versus secure investments) but pensioners will receive at least their paid contributions thanks to a minimum rate of return of 0 per cent (nominal), though this may still be a net loss considering inflation. Also, DB plans might be underfunded due to falling asset prices in which case employer contributions need to be increased and/or benefits for new entrants will be lowered. The situation is similar for Riester pensions, where insurance-based plans have a minimum return of about 2.25 per cent and fund-based plans of 0 per cent. Real investment return of German pension funds fell round about 7 per cent in 2008, relatively low compared to the OECD average of about –23 per cent (OECD 2009: 33). German funds benefit from the (often criticized) investment restrictions (maximum of 35 per cent of assets in quoted and 10 per cent in unquoted shares) together with traditional conservative portfolio strategies.

10. Collective agreements and pension schemes

With the exemption of the public sector, collective agreements on occupational pensions at branch or firm level were an exception until after the recent reforms. But since 2001, the right to earnings conversion is subject to *Tarifvorbe-halt*, stipulating that conversions are bound to an existing collective agreement, if applicable, including flexibility clauses that devolve these decisions to the employer and works council at the firm level (Leiber 2005: 315). Until the 1990s, occupational pensions were just a subordinate field of collective bargaining as unions were more interested in wage increases, while employer-only-sponsored occupational schemes made collective bargaining largely unnecessary. Furthermore, the duration of an occupational scheme exceeds the usual duration of collective agreements irrespective of whether employers were interested in negotiating old age security (Stiefermann 2003: 447f). The new earning conversion has changed the employer's interest towards seeking to find efficient low administration costs solutions, reducing wage costs and reinforcing its attractiveness. Collective agreements govern conditions of earnings conversion, the contributions' rules, and the mode of OP and benefit adjustments. Works councils have the right of co-determination in case of an absent collective agreement; they can also specify and improve collective agreed regulations. Company agreements must be negotiated between the works council and the employer (Kemper 2003: 158ff). But generally, the earnings conversion right (contingent on a collective agreement) shifted the scope for occupational pensions from the company to the interfirm bargaining level and to the individual employee respectively (see also Berner 2008). Schemes with broader coverage exist especially in sectors with high union density and broad bargaining coverage. The Labour Ministry can extend collective agreements on social partners' request, such as happened for 1.2 million employees in construction, agriculture, newspaper, and catering as well as in some food industries (BMAS 2008*b*; BMGS 2004: 4, 21).

Contribution conditions vary across industry. In the construction industry, which includes 1.1 million employees, the employer pays 77 per cent of the contributions if the employee relinquishes capital-forming payments. The employer commonly pays contributions into an occupational pension scheme in the metal industry, in retail, in hotel and restaurants, in chemical, textile and clothing, and electrician industries as well as in painting, varnishing, and roofer trades. The preconditions include minimum contributions of the employee and are often conditional on relinquishing capital-forming or holiday payments. Employer contributions in the service sector like in the retail industry are non-typical. In contrast, in sectors as printing, paper, board, and plastic processing as well as in travel agencies there are no employer contributions. It is the employer who decides about the mode of occupational pension in chemical, printing, hotel and restaurant, textile and clothing, paper, board, and plastic processing industries as well as in travel agencies. In contrast, employer and employee together choose the occupational pension mode in the construction, electrician, steel industry (after consulting with the works council), and retail industry (see Table 5.6). Surpluses of occupational pension assets in

Table 5.6 Selected collective agreements on occupational pensions in the range of earnings conversion (Germany, mid-2000s)

Sector	Employees (mio.)	Employee's contributions	Employer's contributions	Mode of occupational pension	Collective scheme/general agreement
Public sector (VBL)[a]	5.30	1.41% (West) 0.5–2% (East)	6.45% (West) 0.5–2% (East)	PAYGO (West) Partly funded (East)	VBL (public law agency) with equal representation in administration board
Metal and electrician industry	3.41	–4%*, higher after consultation of employer with employee	€319.08 p.a. (instead of former capital-forming payments)	All possible (employer decision)	*MetallRente* with equal representation in executive board
Retail industry	1.62	–4%*, at the request of employee higher contributions are possible	€300 p.a. by abdication of capital-forming payments (+10% earnings conversion value)	All possible (decision of employer and works council)	General agreement with six provider institutions
Construction industry (voluntary earnings conversion)	1.10	min. €110 (West) min. €37 (East) p.a.	€368 p.a. (West) by abdication of capital-forming payments; €123 (East)	All possible (decision of employer and employee); if no agreement: *Zusatzversorgungskasse Bau*	SOKA BAU, collective institution
Hotels and restaurants	0.65	–4%*	€150 p.a. + 16% earnings conversion value (by saved social insurance contributions)	Employer decision; preference of superannuation fund	*Hogarente*, collective institution
Chemical industry	0.59	(+€100)	€614 p.a. (instead of former capital-forming payments) (+€13) (2010: plus €300 p.a.)	All possible (employer decision): *Chemie Versorgungswerk*	Social partners are represented in board of directors and *Anlageausschuss (Pensionsfond)*
Insurance industry (earnings conversion)	0.24	–4%*	€480 by abdication of capital-forming payments	All possible (employer decision); employees are eligible for a direct insurance	BVV with equal representation

Textile and clothing industry (West)	0.19	–4%* min. €240	€120 + 10% earnings conversion value	All possible (employer decision)	Use of *Metallrente* with sectoral name (*Textilrente*)
Electrician trade	0.18	–4%* min. €360	10% of the employee contributions	All possible (employer decision in consultation with employee)	General agreement with occupational pension provider (inter alia *Metallrente*)
Bakery trade		min. €150	€80 p.a.	Superannuation fund	Equal representation in controlling board
Painter and varnisher trade (voluntary)	0.12	–4%*	12% of employee contributions (by saved social insurance contributions)	Collective scheme of painter and varnisher trade (ZVK); other mode in consultation with employee	ZVK (superannuation fund), collective institution
Roofer trade	0.11	–4%*	€399 by abdication of capital-forming payments	ZVK	Collective scheme of roofer trade (superannuation fund)
Steel industry	0.09	–4%*	Earnings conversion of capital-forming payments	All possible (employer decision after hearing works council)	Use of *Metallrente*
Paper, board and plastic processing industry	0.09	–4%*	None	All possible (employer decision); preference of superannuation fund	*Zukunftsfonds Medien* with equal representation in advisory board
Travel agencies	0.04	–4%*	None	All possible (employer decision)	

Notes: p.a.: per annum; a: this mandatory OP is listed (not: earnings conversion) due to the specific characteristics of the public sector; * up to statutory contribution ceiling.

Source: BDA (2008), Bispinck (2004), Stiefermann (2003), WSI (2008).

construction, metal, and textile and clothing industries have to be accrued to the benefit of the insured (IG BAU 2005; IG Metall 2002, 2006). The public sector is a special case (until the 1990s) since it guarantees employees an overall replacement rate including statutory and occupational pensions similar to the civil service final-salary scheme; however, the agreement of 2002 changed the system towards a notional DC benefit, based on the hypothetical outcome of a 4 per cent contribution in a fully funded scheme.

Instruments for the design and governance of occupational pensions for the social partners are, besides collective agreements, self-administered 'pension institutions'. In some sectors, legally independent pension schemes were founded by unions and employers' associations in which the social partners are members of the advisory board. Such agreements and contracts have a broader coverage and risk pooling with lower administration costs than unilateral employer decisions or individual contracts. A prime example is the *Metallrente*, one of the earliest and largest schemes administered by the metal workers' union and the respective employer organization.[6] A parity executive board is responsible for negotiating, controlling, and terminating contracts with the financial companies (IG Metall 2001). The possible modes of occupational pensions are a pension fund (with social and ecological sustainability aims), superannuation funds, and a direct insurance in which financial service providers assume the transaction. The bipartite advisory board has a consultative character in matters concerning development of asset investments, design of pension plans and investment principles (Karch 2002). In the chemical industry, the social partners signed a contract with an insurance company to form *ChemieVersorgungswerk* which includes a pension fund (330,000 insured), the first one in Germany that dates to an initiative of the social partners. Both social partners are represented on the management board and in the investment committee, but the pension fund is part of a commercial insurance group. Furthermore, for the direct insurance, the social partners agreed a group-contract with a consortium of insurance companies.

A special case is the construction industry: a bipartite insurance fund (*Sozialkassen*) provides assistance during the winter time since the 1950s. The *SOKA* pension is set up by the two employer federations in construction and the respective trade union (*IG BAU*). Since 2001, an option for a supplementary occupational pension exists. In 2007, 57,000 employees were insured in the supplementary pension scheme *Zukunft Plus*, a superannuation fund, which is controlled by a supervisory board. The board is responsible to the general meeting and to the three bargaining partners.[7] Several other occupational

---

[6] In 2009, 16,000 firms participated in *Metallrente* (out of 21,500 firms) with about 0.3 out of 4 million metal workers (interview, June 2009), though it is also open for non-metal firms.

[7] About 57,000 out of 600,000 employees in the construction industry make use of *Zukunft Plus* (10 per cent) (Interview, May 2009).

schemes exist in smaller sectors (see Table 5.6). Most notable is a scheme in the printing industry (*Zukunftsfonds Medien*) and a pension institution for the press, dating back to 1926, where editorial journalists of newspapers and magazines not covered by statutory pensions pay 7.5 per cent of their earnings into a (mandatory) pension institution in addition to contributions twice as high by employers (WSI 2001: 63).

The public sector employee scheme is the most regulated collective scheme, based on a mandatory collective agreement since 1967. The *VBL* together with the municipal supplementary pension scheme is responsible for the administration. The *VBL* is a statutory body institution with bipartite representation (VBL 2004: 66). The chairman and eight members of the executive board are nominated by the supervisory authority in consultation with the participating states (*Länder*) and the rest of the eight members are nominated by the unions (VBL 2004: 78). The administrative board in turn consists of thirty-eight members which are one half each appointed by the union and the employers. The main conflict of interests in funded schemes divides beneficiaries who favour long-term security of old age retirement income and pension providers with short-term maximization of returns. Occupational pensions when administered collectively shift responsibility from employees to collective interest representatives (employers and their associations vis-à-vis unions and works councils) that usually have more substantial information and financial expertise to make informed administrative and investment decisions than the ordinary employee or employers in small firms. Negotiating such agreements also provides trade unions with a new role.

11. The outlook

Germany's century-old Bismarckian public pension system has been one of the most path dependent welfare state arrangements among European countries, guaranteeing for most employees status maintenance in old age, thanks to earnings-related pensions paid by employer employee contributions. Occupational pensions were available mainly to those working in core firms or the public sector, allowing them to 'top up' their retirement income. Continued unemployment problems and high labour costs, the ongoing demographic trends and post-Maastricht fiscal restrictions have put additional pressure on the government to reform the German public pensions which had once been hailed as 'safe'. The politically contentious reforms following the 1990s initiated phased-in parametric cutbacks in public pensions, while during the early 2000s subsequent reforms led to a paradigmatic change in the public–private mix, making voluntary private pensions necessary to maintain one's living standard in old age. Public pensions will no longer maintain status but become increasingly rather meagre, particularly for those with insufficient contribution years and low income. The introduction of a minimum pension (*Grundsicherung im Alter*) in 2003 has added a new basic pension element. Although thus far this minimum pension has only a minor impact as most retired people receive contributory public pensions above the minimum limit, in the future political pressures could mount to transfer this into a more substantial tax-financed basic pension. For those low-income groups that will receive the minimum pension, there may be a (perceived) disincentive to save privately, because private pension savings are credited against minimum pension entitlements. However, the unemployment assistance scheme exempts private Riester personal pension from means testing.

In the short term, the recent financial turmoil might lead to higher contributions and lower benefits due to loss of pension savings, but more dangerous are indirect effects of the crisis, in particular insolvencies of banks, financial services and bankruptcies of firms. Occupational pensions are protected against insolvency through reinsurances (PVS and *Protektor*). Providing relief to financially stricken firms like Opel and firm bankruptcies will lead to higher premiums to afford these protection institutions. More long-term risks of the current crisis are rising unemployment rates that lead to higher unemployment expenditures and lower social contributions. Moreover, if net earnings are falling, there will be less space for investments in supplementary pensions. Lower earnings and higher unemployment rates lead to lower revenues for the statutory pensions, which might cause higher contributions or tax grants for state pensions. The increase in public debt will also raise the pressure on cutting back public expenditure, particularly in the light of continued ageing.

One of the most important risks to private old age provision would be a decrease in trust of people in financial markets and funded supplementary pensions themselves. Private pensions, both occupational and personal pensions, will become more important in respect to retirement income given the cutbacks of public pensions in the future. Currently employees are expected to contribute 4 per cent of their earnings to voluntary private retirement savings, which equals one-fifth of the mandatory contributions to the public pension. The share of private pension contribution may need to increase if public pensions lose even more in value or the returns on funded capital does not keep up its expected promises. Yet not everyone will be covered by the voluntary pensions. Approximately one in two employees is covered by an occupational pension for some time and about every one in three employees has a personal pension. But those with low income and unsteady attachment to employment will be less capable of contributing to private old age savings. The tax concessions and subsidies have only had limited impact on increasing the sign-up rate of voluntary personal pensions, while collectively negotiated schemes have increased coverage beyond the public sector more recently but still fall short of the high coverage in countries with collective schemes or a mandated one. Whether an invigorated collective bargaining route will be able to expand occupational pensions or political pressure will gain enough momentum for mandatory private pensions is difficult to predict.

Bibliography

aba (ed.) (2005). *Mit der Betriebsrente in eine sichere Zukunft.* Heidelberg: Arbeitsgemeinschaft für Betriebliche Altersversorgung.

Alber, J. (1986). 'Germany', in P. Flora (ed.), *Growth to Limits: The Western European Welfare States Since World War II. Volume 2.* Berlin: Walter de Gruyter, 1–154.

BDA (2008). *Tarifvertragliche Vereinbarungen zur betrieblichen Altersvorsorge auf der Basis des AVmG.* Cologne: Bundesverband der Deutschen Arbeitgeber (www.bda-online.de).

Berner, F. (2008). 'Steuerungsprobleme im regulierenden Wohlfahrtsstaat'. *Zeitschrift für Sozialreform*, 4: 391–417.

Betriebsrentengesetz (2007). *Gesetz zur Verbesserung der betrieblichen Altersversorgung (Betriebsrentengesetz – BetrAVG)*, 20 April 2007 (BGBl. I S.554).

Bispinck, R. (2004). 'Wie die zweite Säule wächst'. *Mitbestimmung*, 1+2/2004: 11–16.

BMAS [Bundesministerium für Arbeit und Soziales] (2006). *Übersicht über das Sozialrecht.* Berlin: BMAS.

——(2007). *Statistisches Taschenbuch 2007.* Berlin: BMAS.

——(ed.) (2008a). *Ergänzender Bericht der Bundesregierung zum Rentenversicherungsbericht 2008 gemäß § 154 Abs. 2 SGB VI (Alterssicherungsbericht 2008).* Berlin: BMAS.

——(2008b). *Verzeichnis der für allgemeinverbindlich erklärten Tarifverträge.* Berlin: BMAS.

——(ed.) (2009). *Entwicklung der Riester-Rente.* Berlin: BMAS.

BMGS [Bundesministerium für Gesundheit und Soziale Sicherung] (2002). *Bundesrepublik Deutschland – Nationaler Strategiebericht Alterssicherung (NSB) – Anhänge zum Nationalen Strategiebericht Alterssicherung 2002.* Berlin: BMGS.

——(2004). *Der Sozialschutzausschuss – Sonderstudie über Renten – Nachhaltigkeit der Systeme der zweiten und dritten Säule und ihr Beitrag zu einer angemessenen Alterssicherung – Vorläufiger Fragebogen der Kommission – Deutscher Beitrag vom 30.07.04.* Berlin: BMGS.

——(2005a). *Bundesrepublik Deutschland – Nationaler Strategiebericht Alterssicherung 2005 (NSB).* Berlin: BMGS.

——(2005b). *Sozialbericht 2005.* Berlin: BMGS.

Bundesverband deutscher Banken (2007). *Altersvorsorge – Die Herausforderungen der Kapitaldeckung Meistern.* Berlin: Bundesverband deutscher Banken.

Busemeyer, M. R. (2006). 'Moving the Unmovable: Political Strategies of Pension Reform in Germany'. *German Policy Studies*, 3/3: 400–45.

Clark, G. L. (2003). *European Pensions & Global Finance.* Oxford: Oxford University Press.

DRV (ed.) (2006). *Rentenversicherung in Zeitreihen 2006.* Berlin: Deutsche Rentenversicherung Bund.

Ebbinghaus, B., and Schulze, I. (2007). 'Krise und Reform der Alterssicherung in Europa'. *Archiv für Sozialgeschichte*, 47: 269–96.

Esping-Andersen, G. (1990). *The Three Worlds of Welfare Capitalism.* Cambridge: Polity Press.

——(1996). 'Welfare States without Work: The Impasse of Labour Shedding and Familialism in Continental European Social Policy', in G. Esping-Andersen (ed.), *Welfare States in Transition: National Adaptations in Global Economies*. London: Sage, 66–87.

Frommert, D., and Heien, T. (2006). 'Kontinuität oder Wandel? Die Bedeutung der drei Säulen der Alterssicherung im Zeitvergleich'. *Deutsche Rentenversicherung*, 61/2–3: 132–55.

Hinrichs, K. (2005). 'New Century–New Paradigm: Pension Reforms in Germany', in G. Bonoli and T. Shinkawa (eds.), *Ageing and Pension Reform Around the World: Evidence from Eleven Countries*. Cheltenham, UK: Edward Elgar, 47–73.

Hockerts, H. G. (1980). *Sozialpolitische Entscheidungen im Nachkriegsdeutschland: Alliierte und deutsche Sozialversicherungspolitik 1945 bis 1957*. Stuttgart: Klett-Cotta.

IG BAU (2005). *Tarifvertrag über eine Zusatzrente im Baugewerbe (TV TZR)*. Frankfurt a.M.

IG Metall (2001). *Verhandlungsergebnis 'Altersversorgung Metall und Elektro – eine gemeinsame Einrichtung von Gesamtmetall und IG Metall'*. Frankfurt a.M.: IG Metall.

——(2002). *Textil – Tarifvertrag zur Entgeltumwandlung*. Frankfurt a.M.: IG Metall.

——(2006). *Tarifvertrag zur Entgeltumwandlung*. Frankfurt a.M.: IG Metall.

Jackson, G., and Vitols, S. (2001). 'Between Financial Commitment, Market Liquidity and Corporate Governance: Occupational Pensions in Britain, Germany, Japan and the USA', in B. Ebbinghaus and P. Manow (eds.), *Comparing Welfare Capitalism: Social Policy and Political Economy in Europe, Japan and the USA*. London: Routledge, 171–89.

Jacobs, K., Kohli, M., and Rein, M. (1991). 'The Evolution of Early Exit: A Comparative Analysis of Labor Force Participation Patterns', in M. Kohli, M. Rein, A.-M. Guillemard and H. van Gunsteren (eds.), *Time for Retirement: Comparative Studies on Early Exit from the Labor Force*. New York, NY: Cambridge University Press, 36–66.

Karch, H. (2002). 'Die Metallrente'. *Personalwirtschaft*, 4/2002: 24–7.

Kemper, K. (2003). 'Einzelfragen zur Mitbestimmung des Betriebsrates bei einer Pensionskasse', in R. Richardi and H. Reichold (eds.), *Altersgrenzen und Alterssicherung im Arbeitsrecht – Wolfgang Blomeyer zum Gedenken*. München: C.H. Beck, 157–71.

Kohl, J. (2000). 'Der Sozialstaat: Die deutsche Version des Wohlfahrtsstaates – Überlegungen zu seiner typologischen Verortung', in S. Leibfried and U. Wagschal (eds.), *Der deutsche Sozialstaat. Bilanzen – Reformen – Perspektiven*. Frankfurt a. M.: Campus, 115–52.

Leiber, S. (2005). 'Formen und Verbreitung der betrieblichen Altersvorsorge – Eine Zwischenbilanz'. *WSI Mitteilungen*, 6/2005: 314–21.

Leisering, L., Davy, U., Berner, F., Schwarze, U., and Blömeke, P. (2002). 'Literaturstudie zum Projektantrag an die DFG: Vom produzierenden zum regulierenden Wohlfahrtsstaat'. *Regina Arbeitspapier Nr. 2*.

Manow, P. (2000). 'Kapitaldeckung oder Umlage: Zur Geschichte einer anhaltenden Debatte', in S. Fisch and U. Haerendel (eds.), *Geschichte und Gegenwart der Rentenversicherung in Deutschland*. Berlin: Duncker & Humblot, 145–68.

Mattil, B. (2006). *Pension Systems – Sustainability and Distributional Effects in Germany and the United Kingdom*. Heidelberg: Physica-Verlag.

Naschold, F., and de Vroom, B. (eds.) (1994). *Regulating Employment and Welfare: Company and National Policies of Labour Force Participation at the End of Worklife in Industrial Countries*. Berlin: W. de Gruyter.

Neise, M. (2007). 'Flexibler Rentenzugang in der betrieblichen Altersversorgung – Der Kommentar'. *Betriebliche Altersversorgung*, 7/2007: 593–4.

OECD (2005). *Survey of Quantitative Investment Regulations of Pension Funds*. Paris: OECD.

——(2009). *Pensions at a Glance 2009 – Retirement-Income Systems in OECD Countries*. Paris: OECD.

Pfau-Effinger, B. (2004). *Development of Culture, Welfare States and Women's Employment in Europe*. Aldershot: Ashgate.

Pinheiro, V. C. (2004). 'Supervisory Structures for Private Pension Funds in OECD Countries', in OECD (ed.), *Supervising Private Pensions – Institutions and Methods*. Private Pensions Series. Paris, 21–76.

Ricken, O. (2007). 'Modelle zusätzlicher Altersvorsorge'. *Deutsche Rentenversicherung*, 62/6: 366–80.

Riedmüller, B., and Willert, M. (2007). 'The German Pension System and Social Inclusion', in T. Meyer, P. Bridgen and B. Riedmüller (eds.), *Private Pension Versus Social Inclusion? Non-State Provision for Citizens at Risk in Europe*. Cheltenham: Edward Elgar, 139–67.

Rolfs, C. (2007). 'Anpassung betrieblicher Versorgungssysteme an die geänderte Lebensarbeitszeit'. *Betriebliche Altersversorgung*, 7/2007: 599–606.

Rosenow, J., and Naschold, F. (1994). *Die Regulierung der Altersgrenzen: Strategien von Unternehmen und die Politik des Staates*. Berlin: Sigma.

Rothenbacher, F. (2001). 'Die Altersversorgung im öffentlichen Dienst in Großbritannien, Frankreich und Deutschland seit dem Zweiten Weltkrieg.' in B. Wunder (ed.), *Pensionssysteme im öffentlichen Dienst in Westeuropa (19./20. Jh.)*. Baden-Baden: Nomos, 127–52.

Ruland, F. (2007a). 'Die gesetzliche Rentenversicherung im Wandel der Herausforderungen – Zentrale Rentenreformen nach 1957 bis 2007–'. *DRV-Schriften*, 73: 29–46.

——(2007b). 'Die gesetzliche Rentenversicherung im Wandel der Herausforderungen – Zentrale Rentenreformen nach 1957 bis 2007–', in Deutsche Rentenversicherung Bund (ed.), *Die gesetzliche Rente in Deutschland – 50 Jahre Sicherheit durch Anpassungen*. Bad Homburg: wdv Gesellschaft für Medien & Kommunikation, 29–46.

Ruppert, W. (1997). 'Ungünstige Bedingungen für die betriebliche Altersversorgung'. *ifo Schnelldienst*, 50/28: 10–19.

Scharpf, F. W. (2001). 'Employment and the Welfare State: A Continental Dilemma', in B. Ebbinghaus and P. Manow (eds.), *Comparing Welfare Capitalism: Social Policy and Political Economy in Europe, Japan and the USA*. London: Routledge, 270–83.

Schmähl, W. (1997). 'The Public–private Mix in Pension Provision in Germany: The Role of Employer-based Pension Arrangements and the Influence of Public Activities', in M. Rein and E. Wadensjö (eds.), *Enterprise and the Welfare State*. Cheltenham, UK: Edward Elgar, 99–148.

——(2004). 'Paradigm Shift in German Pension Policy: Measures Aiming at a New Public–Private Mix and their Effects', in M. Rein and W. Schmähl (eds.), *Rethinking the Welfare State: The Political Economy of Pension Reform*. Cheltenham, UK: Edward Elgar, 153–204.

Schulze, I., and Jochem, S. (2007). 'Germany: Beyond Policy Gridlock', in E. M. Immergut, K. M. Anderson and I. Schulze (eds.), *The Handbook of West European Pension Politics*. Oxford: Oxford University Press, 660–710.

Schwind, J. (2009). 'Deckungsmittel der betrieblichen Altersversorgung 2007'. *Betriebliche Altersversorgung*, 4/2009: 359–63.

Stevens, Y., Gieselink, G., and Van Buggenhout, B. (2002). 'Towards a New Role for Occupational Pensions in Continental Europe: Elements and Techniques of Solidarity

Used within Funded Occupational Pension Schemes'. *European Journal of Social Security*, 4/1: 25–53.

Stiefermann, K. (2003). 'Wachsende tarifpolitische Bedeutung der betrieblichen Altersversorgung', in R. Richardi and H. Reichold (eds.), *Altersgrenzen und Alterssicherung im Arbeitsrecht – Wolfgang Blomeyer zum Gedenken*. München: C.H. Beck, 445–65.

Streeck, W. (1997). 'German Capitalism: Does it Exist? Can it Survive?', in C. Crouch and W. Streeck (eds.), *Political Economy of Modern Capitalism: Mapping Convergence and Diversity*. London: Sage, 33–54.

TNS Infratest (2005a). *Alterssicherung in Deutschland 2003 (ASID '03) – Tabellenband 3: Deutschland*. Untersuchung im Auftrag des Bundesministeriums für Gesundheit und Soziale Sicherung. München: TNS Infratest.

——(2005b). *Künftige Alterseinkommen der Arbeitnehmer mit Zusatzversorgung 2005: Endbericht*. Untersuchung im Auftrag des Bundesministeriums für Gesundheit und Soziale Sicherung. München: TNS Infratest Sozialforschung.

——(2008). *Situation und Entwicklung der betrieblichen Altersversorgung in Privatwirtschaft und öffentlichem Dienst 2001–2007 – Endbericht mit Tabellen*. Untersuchung im Auftrag des Bundesministeriums für Arbeit und Soziales. München: TNS Infratest.

VBL (2004). *1929–2004: 75 Jahre VBL – Zukunft durch Wandel*. Karlsruhe: Versorgungsanstalt des Bundes und der Länder.

WSI (2001). *WSI-Tarifhandbuch 2001*. Köln: Bund-Verlag.

——(ed.) (2008). *WSI-Tarifhandbuch 2008*. Frankfurt a.M.: Bund-Verlag.

6

Italy: From Bismarckian Pensions to Multipillarization under Adverse Conditions

Matteo Jessoula

1. Introduction

As in other Bismarckian 'social insurance' systems, Italian old age protection was largely congruent with public pension development until the 1990s. Due to a lack of government action, no regulatory framework for private supplementary pensions was established, and employers did not foster occupational pensions 'from below'. The late introduction of supplementary pensions is a clear example of a 'top-down' process, as it was pursued by governments in order to compensate for future reduction of public pensions following reforms of the 1990s. In particular, the regulatory framework for (pre)funded supplementary pensions was first set up by the Amato government parallel to the adoption of the first cost containment reform of public pensions in 1992–3. In fact, given the critical financial condition of pay-as-you-go (PAYG) schemes in a country with a rapidly ageing population, the generous public pensions could no longer be maintained as in the past. Hence, funded supplementary pensions became crucial in order to provide income maintenance for the elderly.

A few other elements characterized the emergence of funded pensions in Italy. First, as this development was pursued in fiscally and economically adverse conditions, these factors amplified the 'double payment problem' of shifting from a PAYG to a partly funded system. Second, in order to overcome these constraints, the development of supplementary pensions relied on the 'exploitation' of a pre-existent, compulsory severance-pay scheme (*Tfr*) – that represented an 'institutional gate' facilitating policy change (Ferrera and Jessoula 2007; Jessoula 2009). The expansion of supplementary pillars in Italy can thus be conceptualized as a case of 'top-down layering' through (voluntary) 'institutional conversion' following Streeck and Thelen (2005). In fact, third, the choice for the *Tfr* as the major source of financing led policymakers to opt for voluntary (and not mandatory) affiliation to the new funded schemes as well as to assign a prominent role – at least originally – to collective occupational pension funds. Over the last fifteen years, however, the 'new politics' that has emerged in the field of supplementary pensions – as a consequence of the entrance in the policy arena of new powerful actors like financial institutions – has led to a peculiar competition between occupational funds and personal pension schemes, thus putting pressure on policymakers for regulatory harmonization.

Part I: The evolution of the public–private pension mix

2. The main features of the pension system

Following Italy's Bismarckian tradition, income maintenance in old age has traditionally been guaranteed by mandatory public PAYG pension schemes providing generous earnings-related benefits (see Figure 6.1). Public old age insurance is compulsory for all employed people, including public employees (since 1864), private employees (since 1919), and the self-employed (since the 1950s–60s). Benefits are relatively high, and they represent the major source of income for current retirees, providing a replacement rate of around 75 per cent (SPC 2006: 61) and about 72 per cent (on average) of the equivalent income of those aged 65 and older – the rest including wages and other social transfers (Ministry of Welfare 2002). Until 1995, a means-tested pension supplement (*integrazione al minimo*) existed for retirees with very low contributory pensions, while all those in need over 65 years received means-tested flat rate 'social pensions' in order to tackle poverty in old age. This minimum provision is tax-financed and, due to the lack of a general social assistance scheme (Ferrera 2005), it constitutes the sole safety-net of the Italian welfare state.

Apart from public pensions, most employees receive mandatory severance-pays both in the private (*Trattamento di fine rapporto* or *Tfr*) and the public sector (*Indennità di buonuscita*). These lump sum payments by employers are due when an employee either changes employers or retires, though, given the long tenure on permanent contracts in the Italian private sector and the job security in the public sector, both programmes *de facto* have traditionally provided supplementary benefits at retirement. Also fixed-term employees receive the *Tfr* when employment ends; by contrast, those atypical workers on project contracts (i.e. economically dependent workers) are not entitled to such a provision.[1]

Over the last fifteen years, however, a series of reforms has radically transformed the institutional architecture from a single-pillar towards a multipillar

---

[1] Though working as dependent employees, they are formally self-employed and that is why they are entitled neither to end-of-service payments nor to unemployment benefits.

	First pillar	Second pillar		Third pillar
		Voluntary – collective agreement (alternative to *Tfr)*	Voluntary – employer commitment	Voluntary personal pension (alternative to *Tfr*)
Third tier				
Second tier (income maintenance)	Public pension (pay-as-you-go): Compulsory: private employees and self-employed (INPS); public employees (INPDAP); other professional categories Contributions: shared (2/3 employers); ceiling (92,000 €) DB benefits for current pensioners; NDC benefits for those insured after 1995; Price indexation	Closed funds (CPF): Default option in the silent-consent mechanism for the transfer of the *Tfr;* industry/group/firm/region wide Open funds (OPF): collective affiliation based on agreement at firm level Both: Funded DC (employees); Funded DB/DC (self-employed) Tax incentives	Pre-existing funds (PEF): mostly PAYG, now shifting to funded DB/DC Tax incentives	PIP Personal plan through life-insurance contracts Open funds (OPF): individual affiliation Both: Funded DC (employees); Funded DB/DC (self-employed) Tax incentives
		Tfr severance-pay: Compulsory coverage of employees (atypical workers on project contracts excluded); 'deferred wage' paid in a lump-sum Can be converted into CPF, OPF, and PIP		
First tier (poverty alleviation)	'Social allowance': means-tested, flat rate old-age pension			

Figure 6.1 Pillars and tiers of Italian pensions

configuration. After these reforms, the public pillar's first tier has been changed only marginally: the so-called 'social allowance' has replaced both the pension supplement and the social pension, maintaining the basic features of the latter.[2]

---

[2] Like the social pension, the social allowance is tax-financed and paid to people over 65 years. The income threshold for receiving benefits is €5,349 per year (single person) or €10,699 (couple), and the level of benefits is €411 per month.

More relevant changes have been introduced in the earnings-related schemes that constitute the second tier. Above all, the 1995 Dini reform has replaced the earnings-related method for benefits calculation with a notional defined-contribution (NDC) system, thus substantially harmonizing the rules for private and public employees as well as the self-employed. Nonetheless, the second tier is still organized along professional lines and most employees pay contributions to one of the two major institutions: the National Institute for Social Insurance (INPS) and the National Institute for Social Insurance of Civil Servants (INPDAP).[3] The former covers around 20 million employees (dependent workers and self-employed) in the private sector providing 10.5 million old age benefits (both contributory and non contributory), while the latter insures 3 million public employees and provided nearly 2 million old age benefits in the mid-2000s.[4] Major funds within INPS are dedicated to employees, farmers, artisans, dealers-shopkeepers, and (since 1996) to 'atypical' workers on project contracts. The first pillar is PAYG financed through social contributions,[5] which are levied on employers (two-thirds) and on employees (one-third). Contribution rates vary from 33 per cent of gross earnings for private employees (32.7 per cent for public) to 26 per cent for project workers and about 20 per cent for the self-employed.

As for supplementary protection, there are different options. Employees in the private sector and those in the public sector employed after 2001 are entitled to the *Tfr* when they retire (or change their employer). The *Tfr* is mandated by law and managed by the employers (by the state in the case of public employees), and it can be paid in a lump sum only, not necessarily at retirement. Therefore, it will be considered here as a 'quasi'-supplementary pension. The Decree 124/93 introduced the first regulatory framework for proper supplementary private pensions. Affiliation to supplementary pension funds is always voluntary and individual, even in case of occupational funds set up by collective agreement, and workers are encouraged to contribute through tax incentives. 'Closed' negotiated pension funds (CPF) and the so-called 'pre-existing funds' (PEF) – as they were already operative before the introduction of the 1993 regulatory framework – are typical occupational pensions (second pillar) for specific groups of employees. Personal pension plans through life insurance contracts (PIP) constitute the third pillar, while 'open pension funds' (OPF) are hybrid institutions (comprising both second- and third-pillar forms

[3] Workers covered by neither INPS nor INPDAP are compulsorily affiliated to the dedicated funds for their professional category: various regimes exist for journalists and entertainment workers, while most free professionals (e.g. architects, psychologists, accountants, and others) have their own independent funds.

[4] Data sources: ISTAT (2006) for coverage, INPS (2007) for pensions paid to private employees, ISTAT (2007) for pensions paid to public employees.

[5] If expenditure for benefits exceeds revenues, the state fills the annual gap with transfers from the public budget.

depending on affiliation modes). In September 2010, 5.2 million people contributed to these private pension institutions (COVIP 2010): this result was mostly due to the possibility of transferring the *Tfr* contributions to occupational funds.

3. The context of the welfare regime, labour relations, and market economy

In order to analyse private pensions, it is useful to briefly sketch the main features of the Italian welfare state as well as the system of industrial relations and the economic structure, as these have strong ties with occupational pensions. Since the 1970s the Italian welfare system has displayed the main traits of the so-called 'Southern model' (Ferrera 1996), characterized by a mixed institutional configuration – occupational income maintenance schemes and universalistic health care – the crucial role of family as well as entrenched particularistic welfare clienteles. The Italian welfare state has also displayed the hypertrophy of the Bismarckian public pensions, siphoning most resources (about 60 per cent of public social protection expenditure) at the expense of unemployment insurance, social assistance, and family policies. Such 'functional distortion' (Ferrera 2006) has played a role in recent reforms. In fact, cutbacks of public pensions were not only motivated by the need to contain costs and achieve financial sustainability (per se, or in order to reduce transfers from the public budget) but they were also justified as a part of a 'recalibration package' (Ferrera et al. 2000) aimed at reducing expenditure for old age while increasing resources for both unemployment protection and social assistance. The challenge for policymakers has thus been how to reform pensions and contain costs while maintaining a high level of old age protection.

The maintenance of adequate pensions was – and still is – one of the most sensitive issues for trade unions, which represent *de facto* 'veto players' in Italian pension policy (Jessoula 2009). Although union density in Italy is not as high as in the Nordic countries and it is slightly declining from about 38 per cent in 1995 to 35 per cent, the bargaining coverage is fairly high between 60 and 70 per cent (Natali 2007). However, the unions' prominent role in pension policy derives from more specific factors. First, Bismarckian pensions have traditionally been considered as 'deferred wages', consequently legitimating union action in this field. Second, since 1969 the unions have been formally engaged (together with employers' representatives) in the management of the major pension institution (INPS). Third, half of all union members are retirees and some unions have specific sections promoting pensioners' interests (e.g. SPI-CGIL), while a separate 'retirees association' does not exist in Italy.

Labour organizations have thus traditionally had a crucial voice in post-war pension policymaking, though their involvement has changed. Until the late 1960s, the unions operated through two different 'channels': they acted as interest groups, by putting pressure on policymakers in order to strengthen and expand the public pensions, and they also relied on 'direct' channels of influence through the parliamentary unionists' groups of the major parties – the Christian Democrats (DC), the Communist Party (PCI), and the Socialist Party (PSI). During the 1960s, trade unions' influence grew and negotiations with the government led to the 1968–9 reforms that accomplished the transition to a fully fledged two-tiered, single-pillar pension system. The year 1969 represented a critical juncture: the unions decided to abandon direct political representation and took seats on the INPS board. During the 1980s, the parliament and political parties were the main actors on the pension stage, but over the last two decades union influence has grown again. In fact, the turn from expansionary-distributive policies to cost containment has given labour organizations the opportunity to present themselves as the bulwark of employees' and pensioners' rights. This has led to two different developments. On the one hand, Italian unions have deployed their high mobilization capacity by organizing strikes and demonstrations in order to block governmental plans of pension reform that jeopardized their interests. On the other hand, although Italy is usually not considered a neo-corporatist country, unions have been involved in concerted processes of policymaking in order to overcome their 'veto power' by crafting consensual reforms.[6] Finally, it should be emphasized that the role of the unions has not traditionally been confined to public pensions only. Unions – with employers – have in fact always been responsible for the management of the *Tfr*. As shown below, this has deeply affected the development of supplementary funded pensions since the 1990s.

In contrast with such a prominent role of the unions, financial actors have never played a primary role in pension politics until the mid-1990s. This was due to both the predominantly single-pillar structure of the pension system and the weakness of national financial institutions. However, things have changed significantly in the last decade following the introduction of the regulatory framework for supplementary pensions. Finally, as we shall see below, two peculiar features of the Italian economic structure are crucial in explaining the current 'state of the art' of private pensions: the high share of self-employed (representing one-fourth of total employment) and the great number of employees working in small firms with less than fifty employees (also about one-fourth of total employment).

---

[6] For a full illustration of both pension policy and the role of the unions in Italy in the period 1980–2008, *cfr.* Jessoula (2009), Ferrera and Jessoula (2007), Baccaro (2002). See also Natali (2007) for a comparative analysis of the role of the unions in pension reform in Italy and four other European countries.

4. The emergence of the public–private pension mix

Italy's early steps in old age protection date back to the late nineteenth century, when voluntary state-subsidized old age insurance for blue-collar workers was introduced in 1898. The shift to compulsory insurance for old age – as well as for invalidity and unemployment – took place after World War I (1919), under the Liberal regime. The first pension scheme was fully funded, covering blue- and white-collar employees,[7] and benefits were contributions-related and rather low. The two decades of the Fascist regime (1922–43) represented a period of consolidation and only limited expansion of social security, the most important intervention being the introduction of survivors' benefits in 1939.

At the end of World War II, a special commission drafted a comprehensive plan to reform the national welfare and pension systems. Though this plan was never implemented as such, most of its fundamental principles and proposals inspired the subsequent development (Jessoula 2009). The commission's proposals essentially aimed at achieving 'Beveridgean goals through typical Bismarckian means'[8] (Jessoula and Alti 2010). Taking full employment for granted, the basic ingredients of this recipe were: the extension of compulsory insurance to all employed people and 'indirect' protection for the non-employed through survivor's benefits and intra-family redistribution. Full coverage for those employed was achieved through various steps: in 1950 all white-collar employees were compulsorily insured, and the self-employed followed in 1957 (farmers), 1959 (artisans), and 1966 (shopkeepers). In the same period, other major interventions regarded the financing method and the type of benefits: since 1945 prefunding was gradually replaced by PAYG until the latter was fully implemented in 1969. As for benefits, a first tier aimed at tackling old age poverty was introduced by a pension supplement for retirees with very low contributory pensions (1952) and a means-tested social pension for all those in need aged 65 and older (1969). The 1969 reform replaced the contributions-related pension formula with a generous earnings-related system for private employees, and introduced seniority pensions for private employees and the self-employed, that allowed retirement after thirty-five years of contributions, regardless of age.[9] After this reform, the public pillar therefore assumed two fundamental functions: *poverty prevention* through the first-tier schemes, and *income maintenance* (at least for public and private employees), which replaced

---

[7] Until 1950, insurance for white collars was compulsory below a wage threshold only.

[8] I owe this idea to Bruno Palier.

[9] Public employees were already entitled to earnings-related pensions; moreover, since 1957 they could retire with very favourable seniority pensions (retirement possible after twenty years of contributions only). By contrast, the earnings-related method would be extended to the self-employed only in 1990.

the original goal of *status* maintenance, through the second-tier occupational schemes.

The gradual, but continuous, expansion of public pensions (see Table 6.1) crowded out private supplementary pensions until the mid-1990s. Nevertheless, in addition to the public system a peculiar end-of-service scheme existed: the *Tfr*. The *Tfr* stands at the final stage of a long-lasting evolution of the severance-pay scheme for white-collar employees (*Indennità di licenziamento*) introduced in 1919, later (between 1942 and 1966) transformed into a 'seniority allowance' (*Indennità di anzianità*) and compulsorily paid to private employees in all cases of employment termination. Meanwhile, labour market transformations substantially modified both the functioning and the rationale of this benefit. The tightening of individual dismissal rules with the 1966 reform and the Article 18 of the 1970 Workers' Statute (*Statuto dei lavoratori*)[10] greatly contributed to Italy's rigid labour market, characterized by the prevalence of permanent contracts, a high level of job security and, as a consequence, few career breaks. The severance-pay thus partly lost its primary function of compensating dismissed workers and rather became an instrument to reward employees for their service, not unlike occupational pensions. Indeed, it increasingly functioned as a supplementary old age benefit, mostly being paid at retirement in a lump sum. In 1982, the 'seniority allowance' was finally transformed into the *Tfr* by Law 297/82, establishing a common method for benefits calculation for all private employees. The *Tfr* was conceived as a 'deferred wage' that firms pay their employees in case of retirement or employment termination, and calculated on a share (*ca.* 7 per cent) of worker's earnings for each year of service. This incremental evolution was the result of a series of convenient 'credit claiming' by policymakers given its 'win-win' character. For the government, it represented an important social protection element for which the state did not bear direct costs.[11] Employees could rely on a 'multi-functional' scheme protecting either against unemployment or old age, which also had a modest but guaranteed return on contributions (fixed 1.5 per cent plus 75 per cent of the inflation rate). Finally, as contributions were only on the book reserves, the *Tfr* represented a substantial and rather inexpensive refinancing source for firms, especially for many small firms that had no access to financial markets.

---

[10] After 1966, individual firing was restricted by law to cases of well-motivated dismissal; Article 18 of the Workers' Statute prescribed that in firms with more than fifteen employees, employers were obliged to re-integrate fired workers if the Court did not accept the motivations for dismissal.

[11] The government was directly involved only in the setting up of a 'Guarantee Fund' that protected workers in case of employers' insolvency, but the Fund was financed with contributions paid by employers (0.03 per cent of gross wages).

Table 6.1 Chronology of major steps for old age protection and the *Tfr*, Italy 1898–1982

Year	Reform	Political context
1898	Voluntary old age and invalidity insurance for industrial workers	Liberal government
	Bipartite contributions, plus state subsidies	
1919	Compulsory old age and invalidity insurance	Liberal government
	Coverage: blue collars and white collars (below wage threshold)	
	Bipartite contributions	
	Fully funded, contributions-related benefits	
	Introduction of a compulsory severance-pay (later developed into the *Tfr*) for white collars	
1939	Introduction of survivors' pensions	Fascist regime
	Retirement age lowered: 60 men, 55 women	
1942	New Civil Code reforms the severance-pay scheme: coverage extended to all employees in the private sector	
	general criterion for benefits calculation	
1945	Pensions partly financed on a PAYG basis	Republican regime Post-war emergency measures
1950	All white collars compulsorily insured	Three-party government DC–PSDI–PRI
1952	Minimum contributory pensions introduced	DC–PRI
1956	'Seniority pensions' for employees in the public sector	DC, PSDI, PLI
1957–66	Extension of old age and invalidity insurance to self-employed: • 1957 Farmers • 1959 Artisans • 1966 Merchants-shopkeepers	Various government coalitions 1963 Centre–Left formula: DC, PSI, PSDI, PRI
1968–9	Reform of the old age insurance for employed workers:	Various government coalitions
	• fully PAYG financing • adoption of the earnings-related system • introduction of 'seniority pensions' for private employees and self-employed • introduction of means-tested 'social pensions'	Negotiations with unions
1982	Reform of the severance-pay: *Tfr*	Five-party coalition: DC, PSI, PSDI, PLI, PRI

5. The changing public–private pension mix

In the early 1990s, the Italian institutionalized old age protection inherited from the golden age faced tremendous challenges as a result of slow economic growth, demographic ageing and contingent shocks – especially the monetary and financial crisis of 1992–5. Italy's situation was particularly critical given its highest pension expenditure in the EU (12 per cent of GDP) and its projected doubling (23.4 per cent) by 2040; moreover, the gap between social contributions and revenues was growing as well as the transfers from the public budget. This could no longer be tolerated given the public budget criteria set by the EU Maastricht Treaty. This external constraint (see Ferrera and Gualmini 2004) – together with the politico-institutional crisis following a major corruption scandal that involved most Italian parties – allowed the shift from golden age distributive policies to retrenchment interventions in the field of pensions.[12] The disappearance of traditional (partisan) veto players led to technocratic governments, which included social partners in policymaking in order to gain the necessary political support to adopt reforms aimed at responding to the massive external pressures. Several public pension reforms were then adopted in 1992, 1995, 1997, 2004, 2007, 2009, and 2010. As a result, and especially due to the 1995 'watershed reform' that introduced the NDC, the public pension's income maintenance role is expected to decline sharply in the next decades (replacement rate for a standard worker around 55 per cent in 2030).

In order to compensate for the reduced generosity of public pensions, policymakers planned to develop supplementary pensions, based on prefunded schemes. Therefore, the income maintenance function was deliberately assigned to the interplay between state and market – public and private actors. What seems 'puzzling' is that, in Italy, the transition from a single-pillar to a multipillar pension system appeared the most unlikely. In fact, new-institutionalist and economic analyses have stressed that such a transition is hampered by the so-called 'double payment problem', which is most acute when public pillars are financially unsustainable and particularly difficult to overcome in mature PAYG systems (Myles and Pierson 2001; Orszag and Stiglitz 2001). In such cases, more resources are needed to honour the PAYG system and to make it sustainable. Moreover, economists emphasize that the development of funded pensions is most unlikely when resources are scarce, that is when public pension contributions are high, the public deficit/debt is high or other constraints on public expenditure exist, and no reserve (buffer) funds are available. As for the Italian situation in the early 1990s, public pension schemes provided coverage to the entire workforce and delivered generous earnings-related benefits, contribution rates were very high (26 per cent in 1992) and raised substantially (33 per cent in 1995), ruling out further increases, and the gap between revenues and expenditures was growing. Other sources to finance the transition to a multipillar system were not available: the public debt was extremely high (117.3 per cent of GDP), the worst rate in Europe in 1992, and the public deficit was at 10.5 per cent (1991). Italy therefore fell dramatically

---

[12] The national and international literature on the topic is vast. See Levy (1999), Ferrera and Gualmini (2004), Natali and Rhodes (2004), Ferrera and Jessoula (2007), Jessoula (2009).

short of the 'Maastricht criteria'. Moreover, there was no reserve fund and no reliable forecast that suggested increasing resources from higher employment or faster economic growth. Finally, Italy lacked any tradition in funded pensions, with less than 5 per cent of private employees covered by occupational schemes in the early 1990s. Nevertheless, Italian policymakers embarked on the path towards a multipillar pension system. How was this possible?

In order to solve the puzzle, special attention must be given to *Tfr*. This has in fact operated as an 'institutional gate' (Ferrera and Jessoula 2007; Jessoula 2009) that facilitated the multipillar reconfiguration. In 1992–3, the Amato cabinet was aware of both the critical situation of public pensions and the acute double-payment problem (see Table 6.2). After the public pension reform was passed (Decree 503/92), the government delivered a plan to develop funded private pensions, which relied on the *voluntary transfer of the Tfr* to the so-called 'closed' occupational funds (CPF) set up by collective agreements. More precisely, the first regulatory framework for supplementary pensions (Decree 124/93) prescribed that, *in case of affiliation* to occupational funds, the *Tfr* was to be fully merged into the latter. This applied to workers employed after April 1993; for those already in employment collective agreements would define the *Tfr* share to be transferred to these funds. Such a 'choice' for *Tfr* as the major financing source of occupational pensions also had an impact on other basic features of supplementary pensions. First, as the government did not want to jeopardize social partners' control over the *Tfr*, its compulsory devolution to pension funds was ruled out and the principle of 'voluntary affiliation' was established; second, the transfer of the *Tfr* to the so-called 'open' pension funds (OPF), which were directly set up by financial institutions, was excluded. A residual role was thus assigned to OPF, as testified also by the provision that allowed workers to become members of these funds only if a 'dedicated' occupational fund was not in place for their professional category.

At this stage, however, public pensions were still earnings-related (though less generous) and the need for supplementary pension coverage was not fully acknowledged. Moreover, the critical situation of public finance did not allow generous tax incentives for supplementary pensions. Hence, no pension fund was set up in accordance with the new rules. But in 1995, the take-off of supplementary pensions became a prominent issue in the concertation process launched by the 'technocratic' Dini government with the social partners, aimed at a consensual pension reform. The decision to replace the earnings-related system with an NDC system made developing funded pensions crucial in order to compensate the expected sharp decline of the replacement rate of public pensions, especially for younger cohorts. Supplementary pensions were included in the concertation also because of the traditional role of the social partners in the *Tfr* management. As two years before, such involvement ruled out the compulsory transfer of the *Tfr* to pension funds, but the government was now aware that more resources were needed to induce the social partners and financial actors setting up pension funds as well as to increase the attractiveness of supplementary schemes for employees. The unions were persuaded that occupational pensions were absolutely necessary to supplement the less generous public benefits. The financial sector, with growing influence in the pension arena, 'voiced' its interest in expanding what could represent a 'mega business'. The final solution (Law 335/95) consisted of a revision of the original tax regime, making it more favourable: (*a*) incentives for employees were made more generous as contributions became deductible (up to 2 per cent of gross annual income with a maximum of about €1,300); (*b*) these incentives were linked more tightly to the transfer of *Tfr* to these funds; and (*c*) taxes on pension funds were reduced. All seemed to be ready for the take-off of supplementary pillars.

After the completion of the regulatory framework by two ministerial decrees, in 1998 four occupational pension funds took effect, all for private sector employees. The expansion of the second pillar continued at a good pace until the financial market crisis following the 9/11 attacks in 2001, which curbed the growth of membership (COVIP 2005). Meanwhile, in order to boost supplementary pensions the Decree 47/2000 further augmented the deductibility of contributions (up to 12 per cent of gross income, and a maximum of €5,000) and extended tax incentives to personal pension plans through life insurance contracts (PIP), thereby enriching the menu of options. An agreement extended the *Tfr* to public employees starting after 2000 with the aim to give these workers a fundamental source to finance supplementary pensions.

Furthermore, in 2001 the Centre–Right government led by Berlusconi drafted a reform proposal aiming at building a fully fledged funded system next to the traditional public pillar. The proposal was based on the full exploitation of the *Tfr*, through the compulsory transfer of the latter to supplementary funds, and on levelling the playing field between the different types of supplementary pension funds with the aim of stimulating competition among them.[13] The first measure would have definitively 'opened the institutional gate' by mobilizing more than €12 billion per year (around 1 per cent of GDP) (Ministry of Welfare 2002). However, the government plan soon became highly controversial as it jeopardized unions' interests (and to a certain extent also that of employers). Only after four years of protest, blockages and revived negotiations,

---

[13] Two major considerations were behind the plan. On the one hand, after the release of projections on the decline of public pension replacement rates (from *ca.* 70 per cent in 2010 to less than 50 per cent in 2030) and figures indicating lower take-up rates of supplementary pensions among youngsters, the cabinet was willing to address the issue of benefits adequacy for younger cohorts. On the other hand, policy arrangements and institutional settings create their own new constituencies: thus financial institutions, that had entered the stage of pension policy during the 1990s, put pressure on the government calling for an expansion of supplementary pensions and a greater role for non-occupational pension funds.

a compromise was eventually found in 2005 with Decree 252/05: the *Tfr* would be transferred to pension funds with a 'silent-consent' formula (see Figure 6.2).

PART II: The governance of supplementary pensions

In accordance with the regulatory framework set up by Decree 124/1993 and subsequent revisions (see Table 6.2), there are currently four different forms of proper supplementary pensions: (*a*) so-called 'pre-existing funds' (PEF), (*b*) closed funds (CPF), (*c*) open funds (OPF), and (*d*) individual pension plans through life insurance contracts (PIP). PEF and CPF are occupational, typically second-pillar funds, PIP are third-pillar personal pensions, while the so-called OPF are hybrid institutions, as they can be classified either as second- or third-pillar funds. PEF are those funds that were already set up by employers, especially in the banking/financial sectors, and by major multinationals before the regulatory framework was introduced in 1993. The other three forms were introduced by (or after) the 1993 Decree. This also assigned a primary role to CPF set up by the social partners through collective agreement. OPF, which are directly set up by financial institutes (banking, insurance, and investment

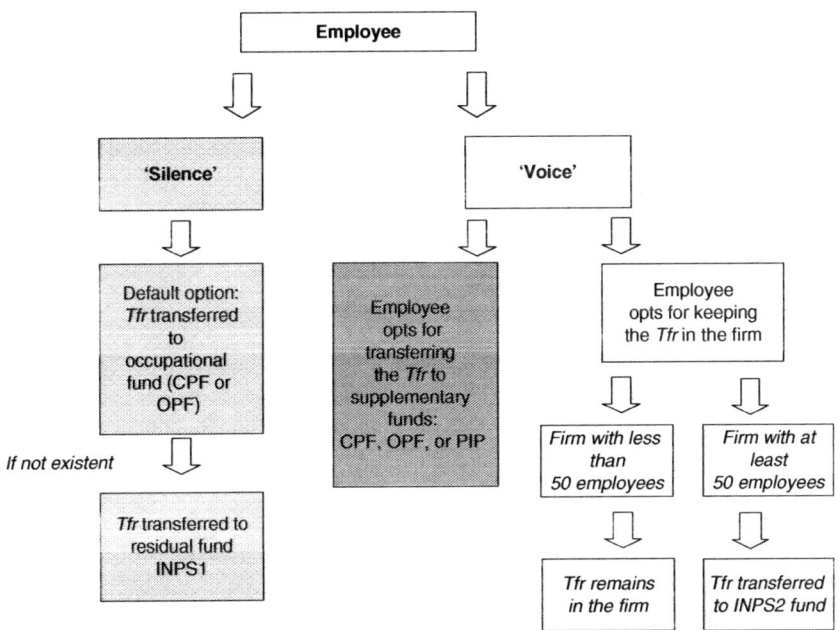

Figure 6.2 *Tfr* and supplementary pensions: the 'silent-consent' mechanism, Italy

Source: Elaboration by the author.

Table 6.2 Chronology of pension system restructuring since the mid-1980s

Reform	Reform measures	Political context
1984	Invalidity pensions reform	Five-party coalition: DC, PSI, PSDI, PLI, PRI
1990	Old-age pensions reform: schemes for the self-employed: • extension of the earnings-related formula	Five-party coalition: DC, PSI, PSDI, PLI, PRI
1992–3	Amato old-age pensions reform 1992 parametric reform of the public pillar: • still earnings-related	Partly technocratic cabinet: DC, PSI, PSDI, PLI Politico-institutional crisis
	1993 Introduction of a regulatory framework for supplementary pillars: • voluntary affiliation • *Tfr* primary source of financing • incentives (deductible contributions)	Negotiated reform with social partners
1995	Dini old-age pensions reform First pillar: • shift to an NDC system (long phase-in) – flexible retirement age 57–65 years	Technocratic cabinet: Centre–Left and Northern League support in the parliament Concertation with social partners.
	Supplementary pillars: • more generous incentives • more favourable tax regulations • collective affiliation to 'open funds' made possible	Employers do not sign the agreement
1997	Prodi old-age pension reform: • adjustment of 1995 reform	Centre–Left coalition
2000	Reform of the regulatory framework for supplementary pillars: • more generous incentives • partial harmonization of closed and open funds • introduction of personal pension plans (PIP)	Centre–Left coalition
2004–5	Maroni-Tremonti old-age pension reform 2004 Reform of the first pillar: • incentives for postponing retirement (2004–7) • tightened eligibility conditions for seniority pensions; retirement age no more flexible: 60 (women), 65 (men)	Centre–Right coalition
	2005 reform of supplementary pillars: • 'silent-consent' formula for the transfer of the Tfr to occupational pension funds (as of 1/2008)	
2006	Reform of the 'silent-consent' formula: • implementation anticipated to January 2007 • different regulations for workers in firms under/over fifty employees	Centre–Left coalition Concerted with social partners
2007	Revision of the 2004 reform of the public pillar	
2009	First pillar: retirement age gradually raised to 65 (by 2018) for women employed in the public sector	Centre–Right coalition Response to ECJ sentence
2010	First pillar: retirement age for women in public sector 65 by 2012; after 2015 automatically linked with life expectancy	

Source: Elaboration by the author.

companies) and managed as 'separate accounts',[14] were originally conceived as personal pension plans. However, after the introduction of the possibility of collective affiliation[15] to these funds in 1995, OPF can be considered as second-pillar institutions in this case, and otherwise as third-pillar forms. Beside these plans, also the *Tfr* may provide supplementary old age protection to most employees in the private sector and to those employed after 2000 in the public sector.

In accordance with the silent-consent mechanism introduced in 2005, private sector employees have six months – either from January 2007 if already employed, or at the time of first employment or when they get a new job – to decide if they want to keep the *Tfr* or transfer it to supplementary pension funds. In the latter case, they may opt for CPF, OPF, or PIP because Decree 252/05 removed all restrictions with regard to first affiliation. By contrast, if they remain 'silent', the *Tfr* is paid by default into an occupational pension fund (CPF or 'collective OPF'). In 2006, the Centre–Left Prodi government made an important adjustment to the silent-consent mechanism (see Figure 6.2). If employees opt for keeping the *Tfr*, two alternative paths are envisaged depending on the firm size where they are employed: the *Tfr* can be actually kept in the firm with less than fifty employees, otherwise it is transferred to an ad hoc fund set up by INPS (see Figure 6.2).[16] This provision has completely cut off bigger firms (with at least fifty employees) from the *Tfr* 'game': in fact, depending on employees' choice, *Tfr* contributions will be paid either in supplementary pension schemes or in the INPS fund, and they may no more be used by firms as a refinancing source.

In the following, we focus on proper supplementary pensions introduced by Decree 124/93, with few remarks on *Tfr* and pre-existent funds where relevant. A peculiar feature is the high standardization of the rules for supplementary institutions in Italy. When policymakers planned to introduce supplementary pensions in the early 1990s, they intentionally designed a system in which most fundamental rules – regarding the type of benefits, entitlement conditions, the funding method, the withdrawal and anticipation of benefits, and, to a certain extent, the sources of financing and the tax incentives – applied to

---

[14] It refers to a pension fund that is legally segregated from the financial institution that acts as the manager of the fund on behalf of the plan member.

[15] Note that affiliation is always individual and voluntary. The term 'collective affiliation' refers to cases in which through collective agreements at the firm level an OPF is identified as the reference fund for employees in the firm.

[16] The 2005 and 2006 reforms have therefore introduced two public funds that do play a role as supplementary institutions in the field of old age protection. Both funds have been established within INPS. The first (INPS1, in Figure 6.2) is a residual fund for those 'silent workers' that do not have a 'dedicated' occupational fund. INPS1 is fully funded and provides DC-benefits. By contrast, the second fund – INPS2 – operates on a PAYG basis. This fund receives contributions by those workers employed in bigger firms (with at least 50 employees) that opt for keeping the *Tfr*. INPS2 consequently pays the *Tfr* to workers on behalf of employers.

both second- and third-pillar institutions. But standardization is also the result of a gradual transformation of the original prescriptions contained in Decree 124/93 that assigned certain privileged conditions to CPF. In fact, the development of supplementary pensions over the last decade can also be told in terms of a growing relevance of individual pensions and increased harmonization of rules between CPF, OPF, and PIP. This has stimulated competition between second- and the third-pillar forms, among which major differences regard the organizational and governance structure.

6. Who is covered?

Despite the existence of three, if not four, different forms of supplementary pensions, CPF play the dominant role (see Table 6.3). PEF are very numerous (411 funds in 2008) but their total coverage is limited (about 677,000 members) and, above all, not increasing. Also OPF are quite numerous, with eighty-one in 2008. They were initially conceived as residual forms and they still play a relatively marginal role, but growing membership (from 440,000 in 2005 to around 800,000 in 2008) seems to indicate a possible change in the near future. These funds are not only the preferred choice for the self-employed, who constitute thus far the majority of OPF members (52 per cent), but more recently assumed also a greater role as collective pension funds for dependent employees (collective affiliations increased from 10 per cent in 2005 to 25 per cent of OPF members in 2008). The same may hold for PIP, after their introduction in 2000, as membership has rapidly grown from around half million in 2003 to almost 1.5 million in 2008, thus overcoming both OPF and PEF in terms of total members. These institutions seem to be capable of attracting both employees and the self-employed, and they are likely to become an important component of the Italian system of supplementary old age protection.

CPF are the preferred choice for dependent workers: 2 million employees affiliate to these funds, in contrast with 648,000 employees affiliated to PIP and 392,000 to OPF. Nevertheless, CPF may be set up not only for employees (both in the private and the public sector) but also for the self-employed. These funds are set up via either collective agreement by social partners or decisions by professional associations of the self-employed. In the first case, they may be established at the industry (e.g. metal workers, chemical workers), group, or a firm level, or set up for employees in a particular region. At the end of 2008, there were thirty-seven funds for private employees – of which only nine were set up at the firm/group level and three were 'territorial' funds (e.g. Valle d'Aosta) – one for the self-employed and one for public employees.

The take-up rate for employees in the private sector is 26 per cent (32 per cent including members of pre-existing funds, COVIP 2008), though this does not capture the actual diffusion of supplementary pensions in Italy, because of

Table 6.3 Supplementary pensions in figures

	Members Private employees (Sept. 09)	September 2009	December 2008	December 2007	December 2006	Variation 2009/ 2006 (%)	Variation 2007/ 2006 (%)	No.
CPF	1,907	2,045	2,043	1,989	1,219	67.7	63.1	41
OPF	392	810	798	747	440	84.1	69.6	81
PEF	648	677	677	681	613	10.4	11.0	411
PIP	753	1,492	1,375	1,189	959	–	–	–
Total[a]	3,702	4,997	4,854	4,560	3,269	56.9	43.2	–

Note: [a]Total excludes double counting.

Source: Adapted from COVIP (2008, 2009a, 2009b).

considerable variation across economic sectors and professional categories. Figures, in fact, indicate extremely varied take-up rates for private sector employees: eight funds have take-up rates over 60 per cent, twelve funds between 30 and 60 per cent, others 'struggle' to reach even 10 per cent of potential members. These differences can be explained by taking into account that the *Tfr* has worked an 'institutional gate' for supplementary pension development. Take-up rates are therefore higher when two conditions are met: first, the *Tfr* is available, which is the case for most employees and, second, the institutional gate is exploited by the social partners, setting up a CPF and then launching informative and promotional campaigns in order to convince employees to become members. But when does this occur? Although the coverage of negotiated CPF is almost universal for private employees, take-up rates are high only in medium or large firms and/or when unions are strong – as in the energy, plastic, chemical, and metal sectors (see Table 6.4). By contrast, take-up rates are low in those sectors with small enterprises and/or weak unions, that are commerce, services, tourism as well as food and textile. In fact, CPFs are 'lite' organizations – in most cases with a small staff – and, consequently, they have to rely on union networks in order to 'capture' employees; therefore, where unions are not present, or very weak, CPFs find it very difficult to promote subscriptions and employees often lack the necessary (and correct) information to opt for the transfer of *Tfr* to occupational funds. The small scale of many Italian enterprises has thus a relevant impact on the actual diffusion of supplementary occupational pensions.

Similarly, it follows that occupational pensions for the self-employed are underdeveloped – only 150,000 subscribers to CPF, 900,000 including members of OPF and PIP with an overall take-up rate around 15 per cent: as the institutional gate of *Tfr* is not available for this category, the primary source of financing supplementary funds is lacking. And occupational pensions lag behind in the public sector too, where just one negotiated fund exists, covering 1.2 million employees in education but attracting 80,000 members only (i.e. 6.3 per cent), while two out of three public employees have no access to a dedicated pension fund at all. This is surprising given that public employees (if employed after 2000) are entitled to the *Tfr* and they may opt for using it to finance pension funds. However, such a choice would have a major direct impact on public finance as the state should pay *Tfr* contributions into pension funds. This has limited the setting up of supplementary funds for public employees and led to the exclusion of public employees from the silent-consent mechanism.[17]

By contrast, the implementation of the latter mechanism started in January 2007 has boosted membership in the private sector. Between 2006 and 2007,

---

[17] Only recently there have been advances, as two agreements have been reached in 2007 creating new collective funds for those employed by ministries as well as regional, local and health-care employees.

Table 6.4 Selected closed pension funds, Italy 2008

| Pension fund (sector) | Sector employed (1000s) | Insured take-up rate (%) | Contributions in % of earnings | | | Portfolio options |
			Employee (%)	Employer (%)	TOTAL* (%)	
FOPEN (ENEL energy)	50	90.9	1.35	1.35	9.61	6
FONCHIM (chemicals)	197	82.5	1.2–1.5	1.2–1.5	9.31–9.91	3
GOMMAPLASTICA (plastic)	100	58.0	1.06	1.06	9.03	3
COMETA (metal)	1,000	47.4	1.20	1.20	9.31	4
LABORFONDS (regional Trentino-A. A))	245	45.9	Variable	Variable	–	4
ALIFOND (food)	300	18.2	1.00	1.20	9.11	3
FONTE (private service employees)	2,000	8.0	0.55–1.00	0.55–1.55	8.01–9.46	4
ESPERO (education – public sector)	1,200	6.9	1.00	1.00	8.91	2
FONDOSANITÁ (health care – self-employed)	800	0.4	1.00	–	7.91	3

Note: *Including *Tfr* (6.91 per cent).
Source: COVIP (2008, 2009a, 2009b).

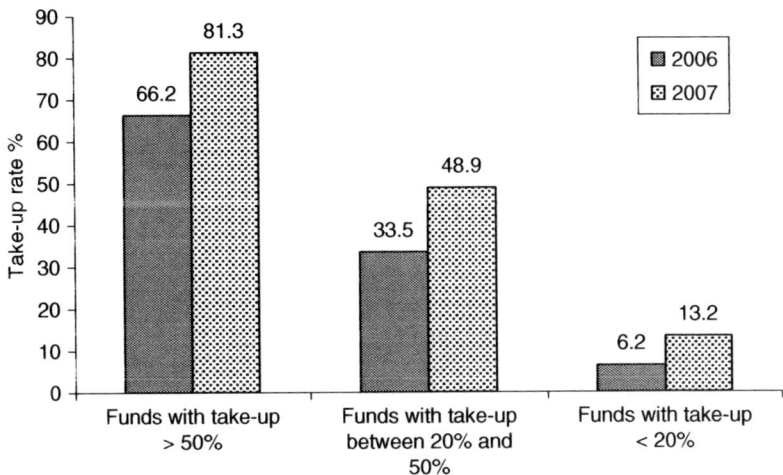

Figure 6.3 The effects of the silent-consent mechanism on take-up rates of CPF for private sector employees, Italy

Source: Based on COVIP (2008).

membership of supplementary schemes for private employees has significantly increased and particularly members of CPF and OPF have rapidly grown, by 64 and 69 percentage points respectively. Nevertheless, such an increase seems to have reinforced the gap between covered/non-covered sectors and categories, and this is also due to the different regulations of the silent-consent mechanism for firms with at least fifty employees and for firms below that threshold. In fact, membership has increased (see Figure 6.3) more in the CPF that had already high take-up rates (+15.1 percentage points) than in less attractive funds (+7 points only).

7. What kind of benefits?

The vast majority of current retirees do not receive supplementary old age benefits – an exception being those formerly employed in the financial sector or in big international firms that receive supplementary defined-benefit (DB) pensions from the so-called 'pre-existing funds'. By contrast, the severance-pay *Tfr* has often functioned as a quasi-supplementary pension scheme, providing lump sum payments calculated as the sum of 1/13.5 of annual earnings for each year of employment, valorized at a state-guaranteed fixed interest rate of 1.5 per cent plus 75 per cent of the inflation rate. However, the *Tfr* is not portable and, in a more flexible labour market, its effectiveness in old age protection is severely limited. Also, the 1982 reform introduced the possibility of partial withdrawal (maximum 70 per cent of the accumulated benefit) for employees with at least eight years of seniority in case of urgent health expenditures or the purchase of a personal or family home. Due to the link between the *Tfr* and supplementary funds, the rules regarding partial withdrawal have been transposed in the regulatory framework for funded pensions.

In future decades, the share of retirees receiving old age benefits from the various supplementary institutions will increase. CPF and OPF provide defined-contribution (DC) benefits, though the regulatory framework allows DB schemes for the self-employed. In case of affiliation via the silent-consent mechanism, DC schemes must provide a guarantee that returns are comparable with those of the *Tfr* through low-risk investments and a minimum guarantee of at least the total contributions paid. Benefits may be delivered as annuities or partly as lump sum (maximum 50 per cent of the total contributions amount). In order to deliver annuities, CPF usually contract with insurance companies. The regulatory framework does not contain detailed prescriptions regarding the type of benefits to be delivered nor their indexation. Therefore, at retirement most pension funds give employees the possibility to choose between different types of benefits – generally including not only old age but also invalidity and survivor's protection – as well as between different kinds of indexation for annuities. However, in most cases such indexation is not sufficient to compensate inflation (Marano 2006) and this will likely entail a gradual reduction of retirees' purchasing power.

Insured employees receive old age supplementary benefits at the standard retirement age of the first public pillar (65 years for men, 60 for women)[18] after a minimum contributory period of at least five years. The age threshold is reduced by five years in case of long-term unemployment (more than four years) and, as noted above, in order to guarantee similar conditions for supplementary benefits and the *Tfr*, employees with at least eight years of insurance may withdraw a maximum of 75 per cent of assets for health expenditure or to buy a home (or maximum 30 per cent for any other reason).

With regard to the portability of accrued rights, employees that change employers may easily move to another fund since all supplementary schemes are DC. Moreover, after two years of affiliation with the same occupational fund, employees are free to transfer their accrued rights to either an OPF or PIP, even if they do not change their employer. This is the result of a long-lasting process aimed at harmonizing affiliation and portability rules as well as the sources of financing between second- and third-pillar forms. The initial Decree 124/93 allowed employees to subscribe to an OPF only if an occupational CPF was not in place. This prescription was later softened by Law 335/95 which permitted the movement from a CPF to an OPF. Five years later, the possibility

---

[18] In the public sector, the retirement age for women will be gradually raised to 65 by 2012.

to transfer accrued rights was extended by Decree 47/00 to movements from a CPF to the newly introduced PIP (Pallini 2007): the transfer was allowed after at least three years spent by employees in a CPF. More recently, Decree 252/05 has drastically reduced limitations on movement through the alternative options by allowing transfers after only two years, thus increasing competition between CPF, OPF, and PIP. In order to facilitate the portability of pensions rights and to allow employees to make informed choices when moving from a scheme to another, the Decree has also imposed an obligation for all supplementary forms to provide their members all information useful to compare the different 'products' in the supplementary pensions market.

With respect to benefits, it is important to note that the interplay between an NDC first pillar and DC supplementary schemes has two major consequences for old age protection for future retirees: first, all demographic, economic, and financial risks will be borne by employees; second, intra-generational redistribution is totally absent (but for contribution credits in first-pillar schemes). This may hamper the effectiveness of the pension system as a whole to provide adequate protection after retirement (i.e. sufficient replacement of past income). The distributive effects of the development of funded pillars also derive from the tax regime for supplementary pensions. Decree 252/05 introduced a very favourable tax regime for annuities that are subject to a single and very low tax rate at 15 per cent (this rate is reduced by 0.3 points per year down to 9 per cent minimum if contribution years are more than fifteen) – differently from first-pillar pensions which are taxed as income from work. In the next decades, the greater role of supplementary pensions in combination with this particular tax regime (if not modified) will therefore affect income distribution regressively and reduce revenues for the state.

8. Who pays?

Before the adoption of the regulatory framework in 1993, pre-existing pension funds were usually PAYG and employer-sponsored, and contribution rates were low (around 4 per cent of gross wages). On the other hand, the *Tfr* was financed through employers' contributions but, as the latter were only *virtually* accumulated, the *Tfr* also represented an important (and relatively cheap) source of finance for companies, which could postpone the actual payment of a share of wages ('deferred wage'). By contrast, all types of supplementary schemes set up after 1993 are (pre)funded. CPF are typically financed on a peculiar tripartite basis: contributions by employers and employees, and the *Tfr*, that constitutes the major source of financing[19] (see Table 6.5). In fact, the average contribution

---

[19] In 2007, the total *Tfr* amount paid into CPF was €1,614 million, out of a total of €2,700 million (€649 million by workers' contributions, €437 million by employers).

Table 6.5 Financial and tax regulation of occupational pensions

	Tax deductions + social insurance contributions	State subsidies	Minimum rate of return	Limited investment
Pre-existing funds	–	–		Yes
Closed funds	Employer contributions deductible/ employee contributions deductible up to €5,164 per year	–	Yes, silent-consent case	Yes
Open funds	Employer contributions deductible/ employee contributions deductible up to €5,164 per year	–	(Yes, silent-consent case)	Yes
PIP	Employee contributions deductible up to €5,164 per year	–	Discretionary	Yes
(Tfr)	None	–	Yes	None (book reserves)

Source: Elaboration by the author.

rate to CPF for employees who entered the labour market after 1993 is 9.29 per cent, of which 6.91 per cent is constituted by the *Tfr*; for older employees the average rate is somewhat lower (4.75 per cent) with the *Tfr* making up about half of it (2.4 per cent). Such figures suggest that occupational pensions, though not equally widespread, are likely to become extremely relevant in income maintenance for younger generations: a contribution level over 9 per cent is in fact high in a comparative perspective, also considering countries with well-developed multipillars systems.[20]

Tripartite financing is also the norm in case of collective affiliation to OPF while, until the 2005 reform, in case of individual subscription to OPF and PIP, contributions were only paid by the worker. This, however, changed with the introduction of the silent-consent mechanism that has allowed employees to transfer their *Tfr* to a supplementary form of their choice (CPF, OPF, or PIP). Therefore, the rules concerning the sources of financing have been substantially harmonized among the various types of supplementary pensions: tripartite financing applies to occupational funds (both CPF and collective OPF), bipartite financing (*Tfr* and employees contributions) to individual affiliations to OPF and PIP. A limited priority to CPF has been maintained with regard to two important aspects: the functioning of the silent-consent mechanism for the transfer of the *Tfr* to supplementary pensions and the portability of employers' contributions when moving from a CPF to either an OPF or a PIP. As for the silent-consent mechanism, in the default option – that is, in case of 'silence' by the worker – the *Tfr* is directly transferred to a CPF. As for the second issue,

[20] See Anderson's contribution on the Netherlands in this volume.

Decree 252/05 has limited the transferability of employers' contributions when passing from a CPF to a third-pillar form only to cases where a collective agreement (on which the CPF is based) explicitly allows such transfer.

A further aspect of regulatory harmonization among the different supplementary institutions has been the tax treatment of contributions paid into pension funds. In fact, the 1993 regulatory framework – that introduced the so-called ETT model – provided the possibility to deduct contributions up to a certain threshold, though limiting this fiscal incentive to CPF. However, the stepwise revisions of the regulatory framework have extended tax incentives to all types of supplementary pensions and made them more generous. By contrast, the long-debated shift to the EET model has never been legislated. Therefore, the state currently supports the development of funded pensions by allowing deductions for social contributions paid to second- and third-pillar institutions: in particular, employers' contributions are fully deductible, while employees' payments can be deducted up to a maximum amount of €5,164 per year.

Paid contributions are then invested by supplementary institutions generally offering their members various portfolio options, in addition to the mandatory option aimed to guarantee returns which are comparable to those of the *Tfr* for the cases of 'silent affiliation'. CPF privilege investment in bonds (around 70 per cent), with equities representing only 15 per cent of the total, while for OPF the asset allocation is more geared towards an active management of invested resources (57 per cent bonds, 33 per cent equities).

Since its adoption in 1993, the national regulatory framework for supplementary pensions provided stringent, quantitative limits on investments in order to contain investment risks and to avoid that pension funds may control the companies they invest in. In particular, there are limits for investments in retail and private funds, and in bank deposits, as well as a minimum investment in the currency in which the benefits will be denominated. Equally for PEF, there are also limits for investments in securities issued by the sponsoring employer(s).[21] Moreover, under the impulse of the EU directive 43/41/EC, in 2007 the government has launched a consultation process with all stakeholders aimed at identifying the guidelines for the revision of investment rules, which has led to the introduction of further quantitative limits on self-investment.

9. Who governs? Who decides? Who manages?

Major differences between second- and third-pillar institutions – but also between CPF and 'collective OPF' that may be both considered second-pillar forms – regard the governance and organizational features. CPFs are non-profit

---

[21] See OECD (2009) for details.

institutions created, as previously discussed, via collective agreement by the social partners which then provide their members with participatory rights. In fact, CPF executive boards are composed of both employers' and employees' representatives, the latter being chosen through elections. The executive board then appoints the fund representative who is charged with control powers. Next to the fund representative, a surveillance board, made up of at least two independent members, is also present: both the former and the latter maintain relationships with the pension funds supervisory commission (*Commissione di vigilanza sui fondi pensione* or COVIP). In particular, the surveillance board controls that the fund is managed in the interest of the members. Despite these complex rules, CPF usually rely on a limited staff (10–20 members maximum). The regulatory framework does not allow CPF to manage assets, thus they have to contract with financial institutions like banks, insurance companies, investment firms, or asset management companies. CPF also contract with insurance companies in order to deliver annuities to retired members, though Decree 252/05 has allowed these funds to provide benefits by themselves.

By contrast, OPF have a light governance structure, but they may count on a much more robust organization for asset management. Employees do not have any right of participation in management boards, and members of the surveillance board are directly appointed by the managers of the financial institution that sets up the fund. Similarly, there is no member representation on PIP; the protection of their interest is delegated to a pension fund agent appointed by the insurance company. Both OPF and PIP are allowed to directly manage their asset.

As for supervision, despite the differences between second- and third-pillar forms, a single independent national authority for supplementary pensions is charged with supervisory competences on supplementary pillars. The pension fund supervisory commission (COVIP) provides authorization to newly established funds (CPF, OPF, and PIP). This commission also controls the activity of supplementary pension institutions and is charged with important regulatory tasks – often clarifying and interpreting rules introduced by law. Furthermore, the commission monitors the development of funded pillars in its Annual Report on Supplementary Pensions. Two other authorities (CONSOB and ISVAP) have some supervisory powers over banks and insurance companies respectively, when these set up OPF or PIP schemes. In particular, differently from other supplementary institutions, PIP must follow the investment criteria defined by ISVAP.

Finally, the regulatory framework has not provided specific protection against pension fund's bankruptcy for the newly established supplementary institutions (i.e. set up after 1993). By contrast, insurance against bankruptcy is mandated by law for those PEF offering DB schemes, while the *Tfr* is state guaranteed in case of firms' insolvency through an ad hoc public fund financed by employers' contributions.

10. The outlook

After several reforms over the last fifteen years, the Italian pension system is currently in transition towards a multipillar configuration. The latest data available for 2010 indicate that roughly 5 million people are members of supplementary pension schemes (CPF, PEF, OPF, and PIP). Due to both the expected decline of public pension replacement rates and the high average contributions to occupational pensions (over 9 per cent of gross earnings), these funded private pensions will play a crucial role in income maintenance in future decades, especially when the public NDC pensions will be fully phased-in by 2035. According to available projections, when younger cohorts retire around 2030–40, their income from pensions will derive three-quarters from public pensions and one-quarter from funded pensions (Ministry of Welfare 2002; SPC 2006).

In spite of these changes, the Italian pension system is also characterized by stability, inertia, and institutional resiliency. If a relevant share of employees has subscribed supplementary schemes – thus creating a new 'welfare clientele' – the majority of the workforce either relies on severance-pay or has no supplementary protection in old age (most self-employed and some atypical employees). As in other Bismarckian countries, the shift from a single public pillar to a multipillar configuration based on voluntary affiliation to supplementary funds is therefore giving rise to coverage problems. These issues may well turn into problems of adequacy in future decades.[22] In Italy, such problems are strictly linked not only to the particularly adverse conditions in which the transition started but also to the peculiar (major) source of financing of supplementary pillars, the *Tfr*. In fact, the latter has actually represented an 'institutional gate' that has allowed the development of supplementary pillars under adverse conditions, that is when no other resources could be used to finance funded pensions. But coverage by collective agreements and individual take-up rates have lagged behind where the *Tfr* was not available and/or it has not been adequately exploited by both employees and social partners.

Taking into account the variation of coverage and take-up rates of supplementary pensions on the one hand, and the different level of protection guaranteed by the public pillar for the various professional categories, substantially different scenarios may be envisaged. Private sector employees will likely receive relatively generous (in comparative perspective) public pensions – with a replacement rate of around 50–55 per cent – though not sufficient to maintain income; therefore, supplementary pensions will likely be necessary in order to replace a part of previous income. The point is, however, that only a portion of private employees (*ca.* 3.7 million) are members of supplementary funds, are

---

[22] See Bridgen/Meyer contribution in this volume.

mostly employed in medium–big firms and/or in highly unionized sectors. The majority of employees in the private sector – employed in micro-small firms – will instead rely on the *Tfr*, and this might represent a problem for at least three reasons: (*a*) the *Tfr* has a guaranteed, but low, return; (*b*) ever more frequent fragmented careers in the labour market reduce the old age protection function of the *Tfr*, as a considerable share is not paid at retirement but when employees change job; (*c*) as already noted, the *Tfr* is paid in a lump sum and not converted into an annuity.

With respect to employees in the public sector, the replacement rate in the first pillar being roughly the same as for private employees, the major problem regards the limited coverage of supplementary schemes. Only 1.3 million employees out of 3.4 million public employees are covered, and the take-up rate is extremely low: around 7 per cent of potential beneficiaries, meaning that only 80,000 public employees are members of a CPF. However, the higher level of job security in the public sector allows long and uninterrupted careers, thus maintaining the old age protection function of the *Tfr* for these employees.

Pension prospects are more alarming for both self-employed and some 'atypical' employees that suffer from *cumulative disadvantages*. First, they pay lower contribution rates in the first pillar and will consequently be entitled to lower pension than employees, with a projected replacement rate of around 30 per cent after forty years of contributions. Supplementary pensions, then, become absolutely necessary in order to maintain an adequate level of income during retirement. Unfortunately, the self-employed and atypical employees on 'project contracts' are not entitled to *Tfr*; therefore they lack a major instrument to finance supplementary schemes. Only 16 per cent of the self-employed are currently members of supplementary schemes, while the take-up rate among atypical workers is negligible. Pension prospects thus appear rather gloomy for a sizeable number of Italian workers. The varying diffusion of supplementary pensions in the various economic sectors and among professional categories contributes to a pension landscape characterized by weak old age protection not only for the self-employed (as in past decades) but also for new social risk groups, like workers employed in small firms in the private sector and, to a more limited extent, public employees.

In addition, three other aspects may be critical for income security after retirement. First, the combination of an NDC first pillar and DC supplementary schemes, which eliminate intra-generational redistribution, may be particularly detrimental for low wage earners. Second, indexation mechanisms both in the first pillar (pensions indexed to prices) and in supplementary pillars (financial valorization of annuities only) will likely produce a sharp reduction of pensions' value after retirement. Third, and very important, in an 'NDC plus DC system' insured workers bear all the risks – that is, demographic, economic, and financial. As to the latter, the recent financial market crisis has raised attention of national policymakers and stakeholders on the consequences of market shocks on DC supplementary schemes, though the effects of the crisis have been more limited in Italy in comparison with other countries. Returns have generally been negative, but CPF, the assets of which have been mostly invested in bonds, have managed to contain losses (about a 6 per cent decrease on average in 2008), while OPF and especially PIP have registered much worse performances (a decline of 14 and 25 per cent respectively). Negative returns have led to a reduction of the share of equities in CPF and OPF portfolios, but the assets of all types of supplementary institutions (but PEF) have increased also in 2008. This is mostly because supplementary schemes in Italy are still 'maturing', that is receiving many contributions and paying very few benefits. That is also the reason why the recent financial crisis has not stimulated an intense debate in Italy thus far.

Instead, the current pension debate has focused on the coverage issue for supplementary schemes. The President of COVIP has recently suggested various strategies in order to expand coverage and increase take-up rates for private employees. In the medium to long run, actions aimed to increase workers' access to information and financial literacy should be pursued. In the short term, two alternative strategies might be effective: either compulsory affiliation at least through the employers' contributions already included in collective agreements, or the periodical implementation of the silent-consent mechanism for those already employed in addition to those entering the labour market. For public employees, a crucial measure would be the introduction of the silent-consent formula. By contrast, remedies seem to be much more difficult to find for the self-employed and atypical workers; without the institutional gate *Tfr*, the resources to finance supplementary pensions remain scarce.

Bibliography

Baccaro, L. (2002). 'Negotiating the Italian Pension Reform with the Unions: Lessons for Corporatist Theory'. *Industrial and Labor Relations Review*, 55/3: 413–31.
COVIP (2003–2009a). *Relazione Annuale*. www.covip.it
——(2009b). *La previdenza complementare: principali dati statistici, ottobre 2009*. www.covip.it
——(2010). *La previdenza complementare: principali dati statistici, ottobre 2010*. www.covip.it
Ferrera, M. (1996). 'The Southern Model of Welfare in Social Europe'. *Journal of European Social Policy*, 6/1: 17–37.
——(ed.) (2005). *Welfare State Reform in Southern Europe. Fighting Poverty and Social Exclusion in Greece, Italy, Spain and Portugal*. London: Routledge.
——(2006). *Le Politiche Sociali. L'Italia in Prospettiva Comparata*. Bologna: Il Mulino.
——Hemerijck, A., and Rhodes, M. (2000). *The Future of Social Europe: Recasting Work and Welfare in the New Economy*. Oeiras: Celta.
——and Gualmini, E. (2004). *Rescue by Europe? Social and Labour Market Reforms from Maastricht to Berlusconi*. Amsterdam: Amsterdam University Press.

Ferrera, M., and Jessoula, M. (2007). 'Italy: A Narrow Gate for Path-shift', in E. Immergut, K. Anderson and I. Schulze (eds.), *Handbook of West European Pension Politics*. Oxford: Oxford University Press, 396–453.

INPS (2007). *Rendiconti generali anno 2006*. www.inps.it

ISTAT (2006). *Gli assicurati alle gestioni pensionistiche invalidità, vecchiaia e superstiti – anno 2004*. www.istat.it

——(2007). *Statistiche della previdenza e dell'assistenza sociale. I trattamenti pensionistici, anno 2005*. www.istat.it

Jessoula, M. (2009). *La politica pensionistica*. Bologna: Il Mulino.

——and Alti, T. (2010). 'Italy: An Uncompleted Departure from Bismarck', in B. Palier (ed.), *A Long Goodbye to Bismarck? The Politics of Welfare Reform in Continental Europe*. Amsterdam: Amsterdam University Press, 157–82.

Levy, J. (1999). 'Vice into Virtue? Progressive Politics and Welfare Reform in Continental Europe'. *Politics and Society*, 27/2: 239–73.

Marano, A. (2006). 'Il mercato delle rendite vitalizie per la previdenza complementare: un commento', in M. Messori (ed.) *La previdenza complementare in Italia*. Bologna: Il Mulino, 587–94.

Ministry of Welfare (2002). *Report on National Strategies for Future Pension Systems*. Brussels: European Union (www.europa.eu.int).

Myles, J., and Pierson, P. (2001). 'The Comparative Political Economy of Pension Reform', in P. Pierson (ed.), *The New Politics of the Welfare State*. Oxford: Oxford University Press, 305–33.

Natali, D. (2007). *Vincitori e perdenti: come cambiano le pensioni in Italia e in Europa*. Bologna: Il Mulino.

——and Rhodes, M. (2004). 'Trade-offs and Veto Players: Reforming Pensions in France and Italy'. *French Politics*, 2/1: 1–23.

OECD (2009). *Survey of Investment Regulation of Pension Funds*. www.oecd.org

Orszag, P., and Stiglitz, J. E. (2001). 'Rethinking Pension Reform: Ten Myths about Social Security Systems', in R. Holzman and J. Stiglitz (ed.), *New Ideas about Old Age Security*. Washington: The World Bank, 17–57.

Pallini, M. (2007). 'Le "altre" forme pensionistiche complementari: I fondi pensione aperti e forme pensionistiche individuali', in A. Tursi (ed.), La nuova disciplina della previdenza complementare: commentario sistematico. *Le nuove leggi civili commentate*, 30/3–4: 766–80.

SPC (2006). *Current and Prospective Theoretical Replacement Rates*. Brussels: Social Protection Committee, European Union (ec.europa.eu/employment_social/spsi).

Streeck, W., and Thelen, K. (2005). 'Introduction: Institutional Change in Advanced Political Economies', in K. Thelen and W. Streeck (eds.), *Beyond Continuity: Institutional Change in Advanced Political Economies*. Oxford: Oxford University Press, 1–39.

Part III

Emergent Nordic Multipillar Pension Systems

7

Denmark: The Silent Revolution towards a Multipillar Pension System

Jørgen Goul Andersen

1. Introduction

Denmark's multipillar pension system has developed gradually. It can be thought of as a silent revolution with little legislation. The tax-financed, flat-rate basic pension – the 'people's pension' – has been maintained, but the pension *system* has been entirely transformed by the layering of 'labour market pensions' – supplementary, fully funded, contributory pensions, typically negotiated in collective agreements. As these occupational pensions approach universal coverage, and as contribution rates have increased, they gradually replace the 'people's pension' as the backbone of retirement income. However, the first pillar has not vanished: The people's pension has become increasingly means tested, but has also been supplemented by other means-tested schemes that guarantee high minimum standards. From an economic perspective, the Danish system comes close to World Bank (1994) recommendations, but the system remains highly redistributive and provides solid protection against poverty. From a social outcome perspective (Andersen 2007*b*), one could speak of a 'Social Democratic' multipillarization. With the benefit of hindsight, these changes might appear designed as adaptations to demographic change, but there was no underlying 'master plan'. Decision-making was incremental and triggered by short-term economic goals. Initially, the government was scarcely concerned with the ageing problem, but welcomed pension savings as a means to improve the balance of payment. Other schemes were introduced and later terminated as means to curb or stimulate private consumption.

Formally, the pension system is highly 'privatized', yet since occupational pensions are typically collective and quasi-mandatory, they function much like a statutory system. This is in line with the Danish tradition of leaving much competence to collective negotiations rather than legislation. Occupational schemes are fully funded and typically sector-wide. Civil servants' pensions are phased out or become similar to occupational pensions. Occupational pension rights are vested, transferable, and unaffected by job change. In addition to old-age pension, occupational schemes typically provide support to survivors and disability pension supplements. Denmark also has a strong tradition of personal pensions which seems unaffected by the expansion of occupational pensions until now. Denmark's pension savings increased to more than 150 per cent of GDP by 2008, investment is subject to regulation, and pension funds are highly skilled in handling risks. Whereas the pension system seems economically sustainable amid ageing populations and volatile equity markets, political pressures to change might emerge as the proportion of pensioners depending on the highly redistributive first pillar is declining.

Part I: The evolution of the public–private pension mix

2. The main features of the pension system

Since 1964 the Danish pension system was dominated by a universal, flat-rate, tax-financed 'people's pension' – supplemented by some occupational and individual pensions. Over decades, but particularly since 1989, there has been a growth of private pensions. This was accompanied by targeting of the first pillar as well as a complex proliferation which ensures high social minima.

2.1 The first pillar

The people's pension is divided into a 'basic amount', provided to everybody (based on forty years of residence), and a 'pension supplement' tested against (household) income. Initially, the supplement was small and obtained by an overwhelming majority. Since 1994, however, the two components (indexed by wage increases) are of the same amount,[1] and the proportion receiving full supplements has declined to 57 per cent by 2007. Moreover, even the basic amount is means tested against employment income above €36,000. This fits well into an overall picture of generous, but more targeted basic pensions. By 2003, a means-tested supplementary pension benefit was introduced for low-income pensioners.[2] The most important element ensuring a high social minimum, however, is a preferential

---

[1] DKK 63,048 and DKK 63,468 annually – roughly €8,500 – for a single pensioner in 2009. For cohabitants, supplement is lower. Indexation is based on *annual* income *less* pension contributions. Due to longer holidays and pension improvements, indexation has lagged markedly behind increases in wage costs (Andersen 2007*a*: 24–5). Besides, indexation technically provides slightly less than full adjustment.

[2] In 2008, coverage was about 27 per cent (230,000 pensioners), see Ministry of Finance (2008: 15). The supplement (up to €1,380) is given independently of real estate assets and housing benefits.

pensioners' housing benefit that often pays more than one-half of the rent (see Andersen 2007*a* for details). In addition, pensioners may receive means-tested heating support, health supplements, and discretionary personal supplements.

The first pillar also includes a mandatory, fully funded, flat-rate labour market supplementary pension (ATP) for all wage earners. For a pensioner with a full-time contribution record of forty years, annual (lifelong) pension from the age of 65 was about €2,800 by 2007. Contributions (about 1 per cent, of which two-thirds are paid by employers, one-third by employees) are decided in collective wage negotiations (€435 for most full-time employed). ATP has become increasingly universal: It was extended to the unemployed (with double contributions) and to people receiving sickness benefits in 1996, and to disability pensioners in 2003. Another funded scheme of roughly the same size – Special Pensions Savings – was introduced in 1998, but suspended by 2004 in order to stimulate consumption. Contributions were announced to be resumed in 2009, but shortly after the scheme was terminated and all savings paid out because of the economic crisis. Even for people receiving no ATP or Special Pensions Savings, minima are very high. For a single resident pensioner who is a tenant and has no supplementary income, net value of pensions and housing benefits is roughly equivalent to maximum unemployment benefits plus ordinary housing benefits (Andersen 2007*a*). Even though nearly the entire complex of first pillar schemes has become means tested, this does not mean that the *system* has become residual. Means testing must be seen in conjunction with the second and third pillar private pensions.

2.2 The second pillar

Danish occupational pensions are second-tier arrangements aimed at income replacement. First and foremost, this includes fully funded 'labour market pensions'. Originally, this referred only to collectively negotiated schemes; it increasingly applies to all funded employment-related schemes (Andersen and Kristiansen 2009), including company schemes and individual schemes attached to the employment contract. Finally, civil servants' pensions also belong to the second pillar. *Labour market pensions* are typically negotiated as part of collective agreements between the social partners. They are normally sector-wide, that is, they cover an educational group or an economic branch across the whole country. In addition or as an alternative to pension funds, unions and employers have formed labour market related insurance companies to exploit economies of scale and keep administration costs low.[3] The schemes

---

[3] These companies and their governance are equivalent to pension funds, and so are the pension schemes, but they appear in statistics in accordance with their formal status as insurance companies. This is a source of confusion in international statistics (e.g. OECD 2009: 50–1).

typically include support for survivors and some coverage of risk of disability. Other second-pillar schemes converge towards labour market pensions. The few remaining firm-based schemes are almost fully equivalent. Firms without collective agreements typically buy a 'standard package' in labour market related insurance companies, or in other financial institutions. *Civil servants' schemes* are phased out, and those that remain have become similar to labour market pensions as calculation of entitlements follow duration of employment quite closely. In short, expansion and convergence are keywords regarding second-pillar pensions. They have expanded to cover the overwhelming majority of the work force, and schemes converge towards contributory, fully funded pensions. When the schemes mature, occupational pensions will provide adequate income replacement and most likely become the backbone of the pension system.

2.3 The third pillar

The third pillar – purely individual pensions – has not been crowded out by the expansion of occupational pensions. Rather, both second- and third-pillar schemes have served to crowd out ordinary savings including savings in owner-occupied dwellings which traditionally reduced current expenses of pensioners. Third-pillar pensions include four arrangements: index contracts, life insurance pensions, capital pensions, and rate pensions.

- *Index contracts* is phased out with generational replacement as signing of new contracts was abolished in 1971. These contracts, introduced alongside the 'people's pension' in 1957, could be signed with a bank or with a life insurance company. They provided tax deductions for contributions to a lifelong payment that was indexed annually by prices.
- *Life insurance pension* (lifelong pension payment) is a classical pension instrument provided by insurance companies throughout the twentieth century. Since 1922, payments have been more or less deductible from taxable income. Life insurance pensions are equivalent to labour market pensions as they provide the insured person with annual payments (lifelong from retirement, or from an agreed-upon age) and often include support for survivors.
- *Capital pensions* are paid out as a lump sum – taxed by 40 per cent – between the age of 60 and 75. Contributions up to a limit are tax deductible. Originally, contributions could only be paid by employers (final taxation being 25 per cent), but from 1987, it also became a purely individual arrangement. In the 1998 tax reform, the tax value of deductions was reduced. This turned people's interest towards rate pensions.
- Contributions to *rate pensions* are deductible, but distributed over several years if they exceed DKK 46,000. This is a cumulative limit for capital and rate pensions and equivalents, but until 2009, payments formally made by

	First pillar		Second pillar	Third pillar
	State pensions and special arrangements for pensioners		Occupational pensions	Personal pensions
Third tier (topping up / replacement gap)				Rent pension Capital pension Rate pension (Index contracts)
Second/third tier (income maintenance)			Semi-mandatory labour market pension Civil servants' pensions (Company pensions)	
First tier (basic security/ poverty protection)	Special Pensions Savings (terminated 2009)			
	ATP: Supplementary Labour Market Pension			
	People's pension	Basic amount		
		Pension supplement*		
	Supplementary pensions benefits*			
	Individual supplements (health, personal, heating)*			
	Preferential housing benefits*			

Figure 7.1 Pillars and tiers of the Danish pension system

Notes: *Means-tested schemes.

the employer were not included. Pension payments must stretch over at least ten years (before the age of 85) and is subject to ordinary income tax.[4] Since deduction was up to 59 per cent until 2009, and since pensioners' marginal taxes are typically lower, this invited to tax avoidance. The 2009 tax reform fixed a cumulative annual limit of deductions for private capital and rate pensions at DKK 100,000, including employer payments. As marginal taxes were simultaneously reduced, both opportunities and incentives were weakened. However, since taxation of current returns is low (15 per cent), an incentive remains. Life insurance pensions are not affected.

---

[4] Pensions and other income transfers are exempted from an 8 per cent gross tax called 'labour market contributions' (which is deductible from taxable income) introduced in the 1993 tax reform.

Capital pensions and rate pensions can be administered by the bank or insurance company, but some people choose to invest the money in bonds or shares themselves. Because these investments are typically supplements to other pensions, some people are less risk adverse with these investments.

3. Flat-rate universalism and the crowding in of private pensions

The Danish welfare state is commonly classified as 'Social Democratic', but this political label is historically somewhat misleading (see Table 7.1). The 1891 reform which introduced tax-financed old age relief for citizens above 60 was mainly initiated by the Liberal Party which was based on middle-sized farmers. The Social Democrats voted against the reform but soon regretted their mistake (Bertolt et al. 1955: 221). The party came to favour larger benefits, broader coverage, and fixed rules rather than discretionary benefits. Ironically, it was a Liberal–Conservative government that introduced fixed criteria of eligibility and entitlements by 1922, alongside a less stigmatizing name ('rent' instead of 'relief') (Petersen 2006). The Social Democrats declined to support the law, as the age limit was raised and benefits were low (Bruus 2004: 82). In 1933, pensions were included in a big social reform, curiously linking eligibility to health insurance fund membership (Bruus 2004: 87). By 1937, the age limit of 60 years was reinstalled, only to be raised to 65 by 1946 (Petersen 2001).

The people's pension reform in 1956 followed the work of a commission appointed to explore the possibility of insurance-based pensions (Rasmussen 1996: 56). The commission responded that this would be impossible due to the 'double payment problem'. Instead, it elaborated a proposal in line with Social Democratic preferences. All citizens became eligible, but entitlements remained means tested until the 1964 reform which introduced flat-rate pensions (with a small means-tested supplement). Bourgeois parties supported both reforms and gained tax-subsidized 'index contracts' in return. Pension age was raised to 67 years.

The 1964 people's pension reform, fully implemented by 1970, was the last big reform adopted solely for pension purposes. The 1964 ATP reform was partly a compensation for a crisis package and government intervention in collective negotiations. Although it carried the same name as the Swedish second-tier scheme, Danish ATP is just a small, flat-rate, fully funded supplement, but its existence hampered the later introduction of an earnings-related second-tier pension. However, the failure to introduce a second tier was hardly an effect of institutional constraint, or of political weakness. Rather, the labour movement was divided (Larsen and Andersen 2004: 67–70). The people's pension was more generous than in the other Nordic countries (Korpi 2002: 41), and significant groups preferred to proceed along this path as they feared that earnings-related pensions would lead to increasing inequality.

Table 7.1 Chronology – the basic pension system in Denmark: from residual to universal to targeted

Year	Pensions	Changes	Political coalition
1891	SP	Tax financed old age relief (residual, discretionary)	C, V
1922	SP	Fixed criteria of eligibility & entitlements (targeted, increasing coverage)	C, V
1956	SP	People's pension I: Universal eligibility, entitlements means tested	All (S, R)
1964	SP	People's pension II: 'Flat-rate': Basic Amount + Small Pens. Supplement (fully implemented 1970)	All (S, R)
1964	(SP/OP)	1964 ATP funded flat-rate supplementary pension (inclusion of unemployed 1996)	All
1977–81	OP	1980 LD funded pension saving based on part of wage increases 1977–9 (only persons employed in 1977–9)	S, R, F
1990	SP	Wage indexation of transfers to households	All
1984/94	SP	Means test of Basic Amount for employment income (annual state budget compromise)	C, V, CD, Chr, R (1984)
1994	SP	Basic amount 50% (part of 1993 tax reform)	S, R
2002		Suppl. Pens. Benefits (annual state budget compromise)	V, C, DPP
1998–2003	SP(PP)	SP, (means-tested) pension supplements 50% (PP). Universal, funded scheme, 1 per cent of gross income	S, R, C, V (1997) S, R, F (1998)
		Temporary measure actuarial 1998	S, R, V, C (1997)
		Permanent, (almost) flat rate 1999–2000	S, R, F (1998)
		Permanent, actuarial 2001–3	C, V, O (2002)
		Savings paid out in 2009–10.	C, V, O 2009

Notes: SP: state pension; OP: occupational pension; PP: personal pension. S = Soc.Dem., C = Cons., V = Liberals, R = Radical Liberals, CD = Centre Democrats, Chr. = Christian Democrats, DPP = Danish People's Party, F = Socialist People's Party. All = broad coalition centre-right + centre-left (but not necessarily all parties). Parentheses indicate driver of reform. Year indicates year of decision, not year of implementation.

Subsequent development was most often triggered by short-term economic concerns. By 1970, the government had to cool an over-heated economy, but preferred the label 'contribution to a Social Pension Fund' for an income tax increase of one (later two) percentage points. This was an act of blame avoidance, but money was earmarked for unspecified pension improvements, and funds accumulated. Decisions were postponed until 1978/81 when the Social Democrats adopted two big reforms about preferential housing benefits and heating support that became essential for minimum standards among pensioners (Andersen 2007a; Ministry of Social Affairs et al. 2003).

Even the decisive step towards a multipillar pension system – the inclusion of labour market pensions in collective agreements 1989–93 – was triggered by the government's need to find remedies against a chronic balance of payment deficit. The Ministry of Finance issued an appeal for pensions in 1984, and the trade union confederation soon elaborated a report about labour market pensions (LO 1985). In 1989, the government accelerated the process by including labour market pensions in all collective agreements in the public sector. This paved the way for an extension to the private sector in 1991. The unions had preferred a statutory scheme whereas employers and the government wanted a voluntary agreement that forced the unions to consider pension improvements as part of the wage increases.

Labour market pensions are in accordance with a Danish tradition of including labour market agreements and supplementary benefits in the collective negotiation system, rather than legislation. Collective agreements have secured *de facto* minimum wages without legislation; some holidays are determined by law, others by collective agreements; a complex interplay between the 'white collar workers act' (dating back to the 1930s) and collective agreements often provides supplementary payment or full wage during sickness absence and parental leave.

Special Pension Savings was introduced in 1997 as an obligatory savings scheme to cool an over-heated economy. In 1998, it was made permanent and redistributive as part of a large economic package. The redistributive element was reversed from 2001 by the Liberal–Conservative government which suspended the entire scheme from 2004 – this time in order to *stimulate* the economy. In October 2008, a re-introduction was announced, only to be cancelled thirteen days later, and in order to stimulate consumption, the March 2009 tax reform package enabled people to withdraw their savings with a tax rebate. As more people than expected *did* withdraw their savings, the programme was eventually terminated and the remaining money paid out.

Only three reforms were motivated mainly by concerns for pensions or for long-term economic sustainability: increased targeting of the people's pension in the 1993 tax reform; introduction of the supplementary pension benefits in 2003 (a concession to the Danish People's Party); and the 2006 welfare reform which will raise early retirement age and pension age from 2019 – and let age brackets follow life expectancy of 60 years olds afterwards (this will probably raise pension age to 70 years for age cohorts born after 1971).

In its 2002 report to the EU (Ministry of Social Affairs et al. 2002), the government could describe Danish pensions as 'adequate and sustainable'. But this had been achieved without any 'master plan', and the main trigger of reform was macroeconomic concerns. The cumulative impact was transformative, but it was a silent revolution as the small, incremental changes were hardly perceived. Intentions could be rationalized post hoc (1) as a relief of financial obligations of the state, and (2) as targeting of the first pillar in order to make it fit with changes in the other pillars. Moreover, it was demonstrated that the 'double payment problem' is surmountable.

Even though many parties joined as architects, distributional outcomes seem as satisfying from a Social Democratic perspective as the outcomes of other Nordic pension reforms (Pedersen 1999; Pedersen and Finseraas 2009). Further, pension rights are safe and transferable. The shortcomings of a pure contributory system were avoided by maintaining and expanding the first pillar so that it provides high minima (except for migrants).

Multipillar pensions make statutory retirement age less important. As defined contribution pension schemes are phased in, a fixed retirement age is phased out. This holds also for early retirement where there is a substantial deduction for other pension income (Andersen 2007a). The 'people's pension' and early retirement allowance remain important for people with low incomes and provide them with an opportunity to retire, but for these groups, changes in age brackets are detrimental as current improvements in health and life expectancy are unequally distributed across social classes (Brønnum-Hansen and Baadsgaard 2008).

4. The emergence of the public–private pension mix

The public–private pension mix in Denmark developed gradually through expansion of individual as well as occupational pensions. Theoretically, 'crowding in' of private pensions is regarded as an inevitable corollary of flat-rate Beveridge-type pensions: As replacement rates are insufficient for the middle classes, private pensions are needed to provide adequate income replacement. Still, even though private pension savings were tax-subsidized since the 1920s, individual pensions only constituted a modest supplement until the 1980s. By 1981, total pension savings in life insurance companies and banks only constituted 22 per cent of GDP (see Table 7.2). By 1990, this had increased to 38 per cent of GDP.[5]

The main driver of change was the growth in collective labour market pensions. They have a long prehistory. Defined benefit schemes had emerged already before 1900, but insurance laws and laws about company pension funds in 1930 and 1935 required that pension rights were transferable (Betænkning no. 1466 2005: ch. 3). The formation of a (non-profit) Pension Insurance Company (PFA) in 1917 also facilitated collective, funded schemes. By 1970, there were some 300 company funds with 40,000 members, and additional 200,000 employees were covered by funded arrangements in insurance companies or sector-wide pension funds (Due and Madsen 2003: 23; Johansen 1996).

---

[5] Most labour market related life insurance companies formed by unions and employers did not emerge until the 1990s.

Table 7.2 Pension savings in Denmark, 1981–2008

	1981	1990	2000	2007	2008
Bill DKK					
Life insurance companies[1]	73.0	221.5	649.5	1,054.2	1,119.0
Banks capital & rate pensions	21.0	95.4	215.3	369.5	308.0
Total banks/insurance companies	94.0	316.9	864.8	1,423.7	1,427.0
ATP (suppl. labour market pension)[2]	20.1	80.4	246.7	388.9	678.0
LD + SP[3]	11.6	28.6	83.9	116.9	104.0
Labour market pension funds[4]	32.5	119.9	312.8	455.3	440.0
Pension funds, total	64.2	228.9	643.4	961.1	1,222.0
Pension savings, total	158.2	545.8	1,507.2	2,384.8	2,649.0
Per cent of GDP					
Banks/insurance companies	21.9	37.7	66.8	84.3	82.1
Pension funds	14.9	27.2	49.7	56.9	70.3
All pension savings	36.8	64.9	116.5	141.3	152.5

Notes:
[1] Includes joint union–employer-owned *labour market related life insurance companies* which are *de facto* equivalent to labour market pension funds. The four largest account for 319 bill DKK in 2008. The two main non-profit (user-owned) institutions specialized in labour market pensions account for 252 bill DKK.
[2] Figures for 2008 include an extraordinary increase by 280 bill DKK due to repo-arrangements during the financial crisis (see www.atp.dk – annual report 2008).
[3] LD administers frozen wage increases 1977–9. SP, Special Pension savings, introduced in 1998, terminated in 2009. Administered by ATP, but could be moved to another institution.
[4] Excluding the funds mentioned in note (1).

Sources: Forsikring og pension (*www.forsikringogpension.dk*); Statistics Denmark (*www.statistikbanken.dk*).

The oldest sector-wide pension funds (for supervisors and bank employees) date back to 1900 and 1912, respectively (Due and Madsen 2003: 31). They were the forerunners of modern, nation-wide, collectively negotiated labour market pensions which cover people with a particular education and/or within particular branches of the economy. From 1945, this model was followed when building occupational pensions, in particular for public employees. In the health-care sector, doctors were the first to obtain a pension scheme (1946), followed by nurses and other bachelor-level professionals in the 1950s, and by lower skilled in the 1960s. Veterinarians (1940) and engineers (1953) were other front runners. Another expansion took place in 1970 when academics in the public sector were transferred from civil servants' pensions to labour market pensions in accordance with a change in employment contracts. In the 1970s, even more public employees included a pension scheme in collective negotiations (Due and Madsen 2003: 29–32; Larsen and Andersen 2004: 78–9).

Around 1980, the development had passed a point of no return (see Table 7.3). It would be impossible to coordinate mushrooming occupational pensions with the introduction of earnings-related public pensions. From 1967 to 1982, the number of sector-wide pension funds increased from twenty to thirty-one, and member figures quadrupled (Henriksen et al. 1987; Vesterø-Jensen 1985). According to a

Table 7.3 Chronology 2 – the development of occupational pensions in Denmark

Year	Reform	Political coalition
1900	The first pension fund for supervisors in manufacture	Collective agreement
1940s–60s	Gradual expansion of pension funds, in particular in the health sector and for academics	Collective agreement
1970	Great transfer of academics from civil servants to ordinary employment	C, V, R
Early 1980s	Reached a point of no return. Public second-tier pension no longer possible	—
1984	Governments signals that it would welcome labour market pensions	C, V, CD, Chr
1985	LO (trade union confederation) publish a report on statutory labour market pensions	—
1988	Labour Market Pension Commission	C, V, R
1989	Labour market pensions in all remaining collective agreements in public sector	Collective agreement
1991–3	Labour market pensions in all large collective agreements in private sector. Long-term target: 9 per cent	Collective agreement
2000	Avoidance of civil servant's contracts in the future	S, R
2004	Target for new schemes typically 10.8 per cent	Collective agreement
2007	Target for new schemes typically 12 per cent (from 2009)	Collective agreement
2009	Contributions normally between 12 and 18 per cent	Collective agreement

Notes: S = Soc.Dem., C = Cons., V = Liberals, R = Radical Liberals, CD = Centre Democrats, Chr. = Christian Democrats, DPP = Danish People's Party.

survey, 34 per cent of white-collar employees in the private sector and 48 per cent of white-collars in the public sector had a pension arrangement (co-) financed by their employers by 1986 (Morgenavisen Jyllands-Posten 3.9 1986). The final breakthrough came when the Conservative led coalition government – due to chronic problems with balance of payment deficits – announced in its 1984 Budget Report that it would welcome an expansion of collective labour market pensions (Ministry of Finance 1984: 35). The trade union confederation (LO) almost immediately produced a proposal which envisaged statutory, funded pensions (LO 1985). The proposal was adopted at the 1986 LO congress, but in order to avoid wage drift the government and the employers insisted on voluntary agreements between the social partners to ensure that pension contributions were calculated as wage improvements. The unions were also attracted by pension funds as a substitute for economic democracy, but the government strongly wanted to avoid a union-controlled central fund (Larsen and Andersen 2004).

There was disagreement and ambivalence within the government. After tripartite negotiations in 1987 which resulted in a general agreement about wage moderation, a fast-working corporative Labour Market Pension Commission was appointed in February 1988 to elaborate a comprehensive analysis.

The report was delivered ten months later,[6] and in the public sector wage negotiations in 1989, government and municipalities took a decisive step by granting labour market pensions to all groups which did not already have such a scheme. This constituted a fait accompli and became the great breakthrough. In private sector negotiations in 1991, labour market pensions were introduced (from 1993) for a majority of employees. Most of the remaining groups were soon to follow. In the beginning, contributions were small (0.9 per cent the first year), but unions typically put up a target of 9 per cent. This target was increased to 10.8 per cent in 2004, and to 12 per cent in the 2007 negotiations (from 2009), close to the level in the 'old' schemes (12–18 per cent).

The new labour market pensions were built on the same principles as previously existing schemes. Pensions are fully funded and fully actuarial. People do not lose pension rights if they leave a job; in most cases, they will not even be required to change pension fund. Nor do individuals need to worry about pensions in the case of bankruptcy of the employer. These conditions converge across a variety of schemes.

When they mature, funded labour market pensions will probably constitute the backbone of the pension system and become the main source of pensioners' income. But some uncertainty remains. First, future pensions depend on the real return rate on investments. Second, they depend on taxation which by 2001 was fixed at 15 per cent of the annual growth of the capital stock, regardless of type of income, for all sorts of funded pensions. Finally, life expectancy is crucial. In 1998, it was estimated that only 30 per cent of the income of pensioners in 2045 would come from the people's pension whereas 21 per cent would be payments from ATP and 49 per cent from labour market pensions (Economic Council 1998: 156; individual pensions not included). Since then, contributions have increased, and so has the projected improvement of life expectancy. As projected return rates were perhaps too optimistic, the 1998 calculation may overestimate the funds-based pension income.

One might have expected that the massive increase in labour market pensions would have a crowding-out effect on individual pensions, but this does not seem to be the case. As figures on life insurance companies include labour market pensions, they give no indication, but it emerges that growth in capital and rate pensions has been at least as strong as the growth in collective arrangements (see Table 7.2). Altogether, the total accumulated stock of pension savings – collective or individual – represented a value of DKK 2,649 billion by 2008, worth more than 150 per cent of GDP. This also represents an implicit asset of the state which can expect to receive nearly one half of this amount in future revenues. As the state's pension expenditure per individual will decline due to means testing whereas tax revenues from pension income will increase,

---

[6] Surprisingly, the report revealed that the *de facto* compensation rate for a single unskilled worker was already close to 100 per cent (Arbejdsmarkedspensionsudvalget 1988).

future pension expenditures is not a matter of serious concern. Ageing provides an economic challenge to elderly care and health care, and to aggregate labour supply, but not to financing of future pensions.

5. The changing public–private pension mix

In Denmark, the debate about the challenges of ageing largely came *after* the changes in the pension system. There was some public debate around 1984 when the first long-term population forecast was published. The fertility rate had reached a low point (1.38) in 1983, and a population decline was pictured. The ageing problem did receive some paragraphs in the trade unions' proposal (LO 1985), but otherwise ageing problems were not discussed much until the 1990s. As fertility increased significantly, and as life expectancy improvements were exceptionally bad until 1996, Danish population forecasts did not reveal dramatic ageing. Besides, the people's pension was inexpensive – spending as per cent of GDP had been declining since 1981 and was even lower in 1970 (Economic Council 2005: 105). A key report of the government (Ministry of Labour et al. 1995: 5–8) estimated the long-term increase in public expenditure due to ageing to about 4 per cent of GDP.

Still, it became a concern of the government to figure out how this expenditure increase could be financed without higher taxes. The answer was constraints on medium-term economic policy. A key element was to reduce interest payments on public debt, by means of increasing employment and constraining public expenditure growth. By April 1997, this was codified in a so-called 2005 Plan (Ministry of Finance 1997) which was updated in 1998 (Ministry of Finance 1998) and later replaced by a 2010 Plan (Regeringen 2001). The plan was taken over by the new government in 2001 and was a key reference point in public policy debates for several years. The plan was too optimistic regarding the means, but prosperity and oil revenues built up a large budget surplus, and requirements regarding the bottom line of public debt were met before time (Ministry of Finance 2006*a*). In a report about 'sustainable pensions' (Regeringen 2000), and in the national strategy report of 2002 to the EU (Ministry of Social Affairs et al. 2002), the government concluded that Denmark could maintain adequate and sustainable pensions without increasing taxes.

This did not kill the discussion about ageing. A Welfare Commission which was set up in 2003 to elaborate solutions actually came up with slightly lower cost estimates, but this time the issue was presented as highly serious, and in 2006, a broad political majority including the Social Democrats agreed to postpone the age of early retirement by two years from 2019 and retirement age five years later. From 2025, age brackets should follow life expectancy for the 60 years old. According to the law, pension age will most likely increase from 65 years for age cohorts born before 1959 to 70 years for age cohorts born after 1971. Early retirement age brackets are elevated correspondingly.

Apart from a long time horizon, the 2006 reform was radical. In particular, the lower educated and lower paid segments of the labour force will have to retire substantially later. Unfortunately, improvement of health and of life expectancy is rather low for this segment. For better off groups, formal age brackets lose importance in a defined contribution pension world. People may choose between early retirement and a lower pension, or continued employment and a higher annual pension. With the exception of the 2006 reform, the discussion about ageing has had little impact on the Danish pension system as the institutional changes were already carried through. The first pillar provides solid poverty protection and is relatively inexpensive. Pensioners are projected to enjoy higher compensation rates, but this will not affect taxpayers much – unlike increasing costs for health care and elderly care, and declining labour supply.

Part II: The governance of supplementary pensions

Apart from civil servants' pensions, second- and third-pillar pensions are fully funded defined contribution schemes. If administered by pension funds or life insurance companies, they are subject to basically the same regulation of financial risks, embodied in a general law regarding financial companies. At first, there were fears of importing 'socialism through the back door' and restrictions regarding investments in shares. Such fears have vanished, and constraints have been focused on risk (where a very high ceiling remains). Apart from risk control, continual surveillance by the fiscal authorities, and a unisex requirement, government interference is small. Funds have generally been risk adverse and prudent in handling risks. So far there have been no financial scandals of importance, and losses during the 2008–9 financial crises were generally small.[7] However, guaranteed return rates of some 4–5 per cent, which were offered previously, have occasionally forced a sell-out of shares at an unfavourable point of time. In order to protect pension funds against a forced sell-out of bonds, the government in October 2008 temporarily made requirements more lenient.[8]

---

[7] See www.forsikringogpension for the return rate of individual funds and companies over time. One fund (for bank employees) had a negative return rate around 20 per cent, but some of the biggest players earned a surplus, and few lost more than 10 per cent.

[8] On October 31, 2008, the government made an agreement with the association of pension funds and insurance companies (http://www.oem.dk) in accordance with the law which gives the Danish Financial Supervisory Authority considerable discretion. A key problem in 2008 was a sudden (and irrational) increasing gap between interest rates on state bonds and on bonds issued by Danish mortgage companies. These companies and funds were allowed to include the

6. Who is covered?

Occupational pensions are quasi-mandatory in the sense that they cover the overwhelming part of the workforce, and in the sense that they are nearly always collective arrangements where there is no possibility for the individual to opt out. Most pensions are collectively negotiated between the social partners. Collective agreements cover some 83 per cent of all employees (Scheuer and Madsen 2000). By 1989, pensions were included in nearly all negotiations for the public sector, and from 1991, pension agreements were included in collective agreements for about 80 per cent of private sector employees covered by the main union confederation and the main employer confederation. At that time it was estimated that two-thirds of the labour force was covered (Betænkning no. 1245 1993: 43). Currently, occupational pensions are included in virtually all collective agreements, and similar pensions are introduced for most workers in firms that are not covered by a collective agreement.

There are some exceptions for particular groups of workers. Part-time employees are normally covered, sometimes with an option to pay additional contributions in order to maintain full-time pension rights. For people with fixed-term employment, there are some exceptions. As a minimum, people have pension rights if they are at least 20 (occasionally 22) years old, are employed for at least nine months, or if they have previously been employed under the agreement and are members of the pension fund. A working time requirement (like 15 hours per week) is often included. This typically excludes teenagers, or students with a side job. Many apprentices are excluded by the age criterion. Otherwise part-time employees and people with fixed-term employment are normally covered. As unionization is high (although declining),[9] enforcement of the agreement (e.g. via the Labour Court) is relatively certain (Andersen and Kristiansen 2009). In short, limitations as regards 'precarious jobs' do not constitute a big problem.

Most companies that are not covered by collective agreements will have pension rights anyway, and pension insurance companies offer standard

---

mortgage bond interest rate in calculation of their obligations with guaranteed return rates and to normalize the calculation of individual solvency requirements. Otherwise they would have been forced to sell out bonds which could have instigated further decline in prices. Some private pension companies and others introduced a temporary exit fee for customers who wanted to change company. Although the problems were solved, the issue with guaranteed return rates remains: Pension funds are forced to sell-out of shares when prices reach the lowest point. This actually contributed to a significant increase of national debt in 2000–3, and again in 2007–8. Over the last years, pension funds and companies have modified or dropped these guarantees and persuaded old members to refrain from them as they are in the long-run detrimental to their pensions. Given their considerable reserves, they have not faced difficulties in meeting their obligations until 2009.

[9] Unions sometimes manage to negotiate collective agreements for companies where unionization is low, but there are no 'erga omnes' principles as in some Continental European countries.

Table 7.4 Persons paying employment-related or personal pensions (in 1000s), Denmark, 1995–2008

Pension schemes	1995	2000	2004	2007	2008
Employment-related schemes					
Index schemes	3.0	1.6	0.9	0.5	0.4
Ordinary labour market pensions	1,319.0	1,676.0	1,818.1	1,971.8	2,081.5
– of which: suppl. lump sum in pension fund	244.0	252.0	266.5	265.3	271.0
Capital pensions	807.0	1,311.0	1,245.1	1,280.3	1,277.7
Rate pension or rate insurance	107.0	606.0	1,037.8	1,310.1	1,383.2
One or more schemes		1,721.0	1,995.6	2,150.9	2,270.9
Personal schemes					
Index schemes	159.0	123.0	92.0	65.0	57.2
Ordinary lifelong pension	252.0	260.0	260.6	238.6	232.6
Capital pensions	968.0	821.0	725.8	802.8	674.5
Rate pension/insurance	114.0	226.0	285.7	413.7	383.6
One or more schemes		1,064.0	1,017.8	1,132.2	1,017.5
Total	2,212.0	2,280.0	2,345.8	2,520.2	2,558.4

Source: Forsikring and Pension (*www.forsikringogpension.dk*).

solutions for small firms. Still, coverage is incomplete, and there has been quite some debate about this issue (Betænkning no. 1466 2005; Jørgensen 2007; Ministry of Economics and Business 2003,2005; Pensionsmarkedsrådet 2007). Empirical findings on coverage depend on the delineation of age groups, on the denominator (population, labour force, or employees), and on whether calculations are based on a single year or a longer interval. According to register data on people 30–66 years old in the labour force population analysed by the Ministry of Economics and Business (2003: 45), only 7.5 per cent of those who had mainly been wage earners 1995–2000, had earned no labour market pension rights at all; additionally, 11 per cent had only been earning pension rights for one to three years. For those who had been mainly unemployed during these years, 36 per cent had earned no pension rights at all, and 48 per cent had earned some pension rights (one to three years). However, these figures omit those who had been outside the labour force. From these figures, at least the government usually concludes that coverage is close to universal and satisfactory.

Most importantly, coverage has increased. As it emerges from Table 7.4, figures have increased from 1.7 million in 2000 to 2.3 million in 2007. This largely reflects a genuine increase in coverage which was 79 per cent of the labour force in 2008.[10] Full employment may also improve coverage indirectly

[10] As most Danish students and pupils have a side job, the labour force figure is rather inflated.

as this will force employers to offer acceptable employment conditions, including pensions. In the 1980s, the unions had demanded a statutory labour market pension. They failed, but the outcome does not seem much different. Coverage is nearly universal. Besides, the ATP pension has been extended to unemployed and disabled persons. The figures above do not include civil servant pensions. Civil servant contracts are phased out and replaced by ordinary employment contracts which are more flexible. Among state employees, few groups are left except top level bureaucrats and a larger group of employees in the defence, the judicial system, and the state church.[11] Municipalities and regions are free to choose. However, including all administrative levels and previously state-owned companies, less than 100,000 persons were eligible to civil servant pensions by 2007 (Ministry of Finance 2006b, fn. § 36).

For people without occupational pensions, personal pensions serve as an alternative (Ministry of Economics and Business 2003: 46–8), alongside ordinary savings. Even though some unemployed have personal pensions, this is infrequent, and contributions are normally small. The largest payments to personal pensions are found among the self-employed. The private pension market offers a broad range of choice and self-employed can make use of the same arrangements as employees if they want to. However, people often prefer payment of personal pensions over a shorter period. Previously, the most popular scheme was capital pensions (paid out in one or more portions between the age of 60 and 75), but because of changing tax rules, rate pensions (paid out over ten years or more before the age of 85) have gained increasing importance.

7. What kind of benefits?

Danish labour market pensions are defined contribution (DC) schemes. Typically, pensions are paid as lifelong annuities (from the age of 60 or later), occasionally as capital- or rate pensions or as life-insurance pensions for a fixed number of years. Some funds offer a choice of a capital pension supplement. Further, some funds offer members the right to choose between a low and a high lump sum payment at the time of retirement (and correspondingly lower annual pensions). Most schemes also cover the risk of disability (as a supplement to universal, flat-rate public disability pensions); this compensation is most generous in the funds with a long history and a high contribution rate. Moreover, a lump sum is typically paid in case of 'critical disease'. Usually, the schemes also include a group life insurance and support for survivors: orphans (up to the age of 21 or 24) and surviving spouse/cohabitant (usually for ten years).

---

[11] Following the recommendation in *Cirkulære om anvendelse af tjenestemandsansættelser i staten og folkekirken*. No. 210, 11.12.2000.

Other types of occupational pensions are disappearing and become increasingly equivalent to labour market pensions. A pension right for a civil servant is not mainly a matter of pensions; rather, it constitutes an employment protection (Kristiansen 2005). Civil servant pensions are defined benefit pensions that fix pensions to a share of final salary. However, in practice they are almost equivalent to DC schemes as entitlements follow duration of employment.[12] People easily move forth and back between employment as a civil servant and ordinary employment (with or without voluntary transfer of pension rights). Moreover, civil servant pensions are often *de facto* funded as nearly all municipalities pay contributions to a pension reinsurance company (KP/Sampension) in order to limit future pension expenditures (www.sampension.dk).

Except for individual contracts for top executive officers and a few employees in some transnational firms, company-based defined benefit pensions are negligible (OECD 2009: 54). Firm pension funds which are based on the same contributory system as other pension funds are also on the way to extinction (Andersen and Kristiansen 2009). Total membership declined from 9,900 in 2003 to 6,800 in 2008 (www.forsikringogpension.dk).

As strict DC schemes labour market pensions, by definition, contain almost no redistribution, still there are basic elements of solidarity (Ministry of Economics and Business 2003): first, the presumption of 'normal health conditions', and second the unisex requirement. Unlike the health presumption, the unisex requirement is statutory. Needless to say, it is important whether people are admitted on same conditions, regardless of health. When the trade unions for manual workers entered the field, they carried with them the presumption that if people were employed, they also by definition had normal health and did not have to take a health test. This presumption has become the rule, but exceptions remain. The unisex requirement requires that survival rates underlying the calculation of pension payments are calculated jointly for men and women. In other words, risks are pooled. As women live longer, this is of course important for gender equality. With regards to gender concerns, however, risk pooling is too low in the Danish system. The unisex requirement only applies *within* a pension fund, not *across* pension funds, and gender composition varies a lot. In PKA, which is a large joint company for eight pension funds (for nurses, midwives, and others), about 90 per cent are women. Other pension funds largely have male members. As women have higher risks, regarding longevity as well as disability, the pension system which reflects a gender-segregated labour market produces outright gender discrimination – *in addition* to what follows from wage inequality and employment attachment. Furthermore, there

---

[12] A small advantage remains. Target is 57 per cent of wage after thirty-seven years of employment after the age of 25. First sixteen years count 1.75 percentage point per year, next sixteen years 1.5, and the last five years 1 percentage point per year (§ 6 in the law about civil servant's pension – L95/Jan.2003, as changed by L1155/Dec. 2003).

is also a highly unequal gender distribution of private pensions, due to tax incentives. It should be added, though, that women are the main beneficiaries of the first pillar schemes: After all, the maintenance of first pillar schemes with high minima means that women with low incomes are well compensated, as compared with pension systems that are more thoroughly based only on the DC principle.

Risk pooling is also low as regards social classes, but in this case the net effect is more difficult to calculate. Manual workers have higher risk of disability and would benefit from risk pooling with higher educated groups. On the other hand, higher educated live longer and would benefit from sharing their risk of longevity with manual workers.

Overall, one could expect that the change towards DC schemes would inevitably lead to increasing inequality among pensioners. The evidence is mixed, but the expectation largely seems disconfirmed. Based on personal incomes of individuals before tax, Gini coefficients among old-age pensioners are calculated to increase from 26.7 in 2001 to 31.7 in 2020 (Regeringen 2005: 14).[13] However, this appears to be a maturation effect, not a system effect: From 2020, inequality is projected to decline and reach a much lower level by 2040 (Gini: 21.4) than in 2001. In other words, inequality will only increase until the funded pension schemes for newcomers mature. Over the entire period, income inequality will remain lower among pensioners than among the economically active population (Regeringen 2005: 12–13). Still, a reservation remains regarding the calculation based on individuals as inequality between singles and couples will increase. The people's pension is substantially smaller for couples, making equivalized disposable incomes roughly similar. However, a couple will enjoy the full advantage of two funded pensions (Regeringen 2005: 12). Hence, we have reservations against projections of less inequality. But it does *not* seem that increasing inequality is to be expected if the current configuration is maintained.

8. Who pays?

All second-pillar pensions except civil servant's pensions are contributory; they are usually based on contributions, ranging between 12 and 18 per cent. Employers usually pay two-thirds, employees one-third, though this is largely a formality as the total contribution is paid to the pension fund by the employer. Apart from civil servant's pensions, second- and third-pillar pensions are fully funded. Previously, pension funds used to have a minimum guarantee of returns (often 4.5 per cent) which still applies to older members. However, as this forces the funds to prioritize low-risk investment (e.g. in bonds rather than

---

[13] The calculation is based on personal income *before* taxes, excluding capital income and tax-free transfers like housing benefits. Figures are not equivalized according to household size.

shares), such guarantees tend to be phased out for new members. Old members are offered a choice to shift to a scheme where promises are smaller but long-run prospects are assumed to be better. Many members choose the latter. The pension funds are required by law to provide an annual account and a projection of future pensions which is sent to the members. It seems that some pension funds, due to the global economic crisis of 2008–9, have to apply their minimum guarantee rules a bit more liberally, for example, by including previous bonuses in the calculation of the guarantee return rate.

Funded pensions – occupational or personal – provide a relief for the state, but they are not neutral in relation to public budgets. They fall under the headline of fiscal welfare since there is a tax subsidy to pension savings. Employment-related pension contributions are fully tax deductible. As the highest marginal tax rate was 63 per cent in 2009 (reduced to 56 per cent from 2010), the subsidy is considerable.[14] However, an 8 per cent gross tax (called labour market contributions and deductible before calculation of other taxes) is levied even upon pension savings. This means that maximum effective deduction was only 59 per cent (declining to 52–53 per cent from 2010). This applies to all pension payments except capital pensions where deduction is around 40 per cent (since 1998). Finally, there is an annual (cumulative) limit to private capital pension and rate pension deduction of 46,000 Danish kroner (and for rate pensions of all kinds, including employer-paid pensions, to 100,000 Danish kroner from 2010).

When pensions are paid out, they are subject to normal taxation but without payment of gross tax/labour market contribution. The exception is capital pensions where taxation is 40 per cent. As people often pay lower marginal taxes after retirement, there is an incentive to postpone taxation by means of pension saving.[15] However, since 1984 there has been a taxation of current returns. After recurring changes, taxation was fixed in 2001 at a simple 15 per cent tax on all revenues regardless of type (annual growth of the capital stock). Taxation of negative revenues follows a 'push forward' principle as they are deducted from future positive revenues. In case of massive equity losses as in 2008–9, this may result in excessive taxation as there is no neutralizing mechanism except time. Accordingly, in the 2009 tax reform, the age limit for taking out capital pension was raised from 70 to 75 years. As people are able to make a 'geared investment' with the full pre-tax amount of money, pension savings compare well with ordinary private savings, but as taxation is much tighter than previously, the tax subsidy is substantially reduced. The expenditure account for government looks even better: As most first-pillar schemes are means-tested, composite marginal taxes on pensions can often become quite high.

[14] http://www.skm.dk/tal_statistik/tidsserieoversigter/1288.html
[15] Pensioners with high pension incomes will temporarily pay an additional tax that is gradually phased out, in order to match previously higher deductions.

9. Who governs?

Supplementary pensions are subject to relatively little regulation except a strong regulation of risk. As regards labour market pensions, collective agreements stipulate which pension fund or institution should administer the money. Pension funds are governed by representatives of unions and employers. Funds for academics which are governed exclusively by the employee side are the only exception. At least one half of board members of pension funds must be elected by the members, directly or indirectly. However, pension schemes are increasingly administered by 'labour market related life insurance companies' jointly owned and controlled by unions and employers. Except for their formal status, they are equivalent to pension funds. Most newcomers have chosen this option (PensionDanmark, Industriens Pension, KP/Sampension).

Some pension funds have formed joint companies to administer assets (like PKA that counts eight formally independent funds; see Table 7.5). PenSam was formed at the same basis but may replace the old pension funds. Another large pension fund for lower level business and office workers has entered into a partnership with PFA – the old non-profit pension insurance company mentioned previously. Motives are obvious: Professionalization of administration and exploitation of economies of scale. The largest companies/funds have low administration costs – down to some €40 per member annually.

Table 7.5 Major labour market pension funds, 2009/10 (in 1000s)

(Pension funds + 'labour market related insurance companies')	Members/customers
Labour market related insurance companies	
Industriens Pension IP (union/employer-owned)	400
PensionDanmark (union/employer-owned)	578
Funktionær Pension (owned by union/employer + PFA from 2006)	110
PFA (shareholding company, user-owned)	n.a.
AP (cooperative, user-owned)	73
Sampension (owned by municipalities, regions and unions)	280
Teachers (industry wide; formal status as company)	120
Pension funds	
Pen Sam (based on four pension funds; public employees)	300
PKA (8 independent pension funds; public employees)	230
JØP Lawyers & Economists	41
MP Pension (M.A.'s, Ph.D's, Psychologists)	75
Doctors' Pension Fund	35
Pedagogues	103
Total of industry wide pension funds (2008)	590*

Notes: * Not including pensioners.
Source: Finanstilsynet (*www.finanstilsynet.dk*) and homepages of the funds and companies.

The Liberal–Conservative government from 2001 onwards has pursued the liberal idea of freedom of choice, and in 2003 a committee analysed the possibilities regarding pensions (Ministry of Economics and Business 2003). Freedom to choose between pension funds was regarded unrealistic, however, as it would run counter to the underlying principles of solidarity (risk pooling). Instead, it was recommended that members were given improved opportunities to design the kind of pension and risk coverage they wanted for themselves. This has gone hand in hand with initiatives by the pension funds themselves, but with a few exceptions, interest has been rather low. Especially in the old funds, people have had the possibility to choose between a long, short, or no survivor protection of spouse, and between a guarantee return rate and one or more investment strategies. Apart from this, take up of choice opportunities has been low.

Over time, the most striking change is the professionalization of administration. Funds and companies typically invest globally (in cooperation with broad networks of financial institutions in several countries), and they have become increasingly skilled in handling any sort of risk – from risks of financial markets to risks of longevity. On average, they have performed well during the financial crisis, with a loss rate below average for most other countries. Moreover, pension fund administrators are not passive investors, and they sometimes criticize shareholding companies for insufficient profits, bad management, and insufficient information. Occasionally, they have even cooperated with hedge funds in seeking new investments. Still, overall strategies are quite risk adverse.

The legal framework for pension funds and for life insurance companies – profit, non-profit or corporatist – is basically the same. It is included in a general law about financial business (*Lov om finansiel virksomhed*, LBK 1413, December 2007, § 115) which covers the whole financial sector, including banks. Most importantly, there are requirements regarding risk exposure and financial security (solvency). The proportion of assets that could be invested in shares has been increased. As pension funds and companies invest globally, restrictions concerning domestic investments have become rather meaningless.

Even though gains and losses fluctuate with the trends on financial markets, there have been no significant instances of major losses. In practice, pension funds tend to be more risk adverse than required. Individual capital pensions and rate pensions, however, are only subject to the regulation that a maximum of 20 per cent can be invested in one particular company. People who administer the asset themselves may invest all in high-risk shares if they want to. As regards the pension funds and companies, the main control by the state is exerted by the Danish Financial Supervisory Authority. Funds have to provide an annual report, and they are subject to rather strict rules that force them to have adequate reserves. Some pension funds had problems in 2001–3 when they were forced to sell shares around the time when the business cycle turned upwards. The pension funds have also experienced losses in 2008, although not comparable to the stock market development as most of the investments are in bonds. The problem in 2008 was quite unique: A sudden and temporary decline in prices of mortgage bonds (which are very safe equities in the Danish system). As guaranteed return rates are phased out, the problem of a forced sell-out of shares will be reduced. There has been a controlled sell-out of shares at an early stage of the 2008–9 crisis, but not been much panic-sales. Funds and companies have survived pretty well, although often with losses close to 10 per cent in 2008. Guarantee rules have been kept by exploiting buffers put aside for future bonuses etc., or by calculating an average rate of return over a longer span of years. In short, the pension funds have proved able to absorb quite substantial shocks in the international financial markets.

10. Outlook

If we make a simple extrapolation, the Danish pension system looks quite satisfactory both from an economic point of view and from a social policy perspective. In economic terms, the heavy emphasis on funding and the weakening of the 'generation contract' (as people co-finance their own retirement) is close to World Bank ideals (Andersen 2004; Green-Pedersen 2007; Ploug 2001). But in social policy terms, the system is different as the minima are unusually high. In spite of a high degree of privatization, at least in a formal sense, the reconciliation between economic and social policy goals seems highly satisfactory. However, the Danish pension system has not reached anything comparable to what Pierson terms a 'deep equilibrium' (Pierson 2004). Just to take the period 1998–2009, Special Pension savings was introduced, changed from actuarial fairness to equality, reversed to actuarial fairness, suspended, and (unintentionally) terminated. Contributions to labour market pensions have increased to a higher level than originally envisaged. A completely new scheme – the supplementary pension benefits – has been introduced. And tax rules regarding deductibility for contributions and taxation of current returns have been changed. Considering all these changes just within a decade, the pension system would seem unlikely to 'freeze' in the near future. Still, apart from the changing balance between basic pension and pension supplements in the 1993 tax reform and a tightening of means-testing of housing benefits in 1998, the 'old' institutions have remained stable.

It is always difficult to predict the future, but potential institutional dynamics need to be considered. In the first place, a smaller proportion of future pensioners will be depending on public pensions. According to some calculations (Economic Council 1998; Ministry of Economics and Business 2003; Regeringen 2000), about one half of the pensioners in the 2040s will only receive the basic amount of the people's pension, not the supplement. Paraphrasing Richard Titmuss' insight that 'services for the poor' inevitably ends up as 'poor services', such narrowing of the social support base must be a source of concern in public pensions too. This could also be the case from a value and framing perspective. Pensioners have traditionally been considered a 'deserving' group (van Oorschot 2000). However, as an increasing proportion of the elderly will have relatively high income, the political framing of discussions about pensioners could change. If pensioners no longer constitute a 'weak' group, there are fewer arguments to maintain special arrangements for pensioners.

There have been suggestions that the basic amount of the people's pension should also be means tested, but mainly from 'outsiders' in various parties. It would be more tempting for critics to suggest that special treatment has become obsolete, and this holds in particular for preferential housing benefits. Special schemes for pensioners should be abolished, the argument would run – perhaps compensated by extra cash benefits for poor pensioners. Some proposals have exactly followed this logic: The Welfare Commission (Velfærdskommissionen 2006) suggested that preferential housing benefits should be abolished and replaced by higher supplementary pension benefits for poor pensioners. The problem is that this increase would have to be extraordinarily high in order to maintain the social minima for pensioners, and the proposal of the Commission only covered a small proportion of the losses. Another potential source of instability is the rather high composite marginal tax rate for pensioners which will affect more and more pensioners. Around 1990, governments focused a lot on such problems and modified the rules of means testing (Andersen 2000). It is likely that people will discover that their net return rate from pension savings is sometimes quite low. This could be a source of dissatisfaction, but outcomes are difficult to predict.

In principle, a heavily funded pension system is vulnerable to economic instability like accelerating inflation or financial crises. The inflation problem is inherent, but the financial crisis in 2008–9 indicates that the system is quite recession-proof. Among those who administer their capital and rate pensions themselves, some have experienced considerable losses, though most of these people have other pensions. The surveillance of pension funds and insurance companies is quite strict, resembling surveillance of banks, and the funds and companies normally exhibit a highly risk adverse behaviour.

With regards to social solidarity, there remains a gender problem. There is a unisex requirement *within* each individual pension fund, but not *between* them. The problem is that pension funds follow a gender-segregated labour market. As men tend to have shorter life expectancy, insufficient risk pooling between men and women is a fundamental drawback of the Danish pension system. Comparatively speaking, low-paid women are compensated very well by the high minima in the first pillar, but otherwise women to a large extent have to carry the expenses of higher life expectancy, longer parental leave, and slightly higher disability rates, *in addition* to the impact of wage inequality in a DC system. It would seem relatively easy to enforce a higher risk sharing through legislation, but this has never been a political issue. Rather, public debate has revolved around the issue of women's inadequate knowledge and neglect of their *individual* pension problems. This is one of the main weaknesses of the Danish system. The strength is that it will remain economically sustainable, and that it has managed to combine the classical ideals of poverty alleviation and citizenship with the ideals of income replacement by simply layering labour market pensions on top of the state protection system.

Bibliography

Andersen, J. G. (2000). 'Welfare Crisis and Beyond: Danish Welfare Policies in the 1980s and 1990s', in S. Kuhnle (ed.), *Survival of the European Welfare State*. London: Routledge, 69–87.

——(2004). 'Pensionsbomber og Pensionsreformer. Danmark som Rollemodel'. *Social Kritik*, 94: 24–45.

——(2007a). 'Ældrepolitikken og velfærdsstatens økonomiske udfordringer. Tilbage-trækning, pension og ældreservice i Danmark'. *CCWS Working Paper* 47.

——(2007b). 'Conceptualizing Welfare State Change. The "Dependent Variable Problem" Writ Large'. *CCWS Working Paper* 51.

Andersen, M. B., and Kristiansen, J. (2009). *Arbejdsmarkedspension*. Copenhagen: Jurist- og økonomforbundets Forlag.

Arbejdsmarkedspensionsudvalget (1988). *Delrapport I fra underudvalg a.* Copenhagen: Arbejdsmarkedspensionsudvalget.

Bertolt, O., Christiansen, E., and Hansen, P. (1955). *En bygning vi rejser. Den politiske arbejderbevægelses historie i Danmark, vol. 1.* Copenhagen: Fremad.

Betænkning no. 1245 (1993). *Betænkning om pensionsoverførsler*, Feb. 1993. Copenhagen: Ministry of Industry.

Betænkning no. 1466 (2005). *Ægtefællers pensionsrettigheder*. Copenhagen: Familiestyrelsen.

Brønnum-Hansen H. and Baadsgaard, M. (2008). 'Increase in Social Inequality in Health Expectancy in Denmark'. *Scandinavian Journal of Public Health*, 36/1: 44–51.

Bruus, P. (2004). 'Om den "Lille" Socialreform i 1920 'erne', in N. Ploug, I. Henriksen and N. Kærgård (eds.), *Den danske velfærdsstats historie*. Copenhagen: Socialforskningsinstituttet. Publ. 2004: 18, 70–89.

Cirkulære om anvendelse af tjenestemandsansættelser i staten og folkekirken. No. 210, 11.12.2000.

Due, J., and Madsen, J. S. (2003). *Fra magtkamp til konsensus. Arbejdsmarkedspensionerne og den danske model.* Copenhagen: Jurist- og Økonomforbundets Forlag.

Economic Council (1998). *Dansk Økonomi. Efteråret 1998*. Copenhagen: Det Økonomiske Råd.

——(2005). *Dansk Økonomi. Juni 2005.* Copenhagen: Det Økonomiske Råd.

Green-Pedersen, C. (2007). 'Denmark: A "World Bank" Pension System', in E. M. Immergut, K. M. Andersen and I. Schulze (eds.), *The Handbook of Western European Pension Politics*. Oxford: Oxford University Press, 454–95.

Henriksen, J. P., Kampmann, P., and Rasmussen, J. (1987). 'Subsidiering og Beskatning af Pensionsopsparing'. *Arbejdspapir 16*. Copenhagen: Department of Sociology, University of Copenhagen.

Johansen, S. (1996). *Arbejdsmarkedspension. Historie, status, problemer.* Rungsted: Forsikringshøjskolens Forlag.

Jørgensen, M. (2007). *Danskernes pensionsopsparinger. En deskriptiv analyse.* Copenhagen: Socialforskningsinstituttet. Publ. 2007: 21.

Korpi, W. (2002). *Velfærdsstat og socialt medborgerskab. Danmark i et komparativt perspektiv, 1930–1995.* Aarhus: Magtudredningen.

Kristiansen, J. (2005). 'Arbejdsmarkedspension i arbejds- og forsikringsretligt perspektiv', *Ugeskrift for Retsvæsen*, 139/2005B: 271–80.

Larsen, C. A., and Andersen, J. G. (2004). *Magten på Borgen.* Aarhus: Aarhus University Press.

LO (1985). *Forslag til en samlet pensionsreform.* Copenhagen: Landsorganisationen i Danmark.

Ministry of Economics and Business (2005). *Pensionsopsparingen i Danmark. Økonomisk Tema 2/2005.* Copenhagen: Ministry of Economics & Business.

Ministry of Economics and Business, Ministry of Employment, Ministry of Finance and Ministry of Taxation (2003). *Større valgfrihed i pensionsopsparingen.* Copenhagen: Ministry of Economics & Business/Schultz.

Ministry of Finance (1984). *Budgetredegørelse 1984.* Copenhagen: Ministry of Finance.

——(1997). *Danmark 2005. April 1997.* Copenhagen: Ministry of Finance.

——(1998). *Danmark 2005. Danmark som foregangsland.* Copenhagen: Ministry of Finance.

——(2006a). *Økonomisk redegørelse. December 2006.* Copenhagen: Ministry of Finance.

——(2006b). *Forslag til Finanslov 2007.* Copenhagen: Ministry of Finance.

——(2008). *Aftaler om finansloven for 2008. Marts 2008.* Copenhagen: Ministry of Finance.

Ministry of Labour, Ministry of Business, Ministry of Finance, Ministry of Social Affairs, Ministry of State, Ministry of Economics (1995). *Pensionssystemet og fremtidens forsørgerbyrde.* Copenhagen: Ministry of Finance/Schultz.

Ministry of Social Affairs, Ministry of Finance, Ministry of Economics and Business, Ministry of Employment (2002). *National strategirapport om det danske pensionssystem, 2002.* Copenhagen: Ministry of Social Affairs.

Ministry of Social Affairs, Ministry of Economics and Business, Ministry of the Interior and health, Ministry of Taxation, and Ministry of Finance (2003). *Ældres økonomiske vilkår.* Copenhagen: Ministry of Finance.

Morgenavisen Jyllands-Posten 3.9.1986.

OECD (2009). *OECD Private Pension Outlook 2008.* Paris: OECD.

Pedersen, A. W. (1999). *The Taming of Inequality in Retirement. A Comparative Study of Pension Policy Outcomes,* Oslo: Fafo-report, 317.

——and Finseraas, H. (2009). 'Towards a European Convergence in Pension Policy Outputs? Evidence from the OMC on Pensions', in R. Ervik, N. Kildal and E. Nilssen (eds.), *The Role of International Organizations in Social Policy Ideas, Actors and Impact.* Edgar Elgar, 190–211.

Pensionsmarkedsrådet (2007). *Pensionsmarkedsrådets rapport om restgruppeanalyser.* Copenhagen: Pensionsmarkedsrådet.

Petersen, J. H. (1985). *Den danske alderdomsforsørgelseslovgivnings udvikling. Oprindelsen.* Odense: Odense University Press.

——(2001). 'Hen til kommoden og tilbaws igen. Et bidrag om socialpolitikkens historie', in Socialministeriet, *Festskrift i anledning af Socialministeriets 75 års jubilæum 2001*. Copenhagen: Ministry of Social Affairs, 9–59.

——(2006). *Den danske lovgivning om alderdomsforsørgelse II 1891–1933. Fra skøn til ret*. Odense: Southern Denmark University Press.

Pierson, P. (2004). *Politics in Time. History, Institutions and Social Analysis*. Princeton: Princeton University Press.

Ploug, N. (2001). 'Det danska ålderspensionssystemet – ful ankunge eller vacker svan?', in J. Palme (red.), *Private och offentliga pensionsreformer i Norden – slut på folkpensionsmodellen?* Stockholm: Pensionsforum, 10–32.

Rasmussen, H. K. (1996). 'Medborgerskabets Standhaftighed?'. MA Dissertation, Department of Political Science, Aarhus University.

Regeringen (2000). *Et bæredygtigt pensionssystem*. Copenhagen: Økonomiministeriet / Schultz.

——(2001). *En holdbar fremtid – Danmark 2010*. Copenhagen: Ministry of Finance/ Schultz.

——(2005). *National Strategy Report on the Danish Pension System*. Brusells: European Union (www.ec.europa.eu/employment_social).

Scheuer, S., and Madsen, M. (2000). 'Mod en ny balance mellem kollektivisme og individualisme: ændringer i overenskomstdækning og i udbredelsen af ansættelsesbeviser', in LO, *Ansættelses- og organisationsforhold 2000*. Copenhagen: LO, 5–52.

van Oorschot, W. (2000). 'Who should Get What, and Why? On Deservingness Criteria and the Conditionality of Solidarity among the Public'. *Policy and Politics*, 28/1: 33–49.

Velfærdskommissionen (2006). *Fremtidens velfærd – vores valg*. Copenhagen: Velfærdskommissionen.

Vesterø-Jensen, C. (1985). *Det tvedelte pensionssystem*. Roskilde: Forlaget Samfundsoekonomi og Planlægning.

World Bank (1994). *Averting the Old Age Crisis. Policies to Protect the Old and Promote Growth*. Oxford: Oxford University Press.

8

Finland: From Statutory Pension Dominance towards Voluntary Private Schemes

Olli Kangas and Päivi Luna

1. Introduction

The story of the public–private mix in Finnish pension policy could be a very short one. There is a mandatory earnings-related pension scheme for the employed and a national pension scheme that guarantees basic security for those who, for some reason, do not have any pension income or whose employment pension is too low to satisfy the minimum income standard. End of the story! But the public–private mix is more complicated. The Finnish pension system is a hybrid: one could argue that 95 per cent of pension expenditure are from the public purse and belong to the first tier, but one also could argue that second-tier occupational schemes comprise of 90 per cent of all expenditure. The crucial issue is how we classify employment-related pensions that are legislated and cover the total labour force, yet they are decentralized and run by private pension insurance companies and are administered by the social partners.

This hybrid character of Finnish pensions has caused much confusion internationally. When compiling statistics on social transfers, the OECD traditionally excluded the Finnish private sector employment pensions but has included them more recently due to their mandatory nature. Moreover, the European Union's classification has not merely attracted academic interest but has major practical and political consequences. According to EU legislation, private insurance should be open to foreign competition, thus if the EU regards the Finnish employment-related pensions as belonging to the private pillar then, in principle, any foreign insurance company could start selling such pensions in Finland. In their EU entry negotiations, the Finnish government referred to the special nature of these pensions and argued that they are genuine social insurance schemes according to EU regulation (EEC 1408/71 Regulation) and therefore they should remain under national jurisdiction and need not be opened to market-based competition. For the time, there is a special clause stating that the Life Insurance Directive is not applied to these employment-related pensions which are run by private insurance companies. If the EU were to treat the Finnish employment-related pensions as second-pillar pensions, it would change pension policymaking in Finland considerably.

The story of the Finnish pension systems could thus be told in two different ways: either it is the story of a country with massive occupational pensions, or a tale of a predominately public pension system. In this chapter, we understand these Finnish pensions in a blurred grey-zone between the public first pillar (due to the statutory mandate) and the second occupational pillar (due to its reliance on partly funded private insurances). Leaving aside the classification question, there are various reasons for the dominance of the statutory schemes and for the lack of contractual non-statutory pensions typical of occupational pensions. First, Finnish earnings-related pensions have no ceilings in respect to contribution or benefits. The principle to calculate pensions on the basis of final salary combined with total earnings-relatedness was beneficial for high-income earners. Therefore, these groups had no incentives to demand alternative occupational pension schemes to make up for relative losses in income replacement as was the case in countries with pension ceilings. Second, in the early 1960s, when employment-related pensions were legislated, occupational pensions provided by pre-existing pension funds and pension trusts were utilized to provide the newly statutory employment-related pensions, this diminished the institutional incentives for any additional benefits as the would-be private insurance carriers were merged into the statutory schemes. Third, the Finnish employment-related pensions are decentralized and run by private pension insurance companies or foundations that are administered by the social partners. Thus, there is a strong element of corporatism in the Finnish pension design. Since the social partners have been the 'owners' of these statutory schemes, they have demanded improvements in pension security through 'their' own schemes, not via non-statutory occupational schemes as in many other countries. In sum, the Finnish story is about a hybrid system combining statutory and private features that effectively blocked the expansion of occupational pensions based on labour market agreements and purely individual schemes. However, this picture is rapidly changing. After the description of the statutory part of the pension design, we focus on the emergence of voluntary occupational and individual pensions and the reasons for the recent expansion of the second- and third-pillar solutions.

Part I: The evolution of the public–private pension mix

2. The main features of the pension system

In Finland, basic universal pensions (national pensions, NP) have been responsible for poverty alleviation. Up to the 1980s, the tax-financed NP was the most important part in the pension design but gradually second-tier (employment-related statutory) pensions, introduced in the early 1960s, began to grow in importance. Today, the NP guarantees pensions to very old women without any work history due to family responsibilities, and to disabled people with early work-incapacity who were prevented from accumulating sufficient employment-related pensions. For the other pensioners, employment-related pensions constitute the main source of old age security.

Finnish employment-related pensions are legislated since the 1960s but they are occupationally decentralized. There are two major public sector schemes: one for state employees (VEL) and one for municipal employees (KvTEL), while there used to be a greater diversity among the private sector schemes as short-term (LEL) and long-term employees (TEL) and self-employed (YEL) and farmers (MyEL) used to have their own programmes. In addition to these main private sector schemes, some special groups (e.g. artists (TaeL), seamen (MEL)) had their own arrangements. In the beginning of 2007 the TEL, LEL, and TaeL systems were merged together under the Employee's Pension Act (TyEL). While there were 165 insurance carriers in 1970, thirty years later there are forty-seven insurance carriers left: private pension insurance companies (seven), pension trusts (thirty), pension funds (eight), or special funds for farmers and for seamen.

In the main private sector pensions (TyEL), there is a decentralized administration, with certain principles of cooperation in an emergency. The administrative bodies of the biggest pension insurance companies consist of the representatives of the employer federations, trade unions, and business in general. Although separately managed and capitalized, the individual insurers operate on common principles and there is a central organization, Finnish Centre for Pensions (ETK), that coordinates the activities of the individual insurers and keeps records on the employees' work histories used for benefit calculations. The Ministry of Social Affairs supervises activities of the TyEL, while the Ministry of Finance looks after the state's pension system VEL, and Ministry of Interior has the final responsibility for the municipal KvTEL pensions. When it comes to the risk-sharing, the companies have joint responsibilities. If a company goes bankrupt, the remaining companies are jointly liable for the payment of pensions from that company. Pensions are partly financed by the employer who pays 17.7 per cent of the payroll, while employees contribute 4.7–6.0 per cent of their earnings depending on their age. The pension contribution for the self-employed is 21 per cent. The pension amount depends on the income insured. TyEL pensions are partially pay-as-you-go (PAYG) as most public pensions, but also partially funded as many private pensions abroad. The PAYG part consumes 70 per cent of revenues and the rest is funded for future liabilities.

Despite the corporatist and decentralized funding, benefits paid from these different schemes are, by and large, the same due to the severely legislated regulation, thus only the administration and insurance carriers differ. Furthermore, the Finnish employment-related pension system is one of the very few schemes in the world that has no income ceilings for benefit purposes, which satisfies the needs of high-income earners. Consequently, high-income earners have had no particular incentive to negotiate on collective occupational schemes on top of statutory programmes as has been the case in countries with pension ceilings. For the same reasons, individual pension policies have not been popular either. Therefore, there are mainly statutory pensions in Finland, that is national pensions safeguarding basic security for those outside the labour force (first pillar), and employment-related pensions for the employed (classified as both first and second pillar, indicating the blurred boundaries, see Figure 8.1).

The pure second-pillar pensions mainly consist of 'supplementary TEL pensions' that employers subscribed to in the 1960s and 1970s for those working generations which, due to their age, had no possibilities to earn full benefits. Supplementary TEL pensions are, like TyEL pensions, partially funded and follow the defined-benefit (DB) principle. Today, as the TyEL system is fully mature and all subsequent generations can in principle accumulate full pensions, there is no need for these additional benefits. Therefore, in the 2000s no new policies have been underwritten and the schemes are gradually winding up (10 per cent of the employees are still covered) as are the pension funds that were set up for them. However, individual pension policies and individual (or group) pensions subscribed by the employer for high-skilled professionals and managers are growing and their coverage exceeds additional pensions. Most of these second-pillar schemes apply the DB principle, though in recent years the amount of new defined-contribution (DC) plans has been growing.

3. The strong corporatist traits of the Finnish pension system

The specific structure of the Finnish pension system is rooted in the political history of social policymaking. Comparatively, Finland has been a latecomer in the field of social policy in Europe, particularly in respect to social insurance (Alber 1982; Alestalo et al. 1985). However, chronological tardiness was compensated by broader extension of the reforms, thus Finland came to develop a universal model of social protection earlier than most other European countries (Kangas and Palme 2005). The explanation for this pattern lies in the peculiar

	First pillar (basic pensions)	Second pillar (earnings-related pensions)						Third pillar (individual policies)
Individual policies								Tax-subsidized individual pension policies (*ca.* 775,000; 15% of labour force)
Third tier (topping up)		Supplementary TEL pensions (closed in 2000; coverage less than 10% of employees) Group pensions, coverage less than 20%						
Second tier (income maintenance)		TyEL: private sector employees	KvTEL: municipal employees	VEL: state employees	YEL: self-employed	MYEL: farmers	OTHER: Church, artists, Åland, seamen (MEL)	
First tier (poverty alleviation)	Universal national pensions (NP); since 1996 NP, tested against pension income from legislated pensions; financed by revenues from taxes.							

Figure 8.1 Pillars and tiers of Finnish pensions

Source: Adapted from synopsis in Kangas (2007).

interaction of structural factors, in particular a significant rural population and relatively small urban/industrial communities, and political factors, in particular a strong agrarian party and a divided political left, inhibiting the development of social insurance until the 1960s.

The struggle over the Finnish welfare state was between the two main political forces, the Social Democrats (SDP) and the Agrarian Party (*ML*, and since 1966 the *Centre*). On the Social Democratic agenda, adequate compensation for income loss was given priority and the concern was with insurance for workers and not particularly with other socio-economic groups. The agrarian party agenda preferred universal flat-rate benefits covering the entire population, including unpaid agricultural family workers and housewives, and providing flat-rate benefits, was more preferable for the rural population, who were still living in a subsistence economy (Alestalo et al. 1985).

The Finnish political left was divided into two competing parties: in addition to the SDP there was a rather strong Communist party that often adhered to the Agrarian's priorities (Pesonen and Riihinen 2002). Up to the late 1950s, the Agrarians had an upper hand in Finnish politics, thus shaping also Finnish social policy. From the late 1950s onwards, the emphasis shifted towards industrial workers, more generally speaking employees' interests. Political dualism is reflected in the institutional set up of the Finnish income transfer system. All major basic security benefits are administered mainly by the National Social Insurance Institution (Kela), while all employment-related benefits – with the exception of sickness insurance which is under Kela – are organized via the labour market. Hence, the Finnish institutional design is characterized by strong dualism, that is, the insider–outsider divide and elements of corporatism. Corporatism has been fortified by centralized wage negotiations between the Employer Federation representing enterprises and the Central Organization of Trade Unions.[1] As a rule, these income policy agreements have included 'social packages' where the state, employer, and employee organizations have agreed upon social policy issues including pensions, occupational health care, and holidays (Kangas 2007). Since the 1990s, the Employer Federation has expressed its willingness to abandon centralized negotiations and conduct decentralized wage agreements which presumably will have consequences for pension policy, increasing the likelihood of enterprise and sectorwide occupational pensions.

---

[1] In Finland, almost 80 per cent of employees are organized in trade unions (Pesonen and Riihinen 2002: 86–96). There are three main labour union confederations: the blue-collar SAK with its 1.1 million members, the white-collar STTK with its 0.6 million members, and the AKAVA for academic employees (0.4 million members). The employers' interests are organized through the Confederation of Finnish Industries (EK) representing larger companies and the Federation of Finnish Enterprises for small companies.

4. The emergence of the public–private mix

4.1 National pensions: from a DC to PAYG system

The first national pension scheme was jointly established in 1937 by the Agrarians and the Social Democrats who formed the cabinet (see Table 8.1). The programme was genuinely an obligatory savings scheme. The insured had individual accounts in the Kela. Those who were covered by the insurance saved in their accounts and at the age of 65 years the claimant could receive benefits. Half of the employee's contribution was paid by the worker and the second half by the employer. The scheme was thus a full-fledged funded DC scheme. The accumulated national pension funds were used to build up Finland's basic infrastructure, mostly power stations and electric networks (Niemelä 1988: 73), providing a solid foundation for the subsequent rapid industrialization of the country. However, three problems of the strictly premium-based system soon became obvious. First, the majority of the elderly were excluded from benefits due to the long maturation period (forty years). Second, with all available supplements, the full national pension amounted to no more than 15 per cent of the average industrial wage (Kangas and Palme 1996). Third, the funded individual scheme required a stable economic environment and when this was not met in the post-war inflationary context, the system collapsed and the state had to take over.

The national pension system was completely revised in 1956. The coalition cabinet (Agrarians and Social Democrats) agreed to complement the universal basic pension by income-related pensions for those in employment, but in the final vote, the Agrarians decided to abandon the income-related part. As the bill was accepted in the form that the Agrarians desired, the funds – mainly paid by the employees and their employers – were distributed on a flat-rate basis to every citizen over 65 years of age. This decision benefited the rural population with no income at all or very little monetary income, and thus with minor contributions to the 1937 scheme. No wonder that the employee organizations criticized the 1956 law for 'confiscating' the employees' funds and redistributing them to the rural population. This dissatisfaction and mistrust with the Agrarians and the Kela had important ramifications for SDP and trade union strategies when employment-related pensions were at stake a couple of years later (Niemelä 1988; Salminen 1987, 1993).

The new National Pension Act of 1956 established universalism. The pension was divided into two separate parts: First, a universal basic amount payable unconditionally to everybody over 65 years of age who had resided in the country for five years before retirement. Second, an income-tested supplementary amount that was inversely related to the claimant's total remaining income. The 1956 scheme was based on the PAYG and DB principles. This allowed immediately paying out pensions, thus those older than 65 years of age de facto became automatically eligible for a national pension. The pension contribution

Table 8.1 Chronology of major pension reforms, Finland 1937–80

Year	Reform measures	Political context
1937	National pension	Agrarian–Liberal–SDP coalition; agrarian-bourgeois hegemony
	• Universal coverage	
	• A fully funded DC scheme	
	• Maturation period of forty years	
	• administered by a semi-public authority Kela (National pension institute)	
	• minimum security for all	
	• pension age 65	
1956	National pension reform	Agrarian–SDP coalition; agrarian interests
	• universal PAYG and DB	
	• citizenship-based basic amount	
	• income tested supplement amount	
1956	Seamen's pension act (MEL)	
	• employment-related pensions for seamen	
1961	TEL	Agrarian government refused to introduce the bill, Parliament (SDP + Conservatives) ruled out the government; SDP interests
	• employment-related pensions for private sector employees	
	• fully legislated, decentralized, run by private pension insurance companies	
	• DB, 40% of earnings after forty years in employment	
	• partially PAYG, partially funded	
	LEL	
	• employment-related pensions for employees in short-term contracts	
1964	KvTEL	Agrarian–Conservative government
	• homogenization of existing municipal pensions	
	• DB PAYG, 66% after thirty years in employment	
1966	VEL	Agrarian–Conservative government
	• DB PAYG pensions for state employees	
	• 66% after 30 years in employment	
1970	YEL and MyEL	Centre–SDP coalition cabinet
	• pensions for self-employed (YEL) and farmers (MyEL)	
1975	TEL reform	SDP–Centre coalition cabinet; SDP interests
	• accrual rate increased from 1% to 1.5% a year	
	• target level 60% after 40 years in employment	

Source: Kangas (2007).

was distributed between the employer (1 per cent of payroll) and the employee (1 per cent of taxable income). Since 1997, the insured no longer pay any national pension contributions, instead employers cover the cost (by 2008 the contribution rates were 0.8–3.9 per cent depending on the size of the firm). In the early 2009, the central organization for employers and the central organization for trade unions agreed upon the 'social income policy package', stating that the Kela-contribution for all employers is 0.8 per cent and from the beginning of 2010 the employer contribution will be abolished. A bit later the government legislated on the issue – once again a good example of the Finnish corporatist way of decision-making in important social policy issues: the social partners agree upon reforms and the government obeys.

4.2 Employment-related pensions: blurring boundaries between the public and private

Some employers provided occupational pension for their elderly workers as a gesture of gratitude for long and faithful service. Despite the rapid growth of occupational schemes towards the end of the 1950s, the actual coverage remained limited (about 20 per cent of employees) and selective (mainly white-collar workers in big firms). Moreover, there was also a portability problem. In case of changing employers, pension rights might be lost. In order to guarantee portability and to extend the coverage to include all blue-collar workers, the trade unions, supported by the SDP and the Conservatives (Kok), insisted on a statutory compulsory scheme. The employer federation proposed a legislated but decentralized scheme with private insurance companies as insurance carriers. For the employees, the most important issue was that of adequate old age security, while the organizational form was less important. Moreover, given the prior experience, the trade unions and the SDP were sceptical against a publicly administrated Kela-based scheme subject to political decision-making (Kangas 2007; Niemelä 1988; Salminen 1993).

The Agrarian government refused to draft a bill on employment pensions and therefore, the main parties in opposition – the SDP and Kok supported by some smaller parties – carried through the bill against the government. Accepted in 1961, the employment-related pensions act for the private sector employees (TEL) provided employers with many concessions since they were paying the whole insurance premium, which amounted to 5 per cent at the beginning of the 1960s (Salminen 1987). A special bipartite organization (Pension Security Institution, *ETK*) consisting of trade unions and the employer federation was established in order to coordinate the activities of the private companies running the insurance. This reform instigated a series of employment-related pension reforms: A separate scheme (*LEL*) was established for employees with short-term employment contracts (1961), and later on, farmers (1974) and other self-employed persons (1974) received their own programmes (*MyEL* and *YEL* respectively). Thus, coverage in the Finnish pension system followed stepwise sectoral and occupational lines.

The Finnish public sector employees at the state and municipal level had their own separate pension arrangements for almost a century, thus predating TEL. The introduction of the TEL system accentuated the need to codify and homogenize the divergent public sector schemes. The local sector pensions (*KvTEL*) run by a special insurance body, the Municipal Pension Institution (*KEVA*), was legislated in 1964, while a separate act on the state pension scheme (*VEL*) became effective two years later (Blomster 2004). Benefits in the public sector have traditionally been somewhat more generous compared to those in the private sector. Both KvTEL and VEL offered 66 per cent of the final salary after thirty years of employment. Hence, the occupational 'bonus' was built into the statutory schemes for the public sector employees and therefore, no additional occupational arrangements were developed (Kangas and Palme 1996).

4.3 Financing statutory employment pensions

The financing of pension schemes varies depending on the scheme. The self-employed MyEL and YEL are PAYG-schemes and the revenues consist of pension contributions collected from the insured and revenues from the state. The TEL scheme is largely PAYG (70 per cent) but also partially funded (30 per cent), the funding aims to mitigate the changes in the size of successive age cohorts. Both of the public sector programmes were initially financed totally on a PAYG basis but in order to confront the challenges arising from the anticipated demographic changes, a substantial degree of funding was introduced to the municipal KvTEL scheme in 1988, and to the VEL state pension scheme in 1990 (Vaittinen et al. 2007: 14). At present, the total pension fund (private plus public pensions) assets constitute about 75 per cent of GDP, which is one of the highest shares in the EU (http://www.tela.fi). Consequently, lots of economic and political power is concentrated in the hands of insurance companies and the social partners administering the funds, while the government and Parliament have often expressed their frustration over the 'lack of democracy' in employment-related pensions (Kangas 2007). In international terms, the funds accumulated by the Finnish legislated pensions are relatively large and needless to say, they are an important actor in the Finnish national economy. Therefore, the investment policy is of utmost importance not only for safeguarding the future pensions but also making the national economy to work smoothly.

The law on the investments of pension insurance companies stipulates that the 'funds must be invested profitably and safely'. In the beginning, priority in investments was given to national objects: The lion's share (one-third) of the investment was directed to Finnish industry, up to the 1980s. In addition to industry, funds were invested in building sector and real estates. Building sector has been an important investments object in the public sector pensions too.

This, in turn, helped to provide houses for those people who had to move from the countryside to the urban areas. In the municipal scheme, precisely as in the TEL, individual municipalities had a possibility to loan back money in reasonable terms from their own centralized municipal pension institute. In sum, both the private and public sector employment-related pension funds were more or less deliberately used in national investment objects to promote the national common good. The rapid industrialization that took place in Finland since the 1960s was greatly facilitated by the employment-related funds that offered capital for the industrial build-up (Kangas 2007; Salminen 1987).

However, the globalization of economies changed the situation and the underpinning commitments to national projects. Towards the end of the 1980s, credit markets were liberalized and pension insurances received more degrees of freedom to act. In addition, as responsible actors hoped for greater profits, they permitted policies that allowed for greater risks tolerance. Foreign investments seemed to offer better profits. As a consequence, the share of national investments dropped markedly. By the year 2000, almost 60 per cent of investments were still made in Finland. By 2008 the share was down to 40 per cent, while the economic crisis that hit the country temporarily increased the popularity of domestic investments (49 per cent by March 2009), but during the latter part of the year 2009, foreign investments have increased more rapidly than the domestic ones. Bonds and convertibles dominate the field in foreign investments (53 per cent in 2009, and 23 per cent for the domestic investments), while real estates are the main domestic object (28 per cent).[2]

Before opening the possibility for foreign investments there was a vivid discussion if it is a correct procedure to place Finnish pension money abroad. That discussion ended up by emphasizing that the main task of the pension scheme is to safeguard future pension promises, and since the foreign investments appeared to give better dividends, they were also regarded as more safe investments. In addition, there were arguments that the risk must be divided into different pools: profits in some pools balance deficit in some other pools.

5. The changing public–private mix

Up to the late 1980s, Finnish pension reforms introduced improvements to the existing statutory schemes and further circumscribed the need for additional occupational and personal pension arrangements. In 1985, means testing was practically abolished for the national pension and it became citizenship-based (Palme 1990). Part-time pensions were implemented within the private sector pensions in 1987 and a liberal early-retirement option was introduced to public

---

[2] http://www.tela.fi/?pid=1181291056

sector pensions in 1989. The economic crisis of the 1990s totally reversed this development, unemployment and early retirement increased considerably. Subsequent pension reforms that were carried out in the 1990s and early 2000s introduced cuts and adjustments in the statutory pensions which opened new windows of opportunity for the second- and notably so for the third-pillar pensions.

The Centre–Conservative Aho government (1991–5) reacted to the economic crisis by increasing the age limit for early retirement from 55 to 58 years (1994), by introducing pension contributions by employees (from 1993), and by cutting off the occupational bonuses from the public sector schemes (from 1995). Previously, all the employment-related pensions had been financed by employer contributions but the 1993 reform made employees responsible for taking part in the financing. Employees' contribution rate was initially 3 per cent of their income. The contribution was deducted from the pensionable salary, resulting in a de facto cut in pensions. The homogenization of private and public sector schemes reduced the target level in public employees' pensions by 10 per cent (from 66 to 60 per cent) and increased the pension age from 63 to 65 years. Since all these reforms were cutting existing benefits, they potentially increased demand for policies supplementing statutory pension by additional private pension arrangements. However, due to the severe economic crisis, the negotiated occupational pathway was excluded and the demand for better income security was channelled through individual private insurance.

The subsequent Lipponen 'rainbow coalition' (SDP–Conservative–Green–Left) (1995–2003) continued reducing pension benefits. In 1995, the government lengthened the calculation period of pensionable wage from the last four to the last ten years in employment. Simultaneously, the universal basic amount was abolished and the whole NP became tested against income from other statutory pensions. Until the mid-1970s, the NP dominated with paying more than half of all pension expenditures. Today, the basic pension has lost its importance due to the maturation of employment-related statutory pensions and partly due to the pension–income testing in basic pensions (see Table 8.2).

In order to carry out a 'big pension reform', the Lipponen government gave a mandate to the social partners to draft a pension reform for the private sector TEL pensions since they financed and administered it and thus were better placed to reform it. Indeed, the role of social partners and pension experts was important, while the politicians played a minor role (Kangas 2007). Previously, each year in employment between 23 and 64 years of age was counted at an accrual rate of 1.5 per cent (for those who were older than 60 years, the rate was 2.5) so that the maximum pension of 60 per cent of final salary was attained in thirty-three to forty years in employment. According to the new TEL pension act, which became effective in 2005, workers can earn pension credits for each year in employment between 18 and 69 years of age. The accrual rate is progressive to discourage early retirement: from 18 to 52 years the rate is 1.5

Table 8.2 Chronology of pension reforms since the 1980s

Year	Reform measures	Political context
1993	Employee's pension contribution introduced	Centre–Conservative cabinet, deep economic crisis
1995	VEL and KvTEL homogenized to the TEL level	
1995	In employment-related pensions, the pension amount calculated on the basis of average income for the ten years in employment (previously the last four)	SDP–Conservative–Green–Left ('Rainbow coalition')
1996	Universal basic amount abolished from national pensions, NP totally tested against other legislated pensions	SDP–Conservative cabinet
2002	TEL pension reform	'Rainbow coalition'
	• target levels abolished	
	• accrual rate 1.5% for employees aged 18–52; 1.9% for 53–62; and 4.5% for 63–67	
	• Pension based on life-time income	
	• Flexible pension age 63–68	
	• Demographic coefficient introduced	
2004	KvTEL and VEL reforms	Centre–SDP coalition cabinet
	• benefits from the public sectors schemes became the same as those from TEL	
2006	TyEL reform	Centre–Conservative coalition cabinet
	• TEL, LEL and TaEL (pension scheme for artists) unified under one Act	

Sources: Kangas (2007); www.etk.fi

per cent, from 53 to 62 years it is raised to 1.9 per cent, and after that to 4.5 per cent. The final salary target level of 60 per cent was abolished. Whereas retirement is flexible between 63 and 68 years of age, early retirement was made less attractive by applying harsher qualifying conditions. A special formula adjusting pensions to the increased life expectancy was introduced, that is, if pensioners are living longer than anticipated, their pensions will be reduced automatically. Finally, the pension amount was calculated on the basis of income over the whole working career. The TEL pension reform was later copied to the public sector schemes and, from 2005, all major employment-related pension schemes have provided the same benefits. The homogenization was further fortified in 2007 by unifying TEL, LEL, and TaeL under one single pension act (TyEL).

Despite its corporatist traits and sectoral divisions, the Finnish pension system is compact and simple in its principles. Up until 1996, the universal basic pension was payable to all pensioners in addition to the statutory earnings-related old age insurance, while a supplementary national pension benefit was paid only to those with insufficient or no statutory insurance benefits (see Figure 8.2). In 1996, the basic amount was abolished, while the employment-related calculation was adopted as the basis for pension

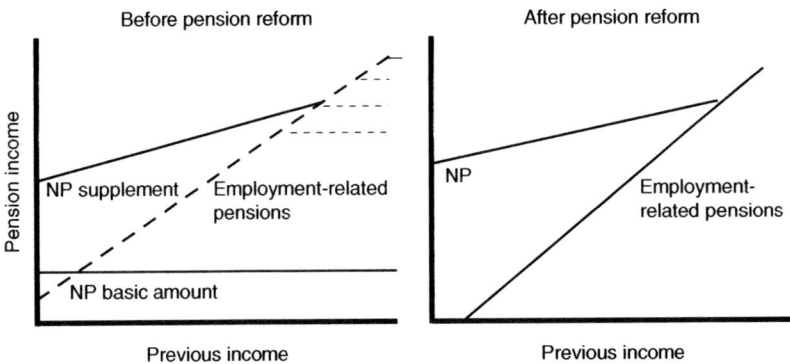

Figure 8.2 The structure of Finnish pension schemes before and after the 1996 reform

entitlements. In principle, the shift as such did not necessarily imply deterioration in benefits. However, in Finland there is a downward trend in the replacement rates of the basic national pension. While the full NP in 1970 was close to 50 per cent of the average income, it equals less that 35 per cent in 2008 and as a consequence, all those elderly who receive only NP have income below the 50 per cent poverty threshold (Kangas and Ritakallio 2008).

The existing occupational pensions were closely integrated into the statutory TEL scheme in two ways. First, the existing pension institutes could acquire responsibility for the running of the TEL scheme together with the private insurance companies. Second, these institutes were given the option of guaranteeing 'supplementary TEL benefits' (indicated by dotted lines in Figure 8.2) for those interim cohorts who, due to their age, had no possibility to accumulate full pensions. Supplementary pensions and the ordinary TEL benefits were coordinated according to different principles. The additional pension filled that gap between the actual pension and the target level of 60 per cent, which automatically included a decreasing trajectory for supplementary pensions, that is, the closer the actual pension is to the target level, the less room for additional arrangements.[3] The development is evident in Table 8.3.

At present, the third (personal pension) pillar is not that well developed. Up until the early 1960s, more than 1 million Finns had savings-based life insurance policies. This was a rudimentary trial to compensate for the lack of sufficient pension security (Kangas 1988). The introduction of employment-related pensions rapidly reversed the picture, and by the mid-1980s the private personal pension pillar was virtually non-existent in Finland again. However, this has changed in recent years.

---

[3] As a rule, most other countries follow a 'floating principle', that is, third-tier pensions float on top of second-tier pensions. Therefore, improvements in legislated pensions do not erode additional occupational pensions, as is the case in Finland.

Table 8.3 Proportional shares (%) of different pension schemes of total pension expenditure in Finland 1950–2005

Year	Total% of GDP	Share in pension expenditure							
		NP	Private sector	State	Municipal	Other	Special schemes and life annuities	Supplementary TEL pensions	Other occupational pensions
1950	1.8	12.0	0.0	30.2	1.0	0.3	55.3	0.0	1.0
1955	2.3	33.9	0.0	32.1	1.3	0.9	29.6	0.0	1.9
1960	3.8	56.1	0.0	21.9	2.5	0.6	14.5	0.0	4.4
1965	4.7	54.7	2.3	19.8	4.7	0.6	13.2	0.0	4.7
1970	6.4	48.9	9.9	19.3	7.1	0.8	9.8	0.3	3.9
1975	8.2	45.4	17.3	17.3	7.2	1.1	7.8	0.6	3.3
1980	9.5	37.7	26.2	16.6	7.8	1.3	6.5	1.0	3.0
1985	10.6	36.7	29.2	14.7	7.8	1.2	6.5	1.1	2.8
1990	10.7	29.4	35.4	15.3	9.1	1.3	5.8	1.2	2.5
1995	13.1	25.0	39.7	15.9	10.5	0.8	5.1	1.2	1.8
2000	10.8	18.9	44.4	16.6	12.1	0.9	4.4	1.2	1.4
2005	11.4	15.4	47.7	17.2	13.4	1.0	3.7	1.1	2.2

Source: KELA (1976: 23–5; 1996: 35–7; 2007: 38–41).

Part II: The governance of supplementary pensions

Second- and third-pillar pensions have a long history in Finland. The first act on pension funds was enacted as early as 1897, though the history of state and municipal pensions is even older, but the state employee pensions were not codified until 1924, and the municipal workers had to wait until the implementation of the KvTEL in 1964. A special law on pension foundations was enacted in 1955 and as a consequence, there was a rapid increase in private occupational and company-based schemes. However, the trade unions were not satisfied and demanded a statutory scheme, which was adopted (TEL) in 1961. The existing pension funds and trusts were institutionally merged into the TEL law framework to guarantee either ordinary TEL pensions (i.e. second tier of the public pillar) or supplementary TEL pensions (i.e. 'semi' second tier). This meant that virtually all of the institutional actors were included in running these statutory schemes, limiting their interest to expand activities beyond the public mandate in private occupational pensions.

The interim arrangements in supplementary TEL pensions included disability and unemployment pensions as well as survivors' benefits and burial grants. Taking out registered supplementary pension insurance was voluntary, but once they were active all activities were regulated by the law, for example supplementary benefits were totally indexed according to the TEL principles, the employee retained the right to the accrued supplementary pension also when the employment contract ended. As stated above, the entry to the supplementary TEL pension scheme has been closed. The proportion of various voluntary occupational schemes of the total pension payments has declined from 6 per cent in 1965 to 2 per cent in 2000. Thus, the main story is about the erosion of voluntary occupational schemes in Finland as these were crowded out by the publicly mandated employment-related occupational pensions.

In addition to group pension insurance, the Finns tried to compensate the lack of adequate social security by individual arrangements before the 1960s, but again the introduction of the TEL ended this development. There are lots of indications that the pendulum is turning back towards voluntary individual and occupational solutions again. There are various reasons for that. First, the public pension reforms described above have cut down the statutory pension promises. According to long-term projections, future statutory employment-related pensions will amount to 35–50 per cent of the final salary provided that the claimant has worked for forty years (see Table 8.4; Lassila et al. 2007: 3; Taloussanomat 2008). However, the general expectation is that a sufficient pension should be equal to 65–70 per cent of final salary (FFFS 2008a); thus, significant additional benefits are needed to meet these expectations. Second, given the growing prosperity there is not only willingness but also more possibilities to rely on private insurance markets to safeguard the achieved

Table 8.4 Pensions (% of final salary) for an individual born in 1987[a]

Length of the career	Average salary (AWI)	Salary (starting 70%, ending 105% AWI)	Salary (starting 100%, ending 200% AWI)
10 years	10.4	8.9	5.8
20 years	21.0	19.1	13.1
30 years	32.0	30.0	22.0
40 years	46.1	44.1	35.3
43 years	55.7	53.8	45.0

Note: [a] The first cohort that will bear the full effect of the new pension system of 2005.
Source: Taloussanomat (2008).

standard of living. The need for mandatory supplementary pensions has been channelled mainly through the third pillar, since pension solutions in the second pillar have been underdeveloped for the reasons described above. Third, there is growing competition among employers for skilled employees, thus occupational pensions tailored to certain groups may play an important role as fringe benefits.

In the early 2000s, the number of group pension policies grew by more than 30 per cent a year, and the premiums paid for those collective policies have increased. In sum, there is room for and, consequently, a boom of private pensions in Finland, taking three forms: collective employer-based group insurance policies, pension policies subscribed by the employer to an individual employee, and individual policies taken by the insured themselves. Thus, employers may provide supplementary pensions for their employees through group pension policy, individual pension insurance, or both. Such benefits are classified to belong to second-pillar pensions (see Table 8.4).

6. Who is covered?

Supplementary occupational pensions were designed for the interim generations to faster accumulate full TEL pensions. In the beginning of the TEL system, such additional pensions were rather popular, but with the maturation of the statutory scheme the importance of supplementary benefits faded away. In the mid-1970s, about 20 per cent of employees were covered by these supplementary occupational schemes, but the share was close to 10 per cent in 2000 (Kangas and Palme 1996: 223), when they were closed to new entrants in 2000, while those already covered maintain their entitlement and employers may still continue contributing.

In 2009, *circa* 31,000 employees were insured in company pension funds plus another 11,000 in sectorwide pension funds. The company pension funds that control the majority of the overall market operate on behalf of groups of employees in different firms, depending on the sector, while pension funds are linked to individual companies. It was hoped that company pension funds would assume a larger part once legislation was changed to allow pension assets to leave insurance companies for a fund, but in many cases the reverse has happened and collective supplementary pension insurance policies are taken through life insurance companies. These supplementary schemes are based on voluntary agreements; they are fully funded DB or DC schemes.

6.1 Second pillar: supplementary group insurance

Access to occupational supplementary pension schemes is linked to employment, but the supplementary second pillar may also include individual provision, that is, the employer can subscribe a policy for an individual worker. In 2008, there were 130,000 such employer-based individual policies. The market for voluntary employee benefits is expanding rapidly and the number of employees covered increases by 20 per cent every year.

Supplementary group pension insurance is always collective. In order to be insured under a group pension policy, certain requirements must be fulfilled. The law on group insurance stipulates that two persons may form a group, but the group covered must be formed according to objective criteria: for example, on the basis of the employee's position, occupation, sector, date of commencement of employment, date of birth, or other pension provision arranged by the employer. The insured group plan can be closed, in which case new employees may no longer be included in the insurance policy. If the employer wants to use subjective criteria, then individual pension insurance must be used.

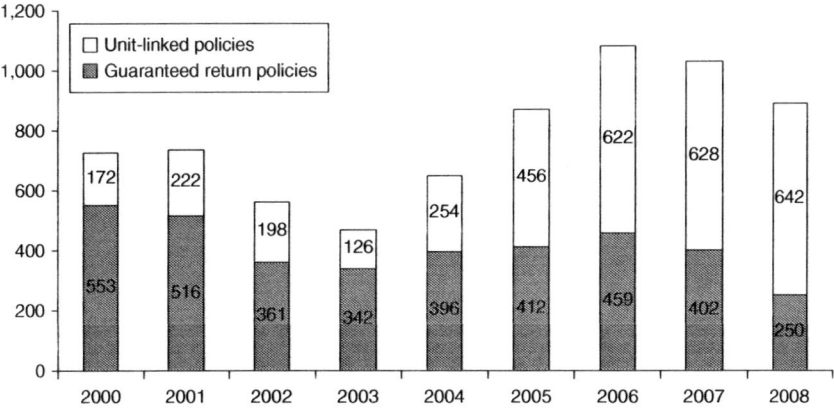

Figure 8.3 Number of new group pension policies, Finland 2000–8
Source: FFFS (2009).

In 2005, there were more than 200,000 group pension policies in Finland, which means that about 10 per cent of all employees are covered. The development has been rapid. In the early 2000s, about 600 new group pension policies were subscribed every year, but about 1,000 policies were added in both 2006 and 2007 (see Figure 8.3), corresponding to about 15,000–20,000 new employees covered by these schemes in each year. Since the number of insured has been growing far more than the number of policies, supplementary group pensions are becoming increasingly common fringe benefits in companies. While guaranteed-return policies can be either DC or DB, unit-linked insurance is only DC. Thus, there seems to be a trend towards DC policies.

A complementary way of seeking answers to why employers are buying additional benefits and to whom these benefits are targeted is to rely on surveys conducted among employers. According to a survey done in 2006, 19 per cent of the private-sector employers had arranged supplementary pensions for their employees and 14 per cent of employers offered a group supplementary pension that covered almost all employees in the firm (Taloustutkimus 2007). Usually, big enterprises are forerunners in company-based benefits. However, a representative survey targeted to small- and medium-sized enterprises (5–250 employees) in industry, trade, services, and construction shows that almost every third (29 per cent) employer regarded supplementary pension as an important way to commit workers to their employer, and consequently, as many as 70 per cent of the employers interviewed had arranged supplementary pensions to at least one key person, such as senior managers and high-skilled specialists, while 15 per cent of the surveyed companies had a pension plan for all workers. There was some variation in the prevalence of this kind of full-coverage benefits – the leading sector with full coverage was retail trade

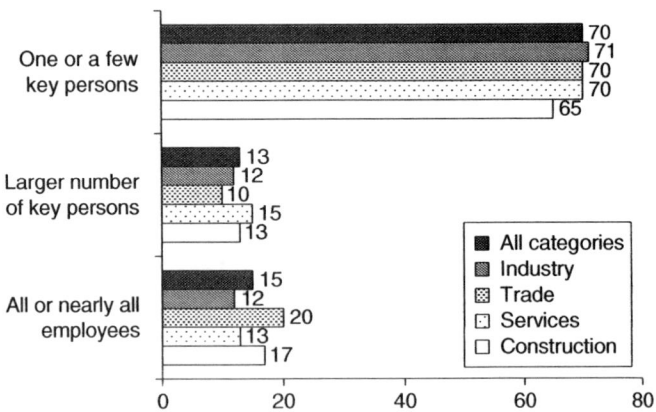

Figure 8.4 Coverage of group pension policies (per cent), Finland 2007

Source: Taloustutkimus (2007).

(20 per cent), followed by construction where 17 per cent of companies had pension plans for all workers. In the other sectors, the coverage was somewhat more limited (see Figure 8.4).

6.2 Third pillar: individual private pensions

Private individual pension insurance is a product devised for supplementing statutory pension either to lower retirement age or to improve benefits or to do both. In principle, everyone has access to individual private pension, which – if not provided by the employer – is directly obtained through a life insurance company. With Finnish life insurance companies becoming increasingly owned by banks, individual pension insurance policies became more accessible for Finns since the mid-1990s as banks aggressively promote their insurance products to the customers. In 2007, 84 per cent of the number of personal pension policies was taken out by the individuals themselves, while the remaining 16 per cent was subscribed by the employer as a part of employment contracts. Benefits are determined by returns and longevity bonus, for example. how long the policyholder actually lives, to be paid out at an agreed retirement age. Pensions may be agreed for payout for a fixed period starting at a certain age or in life annuities. Pension policies are available as individual pension plans and group pension policies. The latter form is typical for some professional groups whose members could voluntarily join a programme with a discount in contributions specifically negotiated by the organization to its members. Tax incentives are given to third-pillar individual insurance policies. Tax deductions

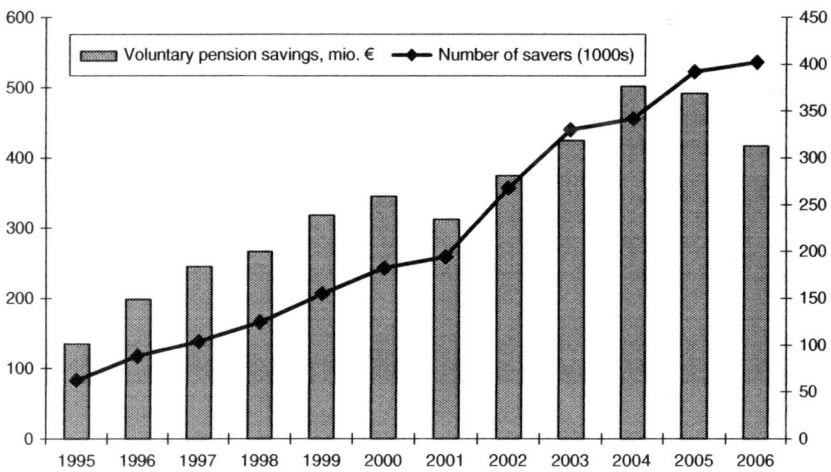

Figure 8.5 Total number of individual pensions plans, Finland 1995–2006

Note: Numbers based on tax returns.

Source: Harju (2008), FFFS (2008a).

are based on tax-deductible savings and taxable withdrawals. The saver must contribute to the saving plan at least for two years in order to get tax benefits.

The prevalence of private insurance policies has grown steadily and in an accelerating tempo in the early 2000s (see Figure 8.5). In the mid-1990s, the number of such policies was less than 100,000 but a decade later the number had already exceeded 400,000. After the turn of the millennium, there was a change in the trend: more and more policies were sold. 2004 was an exceptional year due to the tax reform that was planned for 2005 creating overall uncertainty regarding the tax treatment of private pension contributions. However, the recovery was rapid and the number of pension savers grew sharply, almost by 50,000 immediately after the 2005 reform (Harju 2008). In 2007 alone, the number of personal pension policies sold was more than 71,000. In many cases, the tax exemption promise is an important reason to subscribe individual pension policy: 51 per cent of policyholders say that the tax treatment is an important reason to obtain insurance (FFFS 2003).

It is hard to evaluate the actual coverage since some persons may have several policies. At the end of 2003, approximately 12 per cent of the population

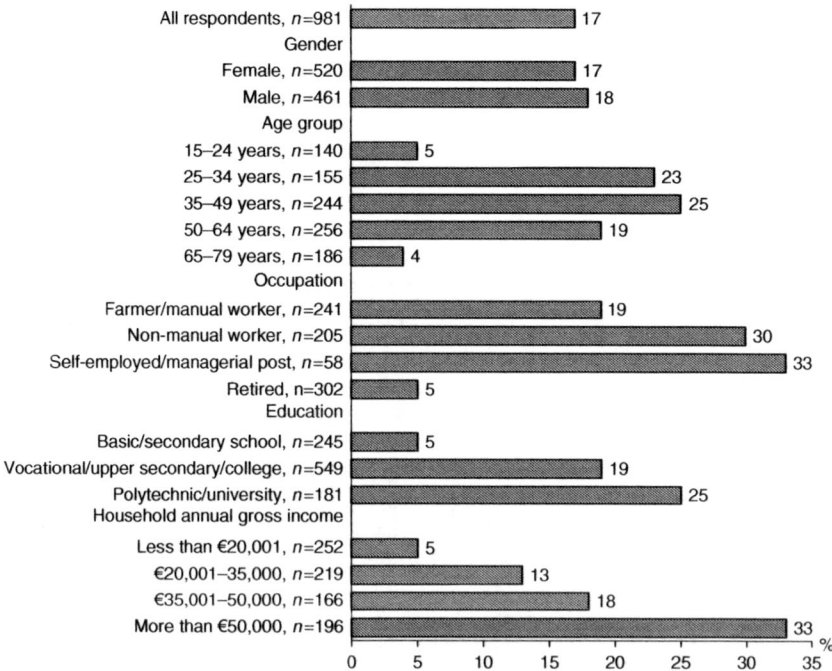

Figure 8.6 Coverage of individual pension policies (per cent) by socio-demographic categories, Finland 2006

Source: FFFS (2008*a*).

230

between 15 and 64 years of age were covered by private pension plans managed by Finnish insurance companies, while in 2008 the corresponding figure increased by 50 per cent (FFFS 2008a; Kuluttajatutkimus 2007).

There is no significant gender bias in coverage (see Figure 8.6) but, not surprisingly, the age of the claimant is of crucial importance. The average age has been declining (in 2002, roughly 30 per cent subscribers were under 35 years of age, whereas in 2006 the figure was 42 per cent) and as a result, the average monthly saving decreased from €100 to €75. There is a strong socio-economic bias in the coverage of private pensions: while 33 per cent in the highest income group had individual pension policy, only 5 per cent in the lowest income group had obtained insurance. Also educational attainment separates subscribers: 25 per cent with university and 5 per cent with basic education have obtained an extra pension. Of socio-economic groups, white-collar employees (30 per cent) and self-employed (33 per cent) are the most prone to subscribe an individual pension, whereas there are no significant gender differences. In the 2000s, 'democratization' has taken place resulting in an increasing number of the middle class paying into personal pensions (Määttänen 2006; Taloustutkimus 2008).

7. What kind of benefits?

In Finland, additional occupational pensions are typically undertaken to complement statutory pensions. The goal of these complementary group pension plans is either to improve the pension level or to lower the retirement age or to do both. Given the projections depicting decreasing replacement rates for coming generations, the improvement of pension benefits presumably will grow in significance. However, there are some other elements in the new pension design that may contradict this trajectory. The retirement age may be agreed to be lower than the statutory pensions retirement age (i.e. flexible 63–68 years of age). If the employee pays part of the contributions to a second-pillar or third-tier group pension plan, the lowest possible retirement age which is entitled to tax deductions is 60 years. The employee can retire earlier only if all the contributions have been paid by the employer. Pension benefits may be agreed for payment during a fixed period of time or, much less frequently, in annuities for life. In order to get tax benefits, policyholders must be at least 62 years of age before taking out the benefit. The benefits are determined on the basis of the accumulated funds (i.e. DC benefits).

In the Finnish life insurance markets, the majority of products are so-called hybrids: you may start with unit-link allocation and reallocate your savings to traditional guarantee-linked benefits later on. In 2007, 94 per cent of the new individual pension plans were typically unit-linked contracts. Since contributions are paid for a relatively long period (average of twenty-three years), the return is often tied to the initial performance of equity funds. Most pension policies include an option to change the targeted return from unit-linked to guaranteed return. The adjustment is typical and strongly recommended at the age of retirement or a few years before. The share of guaranteed return occupational group pension policies accounted for 97 per cent of all plans. Only in the recent years has the proportion of unit-link products increased.

Most of the old group pensions were DB plans, while as a rule all new plans are typically based on defined contributions (DC), though the share of DC schemes in the total portfolio is still rather marginal but rapidly increasing. DB is currently generally considered to be of a higher risk for companies, and DB schemes are largely confined to large and successful enterprises. Due to growing pension liabilities, many employers have shifted from DB to DC plans, thereby shifting retirement risk to individuals in general. This is not only characteristic of private schemes but applies to the statutory earnings-related pension system as well: the life expectancy coefficient, which aims to prevent a growth in pension expenditure as a result of the increased life expectancy of those aged 62 and older, will decrease the amount of old-age pensions starting in 2010 and thereafter.

The guaranteed-return pension insurance plans – in which the life insurer guarantees that a fixed bonus will be added to the sum insured each year – are bound to consumer price index throughout the duration of the policy. The unit-link pension insurance plan is an alternative to a conventional-with-profits policy (guarantee-linked): the value of the investments is mirrored in the price of units. About half of the group insurance plans have vested pension rights depending on the type and conditions of the contract made between the company and the employee, for instance it may depend on the length of the employment contract or it may be only partial, for instance, 50 per cent of the accrued pension rights. In case of job change or termination of employment prior to the foreseen period in the contract, the accumulated funds are either returned to the company or used to benefit other insured.

In respect to the proposed EU directive of vested rights (COM 2005), Proposal for a Directive of the European Parliament and of the Council on improving the portability of supplementary pension rights, which strives to improve the transferability of occupational pension rights both between and within the member states, the Finnish proposition was in line with the Commission's position. The suggestion was that pension rights have to be vested if the employment lasts more than two years. However, the Confederation of Finnish Industries' standpoint was to increase it to at least five years, since Finnish employers seek to provide voluntary occupational pensions to their employees in order to attract skilled labour and to compete with other possible employers. Thus, the individual employer is less interested in schemes that guarantee free portability as this would nullify the whole rationale of the human resource strategy. In contrast to many other EU countries, the vesting of pension rights has never been a major problem in Finland since the statutory pension system (e.g. TyEL) fully guarantees portability.

Persons covered by individual pension plans may start drawing benefits before the statutory pension age if they are disabled for work. If the insured has been unemployed for more than a year, he or she is entitled to the 'surrender value' of the plan, but these practices vary from insurer to insurer. Early retirement on account of disability or unemployment is usually possible only if the assets accrued under the plans are covered by life insurance. The retirement age that qualifies for tax benefits on personal pension plans has been increased several times. The lowest pension age was originally set at 55 years, but the age limit was raised to 58 years in 1992, and additionally to 60 years in 1999. The present limit of 62 years applies to pension plans taken out after summer 2004. The motivation for this increase was the ongoing discussion on policies to prolong working careers and to improve the sustainability of the pension system. Although private pensions were intended to help people retiring earlier, it was difficult to motivate such an option in a political climate that strongly emphasized longer working careers. Moreover, private pensions are mostly regulated via tax legislation that can also attach conditions. There were many changes in tax-deductibility and retirement age in the 1990s. Despite changes in tax-benefits (2004) and a consequent drop in sales in 2004 (from 87,000 to 44,000 plans), voluntary private pensions began to recover.

8. Who pays?

National pensions used to be paid by employer contributions and taxes, but this changed in the spring of 2009 when the social partners agreed that employers' national pension contribution will be abolished and from 2010 the state alone will cover the full cost of basic pensions. The statutory occupational pension remains the most important part of retirement provision, with the average TyEL contribution amounting to 22.4 per cent (of which employees younger than 53 years contribute 4.7 per cent, older employees 6.0 per cent in 2010). In contrast, the payments for voluntary private pensions are more varied. As a rule, individual and collective insurance plans have flexible contributions, and thus higher or lower contributions may be paid than agreed in the plans. In collective group insurance plans, the sums insured vary according to the position of the insured in the company hierarchy. Both the employee and employer may pay contributions. Contributions paid to group pension plans by the employer represent fully tax-deductible expenses for the firm without any maximum amount of the kind applied to personal pension plans, as long as the level of the supplementary pension cover provided is considered reasonable by the tax authority. Employers may also deduct costs for life and disability insurance policies that are often included in pension plans. The tax treatment of supplementary pensions arranged by the employer is the same as that of statutory pensions provided that certain restrictions related to the retirement age are complied with.

The employee can pay a share of group pension contributions but this may not exceed half of the total annual contributions. In the early days of registered supplementary pension insurance, this parity contribution sharing was common in Finland (Pentikäinen 1975). More recent data suggest that contributions paid by employees account for only a few per cent of the total premiums of group pensions, indicating that employers are the main financier of occupational plans (FFFS 2008*b*). The insured contributions are deductible in income taxation up to 5 per cent of the salary up to €5,000 a year (in 2008). However, tax deductibility for an occupational plan does not affect the right to deduct contributions paid to the insured's personal pension plan, whereas occupational individual pension insurance sponsored by the employer does have an effect on the insured's possible private self-acquired voluntary pension plans.

Group pension contributions are entirely deductible expenses for the company, and in contrast to private personal pensions, annual pension contributions have no maximum amounts. The costs for life and disability insurance, which may be included in the insurance policy, are also deductible for the company. Group pension insurance contributions are not considered income for the employee. The subsequent occupational pension that will be paid to the retired will be taxed as normal personal income. Self-acquired voluntary pensions are taxed in the capital income taxation with a flat tax rate, and pension contributions can also be deducted up to a certain amount within the capital income taxation. However, individual pension plans taken out by employers for their employees continue to be covered by the income tax. If the contributions to these plans by the employer exceed a certain limit (€8,500 annually), the excess is treated as income for the employee. In 2004, personal pension plans were transferred from the income tax regime to capital gains taxation. The transfer meant that private pensions are taxed at a lower rate than previously: the capital tax rate is currently 28 per cent, whereas marginal tax rate on income was typically 47 per cent. Most probably, these various tax incentives will increase the popularity of personal and occupational benefits (Kari et al. 2006).

9. Who governs?

While the national pension system is run by the Finnish Social Insurance Institution (Kela), which is under parliamentary supervision, TyEL pension carriers are pension companies where the administrative board consists of representatives of the employee and employer organizations supplemented by insurance and other business experts. Usually the social partners have equal number of board members and their combined number equals the number of experts. The Insurance Supervisory Authority supervises employment pension providers and pension funds by Finnish insurance companies. The Insurance Supervisory Authority, in particular, supervises the solvency of the insurers and pension providers. In addition to domestic life insurance companies, some foreign life insurance companies offer voluntary pensions in Finland. If the policy is underwritten by a foreign company, the supervisor is the authority of the foreign country where that life insurance company is based. The voluntary group pension insurance provided by employers may be arranged with a sector-wide pension fund or with a company pension fund or as collective supple-mentary pension insurance with a life insurance company. It may also be based on the company's own pension regulation, in which case it is not an insurance policy but the employer is committed to paying pensions out of the company's running budget to a defined group of persons (on the book reserves), though there is a risk of insolvency.

In 2009, the Finnish Financial Supervision Authority (FIN-FSA) and the Insurance Supervisory Authority were merged into one single national autho-rity, which supervises financial markets and those who participate in these markets, including banks, investment firms, fund management companies, and the stock exchange as well as other financial institutions. The duties of the new supervisory authority are essentially the same as those of the two existing supervisory authorities: to follow the economic soundness and solvency of companies. The authority is located in the premises of the Bank of Finland. The Ministry of Health and Social Affairs is responsible for legislative issues and presenting the new authority's matters in government. Though the new authority's duties are largely the same as those of the two existing supervisory authorities, there are some important changes. Previously, the supervision of the system was under the Ministry of Health and Social Affairs, whereas the FIN-FSA is under the governance of Ministry of Finance. Thus, the Ministry of Finance has taken a more important position in insurance business in Finland. When it comes to insolvency and potential problems with bankruptcy, there are no guarantees for individual pension policies, but in the statutory TyEl area the joint responsibility guarantees that if one insurance company goes bank-rupt the remaining companies have to cover the costs.

10. Outlook

Up to the 1990s, the history of the Finnish pension design has been a story of the gradual erosion of the importance of voluntary occupational and private arrangements to guarantee old age security. There are a number of reasons for this historical trajectory. One reason is linked to the structure of the pension regime. In Finland, all public and private employees as well as the self-employed are covered by statutory employment-related pensions. Pension rights are based on earnings or income and employment tenure. Since there have been no pension ceilings, the pension amount depends totally on the length of the working career and the pension income was calculated on the basis of final salary. This kind of design has been beneficial to those sectors of employees who usually are the most prone to go for supplementary solutions. The benefits have been adequate for middle- and high-income earners and they were less in need for occupational solutions to top up the relative loss of income as in countries with flat-rate pensions (e.g. Denmark and the Netherlands) or in countries with pension ceilings (e.g. Norway and Sweden). For those who for some reasons have had no possibility to accrue adequate employment-related pensions, national pension was granted on the basis of residence. In sum, the need for guaranteed income in old age has been covered by the statutory pension system. Furthermore, when employment-related pensions were implemented in the 1960s, the pre-existing occupational schemes were coordinated with the statutory pensions according to the 'difference principle': the occupational pension covers the difference between the actual pension level and the target level in the statutory scheme. The narrower the gap, the smaller the allowance for private benefits. Due to the maturation of the statutory systems, the gap is virtually closed, leaving no room for voluntary private pensions.

The landscape, however, is changing rapidly. On one hand, there are problems with the basic security. National pensions are lagging behind the overall income development in society, which may lead to improve basic security by additional insurance policies. Of course, those people who rely on national pensions seldom are among private insurance subscribers. On the other hand, pension reforms since the 1990s have gradually eroded previous pension promises. It had been forecasted that in future statutory employment-related pensions will amount to some 30–50 per cent of the final salary. This fact combined with the general expectation that pensions should comprise 60–70 per cent of final salary, leaving a gap that most probably will be made up by occupational and personal pension arrangements.

The Finnish employment-related pensions are administered by social partners. Since the social partners have been owners of the statutory schemes, they have channelled improvements in pension security through 'their' own schemes, not via various occupational schemes as in many other countries. Also this is changing. Employers are not necessarily as eager as previously in supporting the system, and if the predicted labour shortage will materialize occupational pension plans tailored for specific groups of employees offer new possibilities in the competition of skilled labour. The recent development of group pension schemes gives some evidence that this kind of trajectory is materializing. But not only employers but also employees may be eager to go for occupational pensions plans. If some strong trade unions regard that the statutory pension security has deteriorated beyond the acceptable minimum level, they may in their negotiations demand 'social packages' consisting of extra pensions. If this happens, it certainly would launch an avalanche of voluntary occupational schemes in Finland.

The number of pension savers grew rapidly over the course of several years. People are more eager and they have more monetary resources than previously to supplement their old age security by their own initiatives, and the banks and insurance business are cleverly using the falling pension promises from the statutory schemes to advertise and sell their products. The government took notice of this demand and carried out a new law initiative for long-term saving products in 2009. This new solution is a novel savings vehicle designed to supplement statutory pension benefits. It only applies to new plans beginning in 2010 – previous pension savers can continue to save on previous terms until 2016. A savings account must be created and the provider must invest the assets according to the consumer's wishes: a bank account, mutual fund, or insurance policy. The purpose of this new saving instrument is to increase competition in financial markets by increasing the variety of saving products that consumers can use for pension savings.

Tax benefits for capital gain apply not only to pension insurance but also to other saving or investment products, such as accounts, bonds, and funds within certain conditions. The argument being that there is a neutral tax-treatment for all saving products, not only private pension insurance, regardless of associated risks. In addition, consumers have the right to change from one instrument provider to another, which was not possible earlier. However, this proposal does not recognize the advantages of insurance products but forces them to be equalized with potentially less-secure products, for instance in terms of solvency. In addition, it lacks a solution for longevity risk by not encouraging a longer payout plan (currently ten years) thus not resolving certain problems such as increased health-care cost and long-term care in later life. Sales of individual supplementary pension schemes had decreased by roughly 20 per cent in 2009 (before the introduction of the new saving instrument and the changes to the old contracts) while premiums have not dropped, yet group pension insurance policies have maintained their sales and actually increased in 2010. This new law proposal has already affected the market as well as perhaps even the pension pillars.

Having had strong effects on funds, the 2008–9 financial crisis had a relatively mild effect on the Finnish pension system. Due to the fact that Finland experienced a recession and financial crisis in the early 1990s, there has been increased caution in the financial sector accompanied by structural changes, such as a three to four times higher solvency requirement level in comparison to the European average, which were able to at least attenuate the economic crisis, thus so far severe consequences have been averted. Most supplementary insurance policies currently being taken out have been guaranteed-return policies where companies have taken the risk; therefore, pensioners have generally not suffered loss of assets even if insurance company solvency 'buffers' have been depleted. Such security net would not apply to this new proposed saving instrument. Much political effort has been used to attempt to resolve or at least contain the financial crisis and its underlying causes. Nevertheless, the government must make long term preparations for an ageing society and other challenges in the public sector's financial sustainability deficit that is projected to expand until 2030 due to population ageing. All things considered, it is likely that a considerable shift from the dominance of statutory benefits towards occupational and personal pensions will take place also in Finland. The Finnish pension design would thus include more elements from the first-, second-, and third-pension pillars.

Bibliography

Alber, J. (1982). *Von Armenhaus zum Wohlfahrtsstaat. Analysen zur Entwicklung der Sozialeversicherung in Westeuropa*. Frankfurt: Campus Verlag.

Alestalo, M., Flora, P., and Uusitalo, H. (1985). 'Structure and Politics in the Making of the Welfare State', in R. Alapuro, M. Alestalo, E. Haavio-Mannila, and R. Väyrynen (eds.), *Small States in Comparative Perspective*. Oslo: Universitetsforlaget, 188–210.

Blomster, P. (2004). *Kunnallisen eläketurvan historia*. Helsinki: Keva.

COM (2005). 507 Proposal for a Directive of the European Parliament and of the Council on improving the portability of supplementary pension rights.

EEC 1408/71 Regulation. Council of 14th June 1971 on the application of social security schemes to employed persons and their families moving within the Community.

FFFS (2003). *Eläkevakuutuskysely 2003*. Helsinki: Federation of Finnish Financial Services.

——(2008a). *Vakuutustutkimus 2008*. Helsinki: Federation of Finnish Financial Services.

——(2008b). *Statistics*. Helsinki: Federation of Finnish Financial Services.

——(2009). *Statistics*. Helsinki: Federation of Finnish Financial Services.

Harju, J. (2008). 'Voluntary Pension Savings: The Effects of the Finnish Tax Reform on Savers' Behaviour'. Helsinki: Government Institute for Economic Research. *VATT Working Papers, 7*.

Kangas, O. (1988). 'Politik och ekonomi i pensionsförsäkringen: Det finska pensionssystemet i ett jämförande perspektiv'. Stockholm: Institutet för Social Forskning, Meddelande. *Working Papers, 5*.

——(2007). 'Finland: Labor Markets against Politics', in E. M. Immergut, K. Anderson, and I. Schulze (eds.), *The Handbook of West European Pension Politics*. Oxford: Oxford University Press, 248–96.

——and Palme, J. (1996). 'The Development of Occupational Pensions in Finland and Sweden: Class Politics and Institutional Feed-backs', in M. Shalev (ed.), *The Privatization of Social Policy? Occupational Welfare and the Welfare State in America, Scandinavia and Japan*. NewYork: Mac Millan, 211–40.

—————— (eds.) (2005). *Social Policy and Economic Development in the Nordic Countries*. Basingstoke: Palgrave.

——and Ritakallio V.-M. (2008). Köyhyyden mittaustavat, sosiaaliturvan riittävyys ja köyhyyden yleisyys Suomessa. Helsinki: Kela, Sosiaali- ja Terveysturvan Selosteita, 61.

Kari, S., Kiander, J., and Ulvinen, H. (2006). 'Vapaaehtoinen eläkevakuutus ja verotus'. Helsinki: Government Institute for Economic Research. *VATT-Disucssion Papers, 408.*

KELA (1976) *Statistical Yearbook of the Social Insurance Institution.* Helsinki: Kela.

——(1996) *Statistical Yearbook of the Social Insurance Institution.* Helsinki: Kela.

——(2007) *Statistical Yearbook of the Social Insurance Institution.* Helsinki: Kela.

Kuluttajatutkimus (2007). *Kuluttajien arkipäivän riskit ja turvallisuus. Julkaisuja 8/2007.* Helsinki: Kuluttajatutkimuskeskus.

Lassila, J., Määttänen, N., and Valkonen, T. (2007). 'Vapaaehtoinen eläkesäästäminen tulevaisuudessa'. *ETLA Discussion Papers, 1089.*

Määttänen N. (2006). *Vapaaehtoiset eläkevakuutukset ja eläkkeelle siirtyminen.* ETLA, the Research Institute of the Finnish Economy.

Niemelä, H. (1988). *Suomen kokonaiseläkejärjestelmän muotoutuminen.* Helsinki: Kela.

Palme, J. (1990). *Pension Rights in Welfare Capitalism: the Development of Old Age Pensions in 18 OECD Countries.* Stockholm: Swedish Institute for Social Research.

Pentikäinen, T. (1975). 'A Model of Stochastic Prognosis: An Application of Risk Theory to Business Planning'. *Scandinavian Acturial Journal,* 76: 29–53.

Pesonen, P., and Riihinen, O. (2002). *Dynamic Finland: The Political System and the Welfare State.* Helsinki: Finnish Litterature Society.

Salminen, K. (1987). *Yhteiskunnan rakenne, politiikka ja eläketurva.* Helsinki: ETK.

——(1993). *Pension Schemes in the Making. A Comparatives Study of the Nordic Countries.* Helsinki: ETK.

Taloussanomat (2008). (www.taloussanomat.fi/omatalous/2008/03/11/elake-kertyy-tuskai sen-hitaasti/20087113/139).

Taloustutkimus (2007). *Tutkimus lisäeläketurvasta pk-yrityspäättäjien keskuudessa.* Helsinki: Federation of Finnish Financial Services.

——(2008). *Survey on Private Pensions.* Helsinki: Federation of Finnish Financial Services.

——(2007). *Survey on Private Pensions.* Helsinki: Federation of Finnish Financial Services.

Vaittinen, R., Risku, I., Lindell, C., and Biström, P. (2007). 'Optimising Pension Financing with an Application to the Finnish Earnings-related Pensions'. Helsinki: Finnish Centre for Pensions (ETK), *Working Papers,* 2007:1.

9

Sweden: A Viable Public–Private Pension System[1]

Gabriella Sjögren Lindquist and Eskil Wadensjö

1. Introduction

Sweden, one of the Nordic Welfare States, is known for its universal public pension system, characterized by the social insurance principle with universal coverage and a high replacement rate. For example, every resident is covered by the public old-age pension system. These public pensions are based on the individual's lifetime earnings, but there is an income ceiling as in all public social insurances and a guarantee pension for those with low incomes. In addition to these public pensions, there are also private occupational pensions based on collective agreements and voluntary personal pensions which have often been overlooked in international comparisons. Occupational pensions supplement public pensions for those who have earnings below the ceiling and therefore lower public benefits, and more importantly, compensate for the income gap caused by the public pension ceiling for higher-income groups.

Important changes have been made in the Swedish pension system during the last fifteen years, most notably by the public pension reform decided on in 1994 and 1998 that ended the basic pension (AFP) and earnings-related state pension (ATP), replacing it by an earnings-related social insurance (income pension and premium pension) and a guarantee pension tested against the earnings-related pension. The most important reform component was the switch from a defined-benefit (DB) system to a notional defined-contribution (NDC) system which is sensitive to demographic changes, and the introduction of a funded pension (PPM – premium pension) integrated into the public

[1] We would like to thank Karen Anderson (Radboud University Nijmegen), Per Gunnar Edebalk (Lund University), Agneta Kruse (Lund University), Ann-Charlotte Ståhlberg (Stockholm University), and Annika Sundén (Swedish Social Insurance Agency) for helpful comments on earlier versions.

pillar. Most occupational pensions have also been changed into defined-contribution (DC) schemes but they are still to some extent DB schemes. These changes made pension benefit levels a lot less predictable for the individual, but at the same time the economic outcome is now easier to calculate for public finance.

Part I: The evolution of the public–private pension mix

2. The main features of the Swedish pension system

Since the 1998 reform, the Swedish public pension pillar consists of three parts: income pension (based on notional defined contribution or NDC), premium pension (funded DC), and guarantee pension (tax financed and tested against the income and premium pension). Income and premium pensions are based on the entire working-life income. Contributions are shared by the employer and employee. The contribution rate is 18.5 per cent of pensionable annual income. 16 per cent is paid for the NDC income pension and 2.5 per cent for the funded premium pension. In addition to earnings from dependent employment and income from self-employment, several forms of benefits such as sickness, disability, and unemployment insurance are also credited for pensionable entitlements. University education periods with study assistance, the national service (conscription) and for one parent for the first four years after a child is born, are credited for pension entitlements. Pension entitlements are linked to income development by a special income index. This means that the value of the entitlement follows the average labour income in the economy.

At the time of starting to take up the public pension,[2] predicted economic growth and cohort-specific life expectancy are taken into account in the calculation of the pension. If life expectancy increases, later cohorts will receive a lower income pension than earlier cohorts, while higher economic growth provides higher pensions for later cohorts than earlier cohorts. To ensure that the pension system is financially stable (that the pension liabilities do not exceed assets), a balance ratio is determined every year (Swedish Social Insurance Agency 2008). A balance ratio below 1.0 indicates a deficit (the pension debt (expected future pensions) exceeds the sum of expected future contributions and assets in the buffer funds) in which case the income index will be discounted by the balance ratio in order to restore the balance. The premium pension is invested according to the individual's choice in at most five out of about 800 funds registered by the Premium Pension Authority (PPM).

---

[2] Note that age when retiring, that is ending work, for many individuals differs from age when starting to take up pension.

	First pillar	Second pillar	Third pillar
	State pension (SP)	Occupational pension (OP)	Personal pension (PP)
Third tier (topping up)		4 major OP systems based on collective agreements (quasi-mandatory) Private sector: Separate schemes for white-collar (ITP-1) and blue-collar (SAF-LO) employees; DC Public sector: Separate schemes for government employees (PA03) and for municipal and county council (KAP-KL) employees; mostly DB	Voluntary Traditional insurance Pension funds Individual bank savings
Second tier (income maintenance)	Income pension (NDC; PAYG) and premium pension – PPM (DC; funded), both based on incomes up to the ceiling		
First tier (poverty alleviation)	Guarantee pension (tested against income pension)		

Figure 9.1 Pillars and tiers of the Swedish pension system

Contributions to the premium pension can be shared between spouses or registered partners.

The public pensions (income pension and premium pension) can be drawn at the earliest from age 61. Retirement can be postponed and the pension benefit increases accordingly with each postponed month of retirement. If benefits from the income pension are low, the guarantee pension supplements the income pension from the age of 65. To receive a full guarantee pension, a person must have lived in Sweden for forty years. If the person has lived in Sweden for a shorter period, the pension is reduced proportionally, but a minimum of three years of residency is required. The guarantee pension is not tested against earnings, occupational pensions, or personal pensions but against benefits from the public income pensions as if they had been paid from the age of 65 and similar statutory pensions received from other countries.

Public pensions are complemented by private occupational and personal pensions. For those with high incomes, they are as important as the social insurance pension. There are four main occupational pension systems covering most Swedish employees: two for the private sector (ITP-1; SAF-LO) and two for the public sector (PA03; KAP-KL). They give additional compensation for income parts up to the public pension ceiling and a considerably higher compensation for income parts above the ceiling. For income parts below the ceiling, all four schemes offer DC-type pensions, but for income parts above the ceiling the public sector schemes still offer mainly the DB-type pensions.

Public and occupational pensions are complemented by voluntary personal pensions, which are common among those who otherwise expect a low pension, for example women who have only worked a few years. But they are also popular among those who have high incomes and therefore high pensions under the public pension and occupational pension systems as the contributions are tax-deductible up to an amount.

An overview of the different systems is presented in Figure 9.1. Note that the income pension scheme and the PPM scheme are integrated parts of the same system financed in the same way by employer contributions up to a ceiling and with the same rules regarding the minimum pension age (61). As of January 2010, they will also be administrated by the same authority.

3. The context of the welfare regime, labour relations, and market economy

The Swedish public pension system was established by a Conservative government in 1913 in response to a long political debate. It was further developed by different Social Democratic governments, transforming it into a Beveridge-type basic pension from 1948 and then adding an earnings-related part (ATP) from 1960. Increasing costs led to the transformation of the pension system from a DB into an NDC system during the 1990s. The pension system has always been considered to be the most important part of the Swedish welfare state, especially since the reforms in 1948 (AFP – *folkpension*) and 1960 (*ATP*). The trade unions played a major part in the ATP pension reform.

There has always been a ceiling in the earnings-related pensions. It has led to a development of occupational pension schemes giving compensation for income parts over the ceiling. The schemes have been established as a result of collective bargaining on the national level. The same type of supplementary compensation has also been established for other social security schemes. These schemes are administrated by the social partners together. An important aspect of those systems in Sweden is that they are not related to one workplace or one employer. The right to compensation follows the worker so that they do not hinder mobility as do systems where pension rights are lost if an employee changes employer.

Why do negotiated occupational pensions coexist alongside well-developed Swedish public pensions? One explanation is that individuals want to have a different distribution of consumption over the life cycle than that provided by public insurance. This is of particular interest to those who have income above the ceiling for which benefits are provided in the social insurance system. They may wish to have a high replacement rate above as well as below the ceiling of the public pension system. The question then arises of why this is not dealt with on an individual basis as a part of the individual's choice of consumption over the life cycle. One explanation is that administration costs are lower for collective occupational schemes than for private insurance due to economies of scale and more uniform insurance. A higher benefit level may be purchased with lower flexibility. Another argument is the tax relief provided for the employer contribution to collective occupational pensions in Sweden.

There are also additional arguments. There may be reasons for the employer to defer wages to the future. The wage does not correspond to productivity throughout the entire employment period but is below productivity in earlier years and above during years closer to retirement. One way of postponing the wage is to provide a (particularly favourable) pension for those who remain in the company until retirement (see Lazear 1979). A system of this kind can stimulate additional effort, that is, higher productivity and loyalty to the company. A final salary pension is a typical example. However, a disadvantage of such a system is that it contributes to locking-in effects – leaving an employer entails a cost in pension benefits, and other employers prefer not to employ older persons if the expected pension costs are high. This makes it difficult to find new employment for those wanting to change jobs and for those who lose their jobs due to layoffs. This is an explanation for the development of a few large sector agreements and also for the development of DC schemes, which are easy to transfer when moving from one employer to another or from one sector to another.

The Swedish wage structure is compressed. An additional levelling out occurs through the tax and social insurance system. This levelling out is counteracted by designing pension agreements that provide benefits above the ceiling. This could be interpreted as meaning that the social partners through agreement-based solutions in the area of pensions have opted to counteract the levelling which has taken place by wage agreements and by redistribution by taxes and income transfers.[3]

The pension system is a vital part of the Swedish welfare model. This is the part of social protection which has been visible in the political debate. The earlier political conflicts explain that the major political parties in the 1990s compromised and arrived at a solution acceptable for all of them. Changes made later on have also been supported by the same political parties, the parties forming government as well as the opposition. The great compromise, a combination of NDC and funded premium reserve, is intended as a policy for many decades to come. It has automatic stabilizers for adjustment to the economic and demographic development, incentives to older people to work longer,

---

[3] For empirical results, see Selén and Ståhlberg (2004).

and a guarantee pension financed through the state budget for those with no or low-income-related contributory pension. The social partners have four major agreements regarding complementing occupational pensions, though the last of those four, for blue-collar workers in the private sector, was agreed only in 1973. All of those schemes have been adjusted to the changes in social security pensions even if there still remain some DB parts in the public sector pension systems. The pension system is presently not an issue in the Swedish political debate. The political discussion regarding income transfer schemes is on the rules and level of compensation at sickness and unemployment.

When the ATP pension system was decided in the 1950s, it was expected that savings would diminish as people would save less for their old age. It was therefore decided that relatively large funds, the AP funds, should be introduced to compensate for the expected decline in private savings. The new pension system was designed so that the public pension savings should not decline. The main means for this was the introduction of the premium reserve pensions and the continuance of the AP funds of the former system. But equally important for keeping up the savings level in the economy are the pension funds of the occupational pension schemes. They are at present of about the same size as the premium reserve funds and the AP funds taken together, and they will grow rapidly as a result of the transition from being DB to becoming DC systems.

4. The emergence of the public–private pension mix[4]

The first Swedish pension schemes had already been established in the eighteenth century for state employees.[5] In the nineteenth century, larger municipalities and private firms established occupational pensions for their white-collar employees with permanent contracts. The organization and financing of pensions for tenured central government employees was gradually changed. For a long time, two-thirds of final earnings were paid for civil servants' pensions. Following this model, the municipalities and county councils subsequently developed pensions for their employees as did larger companies,[6] but private sector blue-collar workers were largely uncovered, although some companies introduced pensions for this group as well. As a rule, these pensions were low and were not the result of agreements but came into being as a result

---

[4] See Wadensjö (1997) for a presentation of the Swedish pension mix.

[5] See Harrysson (2000), Schmidt (1974), Sjöfors (1982), and Wadensjö (1997) for some studies of the history of agreement-based occupational pensions; for details see National Social Insurance Board (1999).

[6] Prior to 1960, the municipalities had a premium-based and paid-up policy pension system.

of unilateral decisions by the employers and were thus not protected from changes in the employers' policies.

Most people had no occupational pension coverage at the beginning of the twentieth century. Old people who could not rely on relatives had to be supported by municipalities, which proved particularly challenging for smaller communities. Municipalities with large outmigration and ageing and shrinking populations thus encountered financial problems. This was one of the reasons for the establishment of universal public pensions in 1913 (Berge 1995, 1998). The scheme included old-age and disability pensions. The public pension scheme was contribution-based but for those who received a disability pension there was an income- and wealth-tested supplement. Those with tenured position in the central government sector were not included in the scheme just like some other minor groups with occupational pensions, while other groups with occupational pensions could apply to leave the public system. In 1918, the possibilities to leave the public system were restricted – it was a step in the direction of a universal pension. From 1937, public pension became less contribution-based and all were included in the system, also those employed by the central government. In 1948, the Swedish basic pension became a pay-as-you-go (PAYG) system with no income-/wealth-testing, paying the same flat-rate pension for every resident independent of previous income. See Table 9.1 for the different steps in the development of the pension system.

Many people could supplement the public pension benefit with an occupational pension. Blue-collar workers in the private sector were only covered by occupational pensions to a limited extent, and these were generally less generous than those for white-collar employees. Most self-employed people, including farmers, also lacked supplementary pensions. Already in the 1940s, discussions began about complementing the basic pension with an earnings-related public supplement. Most public employees and also a large share of private white-collar employees were covered by occupational supplementary pensions. In 1959, after an intense political debate during which a referendum was held, a supplementary earnings-related state pension (ATP) was decided in parliament by a majority of one vote. The first contributions were paid in 1960 and the first pensions were distributed three years later. The ATP was a DB system based on the PAYG-financing principle with some reserve funding.

All groups but the blue-collar workers in the private sector already had occupational pensions that aimed at income replacement, thus this new pension was strongly supported by the trade unions of the blue-collar workers (LO), though the other trade unions also welcomed this public second-tier pension. The pre-existing occupational pensions were renegotiated to function as supplements, but such an agreement was not reached for blue-collar workers in the private sector until 1973. The occupational pensions were designed to complement the public pensions by supplementing benefits below the ATP ceiling and compensating the income replacement gap above the ceiling,

Table 9.1 Chronology of major pension reforms, Sweden 1913–90

Year	Reform	Political context
1913	Introduction of public pension system (central government employees stayed outside the system and there was an option for other groups with occupational pensions to apply to stay outside the system)	Conservative government Several arguments were put forward, for example, to alleviate the burden for municipalities with many elderly
1918	Restrictions regarding the possibilities for new groups to leave the pension scheme	Liberal and Social Democratic coalition government
1937 (decided in 1935)	Loosening the link between contributions and benefits; less strict income testing; introduction of universalism; new name: *folkpension* (people's pension) instead of *pensionsförsäkring* (pension insurance)	Social Democratic government
1948	Introduction of basic flat-rate pension equal for all Swedish residents (the decision was taken in 1946)	Social Democratic government
1960	Introduction of statutory earnings-related pension system (ATP)	After a long political conflict, the new pension scheme was decided with a one-vote majority: the Social Democratic government was supported by the Communist party and one Liberal party member
1960	Agreements reached on new occupational pension schemes for white-collar workers in the private sector and for public sector employees	Renegotiations of earlier agreement adjusting to the new ATP scheme
1973	Agreement on occupational pension for blue-collar workers in the private sector All employees in the Swedish labour market were now covered by an occupational pension scheme	
1976	Lowering retirement age for social security pensions from 67 to 65	Social Democratic government Most employees were granted retirement age at 65 under collective agreement, for others and the self-employed it was lowered from 67 to 65 by law; this was an important issue for the Centre party in the 1970s elections

Note: Only the old-age pension system is covered (the disability, part-time, and survivor pension schemes are not covered). No major changes were made in the old-age pension schemes between 1976 and 1990.

Source: Berge (1995, 1998), Elmér (1960), and Molin (1965) on the public pension system and Edebalk and Wadensjö (1989) on the occupational pension systems.

thereby in practice eliminating most of the ceiling effect. The exception was that the agreement for blue-collar workers in the private sector did not include any such compensation above the ceiling, since very few blue-collar workers had such high incomes at that time.

5. The changing public–private pension mix in Sweden

The Swedish pension became the focus of an intense debate in the early 1980s. Several parliamentary and governmental committees have investigated all aspects of the system. The main worries were that slacking economic growth, longer life expectancy, more frequent disability claims and other forms of early exit from work, and the pensioning of the baby-boom generation of the 1940s would lead to very high payroll fees in the first decades of the twenty-first century if the system had remained unaltered. Although the acceptance of ATP pensions had steadily increased since the 1960s, even among the political parties and groups who had previously opposed it, a more critical debate on the pension system began in the 1980s, in particular due to concerns for its long-term sustainability and criticism about unfair income redistribution. The pension costs were expected to increase relative to the contributions for multiple reasons: the economic growth rate was lower than initially expected, the rate of early exit from work increased and thus revenues declined while there were higher costs for disability pensions, and people were living longer, which led to higher pension costs.

The old-age pension scheme was very difficult to change for several reasons. First, the current working population would have made different choices under a new pension system, and a reform would have had to be made in a way which would not alienate large sections of the electorate, especially those close to retirement age. Second, the major political parties tried to avoid a political conflict similar to the one preceding the rather exceptional referendum on ATP in 1959 and the only post-war intermittent general election. As all parties wanted to avoid conflict, the political consensus needed time. A parliamentary committee that had examined this problem for several years presented its final report in 1990, leading to vigorous discussion and criticism. The available parametric option was to increase contributions. In the long run, such a policy would have led to very high contributions and to higher disposable incomes for pensioners than for those employed. On the other hand, a number of stepwise decisions to cut back pension benefits would probably lead to growing distrust in it as stepwise changes would make it easy to see who would be unfavourably affected by the changes.

The government did not put forward a reform proposal but instead appointed a governmental committee with members from all parliamentary parties. The committee presented a report in March 1994, proposing a radically reformed pension system. The four Liberal and Conservative parties of the government coalition at the time (1991–4), and also the main opposition party, the Social Democratic party, supported the proposal. The government presented reform guidelines based on the report, which were accepted by parliament in June 1994.[7]

[7] For political process see Lundberg (2003) and Palme (2001), for aspects of the new system see Anderson and Immergut (2007), Granqvist and Ståhlberg (2003), Palmer (2002), Persson (1998), and Sundén (2006).

A new committee was appointed with members from the parliamentary parties in support of the reform process in order to transpose the guidelines into draft legislation. A first draft was put forward in June 1995 but did not lead to any decisions by parliament as several problems were still not solved. Instead, the committee continued its work. A renewed debate within the Social Democratic Party on the principles of the pension reform started in spring 1996, leading to new negotiations on some parts between the five political parties who supported the reform. A year later, the political parties had reached an agreement regarding the Premium Reserve part. The new draft was presented to parliament in spring 1998, and the decision on the new pension system was taken in June 1998. According to the earlier parliamentary decision in June 1994, the new pension system was to be implemented from January 1996 regarding contributions and accumulation of pension credits, but this date was later changed in three steps to January 1999. The new pension scheme was gradually introduced from 1995 with payments to the premium reserve system, payments to the notional accounts in 1999, and the first payments of pensions in 2001. See Table 9.2 for the different steps in the development.

The public pension reform has also encouraged adjustments in the supplementary occupational pension schemes such as the transition from DB to DC

Table 9.2 Chronology of the public pension system restructuring since 1990s

Year	Reform	Political context
1991	Discontinuation of the option to get a disability pension based on only labour market reasons	Liberal–Conservative government supported by the Social Democratic party
		A part of a policy to increase labour force participation among older workers
1994	Decision by the *Riksdag* on the principles of the new pension system	Liberal–Conservative government supported by the Social Democratic party
		A large majority supported the proposal
1997	Discontinuation of the option to get a disability pension for older workers based on combined medical and labour market reasons	Social Democratic government
		A part of a policy to increase labour force participation among older workers
1998	Decision by the *Riksdag* on the new pension system	Social Democratic government supported by the four liberal and conservative parties
		A large majority supported the proposal
2000	Start of the new income pension	
2000	31 December, last day for new part-time pensions granted from the part-time pension system	A part of the political agreement on the old-age pension agreement

Source: Pensionsgruppen (2009).

Table 9.3 Distribution (%) of pension income on different sources for persons aged 65–69

	Public pensions		Supplementary occupational pensions		Personal pensions	
Year	Men	Women	Men	Women	Men	Women
1996	74.4	80.6	20.3	15.6	5.3	3.8
2002	67.9	76.2	24.2	16.4	8.0	7.4
2006	64.0	72.1	27.7	19.0	8.1	8.9

Source: Based on the database HEK, Statistics Sweden.

schemes and the introduction of possibilities for individuals to choose their investment funds. Table 9.3 shows the relative importance of the three pension pillars (public, occupational, personal) in 1996, 2002, and 2006. The public pension (social insurance) is the most important one but its share of total pension income has declined. The coverage of (collectively negotiated) occupational pensions increased and also the income share above the public pension ceiling. The personal pension share has also been augmented, especially for women with weak labour market attachment who seek to compensate the otherwise low pensions from the other two earnings-related systems.

Part II: The governance of supplementary pensions

In the *second* pillar, there are four large collectively negotiated occupational pension systems:[8] two pension schemes in the private sector, one for blue-collar workers (SAF-LO) and one for white-collar employees (ITP-1/ITP-2); and two schemes in the public sector, one for central government employees (PA03) and one for employees in municipalities and county councils (KAP-KL). In addition, there are some agreements that cover smaller sectors. The *occupational pension for white-collar employees in industry and trade* (ITP) was introduced at the same time as the statutory earnings-related pension (ATP) in 1960 and replaced the previously existing system. The Council for Negotiation and Cooperation (PTK) representing white-collar unions and the Confederation of Swedish Enterprise reached an agreement on a new supplementary pension plan (ITP-1) in 2006. While the old occupational pension scheme (ITP-2) has been continued for those born before 1979, the new scheme is applicable to those born in 1979 or later. White-collar employees have the choice between different placements of the contributions to their pensions: traditional insurance or pension funds.

---

[8] See Edebalk and Wadensjö (1989), Palmer and Wadensjö (2004), Riksdagens revisorer (2002), Sjögren Lindquist and Wadensjö (2006, 2007), and Wadensjö (1990) and collective agreements between parties in the labour market.

The *occupational pension scheme for blue-collar workers* went through several revisions since its introduction in 1973. After renegotiation in 2007, a new system was introduced. This is of the same type as the white-collar occupational scheme. Blue-collar employees have the choice between different placements of the contributions to their pensions: traditional insurance (six insurance companies) or funds (five different funds). It is possible to make extra payments to the pension scheme.

The central government employees had a pension scheme long before the introduction of a public pension system in 1913, and they were not included in that system until 1937. At the introduction of the statutory earnings-related pension (ATP), the system that existed for central government employees was redesigned to become a supplement to the public pension system. The pension scheme for *central government employees* has been revised on different occasions. In January 2003, a new scheme (PA03) was introduced for those who were born in 1943 or later. Those who were born before 1943 are covered by the earlier scheme. PA03 is a combined DC and DB system. For the DC parts, employees have the choice between different placements of the contributions to their pensions: traditional insurance (ten insurance companies) or pension funds (twelve different funds). It is possible to make extra payments to the pension scheme.

The occupational pension scheme for employees in municipalities and county councils was redesigned at the introduction of the ATP scheme in 1960. It has been changed on different occasions. The present *occupational pension system for employees in municipalities and county councils* is the result of an agreement reached in December 2005 (KAP-KL). However, the new pension scheme applies fully only to those born in 1968 or later while those born in 1946 or before are not affected by the new agreement. Thus, there is a relatively long transition period (twenty years) between the old and the new system.

Table 9.4 summarizes the main features of the present versions of the four major occupational pension systems. The four schemes differ in various respects, but there are considerable similarities between the systems – similarities that have become greater with the changes undertaken in recent years. All four systems have changed in the same direction as the public social insurance system, namely from a DB to a DC system. The two private sector schemes for blue- and white-collar workers, respectively, have gone furthest in this direction, being entirely DC systems. In the central and local government systems, there are DB parts for those above the ceiling in the social insurance scheme. However, it should be underscored that many who will retire in the near future will get an occupational pension determined according to the rules of an earlier scheme.

In the *third* pillar, there are three different forms of *personal pension plans*: traditional insurance, savings in pension funds, and individual pension savings in a bank.

Table 9.4 Overview of supplementary pensions in Sweden

Occupational pension scheme	Contributions in 2010		Assets	DB/DC	Financing principle
	On parts up to 7.5 iba	On parts 7.5 iba or more			
Government employees	DC: 4.5%	DC: 4.5% DB: Individual premiums. The government as an employer paid on an average 9.35% of the total wage costs to cover the DB cost in 2005	Funded None	DC; partly DB for income parts over the ceiling	Employer contributions
Public employees (county councils/ municipalities)	DC: 4.5%	DC: 4.5% DB: Means are set aside in the budget when pensions are earned. The DB costs were 1% of the total wage cost for municipalities and 4% for county councils in 2005	Funded None	DC; partly DB for income parts over the ceiling	Employer contributions
White-collar workers (private sector)	4.5%	30%	Funded	DC	Employer contributions
Blue-collar workers (private sector)	4.5%	30%	Funded	DC	Employer contributions

Note: iba = income base amount (51,100 SEK in 2010). The price amount follows income development index.
Source: Sjögren Lindquist and Wadensjö (2006) and information from the occupational insurances.

6. Who is covered?

Occupational pension schemes in Sweden are not mandatory by law, nor are collective agreements required but employers who are covered by collective agreements have to apply these rules and their employees are thus covered. Part-time workers and temporary employees are covered by the occupational pension schemes. In practice, since collective agreements cover almost all of the Swedish labour force, nearly all employees are covered by supplementary occupational pensions. More than 90 per cent of all workplaces have collective agreements in Sweden (Sjögren Lindquist and Wadensjö 2007). As mainly small workplaces lack agreements, the share of employees covered is even larger. The self-employed are the main exception. Many of them are not covered by occupational pension insurance. Even if they are not covered by collective agreements, they may voluntarily join one of the two private sector schemes. The personal pensions are also important. 20 per cent of those aged 65 years or older who received a pension also received a personal pension based on their own savings.

7. What kind of benefits?

The replacement rate is about the same in all four supplementary pension schemes. Adding the statutory pension, about two-thirds of the former income is replaced by statutory and occupational pensions taken together if a person retires at the age of 65. Pension benefits from the occupational pension schemes are indexed by the consumer price index. This means that in periods with real wage growth, the pensions will gradually constitute a lower share of the current wage level as the pensioner becomes older. The rights to a DC pension are generally not influenced by a change of employer or sector. There are, however, some complications regarding the DB parts when changing sector. The DC systems in the private sector are actuarially fair and by that not redistributive. Pension entitlements are fully vested in both private sector schemes immediately. The DB parts in the public sector (central government and municipalities/county councils) are financed by actuarially fair fees paid by the employer. When seen as deferred wage by the employers and the employees and thereby influencing wages setting in collective negotiations, then the DB parts are also non-redistributive. There is no waiting period before benefit entitlements can be acquired for any of the four occupational pension schemes.

- *Private sector white-collar workers* (ITP): The old occupational pension scheme for white-collar employees, ITP-2, is a DB system, covering those who were born in 1978 or earlier. Pension benefits are calculated based on the wage before retirement and an average of commission and production bonus payments during the last three years before retirement. ITP-2 is 10 per cent on wage portions up to 7.5 income base amounts,[9] 65 per cent on wage portions between 7.5 and 20 income base amounts, and 32.5 per cent on wage portions between 20 and 30 income base amounts. The retirement age is 65 although benefits can be drawn from the age of 55 with a deduction of approximately 0.6 per cent for each early month taken. It is also possible to postpone the withdrawal of pension benefits up to the age of 70. The value of the pension then increases by approximately 0.5 per cent per each month postponed.

- The new ITP-1 occupational pension is a DC system. This scheme covers those who were born in 1979 or later. Pension entitlements can be earned between the age of 25 and 65 (if the employer and the employee agree, contributions could also be paid after 65). Pension benefits may be paid from the age of 55 but the standard retirement age is 65. There is an actuarial benefit deduction in case of early retirement in the ITP-1 scheme. The contribution is 4.5 per cent of the wage up to the ceiling and 30 per cent over the ceiling. Pensions

[9] The Swedish social security system is indexed by the use of three different base amounts: the price base amount (SEK 42,800 in 2009), the enhanced price base amount (SEK 43,600 in 2009), and the income base amount (SEK 50,900 in 2009).

are normally paid lifelong but may be taken out during a limited period of five years or more. Those covered can in 2009 make a selection between five insurance companies and five funds for the placement of the contribution.

- *Private sector blue-collar workers* (SAF-LO): The new occupational pension scheme for blue-collar workers is a DC system. Pension benefits entitlements can be earned from the age of 25. The contribution will be 4.5 per cent of the wage up to the ceiling and 30 per cent over the ceiling (it is gradually changed to that level). Pension benefits can be paid from the age of 55, although the pension will be lower if it is drawn before the age of 65 which is the standard retirement age and the upper age limit at the same time. Benefits can be paid as a lifelong annuity or for a shorter period of at least five years. Employees who are covered by the SAF-LO occupational pension scheme can change insurance company once a year even if they do not change employer. Investments made before 2004 cannot be transferred when changing the insurance company. Therefore, employees can have assets with several companies and receive pension benefits from different sources during retirement. Employees choose the pension form themselves, traditional pension insurance with a certain lowest guaranteed yield (six alternatives) or fund insurance (five alternatives), and who is to manage the funds.

- *Central government employees* (PA03): The occupational pension consists of two DC schemes – a basic pension and an additional pension (Kåpan) – and a DB scheme for those whose pension basis is larger than 7.5 income base amounts per year (ceiling of the public pension system). PA03 plans have an upper age limit for the accumulation of benefits but there is no age limit for retirement. Pension entitlements are fully and immediately vested from the first contribution. The basic pension entitlements can be earned from the age of 23. Pension benefits are paid as a lifelong annuity from the age of 65. Entitlements for the additional pension (Kåpan) are earned from age 28 and benefits are usually paid out during a five-year period from the age of 65 but can also be drawn as lifelong annuity. The pension from the DB part is calculated on the average of pensionable wages from the last five years prior to retirement. Pension entitlements are earned from the age of 28. To obtain a full pension, it is required that the employee has worked for thirty years within the area covered by central government pension regulations. The DB pension is 60 per cent of the income between 7.5 and 20 income base amounts and 30 per cent of the income between 20 and 30 income base amounts.

- *County council and municipal employees* (KAP-KL): The occupational pension system for municipalities and county councils has been changed on different occasions. The present scheme is the result of an agreement reached in December 2005. The new pension, KAP-KL, entails significant changes. It should be underlined here that there will be a relatively long period of transition (twenty years) between the old and the new system. Those born in 1946 or before are not affected by the new agreement. Those born in 1968 or later will receive their whole pension according to KAP-KL. Among the major changes can be mentioned: The benefit ceiling is adjusted to the national pension system. The contribution is 4.5 per cent both below and above the ceiling and the same for all groups covered by the agreement. The fact that contributions will be the same above and below the ceiling means that contributions were increased markedly above the ceiling and by that also the DC pension for those with an income above the ceiling. This is counteracted by that the DB pension decreased as a portion of income above the ceiling. The DB pension was reduced to 55 per cent (from 62.5 per cent) between 7.5 and 20 income base amounts and to 27.5 per cent (from 31.25 per cent) between 20 and 30 income base amounts. Pension entitlements are vested after three months of employment.

- *Personal pensions*: There are three different forms of personal pension plans: traditional insurance, fund insurance, and individual pension savings in a bank. The traditional insurance gives a guaranteed yearly accrual, but the pension may also be larger depending on the success of the insurance company's placement of the fees. In fund insurances, there is no guarantee of a minimum growth of the assets. Bank savings plans give no guaranteed interest rate and are not insurance.

8. Who pays?

Private sector occupational pensions are based on employer contributions (see Table 9.4). In the new private sector pension schemes (ITP-1 and SAF-LO), the contributions to be paid by the employer amount to 4.5 per cent of the salary up to 7.5 times the income base amount, and 30 per cent on salaries over that ceiling. Contributions are also paid during periods with benefits due to sickness, parental leave, or for taking care of a sick child. The employees choose how to place their contributions in the new plan. The private sector occupational pension schemes are all funded schemes. The contributions are paid by the employer.

In the public sector, the contribution rate for the *DC part* of the occupational pension for employees in municipalities and county councils is 4.5 per cent both below and above the ceiling. The DB part of the pension is financed by the employer setting aside funds in their books when the pension rights are earned. Reserves corresponding to 1 per cent of the total wage cost were set aside for employees in municipalities and 4 per cent for employees in county councils in 2005. Before 1998, no savings for pensions were set aside, the last employer had to pay the entire cost for the pension. In 2005, municipalities had to pay 3 per cent and the county councils 5 per cent of the total wage costs to finance 'yesterday's' pensions. The costs for DB pensions are higher in county councils than in municipalities since wages are higher in county councils; more county council employees have wages above the ceiling.

The central government finances the *basic part* (DC) of the occupational pension for *government employees*. Contributions are equivalent to 2.5 per cent of the 'pension basis' (all wages paid + other cash benefits including overtime compensation and benefits in kind). Contributions to the *additional part* of the pension (Kåpan) are equivalent to 2.0 per cent of the 'pension basis' up to an annual wage of 30 income base amounts. The DB part of the pension is financed by the employer paying contributions to the insurance administrator, SPV, which is to be used by the central government employer. Contributions are based on earnings, wage increases, age, and retirement age. Since 1998, the employer pays individual premiums for each employee. Prior to 2005, the pensions were paid for by a wage cost supplement of 7 per cent of the gross wages bill. In 2005, the government (as the employer) paid on an average 9.35 per cent of the total wage costs into the scheme in order to cover the PAYG DB part of the pension. The contributions are paid by the employer.

In a formal sense, pension contributions are paid by the employer, but in reality they are paid by the employees as higher costs for pensions are compensated by a lower wage increase. It is the total wage costs including fringe benefits of which the supplementary pensions are a part, which is of interest for both the employers and the employees. Regarding occupational pensions, the employer is able to make a tax deduction of the costs from the profits for pensions up to 35 per cent of the salary up to 10 price base amounts. If the employer pays out the pension directly, that is, pays a pension which has not been deducted in earlier budgets or paid for in the form of fees or placed in a pension fund, the costs are deducted from the profits before taxation the year they are paid out. The employer pays a special wage cost tax for pension costs. It is 24.26 per cent instead of 32.7 per cent (as for wages) as the pension costs are not the basis for the right to social insurance benefits.

A tax corresponding to the employer part of the contribution to the public pension is paid for income parts higher than the ceiling in the social insurance system, even if they are not a basis for rights to payment from those schemes. It means that it is more favourable to be paid in the form of fees to a supplementary pension scheme instead of as a wage given the cost for the employer. A tax of 15 per cent of the value of the increase in pension wealth is paid yearly. This value increase is set to the value of the insurance in the beginning of the year multiplied with the average state-regulated interest rate during the year before the year of taxation. When saving in a fund, the tax is 30 per cent of the realized gain when taking out the money from the fund; when saving in a bank account, the tax is 30 per cent of the interest received during the year. Supplementary pensions are taxed as income from labour when they are paid out.

Table 9.5 Personal pension savings (annual average) by gender and age (% population insured)

Age group	Men				Women			
	2001		2004		2001		2004	
	SEK	%	SEK	%	SEK	%	SEK	%
20–24	2,000	14.2	1,700	14.3	1,700	11.1	2,000	11.6
25–34	3,600	35.4	3,000	40.7	2,900	39.0	3,400	35.1
35–44	5,800	38.7	4,500	49.2	4,300	49.0	5,300	41.1
45–54	8,800	38.1	7,000	51.9	6,300	50.7	8,000	38.5
55–64	11,700	33.1	9,500	43.1	8,700	43.8	11,000	33.4
20–64	7,100	34.4	5,800	43.3	5,500	42.5	6,900	34.7

Source: Statistics Sweden, Hushållens ekonomi, Skatter och taxerade inkomster.

Personal pensions are funded premium reserve systems. The funds are large. In 2006, occupational pension funds amounted to SEK 960 billion and the funds for personal pensions to SEK 390 billion. These figures could be compared with the SEK 1,127 billion in the funds for the statutory pension system (income pension and PPM) in the same year (Swedish Social Insurance Agency 2007). Table 9.5 shows that more than a third of those aged 20–64 pay a contribution to a personal pension scheme. The individual is allowed to make a deduction when paying income tax for the pension fees, but the deduction may not be larger than the income from labour (as self-employed or as an employee) and not higher than SEK 12,000 per year from 2008, except if the individual is not covered by any occupational pension. In this case, the maximum deduction is at most 35 per cent of the income up to 10 price base amounts.

9. Who governs? Who decides? Who manages?

The occupational pension schemes in Sweden are decided by collective agreements, therefore the government is not directly involved in the design and implementation of the schemes. The exception is the system for those employed by the central government. In that case, the government is involved in the design of the pension scheme as one part in the collective agreement and in the implementation as SPV, the entity in charge of the pension administration of the sector, is a governmental authority. The choice is organized by SPV. Government employees can decide how the basic part (DC) of their occupational pension should be managed. However, they cannot decide about the management and investment of the additional part of the pension (Kåpan).

In occupational pension schemes for municipal and county council employees, assets are managed by the insurance company chosen by the employee. The choice is organized through an occupational pension institution called Pensionsvalet. The default setting for individuals who do not choose an insurance company themselves is the placement with KPA, a pension institution within the local government organization. There are no legal insolvency protection rules for public sector schemes, but the state functions as a backup in case of insolvency.

In the private sector, both the employer associations and the trade unions are involved not only in the design of the pension schemes but also in the administration of the pension schemes of insurance companies owned by the social partners. The individual choice of investment is organized by Collectum. There is a Pension Guarantee Mutual Insurance Company (FPG) that protects in case of insolvency of book reserve schemes and pension foundations in the private sector (ITP-2). SAF-LO plan assets are managed by the insurance company chosen by the scheme member. The choice is organized by a company administered by the Confederation of Swedish Enterprises (SN) and the Swedish Trade Union Confederation (LO). Those who do not choose an insurance company are placed by default with AMF Pension, an occupational pension institution. White-collar employees in the private sector covered by the ITP scheme can choose between different funds but at least 50 per cent of pension contributions have to be invested in low-risk funds or a pure unit-linked insurance plan.

Occupational pensions are supervised by a state agency. The Swedish Financial Supervisory Authority, *Finansinspektionen* (FI), was established in 1991 with the aim of creating a single integrated regulator covering banking, securities, and insurance. This was made possible through the merger of the former banking and insurance supervisory bodies. One of the authorities that merged was the Swedish Insurance Inspection (*Försäkringsinspektionen*) which was founded in 1904. FI's role is to promote stability and efficiency in the financial system as well as to ensure an effective consumer protection. FI authorizes, supervises, and monitors all companies operating in Swedish financial markets, while it is accountable to the Ministry of Finance. Among the insurance companies that FI supervises are those that administrate occupational pensions.

10. The outlook for the Swedish retirement income system

The Swedish social security pension has undergone large changes during the last fifteen years. The new system is based on the whole working-life instead of the final salary up to a (yearly) ceiling and is calculated to a major extent by the use of notional accounts and partly based on a premium reserve part (PPM).

A guarantee pension is paid out to those who have had low wages or no wages and therefore low or no income and premium reserve pension benefits. Many more women than men get a guarantee pension. The two parts (the income pension and the PPM) are integral parts of the statutory pension system and they are compulsory and cover everyone in Sweden who is working. Every year, the expected pension for alternative pension ages is sent out in orange envelopes to everyone who is 28 years old or over – the predicted pension is the sum of both parts of the social insurance scheme. To strengthen the relation between the two parts, a special pension authority *Pensionsmyndigheten* (the Sweden Pensions Agency), which will administer both parts of the pension system, started in January 2010 and replaced the PPM authority and the pension division at the Swedish Social Insurance Agency.

The majority of both men and women in Sweden get an occupational pension while collecting a social security pension. All who are covered by collective agreements are also covered by one of the schemes (there are four major ones). The Swedish system is thereby a system which for most people is a combination of statutory pensions and occupational pensions. The occupational pension adds to the replacement rate for income parts above the ceiling and gives a fairly high replacement rate for income parts below the ceiling and by that eliminates most of the effects of the ceiling. In addition, 20 per cent of those aged 65 years or older received a voluntary personal pension based on their own savings.

There are some issues of interest and concern regarding the future development. The guarantee pension is price indexed and not, as the income pension, indexed to the development of the average labour income in the economy. In periods with real income growth, the income situation of poor pensioners will gradually worsen compared to those with an income pension. Sweden's economic history tells us that the politicians sooner or later will increase these benefits. The PPM pension is decided by the value of the funds the individual has selected. If a person has selected funds consisting mainly of shares and the share prices are low, a person may get a much lower pension than expected. The balancing mechanism in the income pension system may also lead to that the pensions and the growth of the pensions become lower than expected in periods of crisis. The funds of the occupational pensions are also to a high extent placed in shares as are much of the funds for the personal pensions. This also leads to that these pensions are sensitive to the variations in the development of the stock market.

The present crisis led at its start to a large decline in the value of the pension funds, both those of the social security system (the AP and the PPM funds) and those of the occupational insurance schemes and the personal pension insurance. A special pension group consisting of members from the five political parties who supported the pension reform and who continually follow the development of the pension system asked the Swedish Social Insurance Agency to conduct a study of possibilities to avoid predicted reductions of the pensions in 2010, for example, by smoothing out the predicted reduction over a number of years. One of the alternatives put in the study, a smoothing over three years, was chosen by the pension group and also by the parliament.

The four large occupational insurance schemes have gradually become DC schemes, but there are still exceptions for those employed in the public sector. The employer side behind one of the two agreements in the public sector – the organization of municipalities and county councils (SKL) – has put forward a proposal in negotiations with the trade unions which started in December 2008 that the system should be changed to a DC system even for those with income parts over the ceiling.

The occupational insurances cover the great majority of employees. However, many of the self-employed are not covered. This is an important issue as the number of self-employed individuals is increasing.

Bibliography

Anderson, K. M., and Immergut, E. M. (2007). 'Sweden: After Social Democratic Hegemony', in E. M. Immergut, K. M. Anderson and I. Schultze (eds.), *The Handbook of Western European Pension Politics*. Oxford: Oxford University Press, 349–95.

Berge, A. (1995). *Medborgarrätt och egenansvar. De sociala försäkringarna i Sverige 1901–1935*. Lund: Arkiv förlag.

——(1998). 'Pensions-separatismen. Frågan om den svenska folkpensionens karaktär 1913–1935'. *Arkiv*, 71: 1–37.

Edebalk, P. G., and Wadensjö, E. (1989). *Arbetsmarknadsförsäkring*. Report to ESO, Ds 1989: 68.

Elmer, Å. (1960). *Folkpensioneringen i Sverige med särskild hänsyn till ålderspensioneringen*. Lund: Gleerups.

Granqvist, L., and Ståhlberg, A.-C. (2003). 'Occupational Pensions from a Gender Perspective', in G. Hughes and J. Stewart (eds.), *Reforming Pensions in Europe: Evolution of Pension Financing and Sources of Retirement Income*. Cheltenham and Northampton: Edward Elgar, 225–46.

Harrysson, L. (2000). *Arbetsgivare och pensioner. Industriarbetsgivarna och tjänstepensioneringen i Sverige 1900–1948*. Lund: Värpinge Ord & Text.

Lazear, E. (1979). 'Why is there Mandatory Retirement?'. *Journal of Political Economy*, 86: 1261–84.

Lundberg, U. (2003). *Juvelen i kronan. Socialdemokraterna och den allmänna pensionen*. Stockholm: Hjalmarsson & Högberg.

Molin, B. (1965). *Tjänstepensionsfrågan: en studie i svensk partipolitik*. Göteborg: Akademiförlaget.

National Insurance Board (1999). *Sammanställning över förändringar i regelsystemet inom socialförsäkringssystemet sedan år 1968*.

Palme, J. (ed.) (2001). *Hur blev den stora kompromissen möjlig? Politiken bakom den svenska pensionsreformen*. Stockholm: Pensionsforum.

Palmer, E. (2002). 'Swedish Pension Reform – How Did It Evolve and What Does It Mean for the Future?', in M. Feldstein and H. Siebert (eds.), *Social Security Pension Reform in Europe*. Chicago: University of Chicago Press, 171–210.

——and Wadensjö, E. (2004). 'Public Pension Reform and Contractual Agreements in Sweden – From Defined Benefit to Defined Contribution', in M. Rein and W. Schmähl (eds.), *Rethinking the Welfare State*. Cheltenham: Edward Elgar, 226–50.

Pensionsgruppen (2009). *Detta är pensionsöverenskommelsen*. Ministry of Social Affairs, Ds 2009: 53.

Persson, M. (1998). 'Reforming Social Security in Sweden', in H. Siebert (ed.), *Redesigning Social Security*. Kiel: Mohr Siebeck, 169–85.

Riksdagens revisorer (2002). *Statens avtalsförsäkringar*. Report 2001/02: 11.

Schmidt, F. (1974). *Allmänna och privata pensioner*. Stockholm: P.A. Norstedt & Söners förlag.

Selén, J., and Ståhlberg A.-C. (2004). 'Wage and Compensation Inequality – How Different?' *FIEF Working Paper*, 197.

Sjöfors, B. (1982). *Historik*. Stockholm: SPV.

Sjögren Lindquist, G., and Wadensjö, E. (2006). *National Social Insurance – Not the Whole Picture. Supplementary Compensation in case of Loss of Income*. ESS Report 2006/5, Ministry of Finance.

—— (2007). *Ett svårlagt pussel – kompletterande ersättningar vid inkomstbortfall*. ESS Report 2007/1, Ministry of Finance.

Sundén, A. (2006). 'The Swedish Experience with Pension Reform'. *Oxford Review of Economic Policy*, 22/1: 133–48.

Swedish Social Insurance Agency (SSIA) (2007). *Orange Report. Annual Report of the Swedish Pension System 2007*. Stockholm.

——(2008). *Orange Report. Annual Report of the Swedish Pension System 2008*. Stockholm.

Wadensjö, E. (1990). 'Ekonomiska aspekter på avtalspensionerna', in SOU 1990: 78.

——(1997). 'The Welfare Mix in Pension Provisions in Sweden', in M. Rein and E. Wadensjö (eds.), *Enterprise and the Welfare State*. Cheltenham: Edward Elgar, 266–308.

Part IV

Mature Multipillar Pension Systems

10

Britain: Exhausted Voluntarism – The Evolution of a Hybrid Pension Regime

Paul Bridgen and Traute Meyer

1. Introduction

Since 1945 the typical features of the British pension system have been a low public benefit and a mature but heterogeneous occupational and personal pensions sector which is far from universal and which leaves many pensioners without additional income to be dependent on the means test. Occupational pensions rest on voluntarism; thus companies have been free to decide whether or not schemes operate. Many large British companies that offer schemes function under a strong shareholder model of corporate governance: employees and therefore unions have until recently had very little impact on scheme development and governance. These traits have led the British system to be viewed as consistent with the liberal welfare and uncoordinated market regime types.

In the following overview of the pension regime and the evolution of the public–private relationship since 1918, we will show that while the classification as liberal market-oriented is appropriate for some elements of the British pension arrangements, the system has, since the Second World War, always had a hybrid nature which has become increasingly evident over time (see also Esping-Andersen 1990: 82–8). From the 1950s onwards, a strong statist side was expressed through the role of the state as employer and as regulator. Significant public sector employment meant that pension coverage has always been broader and benefits more generous for less qualified workers than expected by welfare capitalism theory. Secondly, regulation of occupational schemes has ensured increasingly strict protection of members' benefits, making schemes more inclusive than predicted. This hybridity is a product of the fact that the regime has always been contested politically, a contest that has been particularly evident in recent years. The Pensions Acts of 2007 and 2008 (OPSI 2007, 2008) pledge an increase in the public benefit level from 2012 and introduce a greater element of employer compulsion into the private sector, shifting the regime in a more social-democratic direction.

We will argue that these latest developments followed recognition by all actors that support for the policy of regulated voluntarism set in train in the 1980s had been exhausted. Collective private actors had tolerated increasing regulation for some time, but from the mid-1990s, employers and insurers have retreated significantly from their social policy role. At the same time, public policymakers have not wanted to compensate for private sector withdrawal through an increase in public universal benefits, because the existing regime bestowed on them one of the lowest pension budgets in Europe. The reforms of 2007/8 were a way out of this gridlock between the state and the private sector in the face of a general acknowledgement that the social outcomes of existing arrangements were unacceptable.

Part I: The evolution of the public–private pension mix

2. Main features of the British pension system

The British pension system is generally regarded as consistent with the type of social policy arrangements expected in liberal market economies: it has been characterized by some of the lowest public state benefits in Europe (Bridgen and Meyer 2007b: 229; Ginn 2001: 11–12; 2003: 16; Rake and Falkingham 2000) that have failed to prevent poverty, and mature occupational, earnings-related pensions, supplemented by personal pensions schemes (see Figure 10.1). Means testing has thus always played an important role. In 2006, at least 20 per cent of pensioners, the majority women, claimed the means-tested Pension Credit (DWP 2006; TUC 2004).[1]

Nevertheless, since the mid-1970s the basic state pension (BSP) has been fairly broad in scope and sensitive to social risks. In 2009, it was paid in full to men reaching 65 and women reaching 60[2] who had paid earnings-related contributions on income between a lower and an upper earnings level for at least forty-four (men) or thirty-nine (women) years (IDS 2003: 15). Carers for children, sick, or disabled people received entitlements after at least twenty-two years in employment. Credits were also available for times of unemployment, sickness or disability, and for divorcees, widows, and widowers (Pensions Service 2003: 90). The BSP was complemented by the mandatory, earnings-related State Second Pension, which had replaced State Earnings Related Pension Scheme (SERPS) in 1998, and was set to mature up to 2030, raising the level of state provision for future pensioners significantly above that received by current pensioners (PPI

---

[1] Not all citizens entitled take up this benefit (Evandrou and Falkingham 2005).
[2] Women born after April 1955 will have to retire at 65.

	First pillar	Second pillar	Third pillar
	State pensions (SP)	Occupational pensions (OP)	Personal pensions (PP)
Third tier		Voluntary occupational pension plans	Voluntary personal pension plans
Second tier	State Earnings-Related Pension (SERPS) (1978-2002) State Second Pension (S2P) (since 2002)	National Employment Savings Trust (NEST): mandatory offer by employer with employer contributions of min. 3% from 2012. Employees can opt out of statutory scheme. No contracting out. Contracting-out to approved DB or DC occupational scheme instead of S2P	Contracting-out to approved personal scheme instead of S2P
First tier	Basic State Pension		
	Means-tested Income Support for pensioners, plus housing and council tax benefits and winter fuel allowance; tax-financed.		

Figure 10.1 Pillars and tiers of British pension system

Source: Adapted from synopsis in Schulze and Moran (2007).

2006). However, the State Second Pension excludes the self-employed and those paying into a contracted-out occupational or personal pension (Agulnik 1999). It credits childcare on a lower level and for a shorter time than the BSP.

Non-state provision, the other important element in British pensions, will be left to the voluntarism of the market until 2012. This is dominated by a sometimes very generous occupational pension system which developed quickly from a low base during the post-war period, encouraged by fiscal incentives (Hannah 1986; Sinfield 2000). Coverage has always been concentrated in large firms where the skill imperative has been greatest and costs could more easily be absorbed (Mares 2001) but it has been maintained at a reasonably high level since the mid-1960s because of near-universal coverage in the public sector and industries privatized by the Conservatives in the 1980s. Since the 1980s, this provision has become increasingly tightly regulated, becoming what amounts to a surrogate welfare state (see also Leisering 2003; Marschallek 2005).

Regarding personal pensions, Britain has the largest life insurance market of all OECD countries: in 2004 investments in this area were roughly half of the country's GDP (OECD 2005). However, personal savings schemes have only rarely been used by those on lower to middle incomes. In 1999 Stakeholder Pensions, money purchase personal schemes with limited charges, were introduced to increase private saving particularly among the low paid. Employers had to facilitate access for employees, but they were not obliged to contribute and the large majority did not (Pensions Commission 2004: 93). Thus, take up rates among lower-income groups were low (ABI 2003; Pensions Commission 2004: 92). This situation is likely to change. The Pensions Act 2008 (OPSI 2008) makes it obligatory for employers to enrol employees in a pension scheme which has to meet minimum statutory criteria, and to which employers have to pay contributions.

3. The evolution of the public–private mix

The 2008 reform is the most recent manifestation of a political struggle over the British pension system which has been taking place for most of the post-war period and which is responsible for the hybrid system that developed over this period. As Blake put it, 'the cement never sets on British pensions legislation' (Blake 2003: vii) with public and private pension provision in a particular state of flux since the two systems first became formally entwined in 1959. Tables 10.1 and 10.2 give an overview of these changes.[3] The system has gone through three phases: a liberal one (1945–75) with low benefits, fragmented coverage, and high poverty risks; a brief period of social-democratic reformism (1976–9) resulting in higher benefits broad coverage and significantly diminished poverty risks; and another liberal phase when many of the reforms of the late 1970s were retrenched (1980–2007).

Before 1945, the majority of British citizens over the age of 65 lived in poverty, dependent for their income on either very low public pensions or on the means-tested and much hated poor relief. State involvement in the provision of pensions had begun in 1908 with the passage of the Old Age Pensions Act, which introduced a small means-tested pension for all men and women over 70 who were of 'good character' (Macnicol 1998: 158). Its level was increased slowly over the next decade or so, but in 1925 its role at the heart of British pension policy was supplanted by a new contributory system which was introduced by the Conservatives as part of the 1925 Widows, Orphans, and Old

---

[3] The table is based on our evaluation of the social security legislation, supplemented by academic analyses. It only includes most relevant laws and excludes tax legislation. See Ginn (2001: 11) for an overview of pension reforms since 1975 and their impact on women and Ginn (2003: 18) for an overview of the structure of the British regime in 2002.

Table 10.1 Chronology of major pension reforms, Great Britain 1946–80

Year	Reform	Political context
1946	Introduction of basic state pension below poverty level, patchy, uncontrolled voluntary occupational sector	Initiated: wartime coalition government; passed: post-war Labour government
1946–8	Nationalization of mining, electricity, air travel, gas, iron, steel and transport widens coverage of public sector pensions	Labour government
1959	Small earnings-related pension introduced. Contracting-out rules introduced. Perceived as too complicated, thus no incentive	Conservative government
1973	Protection of rights for early leavers of occupational pension schemes increases employer costs	Conservative government
1975	Introduction of State Earnings-Related Pension Scheme (SERPS). Substantially increased public pension level and increased protection for non full-time employment. Incentives and regulation of voluntary occupational pensions strengthened: state compensates employers for declining value of non-indexed DB payments; reduced national insurance contribution rates; increased state pension offers better foundation. Business costs through 'appalling complexity of the act'; Guaranteed Minimum Pension (GMP) obligatory for contracted-out occupational benefits, not indexed on payment.	Labour government

Source: Acts are on: http://www.opsi.gov.uk/legislation/original.htm; for a comprehensive overview and analysis of British pensions legislation, see Blake (2003), Lynes (1960), and Mesher (1976).

Age Contributory Pensions Act. The Conservatives and the Treasury, the British finance ministry, had come to the conclusion that, given strong public support for state provision, the best option for those wishing to limit public welfare expenditure was to place the system on a flat-rate contributory base. The new system provided a pension for the years 65–69 and was available to those earning less than £250 per year. It was financed by employer and employee contributions and an annual grant from the Exchequer (Macnicol 1998: 214).

Those able to rise above this level could normally do so because of access to additional occupational schemes. Before the war, these were the preserve of a minority – around 13 per cent of workers, mainly public servants and higher paid private sector employees (Hannah 1986). Employers had voluntarily established the schemes and regarded them as a way of improving industrial relations and encouraging the retirement of older workers (see Whiteside 2003: 33). They were also attracted by the tax incentives provided by the state after 1921 (Hannah 1986: 18–30). Defined-benefit (DB) schemes came to predominate because in times of rapidly growing wages, such as the 1930s, they provided a better pension than average wage schemes, and thus better rewarded long-serving workers (Hannah 1986: 38).

Table 10.2 Chronology of pension system restructuring, Great Britain since 1980s

Year	Reform	Political context
1980	Public pension curbed through re-indexing to prices only. Increased costs of occupational pension: Regulation curbs employers' freedom to select scheme members on basis of age. Early leavers can only transfer rights into contracted-out schemes.	Conservative government
1981, 1984, 1985	Increased regulation of occupational pensions. Early leavers have right to transfer rights, and to use greater variety of schemes. Their preserved benefits at level of GMP indexed to inflation. Better information for scheme members.	Conservative government
1986	Cuts in public pension. Increased incentives for private sector voluntarism through contracting-out rules; business costs increase through indexation of occupational pensions: Contracting-out rules extended to money purchase and personal pension schemes. GMP indexed to inflation up to 3% on payment for contracted-out pension schemes, increasing scheme costs; early leavers' full pension rights accrual indexed to inflation.	Conservative government
1989	Private sector costs rise through equality laws: Access of female employees to occupational schemes made easier	Conservative government
1990	Private sector costs rise through extension of early leaver protection and increased regulation: Indexing of rule for early leavers of occupational schemes backdated to include all. Introduction of Ombudsman. Winding up of schemes harder. Tighter restrictions on investment; employee rights strengthened in case of employer insolvency.	Conservative government
1993	Private sector costs rise through reduction of contracting-out rebate for occupational and personal pensions schemes.	Conservative government
1995	Level of public pension reduced. Tightened regulation of occupational pension scheme funding: strict actuarial rules, obligation to appoint professionals to administer schemes, stricter regulation of minimum pension levels; stricter equal rights rules for men and women, strengthening of trustee rights vis-à-vis employers.	Conservative government
1999	Public means-tested pension level increased for very low paid; private sector cost rises slightly through regulation of personal pensions for low paid. Employers must recommend stakeholder personal pension schemes; insurers offering schemes regulated regarding minimum charges, and paying-in mode and scheme funding.	Labour government
2000	Public pension level increased for low earners and carers with employment career. For higher earners, low state pensions increases incentive to contract out. Private sector costs stays constant.	Labour government
2002	Public means-tested pensions for very low paid increased.	Labour government
2004	Private sector costs reduced in some areas, increased in others. Costs reduced through halving of indexation level for pension payments; costs increased through charge for Pension Protection Fund; more regulation regarding information policies and trustees.	Labour government
2007	Public pensions level and scope increased (re-indexed to earnings from 2012 at earliest); retirement age to be raised to 68 (2024–46). Private sector costs increase: Tax incentives for money purchase schemes and personal pensions reduced. DC schemes and personal pensions can no longer contract out of state scheme.	Labour government
2007–8	From 2012 Employers must enrol all employees in a pension scheme and pay contributions (rising to min. 8% for employer/employee of earnings for DC, guaranteed level for DB). Employees can opt out.	Labour government

Source: www.opsi.gov.uk/legislation/original.htm; for a comprehensive overview and analysis of British pensions legislation, see Blake (2003).

After the Second World War, a Labour government reformed the fragmented system of social insurance on the basis of the 1942 Beveridge Report, through the 1946 National Insurance Act. In 1948, the BSP came into immediate effect for all wage earners and their dependants, including the self-employed but it was set at a flat-rate level below that proposed by Beveridge meaning recourse to means-tested benefits continued (Baldwin 1990; Bridgen 2006; Pemberton et al. 2006). This decision, together with a voluntarist approach to non-state provision, made for a strongly liberal system at this stage (Bridgen and Meyer 2007a; Hannah 1986: 54–9; Pemberton et al. 2006). However, there were already elements which ran counter to this, and these were to develop further in the late 1940s and early 1950s. First, the 1946 Act treated married women as dependants and effectively barred them from accruing independent rights even if in paid employment (for details see Ginn 2003: 11–13; Groves 1983: 46; Land 1985: 54, 56). Secondly, a substantial post-war increase in public sector employment as a product of Labour's nationalization programme in the 1940s had important implications for the coverage of occupational provision (Foreman-Peck and Millward 1994: 274–5; Middlemas 1979: 396). Nationalization, in effect, created within the mainly liberal British economy a large corporatist enclave with strong trade unions (Chick 1998: 82; Clegg 1978: 190, 388), which pushed successfully for the extension of pension rights enjoyed by other public sector workers, such as civil servants (Hannah 1986: 4–41; Russell 1991: 128–9).

The basic structure of this public/private mix remained largely intact until the mid-1970s, although a small level of earnings-relation was introduced by the Conservatives as part of the 1959 Pension Act. This reform was a response to a much more ambitious 1957 proposal by the Labour Party that was mainly designed to increase the contributory income of the state scheme by dispensing with the flat-rate contributions favoured by Beveridge and replacing them with earnings related ones (Bridgen 2000). In return, a small earnings-related pension could be accrued but the reform was not meant to undermine the liberal principles of the 1946 Act (Ellis 1989: 16). In addition, the 1959 Act established a greater connection through contracting-out arrangements between the state system and the occupational sphere, which were designed to ensure that the reform did not reduce the ground for occupational provision. Yet, the maintenance of this space came at a cost for employers – greater regulation (Ellis 1989). This was to prove the start of an incremental process of growing state regulation of private sector provision which by the end of the century had created a highly complex public–private pension system.

Notwithstanding these important regulatory implications, the reform was insufficient in terms of benefits to end demands from the left for change (Baldwin 1990: 241–6; Bridgen 2000). However, attempts by the Labour governments of the 1960s to reform state pensions in response to these claims ran into political gridlock (Fawcett 1996; Pemberton 2009), not least because of opposition to change from public sector unions; it took a few more years before another Labour government finally passed the Social Security Pension Act of 1975 (Ginn 2003: 14–16). With this legislation the British post-war public pension system entered a brief social-democratic period, characterized by im-proved protection of private blue-collar workers and married women (Barr and Coulter 1990: 281–2, 295). To raise benefits for employees not covered by occupational schemes, a commitment was made to increase the BSP in line with wages and a new second public tier, the SERPS, was introduced. These changes together guaranteed a pension of 25 per cent of earnings in addition to the BSP (Ellis 1989: 50). SERPS was also open to female employees whose pension levels were calculated in the same way as for men, even though they retired five years earlier and lived longer (Groves 1983: 52; Hannah 1986: 61; Pascall 1986: 211). In addition, SERPS granted a widow's pension (Baldwin 1990: 241–7; Ginn 2001: 11). The Act also phased out married women's option to relinquish pension rights by not paying contributions and it put an end to the other restrictions for wives. All employed women now had to pay social insurance contributions (Groves 1983: 52; Land 1985: 53–62). In addition, through 'Home Responsibility Protection' for the first time care-giving periods were recognized as equivalent to paid work, provided the carer gave up employ-ment and had a contribution record of at least twenty years (Land 1985: 57).

The 1975 Act also increased the state's engagement with the private sector (see Table 10.1). It offered increased incentives for employers to run occupa-tional DB pension schemes, and in turn it tightened regulation: to make occu-pational schemes more attractive for employers, a rebate on national insurance contributions for contracted-out employees and employers was established which remains in place to the present day (Ellis 1989: 48–9). In return, employ-ers who decided to offer contracted-out schemes had to include a widow's pension and they had to pay a similar level of protection to that which members in the new state scheme would receive. This level was specified through the Guaranteed Minimum Pension (GMP). The standard set by the GMP increased employer costs, but they did not have to index payment to inflation. Instead, government took on this role; through public funding it was ensured that contracted-out pension payments would increase in line with inflation, thus protecting benefit levels in occupational and state schemes equally well.

4. The changing public–private mix

The 1970s reforms would have meant a significant move in a social-democratic direction and a more encompassing, more generous public pension. However, this outcome was never achieved. In 1980, the Conservative government re-indexed benefits to prices, and it reduced substantially the benefits accruable under SERPS (Ginn 2003: 15–16; Pierson 1994: 53–73). In the process, a con-certed effort began to dismantle many of the more hybrid parts of the British pension system. Policymakers cut public benefits in successive reforms (1980, 1986, 1995) (see Table 10.2). As compensation, they attempted to encourage private sector expansion, increasingly through the use of individualized personal pensions rather than the more collective occupational forms. In 1986, contracting-out rules were thus extended to money purchase and personal pension schemes, in order to make them more attractive. This policy ran into serious problems in the mid-1990s as a series of scandals hit the operation of non-state provision (Waine 1995). The government's response was greater regulation, such as an insistence on minimum levels of funding, more member involvement in scheme administration (1990, 1993, 1995), and the introduction of a Pension Compensation Board in 1995 (Blake 2003; Clark 2003: 234; Waine 1995; Whiteside 2003: 41–2). All these changes increased company costs, which were made greater by the decision in 1995 to make employers running contracted-out DB schemes responsible for indexation (Blake 2003); and gender equalization changes (1989, 1995) passed largely in response to EU legislation (Cichowski 2004; Mazey 1998).

When Labour came to power in 1997, this policy of expecting the private sector to carry voluntarily a substantial part of the welfare state's responsibility was largely maintained. However, the new government was more concerned to improve the social inclusiveness of the regime, by addressing its two main shortcomings: pensioner poverty and lack of private savings amongst low and middle income groups without employer support (Secretary of State for Social Security 1998: 7). Thus, the means-tested Pension Credit was introduced (1999), regulated forms of personal pensions (Stakeholders) were encouraged (1999), and the second public tier was made more generous for low-income groups and carers (2000). However, by 2002 it had become evident that the steps taken to increase private sector pension engagement had not achieved their aims and the pension system was widely reported as being in 'crisis' (Pemberton et al. 2006). The take-up of Stakeholder Pensions was low, and the early 2000s saw a wave of closure of DB schemes to new members in large private sector companies (see below). Thus, the number of pensioners dependent on the means test was projected to rise strongly in the future, undermining a system based on voluntary savings. In response, the government announced the foundation of an independent Pensions Commission (with three high level members from academia, the employers, and the trade unions), one of whose main tasks would be to question whether private sector voluntarism was still feasible (Secretary of State for Work and Pensions 2002: 5). However, while the Pensions Commission was doing its work, the organized interests of employers, insurers, and pension managers mobilized against greater state intervention in the non-state sphere and pushed for higher state pensions as an alternative (ABI 2002; 2003; CBI 2004; NAPF 2002; 2005). Against this background, the Pensions Commission stretched its remit, and contrary to government's expectations, it recommended fundamental change not only for the private but also the public sector (Pensions Commission 2005: 2, 5).

Even though the government had originally resisted change to the public system, it accepted most of the Commission's recommendations in the face of a broad supportive consensus which included both sides of industry (OPSI 2007, 2008). The Pensions Act commits the government to re-indexing the BSP from 2012 at the earliest and by the end of the parliament at the latest, probably no later than Spring 2015 (OPSI 2007). The means-tested Guarantee Credit will also be linked to earnings, with the costs mediated by a rise in the pension age to 68 by 2046. The Commission's proposal to introduce a residency-based pension was rejected as too costly but the Act broadens the scope for the BSP and the Second State Pension (S2P): qualifying years will be reduced to 30 and credit arrangements for carers and very low earners have improved since April 2010. According to the Department for Work and Pensions as a consequence of this reform, 70 per cent of women will receive the full BSP as opposed to 30 per cent in 2008 (DWP 2008).[4] This change will apply to all pensioners retiring after April 2010, and it will cost an additional 1 billion pounds a year immediately. In total, these reforms would raise the projected cost of pension benefits in 2050 from 4.4 per cent of GDP as envisaged under the old system to 6.5 per cent (DWP 2008). In the realm of private pensions, personal and money purchase schemes will no longer be able to contract out of the state pension. Furthermore, the Pensions Act 2008 makes it obligatory for employers to enrol employees in a pension scheme of their choice, which has to meet minimum statutory criteria and to which employers have to pay contributions.

Part II: The governance of supplementary pensions

5. Who is covered?

British public pensions typically provide a benefit below the poverty line, and therefore occupational and personal schemes are vital for a comfortable retirement. However, these private pensions have only ever been on offer on a voluntary basis, and voluntarism brings with it partial coverage of employees only. Thus, one main feature of the regime has been its large gaps in coverage: in 2007, 47.7 per cent of British employees did not have access to any additional pension scheme through their employer, rendering about half of all adult workers vulnerable to poverty in retirement (see Table 10.3). This number has marginally increased since the late 1960s, when private and public sector pension schemes had the greatest number of members, 12.2 million, compared to 8.8 million in 2007 (GAD 2003: 18; ONS 2008: 15).

---

[4] Such figures are disputed by the Fawcett Society (2006), an independent lobby group for women's interests, but most commentators accept that the changes will significantly improve the situation for women.

Table 10.3 Male and female employment and pension scheme coverage by sector, the United Kingdom, 2007

	Jobs (1000s)	% of total	Jobs (1000s)	% of total	No pension provision with employer (%)			Women/ men ratio
	Women		Men		Women	Men	Total	
Agriculture, hunting, forestry, and fishing	30	0.5	76	1.2	79.9	77.6	78.2	2.3
Mining and quarrying	–	–	13	0.2	–	32.3	31.1	–
Manufacturing	400	6.7	1,060	17.4	53.0	44.1	46.2	8.9
Electricity, gas, and water supplies	13	0.2	18	0.3	31.2	16.6	20.6	14.6
Construction	104	1.7	609	10.0	69.8	66.6	67.1	3.2
Wholesale and retail trade; repair	1,421	23.8	1,366	22.5	70.7	66.7	68.7	4.0
Hotels and restaurants	568	9.5	444	7.3	92.7	91.4	92.1	1.3
Transport, storage, communication	184	3.1	467	7.7	48.2	41.5	43.2	6.7
Financial intermediation	114	1.9	104	1.7	18.8	18.9	18.8	–0.1
Real estate, renting, business activities	984	16.5	1,126	18.5	67.5	58.3	62.3	9.2
Public admin and defence	70	1.2	49	0.8	10.3	7.0	8.6	3.3
Education	723	12.1	249	4.1	25.2	50.2	24.0	–25.0
Health and social work	993	16.7	202	3.3	40.9	32.9	39.3	8.0
Other community, social and personal services	357	6.0	298	4.9	69.4	60.4	65.0	9.0
Total	5,961	100.0	6,081	100.0	47.6	47.9	47.7	–0.3

Source: http://www.statistics.gov.uk/downloads/theme_labour/ASHE_2007/2007_Pensions.pdf, own calculations.

Coverage varies strongly by sector. Public sector coverage has always been high: in 2007, 84 per cent of all workers had access to occupational schemes. In the private sector, only the mining industry (69 per cent), manufacturers (54 per cent), electricity providers (79 per cent), transport businesses (57 per cent), and financial services (81 per cent) offered more than half of their workers access to pension schemes; however, these protected industries accounted for only about 23 per cent of employment in the private sector. Coverage was lowest in the hospitality sector (8 per cent) and it was also low in the two largest private sectors, retail (31 per cent) and real estate (38 per cent). Together, these latter sectors employed roughly 48 per cent of all private sector workers in 2007 (see Table 10.3). Coverage also varies by size of business. In 2003, 60 per cent of workers in large businesses were covered by employer sponsored schemes. In contrast, only a minority of employees was covered by medium sized (44 per cent) and small companies (29 per cent) (DWP 2004: 83; Pensions Commission 2004: 64).

Coverage also varies substantially between income groups, an outcome predicted for occupational systems by Richard Titmuss (1958). Manual workers have always had lower overall levels of access to occupational provision (Russell 1991) and this variation persists today. Thus, in 2007, higher paid workers were covered to a much greater extent than lower paid workers: while 70 per cent of those earning more than £600 a week were covered,[5] only 29 per cent of those earning between £100 and £200 were covered (ONS 2008). This disparity in coverage is made substantially smaller by the broad level of coverage in the public sector. Thus, while in the public sector the coverage gap between these two income groups is 27 percentage points, in the private sector it is 42 percentage points. This reflects a more general sectoral variation in the chances of lower paid workers being covered for occupational provision. While in the public sector more than 65 per cent of individuals earning between £100 and £200 a week are covered, and in finance, where private sector coverage is highest, 66 per cent of this group are covered, in the retail and real estate sectors, where overall coverage is much lower, only 20.2 and 6 per cent respectively are protected (ONS 2008).

The overall story of coverage and decline of employer-related schemes reads very differently from a gender perspective. Indeed, decline affected men strongly, whose pension position had matured in the late 1960s, while women were still catching up until 1995, when both genders were affected by private sector decline. Thus, active male membership in private pension schemes peaked, at 6.8 million, in 1967, it declined to a fairly stable level of 4.5 million during the late 1970s and 1980s, and it went through another phase of steep decline between 1995 and 2007, from 4.1 to 1.8 million. Between 1967 and 2007, private membership had declined by a staggering 74 per cent, but most of this decline took place between 1995 and 2007. Male membership in the public sector had always been lower than in the private and the decline since the mid-1970s was less steep, but it amounted to 62 per cent by 2007 nevertheless (GAD 2003: 17; see Table 10.4).

In contrast, active female membership in the private sector peaked much later, in 1995, at a lower level of 2.1 million, after having risen almost constantly from a very low level in the 1950s and early 1960s, and it also declined steeply, by 48 per cent, from this peak until 2007. In the public sector, in the 1950s and 1960s, membership was as low as in the private sector, but it rose

[5] Coverage includes here defined benefit, defined contribution, and group personal pension schemes.

Table 10.4 Number of active members of occupational pension schemes: by sector and sex, the United Kingdom, 1953–2007

	Private sector		Public sector		Total	
	Men	Women	Men	Women	Men	Women
1953	2.5	0.6	2.4	0.7	4.9	1.3
1995	4.1	2.1	2.0	2.1	6.1	4.2
2007	1.8	1.1	1.4	2.4	3.2	3.5
Peak	6.8	2.1	3.7	2.4	9.9	4.2
Year of peak	1967	1995	1975–9	2007	1967	1995
2007 as % of peak	26.5	52.4	37.8	100.0	32.3	83.3
2007 as % of 1995	43.9	52.4	70.0	114.3	52.5	83.3
2007 as % of 1953	72.0	183.3	58.3	342.9	65.3	269.2

Source: ONS (2008: 15), own calculations.

strongly between 1971 (1.1 mio) and 1975 (1.7 mio) and has increased since, to peak in 2007, at 2.4 million (ONS 2008: 15; see Table 10.4). Therefore, in 2007 there were more female active occupational scheme members (3.5 million) than male (3.2 million), with lower paid women (between £100 and £200 a week) having a better chance of being protected than lower paid men in both the public (62 per cent against 44 per cent coverage) and private sectors (18 per cent against 7 per cent) (ONS 2008).

Examining the share of male and female employees entitled to occupational schemes in the different sectors of the economy for 2007, there were three segments (see Table 10.3): the first consists of manufacturing – it is mainly male – and access to a pension scheme for men was best here overall (above 50 per cent); access was even better in electricity, transport, and social work but these sectors are less significant for employment overall. Those fewer women who worked in manufacturing were significantly less likely than men to have access to a pension scheme. Secondly, and somewhat at odds with the widespread association between women and service employment, there was a mixed-gender segment of private sector services in retail, hotels and restaurants, and business activities. Here, a substantial proportion of men and women worked, and this was the segment with the lowest coverage of non-state pension schemes across the economy, which was even lower for women. Thirdly, there was the public sector, the female part of the labour market. It was far less relevant for men, but pension scheme coverage rates here were highest in the overall workforce.

Sectoral coverage rates and pension scheme quality correlate strongly. In our three segments of the employment structure scheme members in the public sector and welfare sector enjoy the highest quality schemes. In 2007, those members in education, health, and social work were almost always contributing to DB schemes. DB schemes were also strong in manufacturing, but only half of male scheme members had access to one; 32 per cent were reliant on employer-sponsored defined-contribution (DC) or Group Pension schemes, and more than 10 per cent paid into Stakeholder Schemes, possibly without any employer contributions. Finally, in consumer- and business-related services those schemes where the individual carries the risk of market performance, DC, personal pensions, and Stakeholder Schemes, outweighed DB schemes by far among scheme members, and this was true for men and women (own calculation based on official statistics; figures available on request).

Thus, overall, men's access to private pension schemes of high quality is tied to the fate of manufacturing, while women's has been tied to public sector dynamics. Female employees benefited particularly from the strong expansion of public sector services, especially during the Labour governments since 1997 which were committed to improving health and education, and from a public sector ethos that so far prevented the closure of DB schemes in the public sector. In addition, equal opportunity legislation made it possible for female employees to some extent to buck the private sector trend and extend their coverage until the mid-1990s. At the same time, the expansion of consumer and business-related services involved similar proportions of male and female workers, and because of low pension coverage rates and low scheme quality in these sectors for both genders, both increased their poverty risk in similar ways. So far, these three segments have been exposed in very different ways to the most recent pressure on non-state pensions.

6. What kind of benefits?

As shown, benefit types vary strongly by sector, and thus, by gender, and the high-quality DB schemes are concentrated in the public and manufacturing sectors. These schemes are still generally final salary schemes, paying a proportion of last wage calculated in relation to years of service and normally an accrual rate of between 1/60th, the most common, and 1/80th together with a tax-free lump sum (IDS 2006). Average salary schemes have increased in recent years, but are much less common than in other countries such as the Netherlands (IDS 2006: 14).

The high coverage of DB schemes in manufacturing is likely to decline steeply because between 2000 and 2007 the number of occupational schemes still open to new members has fallen quickly, from 250 to 130 in the public sector and from 62,100 to 28,680 in the private sector. Table 10.5 shows that this shift halved the number of schemes open to new members in the public sector and it almost halved those in the private sector. To appreciate the significance of this reduction for workers, it is important to consider the size of these schemes as

Table 10.5 Number of occupational pension schemes by size, the United Kingdom 2007

Members	Open	Closed	Frozen	Winding up	Total	Open schemes % of total
10,000+	370	180	30	10	590	62.7
1,000–4,999	490	510	70	70	1,140	43.0
100–999	940	1,820	870	310	3,940	23.9
12–99	1,210	1,220	. . .	. . .	4,070	29.7
2–11	25,800	15,380	. . .	. . .	44,370	58.1
Total	28,810	19,110	4,410	1,780	54,110	53.2

Note: . . . = cells suppressed to protect confidentiality.
Source: ONS (2007, 2008).

well. Table 10.5 also shows that in 2007 the largest schemes, with more than 10,000 members, were still the most likely to be open to new members (63 per cent), whereas small- and medium-sized companies were the most likely to have closed their schemes.

In a substantial share of businesses, closure indicates that DB schemes have been replaced by less generous DC schemes; between 2001 and 2003, 41 per cent of companies operating a DB scheme changed to a DC scheme for new members (CBI 2004: 13). However, for some new workers the transition means that they will not have access to either (DWP 2004: 56). Increasingly, companies are beginning to close schemes to existing members: 18 per cent of DB schemes closed to new members included in a 2009 survey by the Association of Consulting Actuaries were also closed to future accrual for existing employees, with 34 per cent of those that remained open to future accrual under review (ACA 2009: 3).

Most DC schemes operate on a Group Personal Pension or Stakeholder basis (NAPF 2008), with the company facilitating access to a market provider which supplies pensions on the basis of an individual contract (IDS 2006: 36–8). As is the case with most DC pensions of this type, the size of the benefit is determined on an individual basis by the level of contributions, the performance of the fund, and in most cases the cost of the annuity purchased to provide the pension. However, in recent years the government has encouraged bigger trust-based schemes not to provide pensions on the basis of annuities but fund them instead using the scheme's own resources (DWP 2002). Pensioners can also choose on retirement to delay the purchase of an annuity, but normally only until they are 75 (IDS 2006: 31, 34).

These trends and the variations in pension type by sector mean that there are likely to be significant differences in the benefits employees receive not just by income group but also by cohort, employment sector and company size. These variations will be mitigated over time by the recent reforms but they will be far from eradicated. This can be illustrated by means of policy simulation (for details see Meyer et al. 2007) which can indicate the difference in the projected pensions of individuals with identical work histories and public pension entitlement but varying access to non-state pensions. In Table 10.6, we concentrate on the outcomes for a single biography – a worker on half average wages with a full-working career, whose income on retirement is calculated on the basis of the reformed pension system and access throughout their career to state provision and: (a) a typical DB pension (b) a typical DC pension; (c) a National Employment Savings Trust (NEST; until 2010 called Personal Accounts) pension; and (d) no other form of provision (i.e. they opted out of NEST). Overall outcomes are expressed in 2007 values and in relation to a social inclusion line of 40 per cent average wages.

To illustrate the impact of cohort differences (i.e. the shift away from DB pensions for new company members), Table 10.6 shows the significantly smaller projected pension someone with a typical DC pension receives in comparison to the same biography with access to DB provision. This is mainly a product of the lower contributions paid into the former (see below). Thus, the DC individual is projected to receive £79 a week less in 2007 values, which amounts to 33 percentage points in relation to the social exclusion line. Nevertheless, both are above the social exclusion line, although the DC biography would be expected to fall below it shortly after retirement due to the fact that occupational provision and the state second pension are only indexed to prices. Someone entirely reliant on state provision would be far less fortunate. Their

Table 10.6 Comparison of projected* outcomes for worker on 0.5 average wages by type of pension scheme, the United Kingdom 207

	State only	State/ NEST	State/typical defined contribution	State/typical defined benefit
BSP, 2007 values	82	82	82	82
S2P, 2007 values	38	38	38	none
Non-state, 2007 values	0	65**	124***	241
Total pension, 2007 values	120	185	244	323
Total pension as % of 40% average wages	50	77	102	135

Notes: * Annual inflation, 1.9 per cent; average wage rise, 3.9 per cent.
**. The outcome from NEST is based on the minimum level of contributions (8 per cent of pensionable earnings), a real interest rate of 3.9 per cent after charges and annuity rate of 5 per cent.
***. The figures for the defined contribution and defined benefit pensions are the median outcomes from a range of schemes.
Source: Own calculations.

pension is only projected to be 50 per cent of the social exclusion threshold despite the improvements that have recently been made to state provision. However, their situation would improve significantly if they decided to remain in NEST. This would reduce the gap between them and the DC individual by more than half, although it would still leave them 23 percentage points below the social exclusion threshold (Bridgen and Meyer 2005: 768).[6] Together with the decline in DB pensions, therefore, the recent reform has the potential to diminish over time the inequalities in outcome produced by the British system. However, where DB pensions survive – in larger companies, privileged parts of the private sector (e.g. manufacturing), the public sector, and among older and the most wealthy individuals – workers are likely still to receive a significantly higher pension.

7. Who pays?

Contributions to occupational pension schemes are normally made by employees and employers, although the non-payment of employer contributions to Group Personal Pension and Stakeholder schemes is not uncommon (IDS 2006: 36–40). For contracted-out schemes, the minimum joint level of contributions is determined by the obligation to pay a pension at least equivalent to the state additional pension foregone and to index this to inflation (see Table 10.2). These schemes also receive from the state a contracted-out rebate for each individual, to reflect the cost of the state pension given up. For schemes which are not contracted-out, there is no legally prescribed minimum level of contribution or a contracted-out rebate.

Employee contributions can be fixed rate or age-related for both DB or DC schemes, while for the latter they sometimes operate on a 'matching' basis with the employer paying the same, or doubling, the contribution the employee chooses to pay (IDS 2006: 16, 24). Employer contributions differ markedly between the two types of scheme. For DC schemes they are specified in advance, while for most DB systems, they are determined on an annual basis by the scale of the scheme's liabilities. With liabilities rising in recent years, this has meant a sharp increase in employer contributions to DB schemes. For example in 2004/5, the average employer contribution rose by 42.6 per cent, with the total employer contribution rising by 49.7 per cent (IDS 2006: 15). As a result, employer contributions to DB schemes tend to be much higher than to DC schemes. In 2007, on average, the latter attracted less than half (9.1 per cent) of the contributions of the former (20.5 per cent), which in part explains the shift between the two types.

---

[6] These figures are based on the assumption that the individual is contracted out for both types of provision and that the defined benefit provision worker is only employed by one company. For all other assumptions, see Bridgen/Meyer (2005).

Certainly, employers have used a switch to a DC scheme to reduce payments, with employers' contributions declining on average from 15.6 to 6.5 per cent and employees' falling from 4.9 to 2.7 per cent (ONS 2008: 27). The shift from DB to DC schemes does not only leave scheme members more vulnerable because they are more exposed to the risk of market downturns, but also because their pension pots and thus benefits are going to be significantly smaller. Indeed, many employers have started to worry that DCs will not pay sufficient to encourage older workers to retire (NAPF 2008) and there are some indications that consequently employer contributions to these schemes are beginning to rise (NAPF 2009). The new pension legislation will stop contribution rates for DC schemes from falling below the minimum contribution level of 8 per cent but little will change regarding the pension quality of those currently members of occupational DC schemes.

8. Who governs? Who decides? Who manages?

The governance of occupational pensions in the United Kingdom reflects the broader corporate governance arrangements common among British companies. These arrangements are consistent with the type of strong shareholder model expected in a liberal market economy (Davies 1998: 375, 377). Reflecting this situation, the governance of occupational pensions has until recently been largely in the hands of corporate actors, with little input from employees or unions. Most schemes, particularly DB ones, have operated on the basis of trust law, although with the shift to DC pensions more schemes are operating outside this framework (NAPF 2009). Trust-based schemes must separate the pension fund from the operation of the company with responsibility for the administration of the scheme and the investment of the fund ostensibly lodged with trustees. They must make decisions in the best interest of the beneficiaries (existing and future) on the basis of the trust deeds and rules (Blake 2003: 94–5; Clark 2006: 458; IDS 2005). These protective mechanisms are in place to ensure that the company does not use the pension fund for its own purposes and that its investment strategy is one which advances the long-term financial interests of scheme members.

Companies have considerable discretion over the operation of schemes for four main reasons. First, and in some ways most importantly, the company has always retained the ultimate right to decide whether to offer a scheme or to continue offering an existing one to new members. For example, companies did not need trustee agreement to undertake the recent closure of DB schemes to new members. Secondly, company directors are allowed to be trustees of the company pension fund, and many have been (Blake 2003: 338; Myners 2001: 31). Indeed, it has been seen as useful for the financial director in particular to be a trustee because they have a clear sense of the company's financial position and a high level of financial expertise, both of which are useful for the trust's decision-making. In 2008, most financial directors still felt it was appropriate for them to exercise this role (NAPF 2008). However, this system has operated on the basis that company directors will put aside their company interests when acting as trustees, something which the evidence suggests has not always been the case. Thirdly, the trust deeds of most schemes assign the main power of amendment of schemes to the company, with trustees required to accept such requests (TPR 2007). This amending power might involve, for example, a request to change the benefit structure or accrual rates of existing schemes, generally for future accruals. Trustees are only able to oppose the proposed change if the employer is unlawfully proposing an amendment which affects detrimentally the accrued rights of scheme members (Pensions Regulator 2007) which can only be altered with the agreement of trustees and members (Pickering 2002). Finally, while the trust is ultimately responsible for the administration of schemes, this has generally been an oversight role with the company itself organizing the administration of the scheme either through an in-house pensions team or through a contractual arrangement with professional pensions administrators, such as consultant or actuary companies (IDS 2005). This rather weak position of trustees in relation to companies is accentuated by the fact that most trustees are unpaid and have traditionally met only four or so times a year (Myners 2001). They have for the most part been generalist business executives with no formal training in pension administration or investment and have thus tended to rely on actuaries and investment consultants to advise them on the basis of a contractual relationship (Myners 2001: 66).

Over the last decade, these arrangements for the governance and administration of occupational pension schemes have come under considerable scrutiny. On the one hand, concerns have been raised over whether the trust system sufficiently protects beneficaries' interests, an agenda which has created opportunities for more member and union involvement; on the other hand, the trust system has been criticized in relation to its investment role. As will be seen, these two agendas are to some extent in tension, and debate continues about which is more important. With regard first to the question of beneficiary interest, this agenda rose initially as a consequence of the scandals in the operation of occupational schemes of the early 1990s, most particularly the Maxwell pension scandal. This set in train a legislative agenda on pension scheme governance and funding which started with the 1995 Pension Act and continued up to 2004 when further regulations were enacted. This agenda's main concern has been to bolster the protection of members' interests provided by the trustee system (Clark 2004). The focus has been on the make-up of the trustee board, the funding levels of schemes, and protection for members in the face of company insolvency. In terms of governance, this has led to more member involvement in trusts and an increase in external control and scrutiny by government, operating through a quasi-independent regulator.

With regard to member involvement, the 1995 Pensions Act made it compulsory for at least one-third of trustees (or trust directors) to be member-nominated trustees (MNTs), although alternative selection arrangements could be made with the approval of members. In 2004, this 'opt-out' arrangement was dropped and a commitment was made for MNTs to constitute 50 per cent of trustee board membership by 2009. These developments have been strongly supported by the Trades Union Congress (TUC) which has encouraged union members to become MNTs and has offered training to all individuals who put themselves forward (TUC 2008). Since 2004, trustees have also been encouraged to become more involved in ensuring the financial viability of pension schemes. This issue was initially highlighted by the Maxwell scandal and dealt with by the 1995 Pensions Act through the establishment of a Minimum Funding Requirement which applied uniform rules on funding to all DB schemes, including a requirement for trustees to ensure that an actuarial valuation of the scheme was undertaken at least every three years. It was abolished in 2004 and replaced by a Statutory Funding Framework, in the face of strong disquiet from companies about the inflexibility of the earlier approach. Under the new more company-specific system, trustees are not just responsible for facilitating actuarial valuations of the scheme, they must also prepare a statement of funding principles and put in place a recovery plan for addressing any funding shortfall. They have also been encouraged to keep close tabs on financial developments within companies.

Support and back-up for trustees in the fulfilment of these tasks comes from a new, more powerful government regulator (the Pensions Regulator) which was established by the 2004 Act to replace its predecessor, the Occupational Pension Regulatory Authority, in light of the recommendations of the 2002 Pickering Report. This has greater powers to intervene directly in pension scheme governance in the face of certain specified eventualities. Thus, where the Pensions Regulator determines that trustees or the actuary are unable to meet their obligations under the scheme funding requirement they can: modify future accrual of benefits; direct how liabilities should be calculated; set the time limit within which any deficit should be remedied; and impose a schedule of contributions. An important reason for the strengthening of these regulatory powers is that the 2004 Pensions Act also established the Pensions Protection Fund, which like the Pension Benefit Guaranty Corporation in the United States operates as an insurance system to protect a proportion of members' benefits in the case of company failure. Greater financial oversight of schemes' finances is regarded as necessary, to prevent unsustainable recourse to this new institution and thus preserve its solvency.

The second, parallel, area on which scrutiny of trustees has focused relates to their role as investors. This agenda relates to a broader policy debate – financial decision-making in light of concerns about investment 'bubbles' and irrationality (see e.g. Schiller 2005). Concern about this issue has inevitably focused

attention in Britain on pension funds given their dominant role in the investment industry. This was most obvious in a report on institutional investment
by Paul Myners, a former fund manager, which was sponsored by the Treasury
(Myners 2001) and focused on the role of trustees in investment decisions.
A survey conducted for the report found that 62 per cent of trustees had no
professional qualifications in finance or investment; 77 per cent had no in-
house professionals to assist them; more than 50 per cent had received less than
three days' training when they became trustees; and 44 per cent had not
attended any courses since their initial twelve months of trusteeship (Myners
2001: 5). In response, the 2004 Act stipulated that all trustees must have
knowledge and understanding of the law relating to pensions and trusts, the
principles relating to the funding of occupational schemes and the investment
of scheme assets (OPSI 2004). The Pension Regulator has also strongly emphasized the importance of trustee training in its ongoing monitoring of fund
activities (TPR 2007).

Some commentators have suggested these two policy agendas on pension
scheme governance are not entirely complementary (Clark 2008; Clark and
Urwin 2009; Moss 2009). While the beneficiary protection agenda, for example,
emphasizes representativeness in trust membership, the investment agenda
emphasizes expertise. Some commentators fear that the beneficiary protection
agenda by seeking to ensure the independence of trustees from the company
will put at risk the free availability of company-based financial expertise on
pensions and investment (Clark and Urwin 2009). These problems are not
insurmountable but they have encouraged government to defer its commitment to move to 50 per cent MNTs before 'further research is done' (Stewart
2008a), much to the concern of the TUC which continues to regard
the commitment as 'a priority in order to embed [member] protection and
good governance' (Stewart 2008b). Notwithstanding the government's deferral,
24 per cent of companies have already gone further than the statutory minimum and have in place at least 50 per cent of MNTs (Stewart 2008c). However,
in the face of the financial crisis of 2008/9, pressure has increased on government to place more emphasis on 'expertise' and 'professionalism' (Clark and
Urwin 2009; Holden 2009). This debate is ongoing and will continue to impact
on the governance of DB schemes open to existing members and the comparatively small number open to new members.

Very gradually, however, the number of pension scheme members affected by
these debates looks set to fall with the shift to DC pensions. A 2008 National
Association of Pension Fund's survey found that only 17 per cent of the DC
schemes run by companies in their sample were trust-based; most were either
Group Personal Pension or Stakeholder schemes administered almost entirely
by the financial industry. In these circumstances, investment decisions are left
to the provider; the employer decides which scheme it will recommend to
its employees, whether and how much they wish to contribute and also

sometimes administers the payment of contributions; the employee decides whether they wish to join the scheme and how much they want to contribute, but has no other leverage (IDS 2004: 220–1; see also Blake 2003: 42).

9. Outlook

We have argued above that the British pension regime has entered a more social-democratic phase, involving a change to two of its main liberal elements: the very low level of the public pension and private sector voluntarism. If this reform matures there is a good chance that a heterogeneous regime, with high poverty rates but also very high occupational pensions for some, will be replaced by more homogeneity overall. The bottom level is going to rise, and the share of the population dependent on the means test will stabilize rather than rise dramatically as is currently anticipated (PPI 2006). How likely is the above scenario? Can we expect a more settled phase in British pensions, with greater equality on a lower level for pensioners? There must be doubts.

First, an important imponderable is company's reaction to the implementation of NEST from 2012. Obliged to pay for a much broader range of employees than before, will employers cut their higher rated pensions for all but their very top level employee? This was one point often repeated by business in the debate about the reform. Should this become true, it is likely that average employer contributions per scheme member will fall further. We have seen a similar trend in Switzerland, when government legislated a minimum level occupational pension schemes must offer, top levels declined (Bertozzi and Bonoli 2007). Secondly, after the near collapse of the global financial system in October/November 2008, the government adopted a Keynesian approach to de-freeze credit flows and to bolster domestic demand to prevent a long recession. This has led to record public debts, and thus, the costly re-linking of pensions to earnings from 2012 is threatened under any government, although in May 2010 the new Conservative–Liberal coalition government have committed themselves to the re-link in 2011, but also to a faster rise in the state retirement age. The Conservatives are committed to cost restraints. In the winter of 2008, the shadow cabinet, faced with the credit crunch and sudden recession, rejected Keynesian policies and instead supported the containment of public spending, an approach it has emphasized since the size of the public deficit became apparent. The party has long wished to abolish or reduce further supplementary state provision (Timmins 1995: 402–3), so it is possible that the re-link of the public pension with earnings will be followed by a cutting of the State Second Pension. The Coalition government are also likely to increase the role of the private sector in the provision of the NEST.

Even if the new government decides to leave the current pension legislation untouched, perhaps in order to avoid the rise in means-tested benefit claimants such a move would bring, there is still one explosive area likely to attract more attention in the near future: funded public sector DB schemes. The financial crisis has led to increased pension fund deficits for the remaining DB schemes in many private sector companies, and it is likely that this form of pension is going to be marginal in the private sector. In the public sector, employers still carry the risk of pension fund performance where schemes are funded, such as in local government, and in essence, their costs and losses have to be met by taxes. As we showed above, the number of scheme members has risen sharply since 1997, against the general trend in other areas. In this situation, there is mounting political pressure to change the generosity of public sector DB schemes. In the non-funded public sector, such as the National Health Service, this pressure is even greater. Critics, such as David Cameron, Prime Minister since May 2010, who as Conservative leader called for an end to 'pensions apartheid' (Timmins 2008), maintain that it is not fair to expect private sector employees to face individual long-term risks to their social security, while paying for the safety of public sector workers. This conflict is likely to gather momentum; it is unlikely that public sector workers, among the best organized, will accept cuts without resistance.

Where does this leave the reformed British pension regime as it stands? It seems certain that there is no going back to status quo ante. This was riddled with too many problems – heavy regulation, decline of employer engagement, reluctance of insurers to take on low-wage customers, very low public pensions – leading to high poverty risks and a spreading disinclination to save. Returning to the pre-reform system, therefore, would mean returning to old problems. Against this background, the most likely scenario is that the new pension legislation will become effective, but that policymakers will be looking to reduce further the level of public as well as private benefits stipulated by the legislation. To what extent such cuts will hollow out the social-democratic elements of the reform will depend on what level of retrenchment voters and organized interests will tolerate. Governments, independent of their colour, are likely to try.

Bibliography

ABI (2002). *Closing the Savings Gap. Why the Savings Industry Wants Change.* London: Association of British Insurers.

——(2003). *Simplicity, Security and Choice: ABI Response to the Green Paper.* London: Association of British Insurers (www.abi.org.uk).

ACA (2009). *Twilight or a New Dawn for Defined Benefit Schemes? 2009 Pension Trends Survey.* London: Association of Consulting Actuaries.

Agulnik, P. (1999). 'The Proposed State Second Pension'. *Fiscal Studies*, 20/4: 409–21.

Baldwin, P. (1990). *The Politics of Social Solidarity. Class Bases of the European Welfare State 1875–1975.* Cambridge: Cambridge University Press.

Barr, N., and Coulter, F. (1990). 'Social Security: Solution or Problem?', in J. Hills (ed.), *The State of Welfare. The Welfare State in Britain since 1974*. Oxford: Clarendon Press, 274–337.

Bertozzi, F., and Bonoli, G. (2007). 'The Swiss Pension System and Social Inclusion', in T. Meyer, P. Bridgen and B. Riedmüller (eds.), *Private Pensions versus Social Inclusion? Non-state Provision for Citizens at Risk in Europe*. Cheltenham, UK and Lymes, USA: Edward Elgar, 107–38.

Beveridge, W. (1942). *Social Insurance and the Allied Services*. London: HMSO.

Blake, D. (2003). *Pension Schemes and Pension Funds in the United Kingdom*. Oxford: Oxford University Press.

Bridgen, P. (2000). 'The One Nation Idea and State Welfare: The Conservative Party and Pensions in the 1950s'. *Contemporary British History*, 14/3: 83–104.

——(2006). 'A Straitjacket with Wriggle Room: The Beveridge Report, the Treasury and the Exchequer's Pension Liability 1942–1959'. *Twentieth Century British History*, 17/1: 1–25.

——and Meyer, T. (2005). 'When do Benevolent Capitalists change their Mind? Explaining the Retrenchment of Defined Benefit Pensions in Britain'. *Social Policy and Administration*, 39/4: 764–85.

—————— (2007a). 'The British Pension System and Social Inclusion', in T. Meyer, P. Bridgen and B. Riedmüller (eds.), *Private Pensions versus Social Inclusion? Non-state Provision for Citizens at Risk in Europe*. Cheltenham, UK and Lyme, USA: Edward Elgar, 47–78.

—————— (2007b). 'Private Pensions versus Social Inclusion? Three Patterns of Provision and their Impact on Citizens at Risk', in T. Meyer, P. Bridgen and B. Riedmüller (eds.), *Private Pensions versus Social Inclusion? Non-state Provision for Citizens at Risk in Europe*. Cheltenham, UK and Lymes, USA: Edward Elgar, 223–52.

CBI (2004). *Securing our Future: Developing Sustainable Pension Provision in the UK*. London: Confederation of British Industry.

Chick, M. (1998). *Industrial Policy in Britain 1945–1951. Economic Planning, Nationalisation and Labour Governments*. Cambridge: Cambridge University Press.

Cichowski, R. A. (2004). 'Women's Rights, the European Court, and Supranational Constitutionalism'. *Law & Society Review*, 38/3: 489–512.

Clark, G. (2003). 'Twenty-first Century Pension (in-)Security', in G. Clark and N. Whiteside (eds.), *Pension Security in the 21st Century*. Oxford: Oxford University Press, 225–49.

——(2004). 'Pension Fund Governance: Expertise and Organizational Form', *Journal of Pension Economics and Finance*, 3/2: 233–54.

——(2006). 'The UK Occupational Pension System in Crisis', in H. Pemberton, P. Thane and N. Whiteside (eds.), *Britain's Pension Crisis: History and Policy*. Oxford: Oxford University Press, 145–68.

——(2008). 'Governing Finance: Global Imperatives and the Challenge of Reconciling Community Representation with Expertise'. *Economic Geography*, 84: 281–302.

——and Urwin, R. (2009). 'Innovative Models of UK Pension Fund Governance'. Unpublished paper.

Clegg, H. A. (1978). *The System of Industrial Relations in Great Britain*. Oxford: Blackwell.

Davies, P. L. (1998). 'A Note on Labour and Corporate Governance in the UK', in K. J. Hopt, H. Kanda, M. J. Roe, E. Wymeersch and S. Prigge (eds.), *Comparative Corporate Governance. The State of the Art and Emerging Research*. Oxford, Oxford University Press, 373–86.

DWP (2002). *Modernising Annuities*. London: Department for Work and Pensions.

——(2004). *Income Related Benefits Estimates of Take-up in 2000/2001*. London: Department for Work and Pensions.

——(2006). *Security in Retirement: Towards a New Pensions System*. London: Stationery Office.

——(2008). 'Pension Reform Factsheet'. (www.dwp.gov.uk, accessed: December 2008).

Ellis, B. (1989). *Pensions in Britain 1955–1975*. London: HMSO.

Esping-Andersen, G. (1990). *The Three Worlds of Welfare Capitalism*. Cambridge: Polity Press.

Evandrou, M., and Falkingham J. (2005). 'A Secure Retirement for All? Older People and New Labour', in J. Hills and K. Stewart (eds.), *A More Equal Society? New Labour, Poverty, Inequality and Exclusion*. Bristol: Policy Press, 167–88.

Fawcett, H. (1996). 'The Beveridge Strait-jacket: Policy Formation and the Problem of Poverty in Old Age'. *Contemporary British History*, 10/1: 20–42.

Fawcett Society (2006). *Fawcett Society Response to the Pensions White Paper 'Security in Retirement: Towards a New Pensions System'*. London: Fawcett Society.

Foreman-Peck, J., and Millward, R. (1994). *Public and Private Ownership of British Industry 1820–1990*. Oxford: Clarendon Press.

GAD (2003). *Occupational Pension Schemes 2000. Eleventh Survey by the Government Actuary*. London: The Government Actuary's Department (www.gad.gov.uk/Publications).

Ginn, J. (2001). *From Security to Risk. Pension Privatisation and Gender Inequality. A Catalyst Working Paper* (www.catalyst-trust.co.uk).

——(2003). *Gender, Pensions and the Life Course. How Pensions need to Adapt to Changing Family Forms*. Bristol: Policy Press.

Groves, D. (1983). 'Members and Survivors: Women and Retirement-Pension Legislation', in J. Lewis (ed.), *Women's Welfare, Women's Rights*. London & Canberra: Croom Helm, 18–63.

Hannah, L. (1986). *Reinventing Retirement. The Development of Occupational Pensions in Britain*. Cambridge: Cambridge University Press.

Holden, B. (2009). *Ensuring Pension Fund Governance is Fit for Purpose*. London: IPE/Pioneer Investments.

IDS (2003). *Pensions in Practice 2003/04, From Primary Legislation to Practical Implementation*. London: Income Data Services.

——(2004). *Pensions in Practice 2004/05. From Primary Legislation to Practical Implementation*. London: Income Data Services.

——(2005). *Pensions Trustees and Administration. An IDS Handbook*. London: Income Data Services.

——(2006). *Pension Scheme Design. An IDS Pensions Handbook*. London: Income Data Services.

Land, H. (1985). 'Who Still Cares for the Family? Recent Developments in Income Maintenance', in C. Ungerson (ed.), *Women and Social Policy. A Reader*. Houndmills, Basingstoke: MacMillan Publishers, 50–62.

Leisering, L. (2003). *From Redistribution to Regulation. Regulating Private Pension Provision for Old Age as a New Challenge for the Welfare State in Ageing Societies*. University of Bielefeld.

Lynes, T. (1960). The National Insurnace Act 1959. *Modern Law Review* 23/1: 53–6.

Macnicol, J. (1998). *The Politics of Retirement in Britain, 1878–1948.* Cambridge: Cambridge University Press.

Mares, I. (2001). 'Firms and the Welfare State: When, Why, and How does Social Policy Matter to Employers?' in P. Hall and D. Soskice (eds.), *Varieties of Capitalism.* Oxford: Oxford University Press, 184–212.

Marschallek, C. (2005). 'Weniger (Wohlfahrts-)Staat? Britische Alterssicherungspolitik im Wandel'. *Zeitschrift für Sozialreform,* 51: 416–47.

Mazey, S. (1998). 'The European Union and Women's Rights: From the Europeanization of National Agendas to the Nationalization of a European Agenda?' *Journal of European Public Policy,* 5/1: 131–52.

Meshner, (1976). 'The Social Security Pensions Act 1975'. *Modern Law Review,* 39: 321–6.

Meyer, T., Bridgen P., and Riedmuller B. (eds.) (2007). *Private Pensions versus Social Inclusion?: Non-state Provision for Citizens at Risk in Europe.* Cheltenham: Edward Elgar.

Middlemas, K. (1979). *Politics in Industrial Society. The Experience of the British System since 1911.* London: Andre Deutsch.

Moss, G. (2009). *Essential Governance. Investments and Pensions Europe* (www.ipe.com).

Myners, P. (2001). *Institutional Investment in the United Kingdom: A review.* London: Treasury (www.treasury.gov.uk).

NAPF (2002). *Memorandum Submitted by the National Association of Pension Funds (NAPF) (PEN62).* London: Select Committee on Work and Pensions, House of Commons (www.publications.parliament.uk).

——(2005). *Towards a Citizen's Pension. Final Report.* London: National Association of Pension Funds (www.napf.co.uk).

——(2008). *Finance Directors and Pensions: A View from the Boardroom.* London: National Association of Pension Funds. NAPF Research Report.

——(2009). *Annual Survey 2009.* London: National Association of Pension Funds.

OECD (2005). 'Pension Markets in Focus'. *Newsletter,* December 2005/2.

ONS (2007). *Occupational Pension Schemes Annual Report. No. 14. C. Duffin.* London: Office for National Statistics (www.statistics.gov.uk).

——(2008). *Occupational Pension Schemes Annual Report 2007 Edition.* London: Office for National Statistics (www.statistics.gov.uk).

OPSI (2004). *Pensions Act 2004: Explanatory Notes* (www.opsi.gov.uk).

——(2007). *Pensions Act 2007* (www.opsi.gov.uk).

——(2008). *Pensions Act 2008* (www.opsi.gov.uk).

Pascall, G. (1986). *Social Policy. A Feminist Analysis.* London: Routledge.

Pemberton, H. (2009). *Britain's cross-class alliance against earnings-related pensions in the 1950.* Annual Conference of the Economic History Society, Warwick University, 3–5 April 2009.

——Thane, P., and Whiteside, N. (eds.) (2006). *Britain's Pension Crisis: History and Policy.* Oxford: Oxford University Press.

Pensions Commission (2004). *Pensions: Challenges and Choices. The First Report of the Pensions Commission.* London: The Stationery Office.

——(2005). *A New Pensions Settlement for the Twenty-first Century. The Second Report of the Pensions Commission.* London: The Stationery Office.

Pensions Regulator (2007). *Guidance for Trustees.* London: The Pensions Regulator (www.thepensionsregulator.gov.uk).

Pensions Service (2003). *A Guide to State Pensions*. London: Department of Work and Pensions.

Pickering, A. (2002). *A Simpler Way to Better Pensions – An Independent Report*. London: Department of Work and Pensions.

Pierson, P. (1994). *Dismantling the Welfare State?* Cambridge: Cambridge University Press.

PPI (2006). *An Evaluation of the White Paper State Pension Reform Proposals*. London: Pension Policy Institute (www.pensionspolicyinstitute.org.uk).

Rake, K., and Falkingham, J. (2000). 'British Pension Policy in the Twenty-First Century: A Partnership in Pensions or a Marriage to the Means Test?' *Social Policy and Administration*, 34/3: 296–317.

Russell, A. (1991). *The Growth of Occupational Welfre in Britain*. Aldershot: Avebury.

Schiller, R. J. (2005). *Irrational Exuberance*. Princeton: Princeton University Press.

Schulze, I., and Moran, M. (2007). 'United Kingdom: Pension Politics in an Adversarial System', in E. M. Immergut, K. M. Anderson and I. Schulze (eds.), *The Handbook of West European Pension Politics*. Oxford: Oxford University Press, 49–96.

Secretary of State for Social Security (1998). *A New Contract for Welfare: Partnership in Pensions*. London: The Stationery Office.

Secretary of State for Work and Pensions (2002). *Simplicity, Security and Choice. Working and Saving for Retirement*. London: The Stationery Office.

Sinfield, A. (2000). 'Tax Benefits in Non-state Pensions'. *European Journal of Social Security*, 2/2: 137–68.

Stewart, N. (2008a). 'Gov't Wants "Formal" Research into 50% MNTs'. *Investment and Pensions Europe (IPE)*, 2 July 2008 (www.ipe.com).

——(2008b). 'Unions Call for Full Buyout Review'. *Investments and Pensions Europe (IPE)*, 20 June 2008 (www.ipe.com).

——(2008c). 'Bulk of UK Schemes Meet Trustee Requirement'. *Investments and Pensions Europe (IPE)*, 21 July 2008 (www.ipe.com).

Timmins, N. (1995). *The Five Giants: A Biography of the Welfare State*. London: Harper/Collins.

——(2008). 'The Struggle to End "Pensions Apartheid"'. *Financial Times*, 27 November 2008.

Titmuss, R. (1958). *Essays on the Welfare State*. London: Allen and Unwin.

TPR (2007). *Guidance for Trustees*. London: The Pension Regulator (www.thepensionsregulator.gov.uk).

TUC (2004). *Prospects for Pensions*. London: Trades Union Congress (www.tuc.org.uk/pensions).

——(2008). *The Member Voice in Pensions Governance*. London: Trades Union Congress (www.tuc.org.uk/pensions).

Waine, B. (1995). 'A Disaster Foretold? The Case of Personal Pensions'. *Social Policy and Administration*, 29/4: 317–34.

Whiteside, N. (2003). 'Historical Perspectives and the Politics of Pension Reform', in G. Clark and N. Whiteside (eds.), *Pension Security in the 21st Century*. Oxford: Oxford University Press, 21–43.

11

The Netherlands: Adapting a Multipillar Pension System to Demographic and Economic Change

Karen M. Anderson

1. Introduction

The Dutch multipillar pension system is often regarded as a financially stable, effective way to organize old age protection because it combines a generous flat-rate public pension with quasi-mandatory, funded occupational pensions.[1] The basic pension protects against poverty in old age while occupational pensions provide supplementary benefits related to previous income. This public–private approach is considered to be fairly resistant to the kinds of demographic and financial shocks that affect public pension systems elsewhere in Europe because the risk of old age is shared between the state and the social partners (Haverland 2001; Van Riel et al. 2003). Consociational politics and corporatist industrial relations have substantially influenced the development of Dutch multipillar system (Anderson 2007). The introduction of the flat-rate, PAYG (pay-as-you-go) public pension in 1957 was the culmination of decades of conflict concerning the proper role of the state and corporatist bodies in the area of social policy. In contrast, earnings-related pensions have a long history, and many wage earners were accruing occupational pensions long before the state stepped in to provide public flat-rate pensions.

Dutch political actors agree that occupational pensions cannot be left completely to the market. The state plays a central role by providing the regulatory framework even if the social partners negotiate and administer individual pension schemes. Thus, the Dutch experience is crucial to

[1] The Dutch refer to their second-pillar pensions as 'supplementary' (*aanvullende*) pensions; the terms supplementary and occupational pensions are used synonymously in this chapter.

understanding the dynamics of occupational pension provision because it highlights several core issues associated with regulating an extensive, mature occupational pension system in a period of economic and demographic change. The first issue is the integration of public and private supplementary pensions. The freezing of public pension benefits in the 1980s and 1990s led to pressure on occupational pensions to fill the gap because occupational schemes promised a defined benefit (DB) based on the combined public–occupational benefit. Second, cost control in occupational pensions has been a contentious issue between government and the social partners because pension contributions add to non-wage labour costs and influence labour supply, and because the tax subsidies that finance occupational pensions are substantial. Third, the economic impact of pension funds is pro-cyclical and potentially destabilizing. In an economic upturn, high investment returns lead to lower contributions, thus fuelling inflation. In a downturn, investment losses lead to sometimes painful contribution increases and higher wage costs, thus exacerbating a recession. Finally, the DB ambition of Dutch pension funds has sparked a debate about who really owns pension fund assets and who should bear the burden of investment losses. In the absence of individual ownership, occupational pensioners have begun to stake their claim on asset surpluses, and they have tried to limit the extent to which they pay the costs of pension fund attempts to restore minimum funding levels in the wake of the financial crises of the 2000s.

Part I: The evolution of the public–private mix

2. The main features of the pension system

The Dutch welfare regime is a mix of social democratic universalism and Bismarckian principles (see Figure 11.1). Pensions are the classic example: universal, flat-rate public pensions provide relatively generous benefits to the aged, whereas (nearly universal) pre-funded earnings-related occupational pensions are negotiated by the social partners as part of collective wage agreements. Public and occupational pensions are tightly coupled; the public basic pension serves both as a basic minimum during retirement and as the floor above which supplementary occupational pensions are paid.

The public basic pension (*algemene ouderdomswet* or AOW) pays a flat-rate benefit to all residents over 65 who have lived in the Netherlands for fifty years between the ages of 15 and 65.[2] In January 2010, the pension benefit for a single

---

[2] A deduction of 2 per cent is made for every year of missing residence. Pensioners with a child under 18 receive a supplement, as do pensioners with a spouse younger than 65 with little or no income. The partner supplement will be phased out in 2015.

	First pillar	Second pillar		Third pillar
Third tier	None	Additional voluntary occupational pensions		Voluntary private pension
Second tier	None	Quasi-mandatory subsidized occupational pension: defined benefits above AOW approx. 650 different schemes		Subsidized private pension
First tier	Public flat-rate pensions based on 50 years of residency (*Algemene Ouderdomswet* AOW)	Sectoral pension schemes *bedrijftakspensioenfonds)*	Company pension schemes *ondernemingspensioenfonds).*	Mandatory private pension: none
	Social assistance			

Figure 11.1 The Dutch pension system

Source: Adapted from synopsis in Anderson(2007).

person (€1,114.04 per month including vacation supplements) was 70 per cent of the net minimum wage or about 55 per cent of average gross wages. For married pensioners, the benefit (€776.41) for each spouse is 50 per cent of the net minimum wage.[3] The pension amount is indexed to net minimum wages, set twice a year by parliament. AOW expenditure totals about 5 per cent of GDP (2007), financed by contributions levied as part of the first two income tax brackets (17.9 per cent of income in 2010 up to a ceiling of €32,738). Financing is PAYG, but since the late 1990s there is an upper limit on contributions (18.25 per cent), and any shortfalls are financed from general revenues. The recently established AOW Reserve Fund, financed by annual government deposits, will help to finance benefits starting in 2020 (forecast: €135 billion).

---

[3] Single pensioners pay a monthly health insurance contribution of €74.52; married/partnered pensioners pay €51.87 each.

Occupational pensions negotiated by the social partners currently cover about 90 per cent of wage earners. At the end of 2008, there were 656 pension schemes: 543 company pension schemes, 69 compulsory sectoral pension schemes, 26 non-compulsory pension schemes, and 13 schemes for professions (such as doctors, dentists, and accountants). Until recently, the typical occupational benefit was 70 per cent of the final wage, including the public AOW pension. Since 2005, however, pension funds have overwhelmingly switched to average benefit formulae. Occupational pensions are fully funded in the sense that pension funds are required to possess assets equal to at least 105 per cent of nominal obligations.[4] In early 2008, (before the onset of the financial crisis) pension funds had a combined average funding ratio of 132 per cent (the nearly €500 billion in pension liabilities were backed up by €657 billion in financial assets). About one-third of assets are held in company pension funds and two-thirds in sectoral funds, while the professional pension funds are small in comparison (about 3 per cent of total assets or about €18 billion). In 2005, pension schemes paid nearly €18 billion (or 3.5 per cent GDP in 2005) in benefits, of which €11.5 billion are spent for old-age pensions, €3.6 billion for survivor pensions, and the rest for early retirement and other types of benefits (DNB 2005).

In 2005, the AOW made up slightly more than one half of retirement income for individuals, while supplementary pensions accounted for 40 per cent. As the accumulated pension rights in the second pillar grow, however, this proportion will change in favour of the second pillar. By 2040, second-pillar benefits are forecast to equal 12.9 per cent of GDP and first-pillar benefits 9.0 per cent of GDP (Westerhout et al. 2004: 31).

The advantage of the Dutch multipillar approach is its widespread occupational coverage and strong protection against poverty in old age. Because public pension benefits are based on residence, those with incomplete earnings profiles also qualify for generous income protection. Two groups are exceptions to this, however: first-generation immigrants and Dutch wage earners who worked for longer periods abroad. Means-tested social assistance for the elderly is available for those with insufficient AOW rights, and mobile workers can insure themselves with the Social Insurance Bank for time spent outside the Netherlands. According to the most recent estimates, about 9 per cent of AOW beneficiaries receive a reduced benefit, twice the 1995 level of 4 per cent (Vrooman et al. 2007: 140). However, according to one estimate, only about 70 per cent of those eligible for additional social assistance benefits apply for them (Wildeboer Schut and Hoff 2007: 90–1, cited in Vrooman et al. 2007).

---

[4] Most pension schemes are set up as pension funds and not as life insurance schemes. Regulations governing life insurance require higher capital requirements than what is required for pension funds.

3. The context of the welfare regime, labour relations, and the market economy

As noted, the Dutch welfare state combines the Beveridge and Bismarck models: the impact of Beveridge is present in the basic pension, but most other parts of the welfare state have been, until recently, 'conservative' according to Esping-Andersen's typology. There are traces of the male breadwinner model present even if social security and occupational pension schemes are now based on individual entitlement. In contrast to Scandinavia, women are less likely to work full time and many female part-time workers work relatively few hours in low-paying jobs. But the Netherlands is in transition: it is taking on more and more features of the Scandinavian model such as activation and high rates of female labour market participation, although the public day care that would encourage more women to work (longer hours) is still underdeveloped. And although the public pension provides (residence-based) universal basic benefits, the occupationally fragmented earnings-related occupational pensions rein-force status differentials even if their collective structure provides a modicum of risk redistribution.

Dutch policymakers have grappled with pension reform in the context of societal de-pillarization[5] and the resurgence of corporatist practices. The 1970s were particularly difficult; tripartite bargaining failed to deliver wage restraint and economic growth. The 1980s saw the re-emergence of Dutch consociation-alism with the 1982 Wassenaar Accord. Unions promised wage restraint in return for increased emphasis on boosting employment. The Wassenaar Accord facilitated a period of sustained economic growth and welfare state reform that Visser and Hemerijck (1997) call the 'Dutch Miracle' (see also Cox 2001; Hemerijck and van Kersbergen 1997).

Dutch society is highly organized, and interest groups are important actors in the policymaking process. Despite the recent secularization of Dutch society, pillarization has left a strong imprint on economic organizations. About 30 per cent of Dutch wage earners belong to unions.[6] Union influence is much higher than membership numbers alone would suggest. The mandatory extension of collective agreements to entire sectors means that about 80–90 per cent of all

[5] Societal pillarization refers to the division of society into separate spheres or 'pillars' for different groups. Each sphere included schools, churches, unions, sports clubs, etc. for all members of the pillar. Societal pillarization is not to be confused with the term 'pillar' when referring to different parts of a national pension system. On societal pillarization, see Lijphart (1968).

[6] The Federation of Dutch Trade Unions (FNV) was formed in 1976 after the merger of the Netherlands Trade Union Federation (NVV) and the Netherlands Catholic Trade Union Federation (NKV). Today, the FNV has eighteen affiliates and about 1 million members. The Dutch Christian Trade Union (CNV) remains separate, with sixteen affiliates and 320,000 members. The Federation of Managerial and Professional Staff Unions (MHP) was formed in 1974 and has two affiliates and 160,000 members.

wage earners are covered by union contracts. Employers are also well organized.[7] The bipartite Labour Foundation (*Stichting van de Arbeid* or STAR), established in 1947, advises on policy issues, but its function is more of a negotiating forum for organized labour and business. The STAR has been the scene of some important accords in recent decades: 1982 Wassenaar Accord, the 1993 deal on a 'New Course' in wage formation, and the 1997 covenant on the modernization of occupational pensions.

The occupational pension sector is well organized, with two peak organizations. The Dutch Association of Industry-wide Pension Funds (*Vereniging van bedrijfstakpensioenfondsen* or VB) was established in 1985 with seventy-five member funds representing about 75 per cent of all participants. The Association of Company Pension Funds (*Stichting voor Ondernemingspensioenfondsen* or *Opf*) represents 300 funds with 900,000 active participants and 600,000 pensioners. Together with the social partners, these two pension fund associations are a formidable lobby, usually favouring the status quo and social partner autonomy in occupational pension issues.

Elderly organizations have long been part of the catholic and protestant pillars, and even elderly immigrants have their own organization. An umbrella organization, the Association of Elderly Organizations (CSO), has five member organizations: the Dutch Association of Senior Citizens (ANBO), the Dutch Association for Older Migrants (NISBO), the Dutch Confederation of Pensioners Organizations (NVOG), the Protestant Association of Senior Citizens (PCOB), and the Catholic Elderly Association (KBO).

The density of interest groups representing both occupational and public pension stakeholders means that governments face formidable opposition if they attempt to change the pension status quo (Anderson 2007). For reforms to the AOW, politicians face not only the unions but also several influential elderly organizations. The fragmentation of elderly organizations sometimes hinders collective action, but the sheer number of organized elderly also provides a strong constraint on public pension retrenchment. In the area of occupational pensions, governments face a well-organized, effective pension lobby led by the social partners and the pension fund organizations.

The importance of occupational pensions for the collective wage bargaining system can hardly be emphasized enough. For decades, occupational pensions have been key elements of wage agreements, and the bipartite boards that administer pension funds are a central aspect of Dutch corporatism. This bipartite structure has recently come under attack by pensioners' groups (because they were excluded), and recent reforms increase the influence of pensioners'

---

[7] The Confederation of Dutch Industry and Employers (VNO/NCW) formed from the merger of the Federation of Dutch Industry (VNO) and the Dutch Christian Employers Association (NCW). The VNO/NCW represents about 150 sectoral employers associations and 65,000 member firms.

representatives on these boards. Although occupational pensions are organized as part of collective wage bargaining, several features promote social solidarity. Coverage is nearly universal; unions and employers are equally represented on pension fund governing boards; and risks are pooled within entire sectors (Clark 2003).

4. The emergence of the public–private mix[8]

The multipillar approach to pension provision in the Netherlands is the result of the early emergence and growth of occupational pensions in the context of modest state provision. The 1913 legislation provided public pensions solely to workers, and it was only after WWII that universal entitlement was established (see Table 11.1). The adoption of a universal basic scheme in 1956 represented the victory of Labour and progressive Catholics over conservative confessional groups who favoured corporatist implementation (Anderson 2004; see also Oude Nijhuis 2009). At the same time, the occupational pension system emerged and expanded in tandem with corporatist wage bargaining practices.

Societal pillarization and the consociational practices it produced shaped the emerging division of labour between the state and societal organizations in the provision of welfare. By the time full parliamentary democracy and industrialization reached the Netherlands, the country was home to several distinct groups with their own subcultures: Protestants, Catholics, the secular middle class (liberals), and the secular/social democratic working class. Each group, or 'pillar', had its own unions, employer organizations, schools, newspapers, hospitals, and broadcast media. A crucial principle sustaining societal pillarization was the independence of these separate spheres. The Calvinists called it 'sovereignty in one's own circle', while Catholics called it 'subsidiarity'. Liberals and socialists acquiesced to consociationalism not because they held the same view but because of the realities of Dutch cleavage structure. Neither group, alone or in coalition, was large enough to achieve a majority in parliament, so compromise was inevitable. Thus, the early years of social policy formation were marked by a small state role because it was assumed that each societal group (pillar) should provide welfare functions to its members. This did not mean that the state was irrelevant; the state provided regulation facilitating the fragmentation and decentralization of welfare state programmes that suited confessional conceptions of how welfare should be organized.[9]

---

[8] This section is based on Cox (2001), Jaspers et al. (2001), Veldkamp (1978), and Rigter et al. (1996).
[9] On pillarization, see Lijphart (1968) and van Kersbergen (1995).

Dutch occupational pensions have a longer history than public pensions. Railroad workers were the first to receive occupational pension coverage in the middle of the nineteenth century. The first occupational pension schemes were established by employers to reward employees for loyal service, but the innovation was slow to catch on. By WWI, there were only a few dozen occupational pension schemes, but by 1938 there were more than 750 schemes with more than fifty members each. The state stepped in to regulate the new pension schemes fairly early, adopting the first regulatory legislation in 1908. Among the first items subject to regulation was the requirement that assets be held outside the firm and not be included in the calculation of company assets. In addition, workers were represented on administrative boards. In 1913, one of the Netherlands' largest company pension funds was created, the Philips company pension fund. The first sectoral pension fund was established in 1917, and the 1937 legislation introduced the option for the Minister of Social Affairs to require participation in sectoral pension schemes (Tulfer 1997: 12–16). In 1922, the state established a pension fund for public employees (ABP) that is currently one of the world's largest in terms of assets. In 1942, company contributions to occupational pension schemes were made tax deductible, spurring a wave of occupational pension growth.

In 1949, government passed a legislation allowing the Minister of Social Affairs to declare a sectoral pension scheme binding on all employers in that sector. In 1952, the legislation regulating all occupational pensions (PSW – *Pensioen en spaarfondswet*) was adopted. The PSW was the culmination of government efforts to respond to several decades of occupational pension growth by establishing a regulatory framework that set the ground rules for occupational pension regulation. Because the PSW provided only the institutional framework for second-tier pensions, the social partners have considerable freedom to negotiate the details of their pension arrangements as part of collective wage agreements (CAOs).

By the 1950s, occupational pensions were fairly established, so when the universal public pension was introduced in 1957, policymakers had to deal with the issue of how to treat wage earners who were already covered by occupational schemes. Should wage earners receive both a state and an occupational pension? And what if this combined coverage led to a replacement rate of more than 100 per cent? The 1956 legislation establishing AOW addressed this issue but left it to the social partners to sort things out. Unions and employers settled on tight coupling: occupational pensions would explicitly take the AOW into account by exempting the income covered by the AOW from occupational pension accrual. Occupational pension rights would accrue only for income above the so-called 'AOW offset'. This offset represented the gross AOW benefit, and this amount was subtracted from gross income in order to identify the pension-carrying income for occupational pension purposes. Thus, the 1956 legislation not only established a minimum income for all

Table 11.1 Chronology of main pension system reforms, 1913–80s

Year	Reform	Political context
1913	First public pension law (coverage for workers and their families)	ARP (Calvinist Christian Democrats) and Catholic Party (KVP)
1937	Legislation allowing Minister of Social to declare collective agreements binding for a whole sector	ARP (Calvinist Christian Democrats)
		Catholic Party (RKSP)
		Reformed Protestant Christian Democrats (CHU)
		Left Liberals (VDB)
		Liberals
1947	Emergency Pensions Act	Catholic Party (KVP)
		Labour Party (PvdA)
1949	Law on compulsory participation in sectoral pension funds (Bpf)	Catholic Party (KVP)
		Labour Party (PvdA)
1953	Pension Act (PSW) adopted	Catholic Party (KVP)
		Labour Party (PvdA)
1956	Universal Old-Age Pension Act	Labour (PvdA)
		Liberals
		Catholic Party (KVP)

Source: Anderson (2007).

retirees but it also reduced the obligations of existing pension funds because the AOW reduced the amount of income that occupational pension funds insured.

5. The changing public–private mix

Although the overall structure of both public and occupational pensions has remained fairly stable, both systems have undergone substantial changes since the 1980s in terms of the basis of entitlement, the structure of benefits, and the structure of financing (see Table 11.2). First, both systems have been individualized: the breadwinner basis of the AOW was changed to individual entitlement in 1985, whereas occupational pensions have been slower to change. For both the first and second pillar, EU law was a major force driving change.

The AOW was originally based on the breadwinner principle: married breadwinners paid contributions and received benefits intended for two people. These provisions directly conflicted with European law concerning equal treatment (Directive 79/7/EEC). The Centre–Right government adopted legislation in 1985 that divided the AOW benefit for couples in half and paid an individual benefit to both spouses.

Breadwinner-based entitlement was also common in occupational pension schemes: until the 1980s/90s, discrimination against women was prevalent in occupational pension schemes. The most common types of discrimination were different participation ages for men and women, the exclusion of married women, and the exclusion of part-time workers. The 1990 Barber[10] decision changed all of this. In Barber, the ECJ ruled that occupational pensions were a form of pay and therefore subject to EC law concerning equal pay. The Barber decision would have cost the second-tier pension schemes in the Netherlands an estimated NLG 400 billion (about €180 billion) if pension rights were made retroactive for women previously excluded from occupational pension schemes (Kraamwinkel 1995). Because of the substantial costs involved, the Dutch government (pushed by the pension funds and employers) lobbied successfully in Brussels (along with the United Kingdom) for a protocol to the Treaty of Amsterdam that would limit the retroactivity of the Barber decision. In other words, the new interpretation of EU law would only take effect in 1990.

A second set of changes concerned attempts to control the rising costs of AOW pensions. The real value of AOW benefits has decreased significantly, general revenues now finance a larger share of AOW costs, and a reserve fund has been established to help cover future expenditures. AOW contributions have also increased steadily. The contribution rate has increased from 6.75 per cent of income (up to a ceiling) in 1957 to 17.9 per cent in 2010. Beginning in the 1980s, growing AOW costs prompted ad hoc cuts because of budgetary constraints. Governments began to suspend AOW indexation to wage increases, and what began in 1980 as an ad hoc measure soon turned into a recurring feature of the annual budget negotiations. The 1992 Law on Conditional Indexation stipulates that no indexation will be applied when there are more than 82 inactive for every 100 active persons. Indexing was suspended from 1993 to 1995 (Visser and Hemerijck 1997). The suspension of indexing also had repercussions for occupational pensions because of the tight coupling of occupational and AOW benefits. As the AOW's real value decreased, the pension schemes faced pressure to make up the difference. The pension funds could afford this in the 1980s because they were earning high returns. The Cabinet preferred a more long-term solution, however. In 1997, the Centre–Left government adopted a legislation to improve AOW financing by introducing a special Reserve Fund. The Reserve Fund would be invested in government bonds and would start to help finance AOW pensions in 2020.[11]

5.1 Reforming occupational pensions

Occupational pensions are the prerogative of the social partners, so legislation only provides the legal framework governing access to schemes, benefit accrual,

[10] The Barber decision extended the meaning of Article 119 to include age requirements in occupational pension schemes. This includes both the age of entrance into a scheme and the age of retirement.

[11] In 2007, there was €4.2 billion in the AOW Savings Fund (*AOW Spaarfonds*).

and rules concerning asset investment. If the government wants to influence occupational pension policy, the typical route is to avoid legislation and negotiate directly with the social partners. For more far-reaching reforms, the government may wish to change the regulatory framework. Thus, the development of occupational pensions since the early 1990s has been marked by tripartite attempts to adjust supplementary pensions to changing demographic, economic, and labour market developments. Corporatist bargaining 'in the shadow of hierarchy' (van Riel et al. 2003) has marked this process.

By the late 1980s, rising occupational pension costs were the background to government attempts to get the social partners to implement changes in occupational pension schemes. In particular, the Cabinet advocated switching from final salary benefit formulae to average salary formulae, both for reasons of cost containment and in order to accommodate atypical employment biographies.[12] Negotiations with the social partners began in 1991 and were sealed in a tripartite agreement (so-called 'Covenant') in 1997. The Covenant contained provisions on increasing the coverage of supplementary pensions, and modernizing benefit rules in order to increase flexibility and individual choice (STAR 1997a, 1997b).[13]

The 2001/2 stock market downturn prompted substantial cuts in occupational pension benefits, sharp premium increases, and led to a tense renegotiation about the regulations governing the funding ratio of occupational pensions. Because of their significant investments in equity markets, the reserves of many pension funds fell below the required 100 per cent funding ratio for the first time in 2002. This forced many pension funds to take immediate steps to restore full funding. Most schemes adopted a mix of measures to restore solvency: suspended benefit indexation, non-indexation of accrual, contribution increases, and switching to average earnings benefit formulae. The most striking aspect of this adjustment process is the massive shift from final benefit schemes to average salary schemes. Only 10 per cent of active participants are in final salary plans in 2004, down from 50 per cent in 2003 and 66 per cent in 1998. About 75 per cent now participate in average salary schemes and indexation is overwhelmingly conditional on fund solvency (DNB 2005). Most pension funds restored solvency by 2003.

Regulatory reform had been on the government agenda before the 2001/2 stock market downturn. Policymakers focused on two issues: updating rules for calculating the funding ratio and defining the 'ownership' of both pension fund deficits and surpluses. The new regulatory legislation took effect in 2007 and introduces significant change in three areas: supervision, access, and transparency. The new law clarifies the roles of the social partners, pension funds or

---

[12] In 1987, 72 per cent of participants were in final salary schemes.

[13] In 1994, Parliament passed legislation amending the regulatory framework (rules on the mandatory inclusion of part-time workers and the transfer of pension rights).

Table 11.2 Chronology of main pension system reforms since 1980

Year	Reform	Political context
1980s	Cost containment of the AOW	Christian Democratic Party and Liberals
	• Indexing of AOW pensions suspended in 1983–8 as part of annual budget consolidation measures	
1985	Adapting to European Equal Treatment Law	Christian Democratic Party and Liberals
	• AOW benefit for spouses individualized in response to 1979 EC directive	
	• Supplement available to AOW pensioners with spouse younger than 65.	
1987	• Improvement of portability and protection of accumulated pension rights in occupational pensions	Christian Democratic Party and Liberals
	• Introduction of the SDS (Stichting Dienstverlening Samenwerkingsverband) and other similar organizations for coordinating the transfer of pension reserves for employees between pension schemes	
1992	*Wet koppeling met afwijkingsmogelijkheid* (WKA; Conditional Indexation Act)	Christian Democratic Party and Labour Party
	• Indexation of public benefits like AOW made conditional on moderate wage increases and increased labour market participation; indexing suspended 1993, 1994, and 1995	
	• No indexation if there are more than 82 inactive for every 100 active	
1994	Change in regulatory framework for supplementary pensions (PSW)	Christian Democratic Party and Labour Party
	• Introduction of the right to transfer pension rights	
	• Inclusion of part-time workers in pension schemes	
1997	• Establishment of AOW Reserve Fund to help finance future pensions	'Purple Coalition': Labour Party, Liberal Party, and Social Liberal Party
	• Upper limit on the AOW contribution of 16.5% (later 18.25%).	
2002–4	• Premium increases in occupational pension schemes	Changes implemented by bipartite boards of pension funds in the wake of the stock market downturn
	• Shift to average salary benefit formulae in occupational pensions	
2006	Revision of the PSW	Supported by the Christian Democratic Party, Liberals, Social Liberals, and Labour Party
	• Enhanced transparency in occupational pensions	
	• New solvency rules	

Source: Anderson (2007).

insurance companies, and pensioners; it expands access by decreasing the maximum age of exclusion to 21; and it modernizes the rules governing pension fund solvency. Pension funds will be required to inform participants about their pension accrual, and issues like what to do in cases of under- or overfunding have been clarified. The law also changes how the present value of pension liabilities is calculated. Rather than discounting liabilities at a fixed rate of 4 per cent, funds will use a market rate. The law also introduces a 'minimum test' and a solvency test in order to improve financial risk management. The minimum test is essentially the funding ratio (the ratio of nominal assets to liabilities plus a minimum capital requirement; 105 per cent) while the solvency test is a complicated buffer arrangement.[14] These two provisions mean that pension funds should aim for a funding level of 125 per cent. If the funding ratio drops below 125 per cent (the solvency level), pension funds have fifteen years to restore balance; if the funding ratio drops below 105 per cent, pension funds have three years to restore balance.

Part II: The governance of supplementary pensions

As previous sections discuss, occupational pensions in the Netherlands are primarily DB, average salary schemes. Pension funds are usually set up as foundations legally separate from the employer, while a small number of pension schemes are organized as life insurance. The size and scope of the first and second pillar limit the growth of individual retirement products in the third pillar. Individuals have less incentive to save on their own for retirement because most of their income is insured by the first and second pillar. Moreover, tax deductability for individual savings vehicles is limited to the portion of income not insured in the second pillar.[15] Despite these constraints, the third pillar is not insignificant. However, it is difficult to put a precise number on the size of the third pillar because there is disagreement about which kinds of savings vehicles fall into this category. The most straightforward way to measure the extent of individual pension savings is to look at life insurance savings products, because these are the most common forms of individual retirement savings.[16] In 2008, life insurance premiums amounted to €26 billion, or 4 per cent of GDP (DNB 2009*b*: 21). Of this amount, €17

---

[14] The solvency test and minimum funding test are part of the 'Financial Assessment Framework' (*Financiële Toetsingkader*, FTK) that is embedded in the new pension legislation. The solvency test is a way of assessing whether pension funds can withstand financial shocks and remain at 105 per cent coverage after one year of market movements. There should be more than 97.5 per cent probability that a fund can meet all its obligations in one year (using a standard risk model).

[15] Tax reform in 2001 limited the deductibility of life insurance premiums.

[16] Since 2008, banks may offer tax-preferred individual pension products.

billion flowed into *individual* policies (the third-pillar personal pensions) and €9 billion into collective insurance policies (the second-pillar occupational pensions).[17] Thus, the total level of contributions paid into collective or second-pillar schemes was about €36 million, of which €27 million were contributed for pension funds and €9 million for pension schemes administered by life insurance companies (DNB and CBS). Assets tell a similar story: pension fund investments totalled €650 billion in mid-2008 (109 per cent of GDP) and life insurance (collective and individual products) equalled €283 billion (47 per cent of GDP).

6. Who is covered?

In 2008, there were 533 different occupational pension funds,[18] including company pension schemes (*ondernemingspensioenfonds*), sectoral pension schemes (*bedrijftakspensioenfonds*), and professional pension funds (*beroepspensioenfonds*). Coverage of occupational pensions is very high; about 90 per cent of wage earners are insured. The law on mandatory participation in sectoral pension funds dates from 1949,[19] permitting the Ministry of Social Affairs to require an entire sector to join the same pension fund if a formal request is made. In practice, the Minister seldom refuses such requests given the centrality of this provision for the occupational pension sector. The legislation concerning mandatory participation in sectoral schemes means that new firms must automatically participate in existing sectoral pension funds unless they qualify for dispensation, which in practice means that a firm operates its own pension scheme.[20]

The regulatory framework requires pension funds to accept all employees who are at least 21 years old, and there is no vesting period. Moreover, pension funds may not discriminate against part-time workers. The 1996 Equal Treatment Working Hours Act guarantees equal treatment of full-time and part-time work in terms of wages, working conditions, and fringe benefits such as supplementary pensions.

---

[17] Small occupational pension funds often contract out this service to life insurance companies.

[18] There is a clear trend towards consolidation; in 2007 there were 602 pension funds.

[19] The law was updated in 2000.

[20] The law on mandatory participation stipulates four reasons for dispensation: a firm already had a pension scheme in place that was equivalent to the sectoral one; the firm operates its own pension scheme that meets certain requirements; a firm has its own collective agreement (and not a sectoral one); or if the sectoral pension fund has experienced unsatisfactory investment returns for the past five years.

Table 11.3 Pension scheme types by pension fund category (2004; relative percentages)

	Number of pension funds	Number of active participants	Balance sheet total (EUR millions)
Company funds	*701*	*856,691*	*132,233*
Share (in %)			
DB final pay	50.8	26.4	37.6
DB career average	20.8	31.4	28.3
DC	4.4	6.6	1.5
combined DB/DC	17.4	33.7	32.2
other schemes	6.6	1.8	0.4
Sectoral schemes	*80*	*4,756,913*	*272,786*
Share (in %)			
DB final pay	17.5	10.5	8.5
DB career average	71.3	85.7	91.1
DC	2.5	0.0	0.0
combined DB/DC	5.0	3.4	0.3
other schemes	3.8	0.4	0.1

Source: DNB, www.dnb.nl

7. What kind of benefits?

Until recently, occupational pensions have been overwhelmingly DB schemes, relying on a final salary benefit formula usually equal to 70 per cent of the final wage (including the AOW basic pension) accumulated over thirty-five (or more) years, with a limit of no more than 100 per cent of the final wage. In 1998, 66.5 per cent of active participants (current workers covered by pension schemes) took part in final pay schemes, but by 2005 the number had fallen to 10.5 per cent (Pensioenkamer 2005). Nevertheless, more than 90 per cent are still covered by DB schemes (see Table 11.3). However, most plans combine features of DC with DB, because the indexation of both pension accrual and pension payments is conditional on pension fund solvency (Ponds and van Riel 2007). In other words, the extent to which the DB promise is met is dependent on the performance of the pension scheme's investments, the ratio of current workers who pay contributions to retired members who receive pensions, and interest rate developments.

The public pensions and occupational pensions are closely integrated. However, the majority of pensioners do not achieve the targeted 70 per cent of final salary including the AOW, for several reasons. First, many schemes use an AOW offset that is too high because it is based on the couple benefit. This legacy of the breadwinner-dominated labour market is no longer in sync with the current prevalence of dual-earner couples and singles. Since the late 1980s, Dutch governments have tried and mostly succeeded in getting the social partners to use an individualized AOW offset in occupational pension schemes.[21] A second source of incomplete pension accrual is the increasing tendency of many wage earners to work less than the number of years required for a full pension (usually thirty-five or forty). This holds particularly for women and immigrants. For example, in 2003 the average occupational pension for men was €10,400, while women received on average €3,400 (van der Brug et al. 2005).

The financial health of pension funds is critical for the level of benefits because most schemes make the indexation of pension accrual and payouts conditional on solvency. Before the 2001/2 stock market downturn, the regulatory framework set out in the PSW was somewhat vague concerning how to determine pension fund solvency. The PSW required that pension liabilities be fully funded, but it was silent on the issue of how exactly to calculate assets and liabilities, and this calculation is crucial in the determination of indexation. Until the mid-2000s, pension funds used a rule of thumb: liabilities should be calculated using a fixed discount rate of 4 per cent, and 100 per cent of nominal liabilities should be covered. Under the PSW, if the funding ratio was in danger of falling below 100 per cent, pension funds would raise contributions. This method worked for the post-war period, but the liberalization of financial markets and falling interest rates made this strategy less attractive. Pension funds started to invest more in equities, and interest rates fell below 4 per cent in the 1990s. Low interest rates raised the present value of pension liabilities. When the stock market dropped, pension funds were more exposed to equity risk at the same time that their liabilities became more expensive. The new pension law deals with these realities by introducing a fair market valuation of liabilities and requiring pension funds to state specifically what their indexation policy is.

The emphasis on nominal liabilities is important: the PSW and the new pension law do not require pension funds to index pension accrual or payouts for inflation or wages. The issue of indexation of pension accrual is a relatively recent one because it is irrelevant in a final salary scheme. With the massive shift to average salary schemes, however, indexation of pension accrual became highly salient. The pension benefit level at retirement can be almost 20 percentage points lower in an average salary scheme with no indexation compared to the same scheme with 3 per cent annual indexation. The legally required funding ratio of 105 per cent (ratio of assets to liabilities) is based on nominal pension liabilities, so pension funds aspiring to wage indexation of both pension accrual and payouts need assets equal to about 130 per cent of (nominal) liabilities. Nearly all pension funds aspire to some kind of indexation, but this is a 'soft' promise (unless it is explicitly part of the pension agreement) in contrast

---

[21] In 1998, 30.4 per cent of participants were covered by an AOW offset based on the couple benefit, and this had fallen to 22.3 per cent by 2005. About 60 per cent of active participants are now covered by some sort of fixed AOW offset (DNB 2005).

to the 'hard' promise of nominal pension accrual and payouts. More than 80 per cent of schemes have indexing conditional on pension fund solvency, and if indexing is awarded, about 60 per cent use some form of contract wages (sectoral- or economywide), about 20 per cent inflation, and 20 per cent some other formula (DNB 2005).

The level of indexation often varies widely across pension schemes, as well as between active and dormant members. After the stock market downturn in 2001/2, many pension funds cancelled or decreased indexation of both pension accrual and pension payouts for several years. In 2008, many funds awarded extra indexation in order to compensate for some of the losses in 2001/2. However, according to a survey of the twenty-five largest pension funds by the Dutch Central Bank, most active participants (both workers and pensioners) will receive no indexation at all in 2009 because poor financial performance has caused most pension funds to fall below the required funding ratio (DNB 2009a: 19).

8. Who pays?

Occupational pension contributions are paid only on the salary portion above the public pension benefit. The contributions are set by the social partners (usually the bipartite administrative board of the pension fund). Contributions are typically shared between employers and wage earners, though employers usually pay a higher share, often two-thirds. In 1998, employers paid 6.7 per cent of their wage bill into second-pillar schemes, while employees paid 2.3 per cent of their wages (SZW 2000: 6). Pension premiums have increased dramatically during the last decade; Ponds and van Riel (2007: 6) document that occupational pension premiums have increased by 83 per cent in the period 2000–5. Table 11.4 shows the increase of premiums between 1997 and 2008. The public employees' pension fund ABP is an instructive example: premiums increased from 11.6 per cent of qualifying income (above the AOW offset) in 1996 to a peak of 21.4 per cent

Table 11.4. Occupational pension contributions

	Total contributions (million €)					Employers' share (%)			
	1997	2000	2005	2006	2007	1997	2000	2005	2006
All schemes	6,491	9,516	24,891	23,518	23,844	83.7	82.7	70.3	70.0
Sectoral	4,645	7,368	17,527	16,855	17,926	81.2	82.9	73.0	73.0
Company	1,655	2,140	6,952	6,277	5,488	86.8	74.0	62.9	61.6
Professional	191	8	412	386	430	116.8	2,262.5	78.2	76.4

Source: DNB, www.dnb.nl

in 2005 before falling to 19.2 per cent in 2007 prior to the financial market crisis (ABP: various years).

9. Who governs? Who decides? Who manages?

Occupational pensions are regulated in the Pension Act (PW – *Pensioenwet*) that replaced the previous regulatory framework (PSW – *Pensioen en Spaarfondswet*) in 2007. Until 2004, the Pension and Insurance Authority (PVK, *Pensioen en Verzekeringskamer*) was the supervisory body charged with oversight. In 2004, the PVK was integrated into the Dutch Central Bank and is now called the Pension Chamber (*Pensioenkamer*). Like the PSW before it, the PW provides only the regulatory framework for occupational pensions. The social partners have considerable freedom to decide the details of their pension arrangements, and they are negotiated as part of collective wage agreements (CAOs).

The PW regulates issues such as the funding ratio of pension funds, measures to correct deficits, investment rules, pension portability, and representation on administrative boards. One distinctive feature of the Dutch occupational pension sector is the requirement that funds be held outside of pension schemes and may not be considered company assets. This provision protects pension fund members against the risks of employer bankruptcy. Even if an employer goes out of business, the pension fund should continue to exist and pay benefits because it is legally separate from the employer and its primary obligation is to its members and not to the employer.

The definition of minimum funding has been controversial because it is open to interpretation. The Pension Act states that pension funds must have a regulatory minimum level of funds equal to 105 per cent of nominal (non-indexed) liabilities. If the pension fund falls below this level, it must submit a recovery plan (achievable within one year) to the pension regulator: the Dutch Central Bank. The definition of sufficient funding is stricter: pension funds are considered fully funded if they can guarantee with 97.5 per cent probability that they can meet all obligations, including indexation.[22] This requires a funding level of 125–130 per cent. If a pension fund falls below this level, it must submit a long-term (fifteen years) recovery plan to the pension regulator. Many analysts estimate that a nominal funding level of 150 per cent is required to meet pension promises that are indexed to wages.

The Pension Act requires only that pension funds follow the prudent person principle for their investment strategies. As a result, investments in equities

---

[22] Specifically, a pension fund needs: 100 per cent of nominal liabilities; 5 per cent of liabilities as a risk reserve; an additional 15–20 per cent of nominal liabilities to cover indexation ambitions; and an additional amount to cover investment risks. The latter depends on the precise investment mix. See the Pension Act.

have increased dramatically since the 1980s. Since the stock market downturn of the early 2000s, pension funds have also started to use liability-driven investment strategies. This means that investments should be matched more closely to the type of risks (longevity, biometric risks) that make up the membership of the pension scheme.

The administrative boards of pension funds are classic examples of Dutch corporatism. Pension schemes are components of collective agreements, so they are administered by representatives of employers, trade unions, and sometimes pensioners. Both sectoral and company pension funds must have parity representation by the employer(s) and union(s) active in the sector and company respectively.[23] Employee representatives are elected by the active participants in the pension fund. The issue of pensioner representation has been the subject of much controversy, however. The new Pension Law requires company pension funds with at least 1,000 pensioners to either include a pensioners' representative in the administrative board, or to establish a 'participants council' (*deelnemersraad*) that advises the pension fund board on important issues. Even though participant councils are not obligatory, one-third of pension funds (sectoral, company, and professional) had established them by 2007. The role of the administrative boards in negotiating changes is hugely important: they make annual decisions about whether to award indexation and whether to adjust the contribution rate. In short, they are the key actors when pension funds make decisions about how to deal with fund deficits and surpluses.

9.1 Occupational pensions in practice: ABP, PME, and PMT

This section takes a closer look at three pension funds, one in the public sector (ABP) and two in the metalworking sector (PME and PMT), in order to illustrate the similarities and differences across pension schemes in terms of both basic structure and response to the financial crises of the 2000s. ABP (*Algemeen Burgerlijk Pensioenfonds*) administers pensions for civil servants such as police, the military, teachers, and university employees. ABP has about 2.7 million members, including 1,133,000 active participants, 872,000 dormant members, and 750,000 pensioners. The PMT (*Pensioenfonds Metaal & Techniek*) provides pensions for 400,000 employees in 33,000 firms in the 'small' metalworking sector (*kleinmetaal*). PMT also covers 600,000 dormant members and 150,000 pensioners (see www.bpmt.nl). The Pension Fund for the Mechanical and Electrical Engineering Industries (*Pensioenfonds van de Metalektro*, PME) administers pensions for the firms in the 'big metal' sector (*grootmetaal*). About 1,231 firms participated in the scheme in 2008, with 157,300 active participants (including those on disability). There are 334,000 dormant members and

---

[23] The definition of parity is less strict for company pension funds.

Table 11.5 Main characteristics of the ABP, PMT, and PME pension schemes in 2009

	ABP	PMT	PME
Contributions	20.4% of income above the offset	27.3% of income above the offset to a ceiling of €73,287 −17.7% of income above the ceiling of €73,287	23% of income above the offset with a ceiling of €64,097
	70% employer	50% employer (max)	50% employer (min)
	30% employee	50% employee (min)	50% employee
AOW offset	€10,350	€15,004	€14,843*
Benefits	Average salary; 2.05% of the amount above the offset.	Average salary; 2.236% for the amount between the offset and the ceiling; 1.75% accumulation for income above the ceiling	Average salary; 2.2% accumulation per year for the amount above the offset.
Indexation	• Wage indexation of pension accumulation and payouts if FR** ≥135% • Partial indexation if FR is 105–135% • No indexation if FR < 105%	• Wage indexation of pension accumulation and payouts if FR ≥ 135%; • Partial indexation if FR is 105–135%; • No indexation if FR < 105%	• Wage indexation of pension accumulation and payouts if FR ≥ 135% • Partial indexation if FR is 105–135%; • No indexation if FR < 105%

*Certain categories of older workers fall under previous rules, so they have a higher offset.
**FR = funding ratio.
Source: www.abp.nl, www.pme.nl, www.bpmt.nl.

144,700 pensioners. There is considerable variation across the three occupational pension schemes (see Table 11.5): the only parameter that does not vary is the average salary benefit formula, whereas the contribution rates, AOW offset, and accrual rates are quite different. Moreover, both of the metalworkers' funds use some sort of ceiling for contributions, while public sector fund ABP does not.

These three occupational pension schemes responded differently to the two financial crises of the 2000s. Public sector fund ABP recovered quickly from the 2000/1 financial crisis, boasting a funding ratio of 140 per cent at the end of 2007. In 2008, ABP pensions were fully indexed and the fund paid extra compensation for the years of partial indexation since 2001. By the end of 2008, however, the funding ratio had plummeted by *50 percentage points* from 140 to 90 per cent. Assets fell from €217 billion at the end of 2007 to €173 billion at the end of 2008. It is important to note that about half of the decrease in the coverage ratio is due to the increased value of liabilities because of falling interest rates (ABP 2009). As discussed previously, low interest rates increase the present value of pension liabilities, thereby increasing the size of the denominator in the funding ratio. ABP's liabilities increased from €155 billion in 2007 to €193 billion at the end of 2008. ABP has recovered somewhat in the second half of 2009; the stock market upturn that started in the spring of 2009 has pulled the funding ratio up to 98 per cent. Like many pension funds, the ABP's recovery plan included a contribution increase, starting in July 2009, of 1 percentage point. The plan also called for an additional 2 percentage point premium increase in 2010 until the funding ratio reached 105 per cent. Pension accrual for current workers and pension payouts for current pensioners were also frozen in 2009. By October 2009, the financial market recovery had pulled the funding ratio to 105 per cent, allowing partial indexation for 2010 (0.45 per cent) and the cancellation of contribution increases planned for 2009 and 2010. Despite this recovery, ABP's cancellation of indexation for 2008 (and 2009) comes on the heels of several years of partial indexation following the 2000/1 stock market downturn and only two years of higher indexations of 2.82 per cent in 2006 and 4.05 per cent in 2007 (ABP 2009). Historically low interest rates in the first half of 2010 pulled the funding ratio down again, despite good investment performance. At the end of May 2010, the funding ratio stood at 96 per cent.

The year 2008 was also a disastrous year for the fund of the metal craft sector, PMT. The funding ratio dropped from 141 per cent to 85 per cent (PMT 2009: 17). The value of invested assets fell from €34.7 billion in 2007 to €28.7 billion at the end of 2008, and the value of pension liabilities increased from €24.6 billion to €33.1 billion in the same period. PMT's recovery plan includes freezing both pension accumulation and payouts for five years. The board of PMT also decided to increase contributions from 25.2 per cent in 2008 to 27.3 per cent of qualifying income in 2009. Following the five-year recovery period, pension accumulation and payouts will be indexed and the contributions decreased. The recovery plan spreads the pain across employers (increased contribution), workers (frozen pension accumulation), and pensioners (frozen payouts). The rapid recovery of assets markets in 2009 has improved the funding ratio more quickly than anticipated. Between February and December 2009, the funding ratio increased from 80 per cent to 101 per cent, only to fall to 92 per cent in May 2010 because of low interest rates.

The fund for the larger metal firm sector, PME, also experienced severe difficulties in 2008. PME's funding ratio dropped from 135 per cent at the end of 2007 to 90 per cent at the end of 2008. The value of assets decreased from €22.4 billion to €18.7 billion in the same period. The value of liabilities increased by €4.3 billion (from €16.3 billion to €20.6 billion) in 2008 because of falling interest rates. Like other pension funds, PME's funding ratio has fallen in 2010, to 98 per cent in April. The temporary cancellation of indexation is a central component of PME's recovery plan. The recovery plan foresees a return to the minimum 105 per cent funding ratio in 2012 and partial indexation

(50 per cent of contract wage increases). When the funding ratio reaches 117.5 per cent, the fund plans to increase indexation. PME's board also approved an increase in the contribution rate by 1 percentage point. PME has adopted a maximum contribution rate of 23 per cent and no indexation if the funding ratio falls below 105 per cent. If the funding ratio is between 105 and 115 per cent, the fund grants 50 per cent indexation. Starting at 125 per cent, full indexation is granted, and at 135 per cent the fund starts to repair lost indexation from previous years. Pension payouts are indexed to inflation whereas pension accumulation is indexed to wage increases. During the past eleven years, the indexation of pension payouts totalled 19.5 per cent. Full indexation to inflation would have been 24.5 per cent (PME 2009: 24).

As the three cases show, indexation policy is a core component of pension funds' recovery plans. The shift from final salary to average pay benefit formulae that occurred in the early 2000s is a huge transfer of risk from pension funds to employees because of the way indexation works. Indexation is usually not guaranteed, so in an average wage scheme, an individual's pension accumulation increases each year in line with whatever level of indexation the pension fund awards. This can be inflation, wages, or a mix of both. In a final salary scheme, the indexation of pension accrual is meaningless since only the final salary counts. The Pension Law requires only that pension funds guarantee *nominal* benefits, and the funding ratio is based on the ratio of assets to the present value of *nominal* benefits.

10. Outlook

Until recently, the Dutch multipillar pension system was a model of economic efficiency and social solidarity. However, occupational pensions are currently experiencing their worst crisis ever because of the impact of the 2008/9 worldwide financial crisis. This is not surprising given that occupational pensions are funded schemes that invest significantly in equities. It will take several years, or perhaps a decade, for many occupational pension schemes to fully recover from their losses, and this will have major repercussions for future collective bargaining rounds and retirement incomes. The government has shown some flexibility in allowing the pension schemes extra time to restore solvency but has stopped short of promising any sort of bailout.

The financial crisis provided the first tough test of the new supervisory framework. By the end of October 2008, the average funding ratio for pension funds had fallen to 109 per cent, prompting most pension funds to announce that they would probably have to suspend or decrease the indexation of pension rights and pension payouts. By early 2009, it was clear that the pension funds had sustained massive losses, and it would be difficult to maintain the current level of pension payouts without contribution increases. About 350 of the 650 pension funds had funding ratios below the legally required 105 per cent level. According to the Central Bank's statistics, pension funds' assets totalled €697 billion at the end of 2008, an 8.7 per cent decrease (€66 billion) compared to the previous year. The experiences of ABP, PME, and PMT are indicative of the constraints faced by sectoral pension funds. Company pension funds have also been hard hit by the crisis. KPN (the largest telecom) will make extra deposits totalling €390 million by 2012 and has also frozen indexation. Several smaller company pension funds have actually *reduced* accumulated pension rights and pension payouts.

The problems facing the AOW public pension are potentially as serious as those facing occupational pensions. In 2009, the Centre–Left government (Christian Democrats, Christian Union, and Labour) proposed increasing the retirement age for the public pension from 65 to 67 as part of its emergency packages of measures in response to the economic crisis. The proposal is particularly important because it opens the door to increasing the standard retirement age for occupational pensions to 67, in line with the higher AOW retirement age. Not surprisingly, employers favour the measure (VNO-NCW et al. 2008) because it would decrease pension liabilities by cutting the average pension duration by two years. Unions bitterly opposed the move and accused the government and employers of using AOW reform to introduce cuts in occupational pensions through the back door. The fall of the government (over Dutch participation in the NATO campaign in Afghanistan) in February 2010 gave the unions some respite.

The 2008/9 stock market downturn also prompted another round of discussions about the regulation and content of occupational pensions. Employers entered the debate first by issuing a lengthy position paper in 2008 announcing that contribution rates had reached their natural limit (VNO-NCW et al.2008). The position paper argued that the increased costs caused by financial market volatility, longer life expectancy, and low interest rates would have to be borne by participants (workers and pensioners) and not employers. Employers reiterated the central role of the social partners in running the system, at the same time that they threatened to move to DC schemes if costs continued to increase.

At the same time, the drastic deterioration of the pension fund sector prompted the Minister of Social Affairs to take on a more activist stance concerning occupational pensions. Based on a series of expert reports commissioned during the financial crisis (the Goudswaard and Frijns Reports), the Minister broached the possibility of increasing the number of investment experts on the pension fund boards, increasing the representation of pensioners on the boards, using the real funding ratio rather then the nominal funding ratio to orient pension fund activities, and introducing measures to make pension funds more resistant to demographic and financial shocks (Ministerie van Sociale Zaken en Werkgelegenheid 2010). The Minister's intervention alarmed both unions and employers even if they agreed with many of the

Minister's proposals. Despite their disagreements with each other, the social partners repeatedly emphasized their primacy in the field of occupational pensions. In particular, the social partners intensely opposed any departure from the bipartite structure of the pension fund boards. The subsequent fall of the government gave the social partners time to overcome their disagreements and to present a united front vis-à-vis the government.

Several days before the parliamentary elections (4 June 2010), the social partners announced they had reached an agreement on the AOW and occupational pensions reform. The key elements include an increase in retirement age from 65 to 66 in 2020 for both the AOW and occupational pensions; linking both pensions to life expectancy; introducing flexible AOW retirement; more favourable AOW indexation (real wages instead of contract wages); and making occupational pensions more resistant to financial shocks by making pension rights more conditional on pension fund solvency (STAR 2010).

The 9 June 2010 election produced a shift to the right, and a coalition government led by the Liberals (VVD) is likely to form. The new government will probably adopt most, if not all, of the social partners' proposals. If this happens, the reforms will go a long way towards improving the stability and financial sustainability of occupational pensions. The Dutch are justifiably proud of their extensive system of funded occupational pensions, but the losses sustained in the current crisis threaten to permanently damage the legitimacy of the system. Moreover, the contribution hikes and pension payout freezes required to restore solvency are pro-cyclical in that they exacerbate the effects of the recession. Falling interest rates also threaten the stability of the occupational pension system. As discussed, declining interest rates increase the present value of nominal liabilities. Even if equity values are rising, low interest rates pull down the funding ratio because pension funds need more assets to cover more expensive liabilities.

The pension landscape in the Netherlands has changed substantially in the last decade, not only because of changing labour markets and demographic trends but also because of the repercussions of two financial shocks. However, the deteriorations in occupational pensions resulting from market fluctuations must be viewed in the context of improved coverage since the 1990s for women, younger workers, and non-standard workers. Moreover, Dutch occupational pensions now offer members a level of freedom of choice that was unheard of two decades ago. Thus, the Netherlands enters the 2010s with a modernized, fully funded occupational pension system. Advocates of the multi-pillar approach would surely point to the many advantages of the Dutch system. However, funded pensions also have their risks, as the 2000/1 and 2008/9 financial crises demonstrate. One cannot escape the conclusion that, in many ways, funded pensions are not for the faint of heart. The experience of occupational pensions in the last decade has been a roller-coaster ride as pension funds cycled between periods of over- and underfunding. These fluctuations have unleashed distributive conflict in corporatist decision-making concerning pension fund recovery plans, and they have spilled over into national political decision-making concerning the public pension. Surely, these are issues that the social partners and government prefer to avoid in the future. Another round of reform in 2010 and 2011 is a near certainty, and reforms are highly likely to involve a transfer of risk from pension funds/employers to individuals.

Bibliography

ABP (2009). *Herstelplan ABP naar toezichthouder DNB*. Press Release, March 31, 2009.

Anderson, K. M. (2004). 'Pension Politics in Three Small States: Denmark, Sweden and the Netherlands'. *Canadian Journal of Sociology*, 29/2: 289–312.

——(2007). 'The Netherlands: Political Competition in a Proportional System', in E. M. Immergut, K. M. Anderson and I. Schulze (eds.), *The Handbook of Pension Politics in Western Europe*. Oxford: Oxford University Press, 713–57.

Clark, G. L. (2003). *European Pensions and Global Finance*. Oxford: Oxford University Press.

Cox, R. H. (2001). 'The Social Construction of an Imperative: Why Welfare Reform Happened in Denmark and The Netherlands, but Not in Germany'. *World Politics*, 53/3: 463–98.

DNB (2005). *Pensioensmonitor*, Amsterdam: Den Nederlandsche Bank (www.dnb.nl).

——(2009a). *Statistisch Bulletin maart 2009*, Amsterdam: Den Nederlandsche Bank.

——(2009b). *Statistisch Bulletin september 2009*, Amsterdam: Den Nederlandsche Bank.

Haverland, M. (2001). 'Another Dutch Miracle? Explaining Dutch and German Pension Trajectories'. *Journal of European Social Policy*, 11: 308–23.

Hemerijck, A., and van Kersbergen, K. (1997). 'A Miraculous Model? Explaining the New Politics of the Welfare State in the Netherlands'. *Acta Politica*, 32/3: 258–301.

Jaspers, A. et al. (2001). *'De gemeenschap is aansprakelijk'* . . . *Honderd jaar sociale verzekering 1901–2001*. Den Haag: Koninklijke Vermande.

Kraamwinkel, M. (1995). *Pensioen, emancipatie en gelijke behandeling*. Deventer: Fed.

Lijphart, A. (1968). *The Politics of Accommodation: Pluralism and Democracy in the Netherlands*. Berkeley: University of California Press.

Oude Nijhuis, D. (2009). *Labor Divided. Union Structure and the Development of the Postwar Welfare State in the Netherlands and the United Kingdom*. Ridderprint: Ridderkerk.

Pensioenkamer (2005). *Pensionregelingen*. (www.pvk.nl).

PME (2009). *Jaarverslag 2008*. Stichting Bedrijfstakpenioenfonds van de Metalektro. Velsen-Noord.

PMT (2009). *Jaarverslag 2008*. Rijwijk: PMT.

Ponds, E. H. M., and van Riel, B. (2007). 'The Recent Evolution of Pension Funds in the Netherlands. The Trend to Hybrid DB-DC PLans and Beyond'. *Working Paper*, Center for Retirement Research at Boston College.

Rigter, D., Hemerijck, A., van den Boch, E., and van der Veen, R. (1996). *Tussen sociale wil en werkelijkheid*. Den Haag: VUGA.

STAR (1997a). *Overwegingen en aanbevelingen gericht op vernieuwing van pensioenregelingen*. Den Haag: Stichting van de Arbeid.

——(1997b). *Convenant inzake de arbeidspensioen. Overeengekomen tussen het Kabinet en de Stichting van de Arbeid op 9 december 1997*. Den Haag: Stichting van de Arbeid.

——(2010). *Pensioenakkoord voorjaar 2010. 4 juni 2010*. Den Haag: Stichting van de Arbeid.

SZW (2000). *The Old Age Pension System in the Netherlands*. The Hague: Ministry of Social Affairs and Employment.

——(2010). *Brief aan de Tweede Kamer*. 7 April 2010. Den Haag.

Tulfer, P. M. (1997). *Pensioenen, fondsen en verzekeraars*. Deventer: Kluwer.

Van der Brug, P., Hellenthal, A. J., and Verschuren, L. B. C. (2005). 'Ouderen in het nauw'. *Economische-statitische berichten*, 7 October 2005.

Van Kersbergen, K. (1995). *Social Capitalism: Christian Democracy and the Welfare State in Europe*. London: Routledge.

Van Riel, B., Hemerijck, A., and Visser, J. (2003). 'Is there a Dutch way to Pension Reform?', in G. L. Clark and N. Whiteside (eds.), *Pension Security in the 21st Century. Redrawing the Public–Private Debate*. Oxford: Oxford University Press, 64–92.

Veldkamp, G. (1978). *Inleiding tot de sociale zekerheid en de toepassingen in Nederland en België; Deel I, Karakter en geschiedenis*. Deventer: Kluwer.

Visser, J., and Hemerijck, A. (1997). *A Dutch Miracle. Job growth, Welfare Reform and Corporatism in the Netherlands*. Amsterdam: Amsterdam University Press.

VNO-NCW et al. (2008). *Naar een modern en betaalbaar pensioen*. Den Haag: VNO-NCW, MKB-Nederland, LTO Nederland and WWYN.

Vrooman, C., Gesthuizen, M., Hoff, S., Soede, A., and Wildeboer Schut, J. M. (2007). 'Inkomen en werk', in R. Bijl, J. Boelhouwer, and E. Pommer (eds.), *De sociale staat van Nederland 2007*. Den Haag: SCP.

Westerhout, E., van de Ven, M., van Ewijk, C., and Draper, N. (2004). *Naar een schokbestending pensioenstelsel. Verkenning van enkele beleidsopties op pensioengebied*. CPB Report No. 67.

Wildeboer Schut, J. M., and Hoff, S. (2007). *Geld op de plank. Niet-gebruik van inkomensvoorzieningen*. Den Haag: Sociaal en Cultureel Planbureau (SCP).

12

Switzerland: Regulating a Public–Private Heritage of Multipillar Pension Governance

Giuliano Bonoli and Silja Häusermann

1. Introduction

Switzerland's multipillar pension system has attracted much attention because it combines a universal public basic pension scheme with mandatory semi-private occupational schemes and favourably taxed personal retirement savings. For many international observers, such as the World Bank (Queisser and Vittas 2000), this combination of public pay-as-you-go (PAYG) and (semi-) private funded pensions seems advantageous in the light of current demographic and economic challenges since financial and social risks are spread across multiple pillars. As many west European countries introduced or reinforced supplementary funded pensions over the last decades, Switzerland serves as an instructive case for policymakers looking for lessons in regulatory governance of these schemes. However, the Swiss case does not provide a simple blueprint of effective regulation. As this chapter will show, the Swiss multipillar public–private pension mix is the result of an ongoing and incremental process of welfare state development. Similarly, regulation of supplementary pensions reflects the outcome of political negotiations and it is constantly renegotiated. Finally, the Swiss case also demonstrates the difficulties of effective regulation, because regulatory practice tends to deviate from the formal rules in various ways, both to the detriment and to the advantage of different groups of the insured and benefit recipients. In that sense, the Swiss case also entails lessons about unintended consequences of the (semi-) privatization of old age security.

Part I: The evolution of the public–private pension mix

2. The main features of the Swiss three-pillar pension system

The Swiss pension system is best described as a three-pillar system (see Figure 12.1). The first-pillar public pension (AHV/AVS[1]) covers the basic needs of all retirees. The contributory scheme is moderately earnings-related and includes a means-tested pension supplement (EL/PC[2]). The second-pillar mandatory occupational pensions provide pensioners with a standard of living close to the level experienced during employment. Finally, the third pillar allows people to tailor pension coverage to their individual needs through non-compulsory personal pensions supported by tax concessions. Most pensioners receive income from a combination of the two main pillars. In 2005, outlays of the basic pension accounted for 6.8 per cent of GDP, and those of occupational pensions 7.2 per cent of GDP (OFAS 2007).

The *first pillar* (AHV/AVS) provides universal coverage and is largely a redistributive scheme since there is no contribution ceiling. The amount of the

	First pillar	Second pillar	Third pillar
Third tier		Additional occupational coverage Voluntary coverage (depending on the employer) for earnings above 75,000 CHF p.a.	Voluntary individual pension (No tax concession above ceiling of about 6,000 CHF p.a.)
Second tier		Mandatory occupational pension (*BVG/LPP Obligatorium*): all employees earning 19,350–75,000 CHF p.a.	Voluntary individual pension: tax-subsidized (EET)
First tier	Basic pension AHV/AVS: all residents (20–64)		
	EL/PC (means-tested pension supplement)		
	Social assistance		

Figure 12.1 Pillars and tiers of Swiss pensions

Source: Adapted from synopsis in Bonoli (2007).

---

[1] AHV/AVS: *Alters- und Hinterlassenenversicherung/Assurance Vieillesse et Survivants.*
[2] EL/PC: *Ergänzungsleistungen/Prestations Complémentaires.*

benefit can vary between a floor and a ceiling that is twice as high as the floor. In 2008, the limits are set at CHF 1,105 and CHF 2,210 per month respectively, approximately 20 and 40 per cent of the average wage. Within these limits, the amount of the benefit is related to contributions paid during employment, with about a third of retirees receiving the maximum amount. Benefits are adjusted every two years according to a so-called 'mixed index' (the arithmetic average between inflation and wage increases).

The public scheme is universal for all residents and is contribution-based; those who are not working (e.g. students, housewives) are required to pay flat-rate contributions or, if providing informal care, are entitled to contribution credits. Unemployed people pay contributions based on their unemployment benefit, which is treated as a salary, thus the unemployment insurance contributes 4.2 per cent of the unemployment benefit. The Swiss basic old age security is a compromise between the Bismarckian tradition of earnings-related contributory pensions and the Beveridgean flat-rate poverty prevention approach.

With regard to financing, the basic pension operates on a PAYG basis. It is financed mostly through contributions (8.4 per cent of salary equally split between employers and employees, or up to 7.8 per cent for self-employed). The scheme also receives a subsidy equal to 28 per cent of expenditure in 2008, which includes 1 percentage point of VAT, which has been assigned to AHV/AVS since 1999. The trade unions and employer representatives participate in the administration of some special branch-related funds, but the central fund is managed by the federal administration.

The *second-pillar* occupational pensions have a long history. They were at first granted tax concessions in 1916 and then developed in a wide variety of private schemes (Leimgruber 2008). By the 1960s, only about a third of male workers (mostly the high-skilled) and about a fourth of female workers were covered. This changed in January 1985 when occupational pensions became compulsory for all employees earning at least twice the minimum AHV/AVS pension.[3] In the mid-1990s, coverage was virtually universal among male employees but reached only about 80 per cent of women due to the lower earnings of this group (BSV 1995: 10).

A full occupational pension is granted to employees with a contribution record of thirty-nine years for women and forty for men (to be equalized over the next few years). When occupational pensions became compulsory, many employees were already covered by voluntary arrangements. Therefore, the new legislation needed to take into account the pre-existing occupational pensions. Therefore, it was decided to introduce a compulsory minimum level of provision (known as the *Obligatorium*) calculated on the basis of notional

---

[3] The first BVG/LPP revision, adopted in 2003, lowered this threshold.

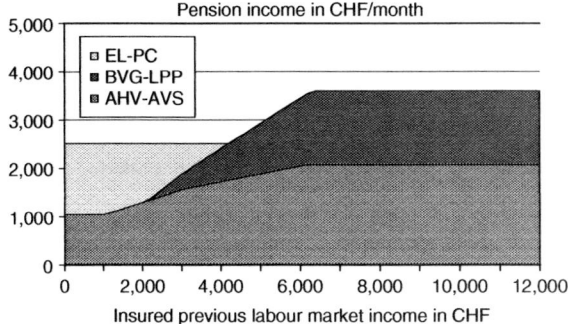

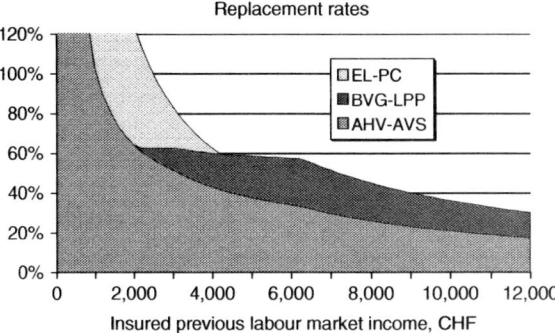

Figure 12.2 Benefits and replacement rates from basic pensions (AHV/AVS), means-tested supplementary pensions (EL/PC), and occupational pensions (BVG-LPP), Switzerland

Source: Nova and Häusermann (2005: 71).

contributions,[4] leaving existing pension funds relatively large autonomy over how to deliver and finance that minimum level of provision. Many pension funds (especially in the public sector or those sponsored by large firms) still offer better conditions than the *Obligatorium* (Bonoli and Gay-des-Combes 2003).

The objective of the new law was a combined (first- and second-pillar) replacement rate of 60 per cent of gross earnings up to a ceiling equal to three times the maximum AHV/AVS benefit. For low-wage workers, this goal could be achieved by the moderately earnings-related benefits provided by AHV/AVS. Those earning between one and three times the maximum AHV/AVS benefits

[4] The notional contribution concept usually refers to PAYG pension schemes (e.g. Italy or Sweden). In Switzerland, occupational pensions are funded, but the calculation method for the compulsory minimum is based on contributions determined by law that do not necessarily reflect actual payments. The use of the term 'notional contributions/accounts' here is consistent with other English-language publications on Swiss second-pillar pensions (see e.g. Queisser and Vittas 2000).

(about 40 and 120 per cent of average earnings) were now guaranteed full coverage. An important characteristic of the occupational second tier is that there are different schemes for employees of the public and private sectors, and that no mandatory second-pillar pension exists for the self-employed.

Figure 12.2 shows the ideal interplay of the benefits and replacement rates of the first and second pillars in 2002 for people with a full contribution record. For people who on an average earned less than about CHF 4,000 per month during their working life, benefits remain low and are complemented with means-tested and tax-financed supplementary pensions, so that up until a previous monthly income of CHF 2,500, the replacement rate remains at least at 100 per cent. It then drops quickly and the second-pillar benefits remain equal from a certain earnings-level (Figure 12.2 includes only the mandatory benefits, i.e. only the pension rights that derive from the insurance of the income up to about CHF 75,000 p.a.), while benefits on top of the mandated provision or private pension savings are not taken into account.

3. A public–private pension system in a conservative welfare state

Most continental welfare states have relied predominantly on a single public pension scheme funded by PAYG. In this respect, Switzerland (next to the Netherlands) is certainly an atypical case, since funded occupational and personal pensions have played an important role throughout the twentieth century. However, despite its peculiar institutional architecture, the Swiss pension system is clearly 'continental' in its effects on social stratification and gender-differentiation when seen in the context of the wider institutional context of a *conservative welfare regime* and a *male breadwinner system*. Consequently, Swiss pension policy faces similar challenges than the other continental countries (Bonoli and Palier 2008).

Recent studies on the Swiss welfare state (Armingeon 2001; Bonoli 2006; Bonoli and Mach 2000; Häusermann 2010a; Obinger 1998) agree that Switzerland must be considered a predominantly *continental welfare regime* despite hybrid features that are not unusual for advanced welfare states. Observers who classified the Swiss regime as liberal (most prominently Esping-Andersen 1990) tended to focus exclusively on state-controlled social insurance schemes, neglecting a variety of public and semi-private schemes that provide social security, such as health insurance or – precisely – supplementary pensions. However, since membership in these semi-private schemes is mandatory at least since the mid-1980s, and since they operate under a legal framework, they are an integral part of the Swiss welfare state.[5]

---

[5] A final problem in classifying of the Swiss welfare regime is that many of the social security schemes were introduced relatively late. In addition to occupational pension, unemployment

Several institutional features of the Swiss welfare state are quite typically continental in their overall structure and effects. As in most continental countries, the Swiss welfare regime emphasizes contribution-related rather than egalitarian benefits. Unemployment-, disability-, and maternity-insurance are all clearly earnings-related schemes. This characteristic also applies clearly to the Swiss pension system: while the first tier provides low but egalitarian benefits, the mandatory second pillar covers only the standard workforce (i.e. employees in stable work relations lasting more than three months and providing an income over 30 per cent of the average earnings). This typically continental focus on employment-related eligibility and earnings-related benefits also fits with the male breadwinner characteristic of most continental welfare regimes.

The Swiss welfare regime also clearly belongs to the conservative variety if one focuses on family- and *gender*-related aspects of social policy. Childcare provision is scarce and most women work part-time, often very short hours. As a result, they incur corresponding losses in their social security contribution records. In 2003, the average income of a single female pensioner household was around CHF 2,500, while a single male pensioner household lived on an average of CHF 3,250 (Bundesamt für Statistik 2003: 48). Moreover, the pension regime has been inegalitarian in respect to gender for a long time. Women lost the right to an individual public pension with marriage, their pension rights being replaced by a couple's pension of 1.5 times the entitlement of the husband. Typically, a woman's occupational pension was also dissolved once married. For these reasons, divorce became a substantial poverty risk.[6]

Switzerland is a Coordinated Market Economy, relying heavily on tripartite concertation, which means that coordination among the state, employers, and trade unions is key to the governance of the welfare state. In the field of pensions, this decentralization of power is particularly strong: for both the first and the second pillars, there exists a specialized tripartite commission, which proposes legislation and supervises the implementation of legislation. In the field of occupational pensions, the role of the social partners is particularly strong, because many of the private and occupational pension funds were initially founded by collective agreements (Leimgruber 2008). With a large share of major pension funds – notably in the public sector – governance is still largely in the hands of bipartite bodies.

---

insurance became mandatory only in 1982, occupational pensions were mandatory for employees since 1985, health insurance was not universal before 1994, and Swiss women even had to wait until 2004 for the adoption of a national maternity insurance programme. This lateness is the result of institutional obstacles to reform (Armingeon 2001; Gilliand 1993) and a long tradition of subsidiary policymaking by the social partners (Trampusch 2008).

[6] For a detailed discussion of the feminization of old age poverty in Switzerland until the 1990s, see Leitner and Obinger (1996).

Given these continental features of the overall welfare state and – more particularly – its pension regime, Switzerland has been facing challenges that are very similar to the ones faced by other continental welfare states since the late 1980s: financial instability and new social risks. Low birth rates and increased longevity threaten the financial stability of pensions, mostly in the PAYG first pillar, but also in the occupational second pillar. In addition, a sluggish economy and the 2008/9 crisis of financial markets have added strain on both PAYG and funded pension pillars. In addition, the strong reliance on the equivalence principle leads to new social risks for people with atypical employment careers. In the public pension pillar, major reforms in the 1990s have rendered the system more gender-egalitarian by introducing the splitting of contributions and benefits in case of divorce, as well as educational pension credits (see e.g. Bonoli 2000; Häusermann 2010a; Häusermann et al. 2004). With regard to occupational pensions, however, the improvements for new risk groups have remained far more modest.

4. The emergence of the public–private pension mix

Social policymaking in Switzerland has been complicated by the country's peculiar constitutional structure. For the federal government to be able to legislate in a new policy area, it must first be identified in the Constitution as an area of federal competence. As a result, every new social law had to be preceded by constitutional change, automatically subjected to a referendum. This resulted in a rather cumbersome and slow process of welfare state building

The first attempt at introducing a national pension scheme failed in 1931, when a majority of voters rejected a government-sponsored proposal for constitutional change in a referendum (Berenstein 1986; Binswanger 1987). As a result, the proposals for a national pension scheme were shelved, and the absence of public old age provision provided room for the expansion of occupational pensions. By the end of Second World War, about 25 per cent of employees had an occupational pension. This meant that a national pension scheme, when introduced, would have to integrate existing occupational provision. This explains the two-tiered character of the Swiss pension system (Leimgruber 2008). The current *basic* scheme (AHV/AVS) was eventually adopted in 1948.

From the point of view of the public/private pension mix, the most important development was the 1971 adoption of a constitutional article establishing the principle of a *three pillar system* with mandatory occupational coverage. The idea of three pillars had been proposed by the government in 1963, though still arguing that the first pillar alone should cover the constitutional goal of providing all citizens with a 'decent standard of living' and the second-cum-third-pillar pensions should complement basic security by maintaining the previous living standard for the middle- and higher-income groups. Hence, initially the government clearly rejected the idea of a mandatory second pillar, even though only a third of the male and a fourth of the female employees were already covered at the end of the 1960s (BSV 1995).

Things were to change in the following years. The first important step in establishing mandatory occupational pensions was a popular initiative sponsored by the Federation of Christian Unions in 1966, demanding mandatory occupational pensions. The government was sceptical and argued that making occupational pensions compulsory would have been 'extremely difficult, both legally and practically'. In addition, the government maintained that such a measure was unnecessary since voluntary occupational pension coverage had expanded rapidly in the previous two decades (FF 1968 I, 1: 682). Eventually, the unions withdrew the initiative.

A few years later, the Communist Party launched its own popular initiative to change the basic pension scheme in a single-pillar Bismarckian direction. According to this proposal, AHV/AVS would pay benefits equal to 60 per cent of average gross earnings during the best five years. Faced with the prospect of such a massively expanded basic pension, the right-of-centre majority worked out a counterproposal that included mandatory occupational pension coverage for all employees. This solution satisfied the Socialists, who joined the government camp. All of a sudden, mandatory occupational pensions had become a politically attractive solution across a wide political spectrum (FF 1971 II, 2: 1624).

In 1972, Swiss voters were asked in a popular referendum to choose between the government-backed multipillar proposal and the Bismarckian scheme favoured by the Communist Party. The outcome was unequivocal: the Communists' initiative was rejected (83 per cent) whereas the government solution was accepted by a large majority (73 per cent). The principle of compulsory occupational pensions was now enshrined in the Constitution: 'the federal government requires employers to insure their staff with a pension fund... [and] establishes the minimal requirements that must be satisfied by such pension funds' (Swiss Federal Constitution, of 29 May 1874, Art. 34, authors' translation). Under the pressure of more radical solutions, key political actors, including employers' associations, agreed to mandatory occupational pension coverage (Leimgruber 2008). Following the referendum, the details of how to achieve this goal, however, still needed to be worked out in the legislative process, and the process would prove to be difficult.

In December 1975, an occupational pension bill was submitted to parliament which provided a compulsory minimum while allowing funds that offered better benefits to maintain these and the bill contained the idea of notional contributions. The bill allowed funds to decide whether to provide defined-benefit (DB) or defined-contribution (DC) benefits and imposed different minimal conditions depending on the option chosen. In addition, the government would set up a central fund, jointly financed by pension schemes, to provide the funds needed to supplement the pensions for middle-aged workers who would not have enough time to accumulate sufficient capital to finance the prescribed benefits. Contribution rates earmarked for the central funds were expected to increase gradually and peak in 1996 at 4.13 per cent of insured earnings. This action was taken to offer older workers better retirement conditions.

The proposal, however, was heavily criticized and modified by the right-wing majority in parliament. First, the minimum requirement (*Obligatorium*) would be established only on a notional defined-contribution (NDC) basis. Second, notional contribution rates were reduced from a career average of 14.625 per cent of insured earnings to 12.5 per cent. Finally, the revised bill did not include plans to establish a central fund, or to provide full benefit indexation (BOAF CdE 1980: 241–301). In this form, the law was adopted and it took effect in January 1985. Parallel to the second-pillar pension law, the government also adopted a decree on the enactment of fiscally encouraged private pension savings (third pillar).

The adoption of mandatory occupational pensions in a country like Switzerland, where employers are extremely influential political actors, can only be understood with reference to the country's direct democratic political institutions, especially the popular initiative. It is difficult to imagine that right-wing parties and employers would have agreed to a mandatory second pillar in the absence of the pressure exerted by the popular initiatives of the Communist and Socialist parties. Support for the multipillar model was reiterated in a government report published in 1995 (BSV 1995). In this report, the government changed its interpretation of the constitutional article: the goal of providing all citizens with a decent standard of living should not be reached within the first pillar *alone*, but the new goal was that the first-and-second pillars should provide together all citizens retirement income with a replacement rate of at least 60 per cent of the last earnings (see Table 12.1).

Table 12.1 Chronology of main pension system reforms, 1948–80s

Reform	Reform measures	Reform coalition
1948	Introduction of the basic pension scheme AHV/AVS • Universal coverage • relatively flat-rate benefit structure • target: cover 'decent standard of living' for all insured	Coalition of all political parties and trade unions, some opposition by employers; bill accepted in a popular referendum
1951	1st reform of the basic pension scheme AHV/AVS • Increase of transitory pensions for pensioners with insufficient contribution record	Coalition of all political parties, employers, and trade unions

1954	2nd reform of the basic pension scheme AHV/AVS	Coalition of all political parties, employers, and trade unions
	• Increase of general pension levels	
	• Employees aged over 65 do not have to pay contributions anymore	
1956	3rd reform of the basic pension scheme AHV/AVS	Coalition of all political parties, employers, and trade unions
	• Harmonization of pension levels across all regions of the country	
1957	4th reform of the basic pension scheme AHV/AVS	Coalition of all political parties, employers, and trade unions
	• Lowering of the age of retirement for women from 65 to 63	
1961/2	5th reform of the basic pension scheme AHV/AVS	Coalition of all political parties, employers, and trade unions
	• Increase of general pension levels	
1964	6th reform of the basic pension scheme AHV/AVS	Coalition of all political parties, employers, and trade unions
	• Lowering of the age of retirement for women from 63 to 62	
1966	Introduction of means-tested supplementary pensions EL/PC	Some opposition by the left against means-testing, but eventually approved by a grand coalition of all political parties, employers, and trade unions
1969	7th reform of the basic pension scheme AHV/AVS	Coalition of all political parties, employers, and trade unions
	• New pension calculation formula, increase of general pension levels	
1971	Constitutional amendment on the multipillar pension regime	Coalition of trade unions, employers, right-wing and moderate left-wing parties. Opposition by the Communist Party
	• Enactment of the three-pillar pension scheme	
	• Introduction of a replacement rate target level in the Constitution	
1972	8th reform of the basic pension scheme AHV/AVS	Coalition of all political parties, employers, and trade unions
	• Pension level increase of 25%	
	• Indexation of pensions on an average of prices and wages	
	• Introduction of a 13th pension benefit per year	
	• Reduction of the tax-financed public contribution to the insurance scheme	
	• Increase of earnings-related contributions to pension insurance	
1976	9th reform of the basic pension scheme AHV/AVS	Coalition of all major parties, trade unions, and some employers; opposition
	• Increase of the minimum contribution to pension insurance	(referendum) by small employers and self-employed
	• Lowering of derived benefits for spouses	

(*Continued*)

327

Table 12.1   Continued

Reform	Reform measures	Reform coalition
	• Increase of tax-financed subsidies to pension insurance	
	• Increase of contribution levels for self-employed	
1985	Reform of the means-tested supplementary pension scheme EL/PC	Coalition of all political parties, trade unions, and employers
	• Increase of means-tested supplementary pension benefits	
	• Increased of means-tested supplementary benefits for long-term care patients	
	• Increase of benefits for house owners	
	• Lowering of complementary benefits for pensioners with own savings	
	• Measures to fight abuses	
1985	Introduction of the law on the occupational pension scheme BVG-LPP (adopted 1982)	Coalition of the main political parties, trade unions, and employers; opposition by the Communist Party
	• Mandatory occupational second-pillar pension insurance for standard employees	
	• Introduction of a combined replacement rate target level for public and occupational pensions	
1985	Introduction of the governmental decree on the third-pillar private pension savings scheme	Coalition of all political parties, trade unions, and employers
	• Tax-favoured contributions to the private pension savings schemes up to about 6,000 CHF per annum	

Source: Année Politique Suisse 1970–2003, www.admin.ch, Binswanger (1987), Kriesi (1980), Häusermann (2010*a*, 2010*b*).

5. The changing public–private pension mix

Switzerland entered the age of pension reform (1990s and 2000s) with a three-pillar pension system that reflected well the dominant consensus on its goals and governance. While the trade unions still privileged public pensions, no major political party seriously questioned the three-pillar architecture anymore. As a result, unlike other western European countries, Switzerland did not experience a major overhaul of its pension system, and the relative weight of public and private pensions was not altered fundamentally. Nevertheless, important reforms within each pillar were enacted. Within the *first pillar*, the most important change was the introduction of gender equality measures in 1995. These included a contribution-sharing mechanism between spouses, credits for child rearing, and the more controversial measure of increasing women's retirement age from 62 to 64 (Bonoli 1999,2000; Häusermann et al. 2004).

With regard to the occupational pension scheme, there have been two reforms over the last two decades. The reform of labour market mobility in the occupational pension scheme (FZG-LLP) of 1994 aimed at adapting the second pillar to the growing flexibility and mobility of the post-industrial labour market. Until then, generous occupational pensions had often been referred to as 'golden chains'. They were very favourable for employees, but they also tied them very closely to their employer, since in case of changing jobs, employees would lose up to half of their savings (employers could retain much of their contributions to an employee's pension savings). This limitation of labour market mobility was not an unintended dysfunction but reflected an explicit goal of the occupational pension scheme, that is, to reward long-term employment relations and to increase employees' allegiance to their employers. In the 1990s, this limitation to mobility had come into conflict with a labour market that demanded increasing flexibility. In addition, this reform enacted some social modernization: first, women's pension savings would not be dissolved anymore in case of marriage and second, the second-pillar pension savings would henceforth be split in case of divorce.

The most important reform of the occupational pension law, however, was adopted through the first revision of BVG-LPP in 2003. The original objective of the reform was to adapt occupational pensions to increasing life expectancy and to improve coverage of atypical workers by lowering the access threshold to compulsory coverage (an option favoured at the time by the unions and by the Socialists). However, the expansion of mandatory occupational pension coverage was firmly rejected by employers and, therefore, the government did not include it in the reform draft presented in parliament in 2000. The proposal dealt mostly with an adaptation of the *Obligatorium* to rising life expectancy. The most important element was a reduction in the rate for converting accumulated capital into annuities (from 7.2 to 6.65 per cent over fifteen years). In order to avoid benefit reductions, the notional contribution rates for determining the amount of capital available to employees were to be gradually increased. This measure would not necessarily have resulted in higher actual contributions. Some pension schemes could have used accumulated returns on capital to finance higher notional contribution rates.

However, left-wing parties, trade unions, but also liberal actors and women's organizations were not satisfied with the bill proposal (Häusermann 2010*b*), and it underwent substantial revision in the lower chamber of parliament. The main criticism against the government's proposal was that it did not improve pension coverage for low-paid, atypical, mainly part-time workers. Eventually, a moderate reduction of the access threshold (from CHF 24,000 to about CHF 18,000 per year) obtained a fair majority in parliament in 2002, including the Left, a majority of Christian-Democrats and Free Democrats, and some Swiss nationalists (SVP/UDC). The upper chamber National Council also introduced a distinction between the access threshold and the amount of non-insured earnings. In the previous system these two parameters coincided, but in the modified version of the bill, non-insured earnings were to be defined as 40 per cent of total earnings.[7] This solution was more favourable to part-time workers who would now see a larger proportion of their earnings insured. Finally, retrenchment was somewhat watered down: instead of 6.65 per cent the new rate would be set at 6.8 per cent.

When the bill was transferred to the upper chamber, the outlook for public finances had worsened, and the lowering of access thresholds was again reversed. The bill went back and forth between the two chambers until October 2003 when majorities in both chambers agreed to a proposal that did include lower-income workers in occupational pensions, but in a somewhat less generous way than in the initial proposal of 2002. The access threshold would be lowered to CHF 18,990 per year, and the amount of non-insured earnings to about CHF 22,155 per year. The conversion rate would be lowered to 6.8 per cent and notional contributions would not increase. The final law was a strong compromise, since both the Left and Right agreed and it was not challenged by a referendum, which is rather unusual for an important social policy reform (see Table 12.2).

Table 12.2 Chronology of main pension system reforms since the 1990s

Reform	Reform measures	Reform coalition
1994	Reform of labour market mobility in the occupational pension scheme (second pillar)	Grand coalition of all political parties, trade unions, and employers
	• Guarantee of individual pension savings in case of labour market mobility	
	• No dissolution of pension savings for women in case of marriage	
	• Splitting of second-pillar savings between spouses in case of divorce	
1995	10th reform of the basic pension scheme AHV/AVS	Grand coalition of all political parties and employers; opposition by trade unions
	• Increase of the retirement age for women from 62 to 64	
	• Flexible retirement age (without public subsidies for lower-income pensioners)	
	• Splitting of contributions and pensions between spouses and educational pension credits	

---

[7] With a floor of CHF 15,450 p.a. and a ceiling of CHF 21,810 p.a.

1996	Reform of the means-tested supplementary pension scheme EL/PC	Grand coalition of all political parties, trade unions, and employers
	• Higher supplementary pensions for house owners	
	• Improved information for pensioners about benefit eligibility	
	• Lowering of waiting periods for supplementary pensions for foreigners	
2003	1st reform of the occupational pension scheme BVG-LPP	Grand coalition of all political parties, main trade unions, and employers; some opposition by part of trade unions and small employers
	• Cutbacks in occupational pension levels (conversion rate)	
	• Increase of the retirement age for women from 64 to 65	
	• Improved occupational pension coverage for low-income earners	
	• Improved occupational pension coverage for part-time employees	
	• Introduction of occupational pension benefits for widowers	
2003	11th reform of the basic pension scheme AHV/AVS (failed)	Right-wing parties and employers against left-wing parties and trade unions; reform failed in a direct democratic referendum.
	• Increase of the retirement age for women from 64 to 65	
	• Cutbacks in the level of widow's pensions	
	• Cutbacks in pension indexation	
	• Increase in contribution levels for self-employed	
	• Flexible retirement age (without public subsidies for lower-income pensioners)	

Source: Année Politique Suisse 1970–2003, www.admin.ch, Bonoli (2000), Häusermann (2010*a*, 2010*b*).

Part II: The governance of supplementary pensions

For historical reasons, the Swiss second pillar – even though mandatory and fully integrated in the social security system – has remained somewhat 'semi-private' because it is run by countless private and semi-private bodies. The law prescribes mandatory insurance, minimum benefits and participatory rights, and regulatory control for providers. As a result, pension funds enjoy a relatively large room for manoeuvre concerning benefit levels and type, financing, and governance structures. Over the past few years, however, regulation has become more stringent, often in response to perceived shortcomings. The 1982 Law on Occupational Pensions (effective in 1985) makes provision for different types of legal structures for pension funds. It is important to distinguish between different types of legal structure according to sector and the fund's sponsors because they generate different regulatory issues.

Employers in the public sector usually rely on publicly chartered pension funds ('öffentlich-rechtliche Pensionskassen'). Unlike in the private sector, these funds are allowed to operate a mixed financing regime (PAYG and funded), since a public entity guarantees their solvency (Pittet 2005: 18). Therefore, public-sector pension funds are not required by law to prove 100 per cent funding of their liabilities. Typically, a funding ratio of 80 per cent is regarded as adequate, though in reality many public-sector pension funds have funding ratios well below this threshold.

Employers in the private sector have to insure their workforce with pension trust funds, called foundations (*Stiftungen/fondations*), there are three main types:

- Medium-sized and large employers tend to have their own 'corporate foundations' independent of the firm and thus protected in case of insolvency of the sponsor.

- Smaller employers tend to insure their employees with the so-called 'group foundations' (*Sammelstiftungen/fondations collectives*). Typically, group foundations are run by private insurance companies and banks. They provide occupational pension coverage for large numbers of firms. Within group foundations, each insured firm has its own pension plan, and firms belonging to the same foundation may offer different conditions to their employees in terms of benefits and contribution levels. Half of the workforce is insured with these collective foundations (Pittet 2005: 24). Group foundations arguably present the biggest governance and regulatory problems, notably with regard to the difficulties in ensuring employee involvement (see below).

- Finally, there are 'joint foundations' (*Gemeinschaftsstiftungen/fondations communes*), created by employer associations and trade unions in a particular branch. Within joint foundations, there is no differentiation of pension plans by employer, thus all firms in the sector offer the same conditions in terms of benefits and contribution levels.

Finally, the state runs a 'default fund' (*nationale Auffangeinrichtung/Institution supplétive*), which provides coverage to those employees whose employers fail to insure them and also to employees and self-employed who are not compulsorily covered but elect to do so on a voluntary basis.

The *third-tier private savings* are divided in two forms: tax concessions for voluntary personal pension plans and free private savings. We look at the governance of personal pensions with tax concessions only, because the other forms of private pension savings do not differ from unspecified other forms of savings, such as savings accounts or life insurance. Tax-deductible personal pensions can take two forms: a special savings account with a bank or an account with an insurance company, but pension funds cannot offer such private savings accounts. In the case of *savings accounts*, individuals can choose between different investment strategies from a normal savings account (with higher long-term interests) to an investment fund (with higher risks for the insured). There is no minimum interest rate and no state guarantee. Individuals are free to contribute as much as they would like up until the ceiling, regularly or at random intervals. Savings contracts with insurance companies differ, since these contracts contain fixed premiums and benefits that cannot be modified flexibly. This form of savings also implies rather high administrative costs (about 11–20 per cent of the annual premiums), but interest rates tend to be 0.5–1 per cent higher than with the bank savings accounts (Saldo 1999).

6. Who is covered?

With the occupational pension reform, since 1985 occupational pension insurance became mandatory for all employees older than 25 and with a yearly income of more than about CHF 24,000 (the 'access threshold'). Their income roughly between 24,000 and 75,560 CHF was then insured according to the mandated conditions stated by the law (*Obligatorium*). Beyond the annual ceiling of CHF 75,560, employers may provide topping-up insurance (*Überobligatorium*), but they do not have to, and they can do so differently from the mandated conditions. In that sense, these voluntary benefits come closer to the private savings in the third pillar, because they are not actually part of the publicly regulated, mandatory old age income system. Since the law specifies minimum conditions only, pension funds are also free to set a lower access threshold.

In the late 1990s, a debate about coverage rates and access thresholds became salient in parliament. Indeed, mandatory occupational pension coverage has remained far from universal, in particular due to the relatively high access threshold. In 2002, 23 per cent of people active on the labour market (15 per cent of men, 35 per cent of women) were not included in an occupational pension plan (SGK-N 2002). More specifically, most self-employed, many part-time or atypically employed, and many persons combining several part-time jobs remained excluded from occupational pension insurance. The coverage is highly gendered due to lower labour market participation among women. In 2004, women represented only 38.7 per cent of the insured in the second pillar, and only 30.4 per cent of the current beneficiaries of occupational pensions, who received only 17.6 per cent of aggregate second-pillar payments. While the average annual occupational pension for men was CHF 29,300 per year in 2004, the women received only 16,968 CHF (BFS 2004). In the wake of the debate about the 'insider–outsider' effects of the occupational pension scheme, the

2003 reform of the occupational pension scheme lowered the access threshold from CHF 24,000 to 18,990 annual income.

The law on Swiss occupational pensions includes also the right for voluntary insurance for self-employed and for employees who combine several part-time jobs, which all – taken individually – fall below the access threshold of the occupational pension pillar. Similarly, if an employee reduces labour market participation to an extent as to fall out of the mandatory insurance, he or she has the right to maintain insurance coverage either with the former insurer or with the public default fund.

Third-pillar personal pensions play a relatively small but increasingly vital role in the Swiss pension system. The number of personal pensions doubled between 1995 and 2003 to approximately 2 million, but the assets held by third-pillar pension providers (banks and insurance companies) amounted to 'only' CHF 30 billion in 1999, or thirteen times less than those held by second-pillar funds (OFAS 2004). Hence, even though these private pensions are very widespread amongst the population, they represent a substantial part of the old age revenues only for the privileged income strata. For the lower-income groups, third-pillar savings are not very important. A study in 2003 (Balthasar et al. 2003) shows that up to a monthly old age income of about CHF 3,000 per month, benefits from the first pillar alone make up for 90–95 per cent of the household income. It is only for incomes of CHF 4,000 per month or higher that second-pillar pensions constitute a substantial part (above 25 per cent) of the household income. Third-pillar pension incomes in no case constitute more than 5 per cent of the pensioner household income.

7. What kind of benefits?

Minimum legal requirements (Obligatorium): The law prescribes only minimum requirements for occupational benefits, thus pension funds enjoy a relatively large degree of autonomy. The minimum requirement can be understood as a test. Once a worker reaches retirement, a pension is calculated on the basis of his or her pension plan. The result must be at least equal to what he or she would have obtained had the minimum requirement rules been applied, otherwise, the legal minimum applies.

The calculation of the minimum benefit is complicated, given three parameters: notional contribution rates, an interest rate applied to the notional capital, and a conversion rate used to transform the accrued capital into an annuity. Pension funds can follow the same rules for the calculation of the minimum, or a completely different set of rules as long as the resulting benefit is at least as high as the minimum legal benefit. The part of exceeding the legal minimum (*Überobligatorium*) is not subject to the same rules concerning interest

Table 12.3 Notional contributions and statutory interest rates for Swiss occupational pensions

Age	Notional contribution rates: proportion of compulsorily insured earnings (%)	Year	Statutory minimum interest rate set by government (%)
25–34	7	1985–2002	4.00
35–44	10	2003	3.25
45–54	15	2004	2.25
55–65 (men)	18	2005–7	2.50
55–64 (women)	18	2008	2.75
		2009	2.00

Source: Federal Social Insurance Office, Switzerland.

and conversion rates. Most pension plans, however, apply the mandatory rates to both the compulsory and the non-compulsory part of the benefit.

Notional contribution rates vary according to age (see Table 12.3) in order that older workers might benefit from relatively high pension rights from the beginning. However, this aspect has been criticized because it incurs higher costs for older workers (as notional contributions need to be financed). This may reduce employment opportunities for those aged between 55 and 65. Notional contributions accrue an interest rate that is set by the federal government, on an annual basis. This rate has varied significantly over the last few years (see Table 12.3). The resulting (notional) capital is then converted into an annuity on the basis of a conversion rate set by law: in 1984, the rate was set initially at 7.2 per cent, but the 2003 reform lowered it to 6.8 per cent (with a transition period until 2013) and the federal government plans to further lower it to 6.4 per cent. Two reasons are mentioned to justify this reduction: longer life expectancy and lower expected returns made by pension fund investments. Changes in both the minimum interest rate and in the conversion rate will result in lower future minimum benefits. Some of these decisions were taken in the wake of the stock market crisis of the early 2000s. At that time, the insurance companies and banks behind the group pension funds were successful in pushing through the reduction in the minimum interest rate first to 3.25 per cent in 2003 and then to 2.25 per cent in 2004 (see Table 12.3). In October 2008, as a reaction to the recent financial market crisis, the statutory minimum interest rate was set at 2 per cent in October 2008, the lowest level ever.

The lowering of minimum interest rates after the stock market turmoils of the early 2000s stirred heated debates, because it revealed problems of regulatory governance. Indeed, the group pension funds had made huge profits between 1985 and 1999 but failed to pass them on to the insured or pensioners. In fact, these insurers obtained rates of return on their investments of 5–10 per cent over the 1980s and 1990s, but they only had to provide the mandatory minimum interest rate of 4 per cent to the insured pensioners. The rest may have been transferred into the balance sheets of the financial companies behind the various group pension funds which are non-profit institutions. They are set up by the key players in the financial industry who then manage these funds. Under this regulatory framework, it is possible to shift profits from the non-profit foundations back to the private financial firms who initiated them. According to trade unionists and left-of-centre political actors, this is what happened throughout the 'golden years' of the 1990s, in a development described as 'pension theft' ('Rentenklau') (PSS 2006). The outcry was particularly strong when the government agreed to lower the minimum interest rate in 2002 and 2003, seemingly as a result of direct lobbying of the private insurance companies (Nova and Häusermann 2005: 38). The crisis of the group pension foundations revealed implementation problems of the non-profit rule stated by the law as these foundations had found ways to circumvent this obligation.

In 2004, the federal parliament requested an audit in order to find out if *Sammelstiftungen* and the financial services companies behind them had actually shifted profits away from the insured towards their balance sheets. The result of the audit was that given the overall lack of transparency in these firms' accounting practices, it was not possible to establish what had actually happened to the profits obtained in the 1990s. The audit report was nonetheless able to show that decisions concerning profit redistribution were based more on marketing considerations than on equal treatment principles. Large employers, that is, the most interesting clients, received more of the profits than smaller ones (Bättig 2005: 8).

7.1 Benefit rules

Most occupational pension providers in the private sector operate on the basis of DC. Many insurers in the public sector (publicly chartered pension funds) traditionally operated on the basis of DB, but since the 1990s, there is a general trend towards DC in all sectors (Pittet 2005: 41). In 2006, about 20 per cent of insured persons were covered by standard DB plans, down from 33 per cent in 1994 (OFS 2008). Beyond the old-age pension insurance payments, Swiss occupational pension funds also pay benefits in case of disability and for survivors. In addition, the 2003 reform introduced occupational pension rights for widowers and for surviving registered partners (for same-sex couples).

A study based on micro-simulation of pension funds rules found that actual benefit levels vary enormously across economic sectors and depending on the size of the employer. The most generous pension plans were found in the financial service sector where one could also find a high level of inequality. The public sector in general provides good pension conditions, while inequality among employers is much less important. The least favourable conditions were found in small manufacturing companies, where only the legal minimum was often applied. These companies tend to produce largely for export markets and may be more strongly subjected to international cost-competition. Regardless of the sector, employer-size also emerged as a powerful determinant of the quality of coverage (Bonoli and Gay-des-Combes 2003).

After the 1982 law on occupational pensions, the transferability of accrued rights in case of job mobility remained a problem, both in the mandatory and the overmandatory parts of the Swiss second-pillar pensions. The 1994 law on occupational pension transferability improved the portability of benefits across funds: the transfer value of a pension is now calculated according to three different sets of rules. One of these being the rules determining the *Obligatorium*, applying the most favourable rules for the employee. There is no minimum vesting period in the Swiss second pillar. Small amounts (less than the equivalent to one year of employee contributions) are paid back in cash to the employee; otherwise transferability rules apply.

In principle, insured employees cannot access their occupational pension savings earlier than five years before the legal age of retirement. However, in 1994 parliament decided to allow people to withdraw their savings early for the purpose of their home. An early withdrawal is also possible for former employees wishing to set up their own business. Third-pillar personal savings can be withdrawn five years before retirement at earliest, or in the following cases: emigration, acquisition of real estate, or self-employment for formerly employed people. Benefits are provided as a lump sum or in annuities. Savings can also be used to buy favourable conditions in the second-pillar pension fund in case of job mobility. This is the only possibility to transfer savings between the pillars.

8. Who pays?

8.1 Contribution payments

Minimum compulsory benefits are calculated on the basis of notional contributions. Depending on the employee's age, individual accounts must be credited with a percentage of insured earnings, ranging from 7 to 18 per cent (see Table 12.3). Pension funds are free to finance the specified amount as they wish, with the provision that contributions must be split at least equally between workers and employers (the latter may contribute more than half). For instance, a pension fund could decide to apply an age neutral contribution rate of 12.5 per cent, or alternatively to charge employees on the basis of their age, thus reflecting the preset notional contributions. The majority of funds (nearly 60 per cent) use age-related contributions (OFS 1999).

Because notional contribution rates are age-related, pension funds with an unfavourable demographic structure are disadvantaged. As a result, the law introduced a demographic compensation mechanism whereby funds with more young employees subsidize those with a less-favourable risk structure. Because of the way notional contributions are calculated and financed, the system is not a 'pure' funded system but includes some intergenerational redistribution, or a PAYG element. The rationale for this was to guarantee adequate coverage to workers who were already employed before the 1985 law took effect and would not have a full contribution record. In theory, this PAYG element should disappear over the next two decades once (and if) all workers mandatorily contribute their entire working life.

For the third-pillar savings, employees who are already covered by an occupational pension can deduct contributions paid into a third-pillar account from their taxable income, up to CHF 6,566 per year (in 2009). These contributions can be made until the age of retirement. Tax concessions are more substantial for those not covered by an occupational pension, such as the self-employed who can deduct up to 20 per cent of their income.

8.2 Investment rules and practice

The regulation of investments has not changed considerably over the last decade. The total assets today reach about CHF 500 billion, which is about 120 per cent of GDP. Switzerland did not follow the lead of Anglophone countries in adopting the 'prudent person' rule for pension funds investment. Instead, federal law prescribes upper limits for various categories of assets as shown in Table 12.4. Swiss pension funds have traditionally been rather cautious investors. In 1992, only 10 per cent of their assets were invested in stocks. Their tendency to invest in companies has increased over the last few years. On

Table 12.4 Maximum limits for different categories of assets

Category	Limit as a % of assets	Actual proportion (%) (2006)
Swiss bonds	100	} 37.0
Foreign bonds	30	
Mortgages	75	2.9
Real estate in Switzerland	50	} 14.2
Foreign real estate	5	
Swiss stocks	30	} 29.1
Foreign stocks	20	
Foreign currencies	25	7.7
Other		7.1

Source: Ordonnance sur la prévoyance professionnelle II, Art. 54; OFS (2008).

average, however, the limits for the most risky assets are not entirely exploited. Swiss pension funds were among those less severely hit by the financial market crisis among OECD countries in 2008 (OECD 2009).

8.3 Minimum funding rules for private sector funds

Private sector funds must be able to fully honour their commitments at all times (i.e. have a 100 per cent funding of liabilities). During the stock market crisis of the early 2000s, several funds failed to reach this level: in 2002, about two-thirds of funds had less than 100 per cent funding and 20 per cent had less than 90 per cent. Many funds had to increase contribution rates (OFAS 2003: 139). By 2005–6, also thanks to the recovery of the stock market, the vast majority of funds, 96 per cent in the private sector, fulfilled the 100 per cent funding requirement (OFS 2008: 20).

The recent turmoil on the financial markets, however, has brought back 'bad memories' of the crisis of the early 2000s. Swiss pension funds have lost between CHF 70 and 90 billion, that is about 12–15 per cent of the capital stock (as of February 2009, see Müller 2009). According to the Swiss association of pension funds, about half of the private pension funds had less than 90 per cent funding (NZZ 2008). The law stipulates that below 90 per cent funding, pension funds need to adopt measures to restore the funding of liabilities.

8.4 The problem of underfunding in public sector funds

A second problem that emerged during the crisis of the early 2000s was the fact that many public sector pension foundations turned out to be underfunded. Underfunding was to a large extent the result of the fact that these public foundations had operated under a mixed regime of PAYG and capitalization. With the privatization of many former state monopolies and parts of the public administration, these pension funds had to switch to a full capitalization at the worst possible moment, that is, when the stock market bubble was highest in the 1990s. In the downturn of the 2000s, this led to underfunding, which had to be compensated by higher contribution rates and lower benefits. This crisis was at least partly the result of lacking regulation of financing modes. In 2007, the government decided that public sector funds must also be fully funded within a transition period of thirty years (BSV 2007).

The stock market and occupational pension crisis of the late 1990s and early 2000s profoundly shook public confidence in the occupational pension scheme. Up to this point, the general diagnosis was that pensions in the *first* pillar were vulnerable, for demographic reasons. But the financial market crisis of the 2000s made two things clear: First, funded pensions are very vulnerable to the financial market performance and – also indirectly – to demographic ageing. Stock market fluctuations destabilize pension funds and this problem is likely to become even more acute in the future.[8] The debates about the actual vulnerability of pension funds have surfaced increasingly strongly over the last years (e.g. Hafner 2004; Schaffner 2007). Secondly, the crisis of 2000 revealed that regulation and control of the Swiss occupational pension market had to be reinforced.

9. Who governs? Who decides? Who manages?

Traditionally, the regulation of financial governance of the Swiss occupational pension funds relied to a rather large extent on self-regulation (Dahlem and Trauffer 2006). Until 2003, the BVG-LPP law only stated that all occupational pension providers must be able to fulfil their legal obligations at any time (Art. 65), that they need to have annual controlling, and that they must appoint a board of trustees with equal representation of employers and insured (Art 50–51), but there were rather few regulations on the implementation of controlling and co-decision. The financial responsibility ultimately lies with the board of trustees of the pension fund, and with its management board. As long as stock markets performed well and the funds made sufficient profits to guarantee current benefits and the minimum interest rate of 4 per cent, regulation was not a very salient issue (Dahlem and Trauffer 2006).

The regulatory arrangement, defined by the BVG-LPP law of 2003, provides the federal government (Art. 64) with the power to delegate its supervisory authority to the following agencies, and regulates their tasks:

- At the level of the individual *pension provider*, each foundation must have a board of trustees that guarantees equal representation of employers and insured (Art. 50–51). Since 2003, the law also states that the insurer must provide the members of this board with the training and information that allows them to perform their supervisory function adequately in order to prevent regulatory capture. In addition to the board of trustees, two external actors are responsible for supervision: a board of control which supervises annual accounting, and a publicly licensed 'expert for occupational pensions', who performs annual checks of whether insurers are able to fulfil their legal obligations (Wernli 2004).

---

[8] As in most countries, funded pensions in Switzerland are still expanding, that is, contribution payments exceed benefits by far. In a rather near future, however, the capital stock of today about CHF 500 billion will have to be liquidated to pay the second-pillar pensions of the retiring baby boomer generation. This massive liquidation of capital may lead to devaluations in capital and real estate markets with still incalculable consequences for the financial stability of pension funds (Zimmermann and Bubb 2006).

- Each of the twenty-six Swiss cantons must designate an administrative *authority*, which is responsible for the supervision of the occupational pension providers (Art. 61).[9] These authorities base their assessment on the reports of the boards of control and the expert reports (Wernli 2004). At the federal level, the Federal Office for Social Insurances and the Federal Office for Private Insurances share the supervisory task for the group foundations (*Sammelstiftungen*). This federalist structure of regulatory supervision has been in place since 1985, but these regulators came under criticism in the 1990s. The Federal Office for Private Insurances, in particular, came under pressure because it lowered minimum interest rates as a result of the direct lobbying of the private insurers, which many observers saw as a clear case of regulatory capture (Wernli 2004). Since then, the office has been reorganized and reinforced with greater resources and staff to ensure more transparency.

- As an additional actor in the regulatory arrangement, we can mention the extra-parliamentary Committee for Occupational Pensions (BVG-*Kommission/ commission* LPP). This permanent committee is composed by representatives of the Confederation, the cantons, employers, trade unions, and the insurance companies (Art. 85). The committee supervises and manages the public default fund (*Auffangeinrichtung*) and the public reserve fund (*Sicherheitsfonds*), which is responsible for the demographic compensation mechanism between insurers and guarantees benefits in case of insolvency and bankruptcy. At the same time, it assures the function of a political advisory committee, which supervises the implementation of occupational pensions, evaluates the need for reform, and drafts reform proposals on behalf of the Swiss government.

The 2003 reform has also sharpened the insurer's obligations with regard to financial control and accountability, until then the law only stated that insurers must be able to fulfil their legal obligations at any time. Since 2003, the standards became more detailed and more specific, even though the means to enforce them have not changed dramatically. Insurers must now follow a *principle of transparency* with regard to the way they calculate contributions and benefits and with regard to financial accounting (Art. 65a), allowing supervisory boards and the insured to request at any time full information. The law also restates what insurers can and must do in case of underfunding, and it authorizes but also obliges the government to define minimum standards as to the required reserves and working capital ratios.

According to the law, pension funds must be governed by a board consisting of equal numbers of representatives of the employers and of employees. Because of the complex legal structures involved, the implementation of this

---

[9] In most cantons, this authority is part of an administrative unit, either in the field of finances, law, or economic affairs.

principle is not always straightforward. Generally speaking, parity representation works well in large companies. Here, employee representatives are elected and can perform an effective control and representation. The situation becomes more problematic with small companies, particularly those that are part of a group pension fund. Technically speaking, each company participating in such a foundation has its own fund and must organize parity representation. However, many companies do not have such committees and the employer negotiates directly with the funds administrators (Bättig 2005: 10).

The parliamentary audit of 2005 found that in individual companies' pension funds, the excessive gains were oftentimes used to lower only the contributions of the employers, not the employees. This last point was clearly illegal, but no supervisory regulatory body controlled these distribution processes due to a lack of data, competence, and an unclear definition of responsibilities. The boards of the group pension foundations were basically called to supervise themselves, and external controls applied only insufficiently and only after the main decisions were taken. At the political level, supervisory regulation failed completely since several offices were in charge simultaneously and in the end, none of them felt responsible for asking for the relevant data and for exercising control. The conclusions of the audit were mainly twofold: first, insurance companies must be forced to separate completely their private insurance business from the pension funds, so that the accountancies for the two are distinct and traceable. And second, the governance structure must be revised in order to clarify competences and responsibilities (Bättig 2005).

Every insured under the Swiss occupational pension law receives an annual report, which details individual savings, the insurance conditions, administrative charges, and the expected annual benefits at age 65. The need for full information is somewhat lighter in Switzerland than in other countries with purely voluntary supplementary pension schemes. The Swiss employees cannot select their insurance fund freely but are automatically insured with the pension fund chosen by the respective employer. Hence, individuals do not have to make informed market-choices with regard to the second-pillar pensions. Claims for the liberalization of this market surface regularly (Econcept 2005), but the government has rejected this demand several times and it is thus not presently on the reform agenda.

9.1 Examples of occupational pension schemes

The high degree of fragmentation of the occupational pension landscape (there are some 2,500 pension funds) makes it difficult to provide examples that would be representative or even typical of a given sector. The study conducted by Bonoli and Gay-des-Combes (2003), which examined about 100 pension plans, shows that sector and employer size are the key determinants of the level of coverage provided. The best plans were usually found in the financial services, even though within this sector one also found the highest degree of variation.

In manufacturing industry, size is a particularly important determinant of plan quality. Large companies, such as the electrical infrastructure manufacturer ABB, provide second-pillar coverage well above the legal minimum. Notional contribution rates increase with age and vary between 8.8 and 34 per cent of insured earnings (the legal minimum is between 7 and 18 per cent). The split between employer and employee is also more favourable than what is prescribed in the law, as the former pays two-thirds of the joint contribution rate. These types of favourable conditions are found in large pension funds (the ABB pension fund has some 2,300 insured persons, of whom 1,100 are retired). Smaller companies in this sector tend to offer the legal minimum only (*Obligatorium*), through a group or in a joint pension fund.

Within the low value-added service sector (retail trade and catering), size also seems to play an important role. Large employers such as the big supermarket chains offer relatively good coverage conditions. Since many work part-time in these branches, some of them take this aspect into account when establishing an access threshold. For example, the pension fund of COOP, a large supermarket chain, insures earnings above 29 per cent of earnings. By expressing the access threshold in relative rather than in absolute terms (as is the case in the law), the pension plans include everyone, including part-time workers with very short hours. Smaller companies, again, will probably not offer this kind of advantages. Gastrosuisse, the peak association of the catering industry, provides a joint pension foundation open to all its members. The foundation offers different types of pension plans, distinguishing basically between low-skill employees and managers. The basic plan for those with lower salaries applies the legal minimum. We can assume that the vast majority of those working for small- to medium-size catering firms will not have access to more than this.

10. The outlook for Swiss supplementary pension reforms

Currently, there is no major restructuring of the Swiss pension system under way. There is still a large consensus with regard to the three-pillar architecture of old age income security, and the recent reforms have to a large extent adapted the first and second pillars to the financial challenges, demographic development, and new social risks. Consequently, the current reform debates revolve around further consolidation and modernization of the existing system, and around a major reform of the regulatory governance. In conclusion, we provide an overview of these ongoing reform processes.

In the first pillar, preparatory studies for an upcoming reform explore mechanisms of financial consolidation which would apply 'automatically' when a certain threshold of demographic or economic strain is reached but under the condition that the cutbacks can be moderated for the most precarious groups of beneficiaries (Bonoli 2008).

In the second pillar of occupational pensions, some reform ideas go in a similar direction of 'de-politicizing' adaptation mechanisms by linking them to the development of particular macroeconomic indicators. More specifically, there is a proposal to define the level of the *minimum interest rate* for beneficiaries not by a political decision but automatically by a formula depending on the performance of the financial markets. Thereby, minimum interest rates would become flexible both downwards when financial market performance is bad, and upwards when pension funds manage to make large profits during the good years. In addition, the government recently improved occupational pension benefits for *atypically employed* workers on short-term contracts (BSV 2008).

The most important reform under way, however, deals with the *governance structure* of the occupational pensions, and it is a direct consequence of the regulatory failures that became apparent after the 2001 stock market crisis. This reform has attracted strong renewed saliency with the current turmoil of the financial markets in 2008/9. In reaction to the 2001 crisis, the government and parliament had already made some changes with the 2003 reform of regulatory governance structure, mostly by implementing stricter rules regarding transparency and accountancies. Currently, a more far-reaching governance reform is discussed. In September 2008, the upper chamber of the Swiss parliament has adopted a reform proposal by the government, which quite fundamentally redraws the regulatory structure (Bundesrat 2007) by reinforcing control competencies and responsibilities, and by stressing the importance of prudential as opposed to *ex post* regulation. There are two new main levels of control: cantons and regions should be solely responsible for the regulation and control of pension funds, including a financial liability for damages that are the result of lacking or insufficient supervision. Some cantons have already started to create new independent regulatory bodies to this effect. The second level of control is at the federal level. In the future, the government wants to create a new independent regulatory agency of seven to nine independent experts with a strong staff, who supervise the cantonal regulators, make the accreditation of official pension fund controllers, and who can intervene directly with particular insurance companies. The new regulatory agency would be independent from political control and its members must have no ties with the pension insurance industry.

The reform proposal of the government was met with mixed reactions: while the left claimed stronger and more centralized supervisory agencies, some parties of the right claimed that the new governance structure would raise the administrative costs of the Swiss second pillar too much (Bundesrat 2007). However, given the current financial crisis, which further shakes the confidence of the insured in the second tier, the prospects for a majority favourable to stronger regulatory mechanisms are rather good. It remains to be seen whether these mechanisms will be effective in stabilizing pension funds and guaranteeing a management of the pension capitals that is responsible and in the interests of the current and future beneficiaries.

Bibliography

Armingeon, K. (2001). 'Institutionalising the Swiss Welfare State'. *West European Politics*, 24/2: 145–68.

Balthasar, A., Bieri, O., Grau, P., Küenzi, K., and Guggisberg, J. (2003). *Der Übergang in den Ruhestand – Wege, Einflussfaktoren und Konsequenzen. Bericht im Rahmen des Forschungsprogrammes zur längerfristigen Zukunft der Alterssicherung*. Forschungsbericht Nr. 2/03. Bundesamt für Sozialversicherungen. Bern: Beiträge zur Sozialen Sicherheit.

Bättig, C. (2005). 'Assurés spoliés: résultats de l'analyse effectuée par le Contrôle parlementaire de l'administration'. *Sécurité sociale CHSS*, 1/2005: 6–12.

Berenstein, A. (1986). *L'assurance-vieillesse suisse, son élaboration et son évolution*. Lausanne: Réalités Sociales.

BFS (2003). *Die schweizerische Altersvorsorge im Spiegel der Einkommens- und Verbrauchserhebung 1998*. Neuchâtel: Bundesamt für Statistik.

——(2004). *Die berufliche Vorsorge in der Schweiz. Pensionskassenstatistik 2002*. Neuchâtel: Bundesamt für Statistik.

Binswanger, P. (1987). *Histoire de l'AVS. Assurance-vieillesse et survivants suisse*. Zürich: Pro Senectute.

BOAF.CdE (Bulletin Officiel de l'Assemblée Fédérale). *Conseil des Etats*. Various issues.

Bonoli, G. (1999). 'La 10e révision de l'AVS: une politique consensuelle de retranchement?', in A. Mach (ed.), *Globalisation, néo-libéralisme et politiques publiques dans la Suisse des années 1990*. Zürich: Seismo.

——(2000). *The Politics of Pension Reform. Institutions and Policy Change in Western Europe*. Cambridge: Cambridge University Press.

——(2006). 'Les politiques sociales', in U. Klöti, P. Knoepfel, H. Kriesi, W. Linder, Y. Papadopoulos and P. Sciarini (eds.), *Handbuch der Schweizer Politik*. Zürich: NZZ Verlag, 763–86.

——(2007). 'Switzerland: The Impact of Direct Democracy', in E. M. Immergut, K. M. Anderson and I. Schulz (eds.), *West European Pension Politics*. Oxford: Oxford University Press, 203–47.

——(2008). 'Rentenreformen in den OECD-Ländern: Beispiele für die Schweiz?'. *Soziale Sicherheit CHSS*, 5/2008: 294–9.

——and Gay-des-Combes, B. (2003). *Evolution de prestations vieillesse dans le long terme: une simulation prospective de la couverture retraite à l'horizon 2040*. Rapport de Recherche No. 3/03. Bern: Office fédéral des assurances sociales.

——and Mach, A. (2000). 'Switzerland: Adjustment Politics within Institutional Constraints', in F. W. Scharpf and V. A. Schmidt (eds.), *Welfare and Work in the Open Economy. Vol. II: Diverse Responses to Common Challenges*. Oxford: Oxford University Press, 131–75.

——and Palier, B. (2008). 'When Past Reforms Open New Opportunities: Comparing Old-Age Insurance Reforms in Bismarckian Welfare Systems', in B. Palier and C. Martin (eds.), *Reforming the Bismarckian Welfare Systems*. Oxford: Blackwell, 21–39.

BSV (1995). *Bericht des eidgenössischen Departementes des Innern zur heutigen Ausgestaltung und Weiterentwicklung der schweizerischen 3-Säulen-Konzeption der Alters-, Hinterlassenen- und Invalidenvorsorge*. Bern: Bundesamt für Sozialversicherungen, Beiträge zur Sozialen Sicherheit.

——(2007). *Mitteilungen über die Berufliche Vorsorge*. 27.9.2007. Bern: Bundesamt für Sozialversicherungen.

——(2008). *Mitteilungen über die Berufliche Vorsorge*. 12.8.2008. Bern: Bundesamt für Sozialversicherungen.

Bundesrat (2007). *Botschaft zur Änderung des Bundesgesetzes über die berufliche Alters- Hinterlassenen- und Invalidenvorsorge*. 15.6.2007, BBl 2007: 5669ff.

Dahlem, S., and Trauffer, C. (2006). 'Das Gleichgewicht der Kräfte – Governance in Schweizer Pensionskassen'. *Schweizer Pensions- und Investmentnachrichten*, 16.10.2006.

Econcept (2005). *Freie Wahl der Pensionskasse. Machbarkeitsstudie*. Bern: Econcept/ECOFIN.

Esping-Andersen, G. (1990). *The Three Worlds of Welfare Capitalism*. Princeton: Princeton University Press.

FF. *Feuille Fédérale*. Various issues.

Gilliand, P. (1993). 'Politique sociale', in G. Schmidt (ed.), *Handbuch Politisches System der Schweiz. Band 4. Politikbereiche*. Bern: Haupt, 111–223.

Hafner, W. (2004). *Im Strudel der Finanzmärkte. Pensionskassen in der Schweiz*. Zürich: Rotpunktverlag.

Häusermann, S. (2010a). *The Politics of Welfare State Reform in Continental Europe: Modernization in Hard Times*. New York: Cambridge University Press.

——(2010b). 'Solidarity with Whom? Why Organized Labor is Losing Ground in Continental Pension Politics'. *European Journal of Political Research*, 49/2: 233–56.

Häusermann, S., Mach, A., and Papadopoulos, Y. (2004). 'From Corporatism to Partisan Politics: Social Policy Making under Strain in Switzerland'. *Swiss Political Science Review*, 10/2: 33–59.

Kriesi, H. (1980). *Entscheidungsstrukturen und Entscheidungsprozesse in der Schweizer Politik*. Frankfurt: Campus Verlag.

Leimgruber, M. (2008). *Solidarity without the State? Business and the Shaping of the Swiss Welfare State, 1890–2000*. Cambridge: Cambridge University Press.

Leitner, S., and Obinger, H. (1996). 'Feminisierung der Armut im Wohlfahrtsstaat. Eine strukturelle Analyse weiblicher Armut am Beispiel der Alterssicherung in Österreich und in der Schweiz'. *Swiss Political Science Review*, 2/4: 1–35.

Müller, R. A. (2009). 'Auswirkungen der Finanzkrise auf die berufliche Vorsorge'. *Blickpunkt: KMU*, 1/2009: 3–6.

Nova, C., and Häusermann, S. (2005). *Endlich existenzsichernde Renten. Erste Säule stärken – 3000 Franken Rente für alle*. Bern: Schweizerischer Gewerkschaftsbund: Dossier 34.

NZZ (2008). 'Krise setzt den Pensionskassen arg zu'. *Neue Zürcher Zeitung*, 28.10.2008.

Obinger, H. (1998). *Politische Institutionen und Sozialpolitik in der Schweiz*. Frankfurt a.M.: Peter Lang.

OECD (2009). *Private Pensions Outlook 2008*. Paris: OECD.

OFAS (2003). 'Mesures destinées à résorber les découverts dans la prévoyance profession-nelle'. *Sécurité Sociale CHSS*, 3/2003: 139–41.

——(2004). *Statistique des assurances sociales*. Berne: Office Fédéral des Assurances Sociales.

——(2007). *Statistique des assurances sociales*. Berne: Office Fédéral des Assurances Sociales.

OFS (1999). *Statistiques des caisses de pensions 1998*. Neuchâtel: Office fédéral de la statistique.

——(2008). *La prévoyance professionnelle en Suisse. Statistique des caisses de pensions 2006*. Neuchâtel: Office Fédéral de la Statistique.

Pittet, M. (2005). *Die öffentlichen Pensionskassen in der Schweiz*. Bern: Haupt.

PSS (2006). *Le vol des rentes continue*. Point de presse du Parti socialiste Suisse, 20.1.2006, Parti Socialiste Suisse.

Queisser M., and Vittas, D. (2000). *The Swiss Multi-Pillar Pension System: Triumph of Common Sense?*. Washington, DC: The World Bank.

Saldo (1999). *Die drei Säulen: gut vorsorgen*. Zürich: Saldo Ratgeber.

Schaffner, U. (2007). *Good Governance von Pensionskassen*. Zürich: Orell Füssli.

SGK-N (2002). *Bericht der Kommission für soziale Sicherheit und Gesundheit (SGK-N) über den Vorsorgeschutz für Teilzeitbeschäftigte und Personen mit kleinen Einkommen, über die Anpassung des Umwandlungssatzes und über die paritätische Verwaltung der Vorsorgeeinrichtungen. März 2002*. Bern: Vereinigte Bundesversammlung, Bern.

Trampusch, C. (2008). 'Von einem liberalen zu einem post-liberalen Wohlfahrtsstaat: Der Wandel der gewerkschaftlichen Sozialpolitik in der Schweiz'. *Swiss Political Science Review*, 14/1: 49–84.

Wernli, S. (2004). *Schweizer Pensionskassen und Corporate Governance. Einflussnahme auf Schweizer Publikumsgesellschaften*. Zürich: Schulthess.

Zimmermann, H., and Bubb, A. (2006). *Das Risiko der Vorsorge. Die zweite Säule unter dem Druck der alternden Gesellschaft*. Zürich: Avenir Suisse.

Part V

Comparing Pension Systems and their Outcome

13

The Governance and Regulation of Private Pensions in Europe

Bernhard Ebbinghaus and Tobias Wiß

1. Introduction

The responsibility for retirement income is increasingly shifted from the state to private actors, in particular employers and employees. Many politicians, policy advisers, and researchers attribute to 'private' pensions a fully funded scheme that is a voluntary individual savings decision without much state regulation or support. But *privatization* is not equal privatization. Given the rather path-dependent evolution of the public–private pension mix, there are considerable cross-national differences in private supplementary pensions as to the responsibility of non-state actors. Private pensions can be negotiated by the social partners, a commitment by the employer or an individual's decision. Private pensions also differ to the degree that they are funded. In some exceptional cases, supplementary pensions are pay-as-you-go (PAYG) schemes or unfunded employer commitments, called 'book reserves'. While many occupational pensions were traditionally *defined benefits* (DB), promising pensions as a share of final salary and service years that was sponsored by employers, increasingly private pensions, including fully funded *defined-contribution* (DC) schemes, depend on the capital returns of savings. Hence, the impact of the shift from public to private pensions depends not merely on the share of private pensions in retirement income but on their design in respect to coverage, benefits, and financing mode (Rein and Schmähl 2004; Rein and Stapf-Finé 2004).

The 'paradox of privatization' (Leisering et al. 2002) lies in the fact that the state partially retreated from the responsibility to finance sufficient and adequate public pensions precisely at a time when the scope for public regulation and societal control of private pensions increased (Hyde and Dixon 2009). The state often intervenes by setting framework regulation and supervision rules, extending collective agreements to non-organized employees or firms, and stipulating tax code regulation for pensions. Moreover, the mode of private pension financing influences the investment risk individuals face. Consequently, state-mandated reinsurances or self-binding reserves for future pension liabilities will lower the financial risk of investments, but it may also increase administrative costs and lower returns on capital. State regulation and codes of practice define whether and to what share pension fund assets may be invested in equities, bonds, real estate, or assets abroad (Blake 2003; Kakabadse and Kakabadse 2004; Musalem and Palacios 2004). These differences in sponsoring and regulation have major repercussions for who is covered and how well. Thus, the governance and regulation of these schemes by state and non-state actors is crucial to understand the way in which the social and participatory rights of the insured are included (Bridgen and Meyer 2009).

Under *supplementary* pensions, we consider all pensions that are non-state pensions sponsored by firms, negotiated by the social partners, or based on individual decisions in addition to mandatory state-provided pensions. We divide in addition to the *first*-pillar public pensions between *second*-pillar occupational pensions (collective schemes or employer-led) and *third*-pillar personal pensions (individual saving plans). However, there are borderline cases. In particular, we include those mandatory quasi-public schemes that are partly administered by the social partners for all employees in Finland and for private sector employees in France, they can be considered to be both first (public)- and also second (occupational)-pillar schemes. For our analysis, we also include the Danish and Swedish mandatory public pensions as third-pillar personal pensions as they are fully funded and allow individuals to choose a mutual fund. Although these are integral part of the public pillar, we include them here because they are similar to personal pensions in Britain or Germany, except that they are not voluntary.

In this chapter, we look at the governance of supplementary pensions in ten selected European countries covering different public–private pension mixes: Belgium, Denmark, Finland, France, Germany, Italy, the Netherlands, Sweden, Switzerland, and the United Kingdom.[1] First, we discuss the principal–agent problem and labour relations conflict of interests in supplementary pensions. Then, we locate the supplementary pensions in the overall public–private pension mix, and in the third section discuss the main cross-national variations of pension fund capitalism. In the following sections, we discuss the questions: Who is included? Who pays? Who controls? And what kinds of benefits are provided? We then return to the question of investment rules and conclude with an outlook into the future, given the current financial market crisis.

---

[1] The analysis of individual countries is based on the country chapters in this volume unless otherwise referenced.

2. The stakeholders in private pension governance

The organization of supplementary pensions always implies *principal–agent* relations as the pension beneficiary relies as principal on an agent – the employer, a pension fund, or an investment manager – to fulfil certain tasks (Besley and Prat 2005: 121; Moe 1984: 756; Ross 1973). As a consequence, problems arise due to asymmetric information and 'hidden' knowledge on the side of the agent(s) vis-à-vis the principal (for incomplete markets, see McCarthy 2006). Especially in the context of highly complex benefit calculations and investment decisions in volatile financial markets, principals are incapable of fully controlling their agents who may engage in their own objectives. Moreover, supplementary pensions differ in the actors who decide on pension arrangements (the *initiators*), who stipulate the governance rules and control these schemes (the *overseers*), who pay into these supplementary schemes (the *sponsors*), and who eventually benefit from it (the *beneficiaries*). In the case of a firm's pension commitment to its employees, the employer may be initiator, overseer, and sponsor, while in other cases some of these tasks are taken on by other actors.

Principal–agent theory analyses relationships in which the principals are dependent on the agents' execution of delegated tasks in their best interests. The principal–agent theory (Shapiro 2005) has been applied to explain the vertical relationships between investor as principal and pension fund manager as agent (Tonks 2006). Given information asymmetries to the detriment of principals, trust plays a crucial role, but so does good governance and foresighted regulation. Further difficulties arise because agents can be principals at the same time or vice versa (Shapiro 2005). Thus, pension funds create *multilevel* principal–agent problems where the trustees are agents of the beneficiaries as well as principals vis-à-vis the managers of pension fund portfolios (Lakonishok et al. 1992). The European Union (EU), the Organisation for Economic Co-operation and Development (OECD), and other international organizations have suggested a range of institutional arrangements and instruments to reduce the risk of mismanagement and fraud by the agents: supervisory agencies, whistle-blowing procedures, code of good practice, and dissemination of 'best practice' models and information rights.[2]

In our analysis, we distinguish three *governance* modes of supplementary pensions based on the sponsor and beneficiary: the individual decision to personal pension, the employer-sponsored occupational pensions, and the collective (bipartite) pensions decided by the social partners (see Figure 13.1). Particularly interesting are 'the individuals and organizations acting on behalf

---

[2] See also OECD and EU reports on private pensions (OECD 2001, 2002, 2004, 2005; SPC 2005).

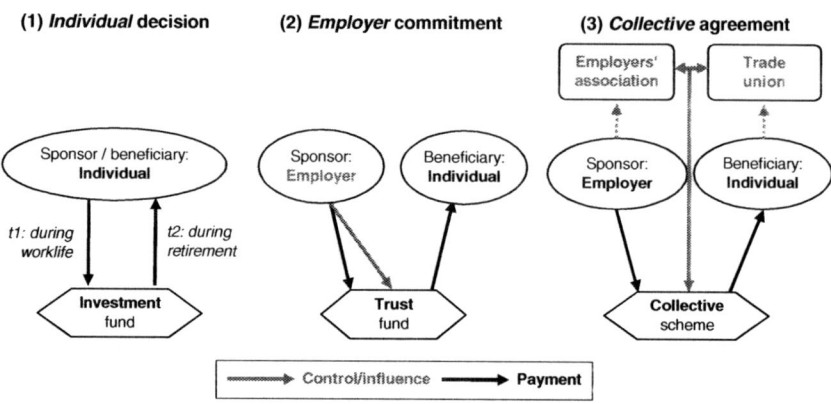

(1) *Individual* decision   **(2) *Employer* commitment**   **(3) *Collective* agreement**

Figure 13.1 Governance modes in supplementary pensions

of those for whom the asymmetries of information, expertise, access, or power are so great that they cannot pretend to control their agents' (Shapiro 2005: 277). Economic theory assumes the importance of 'exit' as a market force, while we will focus here more on the 'voice' mechanism: the participatory rights and regulatory rules in favour of current and future beneficiaries.

Institutional complementarities between corporate governance traditions and pension fund governance can be expected since principal–agent relationships between investors and investment funds (vertical) are embedded in more or less contentious labour relations (horizontal) – the relationship either between employer (sponsor) and employees as well as retirees (beneficiaries) or between employer associations and trade unions (the initiators and overseers). This adds an additional *horizontal* conflict of interests: the negotiations between employers and employees on occupational benefits as part of the individual employment contracts or as part of the collective bargaining on (social) wages. Labour relations may vary in the degree to which they are contentious or consensual, centralized or decentralized (Ebbinghaus 2006: ch. 3), this will have repercussions on private pension governance.

In the case of *individual decisions*, there might be a collective action problem of individuals that have not much power (*voice*) vis-à-vis the investment fund manager, as they might only be able to vote with their feet (*exit*) by switching to a different fund. Here, the regulator will have to intervene to protect the rights of the individual. In the second governance mode, *employers* might be willing to provide DB pensions for human resource strategies to maintain an internal labour market by binding qualified workers to the firm (Lazear 1990). These pensions could be financed by book reserves (directly by the firm), by a trust fund independent of the firm, or by a contract with an insurance company. Employers as sponsors mainly control these plans, while the employees as future beneficiaries have hardly any voice (only through the voice of trustees often picked by the sponsor). Finally, *collective* pensions are negotiated by employer (associations) and trade unions; they will also jointly regulate and govern these schemes. These agreements usually allow for broader coverage and risk pooling, while limiting the voice of stakeholders (sponsors and beneficiaries) to indirect representation through employer associations and trade unions or workplace representatives.

3. Varieties of supplementary pensions

The main stakeholders in private pensions are the employers, the insured workers, the insured retirees, and social partners as well as the state as regulator. Depending on the content of regulation at higher level, that is the state over social partners, the social partners over employers, the employer over employees, there remains more or less scope for discretionary decisions at lower levels.[3] In contrast to the public pension that is solely defined by law, supplementary pensions are regulated by both state and non-state actors. We distinguish between the voluntary decision of an individual, the decision of an employer (the firm), and the collective negotiations between employer(s) and employee organizations (trade unions or workplace representatives). We consider in the following (see Table 13.1) only the most important schemes in these ten countries.

In the case of *collective schemes*, employer and unions agree on jointly managed pension schemes, usually external to the firm and for several firms. The main advantage is the better information capacity of collective schemes in

Table 13.1 Collective, employer-led, and personal supplementary pensions

Collective	Employer-led	Personal
Mandatory quasi-public: France, Finland	*Pension fund*: the Netherlands, Switzerland, Germany (also book reserve), Belgium	*Mandatory public pension*: Swedish Premium P., Danish Special Savings P.
Sectorwide: the Netherlands, Denmark, Sweden, Switzerland, Germany, Belgium, Italy	*Opt-out*: UK *pension fund trusts*	*Voluntary*: Germany (Riester)
		Opt-out: the United Kingdom (Personal, Stakeholder)

Note: Main system in italics.

[3] Not to forget the EU level where hard law (Directives) and soft law (Open Method of Coordination) affects national governments with the main aim of liberalizing the pension markets (Haverland 2007).

comparison to a single employer, particularly a small firm without professional financial experts, or an individual, particularly one without adequate financial knowledge. Collective schemes also allow the pooling of risks, provide better portfolio management, and lower administrative costs than single-employer or individual schemes (Trampusch 2009). Nationwide or sectorwide schemes also allow workers to move between firms without loss of, or disadvantages in, former benefits. In employer-sponsored DB schemes, these can be at risk when an employee moves to another company, depending on vesting rights. Collective schemes, self-administered by the social partners, are quasi-public second pensions in France and Finland, they assume an important second-tier function in Denmark, the Netherlands, and Switzerland, while negotiated occupational pensions are also nationwide 'top-up' benefits in Sweden and are gaining in importance in some sectors in Germany, Belgium, and Italy. However, the decentralized labour relations and lacking state intervention in Britain prevented the evolution towards sector- or nationwide schemes.

Employer-sponsored pension plans (whether pension funds or book reserves) may have higher administrative costs for the firm than collective plans, yet the employer can use these plans for human resource management strategies in order to bind employees to the firm, which would not be the case in collective plans that provide similar benefits across firms. Depending on corporate governance regulation and practice, employees and their representatives may have only limited rights and influence on employer-sponsored plans. Voluntary employer-sponsored occupational pensions play an important role in Britain; they are also a preferred form for Dutch and Swiss larger firms; and Belgium, Finnish, and German firms provide these as voluntary fringe benefits.

In the case of *individual decisions* to save for old age, the responsibility remains solely with the individual, though the state as regulator sets the legal framework and standards, particularly through tax codes and rules for subsidies. An advantage of personal pensions is their portability. Besides the two mandatory personal pensions in Denmark and Sweden, voluntary personal pensions are particularly common in Germany, thanks to tax subsidies (since 2001) and in Britain thanks to an opt-out option (since 1986).

In order to classify supplementary pension regimes, we distinguish the mature multipillar pension systems (the United Kingdom, the Netherlands, Switzerland) with a long funded pension tradition, the Scandinavian countries with substantial supplementary pensions (some of which are integrated as public pensions), and the Continental European countries with dominantly public pension systems and thus far rather limited but growing funded private pensions.

Among the first group of mature multipillar pensions, British occupational pension schemes are pension fund 'trusts'. Employers can decide to contract out their occupational pension from the mandatory state second pension since 1978. In addition, individuals could contract out their personal pensions since

1986. However, the Pension Acts of 2007 and 2008 limit the possibility in the future (by 2012) to contract out DC plans for occupational and personal pensions, and furthermore, employers are required to provide access to the stakeholder pension (as of 2012 compulsory auto-enrolment). The Dutch occupational pensions are mainly sectorwide schemes (liabilities of €500 billion) that are negotiated by the social partners and can be made mandatory by the ministry, and there are also some larger company pension funds (liabilities of €200 billion). In Switzerland, occupational pensions are mandatory but take on different forms: the joint foundations are administered by the social partners for a sector, in group (multifirm) foundations conditions vary across firms, and single-firm plans also exist.

Among the Scandinavian countries with a Beveridge basic pension tradition, Denmark has been a laggard; however, it also boasts the fastest growing private supplementary pension system. The Danish 'labour market pensions' are based on sectorwide collective agreements since the 1990s (similar schemes already existed in the public sector) and the personal pension is mandatory for individuals (suspended since 2004 and terminated in 2010). In Sweden, there are mainly four nationwide negotiated schemes, two for public employees and two for private employees that provide a top-up benefit. These four schemes reflect the main status/sector divisions in union organization and collective bargaining practices (Kjellberg 1992). Following the 1994–8 reform, a funded DC personal pension is part of mandatory public pension contributions, but individuals have the choice of their investment portfolio. A special case is the Finnish collective pension schemes that were made mandatory in the 1960s and allow employers to choose between contracts with pension insurance companies, company pensions, and sectorwide pension schemes. Since benefits of these mandatory occupational pensions are decreasing, there is now room for and a boom of voluntary supplementary pensions, especially collective employer-based group insurances.

Among the Continental European countries, France is a special case due to the mandatory character of the second-tier occupational pensions for 'cadres' (AGIRC) and other employees (ARRCO) in the private sector, based on collective agreements and administered by the social partners. In addition, the newly introduced voluntary funded pensions (PERCO and PERP) give employers and employees more choices. Depending on the model used, German employers are more or less solely responsible for the administration in the case of the 'on-the-books-reserves' and support funds. Large-scale German companies have their own occupational schemes although employers are typically bound to sectorwide collective agreements. Within this frame, they can choose between several modes of occupational pensions regulated since 1972. The 2001 reform introduced voluntary personal pensions, leaving individuals to decide whether or not to sign a state-regulated *Riester* contract (subsidized for low-income groups). In Belgium, three different governance forms coexist, but coverage has increased only recently: group insurance contracts dominate, followed by negotiated sectorwide and single-employer contracts; these are initiated either by a joint-committee or by the employer. In Italy, two modes of occupational pensions are currently possible: closed pension funds are restricted to the employees of the sponsoring employer(s) and open pension funds are accessible for all employees independent of their employer. Closed pension funds are independent legal entities that manage contributions and benefits, based on a collective agreement or a unilateral employer decision.

4. Varieties of pension fund capitalism

Private pensions are considered to foster financial market capitalism through the investment of pension funds and personal saving plans. Whether pensions are funded through investments in shares, bonds or other financial instruments have major implications for the political economy. Pension investment, in particular by larger pension funds, can provide a major impact on financial markets and corporate governance nationally and internationally. Today's level of pension fund assets indicates the importance of funded supplementary pensions for old age income among the elderly, and also the importance of these schemes on financial markets. Based on the Varieties of Capitalism approach (Hall and Soskice 2001), we can assume that there is a relationship between the importance of financial markets in Liberal Market Economies (LME) and a reliance on private funded pensions, while in Coordinated Market Economies (CME) we expect more reliance on PAYG occupational pensions in the public sector and on unfunded 'book reserves' of private sector firms (Jackson and Vitols 2001).

The variations in pension fund assets, financing vehicles, and asset allocation reflect the differences in the design and maturity of funded pensions, including pension funds, personal DC pensions, and public reserve funds (see Table 13.2). The potential impact of pension systems on financial markets is very high for the British LME due to the funded occupational and personal pensions that are allowed to contract out of the (unfunded) state second pension. Also, according to expectation, pension fund capitalism is still relatively low for the CMEs France, Italy, Germany, and Belgium, although in Germany and Italy pension assets are growing with average annual growth rates around 15–18 per cent. However, Switzerland and the Netherlands, both considered to be CME, rank also high in funded capitalism, channelling substantial investments through the Dutch collectively negotiated and the Swiss mandatory pension funds. Moreover, the Nordic CMEs (Finland, Denmark, and Sweden) have by now also substantial pension fund capitalism. We therefore distinguish in the following three types of funded pension capitalism:

Table 13.2 Pension fund capitalism, Europe 2001–8

	Funds % GDP	Funds &c % GDP	Financial assets millions US Dollar		Contributions % GDP	Benefits % GDP
	(a) 2008	(b) 2007	(a) 2008	2001–8 (%)	2008	2008
Mature:						
The Netherlands	113.2	(149.1)	988.1	+13.4	4.0	3.7
Switzerland	99.3	(151.9)	496.6	+9.6	8.7	5.4
Britain	61.8	(96.4)	1,644.8	+6.8	2.8	2.8
Catching-up:						
Denmark[a]	47.4	(140.6)	161.7	+20.6	0.5	0.6
Finland	59.1[b]	(78.1)	159.9	+14.6	10.7	9.1
Sweden	39.1[b, c]	(57.4)	35.3	+9.9		
Latecomers:						
Germany	4.7	(17.9)	172.4	+14.9	0.3	0.2
Italy	3.4	(3.6)	78.5	+17.7	0.6	0.3
Belgium	3.3	(14.4)	16.7	+3.9	0.4	0.3
France	2.7[c]	(6.9)	21.9	−2.3[d]		

Notes: (a) Funds: private pension fund investments (% GDP); (b) Funds &c: total private pensions, including also insurances and book reserves (% GDP). [a] The increase in 2008 is due to semi-public funds (ATP, SP, LD) that experienced a strong increase in the value of bonds and other assets; [b] including funded public pensions (Swedish Premium Pension, Finnish TYEL); [c] including public pension reserve funds (Sweden: 31.7, France: 1.9); [d] France: 2003–8; Germany: only Pensionsfonds and Pensionskassen (no book reserves); France: without AGIRC/ARRCO; Denmark: including ATP; Finland: including TyEL.
Source: OECD (2009a, 2009b).

1. The *mature* funded pension systems of Britain, the Netherlands, and Switzerland with pension fund assets larger than two-thirds if not larger than GDP;

2. The *catching-up* pension fund countries Finland, Sweden, and Denmark with lower but growing pension assets, including occupational but also public pensions (reserve funds in Sweden, Danish and Swedish personal pensions, and Finnish occupational pension YEL); and

3. The *latecomers* with Bismarckian dominantly public pension tradition (Germany, Italy, Belgium, France) and small pension assets, though funded occupational and personal pensions have been fostered in recent years.

There has been a sustained increase in pension fund assets since the 1990s (see Figure 13.2). Among the countries with the highest degree of pension fund capitalism, growth over the last two decades was particularly fast in Switzerland and the Netherlands and somewhat slower and more cyclical in the United Kingdom. Exceptional was the effect of funding in Finland (including statutory

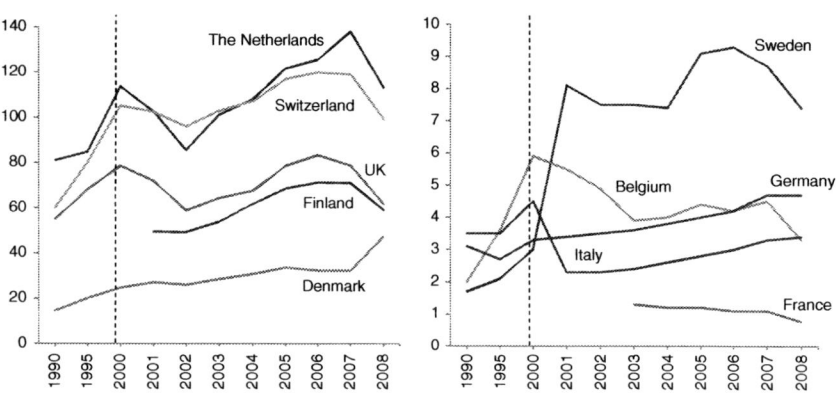

Figure 13.2 Development of pension fund assets 1990–2008 (per cent GDP)

Notes: Funded pensions only, no book reserves; Finland: including statutory OP (private sector TyEL, public sector schemes) and voluntary occupational pensions, group insurance and personal life insurance contracts; the United Kingdom: without stakeholder pension, personal life insurance plans, and OPs for public employees (PAYG); Belgium: without personal savings; Germany: without direct insurance and personal savings (like Riester-plans); Sweden: without personal life insurance plans; Switzerland: without personal saving plans; Denmark: including public ATP fund; the Netherlands: without annuities. The Danish increase in 2008 is due to semi-governmental funds (ATP, SP, LD), which experienced a strong increase in the value of bonds and other assets.

Source: OECD Global Pension Statistics, OECD (2000: 28; 2003: 28), and OECD Pension Indicators 2009 (www.stats.oecd.org).

partly funded pensions) over the last years, coming today close to the British level. Somewhat slower, Denmark has also increased its assets, ranking fifth of the group of countries considered here. A more detailed annual analysis shows that investments in pension funds since 2001 show considerable increase in Germany and Italy, while Germany and Belgium have by now somewhat higher shares than Italy and France, though still far away from countries with pronounced pension fund capitalism. The financial market crisis of 2000/1 also led to a decrease especially between 2001 and 2003 in the Netherlands, Switzerland, and the United Kingdom. The figures for 2008 for those that are already reported by the OECD show again a downward tendency following the onset of the 2008/9 financial market crisis, and this slump should be more pronounced in the next few years.

The scope of pension fund capitalism (see Table 13.2) is measured in the investment of supplementary pensions, thus it is central whether or not pensions are fully funded. Whether or not contributions are channelled to financial markets depends on the financing mode (see Table 13.3). Some public sector occupational pensions are PAYG systems, that is, current contributions are rechannelled to pay benefits of current pensioners. In so far they face the same demographic and sustainability problems as public pensions, thus the state (including public sector companies) have to guarantee long-term

Table 13.3 Funding mode in occupational and personal supplementary pensions

	Mainly unfunded	Funded (DB, DC)
OP	*Book reserves*: Germany, Italy (*Tfr*), Finland (YEL)*, Sweden**	*Defined benefits (DB)*: the Netherlands, Finland (>30%).
	Private sector (PAYG): France (AGIRC, ARRCO)***	*Defined benefits or contribution (DB/DC)*: the United Kingdom (1979)+, Sweden, Germany, Belgium, Denmark, Switzerland, Italy (2000s: open/closed funds), France (PERCO)
	Public sector (PAYG): the United Kingdom, Denmark, Germany, France (*régime spéciaux*), Sweden***	
PP		*Defined contribution (DC)*: the United Kingdom (1986: individual)+, Denmark (1991: Special Savings P.), Sweden (1998: Premium P.), Germany (2001: Riester/Rürup P.), Belgium, France (PERP)

Notes: * for self–employed; ** ITP (private white-collar workers): book reserves (closed since 2007), PA03 (government employees): DB part is PAYG financed, KAP-KL (employees in municipalities and country councils): DB part via book reserves; *** with reserve funds; + UK: opt-out of state second pension (for DC until 2012).

sustainability. PAYG schemes are still common in Germany (VBL), Sweden, Denmark, and the United Kingdom. Nevertheless, increasingly reserve funds are devised or new entrants are insured by partly funded schemes.

Similar problems occur with the book reserves, many larger German private firms profited in the past from credits provided by banks and on the book reserves of their occupational pensions (Jackson and Vitols 2001; Vitols 2003). With increased importance of shareholder value, a reorientation from DB schemes (often with book reserves) towards funded DC schemes occurred. However, these recent changes will not increase assets rapidly due to the often lower contributions and more limited take-up rates (Davis 2003). Moreover, the public sector's occupational scheme is still PAYG in Western part of Germany. French second-tier collective pensions for private sector employees (AGIRC/ARRCO) are largely unfunded (PAYG with a reserve fund). Italy's end-of-service pay (*Tfr*) was a mandatory book reserve system by firms in case of termination of employment but is increasingly being transferred to funded occupational pensions. The contributions to pension funds and benefits paid into pension funds are still very low for these latecomer countries. In these countries, unfunded schemes play a bigger if not the biggest role thus far, a change towards (more) funding could quickly change the impact on financial markets. Thus, PAYG schemes have been common in the public sector in several countries, and in a few cases also in the private sector (French-mandated collective schemes).

In *funded* systems, contributions are invested in capital markets, expecting higher returns. However, in DB pension funds, the employers may be responsible to provide for any underfunding of pension fund liabilities, while they may profit from contribution 'holidays' in times of overfunding. In funded DC schemes, administrative costs and financial charges for investments are higher, while the financial market risks are completely individualized. All occupational pension plans are funded in Switzerland, the Netherlands, and Belgium. In the United Kingdom and Denmark, all plans in the private sector are funded. The financing mechanisms in Sweden, Finland, Germany, and Italy are more mixed. In Sweden, occupational pensions in the private sector are fully funded. In Finland, liabilities of occupational pensions in the private sector are partly funded (30 per cent) but the larger part is PAYG financed. Most of the German private sector occupational pensions are funded (or book reserves). In France, new voluntary PERCO and PERP schemes are funded.

5. Coverage: who is included?

The importance of supplementary pensions partly depends on coverage, the share of the population that is insured by private pensions. We will focus here in particular on the dependent employed, though the self-employed and non-employed (unemployed and other non-employed such as students and house-wives) may not be covered. The coverage of private occupational or personal pensions is largely determined by who decides on supplementary pensions: the state through a mandate, the social partners via a collective agreement, the employer by voluntary commitment, or the individual by choosing a personal savings plan. While mandatory membership by law includes all employees, coverage can also be extensive where collective bargaining is relatively wide-spread due to high union density (Scandinavia), employer organization is relatively encompassing (Germany, Italy) or the extension of collective agreements by the state exists (Belgium, France, the Netherlands). Mandatory pensions enforced by law or quasi-mandatory collective schemes negotiated by the social partners make private pensions more like public pensions by providing broader coverage, often also applying stricter regulation, pooling risks more equitably, using economies of scale, and more professional advice. Wider coverage also reduces social selectivity as well as the moral hazard selection problem, that is, those that are most difficult to cover are not included. Membership in voluntary firm plans is often more concentrated in large firms, which rely on internal labour markets and provide occupational pensions as fringe benefits to bind employees. Smaller firms are less likely to have the expertise and shun the costs of occupational pensions, often only co-financing individual or group insurance contracts. In most occupational pensions, the individual is not responsible for investments, though in some cases personal choice is possible. In contrast, when the individual alone is responsible whether or not to sign a supplementary personal pension plan, the awareness of a possible pension

Table 13.4 Coverage of supplementary pensions (% employees)

	Mandatory/opt-out	Collective	Voluntary
OP	*Mandatory* (>90%):	The Netherlands (1949) >90%	Germany >50%
	Finland (OP 1961)	Sweden (1976) >90%	France (PERCO)***
	Switzerland (1985)	Denmark (1991–) 76%	Italy OP* 11%
	France (OP 1972)	Germany (1969): VBL 20%,	Finland 9%
	Italy (1982: Tfr*)	2001: *Tarifvorbehalt*	
	Opt-out:	Belgium (2003)***	
	Britain (1978) 47%		
PP	*Mandatory public pensions*:		Germany (2001–) 44%
	Denmark (1991: SP**) 89%		Finland 7%, Italy 5%
	Sweden (1999: SP**) 100%		Belgium***
	Opt-out:		France (PERP)***
	Britain (1978) 47%		

Notes: *Tfr*: end-of-service pay (transferable into occupational pensions); **first pillar personal pension (Sweden: Premium Pension, Denmark: Special Savings Pension); ***incl. OP and PP: Belgium: 54%, France: 15%.
Source: GOSPE Project; OECD (2009a: 141).

income gap and the necessary financial knowledge may vary considerably as does the individuals' capability to save, thus creating significant inequalities.

Three main clusters of countries can be distinguished in terms of employees' coverage (see Table 13.4). The *first*, most widespread schemes cover more than 70 per cent of employees due to mandatory state intervention in Finland (since 1961), in France (since 1972), and in Switzerland (since 1985), *erga omnes* extension of collective agreements is common in the Netherlands (since 1949), and, thanks to strong unions, high coverage of collectively negotiated schemes in Denmark (since 1990s) and Sweden (since 1970s). The *second* group covers a substantial workforce share (50–70 per cent) in Britain and Germany. In Britain, it is the 'contracting-out' option for employers and individuals that makes occupational and personal pensions more attractive. In Germany, a negotiated scheme exists in the public sector (since 1969), while more recently the *Tarifvorbehalt* rule gives precedence to collective agreements over individual contracts, leading to a spread across the private sector as well. The *third*, the least organized group (<50 per cent) was late in introducing private pensions (Italy, Belgium) with voluntary but also increasingly negotiated schemes (OECD 2007: 10). The Italian end-of-service pay (*Tfr*) has been mandatory since 1984 and is now partly transferred into occupational pensions, while Belgian occupational pensions have been partly negotiated, partly voluntary firm-sponsored plans (coverage may have reached 50 per cent in recent years).

Among the countries with mandatory occupational pensions, Finland and France have quasi-public occupational pensions that are not fully funded, whereas Switzerland has fully funded occupational pensions. In Finland, these mandatory earnings-related occupational pensions cover all employees in private and public sectors, while 16 per cent of Finnish employees contribute today additional voluntary occupational (9 per cent) or personal pensions (7 per cent). In 2008, in addition to the statutory pension, 15 per cent of French employees have also a voluntary occupational group insurance (PERCO) or individual pension plans (PERP) through their employer. In Switzerland, the occupational pension is mandatory for all employees with at least modest earnings (around €12,500 p.a.).

Negotiated collective pensions can also assume a quasi-mandatory role. This is the case in the Netherlands, Sweden, and Denmark. The Dutch Labour Minister can declare sectorwide agreements as compulsory for all employees in the respective sector on request of employer and employee representatives, this holds for about two-thirds of sectorwide funds (OECD 2008: 267). In Denmark, sectorwide occupational pensions spread since the first important private sector agreements in 1991, though public sector employees already had their own schemes by then. In Denmark and Sweden, these plans are compulsory for all employers and employees covered by the agreement. Unique for European countries are the mandatory personal pensions: Danish individual pensions ('Special Savings Pensions' for employees and self-employed) and the Swedish Premium Pension (funded parts of the first-pillar pension, which provide individual investment choice).

While the coverage rate in the first group of countries with mandated collective schemes is rather high, occupational pension coverage ranks at medium level for the second group of countries: Germany and Britain. Generally, all German employees have the legal claim to postulate an earnings conversion since 2002, with some limitations due to existing collective agreements (*Tarifvorbehalt*). In contrast to the private sector, occupational pensions are mandatory for public sector employees (VBL collective agreement) having advantageous conditions. The funded individual pension (*Riester* pension) was not made compulsory in 2001; instead, high state subsidies were devised to promote coverage among low earners, leading after some initial reluctance to a take-up rate of more than 44 per cent in 2008. Britain also has a relatively high–medium coverage rate, thanks to the opt-out option for occupational pensions (47 per cent) and personal pensions (19 per cent). This option is possible for employers providing an occupational pension (1978) and for individuals signing a personal pension plan (1988). Given the low flat-rate basic pension and the opt-out option, the niche left to non-state pensions was largest in Britain compared to all other non-mandatory private pension systems.

In the last group, with lowest coverage, we find Belgium and Italy, though recent reforms have boosted private pension development. Occupational pensions are voluntary in Belgium, but sectorwide plans based on collective agreements are binding for all covered companies and their employees since 1995. Italy has been thus far the country with the lowest coverage rate. Due to the 'silent-consent mechanism', an automatic enrolment rule for *Tfr* transfers has increased coverage, though not as substantially as expected, particularly in small firms and weakly organized sectors.

In order to evaluate the impact of private pensions, one needs to take a closer look at the interaction of coverage, benefits, and contributions to understand its stratification impacts in overall retirement income. The combination of coverage and benefits shows that countries with higher net state pension replacement rates ($\geq$60 per cent) and different coverage rates of supplementary pensions (e.g. quasi-mandatory in Sweden) have lower levels of total contributions to supplementary pensions (Belgium, Germany, Sweden). In contrast, countries with lower net state replacement rates (<60 per cent) and different coverage rates of supplementary pensions (e.g. mandatory in Switzerland, France, Finland) produce higher levels of contributions to supplementary pensions (the Netherlands, Switzerland, Denmark, France, Finland). A linkage between the level of state pensions and supplementary pension contributions is more significant than a linkage between the level of state pensions and occupational pension coverage rates.

6. Contributions: who pays and how much?

Private pensions, unless made mandatory, are often not considered part of social contributions and payroll taxes, thereby remaining a more hidden part of welfare regimes. The level of contributions indicates the current financial commitment for private pensions and its future importance for old age income; it may also play an (increasingly) important part of overall labour costs and wage negotiations. Thus far, the largest share of retirement income is still financed through public pensions, and mandatory social contributions assume a large part of labour costs, thus leaving less scope for additional private pensions. The highest contributions to public pensions in 2007 (OECD 2009a) are paid in Italy (32.7 per cent), the Netherlands (31.1 per cent, including occupational pensions), followed by France (24 per cent, but including statutory occupational pensions), Finland (20.9 per cent for the statutory occupational pension), Germany (19.9 per cent), Sweden (18.9 per cent, including 2.5 per cent for funded personal pension), Belgium (16.4 per cent) and Switzerland (10.1 per cent). In Denmark, no payroll contributions are directly paid for the public basic pensions, but employers pay into the flat-rate public second-tier pension ATP and withheld 1 per cent for the state personal pension (suspended in 2004 and terminated in 2010). In Britain, National Insurance contributions cover pensions among other social insurance benefits (12.0 per cent by employees and 12.8 per cent by employers above earnings threshold), though a contracted-out DB scheme lowers contributions (the rebate is 2.6 and 3.6 per cent respectively).

In the mature multipillar systems of the Netherlands, Britain, and Switzerland, funded private pensions are an important part of contributions with more than 10 per cent of current salary, but Denmark has also joined their ranks and Finland's statutory (partially funded) scheme is among the high contribution cases. In the Netherlands, contributions to occupational pensions are 15 per cent of payroll, in addition to the relatively high public basic pension that employees have to pay via income tax. In the British contracted-out schemes, contributions are on an average about 20.5 per cent in DB schemes (much larger than the 6.2 per cent contracting-out rebate), but only around 9.1 per cent in DC schemes (the Pension Act 2008 requires minimum contribution of 8 per cent) that are increasingly replacing the former. Statutory contributions define minimum pension rights in Switzerland, as a consequence total contributions vary from 7 to 18 per cent of salary (depending on age). Denmark has reached rates varying between 12 and 18 per cent of salary according to recent collective agreements and has thus reached the level of mature multipillars. Exceptional are the high Finnish contributions (21 per cent) of the statutory pension that is partly funded, while the income-tested public pension is tax-financed.

The medium-level contribution group includes the mandatory French second-tier occupational pensions (AGIRC, ARRCO) ranging from 7.5 per cent (below social security ceiling) to 20 per cent of private employee salaries (above the ceiling). Employer and employee contributions in Italy depend on plan rules, but for the allocation of annual severance pay employers must allocate the whole annual *Tfr* contribution (6.91 per cent of salary) to the pension fund, while the contributions to pension funds are otherwise 4.8–9.8 per cent of gross salary.

In the group with private pension contributions less than 5 per cent of salary, old age income from occupational pensions in Sweden, Germany, and Italy will not be very high (SPC 2005: 18f). Contributions for occupational pensions in Sweden are on an average 4 per cent for DC schemes (albeit up to 30 per cent for high-income earners), while it ranges from 1 to 9.35 per cent for the DB public sector schemes. In addition, the public pension contribution includes a 2.5 per cent contribution for the funded personal pension, thus total supplementary pension exceeds 6.5 per cent for private employees. The German public sector VBL contributions amount to 7.8 per cent of salary, while the maximum publicly supported contribution rate for private pensions is only 4 per cent of the income ceiling. Belgium has the lowest contributions, namely below 5 per cent of salary, though personal pension acquires four-fifths of the overall contributions (see Table 13.5).

The financial burden for employees can be lowered through employer contributions, though this will not alter overall labour costs and may become part of wage negotiations. The highest employer share in contributions is traditionally paid in Sweden, Belgium, and Finland (80–90 per cent of total

Table 13.5 Contributors and contributions to supplementary pensions

Contributors	Contributions		
	High (>10%)	Medium (5–10%)	Low (<5%)
Mainly employers	France (AGIRC)*, Finland (TyEL), Denmark, Britain (opt-out DB)	France (ARRCO)*, Italy (incl. *Tfr*), Britain (opt-out DC), Germany (VBL), Sweden OP & PP*	Belgium, German OP (book reserve)
Mixed	Switzerland*, the Netherlands		(German OP)
Mainly employees	Finland (YEL)*	Britain (opt-out PP)	German PP, Denmark PP*

Notes: OP: occupational pension; PP: personal pension; *mandatory.

contributions). Swedish employers fully pay occupational pension contributions according to the collective agreements, and they also pay 50 per cent of the mandatory Premium Pension. Finnish employers contribute about 85 per cent of the mandatory occupational pension contributions. The employer contributes two-thirds of all contributions in Denmark, France, and the United Kingdom, and in Switzerland at least half. The new voluntary funded pensions in France are paid by employers, except PERCO scheme which are paid by the individual. When contracting out, British employers typically pay 15.6 per cent of salary in DB schemes (employee: 4.9 per cent) and 4.9 per cent in DC schemes (employee: 2.7 per cent). Contributions are typically equally shared in the Netherlands (SPC 2005: 20). German employers traditionally pay firm-level occupational pensions, but the new schemes are jointly or employee-only financed.

7. Governance and participatory rights

The participatory rights of employees and beneficiaries and the way in which the principal–agent problem applies can vary substantially depending on the governance form of supplementary pensions. On the one hand, pension schemes that are *internally* organized such as public sector (PAYG) schemes and employer commitments (book reserves) depend on the trust in the financial sustainability of current and promised future benefits. On the other hand, the pension contributions may be invested by the principal (sponsor) in an *external* independent fund (agent) which is sheltered from the risk of bankruptcy by the sponsoring firm. Thus, we distinguish five modes of supplementary pension governance that internalize or externalize financial responsibility (see Table 13.6): Internal organization for quasi-public guarantees (PAYG) and

Table 13.6 Internal and external governance

	Internal (PAYG)	Internal (book reserves)	External pension fund	(Group) Insurance	Personal pension plan
Mature	Switzerland*, the United Kingdom*		Switzerland+, the Netherlands+, the United Kingdom (trusts)	Switzerland, the United Kingdom (small employers)	The United Kingdom (PP)
Catching-up	Finland (YEL)+, Denmark*	Sweden (ITP)+	Sweden (ITP)+, (Denmark)+	Denmark+, Finland+, Sweden+	Denmark (SP), Sweden (PP)
Late comers	Germany*+, France+ (AGIRC, ARRCO)	Italy (Tfr), Germany (direct commitment)	Germany+, Italy+ (Belgium)+	Belgium+, Germany	Germany (Riester)

Notes: * public sector scheme; + mainly collective; italics: main pension scheme.

employer commitment (book reserves), externalization in pension funds, group insurances, and personal pensions.

Pension schemes with internal governance are those public sector schemes with PAYG financing and those employer commitments that are directly financed from a company's balance sheet (book reserves). An example of the first case is the French PAYG-financed pension institutions for private sector employees. They are managed by a bipartite board, these are supervised by the federations (AGIRC and ARRCO) which also control financial statements and issue regulation (contributions, indexation) and arrange financial compensation between institutions. Public sector schemes in Switzerland, Denmark, Germany (VBL), and the United Kingdom are PAYG organized as the state takes on responsibility for their sustainability.

In the case of book reserves, commercial firms are paying current pensioners, while future liabilities are funded through future returns on reinvestment into the company. In the past, such pensions were less visible to those outside the firm, but with increased importance of shareholder value and the adoption of international accounting standards these employer commitments have to be now fully listed as liabilities (Möllmann 2005). In terms of liabilities, such direct employer commitments are still the most important occupational pension form in Germany and are thus governed by the company management. In case of co-determination of listed companies, a supervisory board with bipartite labour–employer representatives oversees the company, but otherwise only weak rights for works councils exist in respect to occupational pensions. Another example is the Italian end-of-service pay (Tfr) financed via book reserves, though these benefits are increasingly converted into pension funds, at least in larger firms and well-organized sectors. The Swedish occupational scheme for private employees (ITP) also uses book reserves; employers have to register with the Pension Registration Institute, administered by social partners who then manage benefit and pay out pensions.

Most occupational pensions, however, are sponsored by employers and organized externally. This means that pension funds are independent of company balance sheets and shielded from the risk of bankruptcy. In many countries it is possible for employers to participate in multifirm or open pension funds. In addition, employers, particularly small firms, might choose to pay into life or group insurances, even though they have higher administrative costs per insured. In the case of pension funds set up by employers, the administration and supervision is decided by the sponsor according to trust law, whereas in the case of insurance contracts the administration and supervision is outsourced, hence the sponsor and beneficiary need to rely on public supervision and regulation of financial agencies to be ensured of their rights.

External employer-led pension funds dominate in the mature British multipillar system. The boards of directors of British companies are not legally required to have any employee representatives, and pension funds are overseen by trustees appointed by the sponsor (firm). However, by law the trustee must govern on behalf of the interests of the beneficiaries, and one-third of trustees must be member-nominated (employees and retired beneficiaries) and there is pressure to increase the share of member-nominated trustee seats. Pension funds are also increasingly common in German larger firms instead of book reserves following the externalization of liabilities.

Collectively negotiated pension schemes with joint administration balance interests between sponsors and beneficiaries more equally. Such schemes exist in nearly all multipillar systems, except the United Kingdom. It is very common in the Netherlands and Switzerland, but also in Sweden and Denmark. All Dutch pension funds are managed by a bipartite governing board. In this model, employees as well as pensioners can be represented, and on request an advisory board has to be established which holds decision-making power for contributions and benefits. Mandatory Swiss occupational pensions are strictly regulated. Almost all pension institutions take the form of corporate (firm-based), group (multifirm based), or joint foundations (sectorwide). By law these are supervised by bipartite committees, but in smaller companies representative rights are not always taken up. Assets are either administered by the bipartite committee or contracted out to financial institutions, though the bipartite committee remains responsible for investment guidelines. In Danish pension funds, half of the board that governs the pension fund must be elected by and chosen from the plan members, and in most pension funds' administration representatives of unions dominate (Green-Pedersen 2007: 468).

New schemes in Germany, Belgium, and Italy have emerged since the 1990s. In Germany, pension fund associations, superannuation funds, and pension funds must follow the two-tier executive board and bipartite supervisory board structure, while collective pension schemes (e.g. *Metallrente*) are administered jointly by the social partners. In Italy, the executive and supervisory board of closed pension funds are bipartite, overlooking asset managers and investment guidelines. Recent reforms of open pension funds require a supervisory board to assure that it operates in the interest of its members (Stewart and Yermo 2008). Special cases are the French and Finnish mandatory quasi-public pension schemes that are self-administered.

Pension funds as institutional investors can use their voice as shareholders to influence management. For instance, Danish pension fund administrators have been criticizing companies for insufficient profits, bad management, and insufficient information. Especially collective pension funds, which are administered equally by employers and unions, can exert pressure on firms in promoting social, employment, and environmental standards (see for literature: Clark and Hebb 2004: 144). In addition, new 'ecological' or 'social' pension funds might be established in the future for social- and environmental-oriented consumers (already present in the field of banks).

Further external modes of governance are group or individual insurance contracts underwritten by the employer. The personal pension in the United Kingdom (including contracting-out option) provides thus far the choice of private pension companies but no further influence for beneficiaries. Direct insurances are common for German small- and medium-sized companies due to high costs of setting up pension funds. French voluntary funded pensions provide different governance structures with more or less decision-making power to the firm, and no or limited participation of unions. The French PERCO schemes, however, are established by collective agreements and linked to workers' participation schemes. Similarly, Belgian employees participate in company pensions that provide voice to works councils and trade unions.

In Denmark, two-thirds of the sectorwide pension plans are contracts with life insurance companies, though a bipartite board of directors governs the pension institution, which administers contributions and benefits. The mandatory Special Pensions Savings are administered by the bipartite ATP fund, but the individual is able to choose his own fund manager and portfolio. The Swedish pension foundations (ITP) have a governing board with an equal number of employers' and employees' representatives. In the case of insurance plans, special institutions administered by social partners act as intermediaries. A public authority administers the mandatory Premium Pension, but individuals can choose in which mutual funds they invest their mandatory contributions. Most Finnish occupational pension schemes are insurances, though the TyEL pensions are decentralized and have parity administrations, which oversee the asset management strategy.

In sum, in the Dutch and Swiss mature multipillar systems, there is a strong tendency towards bipartite collective schemes with pension funds independent of firms, while in Britain occupational pension funds provide more limited and the personal pensions no participatory right. In the Scandinavian countries, supplementary pensions are increasingly implemented through insurance contracts with parity supervision. In addition, public personal pensions were made mandatory in Sweden and Denmark, allowing the individual choice of financing institutions. The Continental European systems still have a tradition of mainly internal occupational pensions (PAYG and book reserves), but there are signs of growing importance of collective agreements and external independent pension institutions (pension funds and insurance contracts).

8. Supervision

In addition to regulation and governance, supervision is crucial for protecting beneficiaries from non-prudent investment strategies by agents. More effective supervision is possible in the case of collective schemes in Continental Europe than for single-employer pension funds in the United Kingdom (Laboul and Yermo 2006: 517), though much depends on additional state regulation. Particularly, the Dutch quasi-mandatory and Swiss mandatory schemes have substantial supervision, while the United Kingdom exercises more restraint. The Dutch Central Bank supervises occupational pension funds (besides other financial institutes). The Swiss occupational pension schemes are supervised by cantonal and federal supervisory authorities: the Federal agency examines the compliance with federal law and undertakes necessary preventive measures against insufficient funding. Although British pension funds are regulated at arm's-length, following the Maxwell pension fund scandal, regulation has been tightened since 1995. The British private schemes are certificated after passing reference scheme tests for DB and protected rights tests for DC schemes (including personal pensions), while the Pension Regulator is responsible for the supervision of occupational pensions.

The Scandinavian countries have encompassing supervision for both quasi-public and private supplementary pensions. Danish occupational pension funds and insurances must be registered and are supervised by the Danish Financial Supervisory Authority that describes detailed rules, including annual reporting by an approved actuary. The mandatory ATP fund (controlled by social partners) administers a part of the personal pension since individuals are free to invest their contributions via financial institutes since 2005 (Green-Pedersen 2007: 468). The Finnish Social Affairs Ministry authorizes insurance companies and sets the contributions for the different occupational schemes, while the PAYG part of occupational pensions is administered by the Finnish Centre for Pensions, a tripartite agency. The Finnish Financial Supervisory Authority, a public agency, supervises financial institutions, including insurance companies, firm-plans, and collective pensions. The Swedish Financial Supervisory Authority supervises all financial institutions, while the new pension authority administers and manages the social insurances and the Premium Pension.

On the Continent, public pensions have often been self-administered and supervised by bipartite boards, while private pension institutions are supervised by supervision authorities common for the financial sector. The French federations (AGIRC, ARRCO) are self-administered by the social partners, whereas the voluntary occupational pensions are supervised by a public agency. In Germany, BaFin supervises banks, insurances, and pension funds. Led by a board with state and fund representatives, it controls the solvency, transparency, consumer protection, and certification (Riester-pensions) of private pensions. Similarly, the Italian Pension Fund Supervisory Commission can enact sanctions and information requirements, and similar public agencies overlook banks and insurances. In Belgium, a public agency supervises pension funds and insurance companies; it can request information, replace managers, and impose recovery measures. Additionally, EU directives prescribe a supervision framework for pension institutions and supervisory institutions. The payment of outstanding claims to employees in the event of their employers' insolvency should be guaranteed in line with directive 80/897/EEC. In sum, in most of the countries, state institutions exist that are responsible for the supervision of pension provider companies. They might request information, are responsible for stress tests, and they are entitled to carry out on-site inspections. The main thrust behind these regulations is to ensure their financial sustainability and guarantee the underwritten liabilities, thus they are mainly concerned with financial sustainability and not social adequacy of private pensions.

9. Shifting risks: defined contribution versus defined benefits

Of importance for retirement income and the distribution of risks is the way in which benefits are calculated, most importantly whether a private pension is a DB or DC scheme, though there are several mixed forms. DB schemes stipulate predefined benefits based on service years and received earnings during employment with a particular employer, they are guaranteed by the sponsor (employer) and therefore are usually employer-only financed. DB benefits often derive from an employer's strategy to provide fringe benefit and bind workers to the firm, therefore employers have an interest in limiting portability. With DB schemes at firm level, employees can lose all or part of their benefits when changing employers, depending on vesting rights. Financing risks such as underfunding due to less than expected returns on capital, however, remain with the employer (or collective scheme), including the risks of longevity and an increase of life expectancy.

DC pensions are the result of the rates of return on invested capital, depending on the investment portfolio choice. In general, the individual is responsible to contribute sufficiently in order to fill any retirement income gap between expected public pension and acquired living standard; it thus requires long-term foresight and financial literacy from individuals. Individuals bear financial risks like financial market downturns, but they may also profit from higher returns than in PAYG or DB schemes. Another advantage is labour market mobility due to the better portability of DC benefits. However, in contrast to DB schemes, employees who retire will have to transfer their accumulated capital into an annuity or life insurance at some cost, otherwise they might fall prey to the financial market and longevity risks.

In most countries, DC and DB schemes coexist, though there is a general trend towards DC schemes (at least for new entrants), indicating a retreat from employers' commitment and a shift towards individual financial responsibility. A minimum rate of return sometimes eases the establishment of real DC systems. Usually, in the public sector and for high-income earners, DB parts are included in occupational pensions. The majority of all British employees are covered either by contracted-out salary-related schemes (DB) or by public sector plans (prescribed maximum benefits). Many DB schemes have been closed and new employees enter into contracted-out money purchase schemes (DC). The personal pension plans (including stakeholder pensions) are always DC, but with certain prescribed minimum benefits. The Swiss occupational pension schemes must provide a statutory minimum benefit for the more common DC schemes. The majority of German occupational pensions are still DB schemes for current pensioners, but the new Riester pension and some occupational plans since 2002 tend to be DC.

In contrast, quasi-mandatory Finnish and Dutch occupational pensions are DB schemes, and the quasi-mandated French occupational pensions are a notional DC scheme (i.e. a PAYG scheme dependent on point systems). The Dutch industrywide pension plans are DB (some DC), and all plans aim for an overall benefit target (including state and occupational pensions) of 70 per cent of final salary. Unique for occupational pension is the payment of benefits in Finland. The occupational pension scheme with which the employee is insured at retirement pays all benefits regardless of where the employee has acquired benefits, thanks to the Finnish Centre of Pension that traces contributions across pension schemes. In contrast to larger pooled DB schemes (with employer sponsoring), an individual DC pension may be more vulnerable to financial market downturns, this holds especially for pension fund capitalism in Switzerland, the United Kingdom, Denmark, but also Sweden and Italy (OECD 2009a).

10. Indexation and vesting

Indexation rules play an important role for the protection of benefits against inflation risks, though this mainly applies to DB and mixed schemes. In contrast, most DC schemes depend on the returns on capital, thus leaving the inflation risk to the individual. Without proper adjustments, DB pensions will lose their real value in times of substantial inflation. Public pension systems have elaborate rules on indexing set out by government decisions, often leading to political debates. For occupational pensions, the state may also regulate indexation rules as in Finland, Britain, and Germany (see Table 13.7). Finnish occupational pensions are partly adjusted to consumer prices (80 per cent) and wages (20 per cent) in line with public pensions. British DB benefits should be indexed to retail prices up to a maximum of 2.5 per cent (before 2005: 5 per cent). German occupational pensions have to be indexed to consumer prices or net wages of comparable employees in the firm (but at least by 1 per cent), except in cases of economic distress to the firm (a 1 per cent increase is compulsory for earnings conversion and in the public sector).

Apart from these statutory rules, indexation is self-regulated by the social partners or pension institutions in Sweden, Denmark, France, and Switzerland. While Danish DC plans rarely use indexation, the less common DB plans adjust benefits to the consumer price index. Also in Sweden, occupational pensions are usually indexed to consumer prices, based on collective agreements. In Switzerland, the indexation of benefits depends on the pension institution's financial possibilities and calculation methods.[4] The French occupational pension benefits usually are indexed in line with prices. In contrast, no legal indexation requirements are present in Belgium, Italy, and the Netherlands. With increased supplementary pensions, lacking indexation might have long-term consequences for old age retirement income.

Vesting is important in case of job mobility between firms, especially for those groups with high turnover: the low-skilled workers, part-time employees, and temporary employees with interrupted employment careers. Vesting rights facilitate interfirm mobility but reduces an employer's aim to bind qualified employees to the firm. These two opposites together with a potential threat to national negotiated arrangements blocked the EU Directive with the aim to foster employees' mobility and pensions' portability (Mabbett 2009). Whereas DB schemes often require longer minimum contribution periods until benefits are guaranteed and indexed in case of employment termination, DC benefits are automatically vested and thus highly portable. Contributions of employers and employees become immediately vested in France, Italy, the Netherlands, Switzerland, and Sweden. Therefore, employers are unable to use those to bind employees. The conditions for employees are also advantageous in Belgium, where employer contributions become vested after one year (employee contributions immediately). In Britain, vesting starts after two years for DB, DC, and public sector plans but immediately for stakeholder pensions. Danish employee

---

[4] High rates of return during the 1980s and 1990s of about 5–10 per cent have been distributed not to the insured but to the Swiss shareholders ('pension theft').

Table 13.7 Indexation and vesting

Vesting	Indexation		
	Legal requirements	Discretionary/ self-regulation	No special rules
Immediately	Finland (TyEL), Sweden	France, Switzerland	Italy, the Netherlands, the United Kingdom (DC), Germany (Riester)
	Germany (earnings conversion)		Denmark (OP), Sweden (PP)
			Belgium
		Denmark	
	The United Kingdom (DB)		
		Germany	
	Germany (public sector)		
Longer period			

Note: OP: occupational pensions; PP: personal pensions.

contributions are vested immediately, while employer contributions after five years (though immediate vesting is often practiced). The worst conditions for employees are present in Germany, where vesting occurs for employer-financed occupational pensions only after five years of service (in private and public sectors) and a threshold age of 30 (25 from 2009) applies, but vesting is immediate after the first-paid contributions in case of the new earnings conversion rule.

11. Insolvency protection

Insolvency protection is important in the event of a default through bankruptcy of the sponsoring firm; this applies mainly to private sector firm-sponsored occupational schemes. The public sector occupational schemes in Denmark, Germany, Switzerland, and Britain need no special insolvency protection, because they are (partly) PAYG financed and insolvency of the state is assumed to be impossible. However, the asset protection is needed given the asymmetric information between beneficiaries and asset manager or sponsor. Reinsurance of liabilities is often statutorily required or collectively arranged. Due to the moral hazard problem that risk-adverse firms would insure risk-taking ones, conflicts of interests arise in terms of selection of members, the level of insurance premiums, and the share of benefits covered (OECD 2007). Reinsurance incurs higher costs for employers, though they protect rights of beneficiaries. In most countries, no additional insolvency protection rules for independent pension funds exist because there are limited risks in case of bankruptcy of the sponsoring firm, though future DB benefits, particularly indexing, might face underfunding. In case of insolvency of an insurance firm or a pension fund, alternative protective mechanisms usually apply.

In the mature multipillar systems of Britain, the Netherlands, and Switzerland, more developed protection measures may be needed, though this has not always been the case in the past. In Britain, assets of the trust funds are separated from the company. However, the Maxwell affair in 1992 indicated the pension funds' vulnerability in case of imprudent investment into the sponsoring firm. In response, the 1995 Pension Act introduced new regulations, in particular mutual insurance against losses due to fraud (Davis1997). In 2004, the Pension Protection Fund (PPF) was introduced against the background of several scandals concerning underfunding, protecting DB plans in the event of employer's insolvency (Schulze and Moran 2007: 62). In the Netherlands, no legal rules enforce reinsurance, but the Dutch Central Bank may require reinsurance of pension liabilities with a life insurance company, and underfunding rules are relatively strict (OECD 2008: 272). In Switzerland, employer and employee organizations established a default protection fund, which pays subsidies to those with financial difficulties and secures the payment of minimum benefits in the event of insolvency. An extra-parliamentary committee supervises and manages the default protection and the public security funds.

Among the Scandinavian systems, Denmark has no insolvency regulation of the DC schemes (financial risks are individualized), while Swedish and Finnish occupational pensions have particular protective mechanisms. The Swedish occupational pensions for white- and for blue-collar workers have separate guarantee funds, while the public employee schemes are state guaranteed. In Finland, a joint guarantee system for mandatory occupational pensions in the private sector (TyEL) pays benefits in case of insolvency, while the government guarantees the payment of benefits for public employees (VEL), self-employed, and other groups.

On the Continent, Germany and France have more reinsurance protection than Italy or Belgium. Germany's first regulation dates back to 1972, following court cases on bankruptcy of firms affecting occupational pensions. Pension contracts with insurance firms are protected via an extra insurance and all other occupational pensions through the secondary firm liability. Since the highest risk exists for employer commitments (book reserves) and support funds in case of insolvency as well as merger and acquisition, obligatory reinsurance by the pension guarantee fund (PSV) pays benefits in case of bankruptcy. Due to higher investment risks, German pension funds are also mandated to participate in PSV. In France, the mandated occupational pension schemes do support each other in case of financial problems, whereas for voluntary funded schemes an insolvency fund was created (for life insurance companies), but those with DB pensions are risky. Italy has no compensation funds and reinsurance against financial loss, though assets have to be held separately from the sponsoring firm or institution managing the fund. Similarly, there is no legal insolvency protection for occupational pensions in Belgium, but a safety fund for life insurances with a guaranteed rate of return.

Countries with high coverage rates of occupational pensions and mature funding tend to have significant protection and risk-sharing features in plan design (OECD 2007: 17), though the United Kingdom was later and less far-reaching guarantee schemes were often set up in reaction to political events as was the case in Germany in 1972 and Britain in 1995. Generally, insolvency protection funds are the last security net; however, in the case of funded pensions, investment regulations should lower financial market risks and protect minimum rate of returns.

12. Investment rules

Fundamental problems for funded pension schemes are financial market downturns of the severity experienced at the beginning of the millennium and more recently in 2008/9. In DC schemes, downturns might cause substantial reductions of an individual's pension, while in DB schemes it will lead to underfunding and increase liabilities for the sponsor (employer or collective fund). The low and partly negative rates of return after 2001 and again in 2008 point to this fact. The Dutch pension funds lost 11.9 per cent in 2002 and again it dropped by 16.9 per cent in 2008, while the United Kingdom (17.4 per cent), Finland (19.5 per cent), and Belgium (21.6 per cent) had even worse declines in real returns during 2008 (OECD 2009a). Such a downturn may lead to severe underfunding of future pension liabilities and problems to guarantee minimum rates of return, depending on the statutory rules. For instance, Swiss pension institutions lobbied with success for a lower statutory minimum rate, given the financial market downturn in 2000/1, but the earlier high rates of return had been often used for lowering contributions of employers and not for savings during better years. Similarly, in the Netherlands, the 1990s surpluses were used to premium rebates, while the pension funds became severely underfunded during the subsequent financial market downturns. Regulation is appropriate in order to promote benefit security and to boost the national and European financial markets. Funded pension institutions are subject to investment restrictions like rules on currency matching, allocation of assets and investments in the sponsoring company (EU Directive 2003/41).[5] In the field of life insurances, several EU directives include amongst others investment rules and criterions about guarantee funds in the event of insurance companies' insolvency (SPC 2005: 33).

A prudent management can reduce the risk by shifting assets of people nearing retirement into less volatile investments (SPC 2005: 22f). But additional quantitative restrictions that balance portfolios with risky equities and more secure bonds are needed as well as minimum rates of return to protect individuals from undue financial risks. A convergence towards the less-determined 'prudent person' rule in investment regulations and less quantitative restrictions (Laboul and Yermo 2006: 508) which would allow more investment flexibility and higher rates of return (Davis 2003: 126), but with higher risks, does not seem to be prevalent. Moreover, portfolio allocation varies across regimes (see Table 13.8).

Strict state restrictions for investments exist in some cases: Swiss pension funds had only a 12.5 per cent decline in returns and German funded schemes 8.5 per cent in 2008 (OECD 2009a). Swiss mandatory funded schemes invest in different regions and economic sectors, minimum interest rate was 2 per cent in 2008 (compared to 4 per cent in 2002), there is a maximum of 30 per cent in foreign currencies or bonds as well as foreign equities, and a maximum of 50 per cent may be in equities and only 5 per cent in the sponsoring firm (OECD 2008: 432). In Germany, restrictions for direct insurances and superannuation funds are a maximum of 50 per cent in bonds, 35 per cent in investment funds, 10 per cent in shares of non-EU companies, and a maximum of 5 per cent in hedge funds. There are almost no quantitative constraints for pension funds, though a maximum investment of 5 per cent of the assets in the sponsoring firm (OECD 2008: 227). The minimum interest rate for Riester plans based on insurance contracts is 2.25 per cent per annum, while the accumulated contributions are guaranteed by the financial service provider.

Finland also has some restrictions: the minimum rate of return must be 6 per cent in 2006. The insurance companies must contract out asset management (under the responsibility of the board of directors), while company pension schemes may borrow 50 per cent of sponsoring employer if secured by collateral and a maximum of 50 per cent may be in equities, 5 per cent in unquoted shares and 5 per cent in shares issued by a single company. Private and public employment-related pension funds were used in national investment projects, but the share of national investments has fallen (OECD 2008: 357).

Less strict rules of investments exist in Belgium, Denmark, and Italy. In Belgium, for example, a maximum of 10 per cent of assets may be in bonds

---

[5] See for the genesis of IORP Directive including discussion: Haverland (2007).

Table 13.8 Pension fund portfolio allocation (in % of investments) 2007/8

	Cash	Bonds	Loans	Equities	Buildings	Private funds	Other investments
Belgium (2008)	8.5	42.3	0.5	32.8	0.9	–	13.4
Denmark (2007)	0.8	57.2	1.5	14.6	1.2	–	24.8
Finland (2007)	0.6	39.9	3.1	46.8	9.2	–	0.4
Germany (2008)	5.3	38.3	29.3	6.1	2.4	1.0	18.6
Italy (2008)[a]	8.0	46.3	–	10.1	4.8	1.2	30.6
The Netherlands (2008)	4.8	37.5	3.7	37.3	2.7	–	14.1
Sweden (2007)	2.2	53.6	0.0	36.5	3.4	–	4.2
Switzerland (2007)	9.1	38.9	4.6	32.7	9.4	4.5	0.7
The United Kingdom (2007)[b]	3.7	27.1	1.2	45.8	2.8	–	19.4

Notes: [a] Italy: 'Other investments' include 23.4% unallocated insurance contracts, and the rests refer mainly to investments within holdings that own land and buildings. [b] The United Kingdom: Equity share holdings are at market value and all other holdings at book value. Private equity and venture capital are included in equity. 'Other investments' 9.5% unallocated insurance funds, and the rest include security repurchase agreements, commercial paper and contributions receivable.

Source: OECD Global Pension Statistics.

outside the OECD, 5 per cent in bonds and equities issued by single issuer, and the criterions of security, profitability, liquidity, diversification, and dispersion must be respected (OECD 2008: 214). On the other side, minimum rate of returns for employee and employer contributions (3.75 per cent/3.25 per cent) changes DC pensions to more hybrid constructions. Just few investment restrictions are set in Denmark: at least 30 per cent of assets must invest in low-risk investments, and a maximum of 70 per cent may be placed in equities, though only 10 per cent in shares issued outside the OECD (OECD 2008: 221). All Danish pension institutions offer a minimum rate of return. The Italian pension funds have to limit their asset investments up to a maximum of 50 per cent in bonds and equities within OECD, 20 per cent in cash and closed-end investment funds, and 15 per cent in bonds and equities issued by a single issuer, but loans are prohibited (OECD 2008: 247).

Sweden, the Netherlands, and the United Kingdom have the lowest investment regulation in line with the self-governing 'prudent person' rule. In the Netherlands and the United Kingdom, the lowest investment regulation (with higher investment risks) comes along with funded-only occupational schemes (with exception of the British public sector). In fact, in both countries the dangers of financial market crises are highest. Finally, not only truly funded systems are affected by the current financial crisis, for example the PAYG-based AGIRC/ARRCO pensions noted significant losses in their reserve funds.

13. Conclusion

The scope of supplementary pensions varies in Europe: the coverage of private pension and the magnitude of contributions are important to evaluate the importance of private pensions for the future and the retirement income share (see Table 13.9). The British, Dutch, and Swiss mature multipillar systems have (quasi-)mandatory or opt-out options that lead to high coverage but also high contributions to supplement the basic pensions. There are countries with medium contributions in Scandinavia, whereas we find low contributions in the latecomer Continental Europe with voluntary supplementary pensions. There is a substantial increase in occupational pensions in Scandinavian countries, particularly impressive is a fast rise in Denmark, while public basic pensions become more tested (Sweden, Finland) or no state second-tier pension existed. In Continental Europe, the Bismarckian tradition has been altered by public pension reforms, which have 'crowded in' the need for private pensions, though the new private alternatives are still far from being mature funded schemes that will determine a significant part of retirement income.

Although we often speak of pension privatization, the historical evolution shows wide cross-national diversity in respect to the public regulation and governance of supplementary pensions. Whether occupational pensions are collectively negotiated, employer-provided or individual schemes has major consequences for the overall scope of private pensions and the benefits in retirement. The more state or collective regulation intervenes, the larger the coverage of supplementary pensions and the larger is the scope to pool risks and guarantee rights (Bridgen and Meyer 2009). Encompassing coverage and

Table 13.9 Governance of supplementary pensions by funding and contribution

Private pension assets	(Quasi-)Mandatory		Voluntary	
	High contributions	Medium contributions	Medium contributions	Low contributions
High/ mature	*Switzerland, the Netherlands, the United Kingdom* (opt-out OP/PP)			
Medium/ catching-up	*Denmark*, Finland* (OP+)	*Sweden* (OP+PP)		Finland (PP)
Latecomer	France (OP+)		*France* (PP), *Italy* (OP/PP)	*Germany* (OP/PP), *Belgium*

Notes: High = more than 10% of total contributions, medium = up to 10% contributions; low = up to 5% contributions; SP: state pension; OP: occupational pension; PP: personal pension; *statutory funded pension (Denmark: SP, ATP); + mandatory quasi-public pension (Finland: 30% funded; France: limited reserve fund).
Source: Private pensions assets in % GDP (OECD 2009a).

collective regulation depends on bargaining institutions, the willingness of employers to negotiate, and the overall bargaining coverage as well as state support (*erga omnes* extension of collective agreements). In addition, coverage varies strongly by sector and size of firms due to the different strength of unions.

The more funded pensions are growing, the more importance they gain in financial markets including their ups and downs for pensions and old age income. The sensitivity to financial market turbulences, however, depends largely on the scope and portfolio of asset investment. The countries with the largest losses have the highest percentage of equities in their portfolios (OECD 2009*a*: 34). More risky investments, most notably in the United States, but also in the United Kingdom and the Netherlands, lead to higher negative investment returns (from –17 to –26 per cent) than in countries like Switzerland and Germany (–8 to –13 per cent) with more prudent investment in bonds. The main lessons from the two financial crises within the last decade are stricter rules regarding public supervision (e.g. more regular stress-tests), investment restrictions, and partly new benefit protection mechanisms. This indicates that the role of governance of private pensions including (state) regulation continues to gain importance despite the claim of a privatization and retreat of the state.

Bibliography

Besley, T., and Prat, A. (2005). 'Credible Pensions'. *Fiscal Studies*, 26/1 (March).

Blake, D. (2003). *Pension Schemes and Pension Funds in the United Kingdom*. Oxford: Oxford University Press.

Bridgen, P., and Meyer, T. (2009). 'Social Rights, Social Justice and Pension Outcomes in Four Multi-pillar Systems'. *Journal of Comparative Social Welfare*, 25/2: 129–37.

Clark, G. L., and Hebb, T. (2004). 'Pension Fund Coporate Engagement'. *Industrial Relations*, 59/1: 142–71.

Davis, P. E. (1997). 'Private Pensions in OECD Countries – The United Kingdom'. *OECD Labour Market and Social Policy Occassional Papers*, 21.

——(2003). 'Pension Funds and European Financial Markets'. *Focus on Austria: Quarterly Bulletin of the Österreichische Nationalbank*, 2/2003: 124–39.

Ebbinghaus, B. (2006). *Reforming Early Retirement in Europe, Japan and the USA*. Oxford: Oxford University Press.

Green-Pedersen, C. (2007). 'Denmark: A "World Bank" Pension System', in E. Immergut, K. Anderson and I. Schulze (eds.), *The Handbook of West European Pension Politics*. Oxford: Oxford University Press, 454–95.

Hall, P. A., and Soskice, D. (2001). 'An Introduction to Varieties of Capitalism', in P. A. Hall and D. Soskice (eds.), *Varieties of Capitalism: The Institutional Foundations of Comparative Advantage*. New York, NY: Oxford University Press, 1–68.

Haverland, M. (2007). 'When the Welfare State Meets the Regulatory State: EU Occupational Pension Policy'. *Journal of European Public Policy*, 14/6: 886–904.

Hyde, M., and Dixon, J. (2009). 'Individual and Collective Responsibility: Mandated Private Pensions in a Comparative Perspective'. *Journal of Comparative Social Welfare*, 25/2: 119–27.

Jackson, G., and Vitols, S. (2001). 'Between Financial Commitment, Market Liquidity and Corporate Governance: Occupational Pensions in Britain, Germany, Japan and the USA', in B. Ebbinghaus and P. Manow (eds.), *Comparing Welfare Capitalism: Social Policy and Political Economy in Europe, Japan and the USA*. London: Routledge, 171–89.

Kakabadse, N., and Kakabadse, A. (2004). 'Pension Funds Governance: An Overview of the Role of Trustees'. *International Journal of Business Governance and Ethics*, 1/1: 3–26.

Kjellberg, A. (1992). 'Sweden: Can the Model Survive?' in A. Ferner and R. Hyman (eds.), *Industrial Relations in the New Europe*. Oxford: Blackwell, 88–142.

Laboul, A., and Yermo, J. (2006). 'Regulatory Principles and Institutions', in G. L. Clark, A. Munnell and M. Orzag (eds.), *The Oxford Handbook of Pensions and Retirement Income*. Oxford: Oxford University Press, 501–20.

Lakonishok, J. A., Shleifer, A., and Vishny, R. W. (1992). 'The Structure and Performance of the Money Management Industry'. *Brookings Papers on Economic Activity/Microeconomics*, Vol. 1992: 339–91.

Lazear, E. P. (1990). 'Pensions and Deferred Benefits as Strategic Compensation'. *Industrial Relations*, 29/2: 263–80.

Leisering, L., Davy, U., Berner, F., Schwarze, U., and Blömeke, P. (2002). *Vom produzierenden zum regulierenden Wohlfahrtsstaat: Eine international vergleichende und interdisziplinäre Studie des Wandels der Alterssicherung in Europa. Literaturstudie zum Projektantrag an die DFG. Regina Arbeitspapier Nr. 2*.

Mabbett, D. (2009). 'Supplementary Pensions between Social Policy and Social Regulation'. *West European Politics*, 32/4: 774–91.

McCarthy, D. (2006). 'Occupational Pension Scheme Design', in G. L. Clark, A. H. Munnell and J. M. Orszag (eds.), *The Oxford Handbook of Pensions and Retirement Income*. Oxford: Oxford University Press, 543–61.

Moe, T. M. (1984). 'The New Economics of Organization'. *American Journal of Political Science*, 28/4: 739–77.

Möllmann, C. (2005). 'The Making of an EU Internal Market for Pension Funds: From Financial Market Integration to Transnational Social Policy?'. Espanet Young Resarchers Workshop, Paris, July 2005.

Musalem, A. R., and Palacios, R. J. (eds.) (2004). *Public Pension Fund Management: Governance, Accountability and Investment Policies*. Proceedings of the Second Public Pension Fund Management Conference, May 2003. Washington: World Bank.

OECD (ed.) (2000). *Institutional Investors Statistical Yearbook 2000*. Paris: OECD.

OECD (2001). *Private Pensions Systems: Administrative Costs and Reforms*. Paris: OECD.

——(2002). *Regulating Private Pension Schemes: Trends and Challenges*. Paris: OECD.

——(2003). *Institutional Investors Statistical Yearbook 1992–2001*. Paris: OECD.

——(2004). *Supervising Private Pensions: Institutions and Methods*. Paris: OECD.

——(2005). *Guidelines for Pension Fund Governance: Recommendation of the Council*. Paris: OECD.

——(2007). *Protecting Pensions: Policy Analysis and Examples from OECD Countries*. Paris: OECD.

——(2008). *Complementary and Private Pensions throughout the World 2008*. Paris: OECD.

——(2009a). *Pensions at a Glance 2009. Retirement-Income Systems in OECD Countries*. Paris: OECD.

——(2009b). *Private Pensions Outlook*. Paris: OECD.

Rein, M., and Schmähl, W. (eds.) (2004). *Rethinking the Welfare State: The Political Economy of Pension Reform*. Cheltenham: Edward Elgar.

——and Stapf-Finé, H. (2004). 'Income Packaging and Economic Wellbeing in the Last Stage of the Working Career', in M. Rein and W. Schmähl (eds.), *Rethinking the Welfare State: The Political Economy of Pension Reform*. Cheltenham/Northampton: Edward Elgar, 412–33.

Ross, S. A. (1973). 'The Economic Theory of Agency: The Principal's Problem'. *American Economic Review*, 63/2: 134–9.

Schulze, I., and Moran, M. (2007). 'United Kingdom: Pension Politics in an Adversarial System', in E. M. Immergut, K. M. Anderson and I. Schulze (eds.), *The Handbook of West European Pension Politics*. Oxford: Oxford University Press, 49–96.

Shapiro, S. P. (2005). 'Agency Theory'. *Annual Review of Sociology*, 31: 263–84.

SPC (2005). *Privately Managed Pension Provision*. Report by the Social Protection Committee. Brussels: European Commission.

Stewart, F., and Yermo, J. (2008). *Pension Fund Governance: Challenges and Potential Solutions*. Paris: OECD.

Tonks, I. (2006). 'Pension Fund Management and Investment Performance', in G. L. Clark, A. H. Munnell and J. M. Orszag (eds.), *The Oxford Handbook of Pensions and Retirement Income*. Oxford: Oxford University Press, 456–80.

Trampusch, C. (2009). 'Collective Agreements on Pensions as a Source of Solidarity'. *Journal of Comparative Social Welfare*, 25/2: 99–107.

Vitols, S. (2003). 'Varieties of Capitalism and Pension Reform: Will the "Riester-Rente" Transform the German Coordinated Market Economy?'. *Focus on Austria*, 2: 102–8.

Chapter 14

The Public–Private Pension Mix and Old Age Income Inequality in Europe

Bernhard Ebbinghaus and Jörg Neugschwender

1. Introduction[1]

Recent reforms across European welfare states have shifted the public–private mix towards more occupational and personal pensions. This privatization has had and will have major repercussions for the income situation of older people. While public insurance provides more universal and redistributive social benefits by mandating wide coverage and by pooling risks, private pensions tend to reproduce if not amplify market-income inequalities existent during working life in the period after retirement. Unless mandated by law or enforced by collective agreements, voluntary private pensions are less widespread and provide non-redistributive benefits that depend solely on contributions. Furthermore, private pensions are increasingly based not on defined benefits (DB) but rather on defined contributions (DC) that are fully funded and dependent on returns of capital. This shifts financial risks onto individuals. Quite clearly, the financial and economic crises around 2001/2 and 2008/9 indicated the sometimes substantial risk of funded pensions: in countries with high-risk investment strategies, invested assets declined substantially. Across Europe, privatization has thus become a widespread phenomenon that entails major repercussions for today's mature multipillar systems and in the future for those countries that are developing private funded pensions. The choices made in reaction to these economic crises will substantially affect individual old age income situation and overall social inequalities among pensioners.

International organizations and economic policy experts have advised a shift away from pay-as-you-go (PAYG) public pensions to funded private pensions

---

[1] The authors are especially grateful to André Schaffrin for assistance in analysing the SHARE data.

384

for reasons of long-term financial and economic *sustainability* in ageing societies (e.g. EU-EPC 2009; Gruber and Wise 2007; OECD 2000). In the Open Method of Coordination in Pensions and Social Inclusion, the European Union's Social Policy Committee brought the issue of adequate pensions onto the political agenda. In this chapter, we study the *adequacy* of pensions in Europe from a sociological perspective: Does the shift from public to private responsibility increase inequality of retirement income? Which public–private mix and which design of private pension arrangements has more adverse effects? A central concern is that more vulnerable social groups are less likely to be covered by occupational schemes due to non-standard jobs and non-employment periods as well as due to insufficient means and limited foresight or capacity to save voluntarily. This chapter will compare the past and present income situation in old age by looking at the impact of the design of public and private pensions across Europe. We account for institutional differences in the main function of statutory pensions for income security and the varying effects of private pensions that supplement retirement income, particularly for different socio-demographic groups.

The impact of private pensions on income inequality cannot be analysed without understanding the public system's redistributive function. In particular, we need to consider to what degree the public system sufficiently prevents poverty and to what degree it compensates for earnings inequality. We thus analyse the overall poverty rate in old age, the minimum income guarantees provided by public pensions, and the replacement rate of statutory pensions. The main differences between a 'Bismarckian' earnings-related social insurance and 'Beveridge' basic pension tradition (see Chapter 2) help to understand systematic variations in public–private mixes. Among the Bismarckian systems we compare the Continental countries (Belgium, France, Germany, and Italy), among the Beveridge systems we distinguish the Nordic countries (Denmark, Finland, Sweden), and the mature multipillar systems (Britain, the Netherlands, and Switzerland). Our main aim is to contrast the different forms of public pensions for the development of private pensions and the resulting inequalities arising from these core institutions. To evaluate the pension system's impact on old age poverty and inequality, we analyse the degree to which retirement benefits are based on residual means-tested social assistance, on institutionalized universal social rights, or on achievement-oriented earnings-related contributions, following Titmuss' famous triad (1974). The employment linkage may be less important under highly redistributive social security, especially universal basic pensions and social (or minimum) pension insurance systems. Esping-Andersen's de-commodification concept (1990) highlights the degree to which welfare states redistribute so that transfers are independent of market forces, thereby partially reducing social inequality.

As to private pensions, we include all non-state pensions in our analysis, whether occupational pensions by employers, negotiated schemes by the social partners, or individual savings schemes (in British parlance 'personal pensions'). Analysing large-scale surveys of elderly people in Europe, we will compare contemporary differences in public and private pensions across nine of the ten countries covered in this volume (no data are available for Finland). We focus on two aspects that affect old age income inequality: the *coverage* of private pension recipients and the *share* of private pensions in total pension transfers. While recipient rates provide an indicator of inequality in access to private pensions, the private transfer share reveals the importance of occupational or personal pensions in replacing, supplementing, or just topping-up public pension benefits. Analyses by gender, household composition, and income group reveal the social differences in access to and reliance on private pensions. Similar to public earnings-related social insurance, private pensions tend to reproduce market inequalities with respect to employment and earnings during working life. As a previous comparative analysis has argued, 'it is not the mix but the design of the [public–private] mix that is crucial' (Rein and Behrendt 2004: 197).

Systematic cross-national analyses of pension income inequality face several problems, in particular methodological difficulties and data unavailability. Today's income situation of current pensioners reflects the combined effects of past and current regulation governing insurance access, contributions, and benefit rules. There is a long delay between accumulating pension rights (or assets through contributions) over an entire working life of up to 50 years (e.g. a worker who was first employed at age 15) and withdrawing pensions for several years (e.g. after retiring at age 65). Moreover, reforms enacted today may only gradually affect current retirees and most of today's contributors will be affected only in the far future. There are two possible research strategies to cope with the long time-lag between policy changes and its likely effect.

Firstly, by applying today's rules to possible life-course trajectories in estimating future incomes, one can simulate future outcomes, knowing that this is a demanding task and thus rarely done.[2] Such a *prospective* micro-simulation requires us to compile and model detailed current rules, while its results depend on multiple assumptions about future employment careers, demographic changes, future returns on capital, and most importantly the stability of pension rules. The OECD and EU's theoretical replacement rates undertake such an approach, though based on a standard employment case (EU-SPC(ICG) 2009; OECD 2009b), disregarding the increasing diversity in working-life profiles.

Secondly, link outcomes at a point in time with a *restrospective* analysis of the preceding development, which is the common method adopted in most national and comparative studies. Previous cross-national studies on the public–private mix use the Luxemburg Income Study (LIS), which allows us to study

[2] For a simulation study including Britain, Germany, the Netherlands, Italy, and Switzerland, see Meyer et al. (2007).

public transfers as well as private pensions (though mainly occupational pensions) in several OECD countries, sometimes dating back several decades.[3] More recently, EU Statistics on Income and Living Conditions (EU-SILC) provides comprehensive panel data for EU member-states; it is used for the EU's social indicators on social inclusion and pensions. For our analysis of the public–private mix, we opted to analyse cross-nationally the most recent survey data on elderly people (SHARE, ELSA) that allow a breakdown of public and private pensions.[4] We also use poverty and income indicators from LIS and EU-SILC as well as public and private pension recipient data from SHARE/ELSA, interpreting the findings in light of cross-national variations in the changing public–private mix and private pension governance as documented in the country chapters and the two other comparative chapters of this volume.

In this chapter, we first discuss the institutional differences in the public–private mix, distinguishing *mature* from *emerging* multipillar systems and *hybrid* from *dominantly public* pension systems. We then discuss an analytical model that highlights the main sources of inequalities in pension income, in particular the interaction of working-life and pension systems. In the fourth section, we discuss the cross-national institutional variations with respect to the public first tier of minimum income support, the public and private second-tier earnings-related pensions, and the particularities of private pensions. In the empirical analysis, we compare poverty rates over time and across countries, discussing the impact of public pensions. We then analyse in two further sections the recipient rates and income share of private supplementary pensions among the elderly. Although this analysis describes current retirees, conclusions as to the impact of institutional variations in public–private mix and the design of pensions can be drawn for future developments.

2. The public–private mix: the transformation towards multipillar systems

The public–private mix changes with the ongoing transformation towards multipillar systems: the responsibility for income security in old age is shifting from state to private actors (Rein and Turner 2004; Shalev 1996). International organizations, economic policy advisors, and national governments have embraced the idea of shared responsibility for retirement income, advocating a transition away from sole reliance on PAYG-financed public pensions that are

[3] Comparative analyses based on LIS: Behrendt (2000, 2007), Casey and Yamada (2004), Hauser (1999), Korpi and Palme (1998), Pedersen (2004), Prus and Brown (2006), Rein and Behrendt (2004), Smeeding (2001), and Yamada (2002).

[4] Following Callegaro and Wilke (2008), we rely on income data from wave 2 (2006) of SHARE and ELSA wave 3 (2006/7) for the United Kingdom, both survey people aged 50 and older.

viewed as unsustainable in ageing societies. The World Bank (1994) widely propagated a *multipillar* model in which individual retirement income should be drawn from a mix of sources: whereas the first pillar serves essentially redistributive purposes by providing a minimum income in old age, the second is an earnings-related pension tied to employment performance, and the third is a 'topping-up' through individual savings to maintain living standards. First-pillar pensions are expected to come from public schemes, whereas the others should be private provisions (OECD 2007b: 21).[5] The Swiss pension system comes empirically close to this three-pillar model: a contributory public pension for every resident, an earnings-related occupational pension provided by all employers, and voluntary saving schemes offered by banks.

In order to analyse pension systems, we distinguish between three *pillars* according to the main provider (Goodin and Rein 2001) but also discern three *tiers* based on their income function. The concept of pillars captures the public–private mix in governance, while tiers its purpose with respect to income. The first public pillar comprises mandatory state-administered pensions, largely financed as PAYG schemes. The second private pillar subsumes occupational pension schemes set up by the employer or jointly by the bargaining partners (employers and unions). The third pillar is based on the individual's decision, comprising personal pension plans (savings schemes) with financial institutions. We distinguish three tiers according to their goals in income maintenance. The first tier is provided by public basic pensions, means-tested flat-rate benefits, or minimum contributory pensions to secure a minimum income in old age as part of a poverty-prevention policy. The second tier seeks the maintenance of achieved living standards through earnings-related benefits with a strong relationship between contributions and benefits; these can be provided by both public and private pensions. The third tier serves as 'top-up' savings, often particularly relevant for higher-income groups.

Our aim is to relate differences in the public–private mix and the governance of private pensions with poverty and inequality outcomes in old age across the selected European countries. From a cross-national study, Korpi and Palme (1998) concluded that there might be a 'paradox of redistribution': 'The more we target benefits at the poor only and the more concerned we are with creating equality via equal public transfers to all, the less likely we are to reduce poverty and inequality' (681–2). When public pensions are heavily redistributive and target poverty, broad public support may be lacking and minimum benefits may be insufficient to reduce poverty. Moreover, the more a public system is oriented towards minimum security, the more scope there is for private pension

---

[5] In our empirical analysis of private pensions, we focus on occupational pensions since personal pensions still play a minor role (except the United Kingdom) and responses are frequently missing, in which case we presumed that respondents do not have personal pensions.

development, thus often leading to uneven access and unequal benefits above minimum benefits as is the case in basic security systems without fully developed earnings-related state pensions. Korpi and Palme (1998) show that more 'encompassing' pension systems (like Sweden and Finland) combine both poverty reduction and income maintenance, reinforcing broader political support. In 'corporatist' pension systems (Germany and France), the main aim is to maintain living standards in old age, thereby largely crowding out the scope for private pensions. Paradoxically, these systems reduce poverty more than some meagre basic security systems (Britain, but also Canada and the United States), although not as much as the Nordic encompassing systems.

Given the long interval between reforms and their effects, the timing of private pension development is crucial for its impact on old age income. From a comparative perspective, the institutionalization of *multipillarization* varies considerably across Europe: some countries have been early in their shift towards private solutions, while others lag behind. Mature multipillar systems, in particular the basic security *cum* private pensions of Britain, the Netherlands, and Switzerland, will be compared to those countries that maintain a dominant Bismarckian public pillar, such as Belgium, Germany, and Italy. In addition, we discuss some in-between cases: Finland and France with mandatory semi-private pensions as well as Denmark and Sweden with more recently expanded private supplementary pensions. We will look at these four different configurations of public–private mix in order to derive some a priori expectations of their potential impact on poverty and inequality.

The *mature multipillar systems* found in the Netherlands, Switzerland, and the United Kingdom largely follow a Beveridge tradition of public universal (basic) security that seeks to reduce severe poverty, while private pensions emerged in the post-war period to maintain income. The Netherlands was very early in advancing collectively negotiated occupational pensions to supplement the public basic pension, developing a close linkage between both that tends to equalize retirement income. In Switzerland, firm-sponsored occupational pensions, made mandatory in 1985, coexist with the relatively low but universal public old age insurance. In the United Kingdom, funded occupational pensions sponsored by firms coexisted with the rather meagre post-war public basic pension long before employers were allowed to 'contract out' of the second state pension introduced in 1978. A further reform in 1986 extended this opt-out to DC personal pensions, while the State Second Pension (S2P) after the 2002 reform is being transformed into a flat-rate benefit. The share of private pension recipients increased from around 20 per cent of British elderly residents in 1980s to around 60 per cent in 1990s (Behrendt 2000). Thus, we expect to find a rather unequal pattern of pension coverage and private share in pension income in Britain: low-income groups tend to rely on the two state pensions, while the medium- and higher- income groups are likely to have contracted out private pensions. In all three multipillar systems, earnings-related occupational pensions play an important role, supplementing public basic security, particularly for those income groups that expect benefits above the state-guaranteed minimum. As these private pensions are largely funded, their importance can also be seen from the accumulated assets of pension fund capitalism (see Chapter 13).

Among the traditional Beveridge systems, Denmark and Sweden have developed more recently into *emergent multipillar systems*. In Sweden, negotiated occupational pensions played a somewhat limited role, given the encompassing public pension system with a universal basic pension (since 1913) and an earnings-related supplementary pension (since 1960). The 1998 reform replaced the two public pensions by a multipillar system with a public pension guarantee-tested against other transfers, a contributory earnings-related public pension, and a mandatory funded personal pension, while the four coexisting occupational pension schemes negotiated by unions and employers underwent some transformation towards funded DC schemes. In Denmark, the public basic pension remains the main income source. After unsatisfactory attempts to introduce second-tier state pensions, supplementary pensions negotiated by unions and employers became more widespread in the private sector since the 1990s. Both cases constitute interesting alternative paths seen from the crowding-out perspective, leaving more (Denmark) or less (Sweden) developmental scope for private pensions. An analysis with LIS data of the mid-1990s shows that nearly all Swedish elderly residents already had occupational pensions but these contributed only one-fifth of their income, while Danish private pensions were somewhat higher in value but only for every fifth elderly person (Behrendt 2000).

The Bismarckian *dominantly public systems*, found in Belgium, Germany, and Italy, still rely mainly on the contributory earnings-related public pillar, and occupational pensions and private savings coexist particularly for those higher-income groups insufficiently protected by the public scheme. More recently, there have been efforts in all three countries to increase private pensions, while future public benefits will be scaled back. In Belgium, occupational and personal pensions have gained in popularity since the 1990s, not least by reforms and social partner agreements. In Germany, the hallmark of Bismarckian social insurance, voluntary occupational pensions coexisted with public pensions (regulated since the 1970s), while more recent pension reforms added voluntary personal pensions with tax subsidies for low-income groups in an effort to fill the future income gap left by declining public pension benefits. In Italy, recent reforms have also led to the partial transformation of mandatory end-of-service-pay schemes into occupational or personal pensions. These dominantly public pension systems are important cases in order to test the crowding-out thesis, that is, that generous earnings-related public pensions limit the scope for development of private pensions. However, the crowding-out effect might be limited in the case of low contribution ceilings for public pensions, thereby leaving a larger replacement gap for higher-income groups. Moreover, future cutbacks will increase the income gap between former earnings and public pension income, thereby slowly 'crowding in' the scope for potential development of private pensions.

In addition, we consider two *hybrid multipillar systems* that provide mandatory semi-private occupational pensions with a second-tier function: France and Finland. With respect to governance, the second-tier pension schemes in the private sector in France (see Chapter 4) were negotiated by the social partners and made mandatory in 1972, providing the same income maintenance as Bismarckian state pensions elsewhere. Also, Finland (see Chapter 8) has occupational pensions which were made compulsory in the 1960s, these are difficult to classify as either public or private since they are mandatory earnings-related pensions like public contributory pensions but they are partly administered by the social partners and partially funded via private financial institutes. We consider these French and Finnish second-tier pensions as 'hybrid' systems. They indicate that negotiated but publicly mandated pensions can provide income maintenance for medium- to high-income groups, thereby largely crowding out the need for voluntary private pensions, at least until recently. Coverage is nearly universal for the Finnish mandatory occupational pensions; nearly all retired households receive these important pensions already in the 1980s when the basic pension was still in place (Behrendt 2000).[6]

3. From earnings during working life to pension income during retirement

Pension income derives from acquired social rights to public benefits, the promised defined benefits and returns on past contributions for private supplementary pensions. The public–private mix, in particular the redistributive nature of basic pensions, and the inequality-reinforcing character of earnings-related pensions (both public and private ones) are important factors in mediating or reproducing market inequalities in old age. With the help of a stylized analytical model (see Figure 14.1), we analyse how social rights and contributions during the working life are translated into pension income during retirement. Two interacting factors, (*a*) the (non-)employment and earnings profile during working life and (*b*) the intervening rules governing the public and private pension systems, interact to produce the resulting retirement income. Inequalities can arise through market forces, through pension systems' features, and also through early or prolonged work as well as through an interaction of all three. Our interest lies particularly in how the second institutional level (the

---

[6] Unfortunately, the empirical analyses cannot be undertaken comprehensively for Finland because it is not included in SHARE.

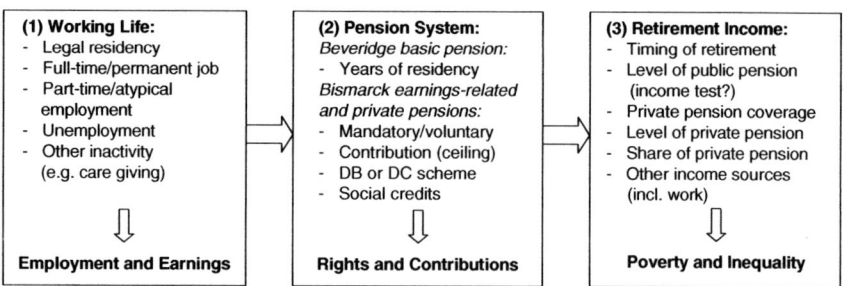

Figure 14.1 Stylized model of retirement income

pension system) interacts with the first and how strong this interaction determines the third stage (retirement income).

3.1 Working-life inequalities

The main sources of income inequality are earnings from dependent work or self-employment, and also profits from investments for those with assets. At the societal level, the overall level of employment and productivity is important in providing the economic resources to support current pension claims in PAYG-systems but also to contribute to funded pensions as savings for the future. For individuals, earnings from employment are important in order to contribute to pension insurance and to additionally save for old age. In most cases, employers contribute to social insurance, and in some cases also to private occupational pensions in order to attract and retain employees. Employment is an important precondition for contributory social insurance but especially for occupational pensions, while sufficient earnings are needed for individual contributions to personal pensions. Employment rates vary considerably across Europe with respect to female and to male labour force participation (see Table 14.1). In the Nordic countries, Switzerland and the United Kingdom, employment rates for both groups are higher, while employment rates are lower in Continental Europe. Not only non-employment but also temporary and part-time employment may increase the risk of poverty during working life and thus lead to insufficient pension contributions.

While unemployment and low pay may have been traditional social risks, 'new' social risks, in particular the problems in reconciling work and family, have increased (Bonoli 2006; Taylor-Gooby 2004). Gender inequality in employment and earnings can be a major cause of later inequality in retirement. In the past, the male-breadwinner model led to low labour force participation of women due to family-care responsibilities with major consequences for their employment attachment and retirement income (Esping-Andersen 2002; Lewis 1992, 2001). The assumption was that the husband's current earnings are

Table 14.1 Labour market statistics by age group, OECD, 1990 and 2008

	15–64						55–64		65+	
	Employment rate		% Temporary employment		% Part-time employees		Employment rate		Employment rate	
	1990	2008	1990	2008	1990	2008	1990	2008	1990	2008
Men										
Belgium	68.1	68.3	3.3	5.9	4.4	5.9	34.3	41.3	1.9	2.8
Britain	82.1	78.5	3.7	4.7	5.3	10.2	62.4	67.7	8.3	10.7
Denmark	80.1	82.4	10.6	7.8	10.2	12.9	65.6	64.2	12.8	9.3
Finland	77.9	73.4	15.6	11.3	4.8	8.2	46.3	57.0	9.2	10.7
France	69.7	69.2	9.4	13.1	4.5	5.2	43.0	40.5	3.7	2.1
Germany	75.7	75.9	9.8	14.3	2.3	8.2	52.0	61.7	4.6	5.7
Italy	69.2	70.3	3.9	12.1	4.4	6.6	51.9	45.5	7.1	6.2
The Netherlands	75.7	81.9	6.1	16.7	13.4	16.2	44.2	60.2	–	7.5
Sweden	85.2	78.1	12.4	13.4	5.3	9.6	74.5	73.6	12.3	16.3
Switzerland	93.4	85.4	11.4	13.4	6.8	9.0	85.5	77.0	26.0	13.4
Women										
Belgium	40.8	55.7	8.6	9.7	28.8	33.8	9.4	24.4	0.6	1.0
Britain	62.8	66.9	7.0	6.0	39.5	37.7	36.7	49.0	3.3	4.7
Denmark	70.6	74.4	11.0	9.5	29.7	23.7	42.4	51.4	3.2	3.1
Finland	71.5	69.0	21.0	18.8	10.6	15.1	39.7	55.8	3.4	4.0
France	50.3	60.1	12.0	15.4	22.5	22.7	28.8	36.0	1.5	1.0
Germany	52.2	64.3	11.6	14.9	29.8	38.6	22.4	46.0	2.2	2.6
Italy	36.2	47.2	7.6	16.4	18.4	31.0	15.2	24.0	2.2	1.2
The Netherlands	47.5	70.2	10.2	20.0	52.5	59.9	15.9	41.1	–	2.4
Sweden	81.0	73.2	16.8	18.7	24.5	19.6	64.7	66.9	5.1	8.1
Switzerland	69.4	73.5	14.3	13.2	42.6	45.9	43.7	60.0	15.1	6.5

Note: * Swiss data from 1991.
Source: OECD (2009a).

393

sufficient to support the whole family during working life and later his social security claims would provide for the couple's retirement, thus women would derive indirect benefits through their husbands' or a widow pension. In recent decades, increased female labour force participation followed social and economic changes; it was also promoted by the European Union's Lisbon strategy. The increase in female employment, however, was in many countries largely made possible by the extension of part-time and temporary jobs, particularly in the service sector (Fagan and Rubery 1996). Furthermore, increased rates of divorce and single parenthood reinforce the problem of insufficient protection in old age.

Moreover, job security has become increasingly unstable in the post-industrial period. As the risk of unemployment and non-standard employment (fixed-term, part-time, and mini-jobs without social benefits) is higher among the less qualified, women with small children, single mothers, and young people, these social risk groups are unlikely to collect sufficient pension contributions to prevent poverty unless minimum social guarantees are provided. Furthermore, reduced pension contributions are often collected during unemployment, non-standard employment, or child-rearing periods even if social credits are provided in some public schemes. Frequent or long periods of low or no contributions thus could lower pension claims in contributory systems, making older people dependent on minimum guarantees or social assistance. Early exit from employment has been partly induced by favourable early retirement options but often also forced upon older workers due to restructuring, affecting particularly those with lower or outdated qualifications. Phases of unemployment close to statutory retirement age have led in many cases to voluntary or even forced early retirement, leading to reduced pension benefits than otherwise, though such 'early exit' policies have now been widely reversed (Ebbinghaus 2006).

3.2 Pension system design

The employment patterns and income differences during working life are mitigated or reproduced by the public and private pension contribution–benefit rules. An important factor is the first-tier function of the public system, while the second- and third-tier functions of supplementary pensions reproduce or amplify market inequalities in old age. All public pension systems provide the *first*-tier function of minimum income security in old age, either through Beveridge universal basic pensions or means-tested social assistance in Bismarckian systems. Not only the Bismarckian earnings-related social insurance but also Beveridge-plus systems that have in addition to public basic pensions a second earnings-related state pension serve the additional *second*-tier function of income maintenance. They help to uphold achieved living standards in old age, particularly for those with previous medium to high earnings.

(1) The public *first*-tier systems – universal basic pensions, means-tested social assistance, or social pensions – provide a minimum income independent of an individual's previous working history, thereby aiming to reduce the risk of poverty. Following the idea of citizenship rights (Marshall 1950), basic pensions require a stipulated period of legal residency, independent of employment history. Basic pensions could thus be reduced if residency years (or contribution records) are not sufficient, a problem particularly for first-generation migrants. For the majority of people, however, residency-based flat-rate pensions are commonly supplemented by public or private earnings-related pensions that depend on contributions during employment. In systems with transfer-tested minimum benefits or means-tested social assistance, these benefits will be reduced or denied when second-tier pensions exceed the guaranteed income minimum.

(2) For *second*-tier earnings-related contributory pensions, individual employment and earnings are of great influence, thus market inequalities are likely to be reproduced in old age for most recipients. However, the effect is mitigated by social and redistributive rules, common in public pensions (Monticone et al. 2008). First of all, earnings-related public pensions are mandatory for all dependent employed. Although all or some groups of self-employed are often exempted, they may voluntarily contribute. In some cases, employment contracts with few hours or low earnings are also exempted from public pension contribution based on the assumption that such 'mini-jobs' are carried out by students, housewives, and retired people who would not need or could not substantially contribute to old age insurance. In case of unemployment, public pension contributions remain mandatory, sometimes paid directly by the unemployment insurance, though often only at a reduced level of former earnings. Interruptions of employment due to family or other caregiving have become increasingly recognized and up to several years can often be credited as contribution years (see Table 14.4). These social rules will mitigate the impact of limited employment periods on final benefits, although given that these regulations are relatively recent, their effect will narrow the gender differences more for future than for current retirees. Depending on benefit levels of the public minimum and earnings-related pensions, the need for additional private supplementary pensions might arise to maintain living standards in old age. This will be particularly the case when public pensions are limited by a low maximum ceiling and thus replacement rates decline with higher income, widening the gap between past living standard and retirement income.

(3) Private *second*- (occupational) or *third*-tier (personal) pensions are supplementing insufficient public benefits or top up already relatively high public benefits. Such incomes are very much linked to employment

status and earnings during working life. In terms of coverage, unless private pensions are mandatory for all employees or a collective agreement stipulates it for a sector, the access to occupational pensions depends on the employer's willingness to provide such schemes for their employees. In addition, personal pensions are voluntary with the exception of the mandatory Swedish Premium Pension. In some systems, self-employed persons have their own (mandatory or voluntary) occupational pensions, otherwise they can choose between voluntary personal pensions. Besides inequality in coverage, the final private pension benefits depend on whether the scheme is a DB or DC scheme or a mix of both (see Chapter 13 for details):

- *Defined-benefit* schemes provide pensions based on the years of employment and past earnings. Occupational schemes are tied to employment with a particular employer, and special rules apply when switching employers (portability) and ending employment (vesting rights), though portability is easier in the case of collective schemes within a sector than between employer schemes. The sponsor (employer or pension fund) will need to assure future liabilities, thus the risk of underfunding remains with the sponsor, while the beneficiary expects the promised benefit, often a share of final salary. In case of employer bankruptcy, special reinsurance or protection measures are commonly provided by law or self-regulation.

- *Defined-contribution* schemes depend on the investment, thus the contribution rate and the rate of return are key variables. Guarantees or prescribed return rates are rarely stipulated by law (Swiss occupational pension and German Riester personal pension are exceptions); otherwise the risk of default and less-than-expected returns depends on the investment portfolio. The 2008/9 financial crisis showed the vulnerability of pension funds with considerable exposure to high-risk equities. Regulation may limit the degree of risky investments, while in some countries no restrictions apply (Denmark) or only a 'prudent investor' convention applies under common law (the United Kingdom). Whereas DB schemes entail risk sharing by the employer, the DC schemes shift the risk to the beneficiary, creating uncertainty and insecurity. While DB schemes require some waiting periods, DC benefits are usually immediately vested and usually easily portable.

Hybrid schemes combine DB and DC features, such as the Italian end-of-service-pay, the French PERCO, and the British Stakeholder Pension (EU-SPC 2008: 11–15). Occupational and personal pensions are often fostered by tax deductions for private pension contributions or direct subsidies (for instance for low-income groups) may be provided. Thus, the state indirectly supports these redistributive goals through hidden tax expenditure. These policies could increase inequality when tax advantages benefit mainly higher-income groups or decrease inequality when only lower-income groups are receiving subsidies in making contributions. However, whether such tax incentives lead to more or less inequality and to which level of tax expenditure depends primarily on the actual take-up rates.

3.3 Inequalities in retirement income

Market income inequality may thus be reproduced in old-age pension transfers through the employment-contribution linkage. It may be reduced by general redistributive public policies (minimum pensions, social assistance, and housing benefits), whereas it is amplified by the earnings-related contribution logic of public and private supplementary pensions. In addition, the availability and level of benefits may also depend on the timing of retirement, thus earlier exit from work than the statutory retirement age may be possible with or without financial penalties (actuarial deductions), while prolonged employment may increase benefits further. Disposable income in retirement is also complemented by other sources of income and savings that are not public transfers or private pensions, such as life insurance contracts, income from rents, or interest on investments, and indirectly influenced by benefits from health-care system regulations. Personal wealth, in particular self-owned housing, could provide substantial value in addition to transfer income, although wealth is even more unequally distributed than past earnings (Gornick et al. 2009). Moreover, earnings from work during retirement are chosen to supplement public and private pensions, depending on income tests, taxation rules, and insufficient retirement income. The phenomenon of working pensioners is well known in the United States but also occurs in some European countries. Some groups of self-employed and professionals tend to work beyond official retirement age, particularly when they are exempted from the Bismarckian contributory public pension (e.g. Germany). The employment rate for men (and to a lesser degree for women) aged 65 and older is still relatively high in Nordic countries, Switzerland and the United Kingdom (see Table 14.1).

In Beveridge countries with basic flat-rate pensions, private supplementary pensions may counterbalance the redistributive effect of the public pension and increase overall income inequality. Given the equivalence principle, Bismarckian earnings-related pensions tend to reproduce inequalities, although private pensions are even more likely to amplify social and gender inequality due to the lack of redistribution or social credits. Past employment practices within firms to secure primarily those in leading positions with occupational 'top-up' plans exacerbate social inequality. Old age income inequality is highly related to primary market inequality measured in both poverty and inequality (see Figure 14.2). There is a high cross-national correlation between severe poverty (less than 40 per cent of the median income) of the working age

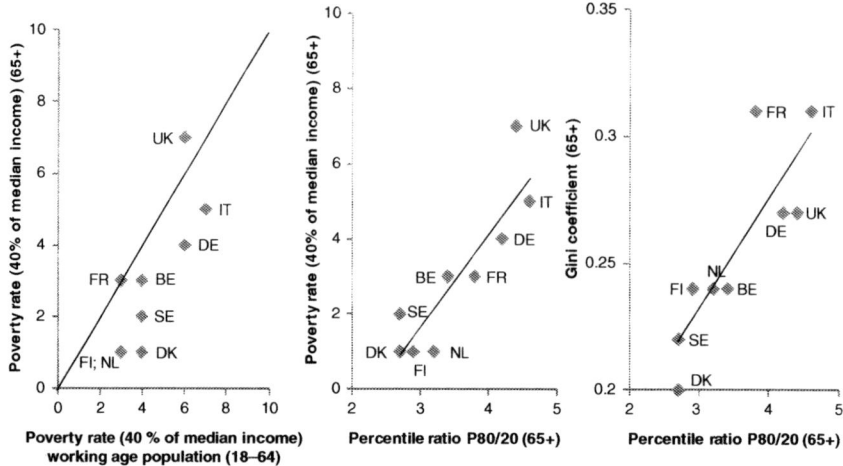

Figure 14.2 Poverty and inequality, EU-SILC 2007, Gini OECD mid-2000s
Source: EU-SILC 2007, OECD Stats.

population (aged 15–64) and severe poverty of the elderly (aged 65 and older), even though poverty tends to be somewhat lower in old age than earlier in the life course. The United Kingdom is the only country where redistribution does not reduce poverty below the percentage of the aged.

Table 14.2 Social benefits of public pensions' first tier (OECD simulation)

Country	Scheme	First tier (% average wage)				First tier (% pension wealth)		
		Total	Tested	Basic	Minimum	Tested	Basic	Minimum
Belgium	EP (min)	28	(22)		28			4.4
Britain	BP*	28	(19)	14	14	0.7	50.0	36.9
Denmark	BP + (GP)	36	(18)	18		13.8	26.3	
Finland	(GP)	(18)	(18)			2.9		
France	EP (min)	23	22		23			4.7
Germany	(assistance)	(19)	(19)			1.5		
Italy	EP (min)				–			
The Netherlands	BP	31		31			41.2	
Sweden	(GP)	(26)	(26)			4.5		
Switzerland	BP/EP	24	24		18	0.2		

Note: (tested); BP: basic state pension; EP: earnings-related pension; GP: guarantee pension (income tested); *including British Second State Pension (S2P).
Source: OECD (2009*b*: 133, 157–8).

The graph in the middle exemplifies that the income distribution of the elderly is also less stratified applying the percentile ratio P80/20. Since there is almost no poverty in the Scandinavian countries and the Netherlands, acquired living standards for the lowest quintile are comparatively high. It is not surprising that the division of the highest income quintile by the lowest income quintile tends to be also lower than in the other countries. Again, Italy and Britain score highest on this inequality indicator.

As a third indicator of income inequality, the Gini coefficient can be linked to the previous graphs. On the right-hand side, we plotted the Gini coefficient for the elderly (65+) against the percentile ratio of the elderly (65+). We find that the Nordic countries and the Netherlands have the lowest scores on both indicators. However, the French Gini coefficient does not match the rather moderate values of the first two indicators: the French income distribution is like other countries that score high on all three indicators (Germany, Italy, and the United Kingdom), characterized by a high poverty gap of those being poor (an indicator not plotted here due to limitations of space). This gap particularly affects the Gini, but not so much the percentile ratio as the poor elderly are a rather small group in France.

4. The minimum income guarantee: public first-tier pensions and poverty

In order to explain these poverty and inequality patterns, we need to analyse the institutional differences between public and private pensions. Our comparative analysis of institutional differences begins with the public *first*-tier pensions (see Table 14.2) that aim to ensure minimum income security – with major consequences for retirement income inequality, in particular poverty. Beveridge basic pensions provide a flat-rate minimum income as a citizenship right (Marshall 1950) to all residents, independent of labour market attachment.[7] While the Dutch basic pension is relatively high (31 per cent of average earnings), the Danish and British basic pensions provide only a relatively low pension for everyone (18 and 14 per cent respectively), though there are additional transfer- or means-tested supplements (18 and 19 per cent) when no other pension income is available. Until the late 1990s, Sweden and Finland provided basic pensions, thereafter they switched to minimum guarantees in case of insufficient earnings-related pension benefits; these are relatively high

---

[7] In the Beveridge (non-contributory) basic pensions systems, fifty years of residency are needed in the Netherlands, in Denmark forty years, while in Finland (since 1996) and in Sweden (since 1998) a transfer-tested guaranteed pension is provided. Full contribution years are necessary in the British basic pensions (44/39 years for men/women) and Swiss public pension (44/43 years), the gender difference will be gradually phased out in the future.

in Sweden (26 per cent) and much lower in Finland (18 per cent). We also count the universal Swiss public pension as a basic security system, even though it is earnings-related but within a rather small band (between 18 and 24 per cent). As a result of the basic pension (or minimum guarantee), pensioners without any earnings-related *second*-tier pensions will still be receiving more than 30 per cent of average income in these countries, except in Britain (19 per cent), Finland (18 per cent), and Switzerland (18 per cent). Among the Beveridge systems, the basic pension remains the dominant income source in the United Kingdom (50 per cent of pension wealth), the Netherlands (41 per cent), and Denmark (26 per cent plus 14 per cent transfer-tested supplement). In Finland and Sweden, the transfer-tested supplements contribute only a small share of overall transfers (less than 5 per cent), thus both systems mainly rely on their earnings-related pensions for income security.

In Bismarckian countries, minimum income protection plays a minor role except for the very few social groups that have insufficient contributory pension claims. In such cases, minimum income security is provided either by means-tested social assistance as in Belgium and Germany or by means-tested supplements as in France. In addition, a minimum 'social pension' for those who have paid into the contributory system for at least some years is provided in Belgium, Italy, and France but not Germany. However, these first-tier pension benefits amount to a rather small share (less than 5 per cent) of all pension transfers. These means-tested assistance or minimum pensions are less important as a result of social credits (or subsidized contributions) granted in contributory social insurance, including periods of unemployment, caregiving, school and university attendance, and civil or military service. Thanks to these credits, social risk groups may receive higher earnings-related pensions than they would have received otherwise. The scope of these non-contributory social benefits is difficult to estimate, although in France and Germany the political debate has highlighted the need for state subsidies of such social insurance policies.

The comparison across countries and time as well as between the elderly and the working population alters considerably when we analyse poverty rates measured at 40, 50 or 60 per cent of median income (see Figure 14.3). A first analysis of *severe* poverty rates in old age (measured at 40 per cent of median income) reveals that Beveridge basic security is not always capable of effectively reducing poverty despite their explicit purpose to do so, while some contributory Bismarckian systems are better suited to reduce poverty, despite focusing on status maintenance. The lowest severe (40 per cent threshold) poverty rates are found in the case of the relatively generous Dutch basic pension as well as at the Danish basic pension (and tested supplement). Until recent reforms, Finland and Sweden showed very low poverty rates for the universal basic and earnings-related pensions (Kangas and Palme 1996), but also the new system with transfer-tested pension guarantees fares very well. In contrast, the United

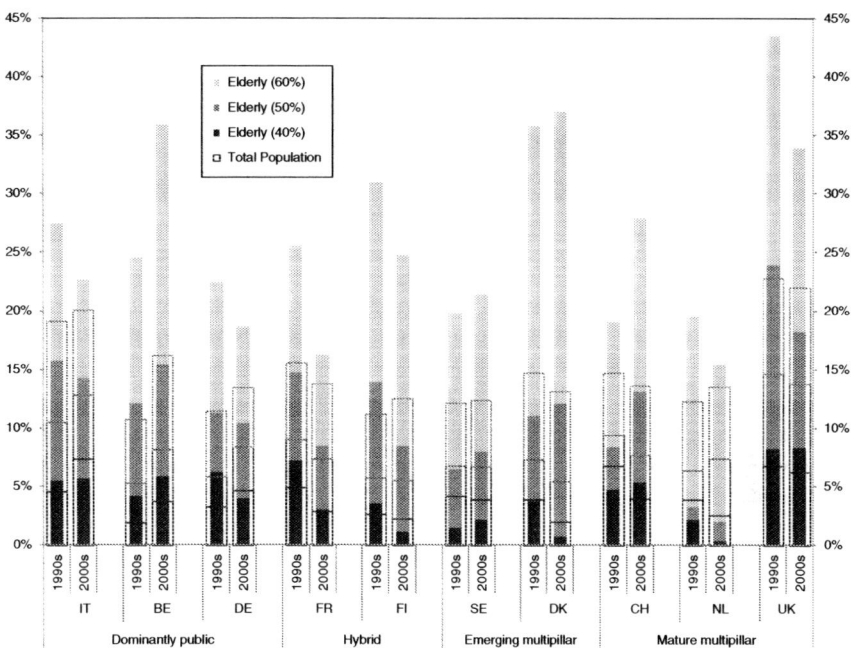

Figure 14.3 Poverty rates for the elderly and total population, LIS 1990s and 2000s

Note: Poverty rates: equivalent disposable household income (square root of number of persons in household) below 40, 50 or 60 per cent median income; elderly: 65 and older; total: total population.

Source: LIS key figures 1988–92; 1998–2002.

Kingdom has had the highest severe poverty rate over the last two decades due to its meagre basic pension. Among the Bismarckian systems, severe poverty was somewhat higher than in the Beveridge systems (except the United Kingdom), though there was also a positive trend since the 1990s, most pronounced in France and Germany (see Figure 14.3). Belgium and Italy reach a medium level of severe poverty (about 5 per cent). In comparison to the working age population, severe poverty is less common today among older people in all countries but in Belgium, Switzerland, and the United Kingdom.

Old age poverty (at the 50 per cent level) exceeds the rate of the working age population in all countries (see Figure 14.3), except in the Netherlands, thanks to its high basic pension. Medium-level poverty rates are achieved by Finland, Sweden, France, and Germany; these are systems with relatively well-developed earnings-related pensions. Some of the other multipillar systems, in particular Denmark, Switzerland, and the United Kingdom, have relatively high poverty rates as do the two Bismarckian systems of Belgium and Italy. When we consider the at-risk-of-poverty rate (at 60 per cent level), the elderly population is in all cases more at risk than the working population, although the difference is less significant and relatively low (up to 20 per cent) in the Netherlands, France (2000s), Germany, and Sweden. In the other countries, whether Beveridge multipillar systems (Britain, Denmark, Switzerland), mixed systems (Finland) or pure Bismarckian systems (Belgium, Italy), the contributory earnings-related elements of public or private pensions lead to significant levels of at-risk-of-poverty for more than every fifth elderly person.

Cross-national differences are revealed by additional disaggregation as to gender and household context when we compare the at-risk-of-poverty rate (60 per cent of median income) for all countries but Switzerland using the most recent EU-SILC data (see Table 14.3). Looking at the age distribution, the elderly population (age 65 and older) has a higher risk of poverty than the working age population (18–64). The difference is less pronounced and relatively low in the Netherlands and Sweden as well as France, Germany, and Italy, while it is substantially higher in Britain, Belgium, Denmark, and Finland. A gender divide is observable in all countries (at least 20 per cent higher for women than men), but poverty is particularly pronounced for women in Sweden (twice as high) and somewhat higher in Germany, Italy, and Finland (40 per cent higher). With their longer life expectancy, women tend to survive their male spouse and are thus more likely to live alone than are men of the same age. As a result of the gender-related employment and earnings-gap, women are more likely to have lower individual pension claims from earnings-related pensions; their survivor benefits or basic pensions may also be relevant. The significance of private pensions may be limited for those with low qualifications, part-time jobs, or fixed-term jobs as they are likely to be excluded from occupational pensions.

The results for those aged 75 and older are primarily driven by the higher female share in this age group and their poor employment histories. A separate analysis of family status also reveals that couples are less likely to be at risk of being poor than those living alone, particularly in comparison to single women who often only receive small widow pensions. With the exception of the Netherlands, single women have a somewhat (40–50 per cent) higher risk of poverty in Belgium, Denmark, and Britain; a substantially (80–100 per cent) higher risk in Germany, Italy, and France; and a risk in Finland and Sweden more than three times higher. Comparatively, single older women in Britain, Finland, and Italy face the highest poverty risk, followed by Belgium and Germany. The relatively high poverty rates for female elderly in Scandinavian countries relate to the fact that a comparatively high share of widowed women stays in single households, while in continental European countries and particularly in Italy a higher share of multigenerational households exists.

Table 14.3 At-risk-of-poverty rate (60% median income) by gender, age group, and household type, EU-SILC 2007

Age group (years)		Belgium	Britain	Denmark	Finland	France	Germany	Italy	The Netherlands	Sweden
18–64	Total	13	15	11	11	12	15	18	9	10
	Men	12	14	11	12	11	14	16	8	11
	Women	13	16	11	11	13	16	19	10	10
55–64	Total	14	17	4	11	10	17	15	7	5
	Men	12	17	4	11	10	16	13	6	5
	Women	15	18	5	11	10	18	16	8	5
65+	Total	23	30	18	22	13	17	22	10	11
	Men	21	27	16	18	12	14	18	9	7
	Women	25	32	19	25	14	20	25	11	14
	Women/Men	*1.2*	*1.2*	*1.2*	*1.4*	*1.2*	*1.4*	*1.4*	*1.2*	*2.0*
75+	Total	26	34	23	28	16	18	23	10	16
	Men	24	32	22	20	14	15	17	10	9
	Women	27	36	23	32	16	20	26	10	20
	Women/Men	*1.1*	*1.1*	*1.0*	*1.6*	*1.1*	*1.3*	*1.5*	*1.0*	*2.2*
Couple 65+	Total	21	26	14	12	9	13	19	9	6
Single 65+	Total	29	40	20	39	18	24	34	10	19
	Single/Couple	*1.4*	*1.5*	*1.4*	*3.3*	*2.0*	*1.8*	*1.8*	*1.1*	*3.2*
	Men	22	35	21	42	17	15	22	7	10
	Women	31	41	20	38	18	28	37	11	22
	Women/Men	*1.4*	*1.2*	*1.0*	*0.9*	*1.1*	*1.9*	*1.7*	*1.6*	*2.2*

Note: Ratios in italics.
Source: EU-SILC 2007 (pension indicators) cit in Eurostat (2007).

5. Reproducing market inequality through public or private second-tier pensions?

The preceding analysis of poverty and first-tier public pensions indicated the importance of second-tier systems for income inequality above the severe poverty line. We therefore now turn to the public and private second-tier systems. Whereas status maintenance is the main purpose of Bismarckian mandatory earnings-related public pensions, in some Beveridge systems a 'second' state pension (Britain, Sweden) was introduced in addition to the basic pension. But in the mature multipillar systems, the second-tier function is largely provided by private pensions (in Britain due to the opting-out of private pensions), thus potentially leading to increased social inequalities, despite first-tier pensions, due to the fact that occupational pensions are less universal and redistributive. The earnings-related public pensions in Belgium, Germany, France, and Italy, and also the reformed systems in Finland and Sweden put particular weight on the linkage to employment. By and large, retirement benefits mirror the years and values of contributions paid during employment. The more the equivalence principle applies to mandatory earnings-related pensions, the more a constant replacement rate is guaranteed for all levels of income (in most cases up to a ceiling).

The overall replacement rate provides an indicator of the relationship between past earnings and current pensions, before (gross) or after taxes (net): the degree of equivalence. If there is an upper ceiling in calculating earnings-related public benefits, a pension gap may arise for those with higher earnings, leaving more scope for private pensions. Only Finland's earnings-related pension has no upper limit (see Table 14.4), thereby crowding out the necessity for voluntary supplementary pensions. Among the Bismarckian pensions, Italy has the highest ceiling (nearly 3.7 times the average earnings), while Germany has a lower upper ceiling (1.5 times), and the Belgian earnings-related pension has a comparatively rather low ceiling (about average earnings). France's public first-tier general scheme also has a low ceiling, but the supplementary pensions in the private sector have higher ceilings, while public employees receive a favourable earnings-related pension. The scope for private pensions is thus larger in Belgium and Germany than in Italy and France.

Since the Beveridge flat-rate public schemes lack status-maintaining elements, the necessity to save was provided either by state earnings-related pensions or private pensions, which was particularly crucial for middle-to-high-income earners. As a consequence, flat-rate schemes without a mandatory second state pension stimulate the crowding in of private second-tier pensions. Britain's mandatory second-state pension (S2P) also has a low ceiling (about average earnings) and increasingly flat-rate character, thus 'contracting out' to occupational (and, since 1986) personal pensions seems a preferable option for

Table 14.4 Public and private second-tier pensions, mid-2000s

Country	Second tier	Coverage	Contribution (% earnings)	Ceiling (%AW)	Benefit	Social credits
Belgium	State	Mandatory	16.4	–118	DB	Yes
Britain	State (1st + 2nd)	Mandatory	23.8	15–105	DB	Yes
	Occupational or personal	Opt-out of S2P			DB/DC	No
Denmark	Occupational	Agreement	11.8		DC	No
Finland	Semi-public	Mandatory	21.4	None	DB	Yes
France	Semi-public	Mandatory	24.0	–99	DBP	Yes
Germany	State	Mandatory	19.5	22–149	DBP	Yes
	Occupational	Voluntary/ agreement			DB/DC	No
	Personal	Voluntary	4.0		DC	(Sub)
Italy	State	Mandatory	32.7	–367	NDC	Yes
The Netherlands	Occupational	Agreement	28.1	None	DB	No
Sweden	State	Mandatory	16.4	–111	NDC	Yes
	State (personal)	Mandatory	2.5	–367	DC	No
	Occupational	Agreement	4.5		DB)DC	No
Switzerland	Occupational	Mandatory	9.8	32–106	DB	No

Note: %AW: average worker earnings; DB: defined benefits; DBP: defined benefits based on contribution points; DC: defined contribution; NDC: notional defined contribution; data for 2004 (Italy after 1995 reform; Sweden after 1999 reform); S2P: State Second Pension (the United Kingdom).

Source: OECD (2009*b*: table III.2, 157–8); OECD (2007*a*: table I.2, 28–30; table II.1.2, 63).

medium- to high-income groups. The mandatory Swiss private occupational pensions have a relatively low ceiling (about average earnings), while the Dutch quasi-mandatory private occupational pensions have no ceiling at all. Given the existence of universal basic security, the Swiss and Dutch occupational pensions are linked to the former and insure only benefits above the expected public pension. The Danish occupational pensions are DC schemes without any ceiling (but varying contribution rates) that provide benefits in addition to the basic pension (18 per cent of average earnings), though insufficient private occupational benefits would be increased by an income-tested supplement (up to 36 per cent of average earnings).

Using the OECD's simulated replacement rates (2009*b*) for an assumed full-time average earner based on current rules in public and mandatory private pensions,[8] the pension gap can be studied. Since gender differences, different

---

[8] These calculations are based on an individual starting her or his employment career in 2006 and retiring in the year 2046 without employment breaks.

household contexts, and special social risk groups are not taken into consideration here, these replacement rates need to be compared across countries with caution. The Belgian and German statutory earnings-related pensions guarantee a relatively low overall replacement rate for an average worker (42 and 43 per cent respectively), declining more rapidly for higher-income groups in Belgium than in Germany (representing the income ceiling effect). The scope for private supplementary pensions is particularly pronounced in both countries, while the Italian replacement rate is higher (68 per cent) and does not decline until relatively high earnings (twice the average earnings). OECD estimates with respect to participation in voluntary systems in prospective employment careers indicate that at least some of the employed may be well covered. However, participation may be primarily linked to sector or tenure, leaving access to such pensions especially problematic for those groups with low income and occupations with no specific regulations on occupational pension plans. The French first- and second-tier pensions in the private sector provide a medium replacement level for those with low-to-medium previous earnings (above 50 per cent), and somewhat lower replacement rates for those earning beyond the median wage earner. The Finnish occupational pension achieves a uniform replacement level (56 per cent) due to the lack of any ceiling, though those people with very low past earnings receive income-tested guaranteed benefits. Additional voluntary private pensions are not considered by the OECD for France and Finland.

The Beveridge or mixed systems combine public first-tier and (public or private) supplementary pensions (see Table 14.5). Denmark and the Netherlands achieve the highest level of gross replacement rates for low-to-median average workers (above 80 per cent), while the other countries are less generous and the United Kingdom seems to be particularly thrifty. However, in contrast to the other countries, the United Kingdom's opting out per se mandates inclusion in occupational and personal pensions (calculated separately in the OECD's model). When including the private pension plans, the British system seems to work quite well in terms of replacement; however, since about half of the workforce currently stays in the second-state pension, one should be sceptical whether replacement levels will increase for the majority of British pensioners in the future. The situation differs from the other multipillar systems, where widespread private pension coverage guarantees a mixed income for most beneficiaries.

In Denmark, the public basic and supplementary pensions are comparatively high for low-wage workers but depend on a test for the pension supplement. State pensions and mandatory private occupational pensions maintain some of the employee's former income, although the share decreases with rising income. This favours, slightly, a crowding in for further voluntary private pensions, despite the comparatively high level of public pension in cross-national perspective. In the Netherlands, the combined basic pension and the

Table 14.5 Gross replacement rates by previous earnings (OECD simulation)

Country	Scheme	OECD gross replacement rate: previous earnings in relation to average earnings					Gap 0.8		Including private	Private only	
		at 0.5	at 0.8	at 1.0	at 1.5	at 2.0	*2.0*		at 1.0	at 1.0	
Belgium	EP	58.1	43.1	42.0	32.5	24.3	*1.8*		58.6	16.6	v
Britain	BP + S2P*	51.0	36.6	30.8	21.3	16.0	*2.3*		70.0	39.2	v
Denmark	BP/(GP) + OP	124.0	94.9	80.3	67.5	63.7	*1.5*		80.3	22.9	m
Finland	(GP) + OP	66.5	56.2	56.2	56.2	56.2	*1.0*		56.2	–	
France	EP (1st + 2nd)	61.7	53.3	53.3	48.5	46.0	*1.2*		53.3	–	
Germany	EP	43.0	43.0	43.0	42.6	32.0	*1.3*		61.3	18.3	v
Italy	EP	67.9	67.9	67.9	67.9	67.9	*1.0*		95.6	27.7	v
The Netherlands	BP + OP	93.4	90.0	88.3	86.6	85.8	*1.1*		88.3	30.2	m
Sweden	(GP) + PP	76.6	64.6	61.5	75.6	81.3	*0.8*		61.5	37.8	m
Switzerland	BP/EP + OP	62.5	62.1	58.3	40.5	30.4	*2.0*		58.3	35.6	m

Note: (tested); BP: basic state pension; EP: earnings-related pension; GP: guarantee pension (income-tested); S2P*: State Second Pension (The United Kingdom); gap: replacement rate for 'low than average' (0.8) divided by replacement rate for high earners (2.0); v: voluntary (not included); m: mandatory (included in OECD gross replacement rate).
Source: OECD (2009b).

supplementary occupational pension maintain a relative high replacement rate for all income groups. In both countries, the quasi-mandatory occupational pension plans contribute more than 50 per cent to the replacement wage of the average earner. Similarly important for the prospective income structures of average earners are the mandatory system in Switzerland and the quasi-mandatory system in Sweden, as both systems contribute one-third of the total replacement rate. The new Swedish public pensions also provide a relatively high level for the lowest income group due to its transfer-test, but the earnings-related and funded pensions will also provide increasingly high levels of gross income replacement, though liable to substantial income taxes.

The OECD prospective replacement rates of (quasi-)mandatory pensions indicate the remaining income gap left for additional private pensions. Systems that already guarantee a high replacement rate even for higher-income earners reduce the necessity of additional private initiatives to maintain living standards. An indicator of this crowding-out potential is calculated by taking the replacement rate of higher-income earners (twice average earnings) in relationship to the below average earners (0.8 times). The need for further private savings is relatively low for Sweden, the Netherlands, and Denmark where quasi-mandatory systems are also quite generous for high-income earners. In Finland and Italy, there is no difference in replacement rates across income groups, thus the need for additional private savings has been less than in systems with earnings-related pensions. However, since the replacement rate is generally rather low in Italy due to the still high relevance of the male breadwinner model, a more general need for a crowding in of private pensions for all income groups can be assumed. Since the replacement rates do not include the voluntary occupational pensions, the gap between higher- and lower-income groups is somewhat higher (20–30 per cent) in France and Germany, and considerably higher in Belgium (80 per cent), though this gap is now increasingly filled. In contrast to the other countries, Switzerland and particularly the United Kingdom provide relatively low benefits for medium to high earners. Whereas the gap in the United Kingdom seems to be filled by contracted-out pensions, the Swiss system seems to offer a broader scope for additional initiatives strengthening private pension plans. An important aspect to consider in the case of private supplementary pension is not only the second-tier income function but also the access to such private plans.

6. The question of access: mandatory or voluntary private pensions?

Given the limited role of public pensions in multipillar systems and the recent retreat of Bismarckian public pensions, private pensions have already and will become more important in maintaining income beyond the minimum guaranteed by public pensions. However, access to such pensions is a crucial precondition for later retirement income as are the years of contributions, the share of earnings contributed, and the ways in which benefits or contributions are defined. Private pension participation depends on the particular governance modes and regulation: it may be mandated by statutory law, self-regulated by collective agreements (sectoral or nationwide), or a voluntary commitment by employers for all or particular groups of employees, and often it is a voluntary individual decision to save for old age. In recent decades, private pension insurance coverage has become more universal in some countries, supported by state mandates or extension of collective agreements. The large variation in coverage across Europe depends not only on these regulations but also on employer willingness and individual capacity to contribute as well as particular employment conditions (see Table 14.6).

Access to private pensions is based on contributions paid by the employer, the individual employee, or both. Coverage of private pensions tends to be highly unequal, resulting from two main processes. First, coverage is generally selective in voluntary schemes and, in the case of occupational pensions, often limited to those in dependent employment. Some employers may provide voluntary occupational pensions as a fringe benefit to some or all employees, while others do not. Where individuals voluntarily contribute to an occupational or private pension plan, some occupational groups are more likely to contribute than others, particularly those in full-time jobs and higher-income groups, especially those with the largest gap left by public pensions in maintaining living standards in old age. Even in collectively negotiated, (quasi-) mandatory systems, some non-standard employment groups are often excluded. Moreover, low-income groups, particularly those with no or limited

Table 14.6 Governance and current coverage rates of occupational pensions

	Mandatory (semi-public)	Mandatory (private)	Collective	Voluntary	Opt-out
High	Finland (second tier: 98%)	Switzerland (95%)	Denmark (95%) The Netherlands (91%) Sweden (90%)		
Medium	France (second tier: 90%)			Germany (64%) Belgium (56%)*	The United Kingdom (47%)
Low					Italy (11%)*

Source: OECD (2007a, 2009b); *recent extension (Italy: transfer of Tfr).

earnings, are less capable (or less foresighted) to contribute to voluntary private pensions, unless substantial tax subsidies are provided. The governance of private pensions directly affects the conditions for access to coverage (see also Chapter 13). We distinguish systems with statutory mandates, collective agreements, employer commitment, and individual decision.

Several of the ten countries considered in this book have mandatory occupational pensions or have extensive coverage due to collective agreements. Switzerland introduced mandatory occupational pensions in 1985 (except those employees earning less than the contribution ceiling for the public pension; about one-third of average earnings). Finland's semi-private earnings-related pensions were made mandatory in the 1960s for all employment groups (including the self-employed), thus covering nearly everyone. In France, the collective agreements on second-tier occupational pensions for private sector employees (AGIRC) and cadres (ARCCO) were declared mandatory in 1972, while public employees profit from generous special schemes.[9] In the Netherlands, since 1947 the Labour Ministry can declare binding collective agreements on occupational pensions for all employers and employees in a sector. Given the high degree of organization of trade unions in Sweden, nearly all employees there have been covered by four collective agreements (private blue-collar, private white-collar, central government, and local public employees) since the 1970s. The Danish metal workers' union struck an agreement on occupational pensions in 1991, which led to similar agreements across the private sector, while such schemes already existed for public employees. In the Netherlands, Sweden, and Denmark, these quasi-mandatory occupational pensions currently exceed coverage rates above 90 per cent of employees, leaving only few workers excluded.

The voluntary pensions in Belgium, Germany, and the United Kingdom include only about half of the workforce, while in Italy private occupational pension coverage has not yet become as widespread. In the United Kingdom, occupational pensions provided by employers have a long tradition, and employers are allowed to contract out of their contribution to the S2P in return for providing their employees with their own occupational pension plan. In addition, since 1986, individuals can opt out of private personal pensions. Given the increasingly flat-rate level of S2P benefits, there is a considerable incentive to opt out, especially as higher rates of return are expected for the DC personal pension. In the three other systems, participation is primarily based on voluntary decisions either by the employer or employee, though collective agreements in some sectors are also possible. Since the 1990s, collective agreements on occupational pensions have been supported by legislation in Belgium, and private pensions have recently spread to more than half of the

---

[9] In France, special schemes exist for agricultural, mining, railroad, marine, public utility, and public sector employees as well as for farmers and the self-employed.

workforce. The comparably high coverage in Germany is a by-product of several collective agreements, particularly for non-tenured public employees and more recently across different private sectors. In addition, since 2001, it has been possible to transfer earnings into occupational pension contributions as tax regulations and collective agreements overrule individual agreements. Italy has the least developed occupational scheme thus far, though the recent developments of transposing the mandatory end-of-service-pay into occupational pensions provide a new avenue. Until then, special occupational schemes existed only in the financial sector, thus covering a small minority of employees outside the public pension system.

7. Private pension beneficiaries: comparing recipient rates across countries

Although private pension coverage among the working population has been increasing recently, the current recipient rate of private pensions may still be lower due to the long time span between contributing and drawing benefits. Analysing survey data for older people aged 65 and older (SHARE 2006 and ELSA 2006/7), the recipient rate (see Table 14.7) provides an indicator of the scope of private pensions among current retirees. Belgium and Italy still show the legacy of the dominant Bismarckian pensions: the current rate of recipients in private supplementary pensions has been very low (around 5 per cent of all residents aged 65 and older). Despite recent changes, Germany's current recipient rate remains at a medium low level (22 per cent), though the recipient rate is considerably higher among men (33 per cent) than women (14 per cent), due to their lower employment rate in the past. Note that German-tenured civil servants (*Beamte*) receive a favourable tax-financed special pension (which is not counted here), while non-tenured public employees are covered by a collective agreement on supplementary pensions (included in the recipient rate). Also in France, the second-tier occupational pensions cover nearly every second older resident (46 per cent of current retirees), thanks to the mandate since 1972, though most French-tenured civil servants receive a favourable public pension based on a special scheme (excluded from the recipient rate). The gender divide is very pronounced in Continental Europe due to the belated rise in female labour force participation; it ranges between 2.5 times higher for men than women in Belgium and only 1.6 times higher in France.

Among the multipillar systems, Sweden and the Netherlands have the highest recipient rates, while Denmark and Switzerland have somewhat lower rates due to the later expansion of coverage. Almost 70 per cent of the Swedish older residents report receiving an occupational pension negotiated by unions and employers, common for all groups since the 1970s. In comparison, the Danish expansion of occupational pensions beyond the public sector occurred only in

Table 14.7 Individual and household recipient rate of private pensions among older people and households

Recipients	Group	Belgium	Britain	Denmark	France	Germany	Italy	The Netherlands	Sweden	Switzerland
% Individuals	Total	5.0	–	33.2	46.2	22.1	5.2	63.6	67.8	44.6
Gender	Male	7.8	–	40.4	58.8	33.1	7.0	80.5	71.4	63.8
	Female	~3.1	–	27.7	37.1	14.3	4.0	51.4	64.9	31.5
	(Gap)	~(2.5)	–	(1.5)	(1.6)	(2.3)	(1.8)	(1.6)	(1.1)	(2.0)
Age group	65–74	4.4	–	39.0	56.2	25.0	5.7	65.4	75.8	49.0
	75+	5.7	–	26.7	34.9	18.8	~4.7	61.6	59.3	40.3
	(Gap)	(0.8)	–	(1.5)	(1.6)	(1.3)	~(1.2)	(1.1)	(1.3)	(1.2)
% Households	Total	8.2	62.8	40.8	63.1	30.5	6.9	74.8	75.3	58.9
Gender	Male	8.9	69.1	44.9	70.6	35.6	7.1	82.0	79.7	69.2
	Female	7.7	58.2	38.1	58.7	27.4	6.8	70.7	72.4	53.6
Age group	65–74	~5.1	68.4	50.4	72.7	33.3	7.8	81.7	84.7	67.7
	75+	9.4	55.1	29.8	50.5	25.9	~6.3	67.4	65.1	49.9
Household	Single	~5.6	48.4	26.0	48.5	19.0	~4.8	65.3	60.2	45.3
	Male	≈6.4	62.7	~26.1	65.0	≈27.1	≈2.4	79.9	64.1	68.6
	Female	~5.5	42.2	26.0	45.5	17.4	≈5.3	61.9	60.3	41.8
	Couple	9.3	71.5	51.2	71.6	37.0	8.0	82.7	86.3	69.4
Income group	Low	≈3.6	27.5	~8.7	42.4	~10.2	≈4.5	33.3	48.8	~12.9
	Middle	9.3	68.3	45.2	73.3	30.1	~5.9	95.5	83.7	80.4
	High	11.5	92.7	68.1	73.6	51.6	10.5	93.4	93.1	83.4

Note: Individuals: persons aged 65 and older; household: at least one person aged 65 and older, partner may be younger but is also retired (households with children or incomplete information were excluded); ~ estimates based on less than thirty observations; ≈ estimates based on less than fifteen observations.

Source: Own calculations based on SHARE 2006; for the United Kingdom: ELSA 2006/7.

the 1990s, therefore only every third Danish older resident currently receives such a private pension. In both Nordic countries, the gender gap is not as large as in Continental Europe, thanks to the earlier and higher female employment rate. Given its early post-war development of collective agreements, nearly two out of three Dutch older residents receive an occupational pension plan. While four out of five older Dutch men profit from it, only every second woman receives a second-tier pension, mirroring the very low female labour force participation until the 1980s. Swiss occupational pensions were made mandatory only in 1985, leading to a substantial share of residents (45 per cent) that currently receive such second-tier pensions but there is a strong gender bias due to the minimum earnings and employment linkage.

The recipient rates are thus in line with the timing of expansion, particularly the introduction of a mandate or the spread of collectively negotiated plans. This timing effect can also be seen when analysing the younger (aged 65–74) and older cohort (aged 75 and older) among current retirees. The largest gap in favour of the younger group can be observed in France and Denmark, though this may not only be a result of the secular increase in coverage but also reflect the composition effect as women are overrepresented in the older age group. While the individual recipient rate is of particular relevance for the impact of labour market attachment, we also need to consider the household context (see Table 14.7) in order to understand the overall impact of transfer pooling among couples. In particular, married (or divorced) women who are not covered by occupational pensions profit from their (former) husbands' occupational pension or indirectly through a widow pension. The pooled recipient rate of private pensions is higher for households than for individuals; particularly in Continental Europe, women profit indirectly from their partners' occupational pension. The incidence rate is higher among couples than among single households, particularly in comparison to single women (mostly widows). As women outlive men for several years (on average), they are overrepresented among single households; they will thus have to rely more heavily on public pensions.

The differential impact of access to private pensions is also observable in the incidence rate across households of different income groups. Low-income households are much less likely to receive an occupational pension than those in the top two-thirds of the income distribution. In general, the higher the overall recipient rate in a society, the lower the differences across the three income groups. Disregarding the two countries with the lowest rates (Belgium, Italy), the differences between the rates of highest and lowest income groups are not as pronounced in high recipient countries (France, Sweden, the Netherlands, and the United Kingdom) than in those where private pensions are less accessible for those with low earnings (Denmark, Germany, and Switzerland). In France and Sweden, the gap between low-income households and the two other income groups is lower than in the mature multipillar systems. The Netherlands and Britain show a substantially lower incidence rate among low-income groups, while in Denmark and Switzerland occupational pensions are infrequent among low-income households. While Denmark, Britain, and Germany show a significant difference between the medium and highest income group households, there are hardly any differences in the other multi-pillar systems.

The British and Danish cases contradict somewhat the crowding-in thesis, which expects the strong development of private pensions in addition to the rather meagre basic pension benefits. In the case of Denmark, we find that the state and social partners had to make major efforts to stimulate occupational and personal pension coverage. Our data analysis shows that currently every second household in the younger cohorts of elderly people (65–74) receives income from private pensions, a strong increase compared to the older cohort. Although the United Kingdom has reached reasonably high recipient rates for the younger cohort of elderly (68 per cent), the system still scores worst according to inequality indicators; this may not only be an effect of the considerably lower recipient rate across those aged 75 and older but also due to less redistributive policies in other social benefits. Hence, the overall rate of private pensions varies not only across gender and household contexts but also according to social strata. These social inequalities are even more pronounced when we consider the share of private pensions in overall transfers in old age.

8. The strength of the non-state pillars: the private share in overall pensions

The importance of private pensions in overall retirement income depends not only on the past coverage (contributors) or current recipient rates (pensioners) but also on the private transfer share. Do private pensions provide merely a topping-up of income for the wealthy or do occupational or personal pensions provide a major part of everyone's pension income? Table 14.8 compares the share of people 65 and older (and their retired partners) who receive a private pension and the private transfer share for those receiving such pensions. Currently, the aggregated private pension share is substantial across the mature multipillar systems of the Netherlands (30 per cent), Switzerland (28 per cent), and the United Kingdom (27 per cent). The French semi-private occupational pensions provide a quarter (24 per cent), while the Swedish (16 per cent) and Danish (15 per cent) occupational pensions are thus far still relatively minor with respect to overall pension transfers. The share is still very small in the Bismarckian systems of Belgium (2 per cent), Italy (4 per cent), and Germany (7 per cent) due to the dominance of public earnings-related benefits. However, given that the recipient rate differs across countries and social groups, the national averages hide the relevance of private pensions for selected groups.

Table 14.8 Share of private pensions in total transfers of older people and households (%)

Groups		Belgium	Britain	Denmark	France	Germany	Italy	The Netherlands	Sweden	Switzerland
% Individuals	Total	32.1	–	41.3	39.7	27.5	65.0	42.8	22.3	50.6
Gender	Male	35.7	–	48.9	44.0	27.9	65.8	49.8	25.2	58.0
	Female	25.2	–	32.4	34.5	26.9	64.0	33.8	19.7	40.7
	(Gap)	(1.4)	-	(1.5)	(1.3)	(1.0)	(1.0)	(1.5)	(1.3)	(1.4)
Age group	65–74	38.0	–	41.4	41.4	28.6	71.4	45.6	24.5	56.7
	75+	27.0	–	41.0	36.4	25.8	56.3	38.8	18.8	45.6
	(Gap)	(1.4)	-	(1.0)	(1.1)	(1.1)	(1.3)	(1.2)	(1.3)	(1.2)
% Households all pension recipients	Total	2.0	26.8	14.9	24.0	7.0	3.8	30.2	16.3	28.1
Only private pension recipients	Total	24.8	40.6	36.1	36.8	22.1	52.5	40.0	21.5	47.6
Gender	Male	25.4	42.3	38.7	38.0	21.3	52.4	42.8	23.1	49.5
	Female	24.3	39.2	34.1	36.0	22.7	52.5	37.9	20.3	46.3
Age groups	65–74	~20.7	40.5	36.2	39.2	21.2	55.7	41.4	23.2	48.8
	75+	20.8	34.7	36.4	34.0	22.5	~49.4	33.9	17.4	43.9
Household type	Single	~26.3	35.1	33.0	35.9	26.3	≈51.6	35.3	18.2	42.9
	Male	–	39.8	47.5	43.2	≈24.7	–	42.8	22.5	47.3
	Female	~23.9	32.1	28.5	34.0	26.8	–	33.1	16.6	41.9
	Couple	24.4	42.8	37.2	37.2	20.8	52.7	42.7	23.3	49.9
Income group	Low	≈15.6	27.3	~17.3	25.5	~20.5	≈66.1	20.2	13.1	~28.4
	Middle	16.8	26.8	24.2	34.6	16.0	~57.7	31.0	15.8	37.1
	High	33.7	54.8	46.5	45.6	26.0	43.1	56.0	31.0	60.8

Note: Individuals: persons aged 65 and older; household: at least one person aged 65 and older, partner may be younger but is also retired (households with children or incomplete information were excluded); private share: private pension income divided by total pension income; ~ estimates based on less than thirty observations; ≈ estimates based on less than fifteen observations.

Source: Own calculations based on SHARE 2006; for the United Kingdom: ELSA 2006/7.

When analysing private transfer shares for those receiving occupational pensions (see Table 14.8), we need to keep in mind the large differences in recipient rates already discussed. Again, there are differences between the perspectives of individual pension receipt and pooled income in the household context. Gender differences are larger when we consider individual pension receipt, while women living with their partners may also indirectly benefit from private pensions. Variations are large across systems with very low recipient rates (see Figure 14.4). For example, the infrequent Italian private pensions tend to be important for those few that receive them (with no significant gender disparity), while the Belgian private share is a relatively low supplement (especially for women). In Germany, private pensions serve to 'top up' about a quarter of transfer income, but only a third of pensioners profit from this (and single women even less). In Scandinavia, a large share of the Swedish older population receives a 'top-up' supplement of about one-fifth of their transfer income (with low gender disparity), while in Denmark the private share is larger than a third of transfers but not as widespread (only 41 per cent) among current pensioners (with lower shares for single women). The other three multipillar systems (the Netherlands, Switzerland, and the United Kingdom) stand out with high recipient rates and substantial shares of private pensions (40 per cent or larger). Together with the French supplementary pensions, these four systems provide more than a third of transfers for about two-thirds of all older people. Women are not only less likely to personally receive a private pension but they also collect a smaller private share, particularly in the multipillar systems of Denmark, the Netherlands, Sweden, and

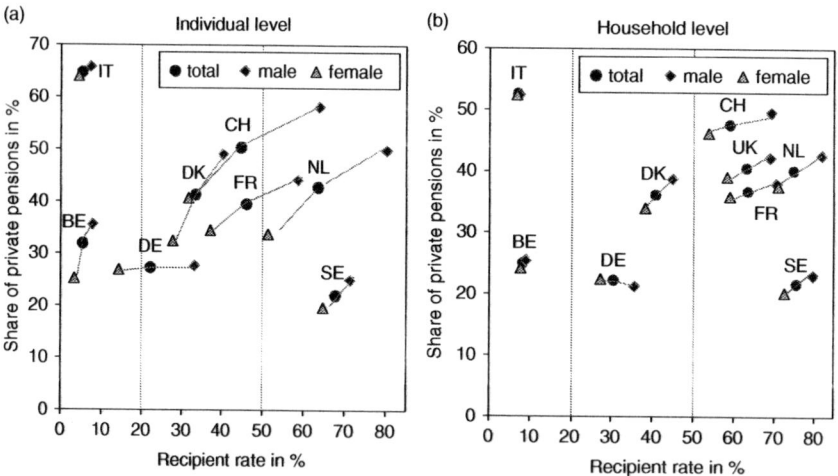

Figure 14.4 Recipient rate and private pension share by gender (SHARE 2006)

Source: SHARE (2006) and ELSA (2006/7), own calculations (see Tables 14.7 and 14.8).

Switzerland (probably also in Britain, although no individual-level data are available). The share of private pensions among single male households is higher than among couples, while the share is smaller among single women than among couples. However, it should be noted that in absolute terms women receive considerably lower transfers than men do.

With respect to age groups, the cohort-related differences in recipient rates are mirrored by the private share in overall transfers: the younger cohort has accumulated a higher share than the group that retired at least a decade earlier. The older age group (75+) has a considerably lower share in the multipillar systems of Britain, the Netherlands, and Sweden, though women tend to be overrepresented in this age group due to longer life expectancy. Figure 14.4 plots the recipient rate and the share of private pensions by gender at the individual level (14.4a) and for household context separately (14.4b). The gender divide exists not only with respect to recipients but also in private transfer shares. With the exception of the Bismarckian countries (Belgium, Germany, and Italy), the share of private pensions at household level tends to be somewhat higher among men than women, although the gender differences in recipient rates are relatively larger. The gender gap is less pronounced at the household level than at the individual level as the former reflects the intra-household redistribution among couples, thus the overall results are driven by the gender discrepancy across single person households.

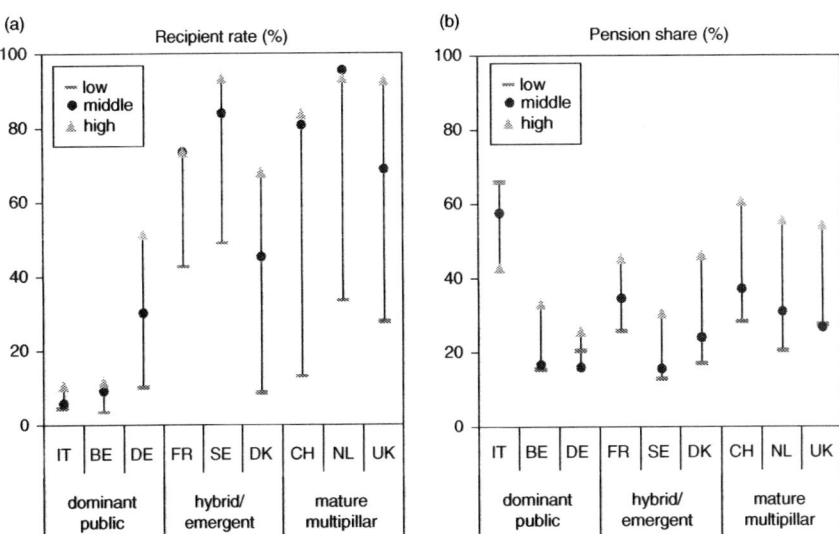

Figure 14.5 Recipient rate and private pension share by household income group (SHARE 2006)

Source: SHARE (2006) and ELSA (2006/7), own calculations (see Tables 14.7 and 14.8).

In terms of income inequality, the private pension share increases from the lowest to the middle to the highest income households (see Figure 14.5). The income group differences are most pronounced in the multipillar systems, while the differences in private shares are less important. While the share is relatively small among the lowest income groups, the share of the highest group is considerably higher than the share of the medium group in the countries with public basic pension traditions: Denmark, the Netherlands, Sweden, Switzerland, and the United Kingdom. France's second-tier scheme similarly shows the importance of occupational pensions for the maintenance of living standards in medium and high-income groups. Occupational pensions in Belgium and Italy are still of importance only to few people in the high-income groups, while in Germany the occupational pensions assume only a top-up function for some, though similarly across all three income groups. Whereas the Bismarckian earnings-related public pensions maintain income even for high incomes (at least up to the contribution ceiling), among the multipillar systems the importance of private pensions is particularly pronounced for the top third of pensioner households receiving a private pension (more than half of transfers in the case of British, Dutch, or Swiss private pensions). These patterns clearly demonstrate the strong contribution of private pensions to retirement income inequality in all countries analysed here. Especially in countries with Beveridge tradition, inequality is an inherent element of the multipillar system, since medium- to high-income earners have an intrinsic interest to maintain a certain level of their former earnings. Since public pensions in multipillar systems do not offer these benefits, occupational pensions are crowded in, yet in most of the Beveridge countries studied here this occurs via (quasi-)mandated plans.

9. Conclusion: exacerbating inequality in multipillar systems?

The impact of multipillar systems in comparison to dominantly public pension systems on poverty and inequality in old age is rather mixed, suggesting that the effect of privatization depends not merely on the public–private mix as such but much more on its design. To reduce severe poverty among those of retirement age, public minimum income security via first-tier pension arrangements, in particular sufficient basic, guaranteed, or minimum pensions, is important. This will become even more crucial given the interrupted and non-standard employment careers of the current and future workforce. In addition, the earnings-related pensions are essential for maintaining living standards for the majority of those who expect more than the minimum provision. While Bismarckian systems traditionally provide such earnings-related public pensions, the Beveridge basic pension systems developed second-tier state pensions or relied on private occupational and personal pensions. While earnings-related state pensions provide some redistributive features, in particular social credits, private pensions rarely achieve social goals, unless tax subsidies, state regulation, or collective agreements intervene. Among current pensioners, most multipillar systems achieve lower poverty and inequality than the Bismarckian earnings-related pensions, though Britain performs badly on both indicators. It should be noted that the poverty and inequality indicators were measured for the total income package also including other social welfare benefits like health, housing, and employment or other capital income. Since pension benefits are the major income source for the majority of retirees, inequalities in old age derive largely from the design of the public–private pension mix.

Access conditions, contribution records, and benefit regulations are all crucial factors affecting the impact of private pensions on old age income inequality. Mandatory supplementary pensions (as in Finland, France, and Switzerland) as well as widespread collective agreements (as in Denmark, the Netherlands, and Sweden and, more recently, in Belgium, Germany, and Italy) are important to increase coverage among current workers. The British 'contracting out' of private pensions and the German tax incentives for personal pensions are also means to increase coverage, but at the cost of tax expenditures. Today's rate of recipients depends on past efforts, thus only the mature multipillar systems have achieved a high and more equal distribution of private pensions with respect to gender, household type, and income group. Among current recipients, the public pillar still dominates in Belgium and Italy, while Germany and Denmark have assumed medium levels and the other multipillar systems already have widespread second- and third-pillar pensions, although some vulnerable groups may be underrepresented.

The analysis of the weight of private pensions in supplementing public pensions revealed that private pensions have considerable importance in the multipillar systems: Britain, Denmark, the Netherlands, and Switzerland. The quasi-private (but not fully funded) occupational pensions in France and Finland are also significant, while such income sources are less important in Sweden and Germany. Alongside these country differences, we found significant disparities with respect to gender, household, and income group: women, single pensioners, and low-income households rely much more on public pensions than do the other social groups. In Britain, Denmark, the Netherlands, and Switzerland, the highest income group profits most from supplementing their public pension. As a consequence, in these countries, private pensions have become a major cause of the reproduction of market income inequalities in old age – at least above the level of public basic security. The Bismarckian systems, designed to maintain status, effectively reproduced inequalities from their early days. Although these countries have increasingly introduced socially redistributive elements, the recent reforms will again reduce public pension benefits, which will provide room for market-induced inequalities through voluntary private pensions, unless state or collective regulation succeeds in increasing coverage and socially redistributive elements.

Although public pensions, particularly in multipillar systems, have reduced the risk of poverty and the degree of inequality in old age, the different combinations of the public–private mix still entail a relatively similar overall reproduction of social inequalities found prior to retirement. Individual pension income and inequalities in resources in old age derive from particular features of the design of pension systems: in the Bismarckian *dominantly public* pension systems via their general equivalence principle, in the *mature* and *emerging* multipillar systems via the major importance of earnings-related pensions for the income of the broad majority in the future, and in the *hybrid* systems via their mixed structure, which also links current labour market integration to later benefits. Recent policy reforms will have major effects, many of which will only become visible in the coming decades. The increased emphasis on occupational and personal pensions results from attempts to offset the costs of public insurance in ageing societies and under fiscal austerity. However, public pensions that provide universal minimum income in old age will become even more important in the future. Moreover, as European welfare states have been challenged by the financial and economic crises of the 2000s, individuals relying on funded pensions have also faced increased financial risks, and these may continue to grow as the reliance on private funded pensions increases. Only broad-based public policies and collectively negotiated self-regulation can pool risks and redistribute social benefits to effectively counteract social inequalities in the lengthening phase of life after retirement. In the future, the ongoing trend of privatization will lead to a gradual convergence of countries as their pension systems become multipillar. As shown in these ten pension systems, the shift towards increasing privatization amplifies the already existing level of social inequality in these ageing societies.

Bibliography

Behrendt, C. (2000). 'Private Pensions – A Viable Alternative? Their Distributive Effects in a Comparative Perspective'. *International Social Security Review*, 53/3: 3–26.

——(2007). 'Pensions and Income Redistribution in a Comparative Perspective: Evidence from the Luxembourg Income Study', in J. Véron, S. Pennec and J. Légaré (eds.), *Ages, Generations and the Social Contract: The Demographic Challenges Facing the Welfare State*. Dordrecht: Springer, 261–77.

Bonoli, G. (2006). 'New Social Risks and the Politics of Post-Industrial Social Policies', in K. Armingeon and G. Bonoli (eds.), *The Politics of Post-Industrial Welfare States: Adapting Post-War Social Policies to New Social Risks*. London: Routledge, 3–26.

Callegaro, L., and Wilke, C. B. (2008). 'Public, Occupational and Individual Pension Coverage', in A. Börsch-Supan, A. Brugiavini, H. Jürges, A. Kapteyn, J. Mackenbach, J. Siegrist and G. Weber (eds.), *First Results from the Survey of Health, Ageing and Retirement in Europe (2004–2007): Starting the Longitudinal Dimension.* Mannheim: Mannheim Research Institute for the Economics of Aging, 222–9.

Casey, B. H., and Yamada, A. (2004). 'The Public–Private Mix of Retirement Income in Nine OECD Countries: Some Evidence from Micro Data and an Exploration of its Implications', in M. Rein and W. Schmähl (eds.), *Rethinking the Welfare State – The Political Economy of Pension Reform.* Cheltenham, UK: Edward Elgar, 395–411.

Ebbinghaus, B. (2006). *Reforming Early Retirement in Europe, Japan and the USA.* Oxford: Oxford University Press.

Esping-Andersen, G. (1990). *The Three Worlds of Welfare Capitalism.* Cambridge/Oxford: Polity Press.

——(2002). 'A New Gender Contract', in G. Esping-Andersen, D. Gallie, A. Hemerijck and J. Myles (eds.), *Why We Need a New Welfare State.* Oxford: Oxford University Press, 68–95.

EU-EPC (2009). *The 2009 Ageing Report: Economic and Budgetary Projections for the EU-27 Member States (2008–2060).* Economic Policy Committee.

EU-SPC (2008). *Privately Managed Pension Provision and Their Contribution to Adequate and Sustainable Pensions.* Brussels: European Commission, Social Protection Committee.

EU-SPC(ICG) (2009). *Updates of Current and Prospective Theoretical Pension Replacement Rates 2006–2046.* Brussels: European Union (Social Protection Committee, Indicator Sub-Group).

Fagan, C., and O'Reilly, J. (1998). 'Conceptualising Part-time Work: The Value of an Integrated Comparative Perspective', in J. O'Reilly and C. Fagan (eds.), *Part-time Prospects: An International Comparison of Part-time Work in Europe, North America and the Pacific Rim.* London: Routledge, 1–31.

Fagan, C., and Rubery, J. (1996). 'The Salience of the Part-time Divide in the European Union'. *European Sociological Review,* 12/3: 227–50.

Goodin, R. E., and Rein, M. (2001). 'Regimes on Pillars: Alternative Welfare State Logics and Dynamics'. *Public Administration,* 79/4: 769–801.

Gornick, J.C., Sierminska, E., and Smeeding, T.M. (2009). 'The Income and Wealth Packages of Older Women in Cross-national Perspective'. *Journal of Gerontology,* 64B/3: 402–414.

Gruber, Jonathan, and David A Wise (2007). *Social Security Programs and Retirement Around the World: Fiscal Implications of Reform.* Chicago: University of Chicago Press.

Hauser, R. (1999). 'Adequacy and Poverty among Retired People'. *International Social Security Review,* 52/3: 107–24.

Kangas, O., and Palme, J. (1996). 'The Development of Occupational Pensions in Finland and Sweden: Class Politics and Institutional Feedbacks', in M. Shalev (ed.), *The Privatization of Social Policy? Occupational Welfare and the Welfare State in America, Scandinavia and Japan.* London: Macmillan, 211–40.

Korpi, W., and Palme, J. (1998). 'The Paradox of Redistribution and Strategies of Equality: Welfare State Institutions, Inequality, and Poverty in the Western Countries'. *American Sociological Review,* 63: 661–87.

Lewis, J. (1992). 'Gender and the Development of Welfare Regimes'. *Journal of European Social Policy,* 2: 159–73.

——(2001). 'The Decline of the Male Breadwinner Model: Implications for Work and Care'. *Social Politics,* 8/2: 152–69.

Marshall, T. H. (1950). *Citizenship and Social Class. The Marshall Lectures*. Cambridge: Cambridge University.

Meyer, T., Bridgen, P. and Riedmüller, B. (2007). *Private Pensions Versus Social Inclusion? Non-State Provision for Citizens at Risk in Europe*. Cheltenham: Edward Elgar.

Monticone, C., Ruzik, A., and Skiba, J. (2008). 'Women's Pension Rights and Survivors' Benefits: A Comparative Analysis of EU Member States and Candidate Countries'. *ENEPRI Research Report, No. 53*.

OECD (2000). *Reforms for an Ageing Society*. Paris: OECD.

——(2007a). *Pensions at a Glance 2007*. Paris: OECD.

——(2007b). *Protecting Pensions – Policy Analysis and Examples from OECD Countries*. Paris: OECD.

——(2009a). *Labour Force Statistics 1988–2008*. Paris: OECD.

——(2009b). *Pensions at a Glance 2009 – Retirement-Income Systems in OECD Countries*. Paris: OECD.

Pedersen, A. W. (2004). 'The Privatization of Retirement Income? Variation and Trends in the Income Packages of Old Age Pensioners'. *Journal of European Social Policy*, 14/1: 5–23.

Prus, S., and Brown, R. (2006). 'Income Inequality over the Later-life Course: A Comparative Analysis of Seven OECD Countries'. *Luxembourg Income Study Working Paper Series, 435*.

Rein, M., and Behrendt, C. (2004). 'The Relationship of the Public/Private Mix with Poverty and Inequality', in E. Øverbye and P. A. Kemp (eds.), *Pensions: Challenges and Reforms*. Aldershot: Ashgate, 187–209.

——and Turner, J. (2004). 'How Societies Mix Public and Private Spheres in Their Pension Systems', in M. Rein and W. Schmähl (eds.), *Rethinking the Welfare State. The Political Economy of Pension Reform*. Cheltenham: Edward Elgar, 251–93.

Shalev, M. (ed.) (1996). *The Privatization of Social Policy? Occupational Welfare and the Welfare State in America, Scandinavia and Japan*. London: Macmillan.

Smeeding, T. (2001). 'Income Maintenance in Old Age: What Can be Learned from Cross-National Comparisons'. *Luxembourg Income Study Working Paper, 263*.

Taylor-Gooby, P. (2004). 'New Social Risks and Welfare States: New Paradigm and New Politics?' in P. Taylor-Gooby (ed.), *New Risks, New Welfare: The Transformation of the European Welfare State*. Oxford: Oxford University Press, 209–38.

Titmuss, R. M. (1974). *Social Policy. An Introduction*. London: Allen & Unwin.

World Bank (1994). *Averting the Old Age Crisis: Policies to Protect the Old and Promote Growth*. Washington, DC: The World Bank.

Yamada, A. (2002). 'The Evolving Retirement Income Package: Trends in Adequacy and Equality in Nine OECD Countries'. *Labour Market and Social Policy Occasional Papers, No. 63*.

Index

Index